The Marketing of Sport

Visit *The Marketing of Sport* Companion Website at
www.pearsoned.co.uk/beechchadwick to find valuable **student** learning
material including.

- Links to relevant sites on the web
- An online glossary to explain key terms
- A comprehensive bibliography

We work with leading authors to develop the strongest
educational materials in marketing, business and finance,
bringing cutting-edge thinking and best learning practice to
a global market.

Under a range of well-known imprints, including Financial Times
Prentice Hall, we craft high-quality print and electronic
publications which help readers to understand and apply their
content, whether studying or at work.

To find out more about the complete range of our publishing,
please visit us on the World Wide Web at: www.pearsoned.co.uk

The Marketing of Sport

Edited by

John Beech
Coventry Business School

and

Simon Chadwick
Birkbeck College, University of London

FT Prentice Hall
FINANCIAL TIMES

An imprint of **Pearson Education**
Harlow, England · London · New York · Boston · San Francisco · Toronto · Sydney · Singapore · Hong Kong
Tokyo · Seoul · Taipei · New Delhi · Cape Town · Madrid · Mexico City · Amsterdam · Munich · Paris · Milan

Pearson Education Limited

Edinburgh Gate
Harlow
Essex CM20 2JE
England

and Associated Companies throughout the world

Visit us on the World Wide Web at:
www.pearsoned.co.uk

First published 2007
© Pearson Education Limited 2007

ISBN-13: 978-0-273-68826-6
ISBN-10: 0-273-68826-X

British Library Cataloguing-in-Publication Data
A catalogue record for this book is available from the British Library

Library of Congress Cataloging-in-Publication Data
The marketing of sport / edited by John Beech and Simon Chadwick.
    p. cm.
Includes bibliographical references and index.
ISBN-13: 978-0-273-68826-6 (pbk.)
ISBN-10: 0-273-68826-X (pbk.)
1. Sports—Marketing. I. Beech, John G., 1947- II. Chadwick, Simon, 1964-
GV716.M364 2007
796'.0698—dc22

2006020025

ARP impression 98

Typeset in 10/12.5 pt Sabon by 72
Printed by Ashford Colour Press Ltd, Gosport

The publisher's policy is to use paper manufactured from sustainable forests.

Brief contents

Contents

9   Managing sport products and services   158

David Harness and Tina Harness

10   Developing and extending sports brands   186

Artemisia Apostolopoulou and James M. Gladden

Figures

Tables

Case studies

About the authors

Artimesia Apostolopoulou

Dr Artemisia Apostolopoulou is an Assistant Professor of Sport Management in the School of Business at Robert Morris University, USA. This work was completed while Dr Apostolopoulou was a faculty member at Bowling Green State University, USA. She teaches *Sport Marketing* at the undergraduate and graduate levels and *Introduction to Sport Management*. She has also taught courses in *International Sport Management* and *Professional Resources in Sport Management*. Her area of research involves brand extension strategies implemented by sport organisations. Her secondary research interests include sponsorship and endorsement issues. She has presented work in numerous national and international conferences, and her publications have appeared in *Sport Marketing Quarterly* and the *International Journal of Sports Marketing & Sponsorship*. She has also served as a consultant for the NBA's Market Research department and the Atlanta Hawks' E-Marketing & Interactive Services department.

Dave Arthur

Dave is a Senior Lecturer in Sport Management at Southern Cross University. His current research interests include sport marketing, sport sponsorship and the interaction between these and relationship marketing. He has worked extensively with industry and recently became a full fledged Australian.

Ann Bourke

Ann lectures in International Business at University College Dublin Business Schools. She is currently Dean of Teaching and Learning and director of the Community of European Management Schools (CEMS) Masters in International Management (MIM) Programme. Her research interests include international trade in services, career issues for sports personnel and governance of sports bodies and organisations.

Susan Bridgewater

Susan is a Lecturer in Marketing at Warwick Business School. Her research interests lie in the fields of international marketing and in sport marketing, especially football and rugby. She is Director of the Certificate in Applied Management course, which Warwick Business School runs on behalf of the PFA, LMA and FA for aspiring football managers and numbers premiership managers. Mark Hughes and Stuart Pearce are amongst her former students.

John Beech (co-editor)

John is the Head of Sport and Tourism Applied Research at Coventry Business School. He teaches on both the MBA (Sport Management) and BA Sport Management degrees and has published widely on the use of internet marketing by soccer clubs. He is a committee member of SPRIG.

Kim Cassidy

Kim (a.k.a. Kim Harris) is Professor of Marketing at the University of Lincoln Business School. She has organised and chaired the UK Services Marketing Workshops in 2003 and 2004. Her current research interests include the measurement of the intended effect of service performance and consumer-to-consumer interactions in service settings. She has written articles in services, marketing and management journals, including *Journal of Service Research*, *European Journal of Marketing*, *International Journal of Service Industry Management* and *Journal of Business Research*. She is co-author of *Services Marketing: Text and Cases* (published by Palgrave in 2003).

Simon Chadwick (co-editor)

Simon works at Birkbeck College, the University of London, where he is a co-Director of the Birkbeck Sport Business Centre. He is Editor of the *International Journal of Sports Marketing and Sponsorship* and founder and leader of the Academy of Marketing's Sport Marketing Special Interest Group. Dr Chadwick has researched, published and consulted extensively in the area of sport marketing and is co-editor, along with John Beech, of *The Business of Sport Management* and *The Business of Tourism Management* (both published by FT Prentice Hall).

Michel Desbordes

Michel is Professor in Sport Marketing at the University Marc Bloch of Strasbourg (France) and at the ISC business school of Paris (France). After completing his PhD on innovation in sporting goods, he became a specialist in sport sponsorship and sport events, earning an MBA in Paris from 1999 to 2005. He took up his current position in Strasbourg in September 2005. In addition to his academic activities, he works as a consultant in sport marketing for MX Sports.

Dominic Elliott

Dominic is a Professor of Strategic Management and Business Continuity at the University of Liverpool Management School, and Head of the Division of Management. He is editor of the journal *Risk Management: An International Journal*. His current research interests include service recovery and service continuity, with particular interest in the football industry. He has publications in a number of management journals, including *Journal of Management Studies*, *Long Range Planning*, *Journal of Contingencies and Crisis Management* and *Journal of Strategic Information Systems*. He is co-author of the books *Learning from Crises* (published by Perpetuity Press, 2005) and *Business Continuity Management: A Crisis Management Approach* (published by Routledge, 2nd edn, 2005).

Ron Garland

Ron is an Associate Professor in the Department of Marketing, Waikato Management School, University of Waikato, Hamilton, New Zealand, where he teaches courses and conducts research in consumer behaviour, market research and sport marketing. He has published several chapters on marketing issues in sport management texts as well as general marketing issues in a variety of journals, including *the European Journal of Marketing* and *Journal of Financial Services Marketing*.

Jay Gladden

Jay is Associate Professor and Graduate Program Director For the Department of Sport Management located in the Isenberg School of Management at the University of Massachusetts. He has published articles related to sport brand management, sport sponsorship and fundraising for sport organisations.

David Harness

David is a Senior Lecturer in the Department of Marketing at Hull University Business School. He has worked at a number of UK universities, including Leeds University and Huddersfield Business Schools. He specialises in teaching and researching in the area of services marketing and strategic customer care. His commercial training and experience are in the field of financial services in which he continues to conduct research and consult. He has played a range of sports and recently has become involved in medieval jousting.

Tina Harness

Tina is a Senior Lecturer in Human Resource Management, Leeds Business School, Leeds Metropolitan University. Her specialist area for teaching and research is strategic human resource management.

Maria Hopwood

Maria is Associate Professor in Public Relations at Bond University in Queensland, Australia. Her area of research is in sport public relations and marketing communications. A keen cricket fan, she is especially interested in the ongoing developments in that sport, but her work also means she enthusiastically follows both rugby codes and soccer.

Paul Kitchin

Paul is course leader for the MA Sport Management Programme at London Metropolitan University. He teaches sport marketing from HND, through Undergraduate, to Masters level. Paul's research interests lie in service quality but he also is keen to disseminate the knowledge of sport marketing to community sport within northeast London.

Rudi Meir

Rudi is a Senior Lecture within the School of Exercise Science and Sport Management at Southern Cross University, Australia. He has worked as an academic for approximately 15 years, and previously worked within the NSW Department of Sport and Recreation and was the founding executive director with the North Coast Academy of Sport. He has conducted a range of market research projects for professional rugby league teams, both in England and Australia.

Leigh Sparks

Leigh is Professor of Retail Studies at the Institute for Retail Studies, University of Stirling, Scotland. At Stirling, he teaches sport marketing at undergraduate and post-graduate levels to students in both sports studies and marketing. His sport marketing research interest is on sports goods distribution and retailing. Leigh has a lifelong interest in sport generally, but particularly in the joys and disappointments of Welsh rugby.

Linda Trenberth

Linda joined the Department of Management at Birkbeck, University of London in 2000 from Massey University in New Zealand. Linda was involved in setting up what is now the leading sport management programme in New Zealand in the College of Business at Massey University. In this area, Linda also contributed to and co-edited with Chris Collins texts in *Sport Management* in 1994 and 1999 and more recently published a sport business management text for the UK. Her research interests include issues around the management of employee–employer relationships, women in management as well as work stress, health and—life balance and sport management.

Paul Turner

Paul is a Senior Lecturer and Director of the Sport Marketing program in the Bowater School of Management and Marketing at Deakin University. He received his PhD from Deakin University in 2005, and his research interests are in the areas of sport broadcasting and technology.

Nick Wake

Nick's experience of sport marketing began at Whitbread as Marketing Controller of leading sports club brand David Lloyd Leisure. Between 2002 and 2005, he was head of marketing with the government agency Sport England, where he was part of the team behind the Everyday Sport pilot campaign in the North East, as well as working with sports governing bodies on other initiatives to drive up participation. He now lives and works in Tring with motivation business Grass Roots.

Preface

The two co-editors of *The Marketing of Sport* have each been teaching on sport marketing and sport management programmes for more than a decade in various UK and European universities. During that time, there have been tremendous advances in the extent and nature of both teaching and learning in this area. A decade ago, sport marketing was an area that a few academics were beginning to enter from the perspective of business and management. While today, there are increasing numbers of students graduating with degrees in sport, sport marketing and sport management or having studied specialist modules in sport marketing, few senior academics can claim to have spent their working life exclusively in that area. It thus became clear to the co-editors that as a result, few texts exist that they felt they could whole-heartedly recommend to students. That is not to say that there was nothing available that they felt they could recommend, merely that the available texts had a highly specific geographic (and so sporting) focus. The underlying aims of this book have therefore been to ground sport marketing in the mainstream business literature and to produce an English language text with broad sporting and cultural appeal.

The main objective of this book is to provide an introduction to key aspects of sport marketing for both undergraduate and postgraduate students. The book will also serve as a useful resource for staff involved in teaching on sport marketing and marketing-related modules and programmes, as well as for practitioners working as sport marketers and managers of sport businesses.

The book consists of 24 chapters that are essentially split into six sections:

- The distinctive nature of sport marketing (Chapters 1–3): This helps the reader work towards an understanding of sport marketing.
- Meeting the needs and wants of the sport market (Chapters 4–10): This helps the reader work towards an understanding of sports markets.
- Communicating with the sport market (Chapters 11–14): This helps the reader to work towards an understanding of how to communicate with sport markets.
- Getting sports products and services to the market (Chapters 15–17): This helps the reader work towards an understanding of how to price and distribute sports products and services.
- Moving sport marketing forward (Chapters 18–22): This helps the reader work towards an understanding of the strategic and global contexts of sports marketing.
- Assessing the future for sport marketing (Chapters 23 and 24): This helps the reader works towards an understanding of the future and the reality facing sport marketers.

Each of the chapters in this book contains the following:

- A statement of learning outcomes
- A chapter overview
- An introduction

- Subject content appropriate to one of the sections mentioned above
- Case studies
- A conclusion
- Guided reading
- A bibliography
- Recommended websites

At the time of writing, all recommended websites were live. However, it may be the case that sites become inaccessible.

Acknowledgements

The editors would like to thank each of the chapter authors for their hard work and commitment in getting the book written.

Thanks are also due to the following organisations that have allowed us to use case material relating to their work in the sport industry: Cotton Traders, JJB Sports, sweatyBetty, Tiso and UNITEC.

Respect is due to the patient staff at FT-Prentice Hall – we are grateful for their continuing support. Special thanks are reserved for Ben, who has worked hard to get the book published, and for Jacqueline, who initiated the project in the first place.

John dedicates his work on the book to Sue.

Simon dedicates his work on the book to Barbara and Tomasz.

Publisher's acknowledgements

The publishers would like to thank all reviewers involved in providing feedback during the writing of this book. In particular:

Dr Allan Edwards, School of Education and Professional Studies, Griffith University, Australia

Glynis Jones, Lecturer, Sports Promotion and Marketing, Department of Management and Marketing, University of Huddersfield, UK

Trevor Hartland, Senior Lecturer in Marketing, Business School, University of Glamorgan, UK

Kari Puronaho, Research Director, University of Jyvaskyla, Finland

We are grateful to the following for permission to reproduce copyright material:

Figure 4.2 from *Principles of Marketing*, Figure 2.6, p.50 (Palmer, A. 2000) by permission of Oxford University Press; Figure 6.1 from *The Economics of Sport and Recreation*, Thomson Publishing Services (Gratton, C. and Taylor, P. 2000); Figure 6.2 from 'The Changing Role of Marketing in the Corporation', *Journal of Marketing*, 5, p.56, American Marketing Association (Webster, F.E. 1992); Table 6.1 from *Industrial Buying and Creative Marketing*, published by Allyn and Bacon, Boston, MA. Copyright © 1967 by Pearson Education. Reprinted/adapted by permission of the publisher (Robinson, P., Faris, C and Wind, Y. 1967); Table 7.1 from 'From carefree casuals to professional wanderers', *Journal of Marketing*, 5, 11/12, p.1265, American Marketing Association (Tapp, A., and Clowes, J. 2002); Figure 7.2 from *Market Segments: How to do it, how to profit from it*, 2nd edition, p.24, Palgrave Macmillan (McDonald, I.M., and Dunbar, I. 1998); Figures 11.1 and 11.2 from *Integrated Marketing Communications*, 2nd edition, Pearson Education Limited (Pickton, D. and Broderick, A. 2005); Case study 12.1 St George Bank triathlon leaflet, reprinted by kind permission of St. George Bank Limited; Chapter 12 screenshots from http://essendonfc.com.au (accessed 4 April 2005) on pages 248 and 249 reprinted by kind permission of Essendon Football Club; Figure 13.2 from *Sponsoring Sportif*, 2nd edition, Editions Economica (Tribou, G. 2004); Table 13.3 from *Les Echos*, 28 March 2001, Les Echos; Figure 14.1 from *Public Relations, Principles and Practice* published by Thomson Publishing Services (Kitchen, P. 1997); Figure 14.4 from *Public Relations; Contemporary Issues and Techniques*, with permission from Elsevier (Baines, P., Egan, J. and Jefkins, F. 2004); Figure 18.2 from *Strategic Sport Marketing*, 2nd edition, Allen & Unwin (Shilbury, D., Quick, S. & Westerbeek, H. 2002); Table 19.1 from www.goodyear.com (retrieved 6 March 2005) with permission from The Goodyear Tire and Rubber Company; Table 23.1 from '10 ways to shake up sport', *Observer Sport Monthly*, accessed 3 October 2004 from http://observer.guardian .co.uk/osm/story/0,6903543,00.html.

We are grateful to the Financial Times Limited for permission to reprint the following material:

Case 1.1 In a red shirt of white, Japan just can't get enough of Bekkamu Sama © *Financial Times*, 19 June 2003; Case 1.2 Star US soccer league struggles to shake off it's second-rate image © *Financial Times*, 3 August 2004; Case 4.1 Silverstone suffers from globalisation © *Financial Times*, 2 October 2004; Case 4.2 Goss in a struggle to keep backers on board: Team Philips' latest failure may prompt investors to jump © *Financial Times*, 15 December 2000; Case 5.1 A rare Scottish success in the beautiful game © *Financial Times*, 27 January 2005; Case 6.1 Renault sees F1 as vital in drive to develop its image © *Financial Times*, 30 May 2003; Case 6.2 Serving data on demand at Wimbledon © *Financial Times*, 24 June 2003; Case 9.2 In search of financial muscle © *Financial Times*, 23 April 2005; Case 9.3 South African blacks begin to bowl, bat… and chat, © *Financial Times*, 12 February 2005; Case 13.1 Deutsche Bank tees off its US branding drive, © *Financial Times*, 28 August 2003; Case 18.4 Adidas: off the pace and more hurdles ahead © *Financial Times*, 10 November 2003; Case 19.2 No style handicap © *Financial Times*, 19 June 2004; Case 21.2 Japanese fans form a new major league © *Financial Times*, 12 November 2004; Case 21.3 Centre court to centre stage © *Financial Times*, 24 May 2005; Case 23.1 China's sports fans open their hearts–but not their wallets © *Financial Times*, 21 February 2005; Case 23.2 On the ropes with Peckham's finest © *Financial Times*, 11 December 2004;

We are grateful to the following for permission to use copyright material:

Case 9.1 Golf gets to grips with a new generation from *The Financial Times Limited*, 26 March 2005 © Iestyn George; Case 13.2 Sponsorship proves its pulling power from *The Financial Times Limited*, 1 June 2004 © Pete Brown; Case 18.3 You've got to know what the goal is from *The Financial Times Limited*, 6 August 2004 © Steve Hemsley; Case 19.1 The ring cycle is complete from *The Financial Times Limited*, 6 August 2004 © Michael Payne

Tag Heuer for an extract adapted from 'Tag Heuer – New Sport and Glamour Ambassador' 6 January 2005, published on www.fhs.ch; The American Marketing Association for an extract adapted from 'MR can be the impetus for business model change' by Gurram Gopal, published on p.60 of *Marketing News*, 1 February 2005; Private Media Partners Ltd for an extract adapted from 'The Success of 20/20 Cricket' by Terry Television, published on www.crikey.com, January 2005.

In some instances we have been unable to trace the owners of copyright material, and we would appreciate any information that would enable us to do so.

Abbreviations

ABF	Australian Baseball Federation
AFL	Australian Football League
ARL	Australian Rugby League
ARU	Australian Rugby Union
ASA	Advertising Standards Authority
B2B	Business-to-business
BASIC	Business-customerising, analysing, strategising, implementing, controlling
BBC	British Broadcasting Association
BIRG	Basking in reflected glory
BRW	*Business Review Weekly*
CACI	California Analysis Center Incorporated
CAFOD	Catholic Agency for Overseas Development
CART	Championship Auto Racing Teams
CASC	Community Amateur Sports Club
CBBE	Customer-based brand equity
CCT	Compulsory competitive tendering
CEO	Chief executive officer
CIPR	Coalition for Intellectual Property Rights
CIM	Chartered Institute of Marketing
CIPR	Chartered Institute of Public Relations
CIS	Customer information systems
CORF	Cutting-off from reflected failure
CPR	Corporate public relations
CRM	Customer relationship management
DMU	Decision-making unit
EB2B	Electronic business-to-business
ECB	England and Wales Cricket Board
ETOP	Environmental Threat and Opportunity Profile
EU	European Union
F1	Formula 1
FA	Football Association
FAI	Football Association of Ireland
FC	Football club
FDI	Foreign direct investment
FFF	French Football Federation
FiC	Fixed cost
FIFA	Fédération Internationale de Football Association
GAA	Gaelic Athletic Association
GDP	Gross domestic product
GM	Gentle member

GO	Gentle organiser
IAAF	International Athletics Federation
ICNPO	International Classification of Nonprofit Organizations
IMC	Integrated Marketing Communications
IMP	Industrial Marketing and Purchasing
IOC	International Olympic Committee
IMC	Integrated marketing communications
IPR	Intellectual property rights
IRB	International Rugby Board
IRL	Indy Racing League
LPF	Liga de Futbal Profesional
MBWA	Management by walking around
MIS	Management information system
MLB	Major League Baseball
MLS	Major League Soccer
MPR	Marketing public relations
MU	Manchester United
NASCAR	National Association of Stock Car Auto Racing
NBA	National Basketball Association
NBC	National Broadcasting Corporation
NBDL	National Basketball Development League
NBL	National Basketball League
NDPB	Non-departmental public body
NFL	National Football League
NGB	National governing body
NPD	New product development
NRL	National Rugby League
NSO	National-based sporting organisation
ODI	One-day international
OEM	Original equipment manufacturer
OFT	Office of Fair Trading
PEST	Political, economic, social, technological
PESTLE	Political, economic, social, technological, legal, environmental
PLC	Product life cycle
PR	Public relations
QUANGO	Quasi-autonomous non-governmental organisation
RFC	Rugby Football Club
RFU	Rugby Football Union
RLFC	Rugby League Football Club
RM	Relationship marketing
RMT	Reward/measurement theory
ROI	Return on investment
SBU	Strategic business unit
SCA	Sustainable competitive advantage
SIMCM	Sports integrated marketing communications mix
SL	Super League
SLEPT	Social, legal, economic, political, technological
SMART	Strategic, measurable, actionable, realistic and timely

SME	Small to medium enterprise
SMPR	Sports marketing public relations
SMS	Short message service
SNCCFR	Sir Norman Chester Centre for Football Research
SNPTV	Le Syndicat National de la Publicité Télévisée
SOCOG	Sydney Organising Committee for the Olympic Games
SRI	Sponsorship Research International
SSC	State-based sporting club
SSO	State-based sporting organisation
SWOT	Strengths, weaknesses, opportunities, threats
TC	Total cost
TF	Tele France
TR	Total revenue
TVE	Television Espanola
TVS	The Virtual Sale Yard
UBA	Universal Boxing Association
UCPA	Union Nationale des Centres Sportifs de Plein Air
UEFA	Union of European Football Associations
UK	United Kingdom
US	United States
USPS	United States Postal Service
VC	Variable cost
WCCC	Worcestershire County Cricket Club
WICB	West Indies Cricket Board
WLAF	World League of American Football
WTA	Women's Tennis Association
WWE	World Wrestling Entertainment
WWF	World Wrestling Federation
WWW	World Wide Web
YOC	Youth-On-Court

General sport marketing websites

As introduction to the book and to areas of sport marketing covered by it, the reader may find the following websites a useful starting point.

Business of Sport Management Blog
http://businessofsportmanagement.blogspot.com

Business of Sport Management Companion Site
http://www.booksites.net/download/chadwickbeech/index.html

ESPN Sports Business
http://espn.go.com/sportsbusiness/index.html

European Association for Sport Management
http://www.easm.org

European Sport Management Quarterly
http://www.meyer-meyer-sports.com/en/produkte/zeitschrift/esmq.htm

International Journal of Sport Management and Marketing
https://www.inderscience.com/browse/index.php?journalID=102

International Journal of Sport Marketing and Sponsorship
http://www.imr-info.com/#goIJSM

Journal of Sport Management
http://www.humankinetics.com/products/journals/journal.cfm?id=JSM

North American Association of Sport Management
http://www.nassm.com

Sport Business International
http://www.sportbusiness.com

The Sport Journal
http://www.thesportjournal.org

Sport Management Association of Australia and New Zealand:
http://www.gu.edu.au/school/lst/services/smaanz

Sport Marketing Association
http://www.sportmarketingassociation.com

Sport Marketing Quarterly
http://www.smqonline.com

Sport Marketing Special Interest Group
http://sportmarketingsig.blogspot.com

SportQuest
http://www.sportquest.com/resources/index.html

Sports Business and Industry Online
http://www.sportsvueinc.com

Sports Business Daily
http://www.sportsbusinessdaily.com

Sports Business Journal
http://www.sportsbusinessjournal.com

Sports Business News
http://www.sportsbusinessnews.com

Part One

The distinctive nature of sport marketing

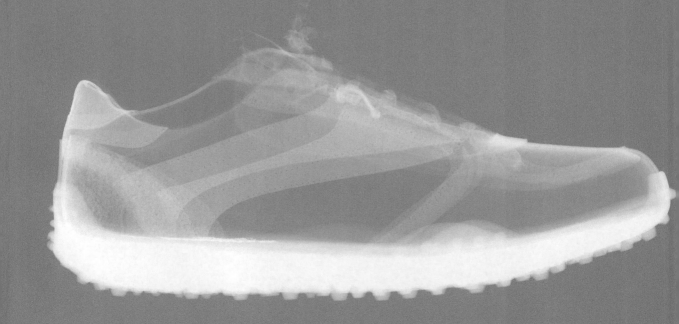

Chapter 1

Introduction: the marketing of sport

Simon Chadwick
University of London
John Beech
Coventry University

'Sport is the only entertainment where, no matter how many times you go back, you never know the ending.'

US playwright Neil Simon quoted in Pickering (2002)

Learning outcomes

Upon completion of this chapter, the reader should be able to:

- Define what is meant by sport marketing.
- Highlight the distinctive characteristics of sport marketing.
- Indicate the scope of marketing in the sport sector.
- Identify a range of challenges facing marketers in the sport sector.
- Explain the layout and structure of the book.

Overview of chapter

The chapter begins by briefly introducing the focus of the chapter and the book, and it then considers the nature of sport marketing. Of particular note at this point is the new definition of sport marketing the chapter proposes. Drawing from this definition, the example of Real Madrid is used to illustrate the range of organisations to which the definition of sport marketing applies. Given the relatively recent development of sport marketing as an area of interest, allied to some scepticism about it amongst academics and practitioners, the chapter then addresses two key issues: Firstly, it dispels some established myths about what sport marketing is and what it is supposed to do; secondly, it highlights the distinctive features of sport marketing. The chapter concludes with two case studies: Beckham mania in Japan and the continuing failure of soccer in North America.

Introduction

Pick up any newspaper or magazine, watch any sport programme on television, walk down any street across the world, and it is likely that you will be exposed to some aspect of sport marketing. Beckham, Schumacher, Kournikova, Nike, Ferrari, Vodafone and Manchester United are names that call out to consumers from billboards, adverts and countless other tools of marketing communication. The big names and the big money they are associated with have become synonymous with sport marketing and the logic amongst some in the commercial world is that, if sports and its personalities can be packaged and sold, then why not do it? But this is only one view of sport marketing because for every Beckham, there are hundreds of other individuals, teams, clubs, businesses and organisations for whom survival or scratching together enough funds to compete is an important part of what they do.

This book therefore sets out to consider the high value end of the market and addresses issues pertaining to, amongst other things, the branding, sponsorship and selling of superstars and hugely popular sports. Yet it also sets out to examine the role marketing can play in tackling, for example, the challenges faced by small sports clubs that may encounter intense local competition from a rival leisure provider and the difficulties that less popular sports may have to contend with in seeking to attract new participants or spectators. The main aim of both this chapter and this book, therefore, is to highlight both the potential for achieving commercial returns and the quest for survival that sport marketing can help to fulfil.

What is sport marketing?

Take a look at any standard marketing textbook such as Kotler, Saunders and Armstrong (2004) or Brassington and Pettitt (2002) and you will find marketing characterised as an exchange process whereby organisations work in order to meet the needs and wants of customers. Definitions of this type often also stress the importance of achieving profitability or efficiency through this process. Later definitions of marketing, such as the one provided by Gronroos (1994), are rather more seductive in the way they emphasise the importance of enduring relationships between customers and organisations. But even these definitions of marketing fail to encapsulate the essence of sport and do not differentiate sport from other products and services. Sport marketers have hardly helped themselves or the sport marketing cause either as most of the definitions (see, for example, Mullin, Hardy and Sutton, 2000; Pitts and Stotlar, 1996; Shank, 2005) generally take generic definitions to which the word 'sport' is inserted. But buying a ticket to watch a game, paying a subscription to a sports internet site or purchasing a piece of sport memorabilia is simply not the same as marketing industrial components or boxes of washing powder. If we are honest, for many people, it is not even the same as going to the theatre or donating money to charity.

The factors that make sport and sport marketing such unique phenomena are considered in detail later in this chapter, but they help in providing the background to the following definition of sport marketing:

> It is an ongoing process through which contests with an uncertain outcome are
> staged creating opportunities for the simultaneous fulfilment of direct and indirect

objectives amongst sport customers, sport businesses and other related individuals and organisations.

So what does this definition mean, and who does it refer to? The first thing to note is the use of the term uncertainty of outcome. In literature on the economics of sport, this is held as being the most fundamental appeal of sport (Dobson and Goddard, 2001). People go to watch a horse race or a tennis match because nobody really knows what is going to happen. This creates a sense of excitement and expectation that is arguably unsurpassed by any other form of human activity. Chris Waddle, an ex-England football player, once suggested that football is even better than sex! Many sports fans might well agree. Take the tension and drama away from sport, and people start to lose interest. If evidence of this is needed, look no further than what happened to Formula One during Michael Schumacher's domination of the sport. This uncertainty leads people to respond in many different ways. Some will attend sporting contests, watch sport on television or read about sport in newspapers and magazines for reasons of pure enjoyment. Others will use them as the basis for associating with success or, perversely in some cases, failure. Some will see 'their' sport as being a way that they can publicly communicate their affiliations, geographic or otherwise, and others will use sport as an expression of their values: 'I like them because of the stylish way they play.'

But the contest is not just about fans; the teams and clubs that create the contests are clearly important as well. At a basic level, there are two ways to assert the significance of the definition for them: Sports clubs and teams need spectators in order to create the excitement and tension that so many associate with watching sport. Without this, the fans will not watch and support, and they may cease to attend sporting contests. For example, the Scottish Claymores American football team recently closed because of lack of local interest in the sport. Sport organisations also need to ensure that large enough numbers of people are watching their contests in order for them to generate revenue that will enable them to survive, if not prosper. Although there may be philanthropic reasons for staging contests, marketing nevertheless serves to heighten the sense of uncertainty by ensuring they remain exciting whilst at the same time ensuring that significant numbers of people are aware of, and have access to, them. The Tour de France may be a national institution to those in France, but careful marketing of the event nevertheless helps to guarantee that an average of 1 million spectators per day watch the race from the side of the road.

For those who follow Le Tour, a characteristic of the event is that a procession called *the caravan* precedes each day's stage. This consists of official sponsors and suppliers handing out free gifts to promote their association with the event. The fact that many stages are hugely unpredictable surrounds these organisations with the same excitement as that which the spectators experience. Being associated with sport therefore enables related organisations, amongst other things, to raise awareness of their products, services and brands; to engage in the public relations activities; and to achieve the benefits of image transfer. To the list of associated organisations can be added newspapers and television companies (sport makes for great reading and viewing), corporate hospitality businesses, local and national governments, kit manufacturers and book publishers. It is then that one begins to appreciate how big an impact the staging of a sporting contest actually has. Sport, the uncertainty it brings, and sport marketing enable the fulfilment of a multitude of objectives amongst a diverse range of individuals and organisations.

The process of marketing sport is a never-ending one; whether for a year-long competition such as league soccer, a one-off event such as the Olympics or a one-day contest such as a cup final, marketers are involved in planning, executing and evaluating their activities. Added to this, maintaining relationships with fans and customers is crucial. After all, if an event only takes place, say, every 4 years, ensuring that it stays in the forefront of people's minds will be a major challenge. For marketers of, for example, the Olympics, the challenges may be even more multidimensional and longitudinal. Before they can even start marketing the event to people, they actually have to market their bid to the appropriate authorities to win the right to host the games.

Within most other definitions of sport marketing, it is implicit that they are referring directly to the commercial activities of sport organisations. Clearly, the definition provided earlier acknowledges that this is an important focus for sport marketing. But smaller and not-for-profit organisations equally benefit from more formal or professional marketing activities. For example, a governing body or voluntary organisation needs to decide to whom their service is being targeted. For example, a project aimed at addressing social exclusion uses sport as a vehicle for promoting the achievement of objectives, knowing who the beneficiaries might be, where they are, what they want and how they can be reached as just as valid marketing activities as selling basketball merchandise in new marketplaces.

To add to this, it is important to note that the definition is not just restricted to those organisations directly related to the fields and arenas where contests take place. The sport marketing domain can be thought to embrace a wide range of organisations to which sport makes a significant contribution. Following the successes of the British cycling squad at the Athens Olympics, it was widely reported that sales of bicycles increased dramatically in the month following the games. The fact that countries actually bid to host Olympic Games in the first place itself indicates how sport marketing has a much wider impact than one might imagine. The successful hosting of an event can be equated with exciting sporting contests but will also lead to the promotion of a country's image, the generation of tourism, multiplier effects on the income of local businesses and the promotion of employment.

In these terms, the domain of sport marketing can therefore be thought to embrace a wide range of organisations and activities; this is illustrated in Table 1.1.

Table 1.1 The sport marketing domain: the example of Real Madrid

Directly related	Indirectly related
▪ Fans (e.g., the people who buy their tickets at the gate on the day of a game) ▪ Individuals (e.g., David Beckham) ▪ Teams (e.g., Real Madrid) ▪ Leagues (e.g., La Liga) ▪ Competitions (e.g., Champions League) ▪ Events (e.g., a Real Madrid tour to China) ▪ Commercial partners (e.g., Siemens, Adidas) ▪ Televised sports coverage (e.g., TVE) ▪ Governing bodies (e.g., LPF)	▪ Place marketing (e.g., the city of Madrid) ▪ Local economic and social development (e.g., profitability of bars and cafes close to the Bernabau stadium) ▪ Magazines and newspapers (e.g., Don Balon) ▪ Betting and gambling services (e.g., Betandwin.com) ▪ Sportswear manufacturers [e.g., football boots (even if no one on the team actually wears or endorses them)]

Why do sport organisations need marketing?

Many people think they know what sport marketing is but probably do not really grasp the fundamental nature of it. Let us consider five of the most popular myths about sport marketing (there may be more, but these seem to be the most popular). In no particular order, they are:

Myth 1: Sport marketing is just about selling things to people

If, for instance, Sport England wanted to introduce a series of initiatives aimed at promoting the grassroots development of sport or a social inclusion agenda, the organisation would need to have a clear vision of what they were trying to achieve, how this could be introduced, to whom it would need to be directed and how the initiative could be communicated to the appropriate audience. This would require the organisation to carefully consider how to market the initiative. Nothing is being sold, no goods change hands and no one necessarily achieves a direct financial return. Some sport organisations may perceive that marketing is solely a commercial activity, but it does not have to be because it can perform a multitude of functions.

Myth 2: Sport marketing is all about putting a gloss on the commercialism and commodification of sport

It is clear that many people love sport and that sport is up against intense competition from other leisure and entertainment pursuits. Moreover, as disposable income levels rise, competition for people's spending comes equally from other goods and services such as washing machines, financial products and furniture. Marketplaces are incredibly crowded, and creating a sense that the sport product is different, if not better than products available elsewhere, is vital. Sport marketing therefore entails building a differential advantage for sport by emphasising the appeal of the core product whilst highlighting its key features. To some, this might seem like gloss, but it is actually more about maintaining the appeal and relevance of sport.

Myth 3: Sport marketing is all about 'money men' taking from supporters in order to make even more money

The first thing to dispel is that *money men* is something of a generalisation because both men and women are engaged in marketing and sport. The purpose of any business is to make money. If a business is not profitable, it will ultimately cease to trade. Industry in general is littered with high-profile examples of such businesses, and sport is no exception (think of, say, the Arrows Formula One team). Marketing therefore contributes to the activities of many sport businesses, helping them maximise the revenue they earn from the products they sell. There is a view that this can be exploitative, but some sport organisations are increasingly receptive to the power of the consumer. For example, Manchester United has placed a customer service charter on their website. This details the minimum standards of service that customers can expect from them. At the same time, the regulatory authorities across a number of countries are working to prevent fans and customers from being exploited, England's Football

Task Force being one example. But above all, marketing is not simply about selling people things they do not want. Rather, marketing entails a process of trying to understand the needs and wants of the marketplace and then producing goods and services that satisfy either actual or latent demand.

Myth 4: Sport marketing is all about leading customers to believe things that sometimes are not true

If one thinks about attending, say, a rugby match one evening in the middle of winter when the rain is falling and the temperature is plummeting, the uninformed may well question the role that marketing plays in sport. No matter how much one might try to 'gloss over' it, watching the game is likely to be a cold, wet experience. But at one level, there may be certain sports fans who enjoy such an experience, and this may form the basis for maintaining and developing this type of contest. The essence of sport marketing is to try to identify whether or not this is the case. If people want something different, trying to convince them that what is currently on offer would be difficult, in which case, developing the product by, for example, providing better facilities would be one role that marketing could perform. Otherwise, the task of the sport marketer might be to make fundamental changes to the product on offer by, for example, moving games to times and locations more conducive to better conditions and bigger crowds.

Myth 5: Sport marketing is a corruption of the purity of sport

If anything, sport marketing is about celebrating the purity of sport. At a time when people's spending patterns are changing, the need for sport organisations to continue being relevant to people's lives is of paramount importance. With higher incomes at their disposal, consumers are faced with an ever-increasing array of leisure goods and services. If sport is to retain its appeal, ensuring it is one of the first spending choices in the minds of consumers is one of the most important functions that sport marketing serves.

What is so distinctive about sport marketing?

The main purpose of this book is to examine the distinctive nature of sport marketing. In so doing, it will implicitly differentiate between sport organisations and products and organisations and products found in other industrial sectors. The definition of sport marketing presented above is intended to encapsulate the differences, but the specific nature of sport and sport organisations means that marketers working within such organisations variously face a number of unique challenges. These are explored below.

Sport is product led

Many sport organisations are currently product led. This means the focus and success of the marketing effort off the field of play is largely determined by what happens on it. This often leads to players and teams dominating what happens in sport organisations rather than fans and customers necessarily having a major influence on marketing.

■ Sport is all about the uncertainty of outcome

This is the core of the sport product and is one of the main reasons why so many people are motivated to consume sport. The uncertainty of outcome induces levels of excitement, stress, emotion and tension rarely, if ever, associated with the repeated purchase of other products. Just how the uncertainty of outcome and the associated *experience* can be marketed is one of the crucial challenges that sport marketers face. Allied to this are the related challenges concerning how sport marketers should set about marketing the tangible, augmented and potential sport products (see Chapter 9 for more details).

■ Sport customers help to produce the product

Visit a supermarket, purchase a financial services product or ask an engineer to install a component for you – it does not really matter who else is there, if anyone, or what they look like or how they sound. Contrast this with sport; soccer is a great game, and some of us might derive immense pleasure from attending a game, even if nobody else is present. But the essence of sport for many people is the atmosphere and excitement generated by other people around them. It is good to win a game by a huge margin, but it is even better if you are watching it with friends, family or other supporters. The marketing of sport is therefore unique in the way that the presence of other customers is a vital element of the product and of the consumption experience. Thus, the individual is of paramount importance in sport marketing, simultaneously representing both a target and a fundamental element of sport marketing.

■ Sport organisations sometimes adopt a strange approach to marketing

Across the world every weekend there are probably thousands, if not millions, of sporting contests watched by small numbers of fans in under-utilised stadia. Why? In most sports, ticket sales constitute the most important source of revenue. To be a net generator of revenue, it would therefore seem obvious that clubs and teams should market themselves more effectively to increase crowd sizes and sell more tickets. Sadly, many sports do not, for example, reduce ticket prices, target particular groups or advertise on television in order to promote attendance at games. Sport marketing is not a panacea for all the ailments of sport, but it could help go part of the way towards a cure for some of them. At the same time, a 'fill your corporate boxes, sell space on your perimeter advertising boards' mentality pervades many sports. Each year there is a consequent dash for cash, the end result of which is that the marketing manager either remains in employment or has their contract of employment terminated. This indicates that the off-field marketing activities of some sport organisations are actually sales driven. But this does nothing to sustain revenue or relationships with partners. Instead of offering high-quality facilities to the corporate market by working with them to understand their needs and deliver appealing products, some sport organisations simply sell space in their boxes 'because it is there' and has to be filled. As any competent marketer will acknowledge, this is an opportunity missed, something certain sport organisations continue to do.

Sport products are socially and culturally embedded

Sport generates a degree of fervour unheard of in relation to other products. One commentator is reputed to have claimed that Tesco customers (the United Kingdom's leading supermarket chain) never ask for their ashes to be spread down the aisles of their local stores (one service many English football clubs now offer is that people, when they die, can arrange for their ashes to be spread on the pitch of the favourite team). The sociocultural basis of most sports is such that it presents strongly distinctive challenges that marketers of other products do not face. Amongst these challenges are the unswerving loyalty that many fans have for their teams and clubs, the parental and peer influences on consumption and the role that geographic identity plays in influencing consumption behaviour. Unlike other products, sport is thus often consumed in an irrational, rather than a rational, economic way. Logic tells us that if a product continually fails to live up to expectations, people will stop buying it. In sport, this logic does not always hold.

Sport businesses have limited control over their products

Given that the uncertainty of outcome is at the heart of sport, the principle focus for sport marketers therefore becomes how to preserve and develop it. As the example of Xtreme football shows (Willoughby, 2003), sports fans nevertheless value the maintenance of established rules and formats in their sport (when US authorities announced that they wanted to increase the size of the goals for the 1994 World Cup so that more goals would be scored – thus making easier to market soccer in the United States – there was an outcry in other parts of the world). This limits how much sport marketers can therefore adapt and change the sporting contest. Moreover, in addition to the raft of rules that inevitably applies to all organisations, the appeal of sport is further regulated by specific criteria that apply to promotion and relegation, player acquisition and the format of a game or match. If, for example, a team gets relegated from a league, literally overnight the nature of the team's marketing is likely to be influenced in a way other businesses are not routinely exposed to.

Sport measures performance in different ways

Marketers working in most for-profit organisations are likely to have their performance measured in terms of, for example, increased market share or a growth in sales. Amongst not-for-profit marketers, measures such as promoting charitable contributions or raising participation may alternatively be important. But in sport, the acid test for most organisations is 'Did we win the league?' In part, such judgements are bound up in the product orientation of the organisations concerned, although what this does is to effectively relegate traditional measures of marketing success to be of only secondary importance. After all, do most sports fans really care about market share in China if their team has just won a play-off final? In one sense, this does make the job of the sport marketer a more difficult one, although one purpose of this book is to help ensure that sport organisations, their employees and the customers who buy from them can ultimately establish the link between on-field achievements and off-field performance.

■ Sport has unique relationships with broadcasters and the media

In some respects, one might argue that sport organisations do not need to market themselves; they should just let others do it for them. Indeed, certain sport organisations actually take this view; for example, why spend on advertising when television channels, newspapers and websites effectively do your advertising for you? If you open a daily newspaper, it is likely that you will be faced with a multitude of sport stories, factual, salacious and otherwise. The role and importance of 'the media' should not therefore be underestimated because it is instrumental in helping to create the tension and excitement surrounding the sport product. Moreover, the media has generated a range of additional opportunities for sport organisations through, for instance, the promotion of sponsorship deals and endorsement packages. This makes sport unlike any other industry we know (with the possible exception of films and music). However, one lesson that sport marketers need to learn is that leaving the media to do your marketing for you cedes control of how your product is presented and packaged to corporations, some of which may be located thousands of miles away. Taking a more active role both in fostering and managing relations with the media and marketing sport beyond this relationship are important tasks that many sport marketers have yet to seriously address.

■ Sports fans are unlikely to purchase products from a rival sport organisation

If one was to ask a fan of the Boca Juniors soccer team, 'Would you buy a River Plate replica shirt or apply for a River Plate credit card?' the answer is predictable. This line of questioning might even turn nasty if you continued with it. In the same vein, when Kevin Keegan (then manager of the Newcastle United soccer team) appeared in an English television advertisement for a breakfast cereal, sales of the product in Sunderland (great local rivals of Newcastle, their stadiums little more than 10 miles apart) reputedly fell dramatically. What does this tell us about sport marketing and the challenges it faces? Clearly, marketing products associated with one club or team probably means the product will be viewed as undesirable by rival fans. This implies that many sport organisations are likely to have strongly constrained and geographically defined marketplaces. For some, this is likely to restrict their development. For others, it may mean the marketing effort has to, for example, adopt an international focus or use a brand name and image completely different to that of the parent. With the possible exception of consumers who have strong national motives for buying products ('we only ever buy from producers in our home country'), this again sets sport and sport marketing apart from the marketing of other products.

■ Sport marketers face organisational obstacles to their acceptance

Sport is ultimately about individuals and teams engaging in a contest, it is not about the internal structure and competence of the organisations responsible for delivering sport products, at least not to fans and other customers. The problem is that some of the people working in sport appear to take a similar view. As such, marketing is an undeveloped activity in certain sports, so the competence of some sport marketers is questionable. Indeed, in certain cases, ex-players serve as the marketers. Although this is not in itself a problem, it sometimes promotes a highly introspective agenda, meaning that clubs and teams continue to think more about the players and performers than they do about their customers. Thus, raising awareness of the need for and the components of sport marketing is an important step forward that many sport organisations need to take.

Sport organisations underestimate the power and value of their brands

Go to Barcelona and ask a fan, 'What does your soccer club mean to you?' and the fan will probably tell you it is a symbol of Catalan resistance, a statement against the centralised control of a Madrid-based government – a way of life. What this person is unlikely to say is that the Barcelona brand is a highly visible one with a good reputation that they trust implicitly to provide a high-quality sport product. This is *brand speak*; although some people are appalled at the reduction of 'their team' to little more than a brand, a commodity to be exploited, there is little doubt that names such as the *All Blacks* and *McLaren F1* are incredibly powerful, evoking images and responses amongst customers in a way that other brands simply fail to do (whether one's purchase of a box of soap powder can ever approach the emotion of watching your favourite team score a goal is not really open to discussion). There has been a consequent growth in the recognition that sports brands are highly valuable and can be used to generate new income streams for sports clubs. It would be easy to dismiss this as being exploitative, but sport has cost burdens (e.g., player salary costs) that other organisations do not face; such organisations have to cover these somehow. But this needs to be set in the context of cultures where sports fans often react with suspicion and distain when faced with 'commercial exploitation' of sports brands. Balancing diverse interests is an important challenge for sport marketers, the loyalty of fans to their 'brands' strongly emphasising the ethical influences upon sport marketers.

Sport organisations can suffer from marketing myopia

The beauty and appeal of the sporting contest is one that probably attracted the people working within sport organisations and their customers to sport in the first place. But this can often blind both to the problems and frailties of the goods and services with which they are both sometimes associated. Therefore, addressing the specific nature of the sport product may sometimes be neglected. Added to this is the unswerving loyalty that many fans have to their team or their sport. Sport marketers may thus tend to be a little blasé when considering the scale of the marketing challenges they face. But most starkly of all, sport marketers can be myopic in the way they fail to account for the broader impact of leisure trends and, indeed, general market changes. As we have already stated, sport competes for the leisure pound, dollar, Euro or whatever, and sport marketers should embrace and respond to this notion if sport is to retain its appeal.

Sport organisations have a strange relationship with other organisations

Established associations with the 'on-field' contest stress the importance of aggression, strength, confrontation and battles. Without these characteristics, sport would not be half as interesting. Think about some of the classic all-time sporting contests: Prost and Senna, Ali and Frazier, Navratilova and Evert. The problem sport marketing currently faces is that many sport organisations have transferred the values of these contests into their off-field operations. In such cases, their cultures are characterised by secrecy, competitiveness and aggression. Clearly, this happens in other sectors as well, particularly when money and/or politics are involved. But where it is most tangible in sport is in the area of collaboration; that is, working in partnership with other organisations to create some sort of advantage for both. A good illustration of this is the relationships that often develop between sponsors and sponsees. Too often a sponsor will approach sponsee, negotiate a deal, the sponsee will then take the money on offer, the sponsor will get its name on, say, a team strip, and so the relationship ends. The sponsor becomes unhappy because they never really are able to secure the full advantages of such a relationship, and the sponsee gets locked into a series of short-term relationships, lurching from one sponsor to another without ever really addressing why. As both the academic literature and practitioners acknowledge, for 21st century organisations to be successful, they must collaborate to compete. Many sport organisations have yet to fully embrace this notion.

What is the down side to sport marketing?

Some commentators seem to think that sport marketing does not exist or that it is irrelevant, unnecessary, a fad or largely the domain of rampant capitalists more interested in money than sport. Think of your favourite World Cup or the joy of seeing your team win a battle with a fierce rival: Does sport really need marketing? Surely it markets itself? Alternatively, think about the NBA, the Ferrari F1 team or Real Madrid. These organisations have nothing to do with sport; they are money-making machines, aren't they? Such observations result in some people thinking that sport cannot be subjected to the same pressures as other organisations; that marketing is divisive, leading to the polarisation of sport organisations; that it is a waste of time and money; that it is nothing more than gloss and so lacks meaning and substance; and that it exploits clubs, players and fans, thereby polluting the purity of sport. Such views are somewhat outdated, inaccurate and inevitably do little to further the development of sport marketing. Moreover, they perpetuate a particular view of sport marketing that is often based more on myth than on reality. This book intends to address and rectify such a view. Sport marketing can be an activity in which large global corporations engage. But it can equally be something upon which grassroots sport organisations, government initiatives, less popular sports or even amateur sports focus their efforts – in some cases, to grow and prosper, and in other cases, simply to survive. In other words, sport marketing is about ensuring that sport remains popular and relevant to fans just as much as it is about making money.

Overview of the book

The book is organised around six themes into which chapters individually fall (Figure 1.1). The first theme (covering Chapters 1–3) establishes the nature of sport marketing and addresses some of the main contextual factors that influence how marketing is

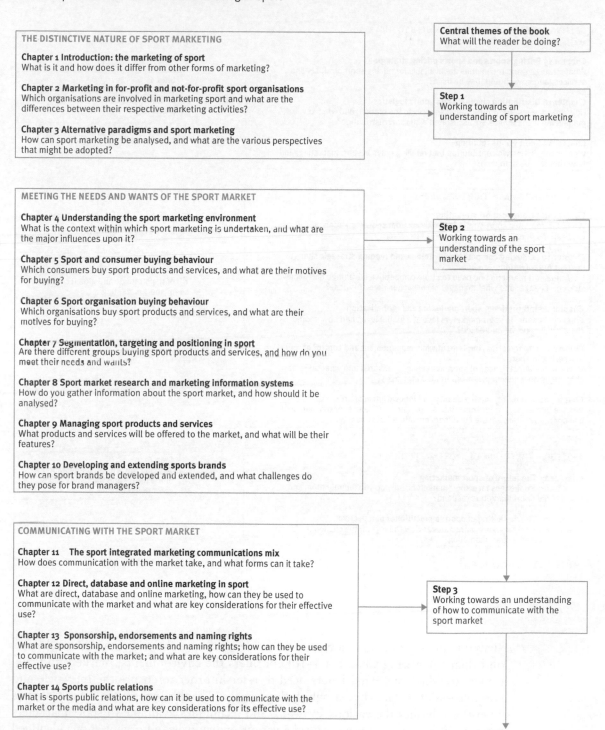

THE DISTINCTIVE NATURE OF SPORT MARKETING

Chapter 1 Introduction: the marketing of sport
What is it and how does it differ from other forms of marketing?

Chapter 2 Marketing in for-profit and not-for-profit sport organisations
Which organisations are involved in marketing sport and what are the differences between their respective marketing activities?

Chapter 3 Alternative paradigms and sport marketing
How can sport marketing be analysed, and what are the various perspectives that might be adopted?

MEETING THE NEEDS AND WANTS OF THE SPORT MARKET

Chapter 4 Understanding the sport marketing environment
What is the context within which sport marketing is undertaken, and what are the major influences upon it?

Chapter 5 Sport and consumer buying behaviour
Which consumers buy sport products and services, and what are their motives for buying?

Chapter 6 Sport organisation buying behaviour
Which organisations buy sport products and services, and what are their motives for buying?

Chapter 7 Segmentation, targeting and positioning in sport
Are there different groups buying sport products and services, and how do you meet their needs and wants?

Chapter 8 Sport market research and marketing information systems
How do you gather information about the sport market, and how should it be analysed?

Chapter 9 Managing sport products and services
What products and services will be offered to the market, and what will be their features?

Chapter 10 Developing and extending sports brands
How can sport brands be developed and extended, and what challenges do they pose for brand managers?

COMMUNICATING WITH THE SPORT MARKET

Chapter 11   The sport integrated marketing communications mix
How does communication with the market take, and what forms can it take?

Chapter 12 Direct, database and online marketing in sport
What are direct, database and online marketing, how can they be used to communicate with the market and what are key considerations for their effective use?

Chapter 13 Sponsorship, endorsements and naming rights
What are sponsorship, endorsements and naming rights; how can they be used to communicate with the market; and what are key considerations for their effective use?

Chapter 14 Sports public relations
What is sports public relations, how can it be used to communicate with the market or the media and what are key considerations for its effective use?

Central themes of the book
What will the reader be doing?

Step 1
Working towards an understanding of sport marketing

Step 2
Working towards an understanding of the sport market

Step 3
Working towards an understanding of how to communicate with the sport market

Figure 1.1 **Structure of *The Marketing of Sport***

GETTING SPORT PRODUCTS AND SERVICES TO THE
MARKET

Chapter 15 Pricing sports and sports pricing strategies
What strategies and techniques are available for pricing sport products and
services, and how should they be used?

Chapter 16 Distribution channels and sports logistics
How do you get sport products and services to the market, and what key
management challenges are associated with sport distribution?

Chapter 17 Sport goods retailing
What is the distinctive contribution that retailing plays in sport marketing, and
how should it be managed?

Step 4
Working towards an understanding
of how to price and distribute sport
products and services

MOVING SPORT MARKETING FORWARDS

Chapter 18 Strategic sport marketing
What differentiates sport strategic marketing from sport marketing, and what
implications does this have for the sport marketer?

**Chapter 19 Achieving competitive advantage and leading strategic change
in sport organisations**
How can sport marketing be used to attain competitive advantage and achieve
strategic change, and what managerial challenges does this pose?

Chapter 20 International sport marketing and globalisation
What challenges do sport marketers face at a global level, and how should
these challenges be addressed?

**Chapter 21 Organisation, implementation, management and control of
marketing in sport**
How can the effectiveness of sport marketing be ensured and what tasks or
challenges does this imply the sport marketer faces?

Chapter 22 Managing service quality and innovation in sport
What is quality, how does this relate to sport products and services, and how
can sport marketers ensure customers are offered best quality?

Step 5
Working towards an understanding
of the strategic and global contexts
of sport marketing

ASSESSING THE FUTURE OF SPORT MARKETING

Chapter 23 The future of sport marketing
What future challenges face sport marketers, how do you identify them and
how should sport marketers respond?

Chapter 24 The marketing of sport: a practitioner perspective
How does a sport marketing practitioner view the role of, the challenges facing
and the future for sport marketing?

Step 6
Working towards an understanding
of the future and the reality facing
sport marketers

Figure 1.1 *(continued)*

viewed in different organisations and the influence this can have on marketers. The second theme (covering Chapters 4–10) considers the environments, markets and customers to which sport marketers need to refer in order to ensure the relevance and
effectiveness of the activities in which they engage. The third theme (covering Chapters
11–14) establishes the various strategies and techniques available to sport marketers
when aiming to communicate with the various individuals and organisations identified
by the second theme of the book. The fourth theme (covering Chapters 15–17) examines how sport products can be priced and distributed to the sport marketplace. The
fifth theme (covering Chapters 18–22) adopts a managerial focus and considers some
of the operational, strategic and global challenges facing sport marketers. Finally, the
sixth theme (covering Chapters 23 and 24) predicts what the future will hold for sport

marketing whilst offering a practitioner perspective of sport marketing, both now and in the future.

After the introduction provided by this chapter, the book goes on in Chapter 2 to compare and contrast the differences in sport marketing between organisations such as Adidas, which have a 'for-profit' orientation and those that operate on a 'not-for-profit' basis such as UK Sport. The theoretical underpinnings to sport marketing are then considered in Chapter 3, including an examination of the differences between different paradigms, such as relationship marketing (a perspective associated with, for instance, the development of fan loyalty schemes).

Chapter 4 sets the environmental context within which sport marketers work and explores some of the numerous factors (e.g., the internet, government policy and social trends) that influence the work that sport marketers do. Amongst the most important influences for any sport organisation are the fans who buy tickets, the customers who buy merchandise and the participants who become members of sports clubs. Chapter 5 examines the motives and behaviour of these people, and then Chapter 6 provides a contrast between this and the motives and behaviour of some of the organisations (suppliers, sponsors, media corporations) with which sport does business. As, say, an event attendee, a television viewer or an ardent collector of sports memorabilia, different people behave in different ways and have different expectations. Chapter 7 therefore establishes the importance of segmentation strategies for sport marketers and establishes how products and services can be positioned to appeal to different customers. How we know what these customers want, where they are and how much they are prepared to pay depend upon the data and intelligence sport organisations have collected. The need for gathering such information and the ways in which it can be collected subsequently form the basis for Chapter 8. As soon as sport marketers have this information, whether it is from a questionnaire or from a record of sport website hits, a key decision will be how to develop appropriate products and services that serve the needs and expectations of different groups. Chapter 9 examines the product management process, and Chapter 10 looks at how existing sports brands can be introduced into new markets or used to create new products.

Although sponsorships and endorsements are routinely associated with sport, they are only two of a number of different techniques that sport marketers can use to communicate with their various markets and stakeholders. Chapter 11 therefore works through the marketing communications mix, highlighting how sport marketers can use, amongst other things, public relations. A further element of the communications mix, direct marketing, is examined in Chapter 12, and this is directly linked to the use by marketers of sport websites and the collection of fan data. Whether through an association with a sport celebrity, the naming of a stadium or the placement of a company name on a team shirt, sponsorships, endorsements and naming rights attract attention and money at all levels of sport. A discussion of motivation, management and evaluation of these activities appears in Chapter 13. A final element of the communications mix, and one to which almost all people are exposed – newspaper stories, press conferences and personal appearances – receives attention in Chapter 14 on public relations, marketing and the media in sport.

Buying tickets to a sporting contest normally means paying different prices depending upon when you buy, where you sit and what you expect to receive for the price. These issues, along with others pertaining to, for example, the pricing of merchandise, appear in Chapter 15. How sport organisations get their products and services to the market, whether it is an online sports information service providing data or a motor sports team selling racing jackets, forms the basis for an analysis of distribution and logistics in Chapter 16. This links in closely to an examination of sports retailing in Chapter 17, which relates to the activities of outlets.

The long-term nature of sport marketing, in which sport organisations establish how they want their product or service to develop, is a strategic decision that requires fundamental decisions to be made by those involved. The nature of strategic marketing is examined in Chapter 18, which is followed in Chapter 19 by an analysis of how sport marketing can help in achieving competitive advantage over rival organisations or in instigating a programme of strategic change within a sport organisation. Many of today's pressing strategic questions have a strongly, although not exclusively, international context. Chapter 20 thus considers the international challenges facing sport marketers. Whether internationally or nationally, the good ideas that sport marketers have about, for example, branding or pricing have to be put into action. The focus of Chapter 21 is an examination of how sport marketers can organise, implement, manage and control their strategies and tactics. In so doing, one of the most important considerations for sport marketers is the need to maintain and improve the standard of products and services. Linking this to the process of innovation, Chapter 22 establishes and explains the importance of service quality management.

In the concluding section of the book, Chapter 23 reflects upon the content of this book and considers some of the lessons of it, as well as speculating on some of the likely developments in sport marketing in the future. The chapter is given resonance by Chapter 24 in which a leading practitioner dissects the reality of being a sport marketer.

An overall structure for the book, indicating the themes and chapters, is presented in Figure 1.1.

CASE 1.1 **In a red shirt or white, Japan just can't get enough of Bekkamu Sama**

Young female pilgrims have for months been worshipping at a 3m-high chocolate shrine of David Beckham in Tokyo's fashionable Shibuya district. Yesterday they got to see the real thing. Hundreds of fans, some already decked out in Real Madrid shirts, greeted Victoria and David – or Bekkamu Sama as he is sometimes reverentially called– as the couple arrived at Tokyo's Narita airport for a promotional tour of Japan.

Beckham, who boarded his flight to Japan a Manchester United player but left it as a Real Madrid all-star, will spend the next three days shooting commercials and attending press events. In Japan, news that the multi-hairdoed soccer sensation had moved clubs played a distinct second fiddle to what, after his World Cup success, was treated like a Second Coming. The change from Manchester to Madrid may be dramatic in Europe, but in Japan, Beckham's fame towers above either club. In a few months, he has single-handedly rebranded J-Phone to Vodafone.

As well as telephones, Beckham is the Japanese face of TBC Salons, which beautifies brides-to-be. He also sponsors Meiji Seika, the confectioner that erected the giant chocolate statue of the footballer as part of its promotion of Almond Choco sweets.

Beckham has been larger-than-life in Japan since last year's World Cup when he converted hoards of female fans to England's (ultimately doomed) cause, and sent thousands of others scurrying to hair salons for his exotic Mohican hair cut.

Sales of Manchester United shirts rocketed, and have peaked again in the run-up to this week's tour, according to World Sports Plaza, a retail chain. It now expects a surge in sales of the white shirts of Real Madrid and a gathering of dust over the red of Manchester United. Soccer fan Masanori Okutomi, who works for an advertising agency, says Beckham's profile is made for Japan. 'There is nothing negative about him. He's a good player, behaves well with his family and has the image of being a good father and husband. That's great for marketing.' Yoshie Izumi, who works at a television company, says: 'I saw him play and I just thought: "Wow, he's cute." I used a picture of him in a bathing suit as my PC screen-saver.' She is unfazed by his Spanish odyssey. 'Who cares if he plays in Manchester or Madrid. He's still sexy.'

Source: D. Pilling and B. Rahman, *Financial Times*, 19 June 2003

Questions

1. Identify and explain how the Beckham phenomenon relates to the definition of sport marketing presented in this chapter.

2. Is Beckham's profile the consequence of sport marketing, sport-related marketing or something else?

3. How else might sport marketers use Beckham or other comparable sport stars to market products and services?

CASE 1.2 Star US Soccer League struggles to shake-off its second-rate image

It was purely by coincidence, of course, that Saturday saw Manchester United square off in New York against AC Milan while in Washington DC Major League Soccer was holding its annual All-Star Game.

But it was also ironic that two of Europe's finest clubs should meet in a preseason friendly on US soil at exactly the moment the best players in America's showcase league were competing in a midseason exhibition. That is because European teams are increasingly looking across the Atlantic with covetous eyes and raiding the fledgling US league for talent. MLS officials insist they are flattered; they have good reason to be flattered, but also to be worried.

The most notable defection to date is Tim Howard, who was in goal for Manchester United during Saturday's loss (on penalties) to AC Milan. Howard joined the Red Devils in 2003 after five years with the New York MetroStars. A number of MLS standouts have made the leap to the European leagues in the past year.

Just last week, DaMarcus Beasley of the Chicago Fire and Bobby Convey of DC United, both members of the national team (as is Howard), were signed by PSV Eindhoven and Reading, respectively.

This could also be the last season in MLS for Landon Donovan, the gifted 22-year-old midfielder for the San Jose Earthquakes. Donovan, who already has 51 caps for the US and two MLS championships to his credit, was loaned to San Jose just over three years ago by Leverkusen, which sent him home to gain added experience but now evidently believes he is ready for the Bundesliga and wants him back.

That MLS now recognised as an excellent incubator of talent is a good thing, but this is not really the role that was envisioned for the league, which began play nine years ago and was created as a condition for the US being awarded the 1994 World Cup. Given the league's shoestring budget (players are paid by the league rather than individual teams) and relatively low profile, it was probably inevitable that MLS would struggle to hold on to some of its marquee attractions. But the league's founders had far greater ambitions for it than merely serving as a farm system for Europe's top leagues.

MLS has a problem on two fronts. Soccer remains a tough sell in the US; most Americans are simply not interested in the sport, and this will likely never change. MLS is at present averaging around 16,000 spectators per game, which is an improvement over its early days but certainly nothing to boast of. However, it is not just the soccer-phobic majority that is depressing attendance figures; it may also be that Americans who actually enjoy soccer have become jaded about the kind of soccer they are willing to watch and do not believe MLS is worth their time and money.

In the decade since it hosted the World Cup, the US has enjoyed unprecedented access to soccer at the highest level. Every World Cup game is now broadcast; Champions League games are shown regularly and, for those couch potatoes willing to pay a supplement, scores of Premiership matches are also on offer. Then there are the annual visits by big European clubs. Last summer, AC Milan, Barcelona, Juventus and Manchester United toured; this summer, it has been Manchester United, AC Milan, Bayern Munich and Celtic.

There is certainly evidence to suggest that Americans who like soccer have grown a little finicky. Saturday's MLS All-Star Game drew just 21,000 spectators; by contrast, 74,000 fans filled the Giants Stadium to watch Man U against AC Milan.

Then there is the Freddy Adu Effect. Adu is the 15-year-old wunderkind now in his rookie season with DC United. Although Adu still spends significant time on the bench, there is clearly a sense among fans that he is from a slightly different mould than other MLS players and destined for greatness. He has thus become a big draw, boosting attendance for United road games by 40 per cent and the team's television ratings by around 50 per cent.

Adu was signed to a four-year deal paying him $500,000 (£274,000) annually, the league's most lucrative contract. In opening its cheque book, the league recognised that it could ill afford not to employ the services of the most touted soccer prodigy the US has yet produced. But even with Adu, MLS is still seen as a second-rate product, and losing players such as Howard, Beasley and Convey only reinforces that impression. Moreover, MLS, which currently has 10 teams, will be adding four more clubs over the next two years, which will stretch the remaining talent even thinner. Of course, given how difficult it has been for soccer to establish a foothold in the US, these are probably not the worst growing pains MLS could be experiencing.

Source: M. Steinberger, *Financial Times*, 3 August 2004

Questions

1. What are the challenges facing the marketers of soccer in the United States?

2. To what extent can sport marketing help to spread the popularity of soccer to North America?

3. What practical measures would you recommend in order to create interest in soccer in the United States?

Conclusions

The diversity amongst 21st century sport organisations is stark. At one extreme, there are sport businesses that actually seem more like multiproduct global leisure brands than basketball teams or football clubs. They are motivated by commercial considerations and operate on a global scale. At the other extreme, there are small and not-for-profit sport organisations that work more closely with the community, are not overtly commercial and have yet to embrace either the managerialism or commercialism evident in the higher echelons of sport. But one thing unites the two extremes: the need to marketing themselves effectively. Whether an organisation operates a small professional cycling team in Belgium, a rugby league team in New Zealand or a basketball club in China, the need to consider the requirements of the marketplace is paramount. The world is an increasingly complex place, and consumers are becoming ever-more sophisticated. As a result, although the romanticism of many sport's histories remains seductive, the reality is that sport organisations increasingly face pressures from, amongst other things, rival leisure products such as cinema, theme parks and even shopping. Sport marketing can be aimed at achieving a commercial return (just think of examples such as the Dallas Cowboys or Manchester United), but it is also about ensuring that all sport organisations and the products they offer are distinctive, desirable and successful. This is when sport marketing comes into its own: Sport is unique, and if marketing means that it continues to be so, then long may it continue.

Discussion questions

1. 'Sport marketing is a necessary evil.' Discuss this statement, referring to examples of when you think sport marketing has been appropriately and inappropriately used.

2. Using a sport business of your choice, chart the development of how this business has used marketing over the past 25 years, providing a commentary on how the marketing strategies and techniques this business has used have changed during this period.
3. To what extent do you think the marketing of sport is any different from the marketing of the arts or charitable causes? What challenges does this pose for those involved in marketing sport?
4. Select either a major international sport star, sport team or sport business and critically evaluate the contribution marketing has made to their achievements, both on and off the field.

Guided reading

As a starting point, the reader may want to refer to *The Business of Sport Management* edited by Beech and Chadwick (2004). This contains chapters on sport marketing, sports sponsorship and endorsements and e-managing sport customers. In support of this book, further readings and cases appropriate to these chapters are presented in both the supporting book website and the Business of Sport Management Blog. Otherwise, the reader's attention is drawn to three journals, all of which have a strong sport marketing focus: the *International Journal of Sport Marketing and Sponsorship*, *Sport Marketing Quarterly* and the *International Journal of Sport Management and Marketing*. Otherwise, reviews of the literature undertaken by Shannon (1999), Pitts (2002) and Chadwick (2003) provide a strong overview of research thus far undertaken in sport marketing. The reader is also referred to the accompanying website to this book for further web links and case material.

Keywords

Affiliations; audience; brands; collaborate; competitive advantage; context; direct marketing; distribution; fans; for-profit; logistics; market share; motivation; motives; not-for-profit; objectives; prices; pricing; product management; products; public relations; relationship marketing; retailing; segmentation; services; spectators; sponsorship; sport marketing; sport marketing domain; sport product; stakeholders; strategic change; strategies; uncertainty of outcome; value.

Bibliography

Beech, J. and Chadwick, S. (2004) *The Business of Sport Management*, Harlow: FT Prentice Hall.

Brassington, F. and Pettitt, S. (2002) *Principles of Marketing*, Harlow: FT Prentice Hall.

Chadwick, S. (2003) Whither sport marketing? Establishing the need for a European research focus, *Proceedings of the 16th Services Marketing Workshop*, Liverpool: Liverpool University Management School, pp. 45–50.

Dobson, S. and Goddard, J. (2001) *The Economics of Football,* Cambridge: Cambridge University Press.

Gronroos, C. (1994) From marketing mix to relationship marketing. Towards a paradigm shift in marketing, *Management Decision* 32(2): 4–20.

Kotler, P., Saunders, J. and Armstrong, G. (2004) *Principles of Marketing: European Edition*, Harlow: FT Prentice Hall.

Mullin, B., Hardy, S. and Sutton, W.A. (2000) *Sport Marketing*, Leeds: Human Kinetics Europe.

Pickering, D. (2002) *Cassell's Sports Quotations*, London: Cassell and Co.

Pitts, B. (2002) Examining sport management scholarship: An historical review of the *Sport Marketing Quarterly*, *Sport Marketing Quarterly* 11(2):84–92.

Pitts, B.G. and Stotlar, D.K. (1996) *Fundamentals of Sport Marketing*, Morgantown, WV: Fitness Information Technology.

Shank, M.D. (2005) *Sports Marketing – A Strategic Perspective,* Upper Saddle River, NJ: FT Prentice Hall.

Shannon, J.R. (1999) Sports marketing: An examination of academic marketing publication, *Journal of Services Marketing* 13(6):517–35.

Willoughby, K. (2003) The inaugural (and only) season of the Xtreme Football League: A case study in sports entertainment, *International Journal of Sport Marketing and Sponsorship*, October:227–35.

Recommended websites

Business of Sport Management Blog
http://businessofsportmanagement.blogspot.com/

Business of Sport Management Companion site
http://www.booksites.net/download/chadwickbeech/index.html

International Journal of Sport Management and Marketing
https://www.inderscience.com/browse/index.php?journalID=102

International Journal of Sport Marketing and Sponsorship
http://www.imr-info.com/#goIJSM

Sport Marketing Quarterly
http://www.smqonline.com/

Sport Marketing Special Interest Group
http://sportmarketingsig.blogspot.com/

Chapter 2

Marketing in for-profit and not-for-profit sport organisations

Paul Turner
Deakin University

Learning outcomes

Upon completion of this chapter, the reader should be able to:

■ Identify the marketing issues that apply to for-profit and not-for-profit sport organisations.

■ Develop an awareness and appreciation of the components of a range of small, medium and large sport enterprises through understanding the revenue or resource implications associated with each type of organisation.

■ Identify the characteristics of for-profit from the not-for-profit sport organisations.

■ Identify the wide range of sport organisation objectives that can be achieved through marketing for-profit and not-for-profit sport organisations.

■ Highlight important issues relating to marketing activities applicable to for-profit and not-for-profit sport organisations.

Overview of chapter

This chapter provides a framework for analysis relating to three major types of sport organisations; the small-to-medium (SME) not-for-profit enterprise, the larger revenue-generating or resource-plentiful not-for-profit sporting organisation and the private or public owned for-profit sporting organisation. Issues that affect the makeup of each organisational type are identified and reviewed. These issues encompass the range of marketing activities and influences that are encountered by each category of sport organisation. The impact of the marketing strategy employed by these organisations is identified through their environment, research, segmentation and targeting approaches undertaken. This approach to marketing is further developed through a review of the marketing mix attributes applicable to each sporting organisation type.

A definition and explanation of the terms *for-profit* and *not-for-profit* will be undertaken, including the linking of the theme of marketing as it applies to these types of organisations. The methods employed through sport organisations' marketing campaigns can be wide-ranging depending upon their profit (revenue or resource) position. These differences are examined and addressed through focusing on the core marketing attributes applicable to each particular organisational framework.

Introduction

The distinction between the not-for-profit and for-profit sectors is made here. Although many of the tools and techniques commonly used in commercial marketing practice are equally applicable to the not-for-profit realm, the ethos that drives their application can be considerably different (Sargeant, 2005). The underlying marketing philosophy that should guide an organisation's approach should be conceptualised and considered in terms of its application in relation to not-for-profit organisations. The critical issue is whether managers need to apply the same criteria to marketing decisions no matter their environment. For a sporting organisation, the marketing approach to volunteer recruitment is quite different than the approach to fundraising, as well as the approach to sponsorship or to the government sector. Each of these (and other) areas needs to be addressed by the sport manager.

Although the whole marketing approach needs to be examined from an organisation- or sector-specific perspective, there is also the question of whether for-profit sporting organisations undertake the same basic approach to marketing as not-for-profit sporting organisations. This is a question that is raised in its context and discussed in the following framework.

There has been much debate about what types of organisations comprise the for-profit and not-for-profit sectors. Labels such as the *third sector, not-for-profit sector, non-profit sector, charitable sector* and *voluntary sector* have been widely used to describe organisations that fit this category (Sargeant, 2005). The complexity associated with this categorisation of not-for-profit organisations is that country by country and organisation by organisation, a wide variety of headings are presented. The first sector that Sargeant (2005) identifies represents the private sector enterprises, which include the commercial sector where the supply of producers with consumer demand for goods and services is matched. The second sector is represented by the public sector. In this sector, the State takes responsibility for organisations and the work that they undertake. These organisations are bound by legislation and supported through the provision of public monies. Within the neglected space represented by organisations that deliver goods and services outside the private or public sectors, third-sector organisations have a role to play. A large component of this sector is that it involves people who voluntarily contribute to support the endeavours required, without significant support from the State. Many government organisations are leaving activities in the public sector to organisations within this third sector (through providing government grants), enabling the service to still be provided to the community.

The initial step is to differentiate between for-profit sporting organisations and not-for-profit sporting organisations. A further step is to identify the role of marketing in each sector. The question has been asked whether non-profit organisations are increasingly becoming more like private (for-profit) firms (Clarke and Mount, 2001). This raises a consideration of whether a shift from financial dependence to commercial sales activity must be employed by all organisations. The debate continues over whether marketing in the not-for-profit sector is different from that of a firm whose sole aim is to make a profit.

Within the for-profit sector and primarily in the case of sporting organisations, the reference is to those organisations in private or public ownership returning dividends in some form to an owner or group of shareholders. These sporting organisations tend to be revenue or resource strong in that they have access to a professional setup and generally extensive media coverage of their activities and events.

In the not-for-profit sector, sport organisations can either be termed *professional*, *revenue generating* or *resource-strong* organisations. Although the term *professional* may be misleading and even invoke different opinions and understanding, the concept used in this instance is really in reference to resources and revenue. Although a not-for-profit sporting organisation may be highly professional in its operations, it may be only of interest to a core support group and thereby unable to generate large revenues. The issue is that within the not-for-profit sector, sporting organisations may in fact generate significant surplus revenues and have access to immense resources and media coverage. The charter of these organisations is one in which wealth is distributed in a different way to that of a for-profit organisation. The difference in marketing of a revenue- or resource-strong not-for-profit sporting organisation against a revenue- or resource-poor not-for-profit sporting organisation can be quite marked. This chapter explores some of the key issues faced by these organisations. It commences by investigating the for-profit sector and then identifying and differentiating between the different organisations in the not-for-profit sector.

The for-profit sport organisation

In a for-profit context, the marketing function is generally concerned with developing goods and services that will then be sold on to customers. The result of these sales will hopefully generate revenue, which can then be used to purchase the raw materials necessary to produce the next generation of goods and services (Sargeant, 2005).

Although the above focus is on marketing sales to specific customer groups, this approach to for-profit organisations is far too simplistic. The argument exists that many commercial organisations draw income from a variety of sources, not just from their primary customer base. For-profit sporting organisations clearly fit this approach. Sporting organisations can attract significant government funding, and they may float a new issue of shares. Sponsorship contracts will be renewed, and broadcasting revenue has increased earnings of for-profit sporting organisations exponentially in certain cases. For-profit sporting organisations must actively market to each of these potential 'customers' in order to continue to be successful.

Within the sport environment, for-profit sport organisations tend to predominate around major league clubs. Many major league clubs across the globe are in the hands of majority share ownership or, in the case of European football clubs, floating on their national share markets. This places these clubs in a position of any other corporation, with stringent reporting and financial guidelines applying to their activities. In some instances, this has had a profound impact on the profitability of certain clubs, with issues relating to player acquisition versus profitability becoming difficult to manage. The result is that some clubs in certain European football leagues have been placed into receivership.

CASE 2.1   TelstraDome

TelstraDome a major sport facility within the heart of Melbourne city opened for business in March 2000 in response to a need for a corporate mid sized stadium. The state-of-the-art venue has enjoyed a patronage of major Australian Football League (AFL) games with 8.2 million footy fans having passed through the gates since the stadium opened. TelstraDome has also hosted some of the biggest performers and staged some of the largest events in an indoor arena including, Robbie Williams, Bon Jovi, Barbra Streisand, Ricky Martin, Bruce Springsteen, KISS and the World Reconciliation Day concert.

Supported with a mix of government and private investment, the facility listed on the sharemarket offering annual membership packages to interested parties. One of these membership types is for interested patrons and corporations to receive membership to the TelstraDome Medallion Club. The Medallion Club Membership provides access to major sporting and entertainment events whilst being convenient with its easy underground car parking and provision of a personal seat to customers. The benefits are also transferable, enabling the membership to be shared amongst employees, clients or family members.

Medallion Club members receive their own dedicated car parking area under the venue, access to fine dining, and a premium reserved seat in a prime viewing location. Access to all public sporting events is assured which includes up to 40 AFL games during the season and finals matches. There is also a guaranteed right to purchase a ticket to the AFL Grand Final at market rates. Monthly newsletters and bulleting are provided and the capacity to list a business through on-line and seat sponsorship is available to Medallion Club members. Members also receive first right of refusal to renew memberships for additional periods. These benefits are widely advertised through direct mail, mass advertising and personal communication strategies undertaken by the facility.

Source: Adapted from http://www.telstradome.com.au and http://www.medallionclub.com.au

Questions

1. Is the marketing of a for-profit organisation any different from that undertaken by a not-for-profit organisation?

2. An obvious marketing strategy employed by an organisation to its core customer base is through the events that it can present. What other methods could be employed by an organisation such as this?

3. Who are the other constituents that are important to an organisation such as TelstraDome? How should they be marketed to?

The not-for-profit sport organisation

The introduction of the marketing concept into the not-for-profit sector was heralded by a paper from Kotler and Levy (1969). Their argument was that the traditional marketing approach used by commercial organisations would provide a useful framework for not-for-profit organisations. The aim was to identify the way that these organisations could implement marketing activities effectively. Because marketing is fundamentally concerned with the exchange process and relationships between people, the perspective of this applying to not-for-profit organisations as well as for profit organisations should apply.

Marketing that applies to not-for-profit organisations is often referred to as *social marketing* (Kotler, 1997). These organisations often aim to achieve social change (improving standards of health and education, increasing recreation opportunities and fitness) within a specific time frame, using marketing practices to motivate the public while at the same time improving the efficiency of the organisation involved. Not-for-profit organisations often deal with marketing issues different than other types of organisations, which can complicate the process. Social marketers often face a situation where there is unlimited demand or excess demand over capacity to supply. These organisations are not often in competition with each other, and there is a limitation on alternatives for customers. The pressures that are experienced by a commercial organisation are not the same.

Not-for-profit organisations have existed for a much greater time than organisations within the for-profit sector. This is especially true for sport organisations. Kinnell and MacDougall (1997) define a not-for-profit organisation as one that, after wages and expenses have been taken into account, is prohibited from dispersing any additional revenue to management or any other controlling personnel such as trustees. There should be no relationship between the control of the operation and the distribution of profits.

The not-for-profit sector comprises a wide range of organisations representing a disparate number and variety of industries. These industries range from arts bodies to healthcare, charities, churches and local authority leisure services. Sporting organisations have been classified separately to take into account their diversity and the fact that the majority of sporting organisations are represented in this not-for-profit category.

Classifying not-for-profit organisations is not an easy task. Hansmann (1980) indicated that not-for-profits should be distinguished according to their source of income and the way that they are controlled. Whereas not-for-profit organisations that derive a substantial portion of their income from donations are termed *donative* not-for-profit organisations, those organisations who derive a large part of their income from the sale of goods and services are termed *commercial* not-for-profit organisations. Hansmann (1980) argues that the classification of not-for-profit organisations is helpful in determining the marketing approach that it might adopt.

The International Classification of Nonprofit Organizations (ICNPO) was developed to enable international comparison to emerge in terms of understanding what organisations constitute the not-for-profit sector. This classification introduces 12 categories of non-profit organisations. The groups are listed in Table 2.1. Concentrating on sporting organisations in the non-profit sector, group 1 is represented by the culture and recreation section, or organisations and activities in general and specialised fields of culture and recreation. For the purpose of classification, there are three subsections of organisations contained within group 1. These are 1.100 culture; 1.200 recreation (which includes sports clubs and recreation and social clubs); and 1.300 service clubs. The other 11 groups represent organisations within the non-profit spheres of education, health, social services, the environment, housing, law, philanthropy, international, religion, business and other. Table 2.1 provides a summary of the categories of non-profit organisations as classified by ICNPO.

Table 2.1 **A summary of the categories of non-profit organisations**

Group 1: Culture and recreation	Media and communications; visual arts, architecture, ceramic art; performing arts; historical, literary and humanistic societies; museums; zoos and aquariums; sports; recreation and social clubs; service clubs
Group 2: Educational and research	Elementary, primary and secondary education; higher education; vocational and technical schools; adult and continuing education; medical research; science and technology; social sciences, policy studies
Group 3: Health	Hospitals; rehabilitation; nursing homes; psychiatric hospitals; mental health treatment; crisis intervention; public health and wellness education; health treatment, primarily outpatient; rehabilitative medical services; emergency medical services
Group 4: Social services	Child welfare, child services, day care; youth services and youth welfare; family services; services for the handicapped; services for the elderly; self-help and other personal social services; disaster and emergency prevention and control; temporary shelters; refugee assistance; income support and maintenance; material assistance
Group 5: Environment	Pollution abatement and control; natural resources conservation and protection; environmental beautification and open space; animal protection and welfare; wildlife preservation and protection; veterinary services
Group 6: Development and housing	Community and neighbourhood organisations; economic development (e.g., building of infrastructure); social development
Group 7: Law, advocacy and politics	Advocacy organisations (organisations that protect the rights of specific groups such as women and children); civil rights associations; ethnic associations; civic associations; legal services; crime prevention and public policy; rehabilitation of offenders; victim support; consumer protection associations; political parties and organisations
Group 8: Philanthropic intermediaries and voluntarism promotion	Grant-making foundations; volunteerism promotion and support; fund-raising organisations
Group 9: International	Exchange, friendship and cultural programs; development assistance associations; international disaster relief organisations; international human rights and peace organisations
Group 10: Religion	Congregations (e.g., churches, synagogues) and associations of congregations (organisations supporting and promoting religious beliefs)
Group 11: Business and professional associations, unions	Business associations (e.g., farmers' associations); professional associations (e.g., medical associations); labour unions
Group 12; Not elsewhere classified	

Source: Adapted from The International Classification of Nonprofit Organizations

The not-for-profit sector is continually undergoing change with the expansion in the number on a global scale, largely due to the changing environmental, social and economic conditions. The changes that are emerging within the sector require many non-profit enterprises to adopt business practices in order to survive. The global reach of organisations, coupled with the emerging contract culture, accountability requirement and need to ensure public trust and confidence require the adoption of sound economic and business principles to be employed.

Sporting organisations, which have traditionally engaged in activities that can be represented by not-for-profit activities, are increasingly being held more accountable for public funds and for distribution of members and shareholders funds. The result is a move towards a more professional enterprise. This has particularly occurred in the professional sports club environment. League and club structures are trending more towards corporate business practices through the appointment of professional boards of management. Clubs are listing on the stock exchange or moving into private ownership arrangements, which in turn makes their level of accountability different and ensures that their focus on traditional not-for-profit outcomes has shifted. This shift from a not-for-profit existence to one of a for-profit existence needs to be considered in terms of a broader marketing focus. Although the marketing activities in managing the sporting organisation may not be dramatically different, the reporting requirements associated with a public company are much more stringent.

Within the not-for-profit sector, a distinction should also be made between the public and the private not-for-profit enterprise (O'Hagan and Purdy, 1993). Although private not-for-profit organisations rely on sales income, donations, grants and volunteers, public organisations are generally supported by public money in the form of taxation from local and other government sources, as well as funding from other public bodies. However, many of the goods or services provided by not-for-profit organisations (particularly in the areas of education and health) often have both public and private aspects.

Sporting organisations represent a particular type of not-for-profit organisation. They are generally organisations that actually do seek to make a budget surplus from their operating activities in order to survive from one year to the next. However, these organisations use these operating surpluses for the ongoing development of their activities. A local amateur netball club will attract playing and membership subscriptions, sponsorship, gate receipts and fundraising activities in order to meet their expenditure obligations. Although operating as a not-for-profit organisation, a club such as this may run profitably year after year, accumulating substantial surpluses (therefore, 'profits'). This approach seems to fly in the face of the definition of a not-for-profit entity. The reality is that these surpluses are usually held in reserve for future infrastructure development or employment of personnel to replace areas traditionally within the domain of volunteer services and are not redistributed directly through payments to the members of the club. The funds may be redistributed to the members through reduced fees or provision of club services, but there is no direct financial incentive presented to specific individuals, owners or members.

CASE 2.2   Compulsory competitive tendering

Does the introduction of compulsory competitive tendering (CCT) into the leisure management sector change the not-for-profit focus of these organisations?

Before the 1990s, most public leisure services such as gymnasiums and swimming pools operated from the perspective of providing a service to the community with little or no thought behind how that would occur (or even if the organisation was required to retain a break-even point [not to mention the horror of retaining a surplus] for services provided). Many of these groups operated under the auspices of local government control, in countries such as Australia, Canada and the United Kingdom. The late 1980s saw the introduction of CCT as a means of creating competition (and thereby improved outcomes) associated with many of the activities undertaken by local government. Leisure facility management and ensuing services was one area that was covered by the introduction of CCT.

CCT was introduced to enhance the review and provision of the services offered and gain greater understanding of the consumers that the organisation wished to attract. Some services received an increase in their budgets to cover the increasing costs of providing enhanced management and marketing activities, and other services were put out to tender in order to achieve the best possible range of outcomes for customers.

The effects of CCT were to make leisure service departments more business oriented, with budget systems being more devolved and results monitored for each delivery area. Effective marketing becomes paramount to the business plan for achieving particular projects or objectives. Contracts that are run in house need to be competitive against privately run enterprises, so managers need to ensure that income is enhanced and centres are marketed effectively to attract customers. In the past, many of these centre managers would wait for the customer to come to them. This has required a shift in the way these facilities were marketed to the public as well as a shift in the way these facilities marketed their services to customers.

The old-style viewpoint that was often associated with sporting facilities in particular regions of 'if you build it, they will come' was replaced by one of being more aggressive in terms of attracting customers. This often required improving the condition and appearance of the facility (place); reviewing pricing strategies associated with program delivery (price); introducing new and improved services, often at a time more suited to the customer (product); and spending time and finances ensuring that people were told about the services (promotion).

Questions

1. What is the impact of the new business environment in which leisure services now operate?

2. One of the major impacts of this move to professional service provision is associated with quality management. Why has quality management become such a significant part of public service provision in recent years?

3. What role does marketing play in supporting the concept of quality development?

4. What has been the effect of CCT on service development? What is the impact of the next wave of service delivery (best practice – next outcome)?

Marketing the for-profit and not-for-profit sporting organisations: is there a difference?

Numerous definitions are presented to describe marketing and the marketing function. Suffice to say, throughout the main themes, the impact of a management process responsible for identifying, anticipating and satisfying customer requirements emerges as a consistent framework. Marketing should be seen as both a concept and a function. At the conceptual level, marketing represents a philosophy or approach that places the customer as a central component of everything an organisation does. At the functional level, it can be regarded as the research, service design, pricing, distribution and promotional activities engaged by an organisation (Sargeant, 2005).

Critical to managing the exchange process between an organisation and its customer base is the actual determination of the key customer groups with which an organisation engages. Although it may be clear to the for-profit organisation who their constituents are represented by, the groups in society that a not-for-profit organisation services might not be quite as clear cut.

Marketing can assist in improving the levels of customer satisfaction attained. Although most sporting organisations cannot affect the outcome of the 'core' product (i.e., the competition or the game), they can certainly support the product 'extensions' in the form of support services (Mullin, Hardy and Sutton, 2000). The provision of a programme indicating player names and numbers is a small undertaking for all clubs, but can provide an immeasurable service to spectators in attendance at the game. Whereas the professional 'for-profit' club would usually undertake this service as a matter of course, with a glossy full-colour production incorporating many extra options, the not-for-profit club may see this as a time-consuming and costly imposition. Although the resource capacity of the small amateur club may be extended initially by the provision of this service, even to the extent that it represents a one-page home-game player list can provide marketing extensions that can be developed over time. Supporters would be grateful for the information on key players, sponsors would appreciate the opportunity to advertise their activities, and the club can promote future events in order to generate interest. The scale might be different between the type of production presented to key constituents, but the outcomes are not dissimilar.

The benefits of activities such as those associated with a club programme are the enhancement of opportunity for resources to be attracted to a not-for-profit organisation. Most not-for-profit organisations need to raise funds to support their work. Marketing tools and techniques can offer fundraisers substantial utility and afford them greater opportunities to fulfil the organisation's mission. The adoption of a professional approach to marketing can assist an organisation in determining its distinctive competencies – in other words, define what the organisation can offer to add value and therefore enhance their service delivery. This framework can be enhanced in terms of a systematic approach towards setting objectives and controlling activities.

One of the key activities undertaken by non-profit organisations is to produce services rather than physical goods. This is a key requirement of most sport organisations whether they can be considered for-profit or not-for-profit. Sargeant (2005) notes a distinction between services and products that makes the marketing process inherently more difficult. The key differences can be broken down into four aspects:

1. Intangibility: Service products are consumed without a physical outcome being presented. Sport services cannot be inventoried or saved.
2. Inseparability: Physical goods are purchased and then consumed. Service products are sold first and then consumed (i.e., production and consumption are inseparable). There is no knowledge that the service delivered matches what was planned and expected.
3. Heterogeneity: The level of pre-inspection or quality control is unable to be determined. The sport product is extremely uncertain, with no idea of the quality of performance or outcome of the contest.
4. Perishability: Services cannot be stored or reproduced in the same way as other products. Sport also presents a limited supply of goods. A team can only perform a limited number of competition games. These vary in quality and outcome and cannot be returned or resold.

Although these aspects are strongly associated with many non-profit enterprises, they are also strongly aligned to the sport product, which is clearly associated with the delivery of a service to consumers. Added to this effect is that sport is often associated with high levels of public scrutiny. This scrutiny can be in the media or through the service provision process to customers.

CASE 2.3   The haves and the have-nots in the not-for-profit sport environment

The Australian Football League (AFL) operates as a resource-rich not-for-profit sporting organisation. Represented by 16 clubs that stretch across the whole nation, combined attendances totalled 6.35m for season 2003, television audiences in the five mainland capital cities was 3.84m people, and over 440,000 registered participants play the game. A record operating surplus of \$AUD114.7m was achieved in season 2003, resulting in a net surplus of \$4.7m following distributions. The AFL provided \$79.6m to the clubs, provided special financial assistance of \$1m to two clubs, paid \$7.7m to the AFL Players Association (for the AFL Players' Retirement Fund and player welfare programs), game development grants of \$16.5m and ground improvements undertaken at a cost of \$6.2m.

This solid financial base that reflects the AFL's position is one which consistent surpluses have been achieved and opportunities to direct these surpluses to specific targeted program can be undertaken. The capacity for the AFL to support player and game development is an integral outcome of the surplus revenues obtained.

The Australian Baseball Federation (ABF) recognises that they are an organisation which does not possess an effective business development scheme. They recognise that the reasons for this are many and varied, but essentially, like other national sporting organisations it is because they are focussed upon administering the sport, establishing policy, organising teams, running competitions and events and enforcing the rules and procedures that govern all of this activity.

The ABF admit to being very sport-specific and program focussed. The ABF sits within the Australian sports system as a medium level not-for-profit enterprise. Their average annual income between 2000–2005 has been in the range of $AUD2.75m. The ABF in the past have depended on government/agency funding for more than 50% of total annual income.

This dependency on government funding support reflects a natural tendency within the Australian sport context. The ABF recognise that while so much of the revenue available to sports comes from government funding agencies who virtually dictate how and where the funds are to be spent: this subsequently directly affects the staff structure and the national sporting organisation's operational activities. The fundamental problem with this syndrome is that the sport becomes overly reliant on government/agency funding and has great difficulty getting out of the funded situation. As a smaller resource-poor national sporting organisation, the aim of the board of the ABF is to address this limiting cycle and to create and implement a business development strategy that can expand the revenue, sales and marketing opportunities for the sport of baseball.

The ABF undertook an extensive review and developed a strategic direction to allow the sport of baseball, at all levels, to create revenue-producing business opportunities without detracting from a well established track record of running quality sport and athlete development programs.

Source: Adapted from Australian Baseball (2003) *The Sport of Baseball in Australia National Business Development Plan*; AFL (2004) *107th Annual Report 2003*

Questions

1. Is it fair that a sporting organisation that can turn over in excess of $100m should be classified as a not-for-profit?

2. How does the sporting organisation struggling to survive in order to provide its service consider undertaking its marketing activities?

3. If you were responsible for managing the affairs of the AFL, how would you conduct your business? In the case of the ABF?

Marketing in for-profit and not-for-profit sport organisations

The approach to marketing is often one in which it is often left to the sales department within an organisation to determine, manage and direct the customer requirements. The purpose of marketing in this sense is not to ensure satisfaction of the organisation's customers, but rather to hard-sell failing products and services (Sargeant, 2005). Having or adopting a professional approach to marketing can assist an organisation in defining its distinctive competencies. Marketing can define what the organisation can offer that other organisations cannot. If an organisation can identify areas in which it can offer value, over and above those offered by its competitors, it can refine those competencies and use them to enhance its service delivery and other activities. Developing a marketing strategy is the first stage in this process.

Marketing strategy

Crucial to any marketing strategy, whether focusing on the for-profit or not-for-profit sectors, is the establishment of common themes or dimensions. The questions of where are we now, where do we want to be and how are we going to get there should be fundamental to any organisation (Sargeant, 2005).

1. **Where are we now?** A complete review of an organisation's environment, its past performance and future direction should be completed. Understanding the current strategic position of the organisation in relation to the audiences that it serves assists in developing meaningful objectives for the future direction of the organisation.
2. **Where do we want to be?** The organisation needs to identify and plan what the direction of the organisation will be. Targets, objectives for awareness, image and sales need to be mapped out to ensure organisation success.
3. **How are we going to get there?** The strategy and tactics to be employed by the organisation to meet targets occurs at this point. The basic marketing approach is formed, including the strategy to achieve the marketing outcomes undertaken.

The planned approach to developing a marketing framework includes establishment of the organisation mission and objectives and scanning the environment to determine the influences on the organisation. This is followed by the development of marketing strategies and tactics applying to the integration of market research, positioning, segmentation and targeting, as well as developing the marketing mix attributes of product, price, place, promotion, people, process and physical evidence. Each of these aspects is briefly introduced in turn, with particular emphasis on the for-profit and not-for-profit sector components applicable to this chapter.

Although these marketing concepts are seemingly straightforward in their context, the difficulty in implementation between for-profit and not-for-profit organisations is often pronounced because of the availability of resources. A not-for-profit organisation often does not have the same level of access to resources to enable a marketing strategy to be initiated.

Environment

The modern marketplace is placing increasing pressure on organisations to become more market focused in their approach. Private-sector management practices have been introduced into many public services such as health, education and local government. This policy is one that propounds that value for money can be achieved through open competition, which uncovers inefficiencies and bad practices. Competitive marketing and contracting out services have existed for many years in the general public environment, but the specific introduction of public policies such as compulsory competitive tendering and best value through local and state government acts have enabled the progression of the competitive environment.

The political, economic, environmental, sociocultural and technological environments should all be determined and mapped out to enable the organisation to determine the aspects of the environment that may be able to be developed or, alternatively, are too difficult to develop. For example, a sporting organisation may determine that the internet (technological environment) offers a cost-effective means of providing members with regular updates and information. This could well be problematic if the types of customers serviced by this organisation belong within a lower socioeconomic part of the community (economic and sociocultural environments) and therefore their access to the internet is not forthcoming.

Research

The development of a comprehensive collaborative review, market analysis and analysis of publics needs to be undertaken. Although competition may be a key strategic issue for all organisations, most sporting organisations will collaborate to deliver their product. Most clubs in a competition, whilst competing with one another, also collaborate in order to ensure the product is delivered. The game would not occur without the input of two teams. Equally, the national governing body may need to collaborate with other governing bodies to ensure that a world championship takes place.

Undertaking a comprehensive analysis of the markets in which an organisation operates is crucial to success for both for-profit and not-for-profit organisations. The framework upon which an organisation perceives itself – and more importantly, how the organisation's stakeholders perceive it – is an important development. The not-for-profit sporting organisation needs to understand who will be interested in supporting its fundraising activity, from sponsors of products that it might raffle, through to volunteers who can distribute and sell tickets. Many not-for-profit organisations are engaging the services of professional fundraising organisations, who, for a fee, will distribute and sell raffle tickets and collect and disburse the funds raised. These professional fundraising organisations have access to large databases of potential salespeople and potential customers. Smaller not-for-profit organisations often need to identify their most significant research needs because they are not in a position to purchase research and do not have the resources necessary internally to engage in research-related activities. An alternative option is to explore the opportunity to develop research through relationships with universities or other institutions where students may support the gathering of data through projects that they are required to undertake for credit.

The development of publics, representing people whose potential or actual needs must be served, embraces many potential stakeholders to be identified by the sporting organisation. The publics may include supporters, members, media, sponsors, staff, facility operators, event coordinators and volunteers. The needs and behaviours of these diverse groups need to be determined by the sporting organisation.

Segmenting, targeting and positioning

The range of interest and motivation of people for sport through participation or viewing or spectating requires a range of marketing strategies to be employed to specifically satisfy diverse ranges and groups of people. These strategies must be developed and targeted towards these groups or market segments. The initial phase is to begin by defining the organisational direction in order to have an understanding of what the organisation is seeking to achieve.

After defining the organisational direction, it is important to define the customers. Market segmentation involves breaking the market into segments that show common properties (Kotler, 1997). The main segmentation strategies involve identifying customers on the basis of demographic, geographic, behavioural and psychographic parameters.

Targeting becomes an important consideration of not-for-profit sporting organisations. The marketing strategies of most organisations are relatively unsophisticated, too often relying on mass marketing, and often this is supplied through community service or charitable sources. Technology brings with it a range of communication channels and possibilities. These possibilities require specific marketing approaches because they are beyond the traditional marketing approaches generally undertaken (Saxton, 2001). The development of the internet and introduction of an increasing array of digital delivery opportunities means that customers are seeking their information through a broader variety of marketing channels. Marketing niches (e.g., younger customers) are displaying an increasing demand for information via mobile telephone text services. The organisation that can extend its marketing to meet these demands is better placed than one that cannot. Although texting services may not be cost effective at present depending upon the country of delivery, the links between the mobile phone, the internet and other emerging delivery opportunities such as podcasting are considerably opening up the boundaries for all types of sporting organisations.

Positioning of an organisation involves the process of gaining an understanding and thereby greater impact on the particular market in which the organisation operates. It is imperative for an organisation to understand how its various customer groups perceive it in relation to other suppliers in the market (Sargeant, 2005). The organisation can map its position in the market against specific criteria and other organisations.

Branding

Not-for-profit organisations traditionally have operated without a'face', focusing mainly on surviving in a turbulent and increasingly competitive environment (Goerke, 2003). With an increase in competition and a greater focus on private delivery in sectors such as health and lifestyle, it has become important for organisations that have been quiet about their presence to instigate competitive measures and create brand awareness and reputation. One way to achieve this is through the creation of a brand personality, which should be created, painted and replicated in everything an organisation does.

A brand can be defined as a name, term, sign, symbol or design, alone or in combination, intended to identify the goods or services of one seller or a group of sellers in order to differentiate them from those of their competitors (Shimp, 2000). A brand is a device that enables members of the public to recognise a particular organisation through the form of a trademark, name, logo or other form. These names can be protected in many industrialised nations in order to ensure that no other organisation can impinge on their intellectual property. A case in point is the requirement for the World Wrestling Federation (WWF) to amend their name to World Wrestling Entertainment

(WWE) in deference to the World Wildlife Fund's (WWF) having a greater global acknowledgement of the trade name WWF. The development of trade names and logos is important for the identity of sporting organisations. The global acknowledgement of not-for-profit sporting organisations such as the International Olympic Committee (IOC) and Fédération Internationale de Football Association (FIFA) is widely accepted and understood. The IOC logo represented by the five coloured rings is one of the most recognised symbols across the world. This branding activity plays a crucial role in supporting the organisation.

CASE 2.4   Cricket in Australia: a rebranding approach

During 2002–2003, Cricket Australia undertook a major rebranding exercise for its organisation. The major emphasis was built upon the move 'from backyard to baggy green', recognising the various stakeholders for which Cricket Australia assumes responsibility. The first stage of this process was a name change from the Australian Cricket Board to Cricket Australia. The new name was part of an overhaul of the organisation's brand structure, which was designed to give all levels of Australian cricket the chance to be part of an integrated look.

The next stage was to develop the symbols and logos associated with Australian cricket. A new corporate logo was designed to appear on elite team uniforms and equipment and was to be incorporated into all advertising, licensing and game development programmes. The only aspect of Cricket Australia branding that remained unaltered was the cherished baggy green cap. After consultation with players and other stakeholders, it was thought that the iconic baggy green should retain its original format, retaining the traditional cricket coat of arms emblem.

The new brand mark that was introduced incorporates a kangaroo and emu from the traditional cricket coat of arms, the southern Cross, the green and gold colours of Australia and a sunburst, designed to represent the traditional relationship between cricket and the Australian summer. Through an extensive consultative approach with cricket's key stakeholders, including players, former Australian captains, directors, state and territory associations, commercial partners, licensees and media, the design was finally agreed upon. Cricket Australia has successfully incorporated this brand into its logo for the organisation, its teams and events. Although this transition has occurred at the national level, the state members have retained their own logo and brand identity, not altering their own logo to match the national body.

Questions

1. Why is a recognisable brand important to a sporting organisation?

2. As a not-for-profit sporting organisation, perhaps operating with limited resources, would it be worth undertaking a rebranding exercise such as that undertaken by Cricket Australia?

3. How does a sporting organisation struggling to survive in order to provide its service consider undertaking its branding activities? What if the outcome does not live up to expectations?

Marketing mix

The traditional marketing mix represents the strategic combination (or mix) of four primary elements represented by the 4Ps. The 4Ps are product, price, place and promotion. Within the services marketing context is the addition of a further 3Ps represented by process, people and physical evidence (or packaging). It is necessary to reach a point where the optimal combination of these Ps is right for a particular product and organisation, whether the organisation is classified as a for-profit or not-for-profit organisation. The organisation should briefly identify the mix of product, price, place, promotion, process, physical evidence and people and then apply the for-profit or not-for-profit focus to these attributes.

Product

Although the key focus on commencing an examination of the marketing mix lies with determining the requirements of the target market (i.e., what needs do the target segments have, and how can they best be satisfied?), as soon as this knowledge is gained, the marketer must then ensure that the organisation's products and services match the needs of its customers.

The components of a product or service have been widely discussed in the marketing literature. Kotler (1997), for example, distinguishes between the core, tangible and augmented aspects of a service. The core service in the case of sport is the game, event or contest. The tangible element is the part that the consumer can take away from the experience. In the case of most physical products, this reflects on the actual item purchased. In the case of sport, however, a consumer may receive a ticket for entry, a programme or an item of merchandise that represents the tangible evidence. The crucial aspect of services, and in particular sport service, is the augmented product or the 'value-added' elements of the service; this is the key to providing a greater experience to the consumer.

The sport marketing literature spends considerable time on differentiating the core product from the product extensions (Mullin et al., 2000; Pitts and Stotlar, 2002; Shilbury, Quick and Westerbeek, 2003). The argument in sport is that it is extremely difficult to control the core product (i.e., the game itself), but the additional services associated with the game play a crucial role in the outcome and perceptions that customers take away from the event. It is extremely difficult to determine the quality of an actual tennis match during a round of a Gland Slam tennis tournament such as the Australian Open. It is unknown who will win, how many sets will be played and how well each player will perform (or even if they will be injured during the contest). The customer purchases a ticket to see the game with a belief that the contest will be a good one. The reality is that the game form itself is beyond the control of the organiser. What can be controlled to a large extent is the extra product features that the customer receives. The food that they purchase, the comfort and sightlines associated with the seat, the merchandise, the cleanliness of toilets and so on all contribute to the customer's satisfaction with the event. Because of the fact that a tangible outcome is not generally associated with the sport product, the augmented part of the service becomes crucial in ensuring success in the eyes of the consumer.

The components of a service are a crucial requirement of any sport organisation. The quality of a service is paramount to ensuring that the values and mission of the organisation are achieved. Ensuring that high levels of quality service are achieved enhances the ability of the organisation to attract and retain service users. Sporting organisations, primarily representing not-for-profit service providers, will always retain a select number of enthusiastic and committed service users for their product offerings. Being able to sustain the organisation in the longer term requires ensuring that a level of service is provided. The core product may be a suitable avenue to achieve customer satisfaction in the short term, but organisations must also be reviewing the core product and associated augmentations that can be applied in order to ensure that the future development can occur. A problem faced by most not-for-profit sport organisations is that they are highly underresourced in terms of funds and personnel to be able to undertake and achieve this process. They must therefore often seek to centrally develop their product.

Price Price plays an important role in any organisation regardless of its status. In a not-for-profit sense, price may be represented through entrance fees, membership charges, equipment and merchandise sales, donations, sponsorships and so on. An approach to pricing in the not-for-profit sector is essentially the same as that taken in the for-profit sector. A major difference that exists regarding pricing is that whereas a profitable outcome would be considered crucial in most instances in which the for-profit sector is concerned, this may not necessarily be the case for the not-for-profit organisation. Although some for-profit organisations may be prepared to reduce prices in the short term in order to achieve market share, they cannot sustain this in the medium to longer term if they wish to remain in business. The not-for-profit organisation only needs to ensure that prices cover costs, however, because they are not dependent upon achieving a substantial profit. They may seek to establish a surplus that can be allocated to future programmes, but there is no need to ensure that their profit margins are reported back to a group of shareholders.

The critical issue that emerges with price for sporting organisations is to gain an understanding of the total package of pricing that can be associated with an activity. If someone is attending a sporting event, the total cost is not simply associated with the ticket to gain entry to the event. The customer has to get to the facility (cost in fuel or public transport), park, purchase a programme and food and beverages, maybe buy some merchandise, pick up a raffle ticket to support their club, pay for the babysitter so that they can attend the event and so on. There is also the opportunity cost of attending the event; what else could the person be doing instead of this? The total cost must be factored in to include all aspects, not just the price paid for entry into an event. Not-for-profit sporting organisations need to consider this when providing a service to customers or seeking to raise funds through fundraising activities.

In the not-for-profit sporting organisation, the price additions need to be managed for customers to believe that they receive value for money through purchasing those additional items above and beyond the entry ticket to an event.

Place Place is associated with the degree of accessibility and distribution of a service. The not-for-profit sector has a number of complexities associated with it. This extends into service accessibility through the choice between market segments that may arise and the potential trade-offs that need to be made. Many not-for-profit organisations rely on the services of volunteers and must be mindful of the geographic and psychographic issues faced by these people. The locality of a particular sporting organisation also has an impact on the accessibility of donations, attendance and interest. The distribution channel needs to be clearly identified and managed, particularly through the presence of electronic channels of communication.

Promotion The process of promotion involves informing, persuading, reminding and differentiating the service in the minds of potential customers. The use of various elements of the promotional mix such as advertising, sales promotion, direct marketing and public relations (PR) are integral aspects of any profit or not-for-profit sport organisation's communications. The key difference that exists is that the for-profit organisation, or the resource-rich not-for-profit organisation, is usually in the fortunate position of having resources available to develop an advertising programme. The resource-poor not-for-profit organisation generally has to achieve its promotional objectives through a variety of mix attributes and some clever approaches to generating interest and publicity.

One of the more influential promotional mix attributes in the context of sport is associated with PR and publicity. Mullin et al. (2000) present the concept of PR as a crucial attribute of any sport organisation, so much so that they identify it as a 'fifth' P of marketing. Whether that is a reasonable assumption or not is largely irrelevant, considering that most professional sports receive widespread media coverage and therefore are in the position of having to manage their PR process.

Although professional sport organisations have to manage their PR appropriately, not-for-profit sport organisations must seek innovative ways of attempting to generate sufficient media coverage of their sports and events. This may be achieved through specific events, emergence of key athletes, support for special developments and such, and then the organisation being in a position to maximise their message through all possible media outlets.

CASE 2.5   Women's sport: not-for-profits seeking promotion

Sportswomen are playing harder, faster and more professionally than ever, developing proven international records, yet they still struggle for consistent, long-term media coverage (Phillips, 1997). Participation rates in women's sport continue to increase, but the media coverage and positioning of women's sport stories has remained a major obstacle to the development of the athletes and their sports.

Added to the lack of coverage, when media does take an interest in women's sport, it often uses language to describe the athletes or the sport stressing weakness, passivity and insignificance. Women are often portrayed as girls no matter what their age (Phillips, 1997).

Consistent media coverage assists a sport in gaining and maintaining a profile, providing positive role models, and ensuring increased interest and spectator appeal and sponsorship opportunities. The credibility that can be achieved by the way the media portray a sport or athlete can be of infinite benefit.

Questions

1. What implications emerge in the case of a resource-poor not-for-profit organisation when dealing with promotion via the media? As a women's sporting organisation, how would you develop or maximise media coverage?

2. Many women's sport organisations and athletes have undertaken the 'sex sells' approach to promotion of their sport. Is this a relevant or useful approach to take?

Physical evidence The physical evidence or packaging within the marketing mix reflects the external appearance of the product or service (i.e., the way in which people look at the organisation) and can often lead to completely different reactions from customers. The physical evidence displayed by the organisation or its products or services applies to everything that the customer sees from the first moment of contact through to the purchasing process and beyond. The customer not only takes notice of the product itself but also all aspects of the organisation, including how the product is packaged and presented through to how the staff are dressed and groomed. Everything can have an impact upon the customer's impressions of the organisation.

The major difference between the not-for-profit sport organisation and the for-profit sport organisation when referring to physical evidence is the resources available for the for-profit organisation to ensure that the presentation is of high quality. The smaller resource-poor not-for-profit sporting organisation may not have the resources to put together an impressive glossy, full-colour programme as part of its event. This obviously impacts on the presentation of the actual event to the public.

Process Within the services industries, an organisation's processes can present greater scope for success. Processes support providing customers to get what they want. Identifying the processes, systems or services that make it easier for customers to do business with the organisation (including the introduction of new systems or new technology) can differentiate a specific organisation from the competition.

It is often the scale of process that will differ between the not-for-profit and for-profit sporting organisation. The critical issue is for all organisations to manage their processes within the resource constraints that face them.

People To an organisation providing service to customers, the people element of the marketing mix is probably the most important. Whether the people are paid employees or unpaid volunteers, they will often make or break the experience that a customer receives. The issue with most sporting organisations is the type of people who represent the organisation. One of the key aspects is to employ people with a background in the sport. This has obvious benefits but can also present many problems to an organisation. In the case of the not-for-profit sporting organisation, a key contribution made to the organisation and the events it runs is through the service provided by volunteers.

Volunteers represent one of the major attributes associated with not-for-profit sport organisation. These volunteers can make or break the event. The process of recruitment involves considerable marketing. It is easier and more cost effective to retain current volunteer staff than to recruit new staff. Understanding the motivations behind volunteers can assist in ensuring that they can be retained. Providing training, opportunity and reward for effort can ensure that people will continue to seek to be involved.

Fundraising A final aspect worth identifying is concerned with fundraising. Many not-for-profit sport organisations must undertake fundraising activities in order to survive. Although charities receive special assistance through governments by way of taxation exemptions and the like, most sporting organisations do not. These sport organisations still have to ensure that they raise sufficient funds to be viable. One of the ways this can be achieved is through fundraising campaigns. How an organisation proceeds to develop its fundraising strategy can have a profound impact on the success of the organisation.

Income from fundraising can arise through individual donations, legacies, sale of goods and services, investments, tax benefits and government grants (Sargeant, 2005). The establishment of a fundraising plan can be the first step in ensuring that an organisation can meet its financial objectives. The approach to fundraising can take a similar approach to that developed by an organisation in terms of its marketing. The organisation can consider the positioning, segmentation and targeting of potential donors in the same way that it would approach its marketing. The tactical marketing approach needs to then be initiated in terms of attracting, retaining and developing donors, similar to the requirements of attracting, retaining and developing customers.

Conclusions

This chapter focused on the impact of marketing for-profit and not-for-profit sporting organisations, including how to define the profit and not-for-profit sporting organisation, what marketing issues apply to the various types of organisations and how these organisations can achieve their marketing objectives in an appropriate way.

The special nature of sporting organisations means that many of them cannot be truly classified as being either for-profit or not-for-profit organisations. A large number of sporting organisations operating in the professional sport market can realistically be termed profitable organisations. Although they operate and are recognised as not-for-profit organisations, for all intents and purposes, they actually turn over significant surpluses (or profits) from their activities. These resource-strong sporting organisations are therefore in a strong position to develop significant marketing activities and approaches. Coupled with this capacity to finance their marketing activities, these organisations are often extremely media friendly and therefore receive a great deal of publicity and promotion to support their activities.

On the other hand, the smaller, more amateur (or resource-poor) sporting organisation has to contend with an entirely different market with which to deal. These organisations must attempt to develop their marketing strategy through developing a loyal customer base, attracting resources and people through a variety of both well-established and innovative means, and endeavour to maximise opportunity through a low budget and planned approach. The actual marketing activities and processes used by the for-profit, the resource-rich not-for-profit and resource-poor not-for-profit sporting organisation may actually not differ greatly. The predominant difference is the resources available to initiate a successful marketing programme and how the organisation endeavours to pursue this process.

Discussion questions

1. Three types of sporting organisation types are a professional rugby league club such as the Sydney Roosters, a venue such as Telstra Stadium and a small state sporting organisation such as the Victorian Little Athletics Association. For each organisation, classify it as a for-profit or not-for-profit sporting organisation and develop a marketing approach that each could initiate in terms of member recruitment.

2. Addressing new media technologies such as the internet, mobile telephony or pod-casting, how could a not-for-profit sporting organisation access and incorporate these new technologies to assist in its marketing approach?

3. What do you understand to be the difference between for-profit and not-for-profit sporting organisations? How would you obtain market research to support your marketing approach for a not-for-profit sport organisation?

4. Look at a resource-poor not-for-profit sporting organisation that you have some involvement with. Why have you defined it as resource-poor, and what marketing activities does it undertake in conducting its business?

Guided reading

Further information relating to the aspects relating to marketing in not-for-profit organisations can be found in the text *Marketing Management for Nonprofit Organizations* by Sargeant (2005). This book provides a comprehensive overview of the not-for-profit sector and the broad concepts associated with marketing in this sector.

Keywords

Brand awareness; controlling; databases; distribution channel; economic environment; heterogeneity; inseparability; intangibility; market research; marketing mix; marketing strategies; packaging; perishability; political environment; positioning; publics; resource-poor; resource-strong; satisfaction; segments; sociocultural environment; target market; targeting; technological environment; trade-offs.

Bibliography

Australian Baseball (2003) *The Sport of Baseball in Australia National Business Development Plan*, Sydney: Australian Baseball.

AFL (2004) *107th Annual Report 2003*, Melbourne: AFL.

Clarke, P. and Mount, P. (2001) Nonprofit marketing: The key to marketing's 'mid-life crisis'?, *International Journal of Nonprofit and Voluntary Sector Marketing* 6(1):78–91.

Goerke, J. (2003) Taking the quantam leap: Nonprofits are now in business. An Australian perspective, *International Journal of Nonprofit and Voluntary Sector Marketing* 8(4):317–27.

Hansmann, H. (1980) The role of the nonprofit enterprise, *Yale Law Review* 89(April):835–99.

International Classification of Nonprofit Organizations (2005) Retrieved April 13, 2005, from http://www.statcan.ca/english/freepub/13-015-XIE/2004000/icnpo.htm

Kinnell, M. and MacDougall, J. (1997) *Marketing in the Not-for-Profit Sector*, Oxford: Butterworth-Heinemann.

Kotler, P. (1997) *Marketing Management: Analysis, Planning, Implementation and Control*, 9th edn, Upper Saddle River, NJ: Prentice Hall.

Kotler, P. and Levy, S.J. (1969) Broadening the concept of marketing, *Journal of Marketing* 33(1), 10–15.

Mullin, B.J., Hardy, S. and Sutton, W.A. (2000) *Sport Marketing*, 2nd edn, Champaign, IL: Human Kinetics.

O'Hagan, J. and Purdy, M. (1993) The theory of non-profit organizations: An application to a performing arts enterprise, *The Economic and Social Review* 24(2):155–67.

Phillips, M. (1997) *An Illusory Image. A Report on the Media Coverage and Portrayal of Women's Sport in Australia 1996*, Canberra: Australian Sports Commission.

Pitts, B.G. and Stotlar, D.K. (2002) *Fundamentals of Sport Marketing*, 2nd edn, Morgantown: Fitness Information Technology.

Sargeant, A. (2005) *Marketing Management for Nonprofit Organizations*, Oxford: Oxford University Press.

Saxton, J. (2001) New media: The growth of the Internet, digital television and mobile telephony and the implications for not-for-profit marketing, *International Journal of Nonprofit and Voluntary Marketing* 6(4):347–63.

Shimp, T. (2000) *Advertising Promotion Supplemental Aspects of Integrated Marketing Communications*, 5th edn, Fort Worth, TX: Dryden.

Shilbury, D., Quick, S. and Westerbeek, H. (2003) *Strategic Sport Marketing*, 2nd edn, Crows Nest NSW: Allen & Unwin.

Recommended websites

Baggy Green
http://www.baggygreen.com.au

Cricket Australia
http://www.cricket.com.au

Medallion Club
http://www.medallionclub.com.au

Statcan
http://www.statcan.ca/english/freepub/13-015-XIE/2004000/icnpo.htm

TelstraDome
http://www.telstradome.com.au

Chapter 3

Alternative paradigms and sport marketing

Dr Susan Bridgewater
University of Warwick

Learning outcomes

Upon completion of this chapter, the reader should be able to:

- Understand the distinctions between relational and transactional perspectives on marketing.

- Identify key issues in sport marketing that arise from use of relational rather than transactional perspectives.

- Understand the key relationships in sports.

- Understand the nature of affiliation between fans and sports brands.

Overview of chapter

This chapter presents the major characteristics of relationship marketing and considers how it can contribute to our understanding of sport marketing. Whereas traditional, transaction-based marketing tends to view customers as passive, relationship marketing views customers and other stakeholders as active participants in the marketing process. Network perspectives on marketing consider clusters of relationships surrounding the central, or focal, organisation. This chapter presents the major stakeholders in sport marketing and considers the key features of some of these relationships such as fan-club relationships. These relationships are intensely emotional but also have a number of other factors that contribute towards creating fan allegiance to the club. The dynamic aspects of relationship marketing are shown in brand experiences that are designed to develop the interaction in relationships with brands over time. The chapter also focuses on co-branding relationships in which a sponsor ties its activities to a particular sports brand. The impact of the actions of one partner on the other is explored to show that the organisations become dependent on each other and are affected by each other's actions.

Introduction

In his introduction to *Culture's Consequences*, Hofstede (1980) says of studying social sciences:

> Social scientists approach (. . .) social reality as the blind men from the Indian fable approached the elephant; the one who gets hold of a leg thinks it is a tree, the one who gets the tail thinks it is a rope, but none of them understands what the whole animal is like. We will never be more than blind men in front of the social elephant; but by joining forces with other blind men and women and approaching the animal from as many different angles as possible, we may find out more about it than we could ever do alone. (p. 15)

Studies of marketing in the 1990s see different parts of this elephant depending on the approach they take. Similarly, Gummesson (1999) suggests that relationship marketing is a pair of 'eyeglasses' that a reader might use to study marketing issues. As soon as the reader puts on these eyeglasses, the same issues look different. New angles are revealed, and greater clarity and valuable insights can be gained. As taking a different approach to the study of sport marketing might, therefore, reveal alternative aspects of traditional marketing challenges, this chapter attempts to provide these by using the lens of relationship and network, rather than transactional approaches, or paradigms, to the study of sport marketing.

Traditional, relationship and network perspectives of marketing

The need to generate repeat business with loyal customers has become central to the study of marketing. Yet despite the importance of ongoing relationships in profit terms, the majority of marketing literature still analyses static marketing situations (Johanson and Mattsson, 1997). There is a tendency to focus on cross-sections of data – for example, how a market is segmented or what types of buying behaviour may be observed – rather than studying marketing phenomena over time. Relationship perspectives, however, study marketing as a dynamic process in which the creation, development and maintenance of relationships between firms, their customers and other stakeholders is of central importance.

A number of strands of literature have contributed to understanding of marketing from a relationship and network perspectives. These are summarised below.

Relationship perspectives have developed from two main bodies of literature. The first strand is that of the European Industrial Marketing and Purchasing (IMP) group (Håkansson and Östberg, 1975; Håkansson and Wootz, 1975). The work of IMP and its associates now represents a considerable and ongoing contribution to understanding of marketing (Axelsson and Easton, 1992; Håkansson, 1982; Turnbull and Valla, 1986). This work either breaks down the web of relationships surrounding the firm and studies the smallest relationship (that between two parties, or a 'dyad'). This simplification permits clear study of the constituents of the relationship and the interaction between the parties.

The second perspective studies the network of direct and indirect relationships as an entirety. Proponents of network studies of marketing argue that this approach captures the complex range of actors and relationships that impact marketing activities. This approach will, from here on, be referred to in this chapter as *network studies of marketing*.

A second stream of relationship literature that has developed in parallel to the IMP's work in recent decades is that of relationship marketing (Berry, 1983; Christopher, Payne and Ballantyne, 1991). The IMP's work studied interactive relationships between industrial buyers and sellers. No such interaction was seen between marketers and final consumers. Developing interactive relationships with such a large number of consumers was held to be impossible. Technological developments have opened up the possibilities of developing 'virtual' interaction with these consumers. A byproduct of, although not to be confused with database marketing, relationship marketing looks at how value can be added in relationships between marketers and a range of other actors.

In relationship marketing, the focus is again on studying each type of relationship separately, rather than in total. Although different in its emphasis, relationship marketing is viewed here as a parallel development to dyadic interaction.

A summary of the main features of relationship and network perspectives on marketing

Interaction studies

Interaction studies are based on the belief that firms do not market to passive customers but that customers interact with marketers. Imagine the scene: Your club is attempting the naming rights to your new stadium in a multimillion pound deal. You have carefully explained the marketing benefits of the deal. You arrive at the final meeting expecting to clinch the deal. Despite your positive expectations and carefully honed negotiation skills, the deal is rejected. You leave wondering what went wrong. . . .

Interaction studies focus on a number of characteristics of business-to-business marketing that may help you to understand. Firstly, business-to-business buyers are very different from final consumers. They tend to be large, professional buyers and have specific requirements for any sponsorship deal. The marketing director to whom you have spoken in previous meetings may now have involved the financial director of the customer. This new stakeholder may consider that your asking price is too high. The chairman may prefer to deal with a different club or be disinterested in your sport. The chances of a successful outcome take an unexpected downturn.

The interaction approach to business-to-business marketing was originally defined in a pan European IMP project (Håkansson, 1982). A valuable overview of the development of this area can be found in Ford (1990).

Four types of variables play a role. Variables that:

- Describe the parties involved, both as organisations and individuals.
- Describe the elements and process of interaction.

- Describe the environment within which the interaction takes place.
- Describe the atmosphere (conflict or cooperation) in which the interaction takes place.

Taking an interaction approach to study of your sponsorship relation is similar to mainstream marketing in that it involves research into the composition of the buying unit. It goes further in that it might explore the individuals and firms involved over a greater period of time to identify past connections between any of the key players. It will look. It may look, not only at the opportunities and threats posed by the macroenvironment (e.g., Is the potential partner suffering a downturn in a key market, has regulation worked against it, and so on), but also at key relationships with stakeholders in this contact. The macroenvironment is no longer 'faceless' and uncontrollable (Porter, 1980); rather, it is made up of actors. Has the firm had a run-in with the local council in the past? Might its business investors see a conflict with the behaviour of your fans? In the case of the US Postal Service's sponsorship of Pro Cycling, is this an appropriate use of taxpayers' money?

In sum, interaction studies consider those involved in relationships to be active rather than passive, study relationships over time and consider the role of individuals and other stakeholders in a 'full-faced' environment as playing a role in the development of relationships.

From the perspective of interaction studies (Ford, 1990), distances between actors in a relationship can be created by:

- Social factors
- Culture
- Technology
- Time
- Geography

Imagine, for example, that the New Zealand All Blacks Rugby Union team is attempting to raise its profile with potential sponsors in Belgium. The language difference is an initial barrier to building a relationship. Depending on the location of the Belgian partners' operations, the New Zealand club may need to speak both French and Dutch. Each partner may have different cultural expectations of good business practice: How formal should the meeting be? What should each partner wear? Geography may limit the number of face-to-face meetings. Time zones make telephone conversations difficult, and electronic communication may be hampered by the two partners using different software. The draft contract arrives but cannot be read. Static approaches to market analysis may not capture the complexities of successful sport marketing in this situation.

Relationship marketing

Relationship marketing goes back to the basics of determining what customers need and want (Christopher et al., 1991; DeBruicker and Summe, 1985; Narus and Anderson, 1995), but goes beyond transactional approaches to look at the development of ongoing relationships with these customers. It is then 'as much about keeping customers as it is about getting them in the first place' (Christopher et al., 1991, p. 1). Berry (1983) describes *relationship marketing* as the development, maintenance and enhancement of customer relationships. In this respect, it is a reinforcement of the central importance to marketing of building ongoing customer relationships.

Gummesson (1999) explains of transactional marketing:

In transaction marketing, the fact that a customer has bought a product does not forecast the probability of a new purchase, not even if a series of purchases have been made. A customer may repeatedly use the same supplier because of high switching costs, but without feeling committed to the supplier or wanting to enter a closer relationship. Transactions lack history and memory and they don't get sentimental. (p. 11)

Relationship marketing is similar to interaction studies in the sense that it studies the interaction between buyers and sellers, but it also broadens the focus from business-to-business into services and also consumer markets. It has its roots in services marketing (Berry, 1983; Gummesson, 1999) as well as the interaction studies discussed in the previous section.

Relationship marketing began with a focus on direct contact with sophisticated buyers who required high levels of service quality. Its central theme is that of building loyal customer relationships. It aims to persuade customers to climb a 'loyalty ladder' (Christopher et al., 1991) from being a prospect, to a customer (first purchase), to a client (recurrent purchases). As soon as a longstanding relationship is established, the client may become a supporter and finally an advocate for the supplier.

As sports as services, the central concepts of relationship marketing are very significant to understanding successful sport marketing, yet there remain few relationship studies of sport marketing (Chadwick, 2004). Because, for example, sale of season tickets to loyal fans, revenue from digital television sports subscriptions and successful sponsorship relationships are central challenges for many sports clubs, relationship marketing appears to have some critical lessons for best practice.

Gronroos (1990) suggests that excellent service may be different at each stage of the relationship. Establishing relationships involves making promises; maintaining them involves fulfilling promises; and enhancing a relationship involves making a new set of promises based on fulfilment of earlier promises. When Newcastle United football club sold fans season tickets on the basis of a particular seat in the stadium but then moved them to accommodate a corporate box, the fans thought that the initial promise had not been fulfilled. Whilst the decision might have made logical business sense in itself, the cost–benefit analysis would have to take into account the potential revenue loss from these fans not developing relationships further and from sending out the message that the club does not value its fan relationships.

The rise of relationship marketing

A common belief of interaction and services relationship marketing was that they involved direct, face-to-face relationships with customers. There were simply too many consumers to make relationship marketing possible. Yet this barrier has been partially overcome by developments in information technology that have made it possible to build relationships virtually with large numbers of consumers (Everett, 1994).

Retailer loyalty cards and databases of buyer behaviour have made it possible for firms to know enough about large numbers of consumers to interact with them. These developments have prompted a growing body of theoretical and practitioner studies of relationship 'value' (Mitchell, 1995; Prus and Brandt, 1995). Chapter 12 studies the issues relating to successful use of customer relationship management (CRM) to create sport marketing relationships. A key challenge for the success of these techniques in sport marketing is the extent to which they can create loyal, value-creating virtual relationships. The growth of web boards and other virtual communities among sports fans suggests that this is possible.

Relationship marketing proposes a series of practical steps for CRM:

■ Prioritising the customer portfolio on some basis to identify those who are most loyal (Prus and Brandt, 1995).
■ Creating communities of loyal customers such as through development of loyal customer clubs (Mitchell, 1995).
■ Providing rewards for loyalty (O'Brien and Jones, 1995).

Network perspectives on marketing

Recognition of the importance of networks in management is increasing. The concept of networks is so widely used that it can be confusing. The term is used for everything from clusters of strategic alliances (Lorenzoni and Ornati, 1988) to the leveraging of social contacts and network marketing, meaning pyramid selling. The first task of this chapter then is to summarise the main strands of network theory that are relevant to this chapter. Marketing focuses largely on:

■ Networks are a type of organisation that a firm may choose to use.
■ Markets as webs or 'networks' of relationships.

This chapter focuses on the latter.

Markets as networks

The 'markets as networks' view builds on the work of the IMP group described earlier in the chapter. From this perspective, markets are made up of a complex web of interactive relationships:

> The markets are characterised by interaction between firms in relationships where the parties have some control over each other and the organisations are not "pure" hierarchies. To us the legal frameworks of the transactions are less important and the boundaries of the networks are unclear. (Johanson and Mattsson, 1987, p. 12)

Different levels of relationship exist in the network. A variety of different terminologies have been used to describe these different levels. Blankenburg (1995) distinguishes between relationships in the broader marketing environment, relationships between organisations and relationships within the firm. The work of the IMP group commonly describes these as macro-, inter-organisational and intra-organisational relationships, respectively. In his synthesis of interaction, networks and relationship marketing, Gummesson (1999) categorises these as *mega* (macro environmental), *market* (competitor, supplier and customer relationships) and *nano* (relationships within the firm). The distinction lies largely, therefore, in the number of relationships taken into account and the fact that network perspectives take into account the impact of indirect as well as direct relationships.

Imagine, for example, that Malcolm Glazer's proposed takeover bid for Manchester United fails because the brand image of Tampa Bay Buccaneers is in some way damaged and the tycoon decides that sports clubs are risky investments. The network of relationships in which Malcolm Glazer is involved would, therefore, play a role in the future of Manchester United's global brand.

Relationship studies of sport marketing

The types of relationships that must be taken into account by sport marketers are many and varied. Some of these are listed below:

- Fans: Clubs or sports brands
- Fans: Sports icons
- Clubs or sports brands: Media
- Clubs or sports brands: Agents
- Clubs or sports brands: International sporting bodies
- Clubs or sports brands: Leagues
- Clubs: Shareholders
- Sports brands: Global broadcasters

Because not all of these can be studied in depth in this chapter, the chapter focuses first on the first of these types of relationship to see what lessons can be drawn. It then draws broader lessons for analysing marketing relationships and considers the extent to which these can be usefully applied to the study of sport marketing.

Analysing sports relationships: the bond between fans and football brands

CASE 3.1   Fan affiliation with English premiership football clubs

Football fans are very loyal to the clubs they support. Whilst some may moan about particular performances, sport markets are unlike those for other products and services in that fans would rarely switch to a competitive brand – few disgruntled Arsenal fans turn to supporting Chelsea or Manchester United fans transfer allegiance to Manchester City. Allegiances are 'tribal' and strongly felt. A study of 2557 fans of 20 Premiership football clubs in the 2001–2002 season identified five components, or factors, that seem to help explain the nature of these intense relationships.

Support for the team

This factor relates to the fans' emotions if the club is successful. This is part of the fans' emotional attachment to the club but may prompt a set of activities. These are referred to as 'increased support for the team'. High scores here indicate that, if their team is successful, fans are more likely to talk about their team, attend matches, take others to matches, wear replica shirts, buy club merchandise, visit official club and fanzine websites, subscribe to a club magazine, become more interested in football as a whole and visit football websites more often.

Match-related activities

This relates to the frequency with which fans attend matches and take part in other activities that are related to match attendance. Fans rating highly on this dimension attend more matches (both home and away) of both league and non-league varieties and go to reserve matches. They are also more likely to participate in official transport to matches and attend events organised by the club. The fans may also participate in informal match-related activities such as sharing transport to matches and making informal swaps of seats.

History, symbols and perceived knowledge

This is the importance attached by the fans to the history and symbols of the club. High scores here mean that fans can identify the team logo, motto, sponsors, mascot and nickname. They also have knowledge of classic victories, goal scorers and opponents in cup runs and other past successes. Fans scoring highly on this dimension have a high self-professed knowledge of the club and its history.

Self-esteem

Linked with the emotional response to team success, this emotional bond relates to how fans feel about themselves if the team is successful. Fans scoring highly here feel better about themselves and feel that they gain respect from friends and colleagues if the team they support is successful.

Organisational ability

This represents the importance attributed by fans to the club's organisational ability. High scores here suggest that fans attach more, rather than less, importance to their club's having financial stability, the availability of a big budget for new players, a strong youth academy, a top manager and coaches, a go-ahead board of directors, honesty and integrity and a good relationship with the community.

Questions

1. What are the advantages and disadvantages for clubs of the highly emotional nature of fan-club relationships?

2. How might clubs attempt to build brand relationships with fans if on-the-pitch performance is not good?

The identification of these dimensions of the bond between fans and football clubs has a number of implications for understanding relationship marketing in sport. In broader relationship marketing literature, social exchanges are considered important to the creation of long-term, stable relationships (Ford, 1990). These sports relationships have a strong social and emotional dimension that may explain their ability to endure.

Fans are also very attached to the symbols and history surrounding the football club. As Coventry City football club recently discovered when its attempt to change the badge resulted in a fan backlash, these symbols are an important part of the relationship between fans and club. Similarly, Liverpool Football Club is keen to gain sponsorship funding from selling the naming rights to its proposed new stadium. Arsenal Football Club have recently gained £100m from a sponsorship deal by naming their new Ashburton stadium in London the 'Emirates Stadium'. Traditionalists, however, are likely to resist any plans to change the name of Liverpool's footballing home, even if the new name incorporates the current name Anfield.

The level of success of the team may not result in fans' switching allegiance to a different football team. It does, however, have an influence on the behaviour of football fans. A later stage of the football fan allegiance study considers the impact of the perceived level of success of the football team on the bond with the brand. Firstly, it should be noted that perceived success bears little relation to the actual level of success of the football club. In 2001–2002 one of the teams perceived to be the most successful was Ipswich, which had just been promoted and was exceeding the expectations of fans, whose main concern that season was to remain in the Premier League. In contrast, high-flying Manchester United, which won the Premier League Championship that season, was perceived not to be doing well. Why? Manchester United had won the treble of the Champions League, the domestic FA Cup and the Premier League in the previous season, a relative lack of success!

When teams were perceived not to be performing as well as expected, fans' level of support for the team went down. They felt the poor performance in lower self-esteem and began to attend fewer matches. They also began to avoid television coverage of football, not just of their team, but of all football and in some cases all sports. This reminded them of the poor performance of their own teams.

Understanding dynamic brand relationships

Transactional marketing tends to focus on brand identity, and brand value and may study the way that advertising plays a strategic role in this process. To date, however, it pays relatively little attention to dynamic interaction between the customer and the brand. One burgeoning field of literature, although still mainly in the practitioner rather than academic literature, is that of brand experiences.

Brand experiences look at creating multiple points of interaction between a customer and a brand in order to develop a more loyal relationship. They have also been proposed as a means of countering the increased ability of customers to filter out traditional marketing messages. Brand experiences often involve the use of technologies such as laser-triggered sound effects, longer events and experiential happenings surrounding particular brands. Examples of brands that have used marketing experiences effectively include ING Bank with its ING Direct Café in New York, Niketown and American Girl, as subsidiary of Mattel toys.

Given the preexistence of venues for many sports brands, brand experiences appear to be a valuable route to creating long-term and valued relationships with fans. Manchester United's description of its Old Trafford stadium as the 'Theatre of Dreams' conjures up images of what this may be like. If history and symbols are an important part of the brand affiliation, the Theatre of Dreams museum will help to reinforce this value experientially. The increasing availability of plasma screens to show bespoke video and audio messages and the potential with 3G mobile telephony to interact with scoreboards and other visual technologies must make the 'match' or sports event a valuable opportunity to create brand experiences.

Marketing strategies for networks in sports

As discussed earlier in this chapter, networks are dynamic, involve multiple types and levels of relationships and mean that the actors in the networks are affected not only by the actions of those with whom they have direct relationships but also by those with whom there is only an indirect link.

The following example of the network of co-branding relationships in the sponsorship of professional cycling will be used to further explore the implications of a network perspective on sport marketing.

CASE 3.2 | The network of co-branding relationships in professional cycling

In 1996, the United States Postal Service (USPS) committed more than £1m to become the official sponsor of the Montgomery Securities professional cycling team. The stated aim of this sponsorship was to make the sport a promotional and image platform in the international marketplace. The sport was chosen for its global appeal (*Brandweek*, 12/4/1995) and for the congruence which USPS perceived between professional cycling and its own brand values. According to Loren E. Smith, chief marketing officer of USPS 'Cycling emphasizes much of the same qualities that the USPS emphasizes: a teamwork, speed, precise movement from point to point.' Moreover, the sport was felt to have a 'good set of demographics for USPS's internationally targeted audience'.

As lead sponsor of USPS, the post office gained signage at events, plus booths at events including the Tour of China, Tour of Switzerland and Tour of Italy through which it could sell its range of collector stamps. Alongside the lead sponsor USPS, the Montgomery team also has a long roster of co-sponsors, including Berry Floors, Nike, Coca Cola, Bissel, Visa USA, Dial Corp, Subaru of America, Yahoo and Trek.

The sponsorship arrangement took effect fully in 1998, when Lance Armstrong – Montgomery's best-known rider – still recovering from cancer, overcame the effects of chemotherapy to win the Tour de France in 1999 and every year since. Lance was subsequently named *Sports Illustrated* Sportsman of the Year (2002), bringing a plethora of positive press coverage and associations to USPS. Benefits for the smaller teams have also been significant despite their relatively smaller financial stake.

Yet the very success of Lance Armstrong may eventually bring the sponsorship arrangement to a close. *Business Week* (6/3/2003) comments 'When someone always wins it gets boring.' Another win, whilst great for the United States, would also be less popular in USPS's increasingly important European markets. Pro cycling has also experienced unfortunate episodes, such as a doping scandal in 1998, that may make it less attractive as a sponsorship target. Given the dominance of Lance Armstrong, sponsorship of other cycling teams has also seen a decline over the period.

Now USPS finds itself under pressure to drop its sponsorship of the Montgomery team (*Advertising Age*, 3/22/2004). This is partly a response to criticism that this may not be an appropriate use of taxpayers' money. More critically, however, as suggested in *B-2-B* (5/3/2004), although Lance Armstrong is an extraordinary brand with which USPS established a link on favourable terms, the majority of business comes from business-to-business customers. Laura Ries, president of branding consultancy Ries & Ries, questions the level of fit between professional cycling and the Postal Service: 'Maybe if he delivered letters on his bicycle,' she said, 'but there is just no connection I can see between Lance Armstrong and the Postal Service. None.'

Questions

1. What are the implications for USPS of linking its brand with Lance Armstrong?
2. Why is USPS under pressure to end its sponsorship deal with the Montgomery team?

This case of the network of sponsors in professional cycling reveals some of the issues that become apparent from this perspective on marketing. Firstly, there is a strong emotional value in the link with Lance Armstrong as a personality. At its peak, this achieved valuable awareness (Gantz, 1981). When he won, Lance Armstrong created a valuable sponsorship association for the USPS brand (Clark, Cornwell and Pruitt, 2002). Ironically, however, this very success has resulted in a reduction in the impact of the sponsorship. Uncertainty and the existence of competition are important in creating continued interest in sports events (Baade and Matheson, 2004). Without this, consumer interest and awareness decline. There are, however, multiple stakeholders in this sponsorship network. Consumers may be most influenced, although some question whether it is appropriate to spend taxpayers' money on sponsorship, so the association has brought some unanticipated negative responses as well as the good. Business-to-business customers see lesser relevance in the relationship: Where is the congruence in values? Furthermore, although US markets associated the sponsorship with winning, European customers make an association with losing.

This suggests that USPS underestimated a number of mutual dependencies created by entering this sponsorship relationship; those between geographic markets, with the broader set of stakeholders (taxpayers and infrastructural relationships) and with events in pro cycling more broadly (such as the doping scandal). These 'unanticipated' outcomes of the sponsorship relationship suggest that a broader analysis of the network of relationships involved in this type of deal should be considered at the outset. Accordingly, a network perspective (Axelsson and Easton, 1992) rather than a dyadic relationship perspective (Christopher et al., 1991) might have captured many of the strategic implications for the brand of entering this relationship.

Conclusions

Different perspectives on marketing provide diverse insights into sport marketing. These are hopefully complementary and reveal new aspects and angles that might not be observed as clearly from a traditional or transactional approach to sport marketing. The chapter focuses on three strands of literature: interaction studies and relationship marketing, which analyse the characteristics of particular types of sport marketing relationships, and network perspectives, which aggregate these relationships and look at the interplay between clusters of sport marketing relationships.

Discussion questions

1. Identify some key business-to-business sport marketing relationships (e.g., club and broadcaster) and analyse the key elements in the interaction between the two 'actors' in this relationship.
2. What characteristics of the external environment are likely to impact on the above relationship?
3. What might cause the existence of 'distances' between the two partners in the relationship?
4. What are the key exchanges that take place within the relationship (e.g., economic, technological, social, informational)?
5. Identify some key positive and some key episodes in a sport marketing relationship and discuss the ways in which these contributed towards the creation or diminution of trust between the partners.
6. Identify a cluster of relationships surrounding a particular sports club. Include as many stakeholders as you can identify in this network. Mark on a diagram the relationships that are direct and those that are indirect.
7. What changes have had an impact on the above network (e.g., reduction in money from broadcasting, the advent of the internet, changes in regulation for the sport)? Who instigated the change? How did this ripple out to affect other actors in the network? Was everyone equally impacted? If not, why do you think some actors were affected more than others?

Guided reading

Axelsson, B. and Easton, G. (eds) (1992) *Industrial Networks: A New View of Reality*, London: Routledge.
The introductory chapter of this book provides an in-depth review of the network perspective on marketing.

Christopher, M., Payne, A. and Ballantyne, D. (1991) *Relationship Marketing*, London: Heinemann.
This provides a useful overview of relationship marketing.

Ford, D. (1990) (ed.) *Understanding Business Markets, Interaction, Relationships, Networks*, New York: Harcourt Brace.
A valuable book which contains the major articles from IMP and its co-researchers on 'interaction' marketing.

Gummesson, E. (1999) *Total Relationship Marketing – Rethinking Marketing Management: From 4Ps to 30Rs*, Oxford: Butterworth-Heinemann.
A useful, more recent overview of relationship marketing.

Keywords

Allegiance; co-branding; dyad; dynamic interaction; interaction; inter-organisational; intra-organisational; markets as networks; network perspectives; relationship perspectives; static marketing situations; transaction.

Bibliography

Axelsson, B. and Easton, G. (eds) (1992) *Industrial Networks: A New View of Reality*, London: Routledge.

Baade, R.A. and Matheson, V.A. (2004) Mega sporting events in developing nations. Playing the way to prosperity, *South African Journal of Economics* 75(5): 1085–96.

Berry, L.L. (1983) 'Relationship marketing', in L.L. Berry, G.L. Shostack and G.D. Upah (eds), *Emerging Perspectives on Services Marketing*, Chicago: American Marketing Association, pp. 25–8.

Blankenburg, D. (1995) 'A network approach to foreign market entry', in K. Möller and D. Wilson (eds), *Business Marketing: An Interaction and Network Perspective*, Norwell: Kluwer, pp. 375–410.

Chadwick, S. (2004) *Determinants of Commitment in the Football Club/Shirt Sponsorship Dyad*, Unpublished PhD thesis, Leeds: Leeds University Business School.

Christopher, M., Payne, A. and Ballantyne, D. (1991) *Relationship Marketing*, London: Heinemann.

Clark, J.M., Cornwell, T.B. and Pruitt, S.W. (2002) Corporate stadium sponsorships, signaling theory, agency conflicts and shareholder wealth, *Journal of Advertising Research* 42(6):16.

DeBruicker, F.S. and Summe, G. (1985) Make sure your customers keep coming back, *Harvard Business Review* Jan–Feb:92–8.

Everett, M. (1994) Database marketing: Know why they buy, *Sales and Marketing Management*, December:66–71.

Ford, D. (ed.) (1990) *Understanding Business Markets, Interaction, Relationships, Networks*, New York: Harcourt Brace.

Gantz, W. (1981) An exploration of viewing motives and behaviours associated with television sports, *Journal of Broadcasting* 25:263–75.

Gronroos, C. (1990) Relationship approach to marketing in service contexts: The marketing and organizational behaviour interface, *Journal of Business Research* 20:3–11.

Gummesson, E. (1999) *Total Relationship Marketing – Rethinking Marketing Management: From 4Ps to 30Rs*, Oxford: Butterworth-Heinemann.

Håkansson, H. (1982) *Industrial Marketing and Purchasing of Industrial Goods: An Interaction Approach*, London: Croom Helm.

Håkansson, H. and Östberg, K. (1975) Industrial marketing – an organisational problem? *Industrial Marketing Management* 4(1):113–23.

Håkansson, H. and Wootz, B. (1975) Supplier selection in an international environment: An experimental study, *Journal of Marketing Research* 12:34–57.

Hofstede, G. (1980) *Culture's Consequences*, London: Sage.

Johanson, J. and Mattsson, L.-G. (1987) Interorganisational relations in industrial systems: A network approach compared with a transaction cost approach, *International Studies of Management Organisation* 17(1):34–48.

Johanson, J. and Mattsson, L.-G. (1997) 'Relationship marketing' and the 'markets as networks approach' – a comparative analysis of two evolving streams of research, *Journal of Marketing Management* 13:447–61.

Lorenzoni, G. and Ornati, O.A. (1988) Constellations of firms and new ventures, *Journal of Business Venturing* 4(2):133–47.

Mitchell, A. (1995) The ties that bind, *Marketing Today* June:60–4.

Narus, J.A. and Anderson, J.C. (1995) Capturing the value of supplementary services, *Harvard Business Review* Jan–Feb:75–83.

O'Brien, L. and Jones, C. (1995) Do rewards really create loyalty?, *Harvard Business Review* May–June:75–82.

Porter, M.E. (1980) *Sustainable Competitive Advantage*, Boston: Harvard Business School Press.

Prus, A. and Brandt, D.R. (1995) Understanding your customers: What you can learn from a customer loyalty index, *Marketing Tools* July–August:10–14.

Turnbull, P.W. and Valla, J.-P. (1986) *Strategies for International Industrial Marketing*, London: Routledge.

Recommended websites

Academy of Marketing's Relationship Marketing Special Interest Group
http://www.academyofmarketing.info/sigrelations.cfm

Brand Channel
http://www.brandchannel.com/features_profile.asp?pr_id=205

CRM2DAY
http://www.crm2day.com/relationship_marketing/

Part Two

Meeting the needs and wants of the sport market

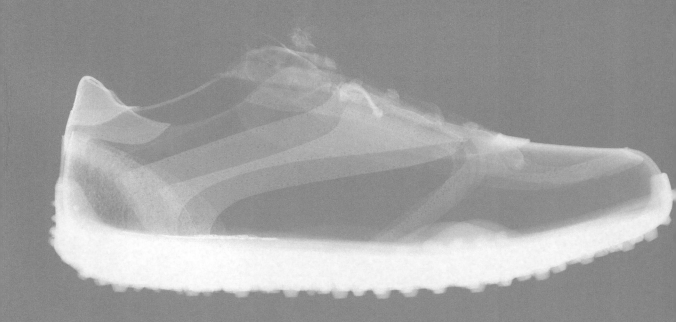

Chapter 4

Understanding the sport marketing environment

Paul Kitchin
London Metropolitan University

Learning outcomes

Upon completion of this chapter, the reader should be able to:

- Define what is meant by the sport marketing environment.

- Identify key environmental forces that may impinge upon sport marketing.

- Highlight techniques for gathering information about the sport marketing environment.

- Locate sources of information needed to understand the sport marketing environment.

Overview of chapter

Central to successful and effective marketing is the identification and satisfaction of the needs and wants of the sport market. By understanding the place of the organisation within the market and the forces that impact on decision making, the sport marketer can gain a better realisation of the context their organisation exists within. A key feature of successful marketing is being flexible to situations arising outside the organisation. Many sporting organisations have to deal with a variety of changing influences and forces that are in a constant state of flux. These are environmental considerations that impact on the way that sport marketers create, implement and analyse their marketing campaigns. This chapter will provide an introduction to the external marketing environment for the sport marketer. This chapter investigates the environmental forces that surround and permeate sport organisations and the sport marketer within them. The first part of this chapter discusses the key principles of environmental analysis, which is that these external forces impact on all organisations, sport and non-sport, that operate within the same environment. Some of these forces can be controlled, but sport marketers have to adapt their practices to other forces. Following a section detailing each of these forces, an examination of market analysis tools and techniques highlights how to carry out environmental analysis. Within this chapter, two case studies are used to demonstrate the interconnectedness of these factors on both sport and non-sport organisations that are involved in the marketing of sport.

Environmental analysis

Marketing within any business environment over the past 20 years has gone through a variety of changes, some intended, some thrust upon the process by changing external forces. If we consider the process of the sport organisation communicating with its members in 1985 as opposed to 2005, the variety of communication tools available then was greatly reduced. There was no email, very few mobile phones and no such thing as text messages, and fax technology was for a limited few. Hence, sport marketers had to rely more on traditional tools of mail-outs and manual databases. Technology has made communication between the sport organisation and their customers, members and stakeholders easier over time.

Technology is one example of an environmental factor that has impacted upon us. Attempting to predict what will happen next can be difficult. Nevertheless, by using information from external sources, organisations can keep abreast of changes. There are a number of general trends that are expected to influence the marketing process for any organisation in the near future. These trends are based on research and extrapolation of current economic and social trends. Westerbeek and Smith (2002) highlight a number of trends that will affect the global sport industry. Some of these trends include:

- The use of sport as programming content for a variety of media agencies
- A need for sport organisations to maintain global reach and focus in order to keep in touch with global sport properties
- An increase in the need for sports to develop as an entertainment package
- An increase in the adoption and understanding of technologies to enable this to occur
- An increase in the economic impact of sport and hence their importance to a wider society
- An increase in the 'westernisation' of sport entertainment. (pp. 48–9)

The need for sport marketers to understand and analyse the potential impacts and opportunities of these forces is vital and should be carried out in a systematic and logical process. The first step is collecting information on the various aspects of the sport marketing environment. Many authors have produced mnemonics such as STEP, PEST, SLEPT, PESTEL and PESTCOM (Kotler, 2000; Shank, 2005; Shilbury, Quick and Westerbeek, 2003) amongst others, to provide for an easy way to remember the range of external environments. The model that this chapter uses is PESTEL, which is a mnemonic for the political, economic, sociocultural, technological, environmental/ethical and legal/regulatory environments (Figure 4.1).

The second step is to assess the potential influences and impacts of each environment through the use of tools designed for environmental analysis. Once this information is collected, step three is to integrate the information into marketing plans, strategies and procedures. The final step of the environmental scanning process is to evaluate its effectiveness in obtaining useful and accurate information.

The external environment

The external environment consists of a number of separate factors and forces that impact on marketing decisions made by the sporting organisation. The model adopted for categorisation of the external environment in this chapter is PESTEL. This

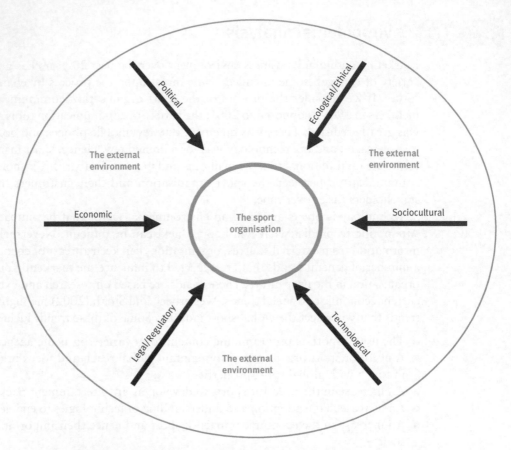

Figure 4.1 **The external environment of the sport organisation**

mnemonic stands for six environmental influences, the first being the political environment which is characterised by the ideology of the party in power and the tier (level) of government. The economic environment is dependent on macro- and micro-economic conditions that pervade organisations and the regions in which they operate. The sociocultural environment is influenced by shifts in society and consumer tastes as well as being characterised by cultural differences and their impact on the marketing process. The technological environment is one of the most revolutionary and rapidly expanding forces over the past 20 years. The technological environment is the impact of technology on the operations of the sport and the impact of technology on the ability of the sporting organisation to carry out its activities, which are the focus of this section.

As capital and investment decisions are now made on global scales, the level of social input into these decisions is limited. From this, the development of environmental and ethical awareness in consumers is growing. Impacts and decisions made in one area of the planet can have repercussions for society in another. These considerations are considered in the section on the ecological/ethical environment. Finally the legal/regulatory environment is the final influence that sport marketers need to take into consideration. All organisations operate within a regulatory environment and are subject to national, state and local legislation. Varying levels of autonomy are allowed for and regulated to maintain. The sport marketer's role is to understand the intricacies of this force and the guidelines it imposes for marketing planning and implementation. Each of these forces can vary in their magnitude and can affect some organisations greater than others. For instance, the changes in the governing political party at a national level can have a more noticeable impact on the marketing of quasi-governmental sporting bodies than for smaller privately owned professional services firms.

The political environment

This environment describes the political landscapes and structures that a sport organisation operates within. An example of this is the political landscape in Britain, where politics has in recent times shifted towards a central political ideology with more compromised views on governance and its role in society (Henry, 2001). The views of political parties from traditional conservative and social reformist viewpoints have been softened to create a third way of government, as evidenced by New Labour's term in office in Britain. Because of the profile and mass appeal of sport, the body politic has been keen to associate itself with successful, popular sport. John Howard, the prime minister of Australia, is one of the leading supporters of Australian cricket, described by some as a cricket tragic. In Britain, New Labour were quick to arrange a formal reception and subsequent photo opportunities with the World Cup-winning English Rugby Union team upon their return from victory.

Political influence has an impact on the operations and administration of sport, as highlighted through two main areas that should be included in the environmental scanning process. The first sphere of influence from the political environment is the ideology and policies of the governing parties involved. This factor can therefore determine the level of involvement and support for sport as an industry or as a pastime. Second, the tier of government and the impact of its operations and influence is an issue for consideration as political bodies operate at international or regional, national, intranational and local levels. Indeed, differences in ideology can exist between the tiers of government, which can also create turbulence for sport marketers and makes the process of environmental scanning increasingly difficult.

Ideology of government

A major influence within the political environment is that of government ideology. Traditionally, most western countries have been dominated by two bipolar ideological themes, conservatism or social reformism. Although a greater analysis of the various approaches is beyond this chapter, it is clear that a certain ideology can create different environments within which sport marketers must operate. Because of the mass appeal of sport, party politics has held less influence over its operations and marketing than, say, health or education, which are cornerstones of policy and ideological difference. Sport, although important to those that participate in it, consume it and work in it, is not as high on the political agenda as some other areas; hence, it is less influenced by the ideology of government.

In Britain, the debate for developing sport has centred on developing sports for the sake of sport or developing sport for the sake of the society that views sport as an important element of society (Hylton, Bramham, Jackson and Nesti, 2001). This is highlighted by the difference in sport policy between the Conservative Major government in their policy *Sport: Raising the Game* and the New Labour policy of *A Sporting Future for All*. The former policy focused on developing sport through school and elite structures because sport was deemed an important aspect of British identity. Conversely, the latter focused on using sport as a tool for developing communities and inclusion, fundamental principles of the New Labour approach. The ramifications for sport marketers offering sport development programmes were substantial. Communication and promotion of sporting programmes under the first policy would need to be rebranded under the new, at the expense of the sport organisation itself.

Furthermore, for elite sport organisations in some western countries, levels of funding are determined by international success. A number of traditionally funded sports are having their funding reviewed on the basis of the contribution they make to participation levels and elite success. For these sports, international success means more funding and hence has an impact on their operations and the number and type of marketing strategies they can employ. If the determinants of international success are based on criteria established through politically sponsored and motivated sporting quangos, then political ideology will have a real influence for sport marketers.

Tier of government

Governments operate on a number of tiers and attempt to coordinate and control people and organisations through a number of spheres of influence. Two of these, legislation and regulation, are discussed in a separate environment below. A third factor is the provision of funding and the influence it brings. Governments operate over a variety of tiers, or levels, and attempt to bring about like-minded change, lately termed *joined-up thinking*, through the flow and restriction of funds for various policies and projects. An example of this is the European Union (EU) regeneration funds that have bought about benefits to sporting facilities and their operators through the region. To obtain the funding for these new developments sport marketers have had to promote EU social goals and objectives, for instance, sport programmes that attract a wide range of participants from underprivileged areas.

UK Sport is a peak agency, quasi-autonomous, non-governmental organisation (quango) that operates throughout the United Kingdom. The agency levers the control of funding to the national governing bodies as a means of achieving common objectives. Many of these bodies have had to embark on a modernisation programme to create more efficient operations and to operate with greater levels of customer service. The bodies have had to do this as they rely on this funding to carry out their business. Sport marketers within these organisations have had to find new ways of communicating objectives to new and existing customers that in turn create a greater likelihood of achieving the funding from UK Sport. Because UK Sport receives its funding from the national government and the National Lottery, through a government department (the Department for Culture, Media and Sport), it is clear that the government can also bring about the change it wants to see, thus demonstrating the impact of national government on national sporting bodies.

Depending upon the political structure of the country within which the organisation operates, there may be other levels of government that also distribute funding. For instance, in Australia, states are supportive of sport event marketing organisations that can attract major events to the particular state. An event that contributes to the economic well being of the state is likely to gain funding support from the state government. Even at the local government level, sporting organisations can obtain greater levels of funding by aligning their development and participation programmes with local objectives. The funding opportunities to these organisations offering social inclusion programmes and, more recently, programmes that make children healthier have increased in the past 8 years in local governments across Britain.

The economic environment

Another external factor that has distinct influence on sport marketing is the economic environment. The economic environment consists of two spheres. The first is the macroenvironment, which is focused on the interactions of the wider economy as a whole. This consists of a range of economic terms that can be affected by (or are affected by) a wide variety of influences. Alternatively, the microeconomic environment focuses on individual decisions made by managers and the structure of the organisations in an industry. In the case of environmental scanning, the macroeconomic environment and its components determine the strength of this environmental force.

The concept of free-market trading has been adopted by a number of countries that believe in the ability of the market to provide goods and services at a fair price for consumers. This has led to the adoption of certain economic policies at a national and regional level, such as the free-flow of international capital and resources, that are impacting globally. In a number of western countries, the period 1995 to 2003 saw stable economic conditions with important indices such as inflation, national incomes and interest rates remaining constant and fairly predictable. This created business cycles of stability and growth. The business cycle is an important indicator of macroeconomic health, and cycles such as recession (trough) and boom (peak) can determine the range and type of marketing strategies used by sport organisations. These cycles affect the levels of consumer demand, which describes how willing consumers are to purchase sporting goods and services. In periods of positive economic growth, organisations and consumers have confidence in the positive aspects of the economic environment and are therefore prepared to spend and invest. Alternatively, in periods of recession, consumers are more concerned with saving because of levels of economic uncertainty. An example of this impact can be seen when considering the trend of professional sporting franchises in the United States and their growing reliance on corporate funds from luxury seat and box sales. This reliance consolidated during the stable periods of the 1990s (Howard and Burton, 2002). But after the attacks on America on September 11, 2001, a period of social and economic uncertainty led the American economy into recession. Looking to protect themselves from a downturn in the economy, the corporate customers of the franchises cut back their spending. This impacted on the franchises' ability to gain funds and market their activities.

National governments can act to influence macroeconomic variables that are linked to the business cycle by initiating fiscal policies. These governments are also concerned with levels of consumption, which can be impacted upon by consumer incomes and saving. Issues such as interest rates, consumer debt and savings are linked to monetary policies initiated by governments and affect economic output and inflation. One method governments can employ is influencing interest rates through the central bank, as is the case in Britain and Australia. Interest rates on loans and mortgages and their subsequent increase or decrease can influence the spending patterns of a country's citizens. Governments can act to increase interest rates if consumer spending is growing at a pace that could impact inflation. This is important because unequal rates of growth and inflation can trigger recession. This highlights the complexity of an external environmental analysis for the sport marketer because both the political and economic environments can be linked. This trend is common with all the spheres of the external environment.

Other economic initiatives taken by governments and regulatory bodies, such as leagues, can also have an influence on the ability of sporting organisations to communicate with their market. Initiatives such as the Community Amateur Sports Club (CASC) status with the Inland Revenue in Britain has allowed sporting organisations to obtain rebates for certain costs, which has freed up other monies to be put into operations and marketing. These initiatives influence the financial health of sport and allow the organisations to invest in marketing opportunities that can further increase the success of the club.

The economic environment in certain geographical areas may also impact the ability of a sporting organisation to operate and market its activities. In the United States, the prospect of economic support for professional sport franchises from local government has lured these organisations to new economic markets. Across the globe in Australia, Australian-Rules Football Clubs based in the city of Melbourne have either relocated, merged or used joint-venture entry into new markets in order to survive the tough economic conditions. These conditions can exist on a macro level, but they can also exist on a micro level. For instance, having too many professional sporting organisations in one economic environment creates hypercompetition, which can destabilise a league, hence affecting all the clubs. This method of economic rationalisation has benefited the Australian Football League as a whole because it has opened up into traditionally untapped markets. An example of a club relocation is that of South Melbourne football club, which moved to Sydney in 1985. Other clubs have been created to allow the league as a whole to enter new markets. Clubs from South and Western Australia, as well as Queensland now compete very effectively in the league. Other clubs such as Hawthorn and the Western Bulldogs play certain home matches in states of Australia that do not have regular teams in the national league. Such moves have also allowed the sport marketers at these relocated clubs to communicate and engage with new consumers, thereby increasing their membership base and ultimately their economic health. This has also occurred on an international level with sports such as Formula 1. The case below highlights the international expansion of the Formula 1 circuit from its traditional European base to a more global scale.

CASE 4.1   Silverstone suffers from globalisation

In 1981, the year Bernie Ecclestone and his Formula One Constructors' Association fought for control of the commercial rights of the sport, there were 15 Grands Prix on the calendar, of which only five were outside Europe.

After 23 years of solid growth in the F1 brand worldwide, Ecclestone looks set to unveil a calendar of 17 dates for 2005 with races in every continent, but with a footprint in just seven European countries. Having added the Bahrain and Chinese Grands Prix in 2004, next year Turkey will make its F1 debut.

Meanwhile, parties from Russia and India are in regular contact with the 74-year-old billionaire, seeking a slot in the coming years. The geography of F1 is changing fast as emerging markets come to the table, all with government backing.

Next year's F1 calendar is not yet finalised, but it looks virtually certain that the British and French Grands Prix will not feature. There has been a British Grand Prix every year since the inception of the world championship back in 1950. Only the Italian Grand Prix can match that.

The British teams, led by Williams and McLaren, will lobby Ecclestone to reconsider his position, but he is unlikely to budge if the numbers don't add up. Ecclestone says the going rate to stage a Grand Prix is now £10m, but the British Racing Drivers' Club, owners of Silverstone, are not prepared to make a loss of about £4m a year and with no sign of the government stepping in to make up the shortfall – sports minister Richard Caborn yesterday reiterated that the government would not intervene – it is hard to see a resolution.

If more money can be found, Ecclestone may offer the teams Silverstone as an 18th race for next year. He had wanted to extend the calendar to 19 races, the teams have said no more than 17, but the travel costs of going to an extra race at Silverstone – seven of the 10 teams are based within 200 miles of the Northampton track – would hardly be onerous.

In its relentless hunger for greater earnings, F1 must decide what store it sets by its history. Races on the 'classic' tracks such as Monza, Spa, Monaco and Silverstone resonate with the audiences. New tracks like Shanghai and Istanbul are very well appointed, but they have no more foundation in the sport's heritage than a Playstation game.

Source: J. Allen, *Financial Times*, 2 October 2004

Question

1. What environmental pressures are impacting on Formula 1, meaning that the relocation of races from Europe to global circuits has become necessary?

■ The sociocultural environment

Every organisation must take into consideration the various beliefs and differences between their members and potential members. Differences along geographical, cultural, societal and ethical lines act to increase the changing composition and nature of this environment. A myriad of aspects could be taken into consideration in the environmental analysis, and each of these can differ again when marketing across local, national and international regions. To simplify this, two aspects will be examined here. The first aspect is shifts in societal tastes, including the changing nature of the dominant market in a particular region. The second aspect is the cultural differences that can be used to understand and include all cultures in a modern sporting provision.

Shift in society and its tastes

Sport has a traditional role in the societies of many countries across the globe. Certain sports have dominated from high participation and high publicity that have allowed those working within them to rely on this traditional link with aspects of society such as class. For instance, rugby league in Australia has strong roots in the working classes of Sydney and north Queensland, and in the southern states of Australia, Australian-rules football has been similarly supported by the working classes (Shilbury and Deane, 2000). From an English perspective, the divide between social class and rugby code has long been established and was until recently highlighted by geographical location. This has led some sports in the past to rely too heavily on this tradition and enter a state of marketing myopia because they believed these links would be everlasting.

The societal makeup in the suburbs of cities such as London and Sydney has changed dramatically over the past 20 years. With these shifts, the traditional customer base of certain sports has altered. The process of gentrification in Sydney and the arrival of new immigrants and the 'white flight' in East London have seen sporting organisations such as Balmain Rugby League Club and Leyton Orient Football Club lose their traditional supporters, and only after readjusting their marketing activities have they been able to appeal to these new social groups.

Another example to highlight changing patterns of taste is in the participation of cricket in the Australian summer. Traditionally, cricket has had strong participation numbers during the summer months. Whereas the Australian states have different football codes during winter, the dominance of cricket as the chosen summer sport has been well documented. Nevertheless, as societal tastes have changed, cricket has come under increased competition from other activities that appeal to one of its key segments, the youth market. The rise of basketball during the 1990s and the shift to lifestyle activities, such as extreme-sports, which are not bound by climactic changes, can be seen as competitive threats. Cricket Australia and the state and local associations need to consider these aspects when designing their marketing activities.

Changes in the demographic makeup of society are another societal consideration. Consumer demographics is one of the categories that sport marketers use to segment their market. Consumers tend to have similar characteristics between each category, which makes it easier for marketers to design marketing strategies. Demographics such as gender ratios tend to remain constant over time, but there is an increasing need in spectator sport to attract more women into a traditionally male-dominated environment. Women are increasingly responsible for and hold considerable influence in household financial decision making. The National Rugby League in Britain is attempting to attract the family market and is adopting its marketing practices according to this changing demographic. Additionally, marketing efforts to appeal to the 'grey market' in community leisure in Britain is also important. This market is characterised by increased leisure time and sometimes secure financial status. Increasing participation from this demographic can be an important step by leisure centres to increase customers during traditional offpeak times between 9:00 am and 4:00 pm and thereby achieve greater economies of scale for their level of infrastructure investment while also satisfying local government objectives.

Sport has also been a popular form of television programming for a number of years and a number of high-profile sports have used revenues from broadcasters to assist in the funding of their operations. According to Mullin (1985), one of the key factors in its appeal to consumers and broadcasters is the unpredictability of the sport product itself. Since the late 1990s, increases in the number of reality-based television shows, such as *Big Brother*, and their appeal to large audiences could pose potential problems for sport on television. Not only does reality television offer unpredictability but also allows viewers to interact with the show, adding to the direction the content will take. Also, reality television appeals to viewers because there is a remote chance that they could actually take part in the show, an option most armchair fans of sport could generally not do at the level they are watching. The sport marketer must examine changes in viewing patterns and preferences to ensure the broadcast of their sport is in tune with current viewer needs. Sometimes these changes may need to be quite dramatic, for instance, to increase the television viewer appeal, the Dutch football league is proposing a series of playoffs to decide European and relegation positions in an attempt to make more games carry more appeal as a spectacle (Marcotti, 2005).

Cultural differences

The movement of people within a country and throughout the world has led to noticeable changes in the cultural makeup of most countries in Western Europe. The arrival of immigrants from the Caribbean, Africa and Asia has not only changed the face of Britain but has also contributed to the development of sports such as athletics, boxing and football. Immigrants to an area bring new tastes, new cultures and new opportunities. Cultural differences can be established from an international imperial perspective that links societies across the globe or through the development of cultures within a country because of forces such as immigration.

On an international scale, the development of colonies by imperial powers throughout the past 300 years has also led to the development of societies with common links to their former colonial powers. The distribution of commonwealth-based sports such as cricket and netball has led to strong emerging nations such as Jamaica (or as part of the region of the West Indies), India, Australia and New Zealand now cherishing their own distinct identities and successes in these sports. An example that exemplifies these cultural differences is the development of cricket and its place within the culture of each of the above nations. All are Commonwealth countries that share a colonial past, but their view of and support for cricket are distinctive. This has implications for the marketing of cricket on a global scale because there is no single global segment of cricketing consumers.

Changes in the cultural landscape within a region can also lead to shifts in patterns of consumption. Increases in international immigration and the rise in the expression of cultural beliefs allow for new sport marketing opportunities. An increase in immigration has the potential to lead to the fragmentation of the sport market. The greater the level of fragmentation, the greater the importance of targeted marketing initiatives and effective distribution techniques needed by sport marketers. Opportunities that could benefit sport marketers in these areas include increases in media distribution channels. In Britain, the launch of the Asian television and radio channels by the BBC attempts to cater for the developing cultural needs of the British-based Asian market. These channels allow sport marketers and their organisations to reach these new emerging markets. For instance, brands can look to tap into successful role models, such as Amir Khan, the British boxer of Pakistani decent, in order to communicate with their key demographics.

The role of religion in the development of cultural life is also an important aspect for consideration by sport marketers. Religious life has certain duties and responsibilities that need to be taken into consideration when marketing sporting tie-ins to religious festivals and events. The operation of sporting facilities has been altered to allow underrepresented people to participate in sport and physical activity. A number of leisure centres from Shepparton in Australia to Luton in Britain are creating environments that allow religious sensitivities to be catered for. The specialised swimming areas staffed by female lifeguards are allowing Muslim women to increase their levels of activity to their benefit and the facility marketer. These new ways of thinking present the marketers of sport with new opportunities. Nevertheless, the importance of marketing research, detailed in Chapter 8, is vital in attempting to understand and ascertain the shifting levels of societal tastes and cultural differences.

The technological environment

The technological environment is probably the most dynamic and uncertain environmental force that faces the sport marketer. Technology influences our daily activities, and although the rate of change of this force has increased in the past 20 years, it has been ever present since the Industrial Revolution. Technology impacts on the ability of sports managers to operate and administer their sport. Hence, technology that has increased the performance of sport and technology that allows for more effective administration are two separate areas of which sport marketers need to be aware.

Sport organisations have used new technologies to improve the playability of their sport for a number of years. In some cases, advances in technology have benefited sport by making it more attractive and hence more marketable to a wider audience. Nevertheless, there are also instances in which advances in technology have taken away from the human error element that has made sport attractive in the past. In the first category, an example of these benefits is the development of stadium technology that has made sport more enjoyable and comfortable to watch. The development of stadia designed for consumer comfort and better viewing, as opposed to the development of stadia for mass spectatorship, has been caused by changes in not only consumer preference but also in technology that allows the modern stadium-goer to sit in relative comfort, out of the elements of the weather, and have the opportunity to receive up-to-date statistical information, internet access and replays on small in-seat information screens. This makes it a very different experience to the days with cold meant pies on a wet and windy terrace. These developments can allow sport marketers to appeal the sport offering to a wider potential audience by using technology to explore new markets and find new income streams.

Although stadium developments such as these may be the exclusive domains of more affluent international sporting organisations, there are still other game-enhancing benefits from technology. The development of racquet material technology in sports such as squash and tennis has allowed many of these sports' participants to use the same types of equipment as the elite players on the international circuits. Technological advances in scoring and timing systems allow a number of local sports teams to equip their facilities with accurate and consistent game-aiding devices that add to the sporting experience for spectators and players. Even advances in micro-processing technology have allowed personal trainers to collect and analyse client information that was once the domain of sports scientists. These benefits have arisen through the rapid diffusion and lowering costs of technology that has placed much of the technology within reach of local organisations and sport participants.

Nevertheless, technology has the ability to reduce some of the predictability that is essential for the marketing of sport. One team and one driver dominated Formula 1 racing in particular. Although Michael Schumacher's success is also because of his superior skills in combination with technology, the domination that he and his Ferrari team exhibited on the track increased the predictability of the sport. Aides such as traction control, race-start programming and automatic gear changes have reduced the driver element to the racing and are reducing the viewing figures (Britcher, 2002). This is requiring those responsible for the marketing of Formula 1 to work harder to highlight the other exciting aspects of the racing and to focus the broadcasts not only on the race leader but the battle for the lower places in order to show a racing element.

All sports have used developments in technology to improve their ability to market and administer their product offerings and extensions. The use of communications technology has allowed sport organisations to communicate with members separated by geographical distances. Whereas onsite meetings and mail-outs are still used, their frequency can be reduced through the availability of cheaper long-distance phone calls, emails, text messages and even video conferencing. For local sports clubs, some of these new technologies are not required, but for organisations working over vast distances in Europe, Asia and Australia, these technologies are proving evermore necessary.

The use of the internet has allowed sport organisations of any size to have a global presence. This alone allows organisations to create a virtual online environment that lets them communicate with members and potential customers, receive feedback, post discussion and news items, watch broadcasts, market merchandise and earn advertising income if they are able to attract sponsors to the site. Although these opportunities are still linked to the ability of the organisation to attract customers from this potentially global area, it does provide sport marketers with a tool for marketing development that is ever advancing.

An increase in technological advances in communication and transport between regions has also created an environment that allows consumer travel on a scale vastly different from the mid- to late 20th century. This increase in travel will open up new opportunities for sport marketers to attract new consumers to their regions for sporting and cultural events. This has implications for sports that regularly operate over international regions, such as Formula 1 racing, powerboat racing and international cricket. For the merchandising arms of sporting events, technology has enabled faster distribution techniques, allowing a virtual-global presence.

The ecological/ethical environment

The ecological and ethical environments have emerged since the early 1990s and are concerned with the interaction of consumers and organisations with the natural and ethical environments. The development of this force has grown from an increase in human consciousness about the importance of how our actions can impact upon interrelated environments, such as the ones discussed so far. Major issues such as global warming, ethical consumerism and sustainable development have arisen from outside the sport industry but are increasingly having an impact on the policies and procedures of sporting organisations.

The increase in concern about global warming and the natural environment has led to changes in the nature of sports consumption. Awareness of the power of the sun, skin cancer and preventative measures to avoid exposure ensures consumers take measures to protect themselves. For instance, an Australian cricket crowd in the late 1970s dressed in a remarkably different fashion than the crowd now in the new millennium. Also, surfers and their spectators across the world now have a good knowledge of the benefits of sun cream and exposure minimisation, and this knowledge creates a safer sporting environment.

Facility operators now implement sustainability procedures to ensure that their levels of waste, noise and other environmental impacts will protect the surrounding ecosystem. The Sydney Olympic Park Trust has a sustainability policy covering a wide range of areas to ensure the effective management of lands, waterways and facilities under the Trust's control. The Trust itself comprises the venues that were part of the Sydney 2000 Olympic Games, which were commended for their level of environmental considerations and awareness. Now cities that are bidding for future Olympic Games have to include a statement in their bidding documents covering the environmental policies to be implemented during the Games period. This highlights the need for sport marketers to locate information on changing trends and include it in the environmental scanning process.

Throughout the past 15 years, charity organisations have looked to sport for assistance in raising the profile of their core issues. The World Wildlife Fund is using sport and community organisations such as the Scouts to involve young people in physical activity and raise their awareness of wildlife issues. Also, individuals attempting to raise the profile of their causes by using their involvement in sport as a promotional benefit are also increasing. In 2004, Michael Long, the indigenous Australian footballer, took part on a walk from Melbourne to Canberra to raise awareness of the plight of indigenous Australian communities. Although initiated by Long, the use of a well-known Australian footballer to highlight social and ethical issues is of great benefit to the affected community at large. These issues are important for sport marketers because it may reflect the changing consumer behaviour.

The development of ethical consumerism as a social trend also has ramifications for marketing practice. The use of cheap labour to manufacture sports goods has an impact on the purchasing decisions of sport shoe and sportswear consumers. Companies such as Nike have come under scrutiny for their outsourcing practices in southeast Asia and Central America. Nike has been required to produce materials explaining the details of its policies in these regions, and the organisation has commissioned research to further investigate these issues. Nevertheless, the complexities of these issues require a combination of educational and public relations strategies to be used by the sport marketers of organisations such as Nike. Hence, the trend towards more ethically responsible footwear is an important issue for which sport marketers need to be attuned. Niche markets are emerging that are demanding footwear that has been ethically traded, such as black-spot (anti-brand) and humanely created and vegetarian (non-leather) shoes. This is in direct response to a growing demographic that is aware of ethically traded and social responsibility issues.

CASE 4.2 **Goss in a struggle to keep backers on board: Team Philips' latest failure may prompt investors to jump ship**   **FT**

Pete Goss flies into Heathrow this morning preparing for a media storm more intense than the North Atlantic tempest that forced the skipper and his crew to abandon Team Philips in the mid-Atlantic on Sunday.

With three mishaps out of three voyages for the radically designed 120ft catamaran, sponsors and supporters are starting to question their loyalty to the £4m project.

At an impromptu dockside news conference in Halifax, Canada, yesterday Goss described the weather conditions that caused the crisis. 'A huge sea built up, some of the worst weather I have ever seen, and we had to run for it. It was really steer for your life.'

The crew had been at sea for eight days practising for The Race, a round-the-world challenge due to start in Barcelona on December 31, when the storm hit. Hurricane-force gusts sent a wave smashing through the central cockpit, making it impossible to steer the boat out of the weather. 'It was very, very sad having to leave her out at sea,' Goss said.

Team Philips continues to drift, 700 miles due west of Ireland and salvage plans are under discussion.

Philips, the Dutch-based electronics company, and British Telecommunications are the principal backers of the team. Both have declined to comment publicly on future support for Goss. John Whybrow, vice-president of Philips Europe, said he hoped to meet the skipper next week for discussions.

Other sponsors are less concerned, for particular reasons. Musto, the British clothing company, has given Team Philips £300,000 as well as equipping the crew with foul weather gear. 'Philips and BT are worried about what this kind of publicity will do to their brands,' said Nigel Musto, head of the company. 'As far as we are concerned, the crew came out of the ocean warm and smiling wearing a Musto survival suit.'

In design terms as well as size, the catamaran is one of the most radical racing yachts ever built. The long, needle-sharp hulls cut through the waves rather than ride over them. The twin windsurfer-style masts are more than 130ft high and without external support.

Both features have already caused big problems. Last April, on the boat's maiden voyage, the port hull snapped in half off the Scilly Isles, causing it to flood and almost sink. After six months of repair work, Goss set off again. On this occasion the mast-housings failed, causing Team Philips to limp back into Dartmouth for another rebuild.

Designer Adrian Thompson has been under a good deal of criticism and yesterday posted his *mea culpa* on the Team Philips web site. 'The boat, which has stretched emotions, budgets and credibility over the last two years, did not, I'm sad to say, provide the basic, safe environment for survival that it should have done and was designed to do.'

'The design elements chosen are not novel for the sake of defying convention, neither were they selected to be sensational. The final design was simply the solution that I was comfortable with, which I thought would combine speed with safety.'

Whether Goss's own reputation for grit and determination will survive yet another calamity remains to be seen. Last month one of his principal crew members resigned, claiming that Goss was obsessed with the project and refused to listen to those with safety concerns.

For The Race itself, the Team Philips fiasco is yet another blow. The prologue races scheduled for this weekend in Monaco were unilaterally cancelled by the authorities when it became apparent that only two of the potential seven Race competitors might appear.

Bruno Peyron, the organiser, and Disney, his principal backer, are praying that fate and the weather will allow the remaining catamarans to arrive in Barcelona to start The Race at midnight on New Year's Eve.

Source: K. Wheatley, *Financial Times*, 15 December 2000

Question

1. From the above newspaper article, discuss the marketing issues for the sport marketer.

■ Legal/regulatory environment

The final environmental force impacting sport marketers is a combination of laws and regulations that may arise from legislators or governing associations. When examining legal considerations, sport marketers are usually subject to act within the law, as specified by legislation, and within codes of practice for a collection of organisations. Governments, trade associations, peak agencies or the operating procedures of the organisation itself generally impose regulations on sport organisations. For instance, if a sport organisation advertises in Britain, the Advertising Standards Authority (ASA) regulates the adverts. This ensures that the adverts are of a certain quality and demonstrates that an industry can implement checks for self-regulation.

Legislation is usually enacted by the national government and affects all organisations and people within its jurisdiction. In 2004, the final component of the Disability Discrimination Act 1995 was enforced in Britain. This legislation specified, amongst other issues, that all businesses would have equal access for all people to their facilities. This has required a number of businesses, both sporting and non-sporting, to adapt the construction and promote the accessibility of their facility. Although legislation binds on all organisations equally, it is beneficial to sport marketers to promote good practice in their operations. Sometimes legislation enacted within an international region, such as the EU, is binding on the operations of all organisations within the region. Legislation to protect competitive practices and equal opportunities can have important ramifications for sport marketers. Because of the special nature of sport, sport organisations have in the past operated in cooperation in order to gain the best access to resources. Anti-competitive legislation can place some of these traditional practices and sources of revenue under threat. For instance, recent investigations by the legislators into the collective selling of television rights could mean that legislation could be enacted to stop this collective selling, hence opening it up to a free market. What this means for sport marketers in the smaller clubs that benefited from the collective selling is that marketing budgets can be reduced. Likewise, anti-tobacco legislation came into effect across Europe in 2006. The loss of this important revenue stream for a number of motor sports will equally lead to cutbacks in marketing budgets to a similar effect as seen in the television revenue.

Governing bodies, to ensure levels of control over the marketing and operations of sport, impose regulations. An international governing body can act to enforce legislation that they believe maintains the unique features of the game. The Fédération Internationale de Football Association (FIFA) enforces a ban on virtual advertising on certain aspects of the television broadcast. For instance, no virtual advertising is allowed on the crowd, which aims to protect the crowd at the televised venue. Without the crowd in the background, the FIFA deems its product altered. For smaller sporting organisations, this would have an impact on their ability to market the broadcasts. Virtual advertising is unique in that it can be tailored for many fragmented markets from the one broadcast, hence increasing total revenue. Likewise, the venue marketing of Croke Park in Ireland is restricted by the regulations imposed by the Gaelic Athletic Association (GAA) that only GAA-affiliated sports can be played at the ground. This limits the scope of sport marketers' ability to secure bookings for the venue.

Through their peak sporting agencies, governments can also regulate to control organisations. Under the New Labour government, UK Sport has required a number of national governing bodies to review their operations to ensure they are modern and customer focused. Although this modernisation policy is striving for efficiency, sport marketers in these bodies need to be aware that poor compliance could lead to funding shortfalls and hence smaller marketing budgets. Once again, this demonstrates the interconnectedness of the external environments and confines sport marketers' ability to scan effectively but addressing one environment at a time.

Techniques for gathering information about the sport marketing environment

As can be seen by the number of external forces that act upon an organisation and sport marketers' role within it, their information needs are extensive. The aim of gathering this environmental information is to assist in predicting the potential impacts and opportunities presented by these forces. As soon as this material is collected, it is integrated by the sport marketer into the plans and strategies of the marketing team. A number of tools can be used for environmental scanning and data collection that are available to sport marketers. For this chapter, we will focus on two techniques. The first technique is the strengths, weaknesses, opportunities and threats analysis (SWOT), in which the marketer analyses the external opportunities and threats alongside the internal strengths and weaknesses of the organisation itself. The second technique is the environmental threat and opportunity profile (ETOP), which develops the SWOT analysis in light of the external environmental forces.

SWOT analysis

The strengths, weaknesses, opportunities and threats faced by the sport marketer vary between organisations. Nevertheless, if the information on external forces and internal characteristics is collected carefully, the SWOT analysis can present the organisation with a tool for developing the business. Zhuang (2002) stressed that SWOT is not really an analytical method but is instead a way of presenting information in an easily accessible way. Furthermore, each factor contained on the table must be supported with evidence. For the purpose of this chapter, strengths are capabilities that an organisation does well. For instance, Lords Cricket Ground in London has strong tangible resources, such as the grounds, stadium and pitch as well as strong intangible resources such as history and tradition. These are noted in the SWOT analysis through comparison with competitors and rivals. Weaknesses, however, are factors that hinder the operations of the organisation, such as customer knowledge. When TelstraDome in Victoria opened in 2001, the major event capability was hindered by the fact that fans of Australian-rules football traditionally arrive 5 to 10 minutes before the start of matches. The stadium, being new, used scanning technology to read the tickets but required the fans to use the tickets in a way they were unaccustomed to. Because of this new method of entering the ground, many spectators were left queued outside even after the game began. The lack of customer knowledge or education led to negative publicity for the stadium mangers and staff and highlighted a weakness in their operations.

In the opportunities and threats section of the SWOT analysis, the sport marketer can begin to use the information contained in the external environment analysis. Therefore, opportunities are any external force that could be favourable to the organisation. The trend towards funding for social and sport development programmes in Britain under New Labour has meant that a number of charities have been able to access increased resources, allowing a greater range of programmes. Increases in technology are allowing microtechnology to be applied to new areas. The development of pedometers and heart rate monitors to mini personal training devices is placing health and fitness knowledge in the hands of consumers.

Alternatively, threats consist of any environmental force that poses a risk to the organisation. Highlighting the variability of these external forces is important because the previous example of nanotechnology can be seen as a threat to personal trainers as their specialised knowledge is superseded. Other threats could take the form of increased regulation in the advertising industry in the promotion of unhealthy food to children, or increases in ecological forces such as regulations for environmental practice (e.g., sun protection) may impede on the ability to organise outdoor sports events.

The range of opportunities and threats that can be compiled from this chapter is extensive, hence the importance of accurate, evidenced information.

ETOP analysis

The ETOP developed by Palmer (2000) allows for marketers to estimate which opportunities have the greatest potential. The greatest potential is whatever factors the sport marketer is attempting to achieve. It can range from the size of the market to enter to the number of new distribution channels available. When Twenty-20 cricket was introduced in Britain using smaller venues, characterised by small- to medium-sized crowds, the England and Wales Cricket Board was able to distribute the Twenty-20 product with an increased feeling of atmosphere. Other organisations such as Nike may release new sportswear in order to tap into a market with greater profitability. Nike's product range in golf and tennis highlights offerings in sportswear markets with higher profit margins than others. Creating an ETOP for each sport organisation can allow the organisation to direct its marketing efforts. Figure 4.2 highlights an ETOP analysis for a National Stadium in any given country.

Although the above shows a basic application of environmental forces on the marketing of a national stadium, it exemplifies how a range of environmental forces can contain both threats and opportunities for sport marketers. For instance, although the structures of the stadium would require adjustments under discrimination legislation,

Factor	Major opportunity	Minor opportunity	Neutral	Minor threat	Major threat	Probability of occurrence
Political						
Conflict arising between local and national government over stadium usage						
				√		0.2
Economic						
Increases in corporate interest tax rates						
					√	0.4
Sociocultural						
Social concerns with declining levels of non-corporate (general admission) seats						
					√	0.6
Technological						
Increases in flat-screen technology allowing better in-stadia experience						
		√				0.8
Ecological						
Increased public concern over disposal of waste materials						
			√			0.4
Legal/Regulatory						
Disability discrimination legislation requiring equal access to all areas						
	√					1.0

Figure 4.2 ETOP applied to national sporting facility

Source: Adapted from Palmer (2000) *Principles of Marketing* by permission of Oxford University Press.

the marketers could use it as an opportunity to highlight the innovations of the stadium and its leadership role in facility management. Alternatively, increasing proportions of the stadium seating to corporate access would benefit the financials of the venue, but it could also generate negative publicity because national stadia are supposedly 'for' the people, and such increases would limit the public's use and access. The probability factor is a means of prioritising which opportunities or threats should hold the most immediate attention of the sport marketer.

SWOT analysis and ETOP are merely two techniques for gathering environmental information and assessing its applicability to the sport organisation. There are more techniques that are beyond the scope of this chapter but central to gathering information is the robustness of the method in which it is collected. As stated, it is imperative that all factors are supported by evidence and research. Failure to do so could place incorrect data into the marketing process and lead to the misapplication of marketing strategies.

Locating sources of information needed to understand the sport marketing environment

Because of the large range of external environmental forces impacting on the sport organisation, it is vital that sport marketers access information sources that are timely and accurate. The concept of timeliness means that the information is current. For instance, the political climate can be generally divided into terms in office. Each party belongs to a certain ideology that structures its reasoning and policies. Therefore, when assessing the political environment, sport marketers must take into consideration which party is in office. Historical details of the opposing party's time in office are generally not necessary because they do not hold the decision-making power at the given time.

The variety and types of information are numerous. A lot of information can be found by using a search tool on the web. This provides sport marketers with a wealth of information on any of the particular environments but should be used with caution. The internet contains information of varying quality; anyone can post a web page with the use of their personal computer, so knowledge of web page suffixes is important. Generally .com sites can be posted by anyone but include businesses in the United States. Sites with .gov are government sites, .edu/.ac is used for educational and academic sites, and .org for is used for not-for-profit organisations. Nevertheless, even organisations and governments have their own collective thoughts and opinions that can contain biases. Sport marketers should take care to add on the suffix of the country that the organisation is interested in for collecting information on. Table 4.1 highlights some of these.

More general environmental trend information can be found through statistical offices such as the Australian Bureau of Statistics (http://www.abs.gov.au) or National Statistics On-line in Britain (http://www.statistics.gov.uk). These sites contain economic and social trends that are of importance to sport marketers. Industry publications and news sites such as *Sport Business* (http://www.sportbusiness.com) and *Sports Business Journal* (http://www.sportsbusinessjournal.com) provide more specific environmental trends and developments in the sport industry. Nevertheless, traditional methods such as searching through industry reports and reference collections at libraries should not be discounted by sport marketers.

Table 4.1 **Internet suffixes by nation**

Country	Suffix	Country	Suffix
United Kingdom	.uk	Greece	.gr
Australia	.au	China	.cn
Germany	.de	Belgium	.be
New Zealand	.nz	Netherlands	.nl
France	.fr	Finland	.fi
Japan	.jp	Norway	.no
Malaysia	.my	Sweden	.se

Conclusions

The process of environmental scanning requires sport marketers to consider a range of external forces and pressures that can be characterised as constantly changing and dynamic. Sport marketers should undertake the environmental scanning process by following four steps. The initial step is identifying the external environmental factors that are most likely to impact the marketing of the sport organisations. Although the external environment is fundamentally similar for all organisations within a given context, some external forces may impact to a greater degree on different organisations. The political environment is concerned with the underlying ideology of the government party in power and the tier of government upon which it operates. The discussion of the economic environment reveals that the macroeconomic business cycle can impact on consumers' willingness to spend and that microeconomic factors can be manipulated to ensure business success or even the survival of sporting leagues.

Shifts in the social makeup of a region and changes in cultural tastes and attitudes can also act as an external force that can be termed the sociocultural environment. Sport marketers who operate over vast regions, inter-regionally or in densely populated regions should be aware of any developments in this area. Advances in technology are creating new communication and administration techniques that can also be of benefit to sport marketers. Keeping abreast of technological change is one method for responding to this environment. Furthermore, increases in ecological and ethical awareness in consumers are creating an increasingly important consideration for sport marketers to promote their sense of public responsibility. Finally, changes in legislation and regulations that impact on the organisation present sport marketers with barriers and challenges that new techniques will need to overcome. Step two uses tools to prioritise the potential impact of these external forces. After prioritisation has taken place, the information is integrated into the marketing process, which eventually establishes the plans and strategies the sport marketer will wield. Measuring the effectiveness of the information gathering is important because the process of environmental scanning is as continuous as the evolving external environments.

Discussion questions

1. Why would two sport organisations, one quasi-governmental, the other private, be influenced in different ways by the political environment?

2. What implications are there for sport marketers if the global economic environment took a downturn?
3. What issues may arise if sport marketers use too many internet sources from general .com websites.
4. Detail some of the potential shortcomings in sport marketers' basing their decisions of too much secondary data.

Guided reading

The varied nature of the environmental analysis requires sport marketers to cover a broad field of enquiry. Political trends are usually covered on a national basis, but comparisons have been made on sport policy by authors such as Houlihan (1997) in *Sport, Policy and Politics: A Comparative Analysis* and Thoma and Chalip (1996) in *Sport Governance in the Global Community*. These authors compare and contrast various European, Australian and North American sporting structures and polices that may provide background information for the sport marketer.

Westerbeek and Smith (2002) in *Sport Business in the Global Marketplace* provide a global perspective on the management and marketing of sport, covering a range of external environmental issues and important trends for the future. Moreover, in their following publication, *The Sport Business Future* (2004), they postulate that advances in technology will have important ramifications for sport marketing and management.

Keywords

Consumer behaviour; ecological/ethical environment; ETOP analysis; feedback; franchises; governance; intangible; legal/regulatory environment; marketing plans; mnemonics; outsourcing; quangos; SWOT.

Bibliography

Britcher, C. (2002) F1 sets sights on eastern promise, *SportBusiness* 76:29.
FIFA (1999) *Regulations for Use of Virtual Advertising*, Retrieved 24 January 2005, from http://www.fifa.com/fifa/handbook/VA/downloads/VirtualRegs_e.pdf
Henry, I. (2002) *The Politics of Leisure Policy*, London: Palgrave Macmillan.
Howard, D. and Burton, R. (2002) Sport marketing in a recession: It's a brand new game, *International Journal of Sport Marketing & Sponsorship* 4(1):23–41.
Houlihan, B.M.J. (1997) *Sport, Policy and Politics: A Comparative Analysis*, London: Routledge.
Houlihan, B.M.J. and White, A. (2002) *The Politics of Sport Development*, London: Routledge.
Hylton, K., Bramham, P., Jackson, D. and Nesti, M. (2001) *Sports Development: Policy, Process and Practice*, London: Routledge.
Kotler, P. (2000) *Marketing Management*, 5th edn, Upper Saddle River, NJ: Prentice Hall.
Marcotti, G. (2005) Welcome to the cheap feats, *Times Online*, Retrieved 24 January 2005, from http://www.timesonline.co.ukprintFriendly/0,,1-31-1455047,00.html

Mullin, B.J. (1985) 'Characteristics of sports marketing', in G. Lewis and H. Appenzellar (eds), *Successful Sport Management*, Charlottesville, VA: Miche, pp. 101–23.

Palmer, A. (2000) *Principles of Marketing*, Oxford: Oxford University Press.

Shank, M.D. (2005) *Sport Marketing: A Strategic Perspective*, 3rd edn, Upper Saddle River, NJ: Pearson Education.

Shilbury, D. and Deane, J. (2000) *Sport Management in Australia: An Organisational Overview*, Melbourne, Australia: Bowater School of Management and Marketing.

Shilbury, D., Quick, S. and Westerbeek, H. (2003) *Strategic Sport Marketing*, 2nd edn, Sydney, Australia: Allen and Unwin.

Westerbeek, H. and Smith, A. (2002) *Sport Business in the Global Marketplace*, London: Palgrave Macmillan.

Westerbeek, H. and Smith, A. (2004) *The Sport Business Future*, London: Palgrave Macmillan.

Zhuang, L. (2002) Making sense of SWOT, *Business Review* 2(9):18–9.

Recommended websites

Advertising Standards Authority
http://www.asa.org.uk/asa

Black-Spot Anti-Corporation
http://adbusters.org/metas/corpo/blackspotsneaker/behindtheshoe.html

CIA Factbook
http://www.cia.gov/cia/publications/factbook/

Sport Business
http://www.sportbusiness.com/home.adp

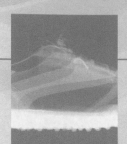

Chapter 5

Sport and consumer buying behaviour

Linda Trenberth
Birkbeck, University of London
Ron Garland
University of Waikato, New Zealand

Learning outcomes

Upon completion of this chapter, the reader should be able to:

- Identify the range of consumers buying products and services in the sport market.

- Explore participant and spectator segments.

- Understand the decision-making process through which consumers purchase goods and services in the sport market.

- Indicate the motives underlying the buying behaviour of these consumers.

- Indicate the influences that will impinge upon these motives.

- Consider the impact of initial and repeat purchase decisions, and retention, for sport marketers.

Overview of chapter

This chapter aims to expand an understanding of consumer behaviour relative to the unique products and services offered in the sport industry. It seeks to explore the range of consumers buying products and services, their reasons for doing so and models of consumer decision-making. The chapter draws on recent and continuing research efforts that aim to reveal the motivations and behaviours upon which marketers can base segmentation models of sport consumption and that allow marketers to customise their marketing communication efforts to sport consumers.

Introduction

Sport is now recognised as an important sector of UK economic activity, accounting for close to 2% of both gross domestic product (GDP) and employment and nearly 3% of consumer expenditure (Gratton, Kokolakakis, Ping Kung and O'Keefe, 2001).

Sport-related marketing has grown enormously as individual sport markets compete for consumers' discretionary income. Therefore, understanding consumption and consumer behaviour in relation to the unique products and services offered in the sport industry is an important and core area of sport marketing. Consuming is a form of activity in which people use consumption objects in a number of ways (Holt, 1995, p. 14). The desire to understand the behaviour of sport consumers is of increasing importance to sport marketers so they can more effectively 'refine marketing activities, redesign sport products, monitor price sensitivities, adjust promotional campaigns and generally customise the sport experience to fit the particular needs of each customer segment' (Stewart, Smith and Nicholson, 2003, p. 206). Although as Gratton et al. (2001) have pointed out, most recent interest has focused on expenditure at the elite level in terms of sponsorship, payments for broadcasting rights, transfer fees and players' salaries, consumer expenditure in the sport market consists in the main of expenditures related to the consumers' own participation in sport rather than to sport spectating. All consumer groups will therefore be considered in this chapter in relation to the consumer buying behaviour of sport products and services, the influences upon participants and spectators and the spectacle, and some of the theories of consumer behaviour that help shape marketers' delivery of sport products and services.

Sport consumer behaviour cannot be reduced to a narrow set of uniform traits as sport consumers come in as many guises as there are sport products. The extent to which people are interested in and follow sport and sport teams, for example, ranges from occasionally watching a televised game or attending a live event to owning season tickets and attending or watching as many games as possible (Funk and James, 2001, p. 119). The sport product has been described as a good, service or any combination that is designed to provide benefits to a sport spectator, participant or sponsor (Shank, 2005, p. 16). Any given consumption product, be it a food item or a sport activity, is typically consumed in a variety of ways for a number of different reasons by different groups, according to Holt (1995). It is incumbent on market researchers to study the variety of ways in which people consume sport products, to understand how these differences vary across groups and situations and to explain the conditions that structure how different groups consume.

Sport consumers

Who are sport consumers? Can sport consumers be neatly compartmentalised into spectators and participants? Customer groups are clearly varied. Meenaghan and O'Sullivan (1999) citing Baker (1982) stated that organised sport activities always involve four groups of people: athletes, spectators, sponsors and commentators. Williams (1994, p. 393, cited in Meenaghan and O'Sullivan, 1999) summarised the increasing significance of the latter two categories due to the impact of commercialism in sport succinctly by stating:

> . . . part of the impact of television, the rise of sponsorship and the growth of the sport business has produced conflicting notions of the client. Who in the days of globalisation is the customer for sport? Traditionally it was the live spectator, now greatly outnumbered by the television viewer. Today sponsorship has become central: if the sponsors are paying for the event they, must implicitly be a customer.

It has been argued increasingly that television produces audiences, which it sells to advertisers, so the advertisers, are a customer and the television audience is merely a 'product'.

Shank (2005) stated that the sport industry seeks to satisfy the needs of three distinct types of consumers: spectators, participants and sponsors. Clearly, the definition of the sport consumer, the motivations of consumption and the identity of the sport product are all complex and despite best efforts, many sport organisations, mostly governing bodies and clubs, still do not know enough about sport consumers, who they are, what are they looking for, what influences their purchasing decisions, what constitutes a high-quality experience and how can they be retained. This, of course, is where market research becomes so important, and this is dealt with in more depth in Chapter 8.

Sport participants

As Gratton et al. (2001) have pointed out, the single most important variable that determines the economic health of the sport market is the level of sport participation. Participants can be broken down into professional, amateur, recreational and online including fantasy games, chat rooms and information/statistics. Many of the subsectors of the overall sport market are dependent on the level of sport participation, including sport clothing and footwear, equipment, admission and membership fees, travel and so on (Gratton et al., 2001). However, although consumers are spending more money than they used to, whatever the activity they participate in, participation levels in the United Kingdom have remained static overall, with growth in some areas such as in the health and fitness area and declines in others such as in squash, and with a worrying falloff in the number of young people participating in physical activity. The evidence suggests that there has been a relative decline in more 'traditional' team and partner sports accompanied by increased participation in a more diversified range of activities such as online activities (Coalter, 1999). This has implications for sport marketers who can influence to some extent the volume and direction of participation in sport.

If participation is the lifeblood of the sport industry, then the role of sport marketers becomes even more important when participation rates fall or remain static. The government in the United Kingdom has recognised the importance of sport participants for a number of reasons with the launching of a sport strategy, *A Sporting Future for All* and an investment of some £750m mainly targeted at youth sport, and the long-term forecast is that the recent decline in young people's participation will be reversed (Gratton et al., 2001). Understanding the sport participant consumer in all segments of the market is vital for such strategies to have any chance of succeeding.

As the number of sport participants grows, the need for sport marketing expertise also increases. For example, as Lough and Irwin (2001) point out, the number of female participants as well as the number of female spectators has escalated at a phenomenal rate in the United States. This trend is borne out in the United Kingdom as well (Gratton et al., 2001). Lough and Irwin (2001) suggest, although their focus is the North American market, that the emerging role of women in sport presents opportunities for funding women's sport sponsorship proposals. As corporations are relying more and more on the merits of sport sponsorship to market their companies' products and services (see below), the sponsorship of women's sport, a growing market, makes it a viable market to tap into. It is important to identify and understand these trends and statistics if the opportunities of such marketplace developments are to be taken advantage of.

| CASE 5.1 | A rare Scottish success in the beautiful game | |

As every sports fan knows, football is a game of two halves. Losing players are invariably sick as parrots, while those on winning side tend to be over the moon.

The latter cliché suits the bullish mood of Goals Soccer Centres' management. Since the five-a-side football centre operator floated on Aim last month its shares have risen from an issue price of 59p to 106p.

Goals, which, is headquartered in Scotland, says the investor demand reflects the growth of five-a-side football, which is booming across the UK and has become more popular than the 11-a-side game. The only problem, it says, is there are not enough places to play it, which is why it aims to open a further 14 facilities in the next three years.

Goals has just opened its 12th centre, which is in the Midlands, and plans to open another five this year, including a complex near Heathrow and one on Teesside. 'This market is big and has hardly been touched,' says Bill Gow, finance director.

Costing about £1.8m a site, typically, each facility has 10 five-a-side pitches and three seven-a-side arenas. All the pitches are floodlit and feature 'rubber-crumb synthetic grass' technology, which is used by many professional clubs in their training centres.

Keith Rogers, Goals' managing director, says the company's synthetic grass differs from other artificial surfaces, which are widely resented by players because they have the potential to leave nasty burns. He says: 'Our grass doesn't burn your knees or elbows if you fall. You can really dive about.'

The group, chaired by Graham Wilson, chairman of Parkdean Holidays, hopes to attract footballers fed up with sub-standard surfaces, tatty changing rooms and other poor facilities by introducing a service designed to set it apart from other five-a-side facilities.

For example, the sound of 80,000 fans shouting and cheering at Real Madrid's Bernebeu Stadium is piped into the changing rooms at Goals Centres to get players in the mood for their match. Mr Rogers says: 'We're trying to reflect the excitement and passion of football throughout what we do. We want to become a nationally recognised brand.'

Finding new locations is difficult, although he adds the group has a good pipeline of sites. Before the floatation Goals estimated the UK could easily accommodate more than 100 sites.

One source of land is schools, some of which have been willing partners in the development of Goals sites. The company is working with six schools – including one in Ruislip, west London – that are willing to act as partners for development in return for free use of the facilities by students. Goals, leases the land from the school and pays an annual rent. With the majority of five-a-side matches taking place at weekends or after 5pm, the arrangement appears to suit everybody. 'It gives the schools a sports facility they don't have to pay for,' says Mr Rogers. 'It gets kids into sport and is a way of the public and private sector working together.'

The group has 45,000 people playing on its pitches every week. It is exploring marketing and sponsorship ideas such as pitch-side advertising with commercial partners across its network of sites. Keith Rogers is adamant the business will not go the way of the health and fitness sector, which grew too quickly, resulting in consolidation and publicly-quoted operators being taken private. 'We think this is a unique industry and don't compare ourselves to health and fitness clubs,' he says. 'We have extremely low levels of attrition – people play (football) because they want to, not because they feel they have to.'

Source: M. Garrahan, *Financial Times*, 27 January 2005

Questions

1. Why do you think there has been such growth in five-a-side football?

2. How might market research on five-a-side football provide information for such constituent groups as providers, governing bodies, government and the consumers?

3. How might sponsors respond to the opportunities the growth of five-a-side football presents?

Sport spectators

'If the sporting event is at the heart of the sport industry then the spectator is the blood that keeps it running' (Shank, 2005, p. 12). As Shank (2005) stated, spectators either observe the event by physically attending or they observe via one of several broadcast media. According to Shank (2005), sport consumers not only become spectators in person or through the media; they can also be individuals or corporations, and because of the power of the corporate consumer, the focus of sport marketers has changed from catering to the needs of consumers at the event to pleasing the media broadcasting the event to spectators in remote locations.

The money associated with satisfying the needs of the media is enormous. For example, News Corporation signed a 5-year broadcasting rights deal worth $323m (US) with the South African, New Zealand and Australian Rugby Unions from 2006, which will include the rights to Super 14 matches and an expanded Tri nations Test series among the three nations plus the rights to all other internationals played by the three countries on their home soil (Lewes, 2004). BSkyB, Rupert Murdoch's pay-TV company will pay £1.02 billion to televise English Premier League's soccer games during the 3 years starting 2004 (*Dominion Post*, 12 August, 2004). These large sums, of course, increase the control of the major media networks over the sport event, such as in the scheduling of events (Westerbeek and Smith, 2003, p. 119).

The spectator market in the United Kingdom is dominated by football, according to Gratton et al. (2001), which accounts for well over half the number of people who watch sports by attending events or by watching them on television. Consumers of sport, whether participants or spectators, are now spending more on their sport consumption than ever before even though the numbers consuming have not risen substantially. Consumer expenditures on subscriptions to sport channels, for example, have grown from nothing to more than £1 billion. People now pay substantial amounts for something they once paid nothing for. Identifying and understanding the different types of spectator consumption is a key consideration for sport marketers when designing a marketing strategy.

Sport sponsors

Other equally important sport consumers are sponsors (in most cases, a business) that exchange money or product for the right to associate their names or products with a sport event. Increasingly, corporations are relying on the merits of sport sponsorship to market their companies' products and services (Howard and Crompton, 1995). Lough and Irwin (2001) showed that in North America, sponsorship expenditure rose 15% in 1998 to $5.4 billion and has reached around $19 billion worldwide in the past decade. For example, the car manufacturer Subaru reported recently (Kurylko, 2004) that the company spends as much as 15% of its marketing budget on events that involve sport participants. Subaru reportedly pays a lot of attention to who their customers are and what they do through market research, and the company targets its sponsorship and advertising efforts accordingly. Subaru and its dealers sponsor about 400 special interest events each year, and the company has a presence at about 1200 gatherings annually.

BMI, a British Midlands-based airline, was signed up as the official sponsor of 2004 Premier league champions Arsenal in its biggest sponsorship deal to date, giving BMI the right to use the club's logo, name, trademark and image across all BMI marketing materials and access to Arsenal's database (*Marketing Week*, 26 August, 2004, p. 12). Carlsberg, in a six-figure tie-up, became Tottenham Hotspur Football Club's sponsor in a three-year deal which saw Carlsberg secure exclusive brand sector rights at Tottenham, including branding on stadium signage, use of club's imagery, tickets for hospitality, signed shirts and player appearances (*Marketing UK*, 18 August, 2004, p. 6). Corporations pursue sponsorship opportunities to achieve enhanced image and awareness in targeted markets or to enhance sales and market share. Sponsors have to decide what sport to sponsor and whether to sponsor events, teams, leagues, male or female individual athletes and level of competition. As securing corporate sponsorship for sport grows increasingly competitive, acknowledging differences based on age and gender of sport properties may be one strategy for enhancing existing relationships and improving the acquisition of new partnerships, according to Lough and Irwin (2001).

Apart from identifying broad groups of consumers, it is also important to be able to identify the key definable demographic, psychographic and attitudinal segments of sport consumers. Developing an understanding of who sport consumers are and what factors influence their consumption behaviour are critical for sport managers, marketers, merchandisers, television networks, advertisers and sponsors who wish to increase the consumption of sport-related products. This chapter will now look more closely at models of consumer behaviour and the motivations of sport consumers.

Consumer behaviour models

Studying consumer behaviour in sport tends to follow the standard decision-making process models prevalent in social and business science. The multidisciplinary nature of research in sport consumption abounds with psychologists, sociologists, historians, anthropologists, geographers, tourism specialists, economists, marketers, communication and management specialists and doubtless several other academic disciplines bringing their own perspectives and contributions to the understanding of sport behaviour. Irrespective of academic background, the core model of consumer behaviour applies.

This model (Figure 5.1) is usually described as having the individual's decision-making process – the 'spine' – at the centre, surrounded by the three major 'influences' upon that decision-making, namely, the consumer's own internal or psychological state; external factors from 'society'; and situational factors such as time, environment and geography. We should remember that models of consumer behaviour are just that – models – and they are used to try to simplify our understanding of complex processes. However, 'to suggest that it is possible to construct a blueprint that is

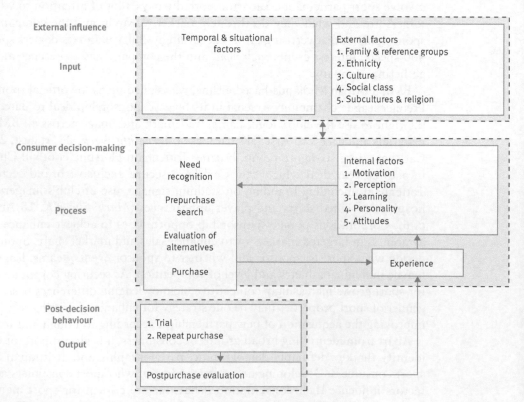

Figure 5.1 **A simple model of consumer decision-making**

capable of determining behaviour is foolhardy' (Shilbury, Quick and Westerbeek, 2003, pp. 38–39). Although academics might debate the influences upon decision-making processes and how decisions are actually formed, the five-step decision-making 'spine' in Figure 5.1 depicting a sequence of steps is relatively universal. These steps are problem recognition, information search, evaluation of alternatives, participation ('purchase') and postparticipation evaluation. How much time we spend in each step is a function of the salience, and level of involvement, we have in the decision and whether we have made such a decision (or one like it) before.

The *problem recognition* stage in the sport domain is rather an unwieldy term. Rarely is sport participation or sport spectatorship a 'problem' in the economic sense – indeed, it is an opportunity! Nevertheless, we can recognise a gap between the *desired* state ('where we want to be') and the *actual* state ('where we are now'). Most sport participants can relate to this situation with their golf handicap, their level of fitness or their club ranking. Next is the *information search* stage, and with it a trawling of our memory (internal source) for any previous experience or the use of external sources to find out more about the decisions we face. Hence, in this step, we try to minimise risk and seek reassurance – in short, become 'more informed'. We seek such information from a variety of sources, some formal (e.g., the media) and some informal (e.g., family and friends).

The *evaluation of alternatives* now follows. These alternative courses of action are assessed by a set of criteria (formed from our search phase, prior knowledge, images, beliefs, attitudes) and perhaps via heuristics or mental rules-of-thumb (e.g., price–value relationships, popularity and reputation of the game to be played or viewed, presence of star players) that we use to help make shortcuts in decision time. Finally, we have reached the time to actually partake or participate – the 'purchase'. Even now other disruptions or irritations can take place in the sport domain. Events can be postponed, tickets can be sold out, sickness can occur, but these instances might merely restart the decision-making process. Assuming a 'purchase' (participation or spectatorship) has been made, the process does not end here. Rather, a post hoc evaluation can occur during which we might weigh up how the 'purchase' performed. Did it meet our expectations? Were we satisfied? The level of satisfaction achieved will form an important factor in propensity to repeat the experience.

Internal and external factors affecting sport decision-making

Although the step-like, sequential nature of the decision-making process is conceptually elegant, not all steps are always followed or with equal emphasis. Impulse or 'snap' decisions can occur, just as elongated, year-long decisions are possible. Obviously, each depends upon the amount of involvement, investment (in both time and money), importance, risk and so on.

It is timely now to review the internal factors that impinge on a sport consumption decision. Also known as psychological factors, these elements of the 'individual' include personality, motivation, perception, learning, beliefs and attitudes. Our *personality* is formed from how we react to the surrounding environment. We all know people with personalities who are just not 'cut out' to be sport participants, just as we know people whose aggressive personalities are well suited to playing rugby or engaging in boxing or motor racing. *Motivation* provides our desire to participate or spectate; *perception* is our own view (of the sport, in this case) based on the images we have and the *beliefs* and *attitudes* we hold; *learning*, whether by reward or punishment (forms of reinforcement) from previous sport participation or spectatorship (behaviourist theory) or by achieving our personal goals (cognitive theory); and *beliefs* and *attitudes*, which are the sum total of previous experience, feelings, opinions, thoughts we have about the sport of interest.

The *external* factors that can influence our sport decision-making processes are many, varied and of unequal weight. Family, social class, age, ethnicity, culture, religion and reference groups can all play a part. *Social class* is not just income related but is also affected by our educational level, occupation and by those with whom we associate. *Reference groups*, which can include family, friends, 'significant others', members of our clubs and teams, and so on, can all influence our attitudes and behaviour. *Culture* includes all the beliefs, mores, traditions, customs and values (and often, shared language) that we pass on from generation to generation. Varying beliefs about the role of fitness in human well being, about diet, about physical appearance, and so on are plain to see across cultures and are especially germane to the role of sport in society, and indeed, individual decision-making about sport participation and sport spectatorship. Also impacting here are various ethnic, racial and religious 'subcultures'.

Finally, various *temporal* and *situational* factors dictate: 'in other words we are always making a decision in the context of some unique situation' (Shank, 2005, p. 154). How we feel at the time (our mood), the 'atmosphere' (affected by others) as well as the weather and our physical surroundings, the presence or absence of *time* constraints, our motivation for participation, and so on all contribute to our decision-making processes. And in the realm of sport, political influences, whether at central, local or club governance levels are noteworthy, too.

Sport spectatorship decisions see many of the same influences as those already discussed. For the active sport participants in the community, there is considerable overlap between participation and spectatorship (e.g., golf is enjoyed by millions, both on the golf course and in front of the television set featuring the British Open). Virtually no sporting code enjoys enough revenue from sponsorship or broadcast media rights to ignore the contribution 'through the turnstiles' – game day attendance by various types of sports fans.

Motivational factors behind sport consumer behaviour

In Sloan's 1985 review (cited in McDonald, Milne and Hong, 2002) of sport motivation, it was suggested that motivational factors traditionally used to explain sport participation could also be applied to sport spectatorship. McDonald et al., (2002) identified 13 motivational constructs in their research measuring motivations for spectating and participant markets. These included physical, fitness, risk taking, stress reduction, aggression, competition, achievement, skill mastery, aesthetics, value development and self-actualisation. The results of their research showed that large variance exists between sports and the complexity of motivations driving sport consumers. For sport participation, four motivational factors that reflect unique aspects of sport consumption were labelled as mental well being, basic sport, social needs and fitness needs. For sport spectators, these factors were mental well being and social, basic sport and personal needs. It is suggested that sport marketers consider using such a set of motivational measures for participants rather than relying on demographics, as has traditionally been the case, to project participation and spectating rates.

An understanding of what motivates spectators to attend sporting events and the factors that influence such attendance are vital for sport administrators. Factors that influence sports fans' game attendance have been researched extensively in the United Kingdom, United States, Europe and Australasia. No longer can sport organisations rely on the 'Field of Dreams' (a popular movie of the 1980s) 'if we build it they will come' mentality. Non-capacity crowds are the norm. Attendance is one of the primary revenue sources for team sport (Hill and Green, 2000; Howard, 1999), and examining the motives that help put fans in the stands has preoccupied sport researchers in the past two decades. Successful professional sport promotion now requires concerted marketing effort. In this context, it is possible to identify and improve areas of the sport marketing mix in the pursuit of more spectators.

Just as with sport decision-making, factors affecting fan attendance have been discussed in several academic literatures, notably social psychology, management, marketing, leisure, tourism and the growing subdiscipline of sport management. Much of the foundation research in sport has been in social psychological contexts, particularly in sports fan allegiance. Comprehensive reviews of this work are covered in, for example, Funk, Haugtvedt and Howard (2000) and Laverie and Arnett (2000). A focus on identity salience and behaviour in the context of fan loyalty is common in such work, which often tests the proposition that higher identity salience results in higher home team game attendance. In turn, the emotions associated with attachment to and involvement with the home team help reinforce and maintain fan self-concept. The enduring involvement with a home team epitomises the 'aficionado or diehard fans' of Wann and Branscombe's (1990) research, in which they gave prominence to the factors of *self-esteem enhancement*: BIRGing (basking in reflected glory) and its corollary CORFing (cutting off from reflected failure). Thus, the role of self-concept in fan attendance has not been overlooked (see, for example, Mahony and Moorman, 1999) and sport marketers, aware of the intricacies of their fans' self-esteem enhancement, have been quick to include aspects of these emotions in their advertising.

As is widely known, sport can provide fans with stress and stimulation. Fun and enjoyable stress, often referred to as *eustress* is a motivational factor for fan attraction (Madrigal, 1995; Mahony and Moorman, 1999). This concept is best exemplified by the fan's heightened anticipation moments before the start of any match. Increasingly, sport can provide *diversion* from the routines of everyday life. Yet sport has an *entertainment* value, too. Enhancing this entertainment value, usually by changing aspects of the basic game (the essential sport product), has been prevalent in most professional sports. Shortening matches, widening goalmouths, changing (shortening) boundaries and allowing technological improvements in equipment are all examples of trying to enhance entertainment value. This trend is demonstrated in the five-a-side football case above.

The introduction of legalised gambling on sports events heralds a new economic value that some fans place on the sport contest. Previously, value was more aligned to the contest itself (quality of the opposition, team record, stage in the competition, type of game [semifinal, final]) and the ticket price (Mahony and Howard, 1998; Mahony and Moorman, 1999). Competitive issues affecting attendance are not only *other sports* and *other leisure activity* but there are also competing forces from within the sport itself. Is the game being televised? If so, should the viewing audience be treated differently than the paying patron?

Sport marketers, like any marketers, encourage their customers to hold a positive disposition or attitude to the sport product so that, in turn, these customers (fans) will buy the sport product. The role of attitude and attitude strength in sports fan attraction and fan intentions has been reviewed extensively by authors such as Mahony and Moorman (1999) and Funk et al. (2000). Yet sport management research on fan attraction has not just been restricted to the social psychological domain: 'Recently, attention has turned to the role that the facility and its service elements play in fan behaviour and satisfaction' (Hill and Green, 2000, p. 146). Obviously, aspects of the sport contest's venue – stadia – impinge on fan attraction – parking, seating, toilets, food and beverage quality and selection, replay screens, prices and so on. Often termed the *sportscape* after the popular *servicescape* (Bitner, 1992), a plethora of studies addressing venue quality in sporting contexts have found their way into the academic literature (e.g., Hill and Green, 2000; McDonald, Sutton and Milne, 1995; Sutton, McDonald, Milne and Cimperman, 1997; Tomlinson, Buttle and Moores, 1995; Wakefield and Sloan, 1995; Westerbeek and Shilbury, 1999). Each of these studies refers to the impact of service quality (usually at the stadium) upon fan satisfaction, fan loyalty and repeat purchase.

Spectators form a key constituent of a sport organisation's success, with greater fan numbers attracting sponsors. A form of double jeopardy exists, however as sports that attract small crowds are unlikely to attract large sponsorship deals or negotiate lucrative television rights, further reinforcing the sport's low profile and its unattractiveness for sponsors. Fans are the demand nodes; differences in demand according to spectator characteristics are recognised. A number of sports fan studies, reviewed by Quick (2000), have suggested that not all fans are motivated by the same factors. Various typologies of fan attendance abound in the sports fan academic literature with many relying on product usage rates (levels of spectatorship) for their classifications. The terms *theatre goers, spectacle whores, fair-weather fans, diehard fans, aficionados and hardcore fans* connote attendance statuses as well as commitment to the sport or team.

Sport marketers recognise that player and spectator attitudes are central to continued participation and spectatorship. Attitudes are our enduring evaluations of 'things', in this case, of our sport codes, events, competitions, leagues, teams and so on. Attitudes serve more than one purpose for us. For example, in sport spectatorship contexts, attitudes may be quite different for different fans as a result of intensity or salience. Any game is likely to draw at least the following types of fans:

■ The *aficionados* or *diehard fans* who are completely entranced with the game, passionate about the sport code and intensely committed to a particular team.
■ The *fair-weather fans* whose support can wax and wane depending upon team results. These fans probably enjoy the spectacle as much as the aficionados but *BIRG* in the good times and *CORF* in the bad times, perhaps even shifting team allegiances during a season.
■ The *theatre goers* or (more cruelly labelled *spectacle whores*) who attend games for benefits exogenous to the contest itself. The occasion, the music, accompanying friends, the comradeship and so on all assume more importance for these fans.

Quick (2000) summarises the heterogeneity of sports fan spectatorship in his statement that

... The tribal, hard-core fan is but a minor figure in the professional sportscape. In recent decades a number of other fan segments have been identified, each having a different expectation of the sport experience. Moreover, each group, whether consuming the sport product at the event, on the street, or over the Internet, has unique value to the sport organisation; because of this, if possible, the needs and experiences of each group must be accommodated. (p. 150)

Implicit in most sport marketing activity is the desire to move spectators up the attendance or participation escalator (thereby turning light users such as 'theatre goers' and 'fair-weather fans' into heavier users).

The strategies used by sport marketers to communicate with each of these fan groups can be quite different. Obviously, information about the sport, teams, players and so on is consumed endlessly by *aficionados* and to a lesser extent by *fair-weather fans*. Buying and wearing team merchandise identifies fans by their displays of loyalty to 'their' team – these consumer bonds tend to be strong, reflecting an enduring attitude. Why do we do this? Psychologists suggest that balance and harmony are desired in our relationships, whether with other people or with our environment. 'Balance theory reminds us that when perceptions are balanced, attitudes are likely to be stable' (Solomon, 2004, p. 238). Hence, in a sporting context, people like to be associated with popular teams or players or even with 'popular' fans or fan clubs. This affiliation is expressed in a number of ways that sport marketers can recognise and use to advantage. For instance, the use of celebrity athlete endorsers has become more common in brand communications, in which marketers rely upon celebrity athletes' fame to transfer to the product or service they are endorsing.

Celebrity endorsement

Considerable research has been conducted into celebrity endorsement. Not surprisingly, the 'source' of the message that marketers wish to convey to their potential customers about their product or service impacts upon acceptance or rejection of that message. 'Sources' – in this case, celebrities – are usually chosen for one or more of their expertise, attractiveness and credibility (in conjunction with their availability, cost and so on). In the early 1990s, Ohanian's research (1990, 1991) combined the dimensions (and the attributes that captured these dimensions) of attractiveness, credibility and expertise into a 15-point, multi-attribute, semantic differential 'source credibility' scale for use in celebrity selection. Matching celebrity athletes with potential endorsement opportunities still remains an intriguing endeavour for advertising agencies and their clients, but using 'star power' in advertising is still popular (Erdogan, Baker and Tagg, 2001). For example, Tiger Woods has now eclipsed Michael Jordan as the richest celebrity athlete endorser (Vranica and Walker, 2002), estimated to have annual earnings from endorsements alone in 2002 of €48m. As the accompanying case on Anna Kournikova's attendance at New Zealand's ASB Women's Tennis Classic 2002 shows, celebrities command these massive sums by capturing media attention and thereby raising awareness, providing 'cut-through' and differentiation from competitors for the endorsed brand.

However, many companies are reportedly beginning to shy away from big names and are dumping celebrity endorsements altogether, according to Duncan (2005), because they say that the brands are not getting the promotion out of the ad campaigns that the stars are getting. Pepsi, for example, has terminated Beyoncé Knowles and Britney Spears as endorsers of their products. Chrysler has dumped Celine Dion from its new ad campaign. Chrysler suggested that the commercials featuring Dion driving a Pacifica produced greater sales for the singer than for the car.

Companies also have to be careful about their choice of celebrity endorser in terms of the risk they present for things to go wrong because the company's image could be tarnished by association with the star in the eyes of consumers. For example, Kobe Bryant's endorsement deals are up in the air, and Michael Jackson's latest legal issues will make it practically impossible for him to gain sponsors for his tours and endorsements as well. Magic Johnson lost his endorsement deals when he announced in 1991 that he was HIV positive. It was not until July 2003 that he landed his first endorsement deal since the announcement. Some companies are finding out multimillion dollar contracts with celebrities are not a surefire way to move products ahead of their competitors despite the obvious success of cases such as that below. Sponsors also have to be careful, especially in very parochial sports such as football, that using a celebrity to endorse their product that is popular with one sector of the industry may have adverse effects in another. For example, there is the 'Kevin Keegan effect': When the then Newcastle United manager agreed to endorse Sugar Puffs, sales of the product fell dramatically in Sunderland.

CASE 5.2   Auckland's adolescents and the Anna Kournikova factor

'Thanks Mum', shouted Auckland teenager Lewis Sinclair as he and three of his 14-year-old mates spilled out of his mother's car. The four teenage boys hurried their way through the turnstiles, taking in the shimmering surfaces of the still vacant outside courts. Jubilant yells greeted them from the practice doubles match on Court 6 along with the low hum of the brightly attired crowd meandering its way to Centre Court. Clutching their $35 uncovered stand tickets, they dodged and weaved their way through the crowd, anxious to get to their seats before the start of the biggest extravaganza in New Zealand's women's tennis. Why were these four teenage boys at an ASB Bank Women's Tennis Classic Tournament in Auckland, New Zealand, on this beautiful summer's day? In two words: Anna Kournikova.

Anna Kournikova, with her athletic figure and alluring looks, has long been a popular cover girl for general, sporting, and certainly, tennis magazines. Although her world tennis ranking slipped to 71 in 2002, following an injury-marred 2001, she had previously risen to No. 8 in the world after enjoying a top 15 ranking throughout 1999 and 2000. Her annual earnings have been estimated at $US18m, an amount surpassed at the time in world tennis only by Martina Hingis and Andre Agassi. However, whereas Agassi and Hingis derived large amounts of their income from prize money, it is estimated that 90% of Anna Kournikova's income is a consequence of her endorsements. Adidas alone is reputed to pay her $US8m annually, while Terra Lycos (internet company), Yonex (sports equipment), Berlei (sports-wear) and Omega (watches) all sponsor Kournikova.

Attracting this tennis star kept Richard Palmer, the ASB Bank Women's Tennis Classic Tournament director, on tenterhooks for weeks as Palmer and his fellow organisers were conscious of not exposing Auckland's tennis clubs to a loss-making event. Luckily Kournikova's performance on court helped reduce this risk. However, as might be expected, Kournikova's presence didn't come cheap. Once her entry was confirmed, prices were set 10–15% higher than previously positioned. In addition, a volume ticket-ing strategy supported this premium pricing strategy. As a consequence, patrons who bought tickets for the Second Round, when they were sure to see Kournikova's first match (she had a First Round bye) were committed to buying a ticket for the following day. This ensured that the tournament came close to covering its costs by end of play Wednesday. Moreover, the previous weekend's qualifying matches, supplemented by the draw card of Kournikova's practice sessions, allowed a $10 daily entry charge when previous years' qualifying matches had been free of charge.

Undoubtedly, Anna Kournikova was the major focus of the tournament, despite the organisers working hard to try and shift some of the attention onto other players with better records and higher rankings. The crowd thinned noticeably once Kournikova left the court. One might ask then, were tennis fans denied the oppor-tunity of seeing the tournament, and its main draw cards, Anna Kournikova and Conchita Martinez (former world number 2 and former Wimbledon champion)? 'No', said tournament director Richard Palmer. 'Prior to tickets going on sale to the general public all tennis club members in Auckland Tennis's affiliated clubs received a two-week preferential period for ticket purchase'.

After the dust had settled and the enthusiasm for Anna Kournikova's presence at the Women's Tennis Classic has subsided, the question that needed to be asked was, how successful was the tournament? Auckland Tennis reported that Auckland's tennis clubs, along with their professional coaching staff, were once again looking forward with optimism. Post-tournament interviews with several Auckland tennis coaches reported unprecedented interest in tennis from all age groups. Court usage was up and membership attrition appeared to have been arrested. Of course, the challenge to Auckland Tennis and its affiliated clubs was to convert this initial wave of enthusiasm for tennis, particularly women's tennis, into ongoing commitment and sustained growth.

ASB Bank remained tight-lipped about the returns from its sponsorship of the tourna-ment. ASB Bank is Auckland's largest sponsor of sport and sport events, meaning that isolating the effect of the event from the overall impact of the bank's sponsorship port-folio is impossible. However, anecdotal evidence suggested that it had received approximately three times the media coverage of past tournaments. Moreover, with the Stanley Street Courts holding 3000 fans per day (including the corporate box crowd), and a Monday–Saturday main draw, there were 18,000 ticketing opportuni-ties. The official attendance figure, including practice days and spectators in corporate boxes, was 22,400. It could be argued that exposure for ASB Bank in this instance was excellent.

EziBuy, a women's catalogue clothing retailer and the tournament's secondary sponsor, indicated that it was well pleased with its first major foray into event sponsorship. Co-owner Peter Gillespie suggested that, 'EziBuy used the Women's Tennis Classic to showcase their brand to the Australasian market' at the same time as providing an excellent platform to further build the brand. Prior to the tournament, EziBuy bought the customer database of Australasia's leading direct mail clothing company, Myer Direct, which added another 2.3 million potential customers (almost all of whom live in Australia) to its existing customer base. Gillespie further opined that the 'move to sponsor [The Classic] was a strategic one and women's tennis was ideal for EziBuy to put its name to as it was synonymous with women's apparel'. Hence they were gratified with the outcome, which was 28 hours of live television coverage and quarter of a million exposures of prominent signage.

Finally, Kournikova used the Women's Tennis Classic to launch her Adidas YOC (Youth On Court) range of tennis wear. The collection was based on Ursula Andress's trend-setting bikini from the James Bond movie *Dr No*. The pro-tennis shop on Stanley Street sold large quantities of the aqua-belted shorts and tops during the tournament, and Auckland's tennis courts have seen hundreds of teenage girls wearing their idol's 'gear'.

All things considered, Anna Kournikova's presence at the Women's Tennis Classic resulted in a resounding success for the tennis tournament itself, New Zealand tennis in general, the ASB Bank, EziBuy, Adidas and undoubtedly, Lewis Sinclair and his three mates!

Source: L. Ferkins (UNITEC) and R. Garland (University of Waikato)

Questions

1. What are the main lessons from this successful promotion?

2. What are the potential short- and long-term limitations of such a promotion?

3. What are some of the mechanisms by which New Zealand club tennis could leverage this promotion?

4. What consumer behaviour theories does this case address?

5. Comment on the advantages and disadvantages of celebrity endorsement for brand managers and tournament organisers alike.

Tomorrow's sport consumer

We have seen that sport consumers come in a range of guises and are motivated by a range of needs. It is one thing to rely on those ever-loyal fans who buy tickets at high prices in good weather and bad. But how do sport marketers reach new sport consumers and turn them into sports fanatics before their attention and disposable income are diverted to other forms of entertainment? Financial pressure within English football, for example, is making it necessary for clubs to start focusing on innovative ways of engendering fan loyalty, generating new revenue streams and reducing costs.

Chambers (2002) shows that clubs have already embraced innovative ways of addressing the issues through the introduction of new card technologies such as sport loyalty cards and introducing promotional campaigns that appeal to emotional rather than transactional relationships through auctioning squad places or allowing access to manager's half-time talks, as two clubs have tried Greater use of the internet and mobile messaging have been used as value-added services to communicate enriched club content and to deliver timely, tailored content to a registered and extended supporter base. Telecom in New Zealand, for example, ran a text messaging campaign to build fan loyalty in New Zealand's national game, rugby, and to cement its position as an innovative and leading developer of SMS applications. The campaign, which involved sending trivia questions on rugby directly to Telecom's mobile networks, attracted 7500 registered users and 5500 daily players and generated 50,000 responses. The mobile sponsorship manager stated that it was a great platform from which to promote the Telecom brand as an active and committed supporter of New Zealand rugby and feed New Zealander's obsession with rugby (http://www.istart.co.nz).

As Kearney (2003) notes, sport organisations are increasingly using technology to communicate with consumers. Arsenal football club provides free web access in Dutch for overseas fans of Dennis Berkamp, for example. But sports bodies are increasingly transforming their internet model from one that is strictly information based to one that generates revenues. According to Kearney (2003), television, the internet and mobile phone technology have the greatest potential for luring new groups of emerging sport consumers. However, as Chambers (2002) notes, any investment in new technologies must support a customer value proposition in which the expected returns are clearly measurable. Again, understanding sport consumers' attitudes is crucial if sport managers and marketers are to take advantage of the range of opportunities in the future and convert new sport consumers.

Conclusions

Sport is a market-driven industry. Managers cannot successfully operate in the industry without a thorough understanding of the marketing concept and its linkage between customers and products. This chapter has focused on understanding consumer behaviour, a vital aspect of marketing. Marketers need to understand the role of involvement and habit, information processing and the concept of life values in consumer behaviour as well as cultural determinants. Motivations have been shown to be important determinants of sport consumer behaviour. Although much interest centres around the spectator market because greater fan numbers attract sponsors, it has to be remembered that the participant market is actually where the greatest consumption occurs and that sport consumption is a complicated activity in which participating and spectating are often intertwined. Understanding consumers is fundamental to the marketing concept.

Discussion questions

1. How would you describe the range of sport consumers?
2. Why is it important to understand consumer behaviour?
3. What are the factors you think are important in 'putting fans in the stands'?

4. Describe the major steps in any sport decision-making model.
5. Outline the steps in the decision-making process for a football player and then an ardent football fan.
6. Discuss how various situational, temporal and environmental factors might influence sport consumption.

Guided reading

For further details on the content covered in this chapter, read the following:

Blackwell, R.D., Miniard, P.W. and Engel, J.F. (2001) *Consumer Behaviour*, Orlando, FL: Harcourt.

Maslow, A.H. (1970) *Motivation and Personality*, New York: Harper and Row.

Shank, M.D. (2005) *Sport Marketing: A Strategic Perspective*, 3rd edn, New Jersey: Prentice Hall.

Shilbury, D., Quick, S. and Westerbeek, H. (2003) *Strategic Sport Marketing*, Sydney: Allen & Unwin.

Solomon, M.R. (2004) *Consumer Behavior: Buying, Having, and Being*, 6th edn, New Jersey: Pearson Prentice Hall.

Wann, D.L. (1995) Preliminary validation of the sport fan motivation scale, *Journal of Sport & Social Issues* Nov:337–96.

Zaltman, G. (2003) *How Customers Think: Essential Insights Into the Mind of the Market*, Boston: Harvard Business School Press.

Keywords

Celebrity endorsement; consumer decision-making; consuming; sport consumers; sport promotion.

Bibliography

Bitner, M.J. (1992) Servicescapes: The impact of physical surroundings on customers and employees, *Journal of Marketing* 56:57–71.

Chambers, N. (2002) 'Increasing fan loyalty in English football', cited 5 March 2005, retrieved 21 May 2006, from http://www.pgw.co.uk/artdec02.html.

Coalter, F. (1999) Sport and recreation in the United Kingdom: Flow with the flow or buck the trends, *Managing Leisure* 4:24–39.

Dominion Post (2003) $2.8B soccer deal, *Dominion Post*, 12 August.

Duncan, A. (2005) 'Companies ditch celebrity endorsements', cited 8 March 2005, retrieved 21 May 2006, from http://advertising.about.com/cs/advertising/a/endorsements.htm.

Erdogan, B.Z., Baker, M.J. and Tagg, S. (2001) Selecting celebrity endorsers: The practitioner's perspective, *Journal of Advertising Research* 41(3):39–48.

Funk, D. and James, J. (2001) The psychological continuum model: A conceptual framework for understanding an individual's psychological connection to sport, *Sport Management Review* 4:119–50.

Funk, D.C., Haugtvedt, C.P. and Howard, D.R. (2000) Contemporary attitude theory in sport: Theoretical considerations and implications, *Sport Management Review* 3:125–44.

Gratton, C., Kokolakakis, T., Ping Kung, S. and O'Keeffe, L. (2001) *Sport Market Forecasts 2001–2005*, Sheffield: SIRC.

Hill, B. and Green, B.C. (2000) Repeat attendance as a function of involvement, loyalty, and the sportscape across three football contexts, *Sport Management Review* 3:145–62.

Holt, D. (1995) How consumers consume: A typology of consumption practices, *Journal of Consumer Research* 22(1):1–16.

Howard, D.R. (1999) The changing fanscape for big-league sports: Implications for sport managers, *Journal of Sport Management* 13:78–91.

Howard, D.R. and Crompton, J.L. (1995) *Financing Sport*, Morgantown, WV: Fitness Information Technology, Inc.

iStart (2005) 'Super 12 text messaging campaigns build fan loyalty', cited 8 March 2005, retrieved 21 May 2006, from http://www.istart.co.nz.

Kearney, A.T. (2003) *The new sports consumer*, Illinois: A.T. Kearney Inc.

Kurylko, D. (2004) Subaru's affiliate marketing pays off, *Automotive News* 78(6099):20B.

Laverie, D.A. and Arnett, D.B. (2000) Factors affecting fan attendance: The influence of identity salience and satisfaction, *Journal of Leisure Research* 32(2):225–46.

Lewes, J. (2004) 'News Corp nabs rugby', *News—International,* cited 23 December, retrieved 21 May 2006, from http://global.factiva.com/en/arch/display.asp.

Lough, N. and Irwin, R. (2001) A comparative analysis of sponsorship objectives for U.S. women's sport and traditional sport sponsorship, *Sport Marketing Quarterly* 10(4):202–11.

Madrigal, R. (1995) Cognitive and affective determinants of fan satisfaction with sporting event attendance, *Journal of Leisure Research* 27(3):205–27.

Mahony, D.F. and Howard, D.R. (1998) The impact of attitudes on the behavioural intentions of sport spectators, *International Sports Journal* 2(2):96–110.

Mahony, D.F. and Moorman, A.M. (1999) The impact of fan attitudes on intention to watch professional basketball teams on television, *Sport Management Review* 2:43–66.

Marketing Week (2004) BMI adds to sponsorship portfolio, *Marketing Week* August 26:12.

Marketing UK (2004) Carlsberg seals Tottenham deal, *Marketing UK* 18 August:6.

McDonald, M.A., Sutton, W.A. and Milne, G.R. (1995) Teamqual™: Measuring service quality in professional team sports, *Sport Marketing Quarterly* 4(2):9–15.

McDonald, M., Milne, G. and Hong, J. (2002) Motivational factors for evaluating sport spectator and participant markets, *Sport Marketing Quarterly* 11(2):100–113.

Meenaghan, T. and O'Sullivan, P. (1999) Playpower – sports meets marketing, *European Journal of Marketing* 33(3/4):241–49.

Ohanian, R. (1990) Construction and validation of a scale to measure celebrity endorsers' perceived expertise, trustworthiness, and attractiveness, *Journal of Advertising* 19(1):39–52.

Ohanian, R. (1991) The impact of celebrity spokespersons' perceived image on consumers' intention to purchase, *Journal of Advertising Research* 13(1):46–55.

Quick, S. (2000) Contemporary sport consumers: Some implications of linking fan typology with key spectator variables, *Sport Marketing Quarterly* 9(3):149–56.

Shank, M.D. (2005) *Sport Marketing: A Strategic Perspective*, 3rd edn, New Jersey: Prentice Hall.

Shilbury, D., Quick, S. and Westerbeek, H. (2003) *Strategic Sport Marketing*, Sydney: Allen & Unwin.

Solomon, M.R. (2004) *Consumer Behavior: Buying, Having, and Being*, 6th edn, New Jersey: Pearson Prentice Hall.

Stewart, B., Smith, A. and Nicholson, M. (2003) Sport consumer typologies: A critical review, *Sport Marketing Quarterly* 12(4):206–16.

Sutton, W., McDonald, M., Milne, G. and Cimperman, J. (1997) Creating and fostering fan identification in professional sports, *Sport Marketing Quarterly* 6(1):15–22.

Tomlinson, M., Buttle, F. and Moores, B. (1995) The fan as customer: Customer service in sports marketing, *Journal of Hospitality and Leisure Marketing* 3(1):19–33.

Wakefield, K.L. and Sloan, H.J. (1995) The effects of team loyalty and selected stadium factors on spectator attendance, *Journal of Sport Management* 9:153–72.

Wann, D.L. and Branscombe, N.R. (1990) Die-hard and fair-weather fans: Effects of identification on BIRGing and CORFing tendencies, *Journal of Sport and Social Issues* 14(2):103–17.

Westerbeek, H.M. and Shilbury, D. (1999) Increasing the 'focus' on place in the marketing mix for facility dependent sport services, *Sport Management Review* 2:1–23.

Westerbeek, H. and Smith, A. (2003) *Sport business in the global marketplace*, Hampshire, UK: Palgrave Macmillan.

Vranica, S. and Walker, S. (2002) Tiger Woods switches watches: Branding experts disapprove, *Wall Street Journal Interactive Edition*, 7 October.

Recommended website

Business of Sport Management Companion site
http://www.booksites.net/download/chadwickbeech/index.html

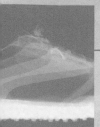

Chapter 6

Sport organisation buying behaviour

Ann Bourke
University College Dublin

Learning outcomes

Upon completion of this chapter, the reader should be able to:

- Identify the range of organisations buying products and services in the sport market.

- Indicate the motives underlying the buying behaviour of these organisations.

- Indicate the influences that impinge upon these motives.

- Understand the decision-making process through which organisations purchase goods and services in the sport marketplace.

- Consider the impact of initial and repeat purchase decisions, and retention, for sport marketers.

Overview of chapter

Sport products and services consist of goods (e.g., apparel and equipment) and services (e.g., coaching, medical services, information, transport, legal) used by sport participants and consumers (individual or organisational). They are provided by sports manufacturers, firms and organisations that aim to meet the needs of consumers. Business-to-business (B2B) marketing focuses on the procedures and processes whereby organisations set out to meet the needs of organisational buyers. Although it is presumed that many organisations have what is termed a buying centre, this may not be applied to a great degree in many sport organisations. Ultimately, an individual makes the decision in relation to purchasing, and that decision maker is influenced by a number of parties, both inside and outside the sports body or organisation. Buying behaviour in sport organisations varies depending upon the organisational mission and objectives (e.g., for-profit versus not-for-profit). The interaction that occurs in the B2B sector is characterised by the complexity of the transaction and the shift in recent years from a transactional approach to a relationship marketing approach. Retaining organisational customers is more cost effective than recruiting (prospecting) new customers, so firms and organisations are now placing a greater emphasis on buyer–seller relationships, taking care to develop and foster them frequently by using a more long-term perspective.

The sport market

The sport market consists of individuals, firms, organisations and institutions associated directly or indirectly with sport participation on a competitive or non-competitive basis. It is an important sector of economic activity that accounts for one quarter of all consumer spending, over ten per cent of total employment in the United Kingdom and brings in over £20bn per annum in foreign exchange (Gratton and Taylor, 2000). According to Hums and MacLean (2003), the various segments of the multinational sport industry include professional sport, universities and colleges sport, youth sport, recreational sport, facility management, event management, sport for people with disabilities, health and fitness, sports club management, the Olympic and Paralympic movements, sport marketing and sport law. King (2002) observes that the value of the US sport industry was estimated at approximately $194bn, higher than the automobile industry and the motion picture industry. Among the components that make up this value are travel; advertising; team expenses; apparel, footwear and equipment; facility construction; sponsorship; gambling; and professional services. Gratton and Taylor (2000) illustrate the elements of the sport market, drawing a distinction between *elite sport* and *sport for all* (Figure 6.1).

In Figure 6.1, the elite sport sector is positioned at the top end of the pyramid, highlighting the reality that it consists of a relatively small number of participants. Money flows into this sector from commercial sponsorship, paying spectators and media

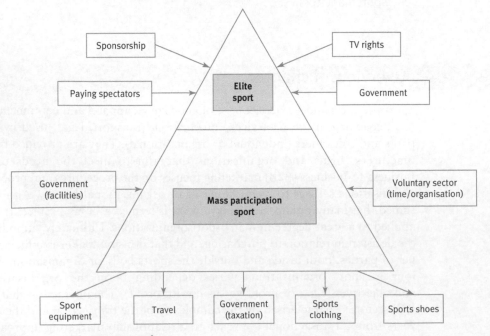

Figure 6.1 **The sport market**
Source: Gratton and Taylor (2000)

companies that wish to purchase the rights to broadcast and report on sports events. In certain countries (e.g., United Kingdom, Australia, Ireland) national or state governments fund this sector, too, by way of grants awarded to sporting bodies (national governing bodies [NGBs], organisations and clubs) or to individual sports people to promote sporting excellence and international success. Part of government financial assistance is usually directed towards providing or upgrading the country's sporting infrastructure to facilitate elite athlete development and achieve international success. During 2004, the Irish government's expenditure on sport (capital and non-capital) amounted to €112.050m. Capital expenditure on sport by the Irish government (via the Department of Arts, Sports and Tourism) comprises of capital grants allocated by the Department and the funding of high-visibility projects such as the National Aquatic Centre (NAC) at Abbotstown (Considine, Coffey and Kiely, 2004). The non-capital expenditure is channelled through the Irish Sports Council.

The bottom part of the pyramid in Figure 6.1 represents individuals and groups who engage in sport for fun, for enjoyment or maybe to get fitter and healthier. These individuals and groups comprise the mass participation sport sector, which is also subsidised by governments but predominantly through local government (Gratton and Taylor, 2000). This funding is often directed towards the provision of community leisure facilities or sports facilities in schools. Another important element in the sport market is voluntary bodies and groups. These organisations provide time without payment and are an important service and support in the sport market. Although governments and the voluntary sector support the recreational end of the market, there are substantial monetary flows from sport participants into the commercial sector on sports equipment, apparel, shoes and accessories. Monetary flows also occur to governments from the sector mainly in the form of taxation receipts (value-added tax, corporate taxes).

Both the demand and supply sides of the sport market are complicated (Gratton and Taylor, 2000). The supply side of the sport market is a mixture of three types of provider: the public sector (government promotes mass participation and the development of elite athletes), the commercial sector (supports elite and grass roots) and the voluntary sector (by way of time providing service and funding activities). Demand within the sport market is composite demand in so much as sport is a demand for free time; the demand to take part in sport; the demand for equipment and apparel; and the demand for facilities and travel. Demanders consist of individual and group participants (clubs, federations and individual personnel) and spectators and government (central or regional). Currently, many educational policymakers (particularly governments) are conscious of the rising levels of obesity among young children and consider it essential that all pupils engage in some sporting activity while attending primary and secondary school. Although state involvement in the provision of educational facilities generates demand for sporting goods and services, it is pertinent to note that the provision of such facilities may also come from the private sector.

In the United States, collegiate sport is very highly structured and operated by paid professional staff (Slack, 1997). Many US universities and colleges (public and private) offer sports (athletic) scholarship programmes designed to attract elite athletes, which allows them develop their sporting prowess while gaining an academic qualification. To offer these programmes, Bok (2003, p. 37) notes that many US universities and colleges have built very modern stadia to attract larger paying audiences; have added luxury corporate boxes to lure corporate sponsors; negotiated lucrative radio and television deals with media firms; and have agreements with leading apparel companies such as Reebok, Adidas and Nike to get free equipment in return for student athletes wearing the company logo. The flow of funds (sponsorship) into these institutions results in a greater number of them having up-to-the minute sports facilities (e.g., running and playing surfaces, well-equipped gyms, medical and training facilities) to meet the needs of their student athletes.

Business-to-business marketing and markets

Industrial marketing is concerned with selling to organisations rather than to final consumers. It is also referred to as B2B marketing, which gives a broad flavour, but its application is wider than that, covering marketing to institutions (e.g., hospitals, schools) and governments (Randall, 1993). B2B marketing covers all activities involved in the marketing of *products and services* to firms that use them in the production of consumer or industrial goods and services (Rogan, 2003, p. 373). Although the fundamentals of B2B marketing are fairly similar to those used for consumer marketing (i.e., the 4Ps, strategic planning, new product development, communication process, relationship marketing and the like), there are a number of differences largely owing to the concentration of the industrial market (golf, yachting) in which single orders can often be quite large.

According to Webster (1991) the differentiating factors of B2B marketing are as follows:

a) **Functional interdependence:** There is a greater need for communication and cooperation between functions, and marketing depends more heavily on other departments for its success.

b) **Product complexity:** Industrial products are more complicated than their consumer equivalents, and this complexity extends to other elements of the relationship between manufacturer and buyer.

c) **Buyer–seller interdependence:** The two are more closely engaged in a relationship that extends beyond the transaction itself.

d) **Complexity of the buying process.**

Although there is some overlap with consumer marketing in terms of products (e.g., sport organisations and households are both likely to purchase footballs and tennis racquets) and in the type of purchases (e.g., sport organisations and households may both purchase fitness equipment), there are many differences, especially in terms of purchasing frequency, size of the transaction and the, importance of the industrial product for the organisation's business. Randall (1993) notes that suppliers (e.g., IBM, Vodafone) are likely to service a wide range of different markets, each with different needs and buying processes, and these markets may react differently to the elements of the marketing mix.

Hutt and Speh (1995) highlight the unique characteristics of *business marketing* practice that distinguishes it from consumer marketing practice. A notable difference stems from that fact that business marketers emphasise personal selling rather than advertising to reach potential buyers. Only a small proportion of business marketers' promotional budgets are likely to be spent on advertising, through trade journals or direct mail. Business marketers' *products* will consist of a complete package, which includes an important service component that the organisational consumer will evaluate, focusing on the quality of the physical entity and the quality of the attached services. Price negotiation is frequently an important part of the industrial buying and selling process. Products are normally made to a particular design and are individually priced. Business marketers find that direct distribution to the buyers strengthens their relationships. Relationships in business markets are often close and enduring; it is repeatedly suggested that when a sale is completed, this signals the *beginning* of a relationship rather than constituting a result.

Hutt and Speh (1998) define business markets as markets for goods and services, local to international, bought by businesses, government bodies and institutions for incorporation, for consumption, for use or for resale. The main differences between B2B markets and consumer markets may be summarised under the following headings: market structure, buyer behaviour, decision-making, products, distribution channels, promotion and price (Rogan, 2003). B2B markets, as noted previously, are often very concentrated and more complex than consumer markets. B2B buyers are normally well informed and unlikely to buy on impulse. Because an organisation is making the purchase, there will usually be multiple influencers offering different points of view on the purchasing decision. In addition, other variables (individual, group, organisational and environmental) that influence organisational buying decisions must be considered (Hutt and Speh, 1995). Anderson and Narus (1999) maintain that whereas customers in business markets predominantly focus on functionality or performance, customers in consumer markets predominantly focus on aesthetics or taste. In each case, most decisions are driven predominantly, but not exclusively, by these considerations. So, when the concept of value is discussed in a business markets context, we refer to the worth in monetary terms of the economic, technical, service and social benefits a customer receives in return for the price it pays for the market offering. Of course, several factors (aside from the product offering) may influence a customer's perception of the value it receives. These factors include:

- The length of customer lead times
- Variation from promised delivery times
- Condition of the product on arrival
- Sales calls and order initiation requirements
- Credit, billing and collection procedures
- Effectiveness of after-sales support
- Product performance, fit and function
- Product downtime frequency and duration
- Maintenance cost and difficulty (Anderson and Narus, 1999)

In *business markets*, as product demand is derived (i.e., goods or services are bought as inputs for other goods or services), the *make-versus-buy* decision must also be considered. Hence, the value provided by the goods or services purchased for the buyer must exceed the price paid (Anderson and Narus, 1999).

Sport organisations as consumers

An organisation is a social entity that is goal directed and deliberately structured (Daft, 2000). *Social entity* means that it consists of two or more people. *Goal directed* means that it is designed to achieve some outcome, such as make a profit, win pay increases for employees or meet spiritual needs. *Deliberately structured* means that tasks are divided and responsibility for their performance is assigned to organisation members.

This definition, according to Daft (2000), applies to both for-profit and not-for-profit organisations. Old (2004) maintains that an organisation is a deliberate arrangement of people to achieve a particular end. He contends that if we are members of an organisation, then our behaviour is not explained by custom, law, tradition or some market arrangement, but by our *membership* of the organisation. Crucially, an organisation may be said to be composed of three elements: members, rules and purpose.

According to Wilson (2000), an organisation is conceptualised as a group of individuals lending support (for whatever reason) to a loose hierarchy of objectives. Chelladurai (2001) observes the characteristics which identify a group of people as an organisation: identity, programme of activity, membership, clear boundaries, permanency, division of labour, hierarchy of authority and formal rules and procedures. Slack (1997), drawing on Daft (2000) and Robbins (1990), defines a sport organisation as 'a social entity involved in the sport industry: it is goal directed, with a consciously structured activity system and a relatively identifiable boundary.' The key elements in this definition are (i) social entity, (ii) involvement in the sport industry, (iii) goal-directed focus, (iv) consciously structured activity system and (v) identifiable boundary.

Slack (1997) confines the sport industry to firms or organisations that have direct involvement (e.g., Nike, International Olympic Committee) in one or more aspects of the sport industry or those that have a substantive involvement in the sport industry (e.g., 3M or Gore-Tex, producer of sportswear and equipment). Slack also maintains that *sport organisations* need to have a relatively identifiable boundary that distinguishes members from non-members, but he acknowledges that clarity may not always exist, particularly for those in the voluntary or non-profit sector. The business opportunities in sport are many and varied, which would suggest that the 'fine line', as asserted by Slack (1997), may no longer apply. For instance, the Middle East sport business market is considered to be at the 'adolescent stage' and apart from the marketing and sponsorship opportunities of particular events (F1, racing, tennis, golf and yachting), other business opportunities now exist, including:

- Sports infrastructure, refurbishment, facilities and surfacing
- Sport venue technology and systems
- Sport goods, licensing and merchandising
- Event planning and management services
- Sports trade fairs, exhibitions and conferences
- Club management, coaching and consumer consultancy (http://www.mindbranch.com)

Although firms and organisations will tender for and complete some of the above projects should they, using the Slack (1997) typology, be classified as sport organisations?

The various organisations that populate the sport industry are local (e.g., Crusaders Athletics Club), national (e.g., Athletics Ireland) and international (e.g., International Association of Athletics Federations). Sport organisations do not exist in a vacuum. As part of the greater society in which they exist, they must anticipate changes in both their external and internal environments. Chelladurai (2001) subdivides organisations' external environment into two categories: (a) the *task or operating environment*, sometimes referred to as the proximal (close) environment and (b) the *general environment*, also called the distal (further removed) environment. Individuals in sport organisations must be aware of what is happening in the external environment and adapt accordingly. Firms and organisations involved in the sport industry must be informed in relation to the latest product and process innovations and developments and must understand the extent, nature and intensity of competition within their sector. Information flows on such matters have been facilitated in recent years by technology developments (e.g., the internet) and with the hosting of an increasing number of sport business forums, conferences, exhibitions and sport business trade fairs.

The internal environment of a sport organisation is created through and influenced by its specific policies and procedures. Such policies and procedures are put in place to achieve the organisation's objectives by reflecting its vision and mission. Organisational objectives are needed to define both financial and strategic direction (Shank, 2005). For example, whereas JJB Sports' principal aim is to supply high-quality branded sports and leisure products to their customers at competitive prices (http://www.jjb.co.uk/corporateinfo/), Celtic Football Club's primary business is as a football club, but it also assumes a broader role of being a major Scottish social institution promoting health, well being and social integration (Celtic Social Mission Statement, 2006). Despite its size, the sport industry is a people-oriented, service-oriented industry in which efforts are made to treat one's customers and employees in a positive fashion.

According to Shank (2005), a sport product is a good or service or any combination of the two that is designed to provide benefits to a sports spectator, participant or sponsor. These goods and services may be intermediary or final products. In Chapter 5, attention is given to sport consumers' buying behaviour; here the focus is on organisations, detailing the various factors that influence the process and the procedures involved in purchasing decision-making. Wilson (2000) questions the validity of such a divide, asserting that organisational purchasing is completed by individuals, who are now working in teams rather than in buying centres.

Commercial enterprises as consumers can be divided into three categories: users, original equipment manufacturers (OEMs) and dealers and distributors (Hutt and Speh, 1998). User customers purchase goods (e.g., computers, photocopiers, training gear and technological equipment) to set up or support their manufacturing or service operation. OEMs buy goods to incorporate into other products sold in the business or to consumers. Dealers and distributors purchase goods (e.g., sports apparel, gym equipment) for resale to users and OEMs.

Goods in the business market have been classified (Hutt and Speh, 1998) as entering goods (e.g., raw materials, manufactured materials and parts), foundation goods (e.g., installations and accessory equipment) and facilitating goods (e.g., supplies and business services). Sport organisations (e.g., Ferrari, Association of Tennis Professionals, Manchester United) purchase these goods and services to acquire the inputs needed to provide goods and services to their final customers (members or fans). The manner of purchase is influenced by cost considerations along with design and quality features of the good or service. The processes used are considered in the following paragraphs.

Purchasing decision-making

Purchasing refers to the acquisition of resources and capabilities by a firm from outside providers. Hutt and Speh (1995) contend that organisational buying processes reflect a history of interaction patterns and a corresponding set of formal and informal relationships that have been nurtured and developed. However, the organisational culture and status of purchasing may vary from firm to firm. In certain circumstances, organisational procurement may be centralised, and in these cases, a separate organisational unit is given responsibility for purchases at a regional, divisional or headquarters level. Centralised purchasing tends to lead to sector specialisation, whereby purchasing specialists display deep knowledge of supply and demand conditions and facilitates the integration of purchasing into the firm's corporate strategy.

Jobber and Fahy (2003) set out the key features of organisational buying. Typically, the number of customers is small and order sizes large. The purchases are often complex and risky, with several parties having input into the purchasing decision, as would be the case with a major IT investment. The demand for many organisational goods is derived from the demand for consumer goods, which means that small changes in the consumer goods market can have an important impact on the demand for industrial goods. Organisational buying is characterised by prevalence of negotiations between buyers and sellers, and in some cases, reciprocal buying may take place.

Three types of buying situations exist: (a) new task, (b) modified rebuy and (c) straight rebuy (Anderson and Narus, 1999; Hutt and Speh, 1998). The *new task* situation is one whereby the problem or need is perceived by organisational decision makers as totally different from previous experiences; consequently, a significant amount of information is required for decision makers to explore alternative ways of solving the problem and to search for alternative suppliers. When there is a continuing or recurring requirement, buyers have substantial experience in dealing with the need, and they require little or no new information. Evaluation of alternative solutions is unnecessary and unlikely to generate major improvements; hence, a *straight rebuy* approach is appropriate. In certain situations, the *modified rebuy*, organisational decision makers may feel obliged to consider alternative product or service features and options and suppliers. This may stem from cost or design considerations or process improvements, and in this case, new information will be sought. A new task situation represents the greatest difficulty for management because it usually represents the greatest risk and uncertainty and thus involves the greatest number of decision makers and buyer influencers. A new task may raise policy questions and require special studies, a modified rebuy is likely to be more routine, and a straight rebuy is essentially automatic.

Organisational buying behaviour is influenced by various environmental variables such as economic, political, legal, cultural, physical and technological. The general condition of the economy is reflected in economic growth; employment; price stability; income; and the availability of resources, money and credit. Because of the derived nature of industrial demand, marketers must also be sensitive to the strength of demand in the ultimate consumer market. When an economic downturn in an economy occurs, the demand for sport, leisure and entertainment products is often the first to suffer a decline in demand. The demand for many industrial products fluctuates more widely than the general economy. Particular events (e.g., Olympic Games, All Ireland Football Final, Formula 1 Grand Prix, Soccer World Cup and Ryder Cup) often stimulate the demand for sporting goods and services (apparel, equipment, coaching). Government regulation may also influence trends and patterns in international trade for sports goods and services and may impact on the buyer–seller relationships. The cultural dimensions (values, mores, customs, habits, traditions) that influence a firm's organisational structure and the manner in which its members conduct business dealings will also have to be considered. Other factors such as the geographic location of the organisation and the supply of labour also influence organisational buying behaviour. Technology is changing rapidly and offers business marketers a unique potential to more accurately predict demand to improve relationships between buyers and suppliers and the distribution of goods and services.

As noted earlier, purchasing managers rarely make a buying decision independent of the influence of others in the organisation. The extent to which individuals are involved in the purchase process varies according to whether it is routine rebuys to complex new task buying situations, in which the group plays an active role throughout the decision-making process. The relevant unit of analysis for industrial marketers is the group decision-making unit (DMU), or the buying centre (Hutt and Speh, 1995). The buying centre includes all individuals and groups that participate in the purchasing decision and that share the goals and risks arising from the decision. The composition of the buying centre may change from one purchasing decision to another and is not prescribed by the organisational chart. A buying group evolves during the purchasing process in response to the information requirements of the specific purchase situation, whether it is establishing a hospital and healthcare facility at a football or tennis stadium or choosing an equipment supplier (timekeeper) for a leading international athletics meeting. Because organisational purchasing is a process rather than an isolated act, different individuals are important to the process at different times. Industrial marketers can often predict decisions in relation to the composition of the buying centre by projecting the impact of the industrial product on various functional areas in the buying organisation. If the procurement decision will influence the marketability of the firm's product offering, then personnel from the marketing department will be actively involved in the decision process. If the procurement will have a substantial economic commitment or impinge on strategic or policy matters, senior management will have considerable influence.

Members of the buying centre assume different roles throughout the procurement process. They may act as:

- **Users:** Personnel using the product
- **Gatekeepers:** Individuals who control information to be reviewed by other members of the buying centre
- **Influencers:** People who affect the buying decision by supplying information for the evaluation of alternatives or by setting buying specifications
- **Deciders:** Individuals who actually make the buying decision
- **Buyers:** People with formal authority to select a supplier and implement all procedures associated with acquiring the product or service (Webster and Wind, 1972)

In many situations, the key influencers are located outside the purchasing department, possibly in a finance department, current customers or external advisors.

Over and over again, the buying centre for highly technical products includes purchasing agents, scientists, engineers and other managers. The factors that contribute to a centre's purchasing strength include its level of technical competence and credibility, base of relevant information, base of top management support and organisational status as an authority in selected procurement areas.

It must be noted that individuals bring to the purchasing situation differing perspectives with regard to evaluative criteria for comparing industrial products and services, motivations with respect to the buying decision [the role of reward and how they are measured – reward and measurement systems], information processing and the perceived level of risk. According to Sheth (1973), various product-specific and company-specific factors determine whether the purchase decision will be a group or an individual one. In deciding whether it should be an individual or group decision, the *product-specific factors* reviewed are the perceived risk, the type of purchase and time pressure. The *company-specific factors* considered are size (larger firms tend to use groups) and the degree of centralisation (the more centralised procurement is, the more likely the purchase decision will be a group one).

Early organisational buying researchers focused on three categories of the organisational buying process: the *buying centre*, the *organisational buying process* and the *factors affecting the buying centre and process*. In essence, these three categories aim to answer the following questions: Who participates? What happens? What causes or influences a specific decision? Tanner (1999) examines the classic approaches to organisational buying: 1) role theory, 2) the BuyGrid analytic framework, 3) reward/measurement theory and 4) organisational buyer behaviour choice, with a view to identifying potential connections with relationship theory. He maintains that little research exists to integrate, synthesise and develop theory.

As noted previously, role theory focuses on the functional areas that participate in the purchasing practices and the roles (user, gatekeeper, influencer, decider or buyer) that each played. Embedded in role theory is the notion that buying and selling are transaction focused. Tanner (1999) argues that although individual roles in the organisational buying process are important, a number of decisions are also involved, such as deciding how to decide (decision rules within groups), and that each decision may involve different forms of governance. This begs the question as to whether some forms of governance support or inhibit the formation of cross-functional or strategic relationships that have a bearing on the operation of the buying centre.

The BuyGrid model is a classic process model that reflects the process through which buyers pass as they make their purchase decision (Table 6.1). The BuyGrid model focuses on two aspects of purchasing: (a) the Buyclass, which is the buying situation, and (b) the Buyphase, which is the activity performed during the procurement process (i.e., the sequence of activities that must be performed in the resolution of a buying situation; Mawson and Fearne, 1997). This model illustrates the *three broad buying situations* and *eight stages* through which the buyer may progress. The speed of the progress depends upon the number of stages and the nature of the buying task.

In organisational buying, decision-making draws upon input from several members of the organisation. Robinson, Faris and Wind (1967) discuss the marketing implications of

Table 6.1 **The BuyGrid model**

	New Task	Modified Rebuy	Straight Rebuy
Need recognition	✓	✓	✓
Determine quantity	✓	✓	✓
Describe quantity	✓	✓	✓
Search for quantity	✓	✓	
Analysis of proposals	✓	✓	
Evaluation	✓	✓	
Selection	✓	✓	
Performance feedback and evaluation	✓	✓	✓

Source: Patrick J. Robinson, *Industrial Buying and Creative Marketing*. Published by Allyn and Bacon, Boston, MA. Copyright © 1967 by Pearson Education. Reprinted/adapted by permission of the publisher.

being an 'in supplier' (on the list) or 'out supplier' (out of the list), anticipating the relationship paradigm. The assumption seems to be that whereas an 'in supplier' would like purchases of its products to be straight rebuys (annual contracts are one way of creating straight rebuys), 'out suppliers' are locked out until the next time the contract comes up for review. There are gaps in the BuyGrid approach when focusing on the open market versus 'in supplier' purchases. Dimensions such as the importance and complexity of the decision need to be considered and understood. Although the concept of a continuum from straight rebuy to modified to new buy may no longer completely reflect the purchasing reality, Tanner (1999) argues that categories of buying processes are still needed using schema that recognise the quality of relationships.

Reward/measurement (RM) theory is a traditional expectancy model of motivation that focuses on the rewards systems of the organisation. According to Hutt and Speh (1998: 89) two types of rewards motivate individual decision makers: intrinsic (being valued) and extrinsic (financial rewards). According to Tanner (1999), little research has been undertaken using RM. He contends that this deficiency may imply a shift away from studying individuals to studying groups.

Behaviour choice theory states that buyers go through a choice process to arrive at decisions of how they will buy, as opposed to the choice process of what will be bought, modelled as part of the BuyGrid. *Organisational buying* involves many people who are not professional purchasing agents, particularly when strategic partnerships are formed and communication must be extended between all functional areas of both firms. Tanner (1999) sees this as a reason to further research focusing on the individual in the organisational buying context. He notes that significant relationships could not be established between reward/measurement and relationship buying activities and asserts that one potentially fruitful area of research may be to find out *what systems do apply* and that behaviour choice theory can provide insights.

Wilson (2000) declares that there are many conceptual and logical weaknesses to the current approach to organisational buyer behaviour theory, the main one being the underlying assumptions. Among these limitations, he lists the following:

1. Organisational marketing has only recently been recognised as encompassing all organisations, not only industrial concerns.
2. Organisational purchasing has been presented as a rational and logical activity of professionals, ignoring the habitual, intuitive and experiential behaviour of purchasing managers and subordinates as being uniquely idiosyncratic individuals.
3. Studies of organisational buyer behaviour tended to fall into one of two broad categories – organisational purchasing (customer was presented as the dominant party) and organisational selling (customer seen as being manipulated by skilful selling staff).

Wilson (2000) asserts that mainstream models and frameworks have conceived organisational purchasing and marketing as discrete occasions characterised by rational and professional reactions to contingently dependent situations.

Jobber and Fahy (2003, p. 66) outline some of the recent developments in organisation purchasing that have marketing implications for supplier firms. They maintain that the advent of just-in-time (JIT) purchasing, electronic marketplaces, the increased tendency towards centralised purchasing, reverse marketing and leasing have all changed the nature of purchasing and the manner in which suppliers compete.

According to Harrison-Walker and Neeley (2004), businesses are increasingly taking advantage of the power of the internet to build relationships with customers in the electronic marketplace. With the growth in the use of the internet, two main categories of marketplaces or exchanges have emerged: vertical electronic marketplaces (industry specific) and horizontal electronic marketplaces (cross industry boundaries). Companies seeking supplies post their offers on the appropriate websites, and potential vendors bid for the contracts electronically. The traditional view of marketing is that supplier firms will actively seek out the requirements of customers and attempt to meet those needs better than the competition. In many firms, purchasing is now taking on a more proactive, aggressive stance in acquiring products and services needed to compete. The process, whereby the buyer attempts to persuade the supplier to provide exactly what the organisation wants, is called reverse marketing. The development has benefits for suppliers who are prepared to listen because it provides the potential to develop stronger and lasting relationships with the customer, and it could be a source of new product opportunities.

Customer retention

According to Anderson and Narus (1999), gaining customers, sustaining reseller partnerships and sustaining customer relationships are the *business market processes* for delivering *value*. Gaining customers is the process of *prospecting* for new business relationships, assessing the mutual fit between prospective customer requirements and supplier offerings and priorities, making the initial sale, and fulfilling the initial order to the customer's complete satisfaction. There are three types of potential customers that supplier firms isolate when prospecting:

a) **Leads** are names of possible clients that business market managers generate from computer databases.
b) **Inquiries** are customer-initiated business contacts with the supplier firm.
c) **Prospects** are *leads and inquiries* that the supplier firm has qualified as having significant sales and profit potential.

Prospecting entails the related activities of internally generating leads from data bases, prompting and gathering inquiries externally from the marketplace and qualifying leads and inquiries as significant prospects. In order to gain from prospecting, suppliers must gain the commitment and support of the sales force. To do so, business market managers must create programmes and systems for the sales force that deliver *four critical elements*: *knowledge, motivation, experience* and *sales support* (Anderson and Narus, 1999). The selling situations vary across each industry and within an industry as a function of each prospect's philosophy of doing business, purchasing orientation, technological sophistication, capabilities and market offering usage and applications.

Sustaining reseller partnerships is the process of a supplier and its resellers fulfilling commitments they have made to one another, strengthening overall channel performance and working progressively together to continue to fulfil changing marketplace requirements. *Sustaining customer relationships* is the process of fulfilling mutually agreed upon customer requirements in a superior way over time and pursuing a targeted share of customer's business through building mutual self-interest. In view of the variations in the selling situation, sales professionals practice *adaptive selling* or 'the altering of sales behaviours during a customer interaction or across customer interactions based on perceived information about the nature of the selling situation.' Two common approaches used in this situation are transactional and consultative selling. *Transactional selling* focuses on gaining an order as quickly as possible. Advocates urge sales persons to structure the entire sales call as a prelude to closing or asking for the order. *Consultative selling* involves the sales representative's becoming a long-term, trusted and value-adding resource for a customer firm by gaining an in-depth understanding of its operations and by contributing analytical expertise to resolve pressing problems. The key distinction between the two selling approaches is that the former focuses on completing the deal (getting or closing an order), whereas the latter emphasise on the longer term perspective.

According to Hutt and Speh (1995), the forces of global competition have reshaped the nature of managerial work and have spawned new ways of structuring organisations and buyer–seller relationships. As illustrated in Figure 6.2, several types of marketing relationships are positioned on a continuum, with pure transactions and strategic alliances serving as the endpoints.

Pure transactional exchange centres on the timely exchange of *basic products* for highly competitive market prices. *Pure collaborative exchange* involves a process in which a customer and supplier firm form strong and extensive social, economic, service and technical ties over time, with the intent of lowering cost, increasing value or both, thereby achieving mutual benefit. Understanding the different forms that relationships take in the business market provides a foundation for developing specific *relationship marketing strategies* for a particular customer.

Robinson et al. (1967), cited by Thompson, Mitchell and Knox (1998), refer to the assertion that the variation in organisational buyer behaviour occurs owing to the level of risk associated with a purchase. *Purchase risk*, according to Robinson et al., is a function of the importance of the (a) particular purchase, (b) complexity associated with the purchase, (c) uncertainty of the purchase and (d) need to reach a decision quickly. Johnston and Lewin (1996) analysed the stream of research on organisational buyer behaviour published during a 30-year period (1966 to 1996), isolating eight propositions that encapsulates their 'risk continuum'. Thompson et al. (1998) question the predominance of the established risk management view of organisational buyer behaviour in marketing textbooks and argue that new process-driven

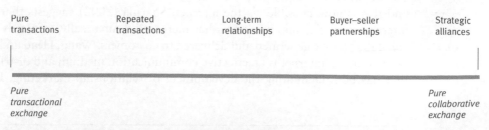

Figure 6.2 **Spectrum of buyer–seller relationships**
Source: Adapted with modifications from Webster (1992)

management styles are changing the way UK buyers and suppliers interact. Their research findings suggest that the risk continuum approach to organisational purchasing is pertinent to some of the cases they discovered. The authors maintain that large high-risk purchasing decision buying centres, laden with the conflicting agendas of the various participants, are being replaced by process-driven buying teams in many organisations. In many leading companies, value is no longer seen to be created by not making mistakes but by suppliers working with customers to create customer value and wealth for both businesses[1]. Because it is now established that customer retention and increasing sales to them is more cost efficient than recruiting new customers, certain companies have shifted their focus towards developing and maintaining stable, long-term customer relationships, with an increasing focus on measuring customer lifetime value (Berger and Nasr, 1998).

Relationship marketing

According to Gronroos (1996), a shift has taken place in recent years from transactional marketing to relationship marketing. Whereas *transactional marketing* focuses on increasing market share, *relationship marketing* focuses on improving customer retention. Relationship marketing and transactional marketing are not mutually exclusive, and there is no need for a conflict between them. Transactional marketing is most appropriate when marketing relatively low-value consumer products, when the product is a commodity, when switching costs are low, when customers prefer single transactions to relationships and when customer involvement is low. When the opposite is the case, as in typical services and industrial markets, then relationship marketing can be more appropriate. Customer retention is at the core of relationship marketing. Relationship building and management involves interacting with customers and satisfying their needs. The term *relationship marketing* has become widely used and covers a disparate range of activities. It has been positioned anywhere between being a set of marketing tactics in which any interaction between buyers and sellers is described as a relationship regardless of the parties' commitment to each other, and a fundamental marketing philosophy that goes to the core of the marketing concept.

Customers also recognise that good buyer–seller relationships are essential for the success of both customers and sellers (Harrison-Walker and Neeley, 2004) and have favoured relationship marketing. Customers often want to be 'relationship customers' and prefer personalised communication with the company representatives. In order to build committed relationships, constant contact must be maintained with both parties, and this is now possible via the internet. Sharma (2002) suggests that the use of the internet in relationship marketing has increased dramatically, primarily because of the value that can be generated and delivered to customers. Wang, Head and Archer (2000) assert that the internet is an effective communication medium and distribution channel that has been facilitating the development of relationship marketing. Learning about

---

[1] While the respondents in their study were drawn from a variety of industry sectors, it must be noted the sample size was relatively small, drawing on interview data only.

customers takes place through relevant dialogues with those customers also known as *customer relationship management* (CRM). As relationships develop, information about the customer is gathered in the customer information systems (CIS): the content, processes and assets associated with gathering and moving customer information throughout the firm. Zahay and Griffin (2004) set out the organisational learning capabilities of customer information management in a strategic context and focus on the key decisions that firms and specifically marketers must make within these firms.

Relationship building may require significant time, technology or personnel investment. Depending on the time and investment needed to develop and maintain relationships, the risk for marketers increases. Relationship building can be limited or restricted by communication and data collection restraints, particularly in the retailing sector. Permission marketing, whereby the customer gives the marketer permission to continue to contact the customer, is one of the tools of relationship marketing. According to Wang et al. (2000), the three stages in the relationship building process are *initial investigation, full range communication* and *relationship network creation*. Harrison-Walker and Neeley (2004) categorise several eB2B practices that can be applied at different stages in the buying decision process to establish and maintain customer relationships. They propose a typology focusing on two dimensions: the level of customer relationship bond sought by the seller (economic, social or structural) and the buyer's phase in the decision-making process (pre-purchase, purchase or postpurchase). The strategies for each buying stage and the level of relationship can be used to advise CRM managers on how to develop new strategies and evaluate current ones.

Tellefsen (2002) examines commitment in B2B relationships from the purchasing manager's perspective. He focuses on the relative importance of organisational and personal benefits in building buyer commitment. The study concludes that suppliers must satisfy the buying firm's organisational needs as well as the purchasing manager's personal needs. In Tellefsen's opinion, industrial marketers must continue to fine tune their organisational benefit bundles (product, price and delivery) for the buying firms and must develop personal bundles (efficiency, power and certainty) for the purchasing managers. Such personal bundles may be supplied via the internet through such things as tutorials, decision support tools and online tracking. Suppliers could also develop a deeper understanding of the purchasing managers' needs. This may involve organising factory tours for purchasing managers and introducing them to employees who influence issues that are of particular concern for purchasing managers.

Anderson and Narus (1999) note that in order to engage in partnering (sustaining customer relationships), it is essential to outline a strategic approach based on fundamental marketing concepts, including segmentation, targeting and positioning. The type of relationship that firms strive to have with customers must match the characteristics of the particular customer. If there is a transactional relationship, then the supplier firm will offer the most basic offerings with few options, but when there is a collaborative relationship, the supplier firm can provide more customised standardised offerings. In many cases, business market managers are now pursuing new business arrangements such as single sourcing, facilities management and outsourcing. Such collaborative arrangements between supplier firms and organisational buyers require constant monitoring and evaluation. IBM, for example, aims to establish supplier relationships that give it access to the latest technologies, supply continuity, speed to market, growth in e-Procurement leadership and retention of best talent within the profession (http://www-03ibm.com/procurement/proweb.nsf).

CASE 6.1   Renault sees F1 as vital in drive to develop its image   FT

Patrick Faure is quite relaxed. The chief executive of Renault's Formula One motor racing team would dearly like to see one of his two drivers – the new Spanish star Fernando Alonso or his Italian team mate Jarno Trulli – climb on the winners' podium at the end of Sunday's Monaco Grand Prix, by far the most glamorous race of the F1 season.

But even if victory proves elusive on Sunday, Mr Faure feels Renault is still well on track to achieve its targets since its full return to the multi-billion dollar global grand prix circus last year after a five-year absence.

The challenge is not merely an expensive exercise in vanity. The French carmaker's return to Formula One is intricately linked with the ambitious commercial strategy to boost Renault's commercial car sales from about 2.5m cars a year to 4m cars by 2010.

'Formula One is one of the vital channels for developing our international reputation and brand image,' says Mr Faure, a 24-year Renault veteran in various senior executive roles.

After amassing six consecutive world championships in the 1990s as the engine supplier of the Williams and Benetton teams, Renault decided to drop out of F1 racing in 1997. But Louis Schweitzer, Renault's chairman, said at the time the French group was not leaving F1 but simply taking a break.

'Schweitzer wanted to come back because F1 was part of Renault's strategy to sell 4m cars by 2010, excluding Nissan (the Japanese manufacturer 44.4 per cent owned by Renault),' says Mr Faure. 'We had no chance of gaining the necessary market share in Europe to reach this sales target. We had no plans to return to the US market. We thus had to go worldwide outside the US.'

Renault needed to build its image in markets where the brand was still unknown, notably Asia, where even the Nissan deal had done little to lift the French company's profile. 'The financial community were aware of our links but most people were unaware,' says Mr Faure, explaining that customer surveys also showed that customers wanted Renault to race under its own autonomous brand rather than in partnership with Nissan.

The F1 comeback occurred earlier than expected. Luciano Benetton, chairman of the Italian family-controlled clothings group, telephoned in 1999 to say he was selling his team because F1 had become a car manufacturers' business, requiring the research and development of an auto producer.

After brief negotiations, Renault bought the Benetton team in April 1999 for $120m.

'We raced under the Benetton name in 2000 and 2001 preparing our comeback under the Renault name in 2002,' says Mr Faure. This time, Renault wanted to be in full charge of the chassis and engine to gain maximum exposure from its F1 investment. 'When we were only the engine supplier we lived in the shadow of the Williams or

Benetton teams even though the engine is the most expensive component for a team,' says Mr Faure.

As a mass manufacturer, Renault's challenge is to leverage the exposure from motor racing into brand awareness rather than develop high-end sports cars from the technology employed. 'Millions of people watch F1 on television all round the world 17 or 18 times a year and the amount it costs is still modest compared to our group's overall advertising budget,' he says.

He declines to disclose the cost to Renault of running the F1 operations.

As part of its drive to sell 4m cars a year, Renault is stepping up plans to build a low-end budget car for developing markets. The X90 vehicle – also known as the '$5000 car' – will be built in Romania by Renault-owned Dacia from late 2004.

The French company also plans to invest €230m ($272m) to produce the car in Russia by the middle of 2005. It is negotiating a joint venture in Iran and considering adding Morocco, Colombia and China to the list.

Mr Faure says F1 is also a 'fabulous tool' for internal motivation for a big company such as Renault with 130,000 employees and extensive dealer and sales networks. But success is also important.

'Mr Schweitzer, my boss, told me we are not simply here to participate but to win the championship in a reasonable number of years.' A win on Sunday at Monaco would be tantamount to winning the entire championship for Mr Faure and his team.

Source: P. Betts, *Financial Times*, 30 May 2003

Questions

1. What is the nature of the relationship between Renault, Benetton and Nissan?

2. Using Webster's (1991) B2B characteristics (noted in the chapter), highlight the significant features in relations between these three organisations.

3. What, if any, are likely to be the benefits of relations between Renault, Benetton and Nissan for each of these three companies and for their customers?

CASE 6.2   Serving data on demand at Wimbledon

On the surface, there seems little to link the lawn tennis championships that opened at Wimbledon yesterday with research into protein structure. But both are supported by the same computers from International Business Machines. When they are not powering Wimbledon's newly re-designed website, they grind away at calculations and simulations needed by IBM scientists to determine how amino acid chains become folded into specific proteins.

This resource management plays to IBM's strengths in the latest networking technology, which it calls 'nodes on demand', and furthers Wimbledon's website ambitions.

'We want to be at the forefront of sports technology,' says Bob McCowen, Wimbledon's marketing director. You may think selling perhaps the world's biggest tennis championship doesn't involve too much work between sets. The 'grand slam' extravaganza pulls in almost half a million paying customers, with five applications for every ticket sold.

But Mr McCowen has other ideas. While he is keen to encourage sales of conventional Wimbledon merchandise – clothing, caps, towels and so on – the main aim is to spread awareness of the championship and bring the Wimbledon experience to those who cannot obtain tickets.

'We owe it to our huge fan base,' he says, 'and it's good for the game.' Since 1995, his principal weapon has been the internet. Wimbledon claims to have been the first big sports event in the UK to use its website as a promotional and marketing tool. This year, new features include a match ticker providing latest highlights, access to the site from personal digital assistants over GPRS networks and a subscription service including match commentaries streamed over the web.

IBM, the championships' technology partner and sponsor, has a long record of developing systems for big sporting events, including the Olympic Games. It maintains a team of six at Wimbledon all year round; in the week before the championships, this expands to 180 as engineers and technicians complete final systems installation and wiring.

The team is managed by Mark McMurrugh, seconded from IBM Global Services in Winchester. To run the website for the two weeks of the championships requires six months of planning and three months of design and implementation. The site claims 2.8m unique users, each spending an average of two hours nine minutes on the site, a degree of 'stickiness' that most commercial organisations would kill for.

But Mr McMurrugh, one of the world's top 100 players of real tennis, says the very unpredictability of sport in general means engineering the site is complex: 'In the past (it) has handled more than 800,000 users in a single day. Unpredictable peaks in users caused by match times, time zones, weather breaks and fans following Wimbledon from all over the world mean an "on demand" environment is essential.'

Last year, for example, when an unprecedented number of seeds failed to survive the first few rounds, US users, who represent about 25 per cent of site visitors, suddenly lost interest.

Some 80 per cent of visitors want up-to-the-minute scores. McCowen is limited in what he can offer because television owns the rights to broadcast live play. The website, therefore, uses IBM's match data service. This involves a team of 80 match analysts chosen from international, national and county junior tennis players.

They work in pairs. One describes the game, much in the style of a radio commentator. The second keys in the details of each stroke and point using a keyboard linked to an IBM laptop computer. (IBM says half a million items of match data will be collected and processed at the tournament.)

The match analysis is delivered to the website scoreboard, TV and radio broadcasters and players.

This year, for the first time, the length of each rally will be recorded in addition to the usual 'speed of service' radar system. And 'Hawk-Eye', the ball-tracking equipment used in international cricket, will be on Centre Court and No. 1 Court, although it will not be used by umpires.

Again for the first time, IBM is installing a WiFi wireless local area network.

Wimbledon is, of course, hostage to the vagaries of the British summer. But if it rains and there are periods when scores are not being processed, at least it will free up some IBM computers to grind away on more protein research.

Source: A. Cane, *Financial Times*, 24 June 2003

Questions

1. What factors are likely to have influenced Wimbledon's decision to acquire new technology from IBM?

2. Who might have been involved in this decision?

3. To what extent do you think the case represents a good example of relationship marketing?

Conclusions

In this chapter, the many issues associated with organisational buying behaviour within the sport market have been outlined and discussed. A variety of organisations (large and small; national and multinational; public and privately owned) with differing cultures, practices and processes in place have been explored. Much attention is given to purchasing decision maker (individual or group) and the factors that have a bearing on the approach taken. Evidence would support the contention that many firms and organisations are actively involved in fostering relationships with key suppliers because over the longer term, they are considered most beneficial from all perspectives (financial and otherwise).

Discussion questions

1. As a sport marketing consultant, advise the CEO of a leading tennis tournament on the procedures to be used in selecting a supplier of timing devices and scoreboards.
2. Cross-functional teams are commonly used in organisational purchasing. Discuss the advantages and disadvantages of such an arrangement.

3. Purchasing strategic inputs for any sports body is influenced by many internal and external variables. As chief buyer for your National Olympic Committee, identify the main inputs to be purchased and detail the approach to be used.

Guided reading

For more detail on organisations, Daft (2000) and Slack (1997) are recommended; Gratton and Taylor (2000) explain the economics of the sport industry. The reader is advised to consult Anderson and Narus (1999) and Hutt and Speh (1998) for deeper insights on business marketing. Rogan (2003) also provides succinct insights on B2B marketing. Gronroos (1996) is suggested for specifics of relationship marketing, and Old (2004) gives insights on organisational behaviour in the sports setting.

Keywords

Buyclass; buyphase; BuyGrid model; buying centre; buying group; concentration; consumer products; corporate strategy; industrial marketing; just-in-time; new product development; organisational buying; reward/measurement theory; validity.

Bibliography

Anderson, J. and Narus, J. (1999) *Business Market Management: Understanding, Creating and Delivering Value*, Englewood Cliffs, NJ: Prentice Hall.

Berger P.D. and Nasr, N.I. (1998) Customer lifetime value: Marketing models and applications, *Journal of Interactive Marketing* 12(1):17–30.

Bok, D. (2003) *Universities in the Marketplace*, Princeton, NJ: Princeton University Press.

Celtic Social Mission Statement (2006) *Celtic View* 41(29):7.

Chelladurai, P. (2001) *Managing Organisations for Sport and Physical Activity: A Systems Perspective*, Scottsdale, AZ: Holcomb Hathaway.

Considine, J., Coffey, S. and Kiely, D. (2004) Irish sports capital funding: A public choice perspective, *European Sport Management Quarterly* 4(3):50–169.

Daft, L. (2000) *Management*, Orlando, FL: Dryden Press.

Gratton, C. and Taylor, P. (2000) *The Economics of Sport and Recreation*, London: Spon.

Gronros, C. (1996) 'The rise and fall of modern marketing – and its rebirth', in S. Shaw and N. Hood (eds), *Marketing in Evolution, Essays in Honour of Michael J. Baker*, London: Macmillan Press.

Harrison-Walker, L. and Neeley, S. (2004) Customer relationship building on the internet in B2B marketing, *Journal of Marketing Theory and Practice* Winter(12):19–35.

Hums, M.A. and MacLean, J.C. (2003) *Governance and Policy in Sport Organizations*, Scottsdale, AZ: Halcomb Hathaway.

Hutt, M. and Speh, T. (1995) *Business Marketing Management*, Forth Worth, TX: Dryden Press.

King, B. (2002) Passions that can't be counted puts billions of dollars in play, *Street and Smith's Sport Business Journal* March 11:25–6.

Jobber, D. and Fahy, J. (2003) *Foundations of Marketing*, Berkshire: McGraw Hill.

Johnston, W. and Lewin, J. (1996) Organization buying behaviour: Towards an Integrated Framework, *Journal of Business Research* 35(1):1–15.

Mawson, E. and Fearne (1997) An organisational buyer behaviour: A study of UK restaurant chains, *British Food Journal* 99(7):239–45.

Old, J. (2004) 'Organizational behaviour in sport organizations', in J. Beech and S. Chadwick (eds), *The Business of Sport Management*, London: FT Prentice Hall.

Randall, G. (1993) *Principles of Marketing*, London: Routledge.

Robbins, S. (1990) *Organisation Theory: Structure, Design and Applications*, Englewood Cliffs, NJ: Prentice Hall.

Robinson, P., Faris, C. and Wind, Y. (1967) *Industrial Buying and Creative Marketing*, Boston: Allyn and Bacon.

Rogan, D. (2003) *Marketing: An Introduction for Irish Students*, Dublin: Gill and Macmillan.

Sharma, A. (2002) Trends in internet-based business to business marketing, *Industrial Marketing Management* 31(2):77–84.

Sheth, J. (1973) A model of industrial buyer behaviour, *Journal of Marketing* 37:50–6.

Slack, T. (1997) *Understanding Sport Organisations*, Champaign, IL: Human Kinetics.

Tanner, J. (1999) Organizational buying theories: A bridge to relationships theory, *Industrial Marketing Management* 28:245–55.

Tellefsen, T. (2002) Commitment in business-to-business relationships: The role of organisational and personal needs, *Industrial Marketing Management* 31:645–52.

Thompson, K., Mitchell, H. and Knox, S. (1998) Organisational buying behaviour in changing times, *European Management Journal* 16(6):698–705.

Wang, F., Head, M. and Archer, N. (2000) A relationship-building model for the Web retail marketplace, *Internet Research* 10(5):374–84.

Webster, F.E. (1991) *Industrial Marketing Strategy*, Englewood Cliffs, NJ: Prentice Hall.

Webster, F.E. (1992) The changing role of marketing in the corporation, *Journal of Marketing* 56:5.

Webster, F. and Wind, Y. (1972) *Organisational Buying Behaviour*, Englewood Cliffs, NJ: Prentice Hall.

Wilson, D. (2000) Why divide consumer and organizational buyer behaviour?, *European Journal of Marketing* 34(7):780–91.

Zahay, D. and Griffin, A. (2004) Customer learning processes, strategy selection, and performance in business to business service firms, *Decision Sciences* 35(2):169–98.

Recommended websites

IBM
http://www.ibm.co.uk

JJB Sports
http://www.jjb.co.uk/corporateinfo/

Mind Branch
http://www.mindbranch.com

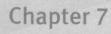

Chapter 7

Segmentation, targeting and positioning in sport

Kim Harris
University of Lincoln
Dominic Elliott
University of Liverpool Management School

Learning outcomes

Upon completion of this chapter, the reader should be able to:

- Understand the nature and significance of segmentation, targeting and positioning in sport.

- Appreciate the advantages of segmentation and positioning in the context of sport marketing activity.

- Identify and evaluate the various bases that might be used by sport organisations to segment markets.

- Evaluate the usefulness of positioning strategies used in sport to develop and maintain competitive advantage.

- Identify the barriers to successful implementation of the segmentation process as experienced by a range of organisations.

Overview of chapter

This chapter explores the meaning and importance of segmentation, targeting and positioning in sport. It begins by outlining the advantages of segmentation experienced by a range of organisations. This is followed by a more detailed discussion of the decisions required at the three stages of the segmentation process using examples from sport marketing. In the initial stage, the selection of the most appropriate base(s) for segmenting the market is critical. Although there are a range of individual bases that can be used to understand customers in a market, the discussion draws attention to the benefits experienced by organisations adopting a clustering approach to develop more meaningful segments. Two cases are used to evaluate the contribution of positioning within the segmentation process. The chapter concludes with a discussion of some of the problems experienced by companies striving to successfully implement the segmentation process.

Introduction

Many academics and practitioners consider segmentation to be one of the most important strategic concepts contributed by the marketing discipline. Supporters of the concept claim that segmentation leads to a better understanding of customers' needs and characteristics and, as a result, allows companies to develop more carefully tuned marketing programmes. As such, segmentation can be viewed as a logical development of the marketing concept, which places the consumer at the heart of the decision-making process (Wind and Cardoza, 1974). It has also been claimed that segmentation has been used most effectively in industries in which customer retention is a primary goal, with firms using their own transaction databases to identify, profile, target and reach segments (Wedel and Kamakura, 2002). This has certainly been the case in one sector of the sport industry, football clubs. Here there has been a growing practitioner interest in the contribution segmentation can make in terms of generating increased revenue from supporter loyalty. Many clubs now have substantial supporter databases, which enable them to segment supporters more easily and consequently carry out more effective direct marketing activity.

According to Kotler (1980), segmentation consists of a three-stage process:

Stage one, termed *segmentation*, consists of splitting customers, or potential customers within a market into distinct groups of buyers that may share common characteristics or buying patterns. In consumer markets, customers are frequently segmented by a range of different criteria, including behavioural, demographic, psychographic and geographic variables. In their recent review of segmentation approaches used in professional sport marketing, Tapp and Clowes (2000) note the use of lifestage, social class, loyalty data and attitudes to winning as bases for segmenting sports supporters. In the same study, the authors illustrate how UK football supporters can be segmented on the basis of elements of overt behaviour, or behavioural segmentation. An extract from their study is provided in Table 7.1.

In business markets, segmentation bases might include type of organisation, benefits sought, nature and characteristics of the buying process as well as personal and psychological variables.

Table 7.1 Segmenting football supporters by 'matchday' behaviour

1. **Mine's a pint:** These are people who like a drink or two either side of the game. These fans arrive early 'to park' and often meet casual acquaintances at the bar or maybe read the programme.
2. **Juggling the kids:** Families trying to fit in two or three events in the day. They may arrive at the ground at the last minute but be high halftime spenders on merchandise.
3. **Thermos at row D:** These are creatures of habit who get into the ground quite late. They are not interested in talking to anyone and may not spend much money at the ground on programmes or food.
4. **Season ticket friendlies:** These people enjoy the social event of meeting fellow supporters by virtue of always having the same seat.
5. **Loyal cash and chanters:** They buy tickets with cash when they get paid and have a good shout at the game. May be 'regular' fans.
6. **Dads and sons:** These are quiet supporters and not part of a group. They are loyal, 'club' rather than football oriented, and critical of disloyal boys being Manchester United fans.

Source: Tapp and Clowes (2002)

Stage two is *targeting*. This involves evaluating each segment's attractiveness in terms of profit potential and deciding how many segments to focus on. In the case of supporters identified in Table 7.1, the club would need to consider whether any group was substantial enough to warrant customised marketing activity. For example, a promotional offer might be developed with a nearby pub to offer the 'mine's a pint segment' a free 'pie and a pint' on match day when they buy any club merchandise. However, if this was such a small percentage of the total fan base, the costs of developing and implementing the promotional campaign might outweigh the potential profit from additional merchandise sales.

Stage three involves developing a competitive *positioning* for the firms' product or service within the segment(s) and developing the appropriate 'marketing mix' to reach the customers. As soon as the organisation has selected the 'segments' it wishes to focus on, it needs to develop a clear positioning in the minds of the target consumers, to differentiate its offer from competitors targeting the same segment. This stage becomes particularly critical in industries with a large number of companies offering very similar product or service ranges. Although it could be argued that the notion of competitive positioning is not as critical in the football industry, in which supporters generally demonstrate high loyalty to individual clubs, it does become more important if you take a slightly broader view about who constitutes 'competition' for the club. In Table 7.1, for example, if the club wished to target the 'juggling the kids' segment, who may represent a growing and potentially highly profitable group of consumers, the club would need to identify the other events that compete with the match for the supporters' time and money. These might include, for example, swimming clubs, cinema showings or simply shopping trips. These could all be viewed as competition for the club. In this extreme case, the club would have to develop a positioning statement that clearly identified the match as a more attractive proposition in the minds of the target supporters. In this case, for example, it might be a strategy that reinforces the exciting or unpredictable nature of the event.

Advantages of segmentation and positioning

Although there are some dissenters, most practising managers recognise the advantages of segmentation and positioning as comprising some or all of the following:

First, the process ensures a closer 'fit' between the customers' needs and the company's products or services. According to Sullivan (2004, p. 128), this fit is the goal of sport marketing: 'The fundamental aim of sport marketing activity is to satisfy the right sport customer needs with sport products or services that offer benefits in excess of all other competitor offerings whilst making the maximum sustainable profit.' To illustrate, Nike has develop a range of products called Nike Pro for Athletes. As the name suggests, this range is clearly targeted at a particular segment of consumers who are interested in optimising their sporting performance and are looking for products that will help them to achieve this. Marketing communications emphasise the advanced technology used in the design of the products. The description of one product in the range, the Nike Pro Vent long Sleeve Top, informs prospective purchasers that it has 'mesh upper back die cut insets that enhance breathability and ventilation and is made of a dri-FIT fabric, which ensures that skin stays cool and dry as moisture is 'wicked away'. Here the technical features of the product are linked directly to benefits that appeal to the serious athlete – that is, maximum ventilation and freedom of movement. The needs of this segment are different from those targeted with another product range, the Nike iD range. Here the company emphasises the design features of the products, which appeal to a very different target segment. Customers in this segment are much more interested in the aesthetic appeal of the products, which they can tailor to their own particular requirements. Sports performance is far less important than image and appearance to these customers.

The second stated advantage of segmentation is that it can lead to opportunities for the development of 'niche' markets. These are generally small but highly profitable segments. In many cases, this can result in segment dominance, something that is often not possible in the total market. For example, the market for package holidays has grown substantially since the 1960s and 1970s, leading to a greater demand for a variety of offerings, including sports-related breaks. Companies such as Hookedoncycling have emerged to meet the needs of a niche segment of consumers, those requiring cycling-only holidays. The basic service offers a package of tour planning, routes, accommodation, travel and bikes. A selection of tours is offered to meet the needs of cyclists with different tastes and diverse levels of fitness, from the first-time cycle tourist or 'softy' leisure cyclist to the most experienced cycle tourist. The company recognises that keen cyclists may wish to bring members of their family on holiday, too, so it offers noncycling members the opportunity to take cookery lessons or to visit historic sites. The company even provides child care facilities.

Third, segmentation and positioning may also be used to gain and reinforce the company's competitive advantage. The notion of market growth through a life cycle is firmly established within the fields of marketing and strategy, despite support and criticism for the concept (Tonks, 1998). As a market matures and competition intensifies, new niches may emerge. For example, within the cycling holiday market, the company Roughtracks has emerged, specialising in mountain biking breaks. These range from long cycling holidays to weekend courses for beginners to cycle maintenance courses. The company's promotional literature emphasises the social dimension of cycling in small groups, making little reference to children and noncycling partners. Another company, Bikecamp.com, founded in 1986 by Olympic gold medallist Connie Carpenter and Tour de France stage winner Davis Phinney, is promoted as 'a vehicle to share their passion for – and knowledge of – road cycling with serious road cycling enthusiasts'. The target segment for this company is serious cyclists, usually taking their own specially constructed bicycles. Where Hookedoncycling caters to noncyclists, too, Bikecamp.com requests that customers check first that a camp is child friendly and that 'independent, well-behaved children are *generally quite* welcome'. As the total market for cycling holidays has grown, companies have attempted to differentiate themselves from the competition by developing distinct positions that appeal to different consumer segments.

Finally, segmentation can also be used to develop expertise in a specific market, to avoid the risks of meeting the needs of all potential customers but not excelling with any group. For example, a cycling tour operator may concentrate on a particular country or region and use its specialist knowledge as a unique selling point. Iberocycle, for example, provides cycling packages in Spain. This expertise is reinforced through all other business decisions to ensure that a consistent message is communicated to target segments. For example, promotional literature emphasises the fact that the company uses expert cyclists recruited for their language and cultural knowledge of the countries visited.

McDonald and Dunbar (1998) identify two additional benefits for organisations that actually work through the segmentation process. First, they argue that the process forces managers in organisations to question some basic assumptions about the nature and size of their market. For example, as noted earlier, a football club that views its competition simply in terms of other football clubs might miss valuable opportunities for service enhancement that appear from an analysis of the positioning strategies of other 'entertainment' venues. Second, these authors found that if the process is adopted at a strategic level, it both improved team building within the organisations and identified 'hitherto undiscovered customer needs' (p. 29).

Stages of the segmentation process

Stage one: Segmentation

As already noted, stage one of the segmentation process consists of splitting customers, or potential customers, within a market into distinct groups of buyers who may share common characteristics or buying patterns. A key consideration at this stage in defining the market to be segmented, is estimating the variation in buyers' needs and requirements at the different product-market levels and identifying the types of buyers included in the market. This process requires extensive market research and data collection. A sport organisation would need to know the actual and potential size of the 'market' and how it divides up between the competing products and services. The organisation would also need to conduct detailed profiling of the different customers within the market in terms of exactly what benefits they are looking for and the relative importance of these benefits.

Most of the common variables used to divide up consumers of sports goods and services fall into one of four general categories: behavioural, demographic, psychographic and geographic segmentation. Many of these have been used to build up profiles of consumers in the sport industry. Table 7.2 identifies these in more detail and provides examples relating to segmentation in the gym and fitness market.

As noted earlier, *behavioural segmentation* is concerned with grouping customers on the basis of product or service usage. There will be differences between high and low users and may well be differences in loyalty. A key feature of many sport markets is high levels of loyalty (e.g., with supporters of local teams). There may be very little switching between supporting one team and another. In such cases, switching may be between sports or other leisure activities, rather than between different teams playing the same sport. Hunt, Bristol and Bashaw (1999) provide a typology of the 'sports fan' based on elements of loyalty. They identify five groups of fans: temporary, local, devoted, fanatical and dysfunctional. The authors use the example of a 'once in a lifetime boxing bout' as an example of an attempt to attract the *temporary fan*. There may be some overlap between segments; the next two identified are *local and devoted fans*. An individual might be both, but whereas the former is attached to a particular area and may differ in levels of consumption, devoted fans display a higher than average level of interest in their chosen sport. *Fanatical fans* are further distinguished by the degree to which their team and the products and services associated with them permeate the different facets of their life. Finally, the *dysfunctional fan* refers to the individual who may indulge in antisocial behaviour around events and also to those

Table 7.2 **Segmentation bases as applied to the gym and fitness market**

Category	Variable	Examples
Behavioural segmentation	■ Benefits sought	■ Gym users differ significantly here. Some go to a gym to exercise to aid weight loss, some for rehabilitation from illness and others for social interaction.
	■ Product or service usage	■ Gym users vary in how often they use facilities. Some may go twice a week for up to 2 hours, some may make five or more shorter visits and others may attend two or three times a month. Usage of the facilities is likely to be linked to the benefits sought.
	■ Occasion or situation	■ Some users go to the gym on particular occasions. Many clubs link health and beauty services to the core gym package and offer 'pampering' packages for groups of women celebrating weddings or birthdays.
Demographic segmentation	■ Age	■ 'Splashtime' for children. Gym times allocated for junior members. Special exercise classes and off peak gym membership for people over 60.
	■ Gender	■ Exclusive use of gym facilities for women at certain times of the day.
	■ Income	■ Gold star gym and leisure packages for those who wish to pay more.
	■ Occupation	■ Corporate membership deals
	■ Family lifecycle	■ Family memberships. Singles-only gym sessions.
Psychographic segmentation	■ Personality	■ Gym sessions for those who do not want to be disturbed by others. Running clubs for 'serious' athletes.
	■ Lifestyle	■ Selection of gym linked to lifestyle. Those who work in town prefer a city centre gym. Opening hours, classes and other facilities would be structured around their busy work schedule.
	■ Motives	■ Fitness, weight loss or social.
	■ Involvement	■ For many, fitness is such a critical part of their life that they could be described as 'highly involved' with the gym. This involvement affects their knowledge about the quality of the services on offer as well as their loyalty to the club.
Geographic segmentation	■ Regional	■ Many fitness clubs open their facilities to local schools and universities to attract consumers in the local area. National chains promote competitions between users of regional clubs to encourage local identity among members.
	■ National	■ National chains of gym clubs such as Living Well, Greens and David Lloyds provide convenience to customers on the move.

for whom devotion interferes with everyday life such as making them regularly miss school or work to attend events, for example. Although it has been suggested that the diversity of sports may undermine the generalisability of any such typology, it does offer some useful insights. In particular, Hunt et al.'s (1999) typology, although deficient in some areas, points towards some of the characteristics of sports fans and highlights how high levels of involvement with a sport can influence all aspects of an individual's life. It is for this reason that so many organisations seek to link their products and services to sports personalities, sports and sporting events.

Demographics may also play a key role in determining the degree to which an individual gets involved with a sport as participator or spectator. Tapp and Clowes' (2002) classification identified in Table 7.1 makes some use of demographic data in its juggling families and dad and son categories. In the United Kingdom, football's championship has recently announced free season tickets to children under 8 years old with the purpose of encouraging youngsters to support their local team from an early age. Other sports, such as cricket, with an ageing spectator profile have sought to attract younger supporters, a case explored in greater detail later. A failure to continually target younger consumers will lead to declining markets as a sporting organisation's target market literally dies out.

Another key basis for segmenting sport consumer is *psychographic* factors such as lifestyle, personality, interests, opinions and attitudes. A characteristic of many spectator sports is the traditional attitudes of their customers towards their sport. For example, a problem experienced by Rugby Union in England after the national side's World Cup victory was the growing attendance of new supporters, many of whom did not fully understand the rules of the game nor the accepted norms of applauding good play from either side. This has also been seen in cricket in which the boisterous behaviour of new supporters was seen to alienate existing ones (Birley, 1999). In golf, Shank (2002) reports from a survey that amongst US golfers, the top lifestyles were regular skiing, tennis, investments, frequent business travel, wine and sailing. Amongst the bottom were Bible study, sewing, healthfoods, science fiction and cat ownership. Such information may be used to determine the types of products and services that might be targeted at golfers and help sponsors decide whether or not to build links with golfing events.

The nature of sport also makes *geographic forms* of segmentation particularly important. Many competitive sports have at their core the notion of local or regional representation, as may be seen in the cases of rugby, football, baseball, basketball, cricket and many other team sports. Individually, particular sports personalities are national representatives, as may be seen in athletics, tennis, cycling and golf. In the form of the Ryder Cup, golf pitches the United States against Europe's best. The physical climate may also play a part in supporting the development of particular sports. Skiing and skating, for example, require cold venues, and surfboarding requires oceanic coastlines.

It has been argued elsewhere that as a sector, sport exhibits a number of unique characteristics, which have necessitated specialist approaches to segmentation (see, for example, Mullin, Hardy and Sutton 2000). Some variables are of particular concern for certain types of sporting activity. For example, within professional spectator sports, issues such as loyalty, attitudes to winning and involvement are vitally important in understanding customers. Loyalty refers to the longevity of commitment between supporter and the team supported. In the case of team sports, such loyalty may be long lived. In the case of individual competitive sports, such as tennis, loyalties may fluctuate in response to the flair or characteristics of the personalities involved. Attitudes to winning may be closely linked to involvement: the higher the degree of involvement (i.e., the more important a club or personality to an individual), the greater the desire for winning. This reinforces the need for us to distinguish between a supporter and a fan (fanatic) as identified in the typology discussed earlier. For example, Luger (2005) reported that rugby in the South of France dominates the local town and great importance is attached to defending your ground. *L'esprit de clocher* (the spirit of the bell tower) means that losing at home is less acceptable than in other parts of Europe; losing away is accepted with less disappointment.

Apart from the basic classification identified above, many organisations have found it useful to cluster different segmentation bases together to divide consumers in a more meaningful way. The geodemographic classification ACORN (a classification of residential neighbourhoods) developed by the California Analysis Center (CACI) is one such example of a clustering approach to segmentation. ACORN analyses not individuals but households using postcode data to distinguish type of property and householder information. This is then combined with a range of other information to provide customer profiles to help companies target more 'meaningful' segments of customers. One product that has been developed from the original ACORN system and is particularly useful for sport marketers in the United Kingdom is Lifestylesuk. This is a database offering more than 300 lifestyle selections from 44 million users in the United Kingdom. It combines real information from questionnaires, share registrations, census data and the complete electoral roll.

A final area for segmentation within the sport sector concerns industrial markets. Although our focus has been concerned with supporters (consumers), commercial customers play an increasingly important part in the financial success of parts of the industry. The influence of television monies can be seen across competitive sport, including American football, soccer, snooker, Formula One and tennis. Sponsors also pay large amounts for links with individuals and clubs from almost every sport. Ellen MacArthur recently broke the round the world sailing record in the B&Q boat, for example. Although this is an area that has not received significant attention to date, observations suggest that much of such sponsorship occurs at the instigation of the sponsor. Sponsor objectives include wishing to raise their profile. Examples include Greenflag's sponsorship of England Football Team to raise awareness of its introduction, and Pringle's request for David Beckham's endorsement to change consumer perceptions of the brand.

According to McDonald and Dunbar (1998), the criteria used for segmentation must have the following characteristics:

1. There must be the ability to distinguish 'unique' segments. The segments must be meaningful in terms of offering profitable marketing opportunities.
2. Each identified segment should have sufficient potential size to justify time and effort devoted to it (i.e., be sufficiently substantial).
3. Each identified segment should be capable of being described or measured by a set of descriptors.
4. Each segment should have relevance (i.e., should be a decision-making factor or affect the process of buying behaviour).
5. The company should be capable of being able to focus resources on that segment.

Stage two: Targeting

As noted earlier, stage two involves evaluating each segment's attractiveness in terms of profit potential and deciding how many segments to focus on. Kotler (1980) suggests three major criteria for assessing the relative attractiveness of market segments: size and growth, structural attractiveness and fit with the company's objectives and resources. Each of these is discussed in more detail below.

Segment size and growth

Tapp and Clowes (2002) research sought to elicit geodemographic and income data, which would help quantify the size and potential profitability of each segment. Although segment size may be an important indicator of current attractiveness, decline and growth rates can provide a pointer towards future profitability. For example, an ageing customer profile would indicate the need to specifically target younger customers.

Segment structural attractiveness

Figure 7.1 depicts a simplistic analysis of the senior British rugby and football industries. Threat of new entrants is low for both because entry into the professional leagues is closely controlled through each sport's governing bodies. The power of buyers in rugby is shown as relatively low because of the more limited influence of television revenues, although this is changing rapidly, especially given the importance of the Heineken European Cup. With the current cap placed upon players' salaries, there are fewer pressures upon the rugby industry's financial resources than is the case with the football industry. In this case, clubs are highly dependent upon revenues from television, as highlighted by the significant impact when ITV digital ceased its contract with the former first division. The dotted line on the power of buyers within the football industry denotes the relative unimportance of paying spectators, although given fan loyalty, this is a reliable source of income for clubs. The threat of substitutes is shown as relatively higher for rugby than for football because the former receives less media coverage and may be more vulnerable to changes in tastes and fashion. Differences in the power of suppliers reflect the success of the Professional Footballers' Association in achieving its objectives, in some cases, against those of the football authorities and clubs. Finally, higher degrees of competitive rivalry within the football industry reflect its greater maturity within the professional era and the well-developed international market for players and supporters. Such structural analyses provide the basis for better understanding an overall industry and the place of specific segments within it. For example, growing television involvement in sports has seen a growth in armchair spectators with less involvement, possibly in a club, and with greater interest in entertainment at the expense of simple results.

Company objectives and resources

Although marketing is largely founded upon the premise that the first step is to identify customer needs and to provide a product or service to meet these needs, this is often idealistic. Organisations rarely begin with a blank piece of paper. For example, Living Well Health Clubs, a part of the Hilton Hotel chain, are frequently located within hotels, offering gym, sauna and swimming pool facilities to guests and local

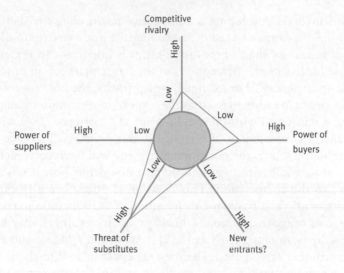

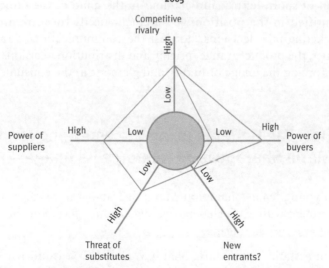

Figure 7.1 **A structural analysis of the senior British rugby and football industries**
Source: Adapted from Porter (1980)

residents. Typically, guests make greater use of leisure facilities at weekends or in the evenings. The pricing policy, therefore, seeks to exclude off-peak members and children from using facilities at these times. Alternatively, for specialist gyms and health clubs, evenings are the busiest times, meaning that off-peak members and children may use facilities before 5 pm on weekdays and weekends. In this way, company resources play a key role in the benefits offered to different segments.

◾ Stage three: Positioning

This involves developing a competitive *positioning* for the firms' product or service within the segment(s) and developing the appropriate 'marketing mix' to reach the customers. As Shank notes (p. 242), it is important to remember that 'positioning is based solely on the perceptions of the target market and how they think or feel about the sports entity'. For example, Roughtracks, the holiday company mentioned earlier, has clearly positioned itself as the 'expert' in mountain biking holidays. This positioning is reinforced with the employment of experienced, knowledgeable staff. However, if target consumers do not recognise this point of difference when choosing between alternatives, then the positioning strategy will have been ineffective. To use positioning successfully, an organisation must first define how it wishes to position itself relative to the competition. This decision is often formally captured in a 'positioning statement'. The bases for differentiation may include particular product or service benefits or usage occasion. A hockey club, for example, may hope to attract new members by positioning itself as the club that offers 'fitness and fun' rather than focusing on winning every game. The message encapsulated in the positioning statement then needs to be communicated regularly and in a consistent manner to an identified segment of consumers. Many organisations use sports personalities to reinforce a particular competitive position. Case 7.1 describes how TAG Heuer has teamed up with a young tennis star Maria Sharapova in an effort to associate its brand with the excitement of sport, luxury and glamour in the mind of the target consumer. The message identified in the positioning statement needs to be reinforced through all of the marketing mix decisions, not just the communications strategy. In the case of TAG Heuer, the products range, pricing and distribution decisions all need to be continually reinforcing the image of luxury and glamour in the consumer's mind.

| CASE 7.1 | How Tag Heuer is using the emerging tennis star Maria Sharapova to reinforce its image |

The young tennis champion Maria Sharapova has signed a long-term ambassador agreement with TAG Heuer, covering product development, advertising, public relations and merchandising.

'I am ecstatic,' says Maria Sharapova, the 17-year-old Russian tennis star and the third youngest Wimbledon Champion in WTA history. 'To represent a brand as legendary as TAG Heuer is a great honor. TAG Heuer has been teaming with the greatest champions in the history of sports, renowned athletes like Carl Lewis, Ayrton Senna or nowadays Tiger Woods. TAG Heuer is the most prestigious luxury partner I can dream of, as legendary and glamorous as the individuals and teams with which it is so closely related, and yet at the same time ultra-fashionable and feminine. It's a perfect fit for me, as I love high tech, glamour and winning. I look forward to building a strong relationship with TAG Heuer in the coming years.'

'In just two seasons Maria Sharapova has made her mark on the WTA pro tennis circuit, quickly advancing to the 4th singles 2004 WTA rankings, and winning two of the most famous tournaments in tennis,' says Jean-Christophe Babin, TAG Heuer's President and Chief Executive Officer. 'Off the court, her beauty and grace have romanced the fashion world, with profiles in leading fashion magazines, and the launch of her own perfume. She is truly a phenomenon. Determined, passionate and audacious, she has shown extraordinary character in taking on the best players in professional tennis and winning. At the same time she is graceful and extraordinarily feminine. Nobody in the world of sports better than Maria embodies the fusion of sport with glamour, and therefore TAG Heuer core positioning.'

Like her fellow TAG Heuer Ambassadors, Maria Sharapova will be directly involved in the development of new TAG Heuer products. In particular, the new ambassador will share her insights on the TAG Heuer Formula 1 and 2000/Aquaracer series, which reflects her sporting allure and distinctively young and feminine appeal. She will also soon be the newest face to be showcased extensively in the TAG Heuer advertising campaign, 'What are you made of?'

Source: Adapted from http://www.fhs.ch/en/news/news.php?id=353

Questions

1. What is the positioning statement TAG Heuer want to reinforce with this marketing strategy?

2. What are the potential weaknesses for TAG Heuer of such a marketing strategy in terms of product positioning?

3. Identify another three companies who have used sports personality endorsement to reinforce their position within the market.

Company/Brand

1.

2.

3.

Positioning statement

1.

2.

3.

At times, declining sales or market share may indicate that an organisation's positioning is no longer meeting the needs of consumers. In this case, a new position may be required rather than strengthening the current position, which may only serve to accelerate the downturn. Case 7.2 illustrates a case of repositioning in the cricket market. As Birley (1999) identifies, English cricket has undergone a decline in terms of spectator numbers and revenues from all sources. A number of factors contributed to this downturn. First, the three-day county match was considered to be too long to fit easily with the lifestyle of many potential spectators. Second, other sports were seen to be offering a more 'exciting' experience, if excitement is measured in terms of uncertainty of outcome. Rugby Union had sought to encourage more spectacular forms of scoring by amending the points awarded for a try from 4 to 5. Similarly Football moved from a system of two to three points for a win to encourage more attacking play. The three-day cricket match might be over in two days, resulting in an empty ground on a sunny Saturday, potentially the busiest day. In 2002 a so-called 20/20 version of the game was introduced, a model quickly adopted elsewhere. The central idea was for each team to bat and bowl for 20 overs each, requiring two or three hours, possibly played in the evening to attract people at work. The aim of the strategy was to reposition the game as a more exciting sporting event in line with actions taken in other sports. Early reports suggest that it has captured the public's imagination and has reversed the declining appeal of English cricket. The question remains how this repositioning will influence the game and whether it will alienate the loyal spectators who were happier with the slower three-day version of the sport. These issues are pursued in the following case study.

CASE 7.2   The success of 20/20 cricket

They're cheering at Willoughby and Cricket Australia after the recent ratings of 20/20 cricket, but equally there'll be a few furrowed brows at both organisations. Why?

Quickie/Quickie cricket, also known as 20/20 cricket

Apart from the Charity one day match last Monday for the tsunami appeal (average more than two million people), quickie cricket has comprehensively defeated the two one day internationals played so far, attracting up to three hundred thousand more viewers than the two One day internationals (ODI) which both involved the audience-grabbing Australian team.

So while there's cheering over the success of the 20/20 game involving Australia A and Pakistan from Adelaide on Thursday night, there's also now fears that it could over-shadow the longer established One Day game in terms of TV audiences. The 20/20 game was a first, so the novelty factor is there, but there's clearly potential. More than 1.380 million people tuned in for the two and a half hours of 20/20 cricket (or twenty/twenty). Compared to the more formal and structured One Day form, quickie cricket resembles beach or backyard cricket. It may have been a trial but it surprised with the big crowd at the ground of more than 21,000 (after more than 20,000 packed out the WACA in Perth the night before for a 20/20 game between WA and Victoria).

In contrast the One Day Game on Friday involving Australia and the West Indies averaged 1.003 million. It was the 5th most watched program, compared to the first place ranking the night before for quickie/quickie. And yesterday's ODI involving Australia and Pakistan from Hobart (a day game so the audience should have been lower) in fact attracted more viewers and averaged 1.087 million people, a good result for cricket and Nine. It was the 6th most popular program. But it was still far behind the first 20/20 game. Now when it's in its 30th or so season of playing and being broadcast, will 20/20 still rank as highly? Will it after the end of next season when we will undoubtedly see more games on TV? It is a quick form of tip and run. That makes it exciting for viewers and crowds and makes it good for TV and broadcasters. This strong audience interest will guarantee that 20/20 cricket is around next year in some way. Perhaps Cricket Australia might want to separate this out of the contract renegotiations about to get underway and offer it to Ten or Seven as a way of getting an auction up to drive more money for the Test and One Day rights from Nine (pay more and we'll throw in the 20/20 rights).

Judging by the performance on the field, the way the crowd reacted and the number of people there, it has arrived as a sporting entertainment form. For how long no one knows. Test cricket has waxed and waned and waxed in popularity over the years with the performance of the national team. It will clearly force Nine and Cricket Australia to launch a televised series next year, perhaps even as part of the ING Cup to preserve that competition and the one day skills it teaches first class cricketers. However 20/20 cricket should not be given the same status as one day internationals or ING Cup, but made into a sort of Australian cricket version of the FA Cup. It is the sort of thing that Pay TV here will want to broadcast to get its foot into the door after broadcasting the Ashes tour mid year.

The 20/20 game was the most watched program in Sydney and Melbourne and was in the top ten in Brisbane, Adelaide and Perth. Its audiences easily eclipsed those for the ODI games in Sydney, Melbourne and Brisbane in particular. For any TV network there's the attraction of running it as a two and a half hour program in mid evening, with a high rating strong program before and after to built the audience and to take advantage of it.

Costs should also be lower for the network as the crewing and broadcast time will be shorter (not up to ten hours, more like half that or even less). While the higher audience numbers should enable higher rates to be charged for advertising.

It makes it an ideal candidate for prime time TV late in Spring and in early summer for Nine (or Seven or Ten if they get their hands on it).

Source: Adapted from http://www.crikey.com.au/media/2005/01/17-0006.html

The evils of 20–20

As I write this column from London, the English over here are going ga ga over their 'new' invention of 20 overs-a-side games at the county level. Well, it's definitely not a new thing, as I have participated in such games when I played league cricket in England in the 80s. In fact they had a tournament that used to start at 6 o'clock in the evening and went up to 9 o'clock. It used to be called a '20 overs slog.' These games were meant for the sheer enjoyment of those who worked throughout the day. Then, before returning straight back home, or instead, having a drink at a bar, they could delight in a game of cricket that did not last longer than three hours.

When the one-day game was introduced, the English initially scoffed at it. Then, they agreed in private that it was very much a reality and here to stay. They accepted it was the lifeline of cricket that fetched in big money as it attracted huge crowds. They even called it 'pyjama cricket' when Kerry Packer ushered in night cricket under floodlights and the game was played with players wearing coloured clothes.

Today, in England, some of the grounds have floodlight facilities and the players also play in colours. Be that as it may, the growth of one-dayers, over the years, proved detrimental to the development of quality cricketers, though this variety of the game became a huge hit with the masses (though not more than was seen at some of the games in Australia). No doubt, it definitely improved running between the wickets and the standard of fielding rocketed sky-high too. The fitness level of players, it must be said, improved considerably too.

But, unfortunately, both batting and bowling standards dropped drastically. Worse, the players began to find it tough to bat for a full day, not to mention one and half days as was the case till the 80s. Though there are less number of draws these days, the hundreds and thousands who came to watch the duels between bat and ball are sadly missing.

Now, with the so-called instant success of the 20-over games, the officials must realise the harm it will inflict on the game in the long-term, for batsmen who are good sloggers will be preferred over technically correct players and the ordinary ones will hog the limelight. In fact, there won't be any place for the kind of artistes who have been delighting spectators over the years and, like the present situation, the game will take an about turn and the longer version will get prominence all over again.

That's precisely the reason why I hail the BCCI decision to ban one-day cricket tournaments for boys up to the age of 17 years so that they can become better cricketers, both mentally and technically. In fact, I was the one who felt that it would be difficult for the Under-14 boys to play for the entire day in the heat of May in Mumbai and started 35 over-a-side tournaments. However, I quickly realised the mistake I had made and changed the format to 90 overs-a-side competitions.

To my surprise, not many teams lasted 90 overs, for they were mentally tuned to playing much shorter versions of the game. In the process, they formed bad habits and those who had better physical growth at that age scored over the physically weaker but technically better boys. I had a similar experience at Bangalore recently, where the inter-zonal academy tournament for Under-19s, which for the last three years or so was a 50-over one, was changed to a 90-over tournament. I found the teams struggled to last the duration of 90 overs. Period.

Whenever I have travelled in India, people have often asked me why Mumbai, which once produced top class batsmen, now struggles to do so. We, at the Cricket Improvement Committee of Mumbai, debated the issue for almost three hours and came to the conclusion that school cricket and college cricket must be played for longer durations of three and four days respectively, with two innings.

Going through the record of the most prestigious school tournaments in Mumbai which, over the years, produced dozens of Test cricketers, like the Harris and Giles Shields, are now being played on one-day or a two-day basis. Whereas I remember a couple of batsmen in the history of these tournaments who have scored more than 400 individually, Nari Contractor and Ramesh Nagdev, while the likes of Sachin Tendulkar and Ashok Mankad scored many a double and triple centuries.

Well, we at the CIC have suggested changes in the format of school cricket and hope it is implemented. For, there's a lot at stake and this level of the game can do wonders in churning out talented cricketers for the country in the future.

Source: Adapted from www1.cricket.indiatimes.com/articleshow/77170.cms

Questions

1. Why do you think 20/20 cricket has been successful?

2. How would you use segmentation to better understand its success?

3. What are the implications of this repositioning strategy for the development of other elements of the marketing mix?

4. What are the potential drawbacks of this repositioning strategy?

Obstacles to successful segmentation

This final section of the chapter highlights two issues that could inhibit the successful implementation of segmentation in sport organisations.

Lack of customer focus and strategic integration

According to Dibb and Simkin (1997), despite the reported benefits of segmentation, management teams wishing to determine and action segmentation strategies often encounter implementation problems (p. 51). These may arise because the market definition and analysis are flawed and incomplete from the outset or because segments chosen are not substantial enough to warrant special attention. However, from experience working with practising managers, McDonald and Dunbar (1998) argue that problems are more likely to arise if the process is neither sufficiently integrated at a strategic level across the organisation or truly customer focused. These two problems are discussed in more detail below and illustrated in Figure 7.2 with reference to a sports/fitness club.

Sales-based segmentation is an approach commonly found in organisations. In this case, the market is segmented on the basis of how the sales function is organised. This may be by geographical region, for example, or by nature of the business. A fitness club might segment on the basis of corporate or leisure business. Separate sales teams would handle the different areas, each with different sales targets and negotiating powers in relation to elements of the marketing mix.

Level of organisational integration

	High	Low
High	**Strategic segmentation** For example: detailed customer analysis reveals profitable professional singles segment. Information would drive all decision making within the organisation.	**Bolt-on segmentation** For example: customers profiled by combination of bases such as usage patterns and demographics. Promotions targeted at these segments to increase frequency of use.
Low	**Structural segmentation** For example: corporate / business divide applied at company head office as well as club level.	**Sales-based segmentation** For example: corporate/ leisure business strategies implemented at individual club level

(left axis label: **Customer driven**, High / Low)

Figure 7.2 Alternative segmentation strategies for a chain of sports/fitness clubs
Source: McDonald and Dunbar (1998)

In the next cell, *structural segmentation* dominates, and again, there is still little consideration of the specific needs of the different groups of customers. In the case of the leisure club, the corporate/leisure divide would apply across all areas of the business at both head office and individual club level. The division would be embedded in all of the organisation's structures and processes.

In contrast, with *bolt-on segmentation*, there is a clear effort to incorporate a high level of customer focus into the process. In this case, the organisation would gather customer data from both within the organisation and externally to develop detailed customer profiles and identify meaningful segments for targeting purposes. In contrast to the previous approaches, this approach is driven by the information held on the customer database as opposed to the structure of the organisation. However, the purpose of the segmentation process is to assist in selling existing products and targeting promotional campaigns as opposed to strategic issues. The danger here is that the company is often unaware of the implications of decisions taken at an operational level for the business as a whole. In the case of the fitness club, the company would develop an extensive database of customer information that might include data on frequency of use, types of activities and time spent in different areas of the club as well as broader demographic data obtained from membership accounts. A significant segment of consumers may only use the bar and restaurant facilities rather than the exercise programmes offered. These customers would then be targeted with promotional offers for meals, drinks or theme night events to increase their usage of these facilities.

In the fourth cell, *strategic segmentation* combines a customer focus and a high level of organisational integration. Here the organisation uses detailed customer information to define specific segments (or segment) that have profit potential and focuses all decision making in a coordinated manner. The segments are defined at the most senior level within the organisation, and all services and communications from the company are developed with their needs in mind. In the case of a leisure club, the customer information might identify an opportunity for a club targeted exclusively at working professionals without children. All aspects of the business could be coordinated to meet these customers' needs, from the ambience and design of club facilities through the strategies for managing interpersonal contact with the company.

Lack of creativity and insight in the implementation of the segmentation process

Tapp and Clowes (2002) study of segmentation in the football industry concentrated upon developing a better understanding of existing supporters. Although there are clearly benefits to developing insights into the motivations and behaviours of current customers, it may be argued that such an approach should be complemented by efforts to better understand latent demand and segments. Thus, although Tapp and Clowes (2002) identified the growing popularity of football amongst women, the segment typology focused upon male supporters. A more creative approach to the segmentation process might ask, what segments might be targeted? Would segmentation based upon gender differences look different? If so, how? A number of cities have large non-white populations. Football clubs could consider using cultural and religious characteristics as a basis for segmentation. An example is to provide food kiosks at which nonmeat products are sold to encourage purchases from those with a religious aversion to beef or pork. The central point is that Tapp and Clowes (2002) argue for attempting a more sophisticated understanding of existing customers, which might be complemented by the search for new customers. As with all marketing strategy, successful implementation of segmentation should be based on a detailed understanding of existing and potential customers. One could argue that for sporting organisations, given the high degree of customer participation and involvement associated with sporting events, this understanding should be relatively easy to obtain. In recent research exploring the supporters' response to a crisis at a Leicester City football club, researchers monitored internet exchanges between fans on the supporters' website chat room. Although the initial focus was the fans' reaction to a particular event, the nature and depth of supporter knowledge about a whole range of issues emerged during the research. If used carefully, this knowledge could easily be used to shape marketing strategy, including segmentation decisions. The really successful sporting companies of the future will be those who recognise the existence and value of the customer information at their fingertips and use it creatively to develop and maintain long-term customer relationships.

Conclusions

This chapter has outlined the key stages in the segmentation process and illustrated some of the key concepts with examples from sport marketing. The advantages of successful segmentation, targeting and positioning are widely documented and for sport organisations can lead to a closer understanding of customer needs (supporters, participants and wider stakeholders), as well as more tightly defined competitive positions within increasingly blurred markets.

For many sporting organisations, the definition of the market they are operating in, the starting point for successful segmentation, is the most challenging task. Many traditional sports have to face the fact that they are competing with a wide range of 'entertainment' venues for customers' loyalty and spending money. As noted at the beginning of the chapter, the Saturday afternoon football match may be competing with destination shopping venues or theme parks for its 'supporters'. The traditional definition of sporting activity is also being challenged with many younger 'participants' opting to use gym and fitness centres as opposed to taking part in traditional more overtly competitive sports.

This changing consumer profile needs to be monitored carefully and systematically if stage one of the segmentation is to be successfully implemented. Theoretically, the internet should facilitate this customer understanding with supporters actively engaging in conversations with both fellow supporters and club officials via web chatrooms. This information should also enable sport organisations to implement stage two of the process, targeting. Here the focus is on ensuring that the segment(s) selected are sufficiently large and attractive to warrant the allocation of the company's resources. Faced with increased competition and rapidly changing customer profiles, sport organisations need to focus on careful consideration of the third stage of the process, positioning.

Many organisations use sports personalities effectively to reinforce their competitive position within their particular markets. However, there does not appear to be the same level of sophistication or thought behind strategies developed by sports bodies to reinforce their position in the market. What are the core values and benefits shared by supporters of 20/20 cricket? What other products and services symbolise these values, and how might they be used to reinforce the position of the game relative to the competition? As with all positioning strategies, success depends on the extent to which the receiver identifies with the core benefits identified in the positioning statement. Again, this needs to be clarified through research. The chapter concludes with a discussion of the importance of maintaining customer focus and strategic integration throughout all stages of the segmentation process. This ensures buy-in from other functional areas and forces the organisation to constantly evaluate its actions from the receiver's perspective.

Discussion questions

1. Which segmentation methods are most commonly used by sport organisations?
2. What are the barriers to using segmentation effectively within the sport industry?
3. How would you evaluate the value of a segment?
4. Consider how you might develop the positioning of a range of sports, including, for example, golf, tennis, soccer and basketball.

Guided reading

For a detailed appreciation of current market segmentation issues and research priorities in marketing, see Wedel and Kamakura (2000). For detailed consideration of practical implementation issues, see McDonald and Dunbar (1998).

Keywords

Behavioural segmentation; business markets; demographic segmentation; geographic segmentation; psychographic segmentation.

Bibliography

Birley, K. (1999) *A Social History of English Cricket*, London: Aurum Press.

Dibb, S. and Simkin, L. (1997) A program for implementing market segmentation, *Journal of Business and Industrial Marketing* 12(1):51–65.

Hunt, K.H., Bristol, T. and Bashaw, R.E. (1999) A conceptual approach to classifying sports fans, *Journal of Services Marketing* 13(6):439–52.

Kotler, P. (1980) *Marketing Management: Analysis, Planning, Implementation, and Control*, New York: Prentice Hall.

Luger, D. (2005) Brits abroad, *Observer Sports Magazine* October:31.

McDonald, M. and Dunbar, I. (1998) *Market Segmentation: How To Do It, How To Profit From It*, 2nd edn, Basingstoke: Palgrave/MacMillan.

Mullin, B., Hardy, S. and Sutton, W. (2000) *Sport Marketing*, 2nd edn, Leeds: Human Kinetics.

Shank, M.D. (2002) *Sports Marketing: A Strategic Perspective*, Englewood Cliffs, NJ: Prentice Hall.

Sullivan, M. (2004) 'Sport marketing', in J. Beech and S. Chadwick (eds), *The Business of Sport Management*, London: Prentice Hall.

Tapp, A. and Clowes, J. (2002) From carefree casuals to professional wanderers, *European Journal of Marketing* 36(11/12):1248–69.

Tonks, D. (1998) 'Exploring the principles of market segmentation', in C. Egan and M.C. Thomas (eds), *The CIM Handbook of Strategic Marketing*, London: Butterworth Heinemann.

Wedel, M. and Kamakura, W. (2000) *Market Segmentation: Conceptual and Methodological Foundations*, Boston: Kluwer.

Wind, Y. and Cardoza, R. (1974) Industrial market segmentation, *Industrial Marketing Management* 3:153–66.

Recommended websites

CACI Information Solutions
http://caci.co.uk

Marketing Teacher
http://marketingteacher.com

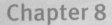

Chapter 8

Sport market research and marketing information systems

Linda Trenberth
University of London
Ron Garland
University of Waikato

Learning outcomes

Upon completion of this chapter, the reader should be able to:

■ Describe the purpose of sport market research.

■ Indicate the techniques that are available for collecting market research.

■ Consider the advantages and disadvantages of each of these techniques.

■ Identify the management information needs of sport marketers.

■ Establish how sport organisations can establish and manage information systems to meet these needs.

Overview of chapter

As noted in Chapter 5 on sport consumer buying behaviour, sport marketing primarily concerns the satisfaction of sport consumer needs with sport products and services that are perceived to provide benefits that cannot be met by other sports or other forms of entertainment that compete for consumers' discretionary incomes. In order to understand customers' needs and how best to achieve customer satisfaction, detailed market research of both the customer and the wider environment is required. This chapter focuses on the tools and techniques available to market researchers with which to gather such vital information. It defines market research and describes the marketing information system (MIS) that is used to store the information collected and the variety of sources available for the development of any MIS. The chapter then describes the steps in the sport marketing research process before exploring the range of approaches to market research, including the importance of determining the most appropriate research design or plan that directs data collection and analysis. The chapter shows that market research and its ensuing MIS are critical to the understanding of the various market segments for sport products and services.

Introduction

Making the right decisions is vital to sport managers and marketers whether they are planning a sponsorship programme or looking for ways of increasing the exposure of a sports club. Market research provides the sort of detailed information on sport markets that is required for such decisions and is an essential element in marketing-oriented organisations. The primary purpose of most market research is to collect, collate and prepare information to help devise marketing plans, establish price points, segment markets, define brands and products and promote teams as well as many other related aspects. Properly conducted sportmarketing research can improve communication flows between organisations and customers and provide the information necessary for the development of promotional strategies and sponsorship proposals. For example, market research recently highlighted the impact and effectiveness of sponsorship by B&Q, a UK home improvement and garden centre retailer. Ellen MacArthur, a yachtswoman, broke the world record for sailing singlehandedly around the world in 2005. She was sponsored by B&Q, and the research showed that in the week following the record, the number of people able to name her sponsor without prompting more than doubled to 58% of the general public. When prompted, this increased to 70% (Geach, 2005).

Sport marketing research that targets consumers' influences and financial implications is an important marketing activity. It is a fundamental tool for understanding and satisfying customers' needs. As noted in Chapter 5 on consumer buying behaviour, each consumer, be they athletes, club owners, managers, sponsors, media or the public, has different needs and expectations, and sport managers and marketers rely on market research to identify these in order to deliver the right product with the right endorsements in the most appropriate way. Market research may provide vital information on both broad and specific questions such as:

- Who are the customers?
- What sports do consumers participate in?
- What new sport products, sport services or sport opportunities would appeal to consumers?
- What demographic, geodemographic and social characteristics are associated with what consumers? Who is playing? Who is watching?
- To what extent do consumers become involved in their chosen sport?
- How and why do consumers choose that sport?
- How much are consumers willing to pay for specific sport events? For a day out with the family to a specific sporting event?
- How do consumers become involved?
- What sports events are watched on television by people of which ethnicity?
- How effective is sponsorship?
- How might sport be promoted? Which promotional methods work best?

These are just a few of the questions that can be answered through market research. Gopal (2005) noted that many organisations find market research expensive, and in their view, unnecessary. However, valid and reliable market research is essential to successful sport marketing strategy and product and service development and even the organisation's business model, as the following case shows.

CASE 8.1   Approaches to and the value of market research

A market survey was conducted for a service that had been developed and which was to be taken to the market. The service was to be delivered to the student market and the market research was directed toward that audience. The research was conducted using both quantitative (online survey) and qualitative methods (focus groups). The research determined that the service in its present form was a better value proposition for medium to large businesses rather than for the college students although useful information was gained on pricing and branding the service. The indications that the service was much better suited to purchase by corporations and the subsequent modifications that needed to be made before the service could be delivered to that market changed the business model that had been envisioned. The modified service was subsequently subjected to a second market research study targeted to potential buyers and users from the corporate sector, which yielded segmentation as well as potential demand and price sensitivity information. The online survey provided usable segmentation and usage information, however it was the directed discussions that took place in physical focus groups that gave the additional information on which the client was able to make the judgment that the service might be better suited to a different market and thus change the nature of the business model.

Source: Adapted from Gopal (2005)

Questions

1. How does the case show the value of organisations conducting market research?

2. What are the pros and cons of using different research methodologies to collect information needed for making marketing decisions?

3. What does the use of both approaches described above serve in market research?

4. Which approach to the collection of information is the most cost efficient, and why?

The above case illustrates that 'marketing research is the systematic process of collecting, analyzing and reporting information to enhance decision-making throughout the marketing process' (Shank, 2005, p. 95). It also shows that in general, there are two primary data collection approaches to market research: quantitative, which produces relatively simple data from a large and varied sample, and qualitative, which produces in-depth information from a much narrower and relatively small sample. These are discussed in more detail below. Most importantly, the Case 8.1 shows that successful marketing decisions are based on good information.

Marketing information systems

One of the reasons for conducting market research is to develop an MIS. For marketers to develop the extensive MIS marketers need to collect general market data, data on individual consumers and data on their competitors and their participants (Shilbury, Quick and

Westerbeek, 2003). By generating demographic, geographic and attitudinal information about customers, sport marketers can begin to enhance the experiences of anyone who attends, hears, sees, participates in or sponsors sport. Using the football club as an example, a competitive response to the threat of a rival leisure alternative might be to differentiate the sport product. After market research is conducted, this could lead to, for example, the installation of better stadium seating, the sale of a wider range of refreshments being sold or the establishment of better media coverage (Chadwick and Thwaites, 2003, p. 214).

General market data include all information that relates to the broad environment in which the sport operates. As Chadwick and Thwaites (2003) noted, sport does not operate in a vacuum, and sport organisations have to consider how potential and actual customers, direct and indirect competition and the wider environment influence their marketing activities. The organisation needs to establish size, demographics, the consumer habits of residents and workers, the ways that individuals use their leisure time and any specific trends that will impact on the sport. After the individual consumer data have been entered into the relevant database, the sport marketer has a large amount of information available from which to develop marketing strategies.

A third source of information for sport organisations relates to competitors and their participants. It is critical that sport organisations are aware of who their competitors are and who the consumers are of a rival's products or services. The major sources of data for any MIS are external data, primary or secondary data, and internal data (i.e., all the information an organisation collects during the day-to-day operation of the business). Wind (2005) notes that marketing, which is at the interface between the organisation and the environment, identifies opportunities that exist to meet the needs still to be met of current customers or new customers for the organisation's current and new products and services (p. 866).

If a sport business is to be successful in meeting the needs of the market within which it operates, then it must always consider how potential and actual customers, direct and indirect competition and the wider environment influence their marketing activities (Chadwick and Thwaites, 2003). There are a range of environmental scanning techniques sport marketers can use that are well documented. One such technique is called STEP, which refers to the sociocultural, technological, economic, and political and legal elements of the environment. Other techniques include PEST, SLEPT or PESTLE analysis and Porter's Five Forces model (1980). Collecting data is merely the starting point for developing an effective MIS. As Shilbury et al. (2003) point out, the information must be then integrated, analysed and stored appropriately for later retrieval for use in decision-making processes. An MIS must be constantly updated and monitored for effectiveness in a constantly changing sport environment. Any MIS is only as good as the data put into it, and the primary data that are collected by way of direct answers to direct questions driven by the organisation itself is often the best source of data. The next section deals with the collection of primary data through the market research process.

The sport marketing research process

As with research in any area, the sport marketing research process includes a series of interrelated steps that are generally followed:

a) Defining the problem or research question
b) Choosing the research design

c) Identifying the data collection methods
d) Designing data collection instruments
e) Designing the sample
f) Collecting, analysing and interpreting data
g) Preparing the research report (Shank, 2005, p. 99)

For small and resource-challenged sport organisations, market research can be expensive, time consuming and expertise intensive. For these organisations, the solution is to find a cost-efficient approach while avoiding the pitfalls of poor research (Smith and Stewart, 2001). Several sport marketing texts already deal in some depth with the research process in terms of sampling, research design, data collection methods and analysis and one of the reasons for conducting market research in the first place, the segmentation of the sport market, which is dealt with elsewhere in this book (e.g., see Chapter 6 and Shank, 2005 and Shilbury et al., 2003). However, based on the series of sequential and interrelated steps already noted, it could be argued that the most important step is the first, problem recognition, for the primary reason that this step shapes what follows. The old saying 'a problem defined is a problem half solved' holds true; too often we try to address symptoms rather than causes in our research.

As soon as the research problem is properly defined, it can be broken down into several research objectives, which form the subsets of information needed to address the (larger) research problem. In turn, these research objectives determine the way, through the choice of research design, one might collect and analyse the desired information. Be aware that secondary information – information that is already available but collected for some other purpose – should inform each of the steps of the sport marketing research process. Next the research instruments data collection methods and analytical procedures can be designed and implemented. Results are interpreted by addressing them to their relevant research objectives. The sport marketer writes reports, and the research process (for the project at hand) has been completed. The rest of this chapter will explore the advantages and disadvantages of a range of approaches to market research and their implications for sport managers and marketers.

Approaches to market research

It is important to consider the range of techniques available to marketers for conducting market research. Valid and reliable research is essential to successful sport marketing. As Garland, Inkson and McDermott (1999) noted, as soon as products, brands and objectives have been clearly defined, managers can use market research to identify the potential consumers, market segments, strengths and weaknesses of the product and develop a marketing strategy. In market research, data collection techniques are either quantitative, which generates superficial data from a diverse and sizeable sample, or qualitative, which produces in-depth information from a narrow and relatively small sample (Smith and Stewart, 2001). This section looks at the relative merits of both these approaches and a mixed-method approach. Firstly though, it explores research philosophy, which underpins the choice of methodology.

■ Research philosophy

According to Saunders, Lewis and Thornhill (2002), there are two dominant views about the research process that influence choice of research methodology. They are positivism and phenomenology. A research philosophy that reflects the principles of positivism works with observable social 'reality', and the researcher will claim to have discovered law-like properties similar to those produced by natural and social scientists. There is an emphasis on a highly structured methodology to facilitate replication and quantifiable observations that lend themselves to statistical analysis, a quantitative approach. There is an assumption that the researcher is independent of the research process. This philosophy underpins much of marketing research to date. Phenomenology on the other hand represents a philosophy of research that argues that generalisability of results is not crucial in business situations that are complex and unique (Saunders et al., 2002). Phenomenologists are more likely to adopt a research methodology that seeks the details of the situation, to understand the reality rather than the numbers, a qualitative approach. A researcher's philosophy of research likely guides his or her choice of research methodology, depending on the nature of the information the researcher wishes to collect and the available resources.

Not withstanding one's philosophy of research the market researcher must choose a research design that is appropriate to the subject under investigation. For example, as Dewhurst (2002) points out, using a qualitative approach provides descriptive information from small physical focus groups. They might, for example, make the observation that more people would buy the product if it was advertised on television. However, the substance of this information might not be very convincing for the marketing director, who needs more detailed information. Using a quantitative research design requires asking more precisely how many items people might buy at a particular price, measuring quantities, for example, and having the observations described in more detail. Of course, a mixed-methodology approach can be used to good effect, and more is discussed about this approach below. In essence, as Shank (2005) notes, research design types emanating from a particular philosophy of research are generally exploratory, descriptive or causal in nature depending upon the clarity of the problem.

■ Quantitative approaches to data collection

Quantitative data refers to all data that could be usefully quantified to answer a research question and can be a product of all research strategies (Saunders et al., 2002). Quantitative approaches to data collection include surveys (the most popular method of data collection), experiments in which the researcher manipulates one variable while holding all others constant (e.g., with time or date of events) and structured interviews (Shilbury et al., 2003). Quantitative studies abound in the marketing literature. Jones (1997) showed the strengths of a quantitative research design through the large survey conducted by the Sir Norman Chester Centre for Football Research (SNCCFR) into the sports fan, which produced broad data across a large fan population at Premier League clubs, allowing the behavioural patterns of the English football fan to be understood. The quantitative design allowed for a simple comparison to be made between clubs, which enabled data to be collected in consecutive seasons and allowed for a longitudinal analysis (over time). Although this approach provides data on the composition of the crowd, their behaviour and their scaleable attitudes towards predetermined question-naire items, the methodology does not allow for information beyond the descriptive level, such as what was it about the experience of attending the game that the spectators enjoyed or not, what they thought of the services provided, why they attended this event and not some other, what they thought of the way their club was managed and so on.

Similarly, each year, the Football Governance Research Centre at Birkbeck College in London conducts a large-scale survey using a quantitative methodology to update the state of corporate governance in football clubs. The report written from the results of this approach can state categorically, for example, that 25% of clubs in the Football Association Premier League and Football Conference have supporter representation on the board (Holt, Michie and Oughton, 2004). However, that fact, although interesting in itself, does not tell us anything about the influence of that board member on the board or anything about the experience of being on the board for that representative.

The strengths of applying a quantitative approach to market research include being able to measure behaviour that is evident, describing events such as the composition of the sport crowd, allowing for comparison and replication, and enhancing reliability and validity (Jones, 1997). Quantitative research designs allow large-scale data collection and analysis at relatively low cost and enhance statistical proof.

The weaknesses of quantitative research designs, however, include failing to illumin-ate deeper underlying meanings, as illustrated above. For example, other factors such as motivation and cognition are as important to the concept of the sport consumer as is measuring quantifiable variables. Quantitative research generally allows for only cross-sectional research or a snapshot at one point in time although surveys can be repeated to show if there have been any changes on the same variables over time. Sports fan attendances may be affected by changes over time such as the team's per-formance which can not be captured in a single quantitative study. As Smith and Stewart (2001) noted, quantitative methodologies that use questionnaires and scaled responses rarely generate the 'hidden', 'deep' or 'elusive' information often necessary to solve the research problem. It takes a qualitative approach to do that.

Qualitative approaches to data collection

Qualitative research designs are associated with interpretive approaches, which seek to explain the behaviours of people in terms of the meaning it holds for them, rather than measuring discrete, observable behaviour (Smith and Stewart, 2001). Saunders et al. (2002) noted that to be able to capture the richness and fullness associated with qualitative data, these data cannot be collected in a standardised way like that of quantitative data. For example, it is generally accepted, rightly or wrongly, based on quantifiable data, that with the exception of perhaps tennis and athletics, most people believe that men's sport provides better quality viewing. Yet what is needed is a thorough qualitative analysis of why this might be so and what needs to change for spectators and sponsors to show more interest in supporting women's sport.

Qualitative market research attempts to capture reality as it is, as seen and experi-enced by the consumers (Smith and Stewart, 2001). Some methods of collecting quali-tative data include focus groups, mail or shopping intercepts (where both quantitative and qualitative data can be collected), observation and in-depth unstructured inter-views. A qualitative research design allows an exploration of how sport consumers view their own situations in greater depth than quantitative designs allow. It allows the respondents to introduce concepts of importance from their own perspective rather than one predetermined by the researcher. It also allows for the identification of longitudinal changes in behaviour rather than the snapshot of quantitative designs. However, as Smith and Stewart (2001) pointed out, qualitative market research has traditionally been unpopular for exploring sport markets. They ascribed this to confusion about the appropriate application of qualitative techniques and uncertainty about the quality of the data they produce.

As with quantitative approaches, however, there are inevitable criticisms and weaknesses of the qualitative approach. Sampling in qualitative research is an issue. As noted by Smith and Stewart (2001), every market research technique requires a structured and duplicable method of selecting who in the market will be questioned. Qualitative research typically uses a small sample representing the key constituents in the market under investigation. This is called *purposive sampling* (Sekaran, 2003) in which it is necessary to obtain information from specific target groups. This can consist of 'judgment' sampling, which involves the choice of subjects who are in the best position to provide the information needed, or quota sampling, which ensures that certain groups are adequately represented in the study through the assignment of a quota.

The main criticism of the qualitative approach is that of validity. Qualitative approaches to collecting data rely on relatively small numbers of subjects, so it is difficult to verify the 'truthfulness' of findings, according to Jones (1997). Validity is the degree to which a method or procedure actually measures that which it sets out to measure. In qualitative research, validity is measured in two ways. The first is face validity. According to Saunders et al. (2002), face validity indicates that on the face of it, the items that are intended to measure a concept look like they do that. Smith and Stewart (2001) indicated that face validity, which is an outcome of the believability of the comments from the participants, is high in qualitative market research. The second type of validity important in qualitative research, according to Smith and Stewart (2001), is convergent validity, which measures the degree to which results are confirmed by future behaviours, experiences and events.

Another issue is that findings may not be generalised to the rest of the population because of the relatively small samples typical of this kind of research. However, Smith and Stewart (2001) point to the fact that limited generalisability may be considered a legitimate price to pay for the depth of insight and quality afforded by qualitative research that cannot be achieved by statistical procedures. The outcome for the researcher is a comprehensive understanding of how the respondent perceives the issue, which in turn allows the researcher to generalise these understandings to other respondents who share similar characteristics.

A mixed-methodology approach to market research

Because a singular approach to market research has inherent weaknesses, Jones (1997) notes that by adopting certain assumptions, combining both methodologies should maximise the strengths of both approaches. For example, qualitative methods such as observation or unstructured interviews could guide the initial phases of market research through developing an overall picture and detail of the subject or area under investigation necessary to frame subsequent quantitative queries. One such study that used a mixed-method approach is that of Recours, Souville and Griffet (2004) in their study into sport participants' motives. First, 12 semi-directed interviews were conducted to gather historical data from sport practitioners about their motivations and emotional rewards regarding their sporting activities. More specifically, the interviews were aimed at exploring the nature of the sensations and emotions elicited by their activities and the localisation of these sensations in terms of place (mental, physical) and time (during activity or afterwards). Phrases from the respondents were analysed for content and developed into a sports motivation scale, which was then tested on a larger sample, revised and then administered to more than 900 people in questionnaire format. This method allowed for inductively generated categories from the qualitative/interpretive interviews of a small sample to be developed into a questionnaire and tested in a quantitative study using a larger sample (Secours et al., 2004). In a similar vein, the case study featured (later) began with brainstorming sessions and preliminary secondary research to identify possible New Zealand celebrity athletes for product endorsement work, proceeded to two focus groups to help refine the list of athletes and then continued into the quantitative phase with a sample survey of the New Zealand general public.

Quantitative analysis may be more appropriate for assessing behavioural or descriptive characteristics, as with components of sports fandom, for example (Jones, 1997). The descriptive analysis, such as the sociodemographic profile of the crowd, may allow a representative sample to be drawn for qualitative analysis. Thus, the mixed methodology ensures that the sample has some representativeness of the population for a sample group for qualitative research. Quantitative analysis may complement findings of qualitative methods by indicating their extent within the population in question.

Data analysis in the quantitative tradition is likely to involve analysis of some form of primary (usually survey) data. Perusal of the initial results involve the researcher 'getting a grasp' of the major themes in the data, usually by studying frequencies and percentages, before proceeding to more complex bivariate and multivariate statistical methods. Irrespective of the type of data collected, statistical analysis should be driven by the requirements of the project.

Statistical power analysis

Related to the use of quantitative methods is statistical power analysis. Parks, Shewokis and Costa (1999) argue, for example, for greater statistical power analysis in sport marketing and management research. This involves designing and interpreting research with attention to the statistical power (i.e., probability) of the study to detect an effect of a specific size. Statistical power analysis is based on the interdependence of sample size, alpha, effect size and power. Parks et al. (1999) show that attending to statistical power is important for a number of reasons. They reviewed 200 sport research articles and found that 93 of the studies reviewed had used statistical significance tests to determine their findings and of those 88 (95%) had reported statistically significant findings but only three mentioned statistical power. Only 24 of the 88 articles had reported effect sizes. Before collecting any data, researchers should know what effect sizes will be meaningful. Effect size refers to (1) the magnitude of a difference between groups expressed in units of standard deviation, (2) the strength of an association and (3) the proportion of variance in the dependent variable that is explained by the dependent variable (Parks et al., 1999).

According to Parks et al. (1999), interpreting effect size is critical because it is possible for a finding to be statistically significant but not meaningful. For example, Parks et al. (1999) noted that if a researcher conducts a study in which sports fans' average annual income accounts for 3% of the variance in their willingness to purchase particular merchandise, only those who know the field can say whether 3% is meaningful or not. Parks et al. (1999) showed in a comparison of two similar studies but with different effect sizes and different sample sizes that, had effect size not been taken into account, the two studies would have been interpreted in much the same way; however, the results taking into account effect size told a different story such that one set of statistically significant results was actually not meaningful. The message here is that sport market researchers must understand the concept of statistical power in order to make their findings much more meaningful, especially when there are often large amounts of money riding on their results. There are simple things to do in order to ensure meaningful results and that should be considered and that may mean increasing sample size, raising the alpha power, increasing the effect size, reducing the variability of the dependent measure, increasing the reliability or validity of the dependent measure, or a combination of these things (Parks et al., 1999).

Additional sources of data for sport market researchers

It is important for sport marketers to keep abreast of new methodologies and data sources. Wyner (2004) states that quite simply, a lot more data are available to help understand customers and markets. The traditional categories of quantitative and qualitative research may need to be updated to reflect the more complicated new realities of today's marketing environment (Wyner, 2004). For example, on the quantitative side, the use of the internet for survey research has grown and generally costs less and takes less time to do than surveys conducted in person or by phone. Online surveys continue to be used to target larger and larger sectors of the market research business. As Sutton, Irwin and McGladden (1998) point out, computerisation offers researchers the opportunity to create interactive, self-directed survey methodologies that permit more than one person to be surveyed simultaneously. Computer models can also be generated to produce sport market forecasts as, for example, that produced by Gratton, Kokolakakis, Ping Kung and O'Keefe (2001).

According to Sutton et al. (1998), community intercepts are an effective form of sport marketing research, especially for ad hoc market research for corporate clients in which central location and mall intercept research are still very important. Community intercepts may include interviewing at shopping malls, theatres, sports bars, event venues and any other area offering a representative cross-section of the community. Community intercepts can be done as surveys or conducted as interviews and are generally used to identify any barriers that are perceived to exist that the marketers can target. Sutton et al. (1998) show that community intercepts can also be used to trace media patterns and to gain information as to the effectiveness of new promotions.

Other changes are occurring that are more qualitative in nature. For example, Wyner (2004) points out new approaches to observing consumers in a broader set of experience contexts include the use of smaller, less costly and more flexible video cameras. Sutton et al. (1998) note the use of video interviews in concert with surveys. The video observations capture not only responses to the question but also respondents' facial expressions, animation and emotions. Behavioural observation in the consumer's natural environment, as at game on match day, can also provide an important balance to self-reported information, in some cases correcting what people say they do. As already noted, however, these more qualitative techniques are based on small and unrepresentative samples, limiting generalisability to the larger population.

Sutton et al. (1998) also point to the use of activity diaries for tracking consumer behaviour, for example. Sport market researchers might like to capture consumers' feelings after events, including their patterns of expenditure, because much of this information is lost in recall or inaccurate. By keeping an activity diary, consumers can record experiential assessments, expenditures and post-event behaviours, thus providing more accurate and reliable results. However, as with any method of data collection, this one has inherent weaknesses. The activity diary is time consuming and requires a significant commitment on behalf of the respondent to log behaviours, and response rates can be quite low. Perhaps this helps explain why the 'recruit at the game; interview later' two-step approach to sport market research advocated by Pol and Pak (1993) is still popular. Most market researchers acknowledge the difficulties of interviewing fans at the game. Therefore, what can be done is to approach fans in the stadium (e.g., by a random or quota sampling procedure using seat numbers as a sampling frame) and invite their participation in a subsequent (a few days later) telephone or internet interview. On acceptance, contact details are recorded and the interview scheduled.

Wyner (2004) has noted a greater use of transactional information in market research. Detailed records can reveal what each customer bought and used at what time, providing a higher degree of external validity. Internal and external customer behaviour data can be trended and modelled against marketing initiatives, as with the market forecasts of Gratton et al. (2001). Behavioural database analysis may be substituted for survey research when the data are readily acceptable and can be tracked internally on a continuous basis.

Whatever the data source the sport marketer decides to tap into, it only yields a partial view of the whole marketing process. Marketers must choose the most appropriate methods for different types of decisions. The sorts of questions Wyner (2004) states need to be asked include which types – qualitative, survey or database research – are needed to assess positioning and which types should be applied in the new product development process at which stage, for example. And then the sport marketer needs to determine how the various pieces of research are synthesised to come to overall conclusions and recommendations (p. 7).

CASE 8.2   Choosing sports heroes to endorse products and services

The benefits of using celebrities and athletes to endorse products and services have been well researched: famous sports stars 'cut through' the promotional clutter and transfer appealing qualities to the products they endorse. But how do advertising agencies choose their celebrity athletes for product endorsement? In New Zealand much depends upon whether the agency's policy accommodates celebrity endorsement, whether sports people are available for a particular commission (depending on previous endorsements, the celebrity's own endorsement plans), what their reputation and image is like and whether the budget is sufficient. However, once the decision is made to choose a celebrity, what happens in terms of researching specific celebrity-product matches? Quite often, some ad hoc questioning around the advertising agency and among 'friends and acquaintances' suffices. At this point selection of endorsers seems to be more an art than a science. While that might suit most purposes it is possible to bring a little science to bear on celebrity athlete selection.

Two focus groups were carried out in late 2003 to discuss, among other topics, celebrity athletes and then to identify (from a 'long list') a short list of four New Zealand celebrity athletes. Those chosen were Bernice Mene (retired netball captain and health sector spokesperson), Justin Marshall (incumbent rugby All Black half-back; former All Black captain), Sarah Ulmer (at the time world champion cyclist – now Olympic champion too) and Stephen Fleming (long serving captain of New Zealand Cricket's Black Caps). In 2004, these prominent New Zealand sporting heroes were put 'under the microscope' with respect to their potential to endorse various products and services via a sample survey (using the electoral rolls) of the New Zealand adult population. Just under half (46% or n = 392) of our sample responded, giving us a maximum margin for error of approximately 5% at 95% confidence. The sample was slightly biased to females (57:43) but was representative of the adult age breakdown in New Zealand. The research was completed before Sarah Ulmer's successful 2004 Olympic Games but during the Southern Hemisphere's Super 12 Rugby competition and New Zealand Cricket's Black Caps' tour of England. Each of the chosen athletes had been featured in promotional campaigns prior to or during the survey – Mene in her health promotion roles; Ulmer in the McDonald's salads campaign; Marshall in general advertising for New Zealand Rugby and Fleming for leading brands Rexona and Fujitsu.

What was found? Table 8.1 shows high levels of familiarity with each athlete. Perhaps the slight female bias in our sample has favoured Bernice Mene. Not surprisingly, fanship, 'involvement' and merchandise purchasing are all predictable – each follows the trend of the celebrity's chosen sport's popularity with New Zealanders (rugby most popular; cycling least popular).

Next, respondents were asked to rate each sports star against a range of possible product endorsement opportunities using the constant-sum scale (which asked respondents to allocate 100 points across the four sports stars for each product). Table 8.2 tells the story.

If you were seeking a celebrity athlete to endorse a brand of isotonic sports drink or bottled water then Sarah Ulmer is probably the best bet whereas deodorant brands

Table 8.1 **Athlete familiarity**

Athlete	Familiar? (%)	Fan of the sport (%)	Involved as player or administrator in that sport (%)	Bought merchandise for that sport in the past 12 months (%)
Mene	89	23	7	7
Marshall	81	44	6	22
Ulmer	82	7	4	4
Fleming	81	31	8	8

Table 8.2 **Endorsement opportunities**

Athlete	Isotonic sports drink (%)	Bottled water (%)	Deodorant (%)	Honey (%)	Bank account (%)
Mene	26	26	28	31	28
Marshall	25	24	22	19	22
Ulmer	29	30	26	30	22
Fleming	21	21	25	20	29

might seek out Bernice Mene. Each of these statements is supported statistically at a 90% level of confidence. Honey is often used by researchers as a commodity type product to act as a control in their product-celebrity match-up research. Both female celebrity athletes have been chosen and by such a margin over the male celebrity athletes that any bias due to the female:male ratio is not an issue. The banking product introduces an interesting twist to the results (and might form fruitful further research) with both captains, Mene or Fleming being chosen. Perhaps sporting leaders are more authoritative? Taking all the results together, one couldn't go far wrong in contracting any of the athletes in an endorsement role but the two female athletes, Mene and Ulmer are particularly appealing. Mene's performance in this survey is especially noteworthy as she has been retired from international netball for several years yet the careful management of her celebrity status in only health promotion roles seems to be reflected in her source credibility. Yet turning to Sarah Ulmer, one can only imagine the impact of Olympic gold on Ulmer's scores if the survey was repeated. Food for thought for players, agents and advertising agencies.

Source: Adapted from a case provided by Ron Garland (University of Waikato), Jan Charbonneau (Massey University) and Lesley Ferkins (UNITEC); reproduced with permission

Questions

1. Why is marketing research important when considering using athletes as endorsers of sport products?

2. What are some of the considerations when using athlete celebrities to communicate messages about sport products?

3. What are the risks involved in using celebrity endorsers, and how can market research minimise such risks?

Conclusions

Marketing research is defined as the systematic process of collecting, analysing and reporting information to enhance decision-making processes. It is important to emphasise that research should be always meticulously organised and as objective as possible so that it is reliable and can be replicated. Following carefully the steps in the sport marketing process noted in this chapter allows researchers to be systematic and unbiased.

In general, there are two different – although not mutually exclusive – philosophical stances on research, positivism and phenomenology. These stances in turn inform the two research approaches of deduction, characterised by the collection of quantitative data and induction, which is more likely to be based on the collection of qualitative data. One of the reasons for conducting market research is to develop an MIS, which essentially is a system of procedures that generates, analyses, disseminates, stores and retrieves information for use in decision-making processes. Another reason for conducting market research is to understand the various market segments for sport products and services.

A number of approaches to data collection were discussed that are contingent on whether the research design chosen is exploratory, descriptive or causal. However, although the method by which the data are collected is important and must be appropriate to the type of research design chosen, it is the making sense of that data that is even more important. Anyone can put data into a computer package and get a print-out of the results, but skilled sport market researchers have the ability to make sense of the data sufficiently enough as to be able to make appropriate recommendations as to how that information can be used or not.

The information gathered through market research is useful at every stage of the sport marketing process, including at the planning stage, during the implementation of marketing plans and during the evaluation stage, in which the effectiveness of marketing and sponsorship objectives might be evaluated. This chapter has given an overview of the sport marketing process and of the tools and techniques that can be used to gather meaningful information from which sport marketers can make intelligent decisions.

Discussion questions

1. Define sport marketing research.
2. What are the steps in the market research process?
3. Describe some of the data collection methods used in sport market research?
4. What factors influence the choice of data collection method?

Guided reading

For further details on the content covered in this chapter, read the following:

Pitts, B.G. (ed.) (2003) *Case Studies in Sport Marketing*, Morgantown, WV: Fitness Information Technology.

Stotlar, D. (2004) *Developing Successful Sport Marketing Plans*, Morgantown, WV: Fitness Information Technology.

Pitts, B.G. and Stotlar, D.K. (2002) *Fundamentals of Sport Marketing*, Morgantown, WV: Fitness Information Technology.

Keywords

Brainstorming; causal research; descriptive research; exploratory research; face validity; marketing information system; phenomenology; positivism; primary data; qualitative data; quantitative data; secondary data; sponsorship objectives.

Bibliography

Chadwick, S. and Thwaites, D. (2003) 'Sport marketing management', in L. Trenberth (ed.), *Managing the Business of Sport* Sydney, Australia: Thomson Learning.

Dewhurst, F. (2002) *Quantitative Methods for Business and Management,* Sheffield: McGraw-Hill.

Garland, R., Inkson, K. and McDermott, P. (1999) 'Sport marketing', in L. Trenberth (ed.) *Sport Business Management in New Zealand*, Australia: Thomson Learning.

Geach, N. (2005) Bulls eye for B & Q!, *Sport Marketing Surveys* February:21.

Gopal, G. (2005) MR can be impetus for business model change, *Marketing News* February:60.

Gratton, C., Kokolakakis, T., Ping Kung, S. and O'Keeffe, L. (2001) *Sport Market Forecasts 2001–2005*, Sheffield: SIRC.

Holt, M., Michie, J. and Oughton, C. (2004) 'Corporate governance and the football industry', in L. Trenberth (ed.), *Sport Business Management in New Zealand*, Sydney, Australia: Thomson Learning.

Jones, I. (1997) Mixing qualitative and quantitative methods in sports fan research, *The Qualitative Report* 3(4), retrieved 24 May 2006, from http://www.nova.edu/ssss/QR/QR3-4/jones.html.

Parks, J.B., Shewokis, P. and Costa, C. (1999) Using statistical power analysis in sport management research, *Journal of Sport Management* 13:139–47.

Pol, L.G. and Pak, S. (1993) The use of a two stage survey design in collecting data from those who have attended periodic or special events, *Journal of Marketing Research* 36(4):315–25.

Porter, M. (1980) *Competitive Strategy: Techniques for Analyzing Industries and Competitors*, New York: The Free Press.

Recours, R.A., Souville, M. and Griffet, J. (2004) Expressed motives for informal and club/association-based sports participation, *Journal of Leisure Research* 36(1):1–22.

Saunders, M., Lewis, P. and Thornhill, A. (2002) *Research Methods for Business Students*, London: FT Prentice Hall.

Sekaran, U. (2003) *Research Methods for Business: A Skill Building Approach,* New York: John Wiley & Sons.

Shank, M.D. (2005) *Sport marketing: A strategic perspective*, 3rd edn, Englewood Cliffs, NJ: Prentice Hall.

Shilbury, D., Quick, S. and Westerbeek, H. (2003) *Strategic Sport Marketing*, Sydney: Allen & Unwin.

Smith, A. and Stewart, B. (2001) Beyond number crunching: Applying qualitative techniques in sport marketing research, *The Qualitative Report* 6(2), retrieved 24 May 2006, from http://www.nova.edu/ssss/QR/QR6-2/smith.html.

Sutton, W.A., Irwin, R.I. and McGladden, J.M. (1998) Tools of the trade: Practical research methods for events, teams and venues, *Sport Marketing Quarterly* 7(2):45–9.

Wind, Y. (2005) Marketing as an engine of business growth: A cross functional perspective, *Journal of Business Research* 58:863–73.

Wyner, G. (2004) Refining data, *Marketing Research* Winter:6–7.

Recommended website

www.booksites.net/chadwickbeech

Chapter 9

Managing sport products and services

David Harness
University of Hull
Tina Harness
Leeds Metropolitan University

Learning outcomes

Upon completion of this chapter, the reader should be able to:

- Define what is meant by sport products and services.

- Identify the key characteristics of sport products and services.

- Differentiate between core, augmented and potential sport products and services.

- Discuss the process through which sport products and services are developed.

- Highlight ways that sport products and services are differentiated.

Overview of chapter

This chapter explores the product concept. It identifies that the sport product exists both as something that is tangible and has physical form, such as a baseball bat, and something that is a service that exists for a very limited time, such as baseball game. The three levels of the physical sports goods are defined and discussed in relation to the benefits consumers gain from owning and using the offering. The chapter considers what makes a sport service different from physical goods. The key differences between the physical sport product and a sport service are based on the four service characteristics of intangibility, heterogeneity, inseparability and perishability. These provide a different management emphasis than exists in the marketing of physical goods, specifically, to use the augmented marketing mix of product, price, place, promotion, people, process and physical evidence. How product managers use each element of the marketing mix to define the nature of the relationship with the user of the offering is discussed. This is related to the product life cycle (PLC) concept. Product life cycle theory highlights the different stages an offering goes through from its launch to its elimination. Finally, this chapter describes how product managers identify new product ideas and develop them to be launched.

Introduction

If asked what a sport product is, most of us would see it as something we take part in such as playing a game of football, skiing or swimming. It is the equipment we buy to facilitate the playing of a sport such as golf balls, walking shoes or a bicycle. We also would see the sport product as something that we watch, either at a venue or on TV. Other types of sports-related product exist, such as replica sports shirts, drinks that help the athlete recover vital fluids lost during training, fitness centres for weight training and medical services such as physiotherapists who treat sports injuries. Each of the examples of sports or sports-related products can be defined as something that is tangible (e.g., a football) or something that is a service (e.g., watching a game of football). This is an important differentiation and one that impacts on how individuals buy and consume the product offering and the ways a business organisation manages and markets the product. What this tells us is that the sport product has to be defined from the standpoint of either the user or the producer and that no single definition of a sport product or sport service exists.

Sport marketing defined: the consumer perspective

The starting point to understanding a sport product or service is to consider how theory defines each of these.

A product is defined as 'anything that is capable of satisfying customer's needs' (Jobber, 2004, p. 60). Often we distinguish between physical goods and service products based on their level of tangibility. A sport product can be very tangible (e.g., a hockey stick, a football or a Formula 1 car). It can also be a service (e.g., playing a game of hockey or watching a car race). We need to distinguish between sport products that are physical and those that are services because each one is consumed and owned differently by consumers.

◼ The sport product

Physical products tend to have the following attributes:

- They consume physical raw materials in their production (e.g., leather to make running shoes).
- Production tends to be separate from their consumption (e.g., running shoes made in China to be sold in Europe).
- Production can be standardised (e.g., each shoe conforms to established UK, US or European sizes).
- The product is usually sold to the consumer via a range of distribution channels (e.g., the sports shop, over the internet and via a catalogue).
- The consumer usually has to buy the goods to be able to use them.
- Ownership is transferred at purchase from the supplier to the customer.

As a consumer, we look at the product and decide if we want to buy it because it satisfies some form of need. This decision is based on factors such as price, brand image, kudos value, peer pressure, celebratory endorsement and fitness for purpose.

We also tend to use the product until it wears out or becomes unfashionable, unwanted or obsolete. At this point, the consumer may start the process of selecting a replacement product.

Each stage of getting the sport product, from production to the final customer, needs to be managed. This tends to be undertaken by product managers or a product management team. Their responsibility is to understand which consumer needs their product will satisfy and then to select the marketing mix (product, price, place and promotion mix) that will best encourage customers to buy the offering. At each stage of the manufacturing process, important marketing decisions have to be taken such as whether the product is aimed at the mass market or a specialist market. This determines the production format – factory or small workshop with skilled crafts people. It also helps define the quality of the product, the materials used, where production takes place and what specific features are incorporated into the offering. For example, a tennis racket for a professional player will be tailor-made to fit the buyer's hand and at a desired weight. The product features and quality levels influence the type of price charged – a mass market product will cost much less than a bespoke one. The product features and quality levels also influence where the product is sold (e.g., in a sports shop or at the sports person's home).

A key decision for the product manager is how to make the target customers aware of a product's existence. A common strategy used by many sports goods manufacturers is personality endorsement (e.g., David Beckham's football boots are sponsored by Adidas). Other strategies are to sponsor teams. Chelsea football club is sponsored by Samsung, which means that every time they play, the company logo is seen by everyone who watches the game at the stadium, on TV or in photographs. Cricket bat manufacturers provide bats to individual cricketers so that their logo, which is on the face of the bat, is seen. A key benefit for these organisations is that for a relatively small cost, the manufacturer gains enormous advertising exposure.

Product managers need to be clear about which consumer needs their product seeks to satisfy. Or to put it another way, they need to consider what benefits consumers will get if they buy and use the product. Marketing theory splits the type of benefits consumers gain from a physical product into three: core product, tangible product and augmented product (Kotler, Armstrong, Saunders and Wong, 1999).

Core product is defined in relation to the customer need that the product answers. For example, a car answers the customer's need for transport. In the same way, a golf club answers the customer's need to hit a small ball a long distance.

The *tangible product* describes the format of the core product (e.g., a football is made out of plastic or leather). The tangible product also describes the features of the offering that we as consumers can see, feel, taste and touch. It includes the brand name, packaging, styling, level of quality and product features. Using golf as an example, drivers (used to hit the ball over long distances) can be purchased made out of wood, graphite or titanium, with offset heads for players who slice the ball, and shafts of varying flexibility (e.g., very stiff) for professionals or whippier for senior players. The width of the grip can also vary depending on the size of the player's hands. The golfer also has an extensive range of manufacturers to choose products from. At the premium end of the market are companies such as TaylorMade, Ping and Calloway, whose products are used by golf professionals; at the entry level are products supplied by companies such as Ryder Group and Ben Sayers.

The *augmented product* is based on the tangible product but includes further services or benefits used to answer additional customers' needs and to differentiate the product from competitors' offerings. These additional services or features include warranties, after- or presales services, payment terms, delivery speed, customising or providing training. For example, the customer may choose one producer of golf clubs over another because of a zero rate credit deal or that lessons with a golf professional are included as part of the purchase package.

The three different levels described in the core, tangible and augmented product are based on the idea that the consumer buys and owns a physical object. Yet, as discussed previously, the sport product can also be defined as a service. To better understand why service-based sport products are different from tangible products, we need to consider the characteristics that makes services unique.

The sport service

Services marketing theory has evolved as a consequence of the failure of traditional marketing concepts to describe how service offerings were produced, consumed and marketed. The development of services marketing theory reflects the increasing importance of services within Western economies whose populations have experienced higher levels of disposable income and more leisure time, which encourage consumers to buy services.

In simple terms, a *service* is anything that is done on behalf of somebody else (e.g., getting your hair cut by a hairdresser). Within this context, Rathmall (1966) very simply defined services as 'a deed, a performance, and an effort'. A deed is something we do for others(e.g., make a meal in a restaurant for a customer), and a performance could be a theatre production or watching a game of football. An effort refers to what has to be undertaken to deliver the service to a customer, for example, training to be an elite athlete. Although this definition captures the essence of what a service is, it fails to take account of variances between different types of services or the role that physical attributes play in their production and consumption. Lovelock and Wirzt (2004, p. 9) incorporate the complexity inherent in producing and consuming services with the following two definitions.

> A service is an act or a performance offered by one party to another. Although the process may be tied to a physical product, the performance is transitory, often intangible, and does not normally result in ownership of any of the factors of production.

> A service is an economic activity that creates value and provides benefits for customers at specific times and places by bringing about a desired change in, or on behalf of, the recipient of the service.

These definitions suggest two important things: 1) that the characteristics of the service product are very important in understanding how it can be produced and consumed and 2) that service producers often undertake the activity to gain financial value from it.

Characteristics of the services product

Service products are described as being different from physical goods because they have four defining characteristics: intangibility, inseparability, perishability and heterogeneity. Each of these four characteristics poses specific challenges for the marketing of service offerings.

Intangibility

Intangibility means that the service offering cannot be seen, touched, tasted or smelled prior to purchase. In essence the nature of a service is defined by the level of tangibility within its existence. Shostack (1977) developed this idea into the physical goods service continuum, which positions goods and services based on the level of intangibility in their existence. For example, a pure physical good would be salt, but a pure service has no tangible elements such as a consultation with a doctor. In between each of these are offerings with a mixture of tangible and intangible elements. For example, a car, which is predominantly a product made of tangible elements such as steel and plastic, is often sold with a warranty (service) and with a hire purchase agreement (service). This concept can be applied to a range of sport products and services (Figure 9.1).

There are a number of benefits to classifying services in this way. Firstly, it enables producers to identify the elements of the product on which to apply their marketing effort. For a pure product, the important features to the consumer may be durability or speed of delivery. But for a pure service such as sports TV, it could be providing different ways of seeing games played such as slow-motion features, replays and alternative camera angles on a game of ice hockey.

A problem posed by service intangibility is that it makes it hard for consumers to evaluate what they are buying. When a customer selects a health club, he or she will

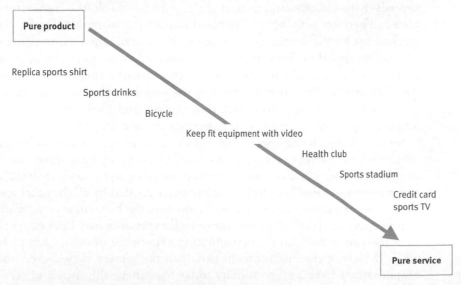

Figure 9.1 **Service/product continuum**

visit the premises; look at fitness equipment such as the weights, running machines and exercise bicycles; and check that the fitness instructors are qualified. Often such clubs charge an upfront joining fee and an annual subscription, forcing the customer to pay a considerable amount of money before being able to experience the service provided by the club. Because these may act as a barrier, which puts potential customers off joining, clubs offer trial memberships or free sessions to encourage new members. Clubs also try to enhance the ownership experience by providing tangible clues to the consumer about the service. For example, a fitness club aimed at premium customers will ensure that its facilities match the expectations of those customers and will provide expensive sweat towels or a personal training portfolio.

Another problem created by intangibility is related to who owns the product when it is purchased. In physical goods, as soon as the consumer has paid for the product, it becomes theirs; ownership is transferred from the producer to the customer. This is not always the case for services because the means of production remains owned by the organisation; it is the output of the production process that is consumed. For example, a sports physiotherapist is the means of production, and the output of the service is the healing that takes place. The consumer buys the service, not the means of production, and because it is intangible, there is nothing ultimately to own. This makes it difficult for consumers to easily evaluate the service's benefits.

Inseparability

Inseparability means that the production of a service and its consumption is often simultaneous. For example, an injured athlete cannot receive the service of a physiotherapist at a distance; rather, both the producer and the consumer have to come together for the service to be produced and consumed. Inseparability also means that the customer becomes a co-producer of the offering. For example, the Manchester United Football club credit card enables customers to purchase goods and pay for them at a later date. This forms the basis of the service; however, the service does not come into being unless the customer uses the card. Production has to occur simultaneously with the consumption of the service to enable the transaction to be completed. There are a number of implications arising from this. Firstly, the production mechanism for the service offering has to be located where customers can access and use it. The appeal of the Manchester United credit card to potential customers would be lessened if it could not be used in an extensive range of commercial outlets. Another aspect about inseparability is the location of sports stadiums. These stadiums need to built near to population centres and have good transport links and ample car parking to ensure that customers can attend games.

Services bring the customer and supplier into direct contact. Other customers can influence the consumption experience. This influence may be positive – for example, part of the experience of a live sports occasion such as horse racing, an athletics meeting or a game of basket ball is to feel the atmosphere created by all the other fans supporting their team. However, if there are problems with the behaviour of supporters, as sometimes happens at football games, the overall experience may be negative. The ability of customers to impact on the consumption experience of others has to be considered when designing the environment in which the service is delivered and consumed. Organisations have a responsibility to try to manage this aspect of service consumption by introducing rules or codes of conduct. For example, managers of a swimming pool may insist that all swimmers shower before entering the pool, or a fitness centre may request that their clients wipe their sweat from the equipment they have used. In the case of football, the segregation of opposing teams' fans is now the norm.

Perishability

Perishability means that the product cannot be produced and stored for future use. From the supplier's perspective, this means that they have to try to ensure that the capacity of the supply matches the demand for the service. Capacity is determined both by the physical infrastructure that surrounds the delivery of the service offering and the number of staff employed who can deliver the service offering. For example, an all-seating sports stadium capacity is determined by the number of seats it has. If a seat is unsold for a game, an unrecoverable financial loss occurs. The ability to increase capacity may also be limited. For sports that have grown in popularity, either at a generic level or because of the success of a club, the existing stadium may be too small, so customer dissatisfaction could occur. Sports clubs can use a number of tools to manage demand for, and the supply of their services. For example, sports clubs may sell season tickets, which helps them predict the number of fans who may turn up. It also means that the income for the club is not lost if the fan fails to go to a game. Demand can be reduced by increasing the entry price of the ticket for high-demand games or charging different prices at different times. For example, a fitness club may provide peak and off-peak memberships, which helps to remove customers from its busiest times. When supply is constricted by the nature of the sport service (e.g., waiting to see a sports physiotherapist, for a coaching session or because a limited number of pieces of equipment exist), the organisation can try to make the waiting process easier for customers. This could be by making the waiting area pleasant, providing a booking system or limiting the time that someone can use a piece of gym equipment. Finally, the sport service provider may only be able to increase capacity by building a new infrastructure.

Heterogeneity

Heterogeneity means that the service provided is likely to vary considerably every time it is performed or delivered. This makes it difficult to standardise. For sport services, this perhaps provides a level of unpredictability within the performance, which makes watching or following a particular sport exciting. For other sports and sports-related services, the inability to standardise the quality of the service may be a problem.

Variability in the delivery of the performance of sports activity is inevitable because its product is based on the actions of an individual, a group or an animal as well as the operating environment (e.g., weather conditions, altitude, time of the day). It is also about the level of expertise required to perform the sport or technical difficulty involved in its delivery. For example, dressage is based on the horse and rider working in unison to perform a set routine. If either the horse or its rider loses concentration or makes a mistake, points will be lost. To reduce poor performance, sports clubs employ managers, coaches and medical staff. They try to 'buy' the best players they can afford and invest considerable time and energy into training. None of this guarantees consistent success. For example, an elite athlete may catch a cold before a big race, a football team may be tired from playing too many matches in a short time scale and lose to a lesser club, or a good cricket team may be bowled by an inexperienced team because of the condition of the wicket. Although fans want to see their teams or the individual win, variability in the performance adds excitement to the activity, which helps to attract customers.

For other sports-related services, the causes of heterogeneity have to be understood and minimised. Variability in the delivery of a service is based on the interaction of two things. First is the level of latitude in the way that an individual can create the product. This means how much flexibility an individual has in making the product. The more a service can be considered 'pure', the more the individual producing it can determine what is produced. For example, a singer can alter the way he or she sings a song in many different ways. However, a fitness instructor teaching someone to use a piece of equipment has to work within the guidelines supplied by the manufacturer; these define the nature of the service delivered. Secondly, customers can also influence the level of variability of a service because of the things they do or what they are. For example, a person's fitness determines how he or she uses a running machine (e.g., if the person is unfit, he or she may only use the walking function). Customers can also alter the service product by the level of questions they ask or what additional services they want or by misbehaving. The challenge for managers is to identify the extent to which these types of issues may arise in their service delivery and identify strategies to deal with them (e.g., training staff in conflict resolution).

CASE 9.1   Golf gets to grips with a new generation

'There's nothing like spending a lost afternoon on the golf course hitting the odd decent shot between lengthy spells wandering in the rough searching for that monster drive that didn't quite come off. Honestly, it's fantastic. You should try it one day.' With this kind of spiel, I've spent many fruitless hours over the years trying to persuade friends that golf really is the new rock'n'roll. Clearly, it's nothing of the sort (thank goodness for that) but when trying to grab the attention of potential golfers, a long ramble about the sporting virtues of the game and the legacy of Old Tom Morris and Harry Vardon just doesn't work.

In the past 12 months, however, something quite peculiar has happened to the image of golf. The players appear to have become trendier – such as Ian Poulter, whose Union Jack trousers, designed by Savile Row tailor William Hunt, were splashed all over newspaper front pages during the Open in Troon last July. The celebrities championing the game also appear to have become trendier – where once there were homespun personalities such as Bruce Forsyth and Jimmy Tarbuck, now there are Hollywood A-list stars George Clooney and Will Smith. Then there's *GolfPunk* magazine. When we were mere striplings working on our own fanzine back in the late 1980s, *GolfPunk* founder Tim Southwell used to drag me on to the golf course from time to time. Little did we know what trouble it would get us into later. The idea for the magazine was formulated during the Open at Sandwich in 2003 – four days of beautiful sunshine, great golf and a little beer (afterwards, I remember Tim telling anyone who would listen: 'It was like Glastonbury! With golf!'). We felt then there was an army of like-minded golfers out there, reared on the fun and games of the men's magazine explosion of the mid-1990s. A year after the first issue, and as the latest 'where have you been all my life' e-mail from a reader is pinned on the office wall, it looks as if we might have been right. (And while British golfers have been keen, the Americans have taken *GolfPunk* to their heart. More than 60 per cent of the traffic to our website has been from the US and when we turned up at the Ryder Cup last year we had our *GolfPunk* caps, visors and shirts virtually torn from our backs.) The most obvious difference people point out when comparing us with other golf magazines is that we have Bunker Babes explaining the rules of the game and a Golf Nurse offering tuition. For us the real difference is that so much rich golfing material had never been written about until we turned up. Despite being outstanding sportspeople, winning millions of pounds on a regular basis and living impossibly luxurious lifestyles, golfers had never been portrayed in anything other than the most mundane terms. Sitting poolside at double Ryder Cup winner Jesper Parnevik's house last year, being treated like one of the extended family of golfing Swedes who hang out in Jupiter, Florida, was remarkable for a number of reasons, not least the fact that he was so much more interesting than the vast majority of Premiership footballers, actors and entertainers I'd previously interviewed. Fortunately for us, the players seem to enjoy *GolfPunk*. There's no doubt that the name made some of the game's establishment pillars initially cautious, but once they realised that the 'Punk' is more wideboy than anarchist, Sandy Jones and Peter Dawson – heads of the PGA and R&A respectively – gave the magazine their seal of approval. Like our other supporters they are hoping that *GolfPunk* may bring new people to the game. At this point in the proceedings, you might quite reasonably ask whether there is a place in golf for young men with vertical hairstyles. The answer, without doubt, is yes. Research conducted two years ago stated that there are approximately 5m golfers in the UK, most of whom are no longer taking the traditional route of applying for membership at a club and buying their clubs from the club pro.

This generation is the future of the game in Britain. Many of them are taking advantage of the fact that too many courses have been built and that clubs are being forced to curtail their membership policies, slash green fees and open up their courses to the masses. Great for those of us who like to play around rather than stick loyally to one club, though not for the people who may have invested millions to turn a patch of land into their own piece of suburban golf architecture. The London Club in Kent, which attracts considerable business from London's Docklands and City areas, is one club that has changed its approach to become successful. 'Our customers are well-travelled people with high expectations,' explains the club's commercial director Heath Harvey. 'That means we've worked hard on setting a high standard of service – quality food and drink – off the course. We concentrate on providing a great all-round experience to fewer people. Instead of having corporate days with 200 people we now have them for 40. The volume of business is down, but the margins of profit are better. In general the elitist reputation of golf has faded. People are no longer intimidated, which means more people are taking up the game. The middle- market is where only the fittest will survive. People just won't accept second-best any more.' An equally competitive approach – also reflective of changing attitudes to the game – has been taken in the equipment world, where companies such as TaylorMade and Nike have challenged the dominance of established names such as Callaway. The availability of discounted name – brand clubs through online retailers such as direct-golf.co.uk and onlinegolf.co.uk is also a constant source of irritation to the club manufacturer looking for higher profit margins, though their popularity with regular golfers is undeniable. In answer to the budget sellers, most manufacturers now offer free 'custom fittings', giving consumers the opportunity to have their clubs made to their own particular technical specifications. There is a shiny universe of technical equipment out there that could keep the most ardent boys' toys fanatic engaged for years. Equipment forums such as bombsquadgolf.com and golf opinions.com feed that addiction with all the latest developments. Another driver for change is travel. It's no surprise to see verdant miles of greenery continuing to sprout all over Spain and Portugal, where golfers have traditionally vacationed for years but other destinations such as Austria and Italy are getting in on the act, with companies such as MW Golf offering golf in summer (skiing in winter once the fairways have been covered in snow). It doesn't end there. In just a few months *GolfPunk* has met the shanty town caddies building their own course in Brazil, played the island with the largest concentration of golf courses per capita in the world (Arran), fought off monkeys in Malaysia and negotiated an awkward chip past a giraffe in Kenya. Hiring a golfing Elvis impersonator in Las Vegas was a blast too. But our best golfing experience to date was on a grey day in Scotland at Prestwick, birthplace of the Open. Walking in the footsteps of the golfing gods on this magically historical patch of grass made us realise that, yes, golf is changing and in some ways needs to change more, but it is also as near perfect as any sport can be. Which other game offers you the chance to play in its greatest arenas and to follow in the footsteps of its greatest players? To play a course such as St Andrews, still open to anyone, remains a genuinely profound sporting experience.

Iestyn George is deputy editor of *GolfPunk* magazine, now available each month. http://www.golfpunkmag.com

Source: I. George, *Financial Times*, 26 March 2005

Questions

1. Identify both the services and physical goods mentioned in the case. Explain why these product offerings can be described as either a service or a physical good.

2. In what ways does the case suggest that the game of golf is changing? Can you identify what is driving these changes?

Services marketing mix

Traditionally, the set of tools used to market a product were defined as the marketing mix. For physical goods, the marketing mix was based on managing an offering's product, price, place and promotion. The development of the four P's marketing mix was supported by research undertaken in the manufacturing sectors and reflected the type of issues important in getting a physical good from a factory to a retail environment for consumers to buy (Borden, 1965). Authors such as Rathmall (1966) and Miracle (1965) questioned whether the underpinning concepts on which the 4 P's were constructed could be applied to the marketing of services. Booms and Bitner (1981) highlighted that because service products were characterised by intangibility, inseparability, perishability and heterogeneity, other components to the marketing mix should be used. Their observations led them to conclude that before the marketing mix concept could be applied to service offerings, it had to take account of other factors. This led to the identification of three further Ps. The first is people, which takes account of the role that employees and customers play in producing and consuming a product. The second is process, which describes the activities involved in delivering the product to the consumer. Finally, Booms and Bitner added physical evidence, described as tangible product attributes used to reduce the risk customers perceive during pre-purchase, consumption and postpurchase (e.g., before buying an expensive golf club, reading an editorial in a magazine written by a professional golfer stating its virtues).

Although service marketing theory was initially based on the identification of a separate paradigm, it is increasingly believed that services and physical goods marketing overlap (Voss, 1992). Increasingly, service elements are important in the marketing of physical goods (Rafiq and Pervaiz, 1995), so much so that many types of physical goods are sold with a service bundle (e.g., hire purchase agreements, maintenance and servicing contracts, warranties, education and training and help lines; Voss, 1992). It is safer when thinking about how to manage sport products and services to use the extended marketing mix and to vary the part played by each element based on whether it is a pure good or a pure service.

Product

Regardless of whether a product is defined as a pure service, a pure good or a mixture of the two, it is used by the organisation to satisfy customers' needs whilst fulfilling corporate objectives. The product links the organisation to its customers and may provide the basis for a relationship. For example, the takeover of Manchester United Football Club by Malcolm Glazer was opposed by a proportion of the fans. The product would be defined as the game of football; however, those fans believe they have a relationship with the club that should give them a say on its future. In a sense, they feel a sense of ownership beyond the price they pay to watch a game or the time frame in which the activity takes place.

Price

Price fulfils a number of functions within the marketing mix. It tells consumers what they have to pay and provides the income for the organisation. A number of issues have to be considered when setting a price. For example, setting the price for a fishing rod would have to take account of what it costs to get the product to market. This includes the cost of purchasing raw materials, manufacturing the product, storing it, distributing it to a retailer and all the expenses involved in the marketing activity such as advertising in a fishing magazine and producing point-of-sale promotional literature.

The organisation also has to factor into the price the level of profit it would like to make. This method of pricing tends to be known as cost-plus pricing. However, it ignores the price levels established in the market by competitors or what different customers segments will pay. Benchmarking the price against what competitors set is known as market-based pricing. For example, the price of replica football shirt of a premier football club is similar for all clubs within that league. The cost will be higher than for replica kit for clubs in lower leagues. Highly relevant to this is the brand image and its power within the marketplace. Sports clubs with strong brand images are able to charge higher prices for their goods and services because these offerings help the consumer identify more closely with the organisation. You only need to watch ice hockey, international cricket, football or baseball to see the many fans wearing the current team strip. Manufacturers of sport products also use their brand image to charge premium prices. For example, sports shoes manufacturers such as Nike and Adidas can charge premium prices because of the association of their brands with successful sports people or organisations (e.g., Nike sponsors six-time Grand Slam champion Serena Williams, and Adidas sponsors English premier football club Chelsea FC).

Setting the price of a service is complicated because often the actual cost of production is unknown. For example, what price should sports physiotherapists charge for providing their services? The time involved in producing the service, the level of complexity of the problem solved, the experience of the physiotherapists and their reputation are all relevant to setting the price. The price for a pure service should reflect the quality the consumer seeks in purchasing the product. The greater the desired quality, the higher the price expected to be paid. A further dimension to pricing is the concept of scarcity. In the context of sports, scarcity is created by an individual's or team's performance in a specific context. For example, Kelly Holmes has increased her commercial value by winning two gold medals at the Athens Olympics. Also, the value of a racehorse that wins the Grand National or consistently wins races also increases greatly, especially for breeding purposes.

Place

Place is concerned with bringing the product and the customer together in a way that facilitates purchase and consumption. For pure products, the location of distribution channels (e.g., retail outlet, sports club, catalogue) is related to the type of market the product is aimed at. Products such as Lucozade sports drink need to be distributed to where the consumer would want to use it (e.g., at the sports venue). It also has to be sold in supermarkets because that provides the most effective channel to get to the mass market. Sports equipment manufacturers may choose to distribute their offerings via specialist retailers that sell only products related to that one sport. A good example is fishing shops that sell only fishing-related products. The advantages this provides over general sports retailers are a much wider range of products to purchase and sales staff with expert knowledge of how to use the offering. The management of the distribution process for sports goods manufacturers is very important and has to be supported by other marketing activity such as ensuring the reliable delivery of products, good point-of-sales promotional material, financial incentives linked to sales output and training about product features.

For sports that are played in stadiums, location increasingly plays an important role in defining what events are held and how many fans can attend. The choice of where the

2012 Olympics are to be held was partly based on the quality of transportation links from the main centres of population and airports to sporting venues. Other location-related issues are based on playing the sports near to where the fan base lives. For many sports, a good proportion of their fans live in the region where the teams are based. Often the clubs include in their name, the town, city or region they are most associated with (e.g., AC Milan, Boston Red Sox, Yorkshire County Cricket Club).

Promotion

Promotion is used to ensure that potential customers know an offering exists, where it can be purchased and how it can be used. The tools used in promotion can be summarised as advertising, sales promotion public relations and personal selling. How these tools are used is determined by the nature of the product and what the organisation wants to achieve through its communication strategy. For tangible sport products, ensuring customers are aware of the offering, where it is sold and the benefits they will gain from buying it are important communication objectives. This may involve TV advertising showing the product being endorsed by an athlete, an editorial in a sports magazine explaining key features, or sponsorship of a sports personality (e.g., Nike and Tiger Woods).

Promotion helps to reduce the risk of purchase by showing what the product does and how consumers enjoy or benefit from using it. This is especially important for services for which the offering is intangible, making it difficult for customers to be sure of what experience they will get. UK football has sought to increase the number of families that attend matches. To achieve this, clubs have had to make their environment safe, add family-friendly facilities and reach out to their local communities with sports initiatives. A key communication objective is to get existing fans to go home and tell their families to attend matches. In services, 'word of mouth' communication can be a powerful tool because it includes a trusted personal recommendation from someone who has experience of the offering we wish to buy.

People

The management of the people element of the marketing mix is especially important in services in which production cannot be separated from consumption. People includes the producers of the service, the staff who support them, the customer consuming the offering and other customers who influence the consumption environment. The organisation's employees fulfil a number of important roles. In one sense, they are the organisation in the eyes of the customer. The extent to which this is the case is determined by the level of personal contact between the employee and customer. In services in which the product is produced on a one-to-one basis (e.g., being coached by a tennis professional), that employee, in the eyes of the customer, *is* the organisation.

It is important to distinguish between employees who produce the product and those that support its production. For example, a fan who goes to watch a rugby game will see the product in terms of the game played by the two teams. In essence, the product is produced by the interaction of the two teams with each other. Supporting the delivery of the product is a whole range of other people, some of whom will be known to the customers, but many will not. The customer may use the club's café and interact with the employee whose job it is to sell tea and coffee but would be unaware of the electrician who waits on call in case the floodlights fail during the game. The management challenge for services is to ensure that the benefits the customer seeks from purchase (e.g., the excitement of watching a game) are delivered. This involves identifying jobs that need to occur within the organisation to support the product, the recruitment and training of staff and the coordination of each. For employees who have a high level of personal interaction with customers, people management skills are highly important (e.g., being responsive to customers' questions).

Physical evidence

The intangibility of services makes it very difficult for potential purchasers of the offering to be sure what they are buying. This adds to the risk that the offering will fail to match their expectations or answer their needs. Service producers try to reduce this risk by promoting the tangible factors related to the offering. This can take many forms:

- The uniforms worn by stewards to reassure customers when they attend large sports occasions
- The display of certificates awarded to coaches, physiotherapists or sports doctors, which tell the client that the person is qualified and experienced
- The promotion literature produced such as a brochure showing customers enjoying the benefits of being a member of a fitness club or the ticket that guarantees entry to watch a game

The quality of the physical infrastructure provides an important clue as to the benefits that can be gained by watching or taking part in a sport. Customers may want to know that there is plenty of car parking, that the sports stadium is safe or that there are places to eat or change a baby. The individuals who participate in the actual sports may want to know that the playing field, sports track, swimming pool or ice rink is well maintained and fit for purpose. They may gain this knowledge from visiting the site, by viewing a promotional film of the facilities or via positive word of mouth from other sports professionals. The existence of these types of tangible clues may encourage sports fans to go to an event or sport participants to play their game at a specific venue. The risks tangible clues cannot reduce is the under-performance by the individual or team being supported. Although this is difficult to overcome, competitive sports tend to be played to win money, medals or cups or gain an improved ranking against other teams or individuals. In a sense, these are surrogate tangible clues of success that may help new fans decide to follow that team or individual. Success in the sports activity also gains media exposure, which reinforces that these clubs or individuals are worth supporting, which in turn helps to reduce purchase risk.

Process

Process describes the way that a service is delivered to its user. In essence, these are the production processes involved in producing a service activity. Service delivery is based on the implementation of a number of steps in a defined sequence. For example, buying a ticket to watch a football game could de divided into the following steps:

1. An individual enquires about availability of a ticket and its cost for a specific game.
2. The ticket agent looks up the information in the database and answers the questions.
3. The individual accepts the answer and agrees to buy the ticket.
4. The ticket agent asks for payment.
5. The customer hands over a credit card.
6. The ticket agent processes the payment and hands the ticket to the customer.
7. The ticket agent reduces the number of tickets available in the database.

All services can be divided into a set of different steps. The number of steps involved in delivery and the level to which each step can be altered enables the supplier organisation to change the quality within the process. So, for example, delivering the services of a sports physiotherapist has few steps within it, but those that are involved are highly personalised to the needs of the client. The ability to vary the service is essential so that the physiotherapist can actually heal the injury that the client has and is based both on consultation and physical examination. This means that no two interactions are the same. This is different from the ticket agent example, in which each step is standardised. Standardisation is based on the ability to define each step and then ensure that the support systems facilitate that activity. In this case, the process is driven by the information technology that holds the database of ticket types, availability and costs. This also enables the service to be delivered remotely by telephone or via the internet.

In designing the delivery format, a number of considerations have to be made. The supplier has to decide on the overall quality of the service. The more that a service is 'customerised', the greater the overall quality within it because it answers the needs of the customer more directly. This is expensive and likely to limit the number of customers that can be dealt with in a given time period. Although it is relevant for specialist sport services, it is perhaps less appropriate for mass spectator sports, which emphasise speed of process. This means that such things as how long a customer will spend in a queue to be served at a café, wait to park their car or the length of time it takes them to get to their seat have to be considered. The management challenge is how to streamline these activities to reduce waiting time or customer confusion by providing stewards to help guide individuals to their seat or by producing maps and signage to direct customers around a stadium. If an organisation fails to create an appropriate delivery process, it could lead to customer dissatisfaction and a reduction in customers' loyalty, which affects repeat purchase and reduces positive word of mouth.

Managing the interactions between customers and employees

The delivery of the service product is a process that brings together the customer and the organisation's employees so that the product can be simultaneously produced and consumed. This is a critical activity in which ultimately, the customers decide if the service they receive meets their expectations. The organisation has to create service delivery systems that support its frontline staff, whose job function is to interact directly with customers. As a way of conceptualising the different roles played by employees in supporting customers, the concept of front office and back office was developed (Chase, 1978). This analogy is used to divide employees between those who have visible direct customer contact and those who work in a support role with no direct customer contact. There are a number of advantages to dividing employees into two groups. Firstly, the organisation has to recruit staff with appropriate skills for their job function. For example, customer contact staff would be expected to have good people skills, but this is less critical for the maintenance engineer at a sports club who would need technical knowledge of how the water, electrical and heating systems worked. Secondly, by identifying the mix of staff required to deliver the service offering, the organisation can evaluate the format of the delivery process to ensure an efficient use of resources, identify potential failures and ultimately decide how to alter quality levels. For example, designing the service delivery process to sell hotdogs at a sports ground is a considerably simpler task than identifying how to manage the front office and back office staff involved in producing and serving food in corporate hospitality.

Measuring service quality

In creating a service delivery process, the organisation has a view about the level of quality it wishes to provide to the customer. However, quality is ultimately determined by the customers' view of what they have received against what they wanted to receive. Customer expectations about quality are derived from the experiences of both the supplier of the service and other service organisations that deliver similar types of experience. The ability to deliver service quality is concerned with how the organisation produces the product and how it manages customers' expectations about what they should receive. Critical to this is that the service delivery process has to be consistent in how it delivers the product to the consumer, which means controlling the interaction between the employees and the customer. To be able to do this, the organisation has to measure the customers' expectations of what service they want to receive against their view of what they have received (perceptions).

One method of doing this is to use a survey research tool called SERVQUAL. This was developed by Parasurman, Zeithaml and Berry (1988) and is based on 22 perception items that evaluate five key dimensions of service quality:

Tangibles – What the physical environment looks like

Reliability – The extent to which performance is accurate and dependable

Responsiveness – Willingness to help; speed of action

Assurance – Being competent and credible

Empathy – Demonstrating understanding of the customer

SERVQUAL measures the difference between a customer's expectations and their perceptions of the service received. If the customer's perception of service quality received is lower than their expectations, they may believe that they have received poor quality.

If poor service quality is identified, the organisation can either improve the delivery of the service or lower customer expectations.

CASE 9.2   In search of financial muscle

Over the past 20 years, the McMahon family has managed to cobble together a group of regional professional wrestling circuits across the US into a publicly listed company, World Wrestling Entertainment, with a market capitalisation of nearly $800 m. Now, as wrestling's first family tries to embark on a new era of growth, it is looking to the international market. The WWE is betting that European fans will shell out for pay-per-view television, tickets to live events and branded merchandise featuring stars such as Kane, a 7 ft, 326 lb giant who likes to finish off opponents with a patented choke-slam. So far, WWE has increased its live events outside the US from just three in 2002 to 31 last year. During that period, foreign revenues have increased from 9 per cent to 17 per cent of total revenues. Yesterday, the company's Smackdown! troupe, featuring reigning champion John Cena and his Chaingang of fans, was touching down in London as part of a tour that will take the WWE to Italy, Germany, Scotland, Ireland and Wales in an effort to drum up more foreign business.

The company is hoping that regular visits will allow it to expand licensing deals with local retailers and better co-ordinate its marketing campaigns. 'There's a lot of growth in Europe,' said Vincent McMahon, WWE's chairman. 'You've got to go where the money is.' The international strategy is being touted not only by WWE but a host of media companies at a time when their share prices have been sluggish, and their domestic growth prospects may have cooled. Walt Disney, for example, has set a goal of generating 50 per cent of its revenue internationally within five years. The Warner Brothers film studio is investing heavily in China. And MTV Networks, the growth engine of Viacom, made its biggest gains in the most recent quarter overseas.

While the WWE has long broadcast its programmes around the world, and occasionally sent its talent abroad, it did not pursue the foreign market in earnest until about five years ago. The strategy has become imperative as its most recent earnings report indicated that the company's audiences were dwindling at home. As a result, its revenues of $248.1m through the first nine months of fiscal 2005 were almost identical to the same period a year earlier.

One thing working in the company's favour is that there appears to be a limitless supply of aggressive young males around the world for the company to tap into. Also, the WWE's product travels easily. 'Our product is one of the very few out there that does not need to change one bit to cross borders,' said Kurt Schneider, WWE's executive vice-president of marketing. 'When you look in the ring, you see a good guy and a bad guy, and someone hits someone over the head with a steel chair, and you get it.'

Like other US sports leagues, such as the National Football League or the National Basketball Association, the WWE tried to find local stars that foreign audiences could identify with when it first sent its show to Japan in the 1980s. But they quickly learned that fans wanted the genuine item. 'When The Rolling Stones tour, Japan does not want to see the Japanese version of The Rolling Stones,' explained Mr McMahon's son, Shane, executive vice-president of global media. About the only concession that the WWE makes to local tastes is to edit its scantily clad divas from television programmes broadcast in the Middle East. 'We have a lot of Mideast fans who don't necessarily enjoy our government,' said Mr McMachon, 'but they love our show.'

Source: J. Chaffin, *Financial Times*, 23 April 2005

Questions

1. Which elements of the service marketing mix can you identify within the case? How are these combined to define the nature of the product?

2. What cultural issues did WWE have to consider in taking its product outside of the United States?

Product management

A critical management activity is to coordinate each development of the marketing mix to ensure that corporate objectives and customers' needs are satisfied. The differences that exist in the physical good and the service offering create diverse marketing challenges for the organisation. In services, more thought has to be given to the role of employees as producers and promoters of the products; for physical goods, the managerial effort has to go into managing the attributes of production, distribution and retailing. Relevant to both the management of physical products and service offerings is the need to ensure the each element of the marketing mix promotes a consistent message to the target customer group. This is a complex task that requires considerable insight into how each element of the marketing mix is viewed by customers. For example, if a fitness club wants to compete in the premium end of the market, its marketing effort should be focused on creating an exclusive image of the organisation. Therefore, the price of becoming a member would be high, the club would be furnished with expensive furniture, it would have top-of-the-range fitness equipment and the number of members for the club would be restricted to reinforce its exclusiveness. This type of fitness club may promote the social benefits of membership such as the bar and restaurant facilities that exist. If the fitness club was aimed at the mass market, then a different marketing mix would be used. Its location may be close to a large population centre, it might not have a membership fee and it would offer the ability to pay monthly with discounts for particular groups such as corporate membership or the over 55s. It will promote the health benefits of being users of the sports facilities rather than other services or facilities.

Keeping a product or service relevant to the target customer group requires an understanding of where it is within its life cycle. Products and service have been conceptualised to go through a number of distinct stages based on the level of customer acceptance and profitability. The different stages have been conceptualised as the product life cycle concept. The product life cycle model has five key stages: introduction, growth, maturity, decline and elimination (Figure 9.2).

Introduction stage

The introduction stage is when the product or service is first brought to the market. This is often a very risky activity in which the offering has to gain growing market acceptance to pay back the costs involved in its launch. Initially, it will experience limited sales whilst potential customers become aware of the offering's existence. An organisation may have a number of objectives driving the launch of a new product to expand the existing market by adding to the range it already offers (e.g., selling swimming goggles to complement its swimming costumes). It may wish to enter a new market (e.g., Nike moving into the supply of golf equipment). An organisation may use its new product development to counter a threat posed by a competitor that brings new offerings to the market. The organisation may have gained new production or service competencies that present different commercial opportunities that can only be satisfied by launching new offerings. If the takeup of the product or service is slow, the company may decide to withdraw it from the market or alter its marketing mix. If the new product succeeds at its launch, it enters the growth stage.

Growth stage

The growth stage occurs when increasing numbers of customers buy the product or service and at a faster speed than during the introduction phase. The marketing objectives for the growth phase may be to rapidly build market share, develop a brand image and create wider distribution channels.

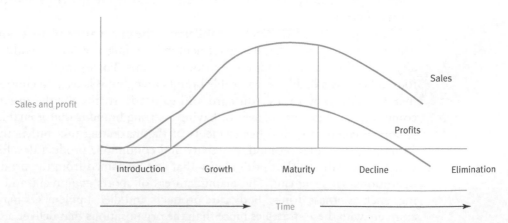

Figure 9.2 **The product life cycle**

An important element to growth is the development of repeat purchase. This may be vital for products that rely on a limited number of customers but who make regular purchases of the offering. For example, an ice hockey club with a small fan base would need a large proportion of them to attend matches on a regular basis to ensure that sufficient income is generated to pay the players and cover other costs. Without considerable repeat purchase, the club may not be financially viable. The growth stage is often characterised by the entry of competitor organisations into the market, which see the ability to make profit. Whilst the market is in growth, this may be beneficial because the size of the total market may expand. This process continues until supply outstrips demand. It is an indication that the market may be saturated and fragmented because of extensive customer segmentation targeted by different competitive strategies (e.g., price, value or location). The impact of this is twofold. Firstly, it makes it harder for organisations to compete effectively and secondly, profit margins reduce. The organisation's response to these challenges may be to try to control and cut costs, seek strategic alliances or withdraw from the market. The end of the growth stage is characterised by a concentration of the number of suppliers in the market, a decline in overall profitability and a reduction in the growth of customer volume.

Maturity stage

The ability to grow sales during the mature phase of the product life cycle is limited because fewer new customers enter the market and competition for existing customers is intense. The marketing challenge is to hold existing market share and grow it by taking share from competitors. Organisations will seek to increase their attractiveness by differentiating the product. Examples include altering the rules of Rugby Union to make the game faster and more enjoyable to watch, making a game of football more attractive to families by providing pre-match entertainment, or involving fans more within the game by using technology such as in cricket, where fans can see on large monitors where the ball hits the stumps or why an LBW decision is not given. Creating different versions of a game to make it more appealing to other customer segments can also increase purchasing levels (e.g., 20/20 cricket appeals to younger fans and those with limited time because the match is shorter than other forms of cricket).

Many sports activities can be considered to be in a mature phase of their existence. This has meant a considerable investment in branding as a way to build customer loyalty and help generate additional income streams. For example, Manchester United football club is a highly recognisable brand name, but it is used to endorse the sales of merchandise, support a credit card and gain advertising for the organisation's TV company. An important benefit of having a strong brand is that it enables the organisation to compete with other elements of the marketing mix rather than having to focus on price, sales promotion activity and continuous product development, all of which reduce the level of profitability that can be gained from the product within its operational environment. The manufacturers of sports equipment and related offerings such as fitness drinks, body care products and diet supplements may be forced to compete with these strategies more than the organisations that deliver a sports activity such as football, cricket or ice hockey.

Decline stage

After a product or service enters a decline phase, it is very difficult for the organisation to reverse it. This is because decline is a symptom that the market has changed. For example, the product may be obsolete, it becomes unfashionable or new and more attractive offerings exist. The marketing objectives may be to gain as much income from as little organisational effort as possible; this is defined as harvesting. The company may cut promotional budgets, simplify the product range, remove product features or decrease the number of suppliers to reduce the total cost of keeping the offering in the market. The organisation may also increase the price of the offering because the customers who remain purchasing the offering may either be very loyal or captured, making it hard for them to switch to other suppliers.

During the decline phase, other competitors withdraw from supplying that market segment, which may increase the speed of market decline. As demand for the product decreases, the organisation is faced with, firstly, the cost of production becoming greater than profit gained and secondly, that its resources could be used more profitably elsewhere. At this stage, the organisation may choose to eliminate the offering.

Product elimination stage

The final stage of a products life cycle is concerned with how the organisation withdraws from the market. This is described as product divestment. For offerings with high levels of tangibility, the issues surrounding the removal activity are based on how best to reassign the attributes of production, such as raw materials, a production plant or stocks of finished goods. For example, when a golf club manufacturer launches a new version of its clubs, it will cease production of the existing ones to create production capacity and will sell any remaining stock at a discount. Service product elimination is less straightforward because of the simultaneous production concept and the idea that ownership remains shared between the suppliers and the user.

In essence, service elimination is about managing customers' ownership experience to encourage them to stop using the current offering and migrate to an alternative (Harness, 2004). The removal of a sports provision such as playing fields or the closing of a squash club may cause a great deal of anger from its users and may affect the reputation of the organisation implementing the activity. This means that service product elimination has to be undertaken with a high knowledge of how the activity will impact on the purchasing intention of the current customers.

Implications of the product life cycle model

The product life cycle concept helps product managers understand what might happen to their offerings over time and how to respond to each change by altering the marketing mix. The model is a conceptual representation of the life cycle of an offering and does not inform about the total life length or the speed with which it goes through each stage. For example, when a football club changes the design of the shirts its players wear, it also necessitates the launch of a new product: the replica football shirt. The time from introduction to maturity may be a matter of weeks because peer group pressure amongst the fans encourages rapid purchase of the replica shirt. The length of time a product is in the mature stage may, as is the case of sports clubs, be a very long time, during which it may go through mini growth phase and decline cycles. For sports such as football, rugby, cricket and Formula 1 car racing, it could be argued that they have moved from being in a mature phase back into a growth because they have global appeal that makes them attractive to companies such as Sky Television. Being shown on Sky TV exposes the sport to a global audience, which helps create a new fan base.

Product life cycle concept emphasises that the product is likely at some point to go into decline and may have to be eliminated. This places two burdens on product managers. Firstly, they need to ensure that they have a good balance in their product portfolio of products in different stages of their product life cycles. Secondly, product managers must spend time and effort searching for new products to replace those in decline or facing elimination.

New product or service development

New product or service development, if successful, provides the organisation with additional or replacement income streams, which helps secure long-term survival. New product development is an inherently risky undertaking. The majority of new products and services fail for many different reasons. There may be no market for the offering, it may be deficient in comparison with other products in the market, the price level may be set too high or too low, there may be production faults with the product or retailers may refuse to distribute the offering. Despite the high level of failure, organisations have to launch new products and services because the marketplace changes.

A key question is what is new product or service development? New products have been defined as existing in four different ways: product replacements, additions to existing lines, new product lines and products that are new to the world (Booz, Allen and Hamilton, 1982). These are highlighted in Table 9.1.

The choice of which form of new product development is undertaken is based on a number of factors. For example, each of the four has different levels of risk attached. Replacing a product that is becoming obsolete is less risky than launching something brand new to the market. The former builds on the organisation's existing knowledge base of market characteristics and consumer purchasing habits. But for the latter, the organisation may be faced with building the market from scratch.

Table 9.1 **Service and physical goods examples of the four forms of new product development**

Form of new product or service development	Physical good example	Service offering example
Product replacements	A golf company produces golf clubs with graphite shafts	A fitness centre trains its instructors to be nutrition advisors
Addition to existing lines	A fishing equipment manufacturer launches a clothing range	A sports club adds an internet booking facility
New product lines	A sports drinks manufacturer launches a deodorant	A football club launches a credit card
New-to-the-world products	A new sports activity is created e.g., snowboarding (snowboard = the physical product; snowboarding = the service)	

The new product development process

It has been identified that organisations that follow formal new product development processes increase their chance of success (Kelly and Storey, 2000). The type of sequence that an organisation can follow is shown in Table 9.2.

Ideas for new services and offerings can come from many different sources. Internal to the organisation, the idea may come from teams tasked with identifying new opportunities for existing offerings or from staff suggestion boxes. New product ideas can be identified by looking at what competitors and other organisations outside of the market do. An important source of new ideas comes from customers who, through suggestion schemes, formal market research and complaints, may generate new insights into what an organisation has to do to answer their needs more fully.

The selection of the best ideas is undertaken to identify the commercial worth of the concept. It is also evaluated to ensure that precious organisational resources are not wasted on ideas that have no chance of succeeding. A key question to be considered is whether the new product idea fits the organisation's core capabilities and the markets in which it competes.

Testing of the concept occurs when the new product idea is translated into an offering that consumers can evaluate. The consumers are shown the product or have the service described, and then they have the opportunity to discuss what merits or problems they see. The customers may also be asked what their buying intention would be. This may be an important filter used to determine if the product idea is given further development.

Business case evaluation involves analysing market potential and identifying costs and likely profit levels. This helps the organisation to judge whether further development of the product concept should take place, such as a building a working prototype.

The development and testing of a product occurs when the concept is translated into either the physical offering or when the service is created. The role of this stage is to identify how the offering functions and the level of likely consumer acceptance. This stage is designed to remove any bugs that may exist in the product or gaps in the service provision.

Market testing takes the offering or service and exposes it to a limited number of customers. This is the first time that potential customers have to make the decision about whether to buy the offering or not. This in itself is an important test of the product's sales potential, and it enables the organisation to identify, in a real sense, likely

Table 9.2 **Stages a new product may go through from development to launch**

Stage	Process
1	Idea generation
2	Selection of best ideas
3	Testing of concept
4	Business case evaluation
5	Development and testing of product
6	Market testing
7	Product launch

customer groups and gauge overall levels of demand. Market testing also helps the organisation determine if the marketing mix selected is successful in attracting the targeting customer segment. A downside of test marketing is that competitor organisations get to see the new product and may have time to react by launching their own new product or distorting the test by some form of promotional activity. This potential disadvantage has to be considered against the reduction in risk achieved by test marketing, which reduces the level of loss the organisation may sustain if the new product fails.

The last stage of the new product development is full market rollout. The final decision as to whether to launch a new offering is based on the results of the test market and may be a direct copy of this, or it may be amended based on any identified weakness.

CASE 9.3   South African blacks begin to bowl, bat ... and chat

One afternoon in Johannesburg last week, I passed a group of black men dancing in the road outside Houghton golf club. It was a protest dance and they turned out to be workers at the club picketing over pay.

They waved their placards at every passing car. One driver swayed in his seat in solidarity, while a black man turning his BMW into the club's driveway grinned uneasily. Later two workers sang a jocular appeal to the president of Zimbabwe: 'Mugabe, come and save us.' Simultaneously, at the other end of the country, the South African cricket team were beating England in a one-day game. The point is that most South African blacks seem to have other things to worry about than cricket. Black Africans – as distinct from 'Coloureds' or 'Asians' – make up three-quarters of the country's population, but few of them have been spotted in the stands during the series that ends tomorrow. Black newspapers have mostly ignored the matches. Cricket still appears far removed from the 'new South Africa'.

In fact, appearances are deceptive. South African blacks are discovering cricket, and this is good for the country. Blacks here have played cricket since the 1850s, when the British began sending the sons of chiefs to schools that used the game as a 'civilising' influence. Many blacks learnt cricket at mission schools. However, after apartheid arrived, little more was heard about this tradition. J.M. Coetzee, reviewing a book of pre-1910 photographs from South Africa, concludes: 'Many of [the pictures] are poignant, less for what they represent than for what they promise and what failed to arrive. A snap (dated 1900), for instance, of ragged black children playing cricket (untutored, unsupervised) in the veld outside Aliwal North.' Coetzee is too dismissive. Many blacks played cricket throughout apartheid, particularly in the eastern Cape. The great-grandfather of the current Test player, Monde Zondeki, founded a black club in King William's Town in 1939.

The game was most popular among better-educated blacks. Andre Odendaal notes in his magnificent Story of an African Game that black cricketing and political families often belonged to the same small African elite. It's no coincidence that Zondeki's uncle, Steve Tshwete, was a senior ANC figure and later sports minister. Further north, the cricket-loving former mission schoolboy Mugabe is another example.

But black matches under apartheid were not televised, not often reported, and not played against the world's best teams, and so they were forgotten. It came to appear as if only whites played. Twenty years ago, visiting my grandparents in Johannesburg, I attended a cricket camp where every kid was white except an Indian boy. All the others called him 'Ranji', after the great Indian cricketer Ranjitsinji. To these boys, the notion that blacks might play cricket was as foreign as the notion that women might. Then, 15 years ago yesterday, Nelson Mandela walked out of Victor Verster prison and the transition began. The whites who ran cricket spread the game. Pitches were built in townships, and black kids learnt the forward defensive.

Watching the series against England, you'd think little had changed. South Africa's sole regular black inter-national is Makhaya Ntini. Only three other black Africans have played Test cricket, none for more than four matches. Yet the blacks are coming. On the playing fields of the posh white schools that traditionally produce South Africa's international cricketers, you now see a few flannelled black boys. Give it a couple more years and this generation should start breaking into the national team.

Already blacks watch cricket on television. The golf club workers do, for instance. If they don't go to games, it's partly because the grounds are in white neighbourhoods and the tickets expensive. But BMI-Sport Info, a market research company, found that since 1992 the number of adult South Africans who followed cricket had grown by 4 per cent a year. Cricket is the second most popular sport among South African fans, after football, and the third most popular among black men, after football and boxing.

Silly as cricket may be, this is good news for South Africa. First, everyone should have the right to discover this maddening game and waste years of their life on it. Second, in every country, sport is part of the national conversation. One of South Africa's problems is that blacks and whites have little in common to chat about: their life expectancies, neighbourhoods and chosen sports don't overlap much. If only blacks could join whites in moaning about Kevin Pietersen playing for England instead of South Africa, it would help to build the nation.

Source: S. Kuper, *Financial Times*, 12 February 2005

Questions

1. Where on the product life cycle would you place South African cricket before the end of apartheid, and why?

2. Where would you now place South African cricket, and why?

3. How could South African cricket be made to appeal to the wider South African population?

Conclusions

The relationship of the sports provider and the sport participant based on their direct or indirect consumption of the product offering (direct = playing a game; indirect = watching the game) is more complex than normally associated with most goods. The relationship is based on how the customer views the benefits they gain from purchase and its use within a specific situation. In the case of dedicated sports fans, the actual game they attend provides only a small part of the product they consume. For those fans, the product also includes the lengthy discussions they have with other fans as to tactics, result and questionable decisions made by the referee or line judge during the game. That fan may also want to demonstrate his or her strong association with the club by buying merchandise such as replica shirts, hats or scarves; using an affinity credit card; and subscribing to sponsored magazines or a TV station. This makes them highly loyal and as a combined body of consumers, very powerful in the sense that they can show discontent via protests or by not attending future games if dissatisfied by the actions of the club. The challenge for those marketing sports clubs and their related offerings is to deal with the consequences caused by failure to gain sporting success. Because of the powerful link between success on the field by a team or an individual, the marketing of such sport products has to be undertaken differently to that described in other product sectors. For example, the strategies highlighted for each stage of the product life cycle cannot overcome a decline in ticket sales caused by consistent sporting failure. For these types of organisations, marketing effort must be directed at managing customers' expectations and ensuring consistent quality of service. This means understanding the total experience of a sports fan or user of the sporting facilities and how it is shaped by the service provided by the organisation.

For other sports-related offerings, the type of marketing activities seen in managing general consumer products is much more relevant. These are products that are less influenced by the success of one team or an individual. Such products tend to be purchased because they enable a hobby to be conducted (e.g., buying a fishing rod) or are related to an individual's desire to be seen as sporty (e.g., drinking a fitness drink, using a sports branded deodorant, wearing sports fashion clothing). These products progress through the various stages outlined in the product life cycle concept. Product managers have to continually realign these offerings to ensure that they fit the ever-changing needs and wants of customers. This means adapting each element of the marketing mix based on where the product is within the product life cycle. Organisations that supply such offerings have to continually seek new products to develop and launch as existing ones lose market share and decrease in profitability.

Consumers evaluate the quality of a service based on their experiences of other services. A key aspect of this is based on the particular consumer's view of what quality is and how the supplying organisation delivers it. As other service providers compete on the quality of their service, consumers' overall expectations of what is acceptable is likely to increase. For example, betting shops have moved into the retail high streets in the United Kingdom and have adopted sales environments similar to travel agents and other retail outlets. This has helped move them from something being considered as 'seedy' organisations into the main stream of retailing, which in turn has enabled them to attract different customer segments. The challenge for organisations that are skilled in delivering sporting excellence is how to develop infrastructure of the same quality, complemented by a range of service offerings that add to the overall consumption feeling. The joining of both elements of the sport product is a financial challenge as well as an activity that requires the application of service product management technique. Sports clubs that fail to do this successfully will inevitably limit the range of customer segments that may wish to attend their events.

Discussion questions

1. From the perspective of a fan, describe how you would define a sport product, such as watching a game of football, ice hockey or cricket.
2. How do the fans' perspective of what a sports activity is differ from the supplying organisation's perspective?
3. Advise a sports governing body, such as the Union of European Football Associations or the World Lawn Tennis Association, on how they could generate new product ideas.

Guided reading

To gain a more detailed overview of the physical marketing products, read Chapters 8 to 10 of *Principles and Practices of Marketing*, 4th edition, by Jobber (2004). In these chapters, Jobber covers the product concept, physical goods marketing mix, branding, portfolio management and new product development.

To understand the challenges facing service producers in marketing their offering a good source is *Services Marketing, People, Technology, Strategy*, 5th edition, by Lovelock and Wirzt (2004). Particularly relevant chapters to understanding the type of issues facing sport marketers can be found in Chapter 4, which explore the planning principles of creating the service product; Chapter 9, which looks at how demand and supply capacity can be balanced; and Chapter 11, which highlights the critical role that employees have in the service delivery process.

For a holistic overview of sport marketing, read Chapter 6 by Sullivan in *The Business of Sport Management*, edited by Beech and Chadwick. This chapter links key marketing concepts such as who the sports customer is, what different types of customer segments can be identified and how their needs can be satisfied by various forms of sports offerings.

Keywords

Competitive strategies; format; product life cycle (PLC); pure product; pure service; SERVQUAL; shop; specialist retailers; standardisation.

Bibliography

Booms, B.H. and Bitner, M.J. (1981) 'Marketing strategies and organisational structures for service firms', in J.H. Donnelly and W. R. George (eds), *Marketing of Services*, Chicago: American Marketing Association, pp. 47–51.

Booz, Allen and Hamilton (1982) *New Product Management for the 1980s*, New York: Booz, Allen and Hamilton, Inc.

Borden, N.H. (1965) 'The concept of the marketing mix', in G. Schwartze (ed.), *Science on Marketing*, New York: Wiley, pp. 386–97.

Chase, R.B. (1978) Where does the customer fit in a service organisation?, *Harvard Business Review* 56:137–42.

Harness, D.R. (2004) Product elimination: A financial services model, *International Journal of Bank Marketing* 22(3):161–79.

Jobber, D. (2004) *Principles and Practice of Marketing*, 4th edn, London: McGraw-Hill.

Kelly, D. and Storey, C. (2000) New service development: Initiation strategies, *International Journal of Services Industry Management* 11(1):45–65.

Kotler, P., Armstrong, G., Saunders, J. and Wong, V. (1999), *Principles of Marketing*, European edn, London: Prentice Hall.

Lovelock, C. and Wirzt, J. (2004) *Services Marketing, People, Technology, Strategy*, 5th edn, Englewod Cliffs, NJ: Prentice Hall.

Miracle, G.L. (1965) Product characteristics and marketing strategy, *Journal of Marketing* 29:18–24.

Parasurman, A., Zeithaml, A. and Berry, L. (1988) SERVQUAL: A multiple item scale for measuring consumer perceptions of service quality, *Journal of Retailing* 64:12–40.

Rafiq, M. and Pervaiz, A.K. (1995) Using the 7Ps as a generic marketing mix: An exploratory survey of UK and European marketing academics, *Marketing Intelligence and Planning* 13(9):4–15.

Rathmall, J.M. (1966) What is meant by services?, *Journal of Marketing* 30:32–6.

Shostack, L.G. (1977) Breaking free from product marketing, *Journal of Marketing* 21(2):73–80.

Sullivan, M. (2004) 'Sport marketing', in J. Beech and S. Chadwick (eds), *The Business of Sport Management*, Harlow: FT-Prentice Hall.

Voss, C. (1992) Applying service concepts in manufacturing, *International Journal of Operations and Production Management* 123(4):93–9.

Recommended websites

Lucozade Sport
http://www.lucozadesport.com

Manchester United Football Club
http://www.manutd.com

The Sports Industries Federation
http://www.thesportslife.com

The Sports Journal
http://www.thesportjournal.org

Chapter 10

Developing and extending sports brands

Artemisia Apostolopoulou
Robert Morris University
James M. Gladden
University of Massachusetts, Amherst

Learning outcomes

Upon completion of this chapter, the reader should be able to:

- Define what is meant by brand development and brand extension.

- Identify the key characteristics of brand development and brand extension.

- Discuss the advantages and disadvantages for sport businesses seeking to develop and extend their brands.

- Highlight challenges for managers seeking to develop and extend their brands.

- Indicate strategies and techniques that may be used to address these challenges.

Overview of chapter

This chapter looks at sport organisations as brands and examines opportunities and challenges in their development and extension. The chapter is organised in two sections: The first section focuses on developing sports brands and includes a comprehensive discussion of brand equity theory as it applies to sport organisations. Strategies and techniques for brand development are also illustrated. The second section focuses on extending sports brands and discusses topics such as the benefits and challenges of using brand extension strategies, variables that can assist sport organisations in succeeding with their brand extension efforts and the role of fan identification in extending sports brands. Both sections include definitions and examples of key terms.

To further illustrate the points discussed in the text, this chapter also includes two case studies. The first one explores brand development issues by studying the NASCAR organisation and the second case study examines brand extension techniques through the study of the NBA's Jam Session.

Introduction

If the 20th century solidified for sport managers the need to run sport organisations as businesses, then the 21st century has certainly taught us to look at sport organisations as brands that can be developed and extended. Professional clubs, athletes, sporting competitions and sport governing bodies are considered brands, and they offer many opportunities for exploitation. Similar to mainstream brands, sports brands need comprehensive brand management programmes for the creation of brand equity and the implementation of extension strategies in order to maintain success and profitability.

Definitions

Before exploring how to develop and extend sports brands, it is important to understand what a brand is. A *brand* consists of the name, logo, symbol and other marks associated with an organisation, company or person that distinguish that entity from others in the same category (Aaker, 1991). Entities such as the National Basketball Association (NBA), FC Bayern Munich, Maccabi Tel Aviv, the International Olympic Committee (IOC), FIFA, Asics and David Beckham are a few examples of sports brands. At a time when consumers have increased choices, information and bargaining power, brands serve as a 'shorthand' for quality and are used to project a certain image about those who consume them (D'Alessandro, 2001, p. 17).

With the brand as a starting point, Keller (2003) discusses the idea of *strategic brand management*, which refers to 'the design and implementation of marketing programs and activities to build, measure, and manage brand equity' (p. 44). He proposes four steps in strategic brand management:

1. Determining the desired positioning for the brand as well as the brand's core values
2. Designing and executing brand-building marketing programmes
3. Measuring the performance of the brand
4. Growing the brand by using extension strategies

A term that has been used extensively to describe the strength of a brand is *brand equity*. Brand equity refers to the 'added value' that a brand name provides to a product (Farquhar, 1989, p. 24). Brand equity can also be seen as the strength of the brand. Boone, Kochunny and Wilkins (1995) describe brand equity as '. . . the premium a purchaser would pay for a branded good or service compared to the amount that would be paid for an identical unbranded version of the same item' (p. 33). Consider, for example, a consumer shopping for running shoes; he could potentially find a pair of unbranded running shoes for €25–€40. A similar pair of Nike running shoes would probably cost that consumer anywhere between €80 and €120. The difference in price claimed and collected by Nike is a result of the equity of its brand.

In his discussion, Aaker (1991) describes brand equity as positive or negative elements that enhance or take away from the value of a brand. He also outlines four components that play a role in creating equity for a brand: perceived quality, brand awareness, brand associations and brand loyalty:

- *Perceived quality* refers to consumers' evaluation of a brand when considering the overarching purpose of the product as well as alternative options (Aaker, 1991). There is a perception of high quality when fans think that in a given season their favourite club will win the championship (which serves as the team's intended purpose).

■ *Brand awareness* is consumers' ability to recall a brand when the competitive landscape in which the brand competes is mentioned (Aaker, 1991). For example, a franchise that is well known regionally, nationally and internationally enjoys high levels of brand awareness.

■ *Brand associations* are the feelings and thoughts consumers hold for a brand (Aaker, 1991). A club whose following demonstrates high levels of fan identification enjoys positive brand associations.

■ Lastly, *brand loyalty* refers to a brand's ability to attract consumers and to keep them and indicates how connected consumers are to a brand (Aaker, 1991). A club with high levels of brand loyalty is one that consistently sells out and one that also has a loyal media following. Thus, having a strong brand opens up a number of opportunities – and profit sources, of course – for any organisation or individual.

Brand development

According to Aaker (1991), 'Brand equity does not just happen. Its creation, maintenance, and protection need to be actively managed. Further, it involves strategic as well as tactical programs and policies' (p. 275). Keller (2003) proposes three steps in building brand equity.

1. Choosing the elements of the brand. In the sport context, a sport organisation looking to develop its brand should carefully select its name, logo, colours, other marks, slogan, mascot and so on. For example, the Charlotte Bobcats, a new team in the NBA, held a public contest to identify the team's nickname (Bobcats) and selected orange as one of the team colours because of its popularity and uniqueness.

2. Creating marketing programmes involving the brand with tactics relating to each of the 4Ps (i.e., product, place, price and promotion). For example, sport organisations can develop different ticket packages, place merchandise stores in strategic locations and use sales promotions to attract fans to the games.

3. Exploiting relationships that a brand might have with other entities. In the sport setting this means leveraging a club's participation in European Cup competitions or Final Four tournaments, promoting a brand's relationships with celebrity endorsers or using retired players as spokespeople for the club.

In an effort to understand and manage them better, sport organisations are increasingly being looked at as brands with elements that can be exploited for the benefit of the organisation and their stakeholders (e.g., owners, athletes, fans, sponsors, media partners). In the first research endeavour looking at sport organisations as brands, Boone et al. (1995) argued that measuring the equity of professional teams might be a rather challenging task because teams constitute 'non-traditional products' (p. 34). Their effort to measure brand equity of US professional baseball clubs included calculating the franchise value of Major League Baseball teams, only to conclude that because of inadequate efforts and practices from management, those franchises are not meeting their potential.

Gladden, Milne and Sutton (1998) followed this up by providing a framework for understanding brand equity at the collegiate level. The authors argued that brand equity is developed from a number of antecedents relevant to that particular organisation that lead to certain marketplace consequences. In turn, those outcomes can later influence the antecedents of that organisation in a cyclical process.

In the case of a North American Division I collegiate athletic department, antecedents that can create brand equity include the on-the-field success of the programme, the head coach, star player(s), the tradition and reputation of the programme, the conference and schedule, game entertainment, local and regional media coverage, the location, competition and fan support. Consequences include national media coverage, ticket sales, merchandise sales, sponsorships, donations and the atmosphere (Gladden et al., 1998).

In a follow-up study, Gladden and Milne (1999) adapted the brand equity framework to the professional sport setting by including two new antecedents – the team's logo and the venue in which the team competes – and replacing the consequence of donations (which is more relevant to collegiate sport) by additional revenues. In this study, brand equity was seen as a function of a franchise's value or as a function of a club's ability to charge high prices for their tickets in addition to considering a club's sell outs and winning percentage over the past 25 years. The results indicated that brand equity – as well as success – played a significant role in generating merchandise sales for a professional team. This study was important because it dispelled the notion that only winning leads to positive marketplace outcomes. For, it documented the fact that brand equity had a unique predictive relationship with positive marketplace consequences.

Even though the existing literature has not examined every single setting and level of sport competition, all sport managers could adapt the brand equity framework (suggested by Gladden et al., 1998) to their organisation and identify the antecedents that are relevant in their setting, as well as the consequences that are most favourable for that organisation. After that happens, the sport manager should focus his or her efforts on manipulating the antecedents in order to achieve favourable outcomes.

Strategies and techniques for developing a brand

In developing brand equity, there are two important considerations: (1) which of the four components of brand equity (i.e., perceived quality, brand awareness, brand associations, brand loyalty) *can* a sport manager influence and (2) which of the four components of brand equity *should* a sport manager influence given the situation the organisation is in. The following section discusses each of the four parts of brand equity (as presented by Aaker, 1991) and provides tactics that could be implemented by sport organisations in order to strengthen each part.

Perceived quality

Of the four components of equity, *perceived quality* is probably the one that a sport manager can control the least. Fans' perception of quality is tied primarily to the on-the-field success and other team-related aspects of a club. For example, if a team wins the Euroleague championship or resigns its top player to a multiyear contract one season, fans' perception of the team's quality for the following year will most likely increase. However, the sport marketer has limited control over those team-related aspects, at least in terms of decision-making. As Mullin, Hardy and Sutton (2000) argue, the core sport product is out of the control of the sport marketer.

What the sport marketer *can* do, however, is use brand elements such as a star coach and players – that are uncontrollable otherwise – and market them to create a perception of a quality organisation. For example, promoting Jurgen Klinsmann's appointment as the new head coach of Germany's national football team could create a high perception of quality for the team. Special promotions and offerings tied to a winning season could prove quite effective in reinforcing the image of a quality organisation. In addition, a promotional campaign involving the coaching staff and the players (e.g., advertising spots, talk shows, profiles, bios), as well as a comprehensive community relations plan (e.g., visits to schools, hospitals and children's institutions, lectures series, sport camps, autograph sessions, fundraisers) could help to portray coaches and players as quality individuals.

Another team-related element that could be used by a sport marketer to create a perception of organisational quality is the ownership group of the club. It has been implied that team owners might be another aspect of the sport product from which fans derive feelings and thoughts about the team (Gladden and Funk, 2002). For example, Dominique Wilkins is one of the investors and executive staff members of the Atlanta Hawks of the NBA. This fact could work favourably for the Hawks organisation if people who supported and admired Wilkins as a basketball player transfer those feelings to the Hawks basketball club to create a perception of quality.

Even though, as mentioned above, the sport marketer cannot promise a win, he or she can guarantee a quality experience at the game. The sport marketer's leverage lies in his or her control over the peripheral elements of the game, such as the services provided from team employees, the venue, the concessions, the merchandise items and game delivery, just to name a few (Mullin et al., 2000). The sport marketer can create an environment that is fan-friendly and can offer a great overall experience for the fans – even if the final outcome of the game is not favourable for the home team – by guarantying high-quality service from all team employees, cleanliness and safety of the venue, variety and affordability of concessions, adequate selection and high quality of merchandise items and memorable game entertainment. All those elements could increase fans' perception of quality of the parent brand and the core product.

Brand awareness

Budget permitting, *brand awareness* might be the easiest component for the sport marketer to control. Even though regional and especially national media coverage typically comes as a result of high brand equity, a sport manager could design a comprehensive promotional plan to increase awareness levels of the organisation. That plan could use multiple elements of promotion (e.g., advertising, personal selling, sales promotions) to create a buzz around the organisation and familiarise people with the various programmes and services offered by the club. For example, information about the schedule, the opponents (including existing rivalries), player transactions, community relations initiatives (e.g., player appearances, autograph sessions), extension products or services and anything else relating to the organisation should be communicated to the public to encourage involvement with the team and to increase their excitement and affinity for the organisation.

One of the unique elements of the sport product is the amount of publicity (i.e., free exposure) that sport organisations and sport celebrities receive (Mullin et al., 2000). In a way, that makes the job of the sport marketer easier. However, because publicity – unlike advertising – is not sponsored or paid for, it can be positive *and* negative. To use this tool to the benefit of the organisation, the sport marketer should develop positive relationships with the media by initiating communication with media representatives, providing them access to club-related information, including them in team functions and maintaining honesty and integrity in their interactions. By doing this, the organisation can reap the benefits of widespread coverage from the press while possibly protecting the team from negative publicity if unfortunate incidents (e.g., scandals) occur.

Brand associations

Brand associations include all feelings, emotions and ideas that fans might have about a sport organisation. Keller (1993) proposes that the three types of brand associations are attributes, benefits and attitudes. *Attributes* include elements or characteristics of a brand and can be *product related* and *non-product related*. *Benefits* refer to the value consumers seek in a brand and can be *functional*, *experiential* and *symbolic*. Finally, *attitudes* include the overall perception consumers hold about a brand and result to a great extent from consumers' perceptions of the brand's attributes and benefits.

In an effort to explore brand associations in the professional team setting, Gladden and Funk (2002) identified 16 dimensions as possible sources of brand associations and tested those to create the 'Team Association Model'. This model includes the following dimensions:

- **Attributes:** Success, star player, head coach, management, logo design, stadium, product delivery and tradition
- **Benefits:** Escape, fan identification, peer group acceptance, nostalgia and pride in place
- **Attitudes:** Importance, knowledge and affect

The challenge but also the opportunity for the sport marketer lies in identifying which of these brand associations are significant for fans and creating programmes to satisfy those. For example, knowing that *nostalgia* is considered by fans as an important element of the game experience could lead the marketer to plan events with retired players, produce a video with past successful seasons of the team, offer merchandise with past team logos or design appropriate theme nights.

According to Keller (2003), brand associations are instrumental in forming the *image* of a brand, an important component of *customer-based brand equity* (the other component of CBBE is *brand awareness*). The author also argues that brand associations are evaluated based on their strength, favourability and uniqueness.

- *Strength* of brand associations can be created by consistently providing consumers with relevant information about the organisation (brand; Keller, 2003). In the sport setting, this means conveying information about the club – preferably, information that has personal significance to consumers – on a regular basis through various communication media (e.g., TV shows, newspapers, magazines) and letting the fans in on inside information about the organisation. For example, one of the NBA's newer initiatives includes placing microphones on coaches and sharing with fans information that is conveyed during time-outs. Another initiative involves the league's development league, the National Basketball Development League (NBDL), and a reality sports show entitled 'Life on the Down Low: The D League', which featured one of the NBDL's teams and focused on the creation of the franchise and the life and dreams of its players.

- *Favourability* of brand associations is created by relating to consumers that the brand offers them desired and valued benefits (Keller, 2003). In sport, that could be achieved by on-the-field success (which, of course, cannot be controlled by the sport marketer) or fan and community initiatives, such as player appearances and meet-and-greet sessions that have a direct impact on how fans feel about the sports club. The goal in all of these activities is to have the sport consumer think positive thoughts when various team associations occur. What makes this challenging is that the associations vary from market to market and team to team. For example, Manchester United of the Premiere League has associations tied to success on the playing field, the red colour in their kits, and with their historic stadium, Old Trafford. Meanwhile, the Chicago Bulls of the NBA probably have their most significant association with a former player, Michael Jordan.
- Lastly, *uniqueness* of brand associations serves to distinguish one brand from another and creates an image of superiority for a brand (Keller, 2003). In the sport context, emotions and thoughts that are linked to the tradition of a particular club can serve to differentiate that organisation from others and to create *unique* brand associations. In the greater leisure and entertainment context, sports brands often have an advantage creating unique associations given the highly emotional nature of sport. Not many other entertainment options evoke such emotion.

Brand associations – especially those that are strong, favourable and unique – are very important because they can strengthen other components of equity such as perceived quality and brand loyalty. Research has shown that fans' brand associations – more particularly, attributes and benefits – can help explain almost half (47%) of the variance of fans' loyalty to their favourite team (Gladden and Funk, 2001). Sport marketers should create marketing and promotional plans to strengthen the associations that are more relevant to fans in hopes of creating a loyal fan base.

However, brand associations are not always controllable by the sport marketer. Many things can happen that could impact the strength, favourability and uniqueness of brand associations and subsequently impact how a fan thinks or feels about a sports club. For example, a player caught using steroids or arrested for driving under the influence of alcohol, a coach involved in a gambling scandal and the practice of illegal or unethical operations can cause fans to develop negative associations about that brand. The job of the sport marketer is to create enough goodwill through marketing and branding programmes that can protect the brand when unfortunate incidents occur (D'Alessandro, 2001).

Brand loyalty

The fourth component of brand equity is *brand loyalty*, which is the ability of a team to develop and keep fans (Aaker, 1991). Loyalty is illustrated by the things consumers do (*behavioural loyalty*), as well as consumers' perceptions and attitudes towards the brand (*attitudinal loyalty*). In the sport context, behavioural loyalty is demonstrated through fans' attendance of team games, their purchase of team merchandise and the length of their loyalty to a particular team (Gladden and Funk, 2001). Attitudinal loyalty, on the other hand, involves fans' commitment to and affiliation with their favourite team, as well as their willingness to follow that team (Gladden and Funk, 2001). Both types of loyalty are necessary in order to maintain a steady stream of loyal fans.

Loyalty is important because it protects a brand from competition and allows the brand a chance to charge increased prices, creating a stream of revenues (Aaker, 1996). Aaker (1996) proposed two measures of brand loyalty: price premium and customer satisfaction. *Price premium* is 'the amount a customer will pay for the brand in comparison with another brand (or set of comparison brands) offering similar benefits' (Aaker, 1996, p. 106). Furthermore, Aaker suggests that brand loyalty can also be measured through consumers' level of satisfaction with the brand, their intention to purchase the brand (over competitors' brands) and their willingness to recommend the brand to other consumers (Aaker, 1996).

Sport might be unique compared with other brands in that its consumers become loyal at an early age and rarely shift their loyalty to support a competitor team. For example, the two most popular Greek clubs, Olympiakos and Panathinaikos, have sworn fans who have been following their favourite team for most of their lives and would never consider supporting the rival team. However, the biggest mistake a sport marketer could make would be to take fans' loyalty for granted. Even if it is highly unlikely that fans of Olympiakos would cheer for Panathinaikos, the extent to which they invest in *their* team (e.g., by buying season tickets, attending games, purchasing merchandise, patronising other team-sponsored initiatives) has a great impact on the success of the organisation.

A sport marketer can enhance fans' loyalty in several ways. Such efforts should be geared towards increasing both behavioural and attitudinal loyalty, as well as increasing fans' satisfaction levels. Promotional and communications tactics should be implemented to encourage fans to follow their favourite team by attending games, watching broadcasts or reading about the team. Efforts to provide a superb experience at the game through excellent service, entertaining product delivery, perks and fan appreciation initiatives, and quality of concessions and other venue-related aspects could increase fans' satisfaction and encourage them to repeatedly attend team events. Also, access to the team through opportunities for fans to directly interact with the coaches and players could significantly strengthen fans' identification with the club, leading to increased brand loyalty.

Advantages of brand development

Enhancing each of the four elements discussed above, as well as the overall equity of a brand is critical for the long-term success of sport organisations. Keller (2003) has discussed a number of positive outcomes of brand equity. Brand equity can lead to increased loyalty and protection from competition, which translates into retaining sports fans and protecting the club from competition from other sporting and entertainment options, thus claiming a greater share of fans' discretionary income. Brand equity can protect a club from crises, such as scandals with coaches and players that can result in negative publicity for the organisation.

Furthermore, brand equity can allow a club to increase ticket prices and the overall cost of attending games without the risk of losing its consumers. Brand equity can assist the sports club in negotiating more favourable deals with media and licensing partners and making the organisation an attractive property for corporate sponsors. Finally, high equity allows a club to grow by engaging in brand extension strategies and successfully introducing a variety of sport- and non-sport-related products and services.

■ Challenges of brand development

However, developing a sports brand and creating brand equity is no easy task. Several challenges can hinder this process, not the least of which is the marketing and management expertise and skill level of team executives. Limitations in staff members' experience in running their organisations as businesses could limit their ability to realise the needs and potential of their organisations (brands). Efforts such as the Union of European Football Associations' new guidelines and regulations regarding team personnel and organisation could encourage – by requiring – a new approach in club management, possibly creating the conditions for a more sophisticated approach in brand development.

Another challenge is the short-term approach often adopted by sports clubs steered by an almost exclusive focus on winning. However, building a strong brand is a long-term process (Aaker, 1991). For sports clubs to benefit from brand development, they need to shift their focus from short-term outcomes to long-term design and efforts to build a strong brand that will go beyond the on-the-field success of the team. Lastly, in the process of developing a strong brand, it is important for sport marketers to balance their efforts to continually refresh their brand's message while maintaining a consistent image of what their brand represents (Keller, 2003).

Extending sports brands

The multiple pressures facing sport organisations in the new millennium – the need to increase profits and to strengthen their relationship with their fans – have forced many organisations to look for new avenues to generate revenues. Using their brand to offer a wide array of new products or services – in other words, *extending* their brand – is one way to enter existing or new markets and create new monies.

From a financial standpoint, sport organisations are realising the opportunity that exists in the *equity* associated with their brand name. That equity can be translated into financial success in other endeavours the organisation undertakes. The appeal of a sport team and fans' affinity with that team can provide a platform for new products and services to be introduced.

In their discussion of the sport product, Mullin et al. (2000) argue that the core sport product consists of the players and coaches, the venues, the equipment and the rules of the game. Everything else is part of the extensions of the core product. In that category, they include memorabilia, fan fests, fantasy camps and cruises, the ticket, personnel and the organisation – in general, anything that helps *extend* the experience of the fan. With that in mind, programmes, products and services that are introduced under the umbrella of a sport organisation (and are different from the core product) can be considered extensions of that organisation.

■ Definitions

When expanding, a brand can use its name on new products and services in a category that is already being served by that brand or in a different category. The new offerings in the first case are considered *line extensions* and the ones in the latter case are considered *brand (category) extensions* (Keller, 2003). Examples of line extensions include products that differ from the core product in terms of their flavour, texture, intended use and so on. For example, Coca-Cola has introduced several variations of its cola product, such as Diet Coke, Vanilla Coke, Cherry Coke, and, more recently, C2. However, Coca-Cola also offers a variety of other products (collectibles) that bear the Coca-Cola brand name and marks but are not part of the caffeinated beverage category, such as posters, containers and glasses. Those products are considered brand extensions. In the sport setting, ESPN's *ESPN2*, an affiliate television station, is a line extension; however, *ESPN: The Magazine* is a brand extension of the network.

In the recent years, sport organisations have extended their brands to offer a number of peripheral products and services. Research in the area of sports brand extensions suggested that most of the extension products that are introduced by US professional teams are sport related, entertainment related, media related or information related (Apostolopoulou, 2002b). A number of other extensions have been introduced by sports clubs that are conceptually more distant from the parent brand (low perceived fit). Examples of those include toiletries, health and fitness clubs, art galleries and credit cards (Apostolopoulou, 2002b; Chadwick and Clowes, 1998).

To enter new markets and capture different groups of consumers, brands can also expand vertically by manipulating their price and quality. This technique, known as vertical extension, can involve an upward or downward direction. A *step-up* extension involves a product of higher quality and higher price than the original offering of the brand; a *step-down* extension is a product of lower quality and lower price (Kim and Lavack, 1996).

Although that technique has not been very prevalent in sport, the NBDL, a minor league of the NBA, has been examined as a step-down extension of the parent league (Apostolopoulou, 2005). That case discussed a number of *distancing techniques* that were used to create a close connection originally and a conceptual distance later on between the parent brand and the extension.

Using brand extensions as a brand-building tool

In his discussion of building and managing brands, Keller (2003) argues that one way to grow a brand and to maintain brand equity is through brand extension strategies. He suggests that brand extensions can be used to revive a brand and to 'renew interest and liking' for the brand (Keller, 2003, p. 589).

In 1991, when the US-based National Football League (NFL) introduced the World League of American Football (WLAF), an intercontinental extension football league (renamed NFL Europe in 1998), it was seen as a strategy to grow the parent brand (i.e., NFL), which was maturing (Campbell and Kent, 2002). Having succeeded in and captured a great share of the US market, the NFL used this particular extension as an inroad to new markets (i.e., mainly European) and as a stage to expose new consumers to its core product, American football.

In addition, brand extensions assist the building of a brand by broadening the meaning of that brand to include more product or service categories and possibly the opportunity to compete in a different industry (Keller, 2003). For example, until recently, attending a professional basketball game in Greece was exactly that: attending a professional basketball game; the game was the appetiser, the entrée and the dessert. That restricted offering limited the meaning of the team to a *sport* brand. However, attending a Major League Baseball (MLB) game is more than a game; it is food, drinking, music, announcers, mascots, games, promotions, giveaways and auto-graph sessions. All those extensions broaden the meaning of the sport team to include entertainment elements – in addition to the core product (i.e., the game) – promoting it to an *entertainment* brand.

Advantages of brand extensions

Consumer brands use brand extensions as a strategy to grow and diversify. Either by identifying a need in the market or by creating one, they introduce new products to their brand portfolio. In doing so, companies need to decide whether they will offer that new product under their parent brand name or a new brand name. Enough evidence in the literature suggests that introducing a new product under an existing brand name could be beneficial in a number of ways.

One of the advantages of brand extensions is that consumers can use their prior knowledge of and experience with an existing brand to judge an extension of that brand (Keller, 2003). Positive associations that consumers might have about the parent brand could transfer to the extension, more so if consumers are able to link the two products on some basis (Aaker and Keller, 1990). Furthermore, it has been shown that extensions require lower promotional investments than new brands (Smith and Park, 1992) and are in a more favourable position with retailers in terms of negotiating shelf space (Keller, 2003).

Another advantage of introducing brand extensions is their potential benefit to the parent brand. Successful extensions can work in favour of the parent brand if they serve to satisfy a variety of needs consumers might have and may retain consumers who might have otherwise switched to another brand to satisfy a particular need (Keller, 2003). Given that the consumer has a good experience with the extension, it can lead to positive associations towards the parent brand or bring to the company new consumers who had no past experience with the parent brand (Keller and Aaker, 1992; Swaminathan, Fox and Reddy, 2001).

In the case of sports brands, in which fans already have an established relationship with a particular team and demonstrate varying levels of fan identification, extensions can serve to provide more opportunities to fans to interact with the franchise or to enhance fans' experience with the team (Apostolopoulou, 2002b; Sutton, McDonald, Milne and Cimperman, 1997). Conversely, fans' affinity towards that organisation encourages their patronage of team-related line or brand extensions. As Wann and Branscombe (1993) illustrated, fans experiencing high levels of identification with a sport team invest more resources in support of that team, which could easily mean supporting that team's extensions.

Reasons for introducing sports brand extensions

Although a prime reason for which consumer brands introduce brand extensions is to build the brand by capturing a larger share of the market and strengthening the company's bottom line (Aaker, 1990), the same might not always be true for sport organisations. Some of the extensions introduced by sport teams can indeed serve as additional revenue sources for the organisation. However, there are a number of other extensions that even though they do not add much to the team's cash register, they assist the efforts of the parent brand to connect with core consumers, expand its reach, enhance its presence in the community, strengthen a positive image and give people more opportunities to experience the brand (Apostolopoulou, 2002b).

The NBA's Jam Session initiative (discussed more extensively as a case study in this chapter) is run in conjunction with the NBA's All-Star Game and is a great example of a brand extension that can achieve all those objectives while possibly also creating some direct or indirect revenues for the league. For a small fee, basketball fans have the opportunity to experience a number of league-related programmes and games, interact with NBA players and other celebrities, enjoy a fan-friendly and festive environment sponsored by the league and hopefully connect with the parent brand in a positive way. This initiative expands the reach of the NBA to people who might not be in a position to afford NBA games, while positioning the league as a caring organisation.

Variables affecting the success of brand extensions in the sport industry

Both the mainstream marketing and sport marketing brand extension literature (e.g., Aaker and Keller, 1990; Apostolopoulou, 2002b; Boush and Loken, 1991; Chadwick and Clowes, 1998; Dacin and Smith, 1994; Keller and Aaker, 1992; Park, Milberg and Lawson, 1991; Smith and Andrews, 1995) suggest that certain variables play a role in whether brand extensions will be successful or not. The most common of these include:

- The strength of the parent brand
- Perceived fit
- Expertise of the parent brand in the extension category
- Location and distribution strategy
- Promotional support
- Quality of the extension
- Management of the extension

These variables are briefly discussed below.

Strength of parent brand

One of the primary reasons for introducing extension products instead of products under a new brand name is that the existing brand name carries certain equity and brand associations that can be beneficial for the extension. Crimmins (2000) argues that, 'Many factors need to be considered in deciding whether to extend a brand name into a new category. One of the key factors is the perceived value the brand name automatically adds for consumers in the new category' (p. 143).

In the case of sports brands, certain athletes (e.g., Zinedine Zidane), professional teams (e.g., AC Milan), leagues (e.g., National Football League) and events or competitions (e.g., Champions League) carry more weight, which could stem from superior skill, popularity, success on the field, history and tradition and competition levels. That weight gives them more clout to introduce successful extension products. Evidence of that is the recent deal signed between the tennis star Andy Roddick and Parlux Fragrances to introduce a fragrance line possibly named 'Andy' (Kaplan, 2004).

The strength of the parent brand becomes particularly important when the category in which the brand is extending is dissimilar from the core category of business.

Literature has suggested that strong brands have more latitude when extending in dissimilar categories than average or weak brands do (Keller and Aaker, 1992). For example, introducing theme restaurants in another continent might be something appropriate for a team such as Manchester United but not a wise investment for a less successful organisation. Capitalising on their popularity and tremendous following, Manchester United has expanded by opening their own chain of Manchester United Reds Café Restaurants in a number of East Asian locations (Stuart, 2002).

Also, as long as there is some meaningful connection between the parent brand and the extension, prior experience and relationship with the parent brand can provide familiarity and a safety net for the consumer who decides to try the extension product (Aaker, 1990). That might be NASCAR's rationale for offering its own branded produce, the first licensed by a league. NASCAR signed a deal with the Castellini Group (a US produce distributor) to allow for their marks to be displayed on the packaging of fruits and vegetables (Lefton, 2004).

Perceived fit

Fit is defined as the extent to which a consumer sees the extension as a logical offering of the parent brand (Tauber, 1988). Most of the studies have examined perceived fit as similarity between the features of a brand's core product and its extension (Boush, Shipp, Loken, Gencturk, Crockett, Kennedy et al., 1987), consumers' evaluation of the two products as substitute or complimentary products (Aaker and Keller, 1990), consistency between the concepts of the two products (Park et al., 1991) and fit between the image of the parent and extension brands (Bhat and Reddy, 1997).

For the extension product to benefit from the existing equity and positive associations of the parent brand, consumers (in this case, the fans) should be able to link the extension to the parent brand. Consumers are able to transfer positive thoughts and impressions that they hold about the parent brand to the extension as long as there is some degree of fit between the two (Aaker and Keller, 1990). When the NFL's extension league was first introduced, its original name, *WLAF*, did not make it obvious that the league was connected to the NFL. The change of name to *NFL Europe* made it easier for fans to trace the extension back to the parent brand and use any perceptions they might have had about the NFL to judge the quality of the extension.

Sport-related research has suggested that when perceived fit is high, fans are more likely to endorse a brand's extensions (Papadimitriou, Apostolopoulou and Loukas, 2004). This research examined a number of extension products and services of the Greek professional club Olympiakos and found that the team's fans were more willing to purchase extensions that had higher perceived fit with the team (i.e., sport-related extensions).

Expertise of parent brand in the extension category

In their study of the role of perceived fit in consumers' evaluation of brand extensions, Aaker and Keller (1990) suggest that another way in which perceived fit can be examined is as consumers' sense of the parent brand's ability to develop a quality product in a different product category. In other words, consumers need to believe that the parent brand has knowledge in the extension category and is able to deliver a product of value.

Especially when introducing extensions that are not sport related, it is important for fans to trust that the team can provide a quality product or service in the new category.

To facilitate expansion into dissimilar product or service categories in which the sports brand has no expertise, relationships could be formed with companies that are experts in that particular area of business. A great illustration of this is provided by Manchester United, which offers an array of non-sport financial services under their MU Finance division in cooperation with a number of other non-sport businesses. Manchester United fans can sign up for a MU credit card provided by MBNA Europe Bank Limited, book their next vacation through Travelcare Direct (the team's official travel partner) or get a MU Finance Insurance Policy promoted by Endsleigh Insurance Services Ltd. Furthermore, to project to fans that these are quality services, the motto on the FU web page reads, 'You support the best team in football. Now let the best team in finance support you!' (Manchester United, 2005).

Location and distribution strategy

Another factor that may play a role in the performance of brand extensions is distribution and location. Placing an extension geographically close to the parent brand by making it available, for example, inside the venue could facilitate the connection of the extension with the parent brand (Apostolopoulou, 2002b). Sports clubs have been doing this for years with venue-based merchandise stores. Similarly, a club could have tables or booths in the concourse of the facility or visible links on the club's website where fans can get information about team-sponsored services and sign up for a team sport camp, a team mobile phone, a team cruise, a team loan or a team fitness centre.

Promotional support

As with any other aspect of sports clubs, supporting team brand extensions through promotional media or through team corporate and marketing partners is imperative for the success of those extensions. Various forms of advertising, sales promotions and public relations should be used to communicate information about the team's extensions and also to create excitement among team supporters. Fans need to not only be informed about the various offerings but also be given reasons to support them. Promotional messages should highlight to fans issues of connecting with the club and demonstrating loyalty and support to the club through the patronage of team-sponsored brand extensions. For example, on its MU Finance web page, Manchester United presents its MU Finance Home Insurance Policy with the line, 'Another way to support your club'. This promotional message also highlights how by signing up for a number of services, fans make a financial contribution to the club and can increase their involvement with the club (e.g., get a team loan and have money to travel to all the away games or to buy a new big-screen TV to watch the team's games).

Promotion could also be used to highlight the relationship between the parent brand and the extension – if it is not already obvious. The team could initiate promotional and communication efforts such as press conferences, launch parties and in-game promotions, just to name a few, to create a buzz around the extension and communicate to fans that the team is involved in the initiative. After introducing its development league (NBDL), the NBA made sure to use promotion to highlight the relationship between the two leagues. Some of the activities included promoting the NBDL on the NBA website, involving the NBDL in NBA community relations programmes, holding NBA games in NBDL arenas, highlighting call-ups of players and coaches to the NBA and so on.

Quality of extension

The literature has suggested that an unsuccessful brand extension can hurt the parent brand by creating negative brand associations (Aaker, 1990). Especially for consumers whose only interaction with a brand is through its extensions, having an unpleasant experience might be enough to alienate them from both the extension and its parent brand. Quality – or lack of – can lead to a negative experience. Consequently, it becomes very important to provide a quality product or service to fans, especially when the name of the sports club is used on that product. Every interaction of the fans with the team or its extensions needs to be a positive experience that enhances fans' relationship with the club and leads to positive perceptions about the franchise.

In the sport setting, fans' affiliation with their favourite team might encourage them to support a number of extensions of that franchise at least once – even those that are quite dissimilar from the core product (e.g., credit card, mobile phone). However, a poor-quality product or service might deter even the most loyal of fans from purchasing that product again and might even cause negative feelings towards the team. For example, a fan might decide to invest in sending her child to a camp run by their favourite team, only to realise that there were no players or coaches participating in the camp, her child ate poor food and her child was given very little instruction over the duration of the camp. No matter how much the fan supports that team, she would most likely not send her child to that camp again and might even go as far as to talk negatively about the franchise.

Management of extension

Another issue, which also speaks to the quality of the extension, relates to the way the brand extension is managed. Because some brand extensions might be very different from the core business of the brand, the organisation might choose to outsource the management of those extensions. In that case, it becomes important that whoever is managing the extension does a professional job and protects the image of the core brand. Using a thorough screening process when choosing business partners to produce, promote, distribute or manage the extension and tying their compensation to the successful performance of the extension are strategies to avoid problems (Apostolopoulou, 2002b). Similarly, if the extension is managed internally, it is crucial that the club staff members involved have the necessary skills and expertise to help the extension succeed.

▪ The role of fan identification in sports brand extensions

Many scholars have examined the construct of *fan identification* and its role in the behaviour of sports fans (e.g., Branscombe and Wann, 1991; Sutton et al., 1997; Wann and Branscombe, 1993; Wann and Dolan, 1994; Wann, Dolan, McGeorge and Allison, 1994). Fan identification refers to fans' psychological connection to a sport team (Wann, Melnick, Russell and Pease, 2001). Sutton et al. (1997) suggest that depending on their investment in the team, fans can be part of one of three groups: *vested*, *focused* and *social* fans. Each of these groups demonstrates varying levels of fan identification, with *vested* fans having the highest levels of identification and increased emotional and financial investment in the team.

Fan identification may play a significant role in fans' response to extension products introduced by their favourite team. Whereas, for the most part, consumer needs drive the purchase of extensions of consumer brands, the need to connect with the team on more levels and to express their affinity towards that team might be the drivers for the purchase of sports brand extensions. It has also been shown that fans with high levels of identification are more willing to spend money and time to follow a team (Wann and Branscombe, 1993), a behaviour that could extend to supporting team-related brand extensions.

In addition, the role of some of the factors that were discussed earlier, such as the strength of the parent brand, might be mediated by the degree to which a fan feels connected to the organisation (Apostolopoulou, 2002a). In other words, high levels of fan identification might compensate for lack of parent brand strength or, in some cases, perceived fit, suggesting that even extensions of weak sports brands can be successful as long as the team has a loyal following willing to support team initiatives. In an effort to explain why fans purchase brand extensions of sport teams, Papadimitriou et al. (2004) found that having fit between the parent brand and the extension explains only part of fans' purchase intention. In their discussion, the authors imply that other variables, such as the level of identification that a fan has with his or her favourite team, might be the main driver for endorsing team-related brand extensions.

If fan identification is a desired condition for successful extensions in the sport setting, then it could also be argued that, by providing more opportunities to fans to experience the team, brand extensions could enhance the symbolic (e.g., fan identification) and experiential (e.g., nostalgia) benefits fans receive from their interaction with the franchise. Furthermore, extension offerings give fans a chance to broaden their involvement with a team by engaging in a variety of team-sponsored initiatives (besides attending games), hence strengthening their loyalty to that brand.

Potential risks of brand extensions

Even though brand extensions can be very beneficial for sport organisations, certain risks should be considered, not the least of which is the possibility to harm the parent brand if the extension performs poorly (Aaker, 1990). An unsuccessful brand extension may lead to financial costs, or, even worse, negative associations towards the parent brand. For example, if a fan eats at a team restaurant and suffers food poisoning, that might reflect poorly on the parent organisation and generate negative associations towards that team.

Another risk of introducing brand extensions is the opportunity cost incurred had an investment in another endeavour or in a new brand produced more beneficial results for the organisation (Keller, 2003). For instance, if, instead of introducing the WLAF/NFL Europe, the NFL had invested that amount in community improvement projects, the league might have received more favourable (monetary and other) returns from its investment. Another alternative could have been for the league to invest in a development league that would appear as a stand-alone brand and not an extension of the NFL.

A major risk associated with the use of brand extension strategies is the possibility of overextending a brand to the point where it is not clear anymore to consumers what the brand stands for (Keller, 2003). Offering a number of new products and services can be beneficial for a team, provided that the team does not lose its focus and that fans do not become confused about the brand's core business. Furthermore, this risk is heightened when teams decide to enter very distant (dissimilar to their core) product categories and introduce offerings such as dairy products (Minnesota Vikings) or produce (NASCAR).

Finally, the chance of hurting (cannibalising) the sales of the parent brand with the brand extension (Aaker, 1990) is something that sport marketers should be aware of, especially if the extension introduced (e.g., another sport league) is directly competing with the parent brand for fans and fans' resources (e.g., money, time).

CASE 10.1	The new NASCAR: in the 'chase' for more revenue, will NASCAR harm its brand?

For an organisation that was founded by on the backs of former 'moonshiners' (people that transported illegal alcohol during the prohibition era in the United States) who raced on dirt race tracks, the National Association of Stock Car Auto Racing (usually known as 'NASCAR') has come a long way.[i] Today, NASCAR's 36 marquis races earn NASCAR an average of $420m (US) annually from two primary broadcast rights holders.[ii] Originally limited to the Southeast portion of the United States, NASCAR has grown into a national phenomenon over the past 10 years. For example, the 2005 season featured 20 races outside of the Southeast, a nearly 100% increase in races outside of the traditional hotbed.[iii] This expansion has been targeted towards increasing NASCAR's presence in traditionally non-NASCAR markets like Chicago, Las Vegas and Southern California.[iv] There is even talk of building a NASCAR track proximate to New York City!

NASCAR also enjoys tremendous sponsor support because of its ability to differentiate itself from the other major sports competitors. For one, NASCAR fans appear to be very inclined to purchase the products of NASCAR sponsors. In one research study, 72% of NASCAR fans indicated that they purchase the products of NASCAR sponsors because of their affiliation with the sport.[v] Secondly, NASCAR has been able to connect its fans with its drivers. NASCAR drivers are well known for two things: interacting with NASCAR fans around the garages where their cars are housed, and regularly thanking the sponsors of their race teams. Finally, NASCAR drivers have not been beset by scandals associated with breaking the law or using performance enhancing (or mind altering) drugs. Thus, if a sponsor is image conscious, they don't have to worry about their brand name being associated with scandalous behaviour.

Beyond the above stated reasons, interest in NASCAR has grown for several reasons. First, it is easier for the average fan to relate to a NASCAR driver because the NASCAR driver is not uniquely large or athletic. Rather, they are just driving cars fast, something most people can relate to. Second, NASCAR's success and popularity has been driven by its ability to convince its popular and powerful drivers to work together over a long and grueling season. As evidenced by the fractioning of Indy Car racing into two racing organisations – the Indy Racing League (IRL) and Champ Car (formerly CART) – it is not always easy to get drivers to work together.

But NASCAR is evolving, and some are questioning whether change is for the better. Related to broadcasting and sponsorship, two significant changes have recently occurred that are significantly changing the face of NASCAR. Both of these changes occurred prior to the 2004 season. First, long-time sponsor Winston (cigarette maker) ended its sponsorship of the points standings ('Winston Cup') that determined who was the best driver of the year. In its place, NASCAR signed a 10 year, $750m (US) with technology provider Nextel.[vi] In its first two years of the agreement, NEXTEL has integrated its product throughout the NASCAR experience. For example, NEXTEL has created 'FanScan', an audio service that allows fans anywhere to listen to communications between drivers and their 'pit crews' during actual races.[vii]

The second change implemented completely revamped the way that the driver of the year was crowned. Beginning in 1975, the driver of the year was decided by a championship points system which allowed drivers to accumulate points over the course of a season. The system was devised in such a manner that consistently good performance over a lot of races was more important than excellence in a few races.[viii] The points system was good for NASCAR in that it made participation in every race important. Because of this, the marquis drivers were racing every weekend, unlike professional golf or tennis, where players pick and choose the tournaments they compete in. Yet, the system sometime resulted in the point winner being determined long before the final race of the season occurred. This had negative implications for the broadcasters, who are now paying hundreds of millions of dollars to televise NASCAR events.

In an effort to ensure significant interest in the final part of the season, the 'Chase for the Nextel Cup' was introduced prior to the 2004 season. In the 'Chase', drivers accumulate points for the first 26 races of the season. After the 26th race, the top 10 drivers are identified and granted a clean slate for the last 10 races of the year. The 10 selected drivers then accumulate new points through participation in each of the final 10 races.

Proponents of the Chase argue that the new system keeps the race for driver of the year going until the final race. In fact, five drivers had a shot at the Nextel Cup entering the final race in 2004.[ix] Because of the increased competition, television ratings for the final race improved 38% in 2004.[x] Meanwhile, opponents of the Chase argue that it does not substantially increase interest in the sport over the entire course of the season. In support of their argument, opponents cite the fact that television ratings for the entire NASCAR season only increased 2% in 2004.[xi] Opponents also suggest that corporate sponsors of cars that do not make the top 10 will be either less likely to renew their sponsorship or look to decrease the dollars they commit to a race team if it finishes out of the top 10. Thus, ultimately they argue that the Chase will be bad for the sport because it could decrease corporate sponsorship dollars overall.

[i] Information on NASCAR's origins pulled from Lipsyte, R. (2001) Perspective: Earnhardt Jr. helps NASCAR find its way back, *New York Times* 15 July, p. 11.
[ii] Bernstein, A. (2004) Dinner conversation: NASCAR renewal talk may come up at banquet, *Street & Smith's SportsBusiness Journal* 29 November, p. 13.
[iii] King, B. and Warfield, S. (2005) Should you believe all you hear about NASCAR?, *Street & Smith's SportsBusiness Journal* 14 February, p. 19.
[iv] Ibid.
[v] Ibid.
[vi] Warfield, S. (2005) Nextel puts its products on starting line, *Street & Smith's SportsBusiness Journal* 14 February, p. 4.
[vii] Ibid.

viii Poole, M. (2004) Successful 'Chase' would reward NASCAR with year round attention, *Street & Smith's SportsBusiness Journal* 6 September, p. 15.
ix Bernstein (2004).
x Ibid.
xi King and Warfield (2005).

Questions

1. The chapter describes how brand equity is developed for a sport team. Does this model apply to auto racing? Please explain.

2. What are the implications of sponsorship on brand management?

3. Does the new title sponsorship with Nextel help or hinder the NASCAR brand management efforts? Please explain.

CASE 10.2   The National Basketball Association and Jam session: it's *all* stars!

The All-Star Game is the NBA's hallmark event; it provides a unique opportunity to celebrate the best players in the game and make teammates out of sworn opponents. Along with the NBA Playoffs and Finals, the All-Star Game draws tremendous attention from the public and the media all over the world. And what an 'All Star' event it is! From basketball phenomenon LeBron James to basketball legend Earvin 'Magic' Johnson, and from rappers Nelly and Ice Cube to television stars Danny Masterson and Donald Faison, the NBA All-Star Weekend is nothing short of fabulous. Sport and entertainment celebrities gather each year at the host city to celebrate the game of basketball and partake in a number of league-organised activities.

But the NBA All-Star Weekend is not just for players and other celebrities; it is also for the fans. Although the All-Star Game tickets are hard to come around, the league offers other options more accessible and much more affordable for the average fan. One of the main attractions of the All-Star Weekend is the NBA Jam Session, a large area full with basketball courts, games, and interactive activities held at a centrally located facility in the host city. This five-day event, which has been part of the league's All-Star Weekend 12 times, offers games and community programmes, food, player appearances and autograph sessions, photograph opportunities, artists' appearances and concerts, and – what else? – *All-Star* basketball![i]

With the 2005 NBA All-Star Game held in Denver, Colorado, the Colorado Convention Center played host to the latest NBA Jam Session, offering 350,000 square feet of fun and employing 2000 volunteers.[ii] Some of the year's attractions included: the NBA Rookie and Sophomore practice, the East and West All-Stars practice, the NBA All-Star Celebrity Game (with athletes and entertainers comprising the teams) as well as a Celebrity Shootout and Slam Dunk contest, the Mascot Slam Dunk, musical performances at the NBA Club and Jr. NBA/Jr. WNBA games.[iii] What a show! And all that for the price of $20 for adults and $12 for kids, seniors and military staff[iv] – although a separate ticket was required for some of the most popular events.

The NBA Jam Session is an extension of the league that not only adds to the festive atmosphere of the All-Star Weekend, but more importantly provides fans with opportunities to experience the parent brand and interact with their favourite basketball and other stars. The league has successfully extended a single game-celebration of its best players to a five-day event, providing an affordable alternative to those basketball fans who cannot pay a couple hundred dollars for a ticket to the NBA All-Star Game.

At the same time, Jam Session provides additional opportunities for NBA sponsors to leverage their relationship with the league and get their brands in front of thousands of fans in a most positive way. One example in this year's Jam Session was Federal Express. The company created a special section, the FedEx Global Village, which hosted special appearances and basketball clinics from some of the league's most popular international players, including, among others, Steve Nash of Canada, Peja Stojakovic of Serbia and Montenegro and Pau Gasol of Spain.[v]

[i] Montero, D. (2005) Hey, maybe a scout will see you dunk; public can frolic, show off its skills at popular Jam Session, *Rocky Mountain News*, p. 15N, retrieved 13 April 2005, from Lexis Nexis database.

[ii] Ibid.

[iii] Briggs, B. (2005) An All-Star tipoff: Celebs descend on Denver as hoops fans get in on action, *Denver Post*, retrieved 20 February 2005, from Lexis Nexis database.

[iv] Montero (2005).

[v] FedEx delivers 'Global Leaders of the Game' lineup for NBA All-Star 2005; Nash, Stojakovic, Kirilenko, Gasol, Nene, Mutombo, Najera to be featured (2005) *Business Wire*, retrieved 13 April 2005, from Lexis Nexis database.

Questions

1. What characteristics has the NBA used in the design of Jam Session to ensure the success of its brand extension?

2. Based on your understanding of brand extensions in the sport setting, please discuss potential benefits and risks for the NBA from this brand extension initiative.

3. Are there other ways for the NBA to extend its brand?

Conclusions

Using brand equity theory to develop and manage sports brands can provide a powerful tool for sport managers. Part of developing a brand includes analysing the organisation and identifying its strengths and weaknesses. The brand equity framework can serve as a guide to identifying the antecedents that enhance the equity of an organisation, as well as those that need improvement in hopes of achieving favourable consequences and a positive marketplace perception.

Furthermore, brand extension strategies can play a strategic role in the growth of sports brands. Creating additional revenue streams and connecting with fans are two of the possible benefits of extension offerings. A successful implementation of brand extension strategies requires the manipulation of the strength and expertise of the parent brand, perceived fit, promotional support and quality, distribution and management for the selection, design and launch of sports brand extensions.

Discussion questions

1. Which of the four components of brand equity is more important for the success of a sports brand? Why?
2. Select a sport organisation and provide specific examples for each of Keller's (2003) three steps on building brand equity.
3. Adapt Gladden et al.'s (1998) brand equity framework to a professional sport league. What are the antecedents of brand equity? What are the consequences? What are the areas that the league should work on in order to create strong brand equity and a favourable marketplace perception?
4. Do you agree with Keller's (2003) view that introducing brand extensions is imperative for the growth of a brand? Should sport organisations spend resources in designing and implementing extension strategies? Justify your response.
5. Choose a sport organisation and identify at least five line/brand extensions that you think could be successful. Who would be the target audience for each of your five proposed extensions? What are some possible benefits for the organisation?

Guided reading

The *Harvard Business Review on Brand Management* (1999) includes a collection of articles on building and growing a brand. Some of the topics discussed include building brands through mass media communications and using vertical extension to grow a brand.

See Aaker and Joachimsthaler's *Brand Leadership* (2000) for a discussion on developing athletic footwear brands Adidas and Nike (Chapter 6) and the role of sponsorship in brand building (Chapter 7).

Interesting branding issues are discussed in *Emotional Branding: The New Paradigm for Connecting Brands to People* (Gobé, 2001), *Emotional Branding: How Successful Brands Gain the Irrational Edge* (Travis, 2000) and Bedbury's *A New Brand World* (2002).

Keywords

Brand associations; brand equity; brand extension; brand loyalty; brand management; fan identification; line extensions; parent brand; perceived fit; perceived quality; vertical extension.

Bibliography

Aaker, D.A. (1990) Brand extensions: The good, the bad, and the ugly, *Sloan Management Review* Summer:47–56.

Aaker, D.A. (1991) *Managing Brand Equity*, New York: The Free Press.

Aaker, D.A. (1996) Measuring brand equity across products and markets, *California Management Review* 38(3):102–20.

Aaker, D.A. and Keller, K.L. (1990) Consumer evaluations of brand extensions, *Journal of Marketing* 54(January):27–41.

Apostolopoulou, A. (2002a) *The Role of Parent Brand Strength, Perceived Fit, and Fan Identification on Consumers' Evaluation of Brand Extensions in the Sport Setting*, unpublished dissertation, Amherst, MA: University of Massachusetts.

Apostolopoulou, A. (2002b) Brand extensions by U.S. professional sport teams: Motivations and keys to success, *Sport Marketing Quarterly* 11:205–14.

Apostolopoulou, A. (2005) Vertical extension of sport organizations: The case of the National Basketball Development League (NBDL), *Sport Marketing Quarterly* 14:57–61.

Bhat, S. and Reddy, S.K. (1997) Investigating the dimensions of the fit between a brand and its extension, *American Marketing Association* 8(Winter):186–94.

Boone, L.E., Kochunny, C.M. and Wilkins, D. (1995) Applying the brand equity concept to Major League Baseball, *Sport Marketing Quarterly* 4(3):33–42.

Boush, D.M. and Loken, B. (1991) A process-tracing study of brand extension evaluation, *Journal of Marketing Research* XXVIII(February):16–28.

Boush, D., Shipp, S., Loken, B., Gencturk, E., Crockett, S., Kennedy, E., Minshall, B., Misurell, D., Rochford, L. and Strobel, J. (1987) Affect generalization to similar and dissimilar brand extensions, *Psychology & Marketing* 4(3):225–37.

Branscombe, N.R. and Wann, D.L. (1991) The positive social and self concept consequences of sports team identification, *Journal of Sport and Social Issues* 15(2):115–27.

Campbell, R.M. and Kent, A. (2002) Brand extension evaluation: The case of NFL Europe, *Sport Marketing Quarterly* 11(2):117–20.

Chadwick, S. and Clowes, J. (1998) The use of extension strategies by clubs in the English Football Premier League, *Managing Leisure* 3:194–203.

Crimmins, J.C. (2000) Better measurement and management of brand value, *Journal of Advertising Research*, November/December:136–44.

Dacin, P.A. and Smith, D.C. (1994) The effect of brand portfolio characteristics on consumer evaluations of brand extensions, *Journal of Marketing Research* XXXI(May): 229–42.

D'Alessandro, D.F. (2001) *Brand Warfare: 10 Rules for Building the Killer Brand*, New York: McGraw-Hill.

Farquhar, P.H. (1989) Managing brand equity, *Marketing Research* Sept: 24–33.

Gladden, J.M. and Funk, D.C. (2001) Understanding brand loyalty in professional sport: Examining the link between brand associations and brand loyalty, *International Journal of Sports Marketing & Sponsorship* 3(1):67–94.

Gladden, J.M. and Funk, D.C. (2002) Developing an understanding of brand associations in team sport: Empirical evidence from consumers of professional sport, *Journal of Sport Management* 16:54–81.

Gladden, J.M. and Milne, G.R. (1999) Examining the importance of brand equity in professional sport, *Sport Marketing Quarterly* 8(1):21–9.

Gladden, J.M., Milne, G.R. and Sutton, W.A. (1998) A conceptual framework for assessing brand equity in Division I college athletics, *Journal of Sport Management* 12:1–19.

Kaplan, D. (2004) New Roddick deal passes sniff test, *Street & Smith's SportsBusiness Journal* 7(32):4.

Keller, K.L. (1993) Conceptualizing, measuring, and managing customer-based brand equity, *Journal of Marketing* 57(January):1–22.

Keller, K.L. (2003) *Strategic Brand Management: Building, Measuring, and Managing Brand Equity*, 2nd edn, Upper Saddle River, NJ: Prentice Hall.

Keller, K.L. and Aaker, D.A. (1992) The effects of sequential introduction of brand extensions, *Journal of Marketing Research* XXIX(February):35–50.

Kim, C.K. and Lavack, A.M. (1996) Vertical brand extensions: Current research and managerial implications, *Journal of Product & Brand Management* 5(6):24–37.

Lefton, T. (2004) NASCAR's fresh idea: Its own branded produce, *Street & Smith's Sports Business Journal* 7(23):1, 34.

Manchester United (2005) MU Finance brings a range of competitive financial products to all United supporters, Manchester United official website, accessed March 2006, from http://www.manutd.com/mufinance.

Mullin, B.J., Hardy, S. and Sutton, W.A. (2000) *Sport Marketing*, 2nd edn, Champaign, IL: Human Kinetics.

Papadimitriou, D., Apostolopoulou, A. and Loukas, I. (2004) The role of perceived fit in fans' evaluation of sports brands extensions, *International Journal of Sports Marketing & Sponsorship* 6(1):31–48.

Park, C.W., Milberg, S. and Lawson, R. (1991) Evaluation of brand extensions: The role of product feature similarity and brand concept consistency, *Journal of Consumer Research* 18(September):185–93.

Smith, D.C. and Andrews, J. (1995) Rethinking the effect of perceived fit on customers' evaluations of new products, *Journal of the Academy of Marketing Science* 23(1):4–14.

Smith, D.C. and Park, C.W. (1992) The effects of brand extensions on market share and advertising efficiency, *Journal of Marketing Research* XXIX(August):296–13.

Stuart, J. (2002) Man U wants bite of Asian dining market, *Street & Smith's SportsBusiness Journal* 5(3):20.

Sutton, W.A., McDonald, M.A., Milne, G.R. and Cimperman, J. (1997) Creating and fostering fan identification in professional sports, *Sport Marketing Quarterly* 6(1):15–22.

Swaminathan, V., Fox, R.J. and Reddy, S.K. (2001) The impact of brand extension introduction on choice, *Journal of Marketing* 65(4):1–15.

Tauber, E.M. (1988) Brand leverage: Strategy for growth in a cost-control world, *Journal of Advertising Research* August/September:26–30.

Wann, D.L. and Branscombe, N.R. (1993) Sports fans: Measuring degree of identification with their team, *International Journal of Sport Psychology* 24:1–17.

Wann, D.L. and Dolan, T.J. (1994) Attributions of highly identified sports spectators, *The Journal of Social Psychology* 134(6):783–92.

Wann, D.L., Dolan, T.J., McGeorge, K.K. and Allison, J.A. (1994) Relationships between spectator identification and spectators' perceptions of influence, spectators' emotions, and competition outcome, *Journal of Sport & Exercise Psychology* 16:347–64.

Wann, D.L., Melnick, M.J., Russell, G.W. and Pease, D.G. (2001) *Sports fans: The psychology and social impact of spectators*, New York: Routledge.

Recommended websites

BRANDTHINK Sports Marketing & Management Consulting Firm
http://www.brandthink.com

BuildingBrands
http://www.buildingbrands.com

Interbrand Branding Forum
http://www.brandchannel.com

Interbrand Corporation
http://www.interbrand.com

Journal of Brand Management
http://www.henrystewart.com/journals/bm

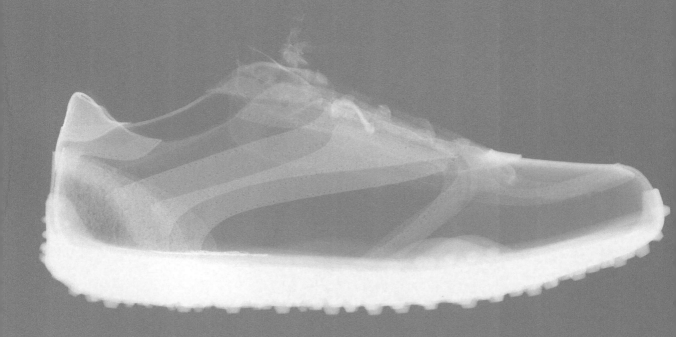

Part Three

Communicating with the sport market

Chapter 11

The sport integrated marketing communications mix

Maria Hopwood
Bond University, Queensland

Learning outcomes

Upon completion of this chapter, the reader should be able to:

■ Identify each of the components of the sport integrated marketing communications mix (SIMCM).

■ Consider the importance for sport marketers of using the SIMCM.

■ Indicate how each of the components can be used by sport marketers.

■ Note the advantages and disadvantages of using each of the components both in isolation and in conjunction.

■ Address issues pertaining to the management of a SIMCM.

Overview of chapter

This chapter introduces the reader to one of the 4Ps of the traditional marketing mix: promotion. The chapter begins with an overview of the contemporary integrated marketing communications mix with specific emphasis on the sport product. The sport integrated marketing communications mix (SIMCM) is briefly contextualised within the contemporary sport marketing mix in order to enable the reader to begin to conceptualise the unique nature of sport marketing communications.

Each of the five major strategic components of the mix and their subsidiaries are then analysed in terms of their promotional validity to sport whilst offering suggestions as to how they can be applied within actual contemporary sports situations. Some of the advantages and disadvantages of each component are considered together with a discussion on the benefits of adopting a fully integrated communications strategy. The final part of the chapter addresses some of the management issues and challenges presented by the SIMCM. The chapter concludes with a summary of the key points.

Introduction

Taking the view that contemporary sport, as a multimillion pound global industry, is here to stay and acknowledging all the indications that the only way for the industry to go within the foreseeable future is up, it is suggested that a critical success factor in this hugely competitive environment is a keen business acumen. In the United Kingdom, there has been a traditionally reticent attitude towards engaging in business behaviour in sport, but in the world's successful sporting nations such as the United States and Australia, it has long been recognised that being a winning team at whatever level and in whatever sport involves having, amongst many other things, a shrewd business focus.

Now, at the beginning of the 21st century, the most popular leisure pursuits in the Western world are sport related, involving countless numbers of individuals as partici-pants or observers and many more in the highly profitable business of satisfying innu-merable sport-related needs and wants. Although modern sport's contribution to the global economy is indisputable, it comes as something of a surprise to learn that the overriding feature of much sport is precisely that it is not organised as a business (Hopwood, 2003). The main reason that most sports seem uncomfortable with the associations of capitalism and entrepreneurship is that they remain heavily influenced by their historical development traditions.

However, although history and tradition are both important values within the context of sport marketing, even more important for long-term business success in contemporary society is an understanding of the techniques and tools needed to create a competitive marketing orientation for the sport product. A key weapon in this armoury is learning the benefits of establishing a SIMCM and applying it effectively. This, then, is the primary focus of this chapter.

Sport as a consumer product

Until very recently, it would have been anathema to athletes to consider that their per-formance on their chosen field of play might be regarded as a consumer product. It is inconceivable that the men sitting in the Three Tuns Hotel in Durham on 23rd May 1882, in the process of founding Durham County Cricket Club could have envisaged that more than a century later, their fledgling club would host an International Test Match televised to a global audience and be involved in the fast-paced Twenty20 Cup, which would completely change the face of the sport of cricket for ever. Yet there can no longer be any doubt that modern sport is regarded as a product. In a recent article in *The Times*, Simon Barnes, the Chief Sports Writer, notes:

> Modern sports marketing is always talking about product. Well what happens when you offer an inferior product? At the moment, sport is carefully and precisely organised to give us increasingly inferior goods.

The focus of this particular article, which was written immediately following the England Cricket Team's first Test defeat in 14 matches, is on the physical demands made on elite international sports people having to fulfil the insatiable appetite of tele-vision and sporting organisations demanding more international sport. Quite simply, the quality of the product (the performance) will get diluted because the excellent players will not be able to maintain the high standards of excellence required. If the product quality is compromised, the end consumers (the spectators and supporters) will show their dissatisfaction:

> ...less excellent sport is less interesting to watch...we will become less interested, less committed to watching. We will start, in short, to switch off. (Barnes, 2005)

This is clear evidence of a fundamental truth in contemporary sport: Sport has evolved into a consumer product and, as such, must be handled in much the same way as any other consumer product. However, sport, unlike many other consumer products, is multifaceted and multidimensional, meaning that although many of the same marketing and promotional techniques can be applied successfully to the sport product, its unique characteristics must be understood and appreciated in order to market it effectively.

Marketing communications: an overview

No matter what organisations do, whether they are large or small, profit or non-profit making, commercial or governmental, educational or sporting, they all have one thing in common: In order to be successful and to survive, they have to engage in communication. Communication can take place within and between organisations and a whole range of other 'publics' or 'audiences' with whom the organisation would like to have a relationship. In today's hugely competitive and 'noisy' marketing environment, those marketing communications messages that get noticed and listened to are those that are precisely targeted and of relevance to the person or persons on the receiving end and that have some degree of originality and memorability about them. For a whole range of reasons, audiences nowadays are proving increasingly difficult to reach, so it is a constant challenge for organisations to try to make and maintain contact. The primary way that organisations make contact is through marketing communications, a process that, at the beginning of the 21st century, is moving towards greater integration in order to attempt to achieve coherence and consistency of the message.

Traditionally, the marketing communications mix consists of five main tools: advertising, sales promotion, public relations, personal selling and direct marketing. This combination of tools is also sometimes more narrowly referred to as the promotions mix and also includes the range of different media via which messages are delivered to targeted audiences. To attempt to understand how marketing communications works and what it does, it is useful to have a definition of the process as a starting point. Perhaps as a reflection of the intangible qualities of the process, there is no single universal definition, and there is a wide range of interpretations of the discipline. Here is a simple one:

> Marketing communications – communications with target audiences on all matters that affect marketing performance. (Pickton and Broderick, 2005, p. 4)

Although this definition is useful as a starting point, it does not take into account the wider function of marketing communications. For example, as a Newcastle Falcons rugby team supporter, you may have got used to and started to look forward to receiving your monthly e-newsletter from the club, but have you thought about why those newsletters have started arriving in your email inbox and whose idea was it to start sending them and for what purposes? Perhaps this definition of marketing communications will aid a better understanding:

> Marketing communications is a management process through which an organisation enters into a dialogue with its various audiences. Based upon an understanding of the audiences' communications environment, an organisation develops and presents messages for its identified stakeholder groups, and evaluates and acts upon the responses received. The objective of the process is to (re)position the organisation and/or its products and services, in the minds of the members of the target market, by influencing their perception and understanding. The goal is to generate attitudinal and behavioural responses. (Fill, 2002, p. 12)

Now things begin to make sense. As a loyal Newcastle Falcons supporter, you are a stakeholder of the club. You might be a season ticket holder, or you might only attend every home game. You or someone you know who might have done it on your behalf, are highly likely to have made a purchase in the club shop. Either way, the club has your details on a database, probably because at some point in your relationship, you have divulged that information. They know the extent of your support and engagement with the club and have decided that you will be receptive to the e-newsletter. Besides giving you regular updates on what is happening at the club and information about the players, the e-newsletter contains specially targeted offers to which you are quite likely to respond favourably, thereby continuing a highly mutually beneficial relationship from which both you and the club gain a great deal. This then, is one example of how marketing communications strategies work in sport and why time, effort and resources need to be spent on them.

The sport marketing communications process

In order to get a better understanding of sport marketing communications, it is necessary to understand the sport marketing communication process, which is founded on the basic human communication process. How we communicate and why our attempts at communication either succeed or fail are subjects of constant interest to psychologists and behaviourists, and much research has been conducted into human communications research over many years. It is obviously necessary that some aspects of communications theory underpin marketing communications in order to create both a framework and a direction for a whole range of communications strategies, but for our purposes, an understanding of a basic communications model is sufficient.

In 1960, Wilbur Schramm developed a concept of communication based on a two-way process model that is entirely relevant to contemporary sport marketing communications. His communication process involves four key elements, which are shown in Figure 11.1.

The premise of this model is that communication is a reciprocal process during which signals are exchanged with the intention of informing, instructing or persuading based on shared meanings and the existence of feedback mechanisms. This a sequential process, meaning that the receiver of a message has to have gone through the informing and instructing phases before being capable of being persuaded.

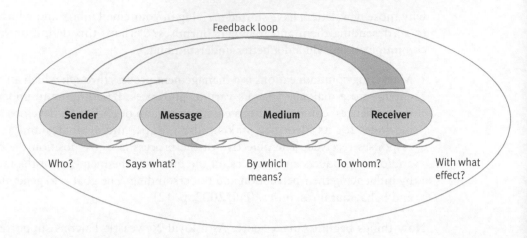

Figure 11.1 Schramm's communications process
Source: Adapted from Pickton and Broderick (2005)

Sport marketing communications messages are no different from any other type of marketing communications messages. If we want to attract customers to our newly opened sport and leisure facility, we have to communicate the benefits and make the offering attractive and superior to that of our competitors. The only way to achieve this is to instruct, inform and persuade. A successful product is created primarily through an understanding that communications is at the heart of the marketing exchange process, so it is helpful to develop an understanding of what each of these stages entails.

Informing, that all-important first stage, is a combination of four distinct steps: 1) attracting attention to the communication and the message and, by association, the product; 2) gaining acceptance of the message; 3) ensuring that the message is interpreted as intended; and 4) getting the message stored away for later use.

Instruction is a much more demanding process that adds a crucial fifth step, which Cutlip, Center and Broom (2000) identify as the stimulation of active learning and practice, both critical success factors in long-term sports relationship management. Chapter 14 contains a more in-depth discussion of sports relationship management.

Persuasion is the process that takes the receiver of the message beyond active learning to the final sixth step of accepting and engaging with change which could be behavioural, attitudinal or both. In sport marketing communications, this means accepting the wishes or point of view of the sender. Achieving successful sport business outcomes to each of these steps is beset by challenges and difficulties, which, in communication terms, are generally known as barriers to communication.

As in all communications situations, barriers are highly detrimental to a successful sport marketing communications exchange process. If we consider our earlier example of the new sports and leisure facility, imagine that one of its objectives is to attract people to use the gym facilities during the quieter times in the week. Because the likely target audience here would be potential customers who are at home during the day, perhaps working from home or parents (usually mothers) of school-age children who perhaps do not have a large disposable income or who are not confident about going to the gym, it is obvious that high membership fees together with reams of pictures of athletic and supremely fit bodies will not have the desired effect in persuading them to join. There are too many barriers in the communication that have already resulted in the receiver's not moving beyond the information stage of the sport marketing communications process. However, if appropriate sport marketing research had been conducted into the kind of messages that would appeal to the target audience, then the outcome would have been very different.

Because the sport product, in all its ramifications, has distinct characteristics that need to be taken into account if sport marketing communications is to be effective, it is proposed that an extended version of the communications process model should be applied to sports. This model is shown in Figure 11.2 and is based on Pickton and Broderick's IMC Process Model.

To reflect the unique characteristics of the sport product, there are more key elements in the SIMC process model than in the standard IMC process model that need clarification. The sender, message, media and receiver are the same as in Schramm's model, but the receiver in the SIMC process model is regarded somewhat differently. In our more inclusive communications model, it is recognised that the receiver may not solely be members of the target audience. In sport marketing communication, the receiver of a message, especially in these times of global mediated communication, could be any number of people who have an interest in a sport or sports for all manner of reasons. For example, Manchester United Football Club's official website homepage at http://www.manutd.com has a single link in the Global Man U section to the Chinese Manchester United's website, no doubt because China is the home of the largest number of Manchester United supporters in the world. It is clearly mediated devotion to this particular football team that motivates these members, not attending the matches in person week in and week out. Special early bird offers on buying an annual season ticket to 'The Theatre of Dreams' are unlikely to be of interest, but receiving regular personalised email communications and the opportunity to buy merchandise from the online club shop are both ways that loyalty and long-term relationship building can be assured.

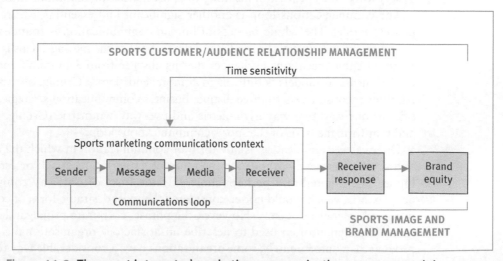

Figure 11.2 **The sport integrated marketing communications process model**
Source: Adapted from Pickton and Broderick (2005)

The end receivers of the message may also be people who have absolutely no interest in sport or a sport organisation but because someone close to them is an avid fan or participant, they need to be engaged with in order to encourage them to visit websites in order to buy merchandise as gifts at various times throughout the year, for example. As Pickton and Broderick (2005) observe when marketing communications are noted, receivers may give a variety of responses from buying and consuming the product and telling others their opinion of it to doing nothing at all. Something that has to be accepted in sport marketing communications is that the actual communications message, if it is not carefully constructed, could fall short of its mark and therefore be received by considerably fewer receivers than was originally intended.

Another feature of the SIMC process model is the sport marketing communications context. The external and internal (macro and micro) environment has a considerable influence in sport marketing communications, and this must be taken into account when planning sport marketing communications strategies. Sport, perhaps more than most other products, is associated with high emotion and deeply held beliefs and ideologies. Bill Shankly, the greatly admired and now legendary one-time manager of Liverpool Football Club, famously said in the 1960s:

> Some people believe football is a matter of life and death. I'm very disappointed with that attitude. I can assure you it is much, much more important than that. (http://www.shankly.com/lifeanddeath.htm)

This quotation has, of course, become part of football's folklore, and although it might have been delivered with Shankly's tongue firmly in his cheek and a knowing twinkle in his eye, it perfectly reinforces the point that it is the *intangible* elements such as loyalty, pride and emotion that wield the greatest power and influence in sport marketing communications. For example, the strap-line in Coca-Cola's advertising campaign during the 1996 football World Cup was 'Eat football, Sleep football, Drink Coca-Cola'. Nationwide, official sponsor of the England football team, uses the words 'Pride. Passion. Belief' on their sponsorship information web page (http://www.nationwide.co.uk/football/default.asp?). Clearly, the environmental context can deeply affect the nature and meaning of sport marketing communications.

The communications loop is another significant and essential feature of the SIMC process model. The whole process of human communication is founded on two-way communication between the sender and the receiver of the message. This is so fundamental to all communications exchanges that its absence from Schramm's and other earlier communications models is difficult to comprehend. James Grunig, an American public relations theorist, refers to three distinct business communication strategies that he identifies as one-way, two-way asymmetric and two-way symmetric (Grunig, 1992, p. 285) and that form the basis of the sports communications loop.

One-way communication is any form of communication in which the sender creates and sends a message without the intention of gathering feedback or establishing dialogue. The original and perhaps most extreme form of one-way communication is propaganda, which would not be considered the most desirable form of communication in today's pluralistic society. However, the phrase 'corporate propaganda' is an unflattering description often used to describe unsatisfactory organisational communication proving that, unfortunately, some organisations have a considerable way to go to engage with their audiences successfully. Many advertising messages were originally created in this way, although it can be argued that if someone buys or engages with a product after seeing an advertisement, then this could constitute feedback, which would then make this *two-way asymmetric communication* because although this feedback might be delayed, it has occurred in some form. Such communications do not allow for true dialogue, and the balance of power in the communications relationship is very one-sided in favour of the organisation. Excellent contemporary sport integrated marketing communications takes a very different approach.

Nowadays, increasing numbers of sport organisations are recognising that the creation and maintenance of long-term relationships is becoming a critical success factor and that engaging target audiences in dialogue is crucial. The Bradford Bulls Rugby League team is an example of a club intent on using proactive relationship-building strategies in its sport marketing communications armoury. Stuart Duffy, the club's media and public relations manager, is adamant that the customer should form the focus of the Bulls' marketing communications strategies. He describes how the general approach used to be very inward looking, neglecting the fact that if the paying customer was not satisfied, then this could have serious negative consequences for the well being of the club. Using CRM (customer relationship marketing/management) strategies, the Bradford Bulls now actively engages in research to find out what its customers want and communicates with them regularly on all manner of issues. This is an actual example of two-way symmetrical communication in which a direct dialogue exists between the sender of the message and the receiver. Two-way symmetrical communication is generally considered to be the 'richest' form of communication because the main objective of both parties in the exchange process is mutually beneficial: long-term relationship building upon which future communications transactions will be founded.

It is worth pointing out that two-way symmetrical communication has been widely criticised by some academics recently as being rather idealistic and not truly representative of marketing communications. There might be some good reasons for doubting its efficacy within the general business context but as far as sport organisations are concerned, there are plenty of instances where two-way symmetrical communications definitely does exist and where it is considered vital for the long-term success of the sport. Apart from the Bradford Bulls example mentioned above, look at the case study on Twenty20 Cricket at the end of the chapter for further evidence.

Research amongst contemporary sport organisations shows that 'new media' (digital communications, e-communications) communications tools (the internet and email) play a significant role in their communications armoury and that successful two-way symmetrical communication can be achieved just as well by using these methods. Personal selling and other face-to-face communications are instances in which two-way symmetrical communications were traditionally very successful. But although 'new media' communications are mediated, there is clear evidence, as demonstrated by the Bradford Bulls example mentioned earlier, that important one-to-one relationship building is thriving. During the first Frizzell County Championship match of the 2005 domestic cricket season in April 2005, Durham County Cricket Club capitalised on its email database contacts by sending out a number of emails informing readers of the tremendous start new Captain Mike Hussey was making with a match-winning innings of more than 200 runs. The fixture was an away one, so this communications technique allowed those supporters who could not get there in person to feel part of the occasion.

The Football Association (FA) is another example of a sporting organisation that uses its website for relationship-building purposes. Adrian Bevington, the current head of media relations at the FA (in conversation with the author on 25th February 2005) explains how the FA website (http://www.thefa.com) has become the most widely used tool in that organisation's media relations strategy. Excellent long-term relationships with journalists and other news media are critical to the FA, and much of Adrian's role is involved with building and maintaining such relationships. But he says that the website has improved this task greatly because it is now used as the first point of contact for anyone wanting up-to-the-minute news and information. Four full-time members of staff are employed to maintain the website with instant news, which is probably one reason why the FA has become the third most quoted organisation in the United Kingdom after the government and Buckingham Palace!

One of the most significant advantages to sport organisations in developing reliable two-way symmetrical communication is that it can enhance the SIMC process model and limit the potentially damaging effects of noise and misinterpretation in the communications loop through the establishment of direct dialogue. In the SIMC process model, *receiver responses* to the communications have to be carefully considered because things like receiver attitude, behaviour and associations with the sport organisation and product create *brand loyalty* and brand equity, which are just as critical to sports as they are to consumer products generally. Shank (2005) describes brand equity as the value that the brand adds to a product in the marketplace. Within the context of sport, consumers who believe that a particular sport product has a high degree of brand equity are more likely to be satisfied with the brand, which, in turn, makes them more likely to become repeat purchasers and eventually, heavy users (season ticket holders or members) desired by most sporting organisations.

The time sensitivity variable in the SIMC process model is included to illustrate that brand equity and user behaviour are built and change over time and that they are susceptible to influences on the consumption experience. Exposure and response to a sport marketing communications message can influence future engagement in the process and impact of messages. Mark Newton, chief executive of Worcestershire County Cricket Club, says that when one supports a team, it is quite likely to be for life. Therefore, it is obvious that one's response to sport marketing communications will not remain constant and that time and experience impact on future response and behaviour as far as marketing communications is concerned. This, clearly, has important implications for all sport marketing communicators.

Finally, two key strategic elements of the SIMC process model are external to the central components of that model: (1) sports customer or audience relationship management and (2) sport image and brand management. These two elements have special significance because their success or failure occurs as a direct result of all the planned, unintended, controlled and uncontrolled communications between the sport organisation and its audiences. If long-term, mutually beneficial exchange relationships are established and nurtured, then the potential for repeat and more frequent buying behaviour becomes a reality. This is where the implementation of one-to-one, two-way symmetric CRM strategies comes into play. Sports public relations strategies can be really useful in this regard. Sports image and brand management tend to be more associated with mass communications strategies targeted at many audiences, such as advertising and sales promotions and other one-to-many communications. So, to get a true dialogue established, specifically targeted communications strategies will reap greater rewards for the sport organisation.

Components of the sport integrated marketing communications mix

Having acquired an understanding of the significance of the sport marketing communications process, the next stage is to examine the various components and techniques that are used in sport and by sport organisations. It is worth pointing out at this stage that in both the marketing and sport marketing literature, the term 'the integrated marketing communications mix' is synonymous with 'the marketing communications mix' and 'the promotions mix'. The preferred emphasis on 'the integrated marketing communications mix' is in reference to the contemporary trend within business to use each of the components of the mix synergistically, a trend that seems to be particularly suited to the business of sport.

Irwin, Sutton and McCarthy (2002) define sport marketing communications activity (or promotional activity as they prefer to call it) as all means available to the sport organisation for communicating and persuading defined consumer groups. Sport marketing communications has to be considered differently from traditional or consumer marketing communications because of the unique nature of the product. As Mark Newton of Worcestershire County Cricket Club (CCC) says, 'Marketing communications here is different to what's normally used in business' (in conversation with the author, February 2005). The primary objectives for marketing communications at Worcestershire CCC, according to Mark Newton, are as follows:

> . . . to raise the profile and awareness of future events . . . to engage as many of the population as possible and persuade them to come to matches or join as Members.

These real-life sport marketing communications objectives agree, almost exclusively, with the theoretical concepts addressed in the sport marketing literature. Knowing what the objectives for sport marketing communications are means that it is then possible to decide which particular techniques are best suited to achieving those objectives. It is here that the differences between the sport communications and consumer product communications become apparent. Although the principles of communication remain the same, the execution is quite different. This next section of the chapter considers techniques commonly used in sport marketing communications and promotion.

A variety of sport marketing communications, or promotions, mixes can be found in recent sport marketing theory. They each have their strengths and weaknesses, and some are much more comprehensive than others. It is suggested that when a sport marketing communications mix is founded exclusively on the traditional marketing communications mix, then it is likely to be too limiting and largely inappropriate for the sport product. There are many reasons for this, and most of them have to do with the special nature of the sport product. For example, not all promotional activity in sport is intended to result in a transactional sale. Also, some of the traditional communications mix tools such as sales promotion do not adequately describe the methods that could be used to attract people to engage with sport. It becomes clear when developing a specific sports communications mix that the five traditional tools of marketing communications – advertising, sales promotion, personal selling, public relations and direct marketing – although they can be applied in sport marketing, are, or should be, used in very different ways for very different outcomes. In addition, it is important to understand that current thinking in marketing communications recognises that the most effective communications strategies are increasingly those that adopt an integrated approach in which each of the tools of the mix are used synergistically. Also, it is argued, because of the likely lifelong or at the very least long-term nature of sport engagement, it becomes imperative that relationship building and management form the foundation from which all other communications activities follow. Figure 11.3 provides an eight-stage SIMCM as a useful framework for contemporary sport business:

The 21st century SIMCM is an amalgamation of Kotler's (1982) non-profit promotion mix and Irwin et al.'s (2002) sport promotion mix. Kotler's mix incorporates advertising, publicity, incentives, personal contact and atmospherics and is considered to be a useful foundation for the 21st century SIMCM because the content of the different categories, and their labels are a more accurate reflection of the promotional techniques used in sport business. Irwin et al. add licensing and sponsorship in order to produce what they describe as a complete contemporary sport promotion mix. However, it is thought that to fully represent current thinking in sport communications, it is essential that the additional dimension of relationship building and management is incorporated. In fact, this dimension is considered so fundamental to the SIMCM that the author has positioned it as the first element in the mix. The next stage will be to break down the mix into its constituent parts and look at each in more detail.

Relationship building and management

A fundamental shift in marketing thinking has been developing during recent years, the outcome of which has seen the emergence of two new marketing concepts which are very different in essence to that of traditional transactional marketing: Relationship marketing

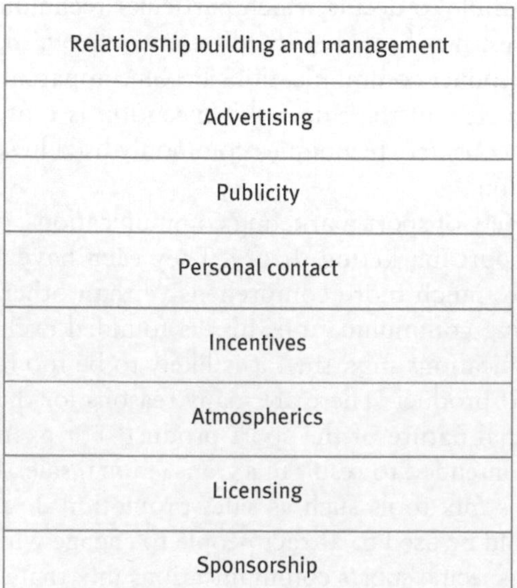

| Relationship building and management |
| Advertising |
| Publicity |
| Personal contact |
| Incentives |
| Atmospherics |
| Licensing |
| Sponsorship |

Figure 11.3 **The 21st century sport integrated marketing communications mix**
Source: Adapted from Irwin et al. (2002)

(RM) and Customer Relationship Marketing (CRM). RM is defined by its creator, Gummesson (2002), as '...marketing based on interaction within networks of relationships.' CRM is defined as '...the values and strategies of relationship marketing – with particular emphasis on customer relationships – turned into practical application.' These basic principles are integral to the SIMCM component of relationship building and management. Gummesson (p. 9) states that 'relationships are at the core of human behaviour' and relationships are vital to successful sport business.

However, it is suggested that to confine relationships to marketing is too limiting within the context of sport marketing. Relationship building and management are intrinsically entrenched in contemporary public relations practice that, the author believes, is at the heart of successful sports communications; this is discussed in Chapter 14. In an article written for *Public Relations Quarterly* (Fall, 2000) Ledingham states that a relationship approach to public relations is vital for any organisation 'seeking to initiate, nurture and maintain positive, mutually-beneficial relationships between their organisation and its key publics'. Sport organisations are intent on getting and keeping their customers because their livelihood depends on it, just like any other business. However, loyalty, tradition and emotion are characteristics of the sport product that are rarely manifested in other consumer products. Consider the numbers of loyal football supporters, often in family groups, who, from one season to the next, doggedly follow their team through the good times and the bad and who will, if it comes to such a pass, weep copiously and openly display their emotions to a global audience. Yet, the next season, they will pay the increased price for their season ticket, all for the love of their team. Many other organisations would kill for such loyalty and devotion, so it comes as something of a surprise to hear some supporters say that they are not happy with the way their football club treats them, that they sometimes feel they are taken for granted. Yet would they transfer their allegiance to another club? That is highly unlikely. The idea that Sunderland AFC supporters would suddenly don the black and white colours of Newcastle United is inconceivable, although they would, without a second thought and in huge numbers, withdraw their savings from the building society that switches its sponsorship from their club to that of their bitter rivals.

Just as with any relationship, it has to be nurtured and worked at over the years. An excellent example of how sporting relationships can be managed and improved is the new Twenty20 Cricket tournament. In recent years, the ECB (England and Wales Cricket Board) came to realise that the traditional 4-day County Championship was losing its appeal and beginning to create a negative image for professional cricket. Pictures of almost empty grounds apart from the stereotypical 'one man and his dog' and comments from players, who were increasingly disappointed by not having an audience to whom they could display their hard-earned skills, were beginning to have an impact. Consequently, the ECB launched a comprehensive market research campaign, the direct outcome of which was the Twenty20 Cup. The research findings told the ECB that their core audience was on the wane and that for cricket to become more meaningful and to attract the players of the future, it would have to make some fundamental changes. In June 2003, the first twenty over per side games were played with resounding success. Intended to appeal to a different demographic, the matches started at 5.30 pm (6.00 pm at Durham's ground at Chester-le-Street in North East England because of extended daylight hours) and lasted around 3 hours. There was atmosphere, excitement, music, entertainment and big-hitting cricket, and the crowds, liberally sprinkled with women and children, came in sell-out numbers. The success that Twenty20 cricket has now become throughout the world is testament to the understanding that if you talk to your customers, listen to what they say and give them what they want in a format that suits them, then they will respond favourably. To keep up with demand, more Twenty20 fixtures will be played during the summer of 2006, and some of these have been sold out months in advance. Perhaps the cricket purists have yet to be persuaded of the virtues of Twenty20 cricket, but the players and spectators are coming back for more. Relationship management in 21st century UK cricket is alive and well and proving its value within the sport context. You will read more about Durham County Cricket Club's sport integrated marketing communications strategy in the case study at the end of the chapter.

■ Advertising

It used to be the case that advertising was the predominant and most popular marketing communications tool; however, in recent years, the reliance on advertising has diminished in favour of the application of other techniques. There are a number of reasons for this, but the most obvious is to do with cost. Advertising is still widely used because of what it can achieve – it has the potential to reach global audiences with attention-grabbing and persuasive messages. But in certain situations, advertising has become prohibitively expensive and audiences have become resistant to its appeals.

In sport integrated marketing communications, each available technique should be used for the things it is good at doing, and advertising's strength in sport is that it is highly visible and therefore widely used by sport marketers. Advertising achieves a wide range of sport marketing communications objectives: It can create and maintain brand awareness and brand loyalty and it can create a strong identity for sport products and services. Although there is much academic debate surrounding the issue of how advertising works, there is no doubt that advertising can directly affect how consumers behave. We can be encouraged to attend a sporting event through advertising, we can be persuaded to buy that particular brand of football boots through advertising or we can be encouraged to watch the winter Test Matches in South Africa through advertising.

But what exactly is advertising? The meaning of advertising is often confused, and the term is frequently used as a 'catch-all' phrase to describe a whole range of different promotional activities such as sales promotions and direct marketing, which are well beyond the scope of advertising. There are many definitions of advertising, but one of the most helpful is this one by Duncan:

> Advertising is *nonpersonal, paid announcements by an identified sponsor.* It is used to reach large audiences, create brand awareness, help differentiate a brand from its competitors, and build an image of the brand. (2005, p. 9)

From this, we can see that advertising is always paid for; we know who has generated the advertisement; and we are exposed to it through the press or broadcast media and are then persuaded or influenced by it. However, as with all good definitions, this one can be developed further. For example, in sport, other methods of communicating the advertising message are used in addition to the mass media. Stadium signage and naming rights, such as the Reebok Stadium, have become a familiar way of getting advertising messages across to specific target audiences. Perimeter advertising at football matches, corporate advertising in match day or tournament programmes, branding and logo on the pitches during televised rugby and cricket matches, athletes as product endorsers and sponsors' logos on kit and equipment – all of these have become accepted ways we are exposed to sports advertising. Sports audiences are captive and willing audiences, so it is not surprising that advertising is a major element of the SIMCM.

For contemporary sport marketers, the internet is taking a significant role in sports advertising strategies. The internet is another example of how the traditional definitions of advertising have become too narrow and how the predominance of mass media usage in advertising is being challenged. Internet advertising is a product extension to traditional advertising in that it has allowed this usually non-personal communications technique to become interactive and much more personalised. There are a number of advantages in using the internet such as flexibility, currency and cost effectiveness. The FA employs four full-time staff members to work constantly on keeping the FA's website (http://www.thefa.com) up to date because it has become such an important advertising and communications medium. Sport organisations work hard at making their websites attractive because they provide the distinct possibility of attracting a worldwide audience that could potentially become long-distance supporters delighted by the prospect of being able to buy team merchandise and to become part of the club's active fan base. Advertising as an element of the SIMCM has many distinct advantages that, when used in combination with the other elements of the mix, create a powerful mechanism for encouraging customer loyalty.

Publicity

Like advertising, the true meaning of publicity is frequently misunderstood, and the word tends to be used in all manner of incorrect ways. According to Marconi:

> Publicity is a process of managing information and bringing it to the attention of the public...the task of generating publicity does not have to be loud and excessive to be effective. (2004, p. 137)

Managing information and bringing it to the attention of the public in a way that is appealing to them is a distinct skill because it is something that has to be done properly if the public is to be prevented from thinking that all publicity is hype and all publicists are liars. Media decision makers and influencers such as editors, journalists and commentators have to be persuaded to take an interest, so publicity has to be shaped to suit their requirements, and relationships built on trust, openness and honesty are critical success factors. Publicity is a great way of generating goodwill and understanding at no financial cost to the organisation, so it is not surprising to learn that it is a tool widely used in public relations practise. The limited financial resources of many sport organisations mean that there is a considerable reliance on publicity. News stories are examples of the type of publicity that is widely used in sports. The back pages of almost all the national and local newspapers are where we turn for our daily update on what is going on in the world of sport. In our contemporary time-poor lifestyles, many sport consumers are increasingly turning to the internet for the same news stories that can be found in the online versions of the daily newspapers, designated internet news sites and the proliferation of dedicated sports websites. An example was given earlier of how Durham County Cricket Club trialled 'e-publicity' at the start of the 2005 season and the fact that, if you want to pay for them, you can get sports results and updates via SMS text messaging on your mobile phone is a further indication of how such forms of publicity are developing.

Because many sport organisations have limited financial resources, publicity is a tool upon which they have come to rely. Publicity undoubtedly has many distinct advantages, but it is disingenuous to think that it is an entirely free form of communication. Much time and energy has to be expended on developing excellent media relations (i.e., relationships with journalists) by designated personnel in sport organisations in order to ensure constant adequate and accurate media and press coverage. Stuart Duffy, media and public relations manager at Bradford Bulls rugby league club, says that much of his job is concentrated on developing excellent media relationships, particularly with journalists from the local press and broadcasting organisations. Local media are crucially important to sport organisations such as the Bradford Bulls because they are the ones to whom the vast majority of the local target population turns for information. Stuart cites the example of competitions for free tickets to Bulls matches on local Pulse Radio's breakfast show as a highly successful technique for reaching people who have never previously attended a game or visited the Odsal Stadium. The potential for converting first-time visitors into regular supporters should be a key objective for sports publicity.

■ Personal contact

In a very well-known study into international business organisations, Peters and Waterman (1982) identify a range of organisational activities that set excellent organisations apart from the rest. One of these activities is what they describe as staying close to the customer (p. 156), which is another way of describing personal contact. Personal selling is one of the five major components in the traditional integrated marketing communications mix, but this, in its commercial sense, does not work particularly well for sport organisations because, as mentioned previously, a sale is not always the intended or desired outcome. For sport organisations, the words *personal contact* are much more applicable.

According to Irwin et al.:

> Personal contact is critical to the success of an effective promotional campaign. Whereas advertising is very public, indiscriminate and impersonal, personal contact can be tailored to the target customers' interests and needs. (2002, p. 8)

As with relationship building and management, the concept of personal contact is rooted firmly in the practice of public relations. Personal contact adds the human element to the relationships that are developed between the sport organisation and the customer which, in turn, are the foundation for the creation of dialogue and that all-important two-way symmetrical communication mentioned earlier in the chapter.

The principles of relationship marketing are integral to sports personal contact because long-term contact is so characteristic of the majority of sport organisation and public relationships whose ultimate goal is to engender loyalty. In sports relationship marketing, there are three distinct levels of loyalty (shown in Figure 11.4) that need some explanation and clarification.

The lowest level is financial bonding, which is 'bought' through a range of financial rewards or sales promotion initiatives such as reduced price gym memberships for a limited period after Christmas or buy one ticket for a game, get another half price. Although such techniques are attractive and designed to appeal to customer requirements,

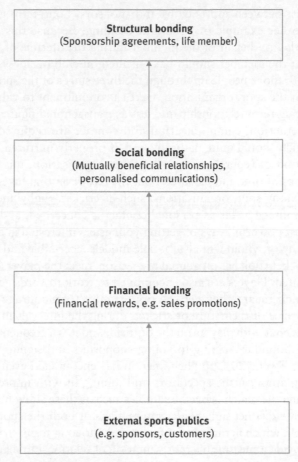

Figure 11.4 The sports loyalty scheme
Source: Adapted from Irwin et al. (2002)

they do not focus on long-term loyalty building; after the offer has passed or expired, the customer will go elsewhere.

The middle level of the sports loyalty scheme is social bonding, which is aimed at developing mutually beneficial relationships between the sport organisation and the customer. At this level, contact needs to be much more personalised because there is the very good chance that when customers are happy with this level of their relationship with the sport organisation, they will move up to the desired final loyalty level. Communications at the social bonding level should be personalised. For example, when you buy your first season ticket from your favourite football club, you might expect to receive preferential treatment or special offers that are particularly targeted at you and your interests. Many sporting organisations use their database information to send out personalised birthday cards or Christmas cards, which make the customer feel that the club has a genuine interest in them and that they are not just another anonymous number. If such a relationship is achieved, then the step up to the final level of loyalty, known as structural bonding, is a small one. At this level, each party has an equal role in the relationship, which is particularly evident in relationships that exist between sports clubs and sponsors. Long-term membership of a cricket club is another example of structural bonding. Because this involves considerable financial outlay on behalf of the member during the lifetime of the relationship, it is only right that the member should be consulted on club business and development.

To move people up through the three stages of the sports loyalty scheme, it is essential that the sport organisation makes a commitment to value the publics more as equals in a long-term relationship and less as transactional figures. Regular, high-quality personal interaction, communication and contact are required to maintain the relationship, which should quite naturally and, if properly nurtured, increase purchase and the like-lihood of repurchase. For the sport organisation, this requires a heavy investment in terms of time and resources, but the return on that investment is high.

Many sport organisations, such as cricket, rugby and football clubs, have a distinct advantage as far as personal contact is concerned, and that is the players. One of the most powerful ways of getting youngsters interested in a sport is by making the players, many of whom will also be role models, accessible and approachable. Durham County Cricket Club has an annual pre-season 'meet the players' night to which all members are invited. Players are also encouraged to work towards acquiring coaching qualifications, which means they get the opportunity to encourage keen youngsters in the sport. Because of the nature of cricket, during the intervals in matches, spectators can mingle and chat with players on the outfield, and it is a frequent sight to see players standing on the boundary talking to young supporters and signing autographs during quiet times. The Twenty20 Cup phenomenon has encouraged even closer contact with players sit-ting amongst the spectators and joining in with impromptu games with the children when the match is over. Examples such as these show how personal contact in sport can create distinct stakeholder impressions of both the sporting organisation and the sport itself, which in turn can be translated into long-term, structural bonding, which can then provide a measurable representation of relationship management.

Incentives

Just as personal contact has been described as an extension of personal selling, incen-tives in sport can be thought of as an extension to the sales promotion component of the traditional integrated marketing communications mix. Incentives, to Kotler (1982), incorporates all the emotional, social, psychological, functional or financial conditions that serve to encourage some overt behavioural response, or, as Irwin et al. say (2002, p. 13), all activities that act to stimulate quick buyer action. However, within the SIMCM, it must be realised that not all sporting consumption experiences are of a transactional nature, meaning that incentives are not only used in order to generate sales. Understanding how to best use incentives also requires an understanding of what motivates sports publics and how they behave. This is of particular relevance during the development of sponsorship agreements because it is known that potential sponsors are interested in engaging in sponsorships with sports or sport organisations that offer a distinct fit to the sponsor's marketing public relations objectives such as image and reputation management.

As with many things associated with sport, there is a distinctly intangible element to incentives that is extremely difficult to quantify. For example, an incentive for the young cricketers mentioned earlier might be self-actualisation, which could take many years to fulfil or that might never happen but that, in any event, will result in a lifelong devotion to the sport. Although the returns on self-actualisation are not as immediate and obvious as they are from the sale of this season's early bird price offer on a replica shirt, they are arguably more valuable in the long term.

Atmospherics

This component of the SIMCM consists of everything that is done to ensure that the place of purchase or consumption of the sport product is designed to create specific behavioural or emotional effects in the consumer. This includes everything that appears at the point of sale, such as posters, displays, signs and other promotional material, such as athlete endorsements, that is intended to persuade people at the point of purchase. Atmospherics also includes features that are intended to influence choice or outlet in which the sport product is to be consumed. So, the actual place where a sporting event occurs becomes an integral element of the overall promotional strategy.

Another unique characteristic of the sport industry is the simultaneous production and consumption of the product or service. It is frequently said that nothing quite matches the experience of attending a live sporting event; it is something that is long remembered, even by people who do not particularly follow the sport. During the 2004 Easter holidays, the author and her family visited Antigua to watch the final Test Match between England and the West Indies. Three of the four family members are cricket fans, but one has no interest in cricket or any sport, for that matter. However, having reluctantly attended the first and final day's play, he is often heard reminiscing about the fantastic time he spent singing along with the Barmy Army anthems, buying a CD from Curtly Ambrose ('He was a cricketer, was he?') who came into the stands to promote his band, dancing along with the home supporters to Chickie's disco and generally having a wonderful 'sporting' experience. As far as he was concerned, the fact that there was a game being played and that England won was incidental. The memories of just being there in the West Indies Oil Lower Stand in April 2004 will stay with him forever.

The Bradford Bulls have seen their attendance figures rise year on year recently, and there is no doubt that one of the reasons for this is that match days have become events with more than just the game to interest the supporters. Music, dancing girls, entertainers, academy matches, fairground attractions, family-friendly activities and international cuisine have all become part of the match-day experience at the Odsal Stadium. Much of the appeal of cricket's Twenty20 Cup is off the field of play – hot tubs, pizza delivery, £1000 for catching a six ball in the stands, music, fireworks, colour, bouncy castles and face painting all designed to create a memorable event and to get the customers coming back for more and spreading positive word of mouth messages. A great advantage for sport is that atmosphere is intrinsic to the product, and because of the uncontrollable nature of the sport product – that is, there is no control over what is happening on the field of play – it makes sense to capitalise on this feature as much as possible to create competitive advantage.

Licensing

According to Irwin et al. (2002, p. 14), licensing has emerged as the fastest growing component of the contemporary sport promotion mix. Just as with a corporate brand or logo, a recognisable symbol for a team or event increases consumer awareness and creates an identity in the marketplace. Such globally recognised logos as the Nike Swoosh and the Adidas Stripes are emblazoned on a whole range of consumer products, not all of which are immediately sports related. Many of these logos and brands have achieved iconic status. For example, an advertisement for Nike is immediately recognisable by the Swoosh; there is no need for the company to include the name as well.

In buying and wearing a favourite team's shirts, supporters are not only demonstrating their allegiance but are also extending the promotional opportunities for any sponsor or corporate logo that might be emblazoned on the replica shirt. Royalty fees are paid by second parties in return for the right to use a logo, name, symbol or mark associated with an event or an athlete. In these days of satellite and cable broadcast sporting events, even the cricket stumps present opportunities for the likes of Pepsi to get their logo seen by a global audience. It is now the norm to sell stadium naming rights to corporate sponsors as in the Reebok Stadium, the TelstraDome (Melbourne) and the McAlpine Stadium (Huddersfield FC). This important aspect of sports promotion is discussed in more detail elsewhere in the book but it is relevant at this point to see this as a fundamental aspect of the integrated sport marketing communications mix. Clearly, sport presents unique opportunities for companies to break through the clutter and noise surrounding conventional advertising so the vast sums of money invested in licensing strategies must be worth it.

Sponsorship

Sponsorship within contemporary sports is probably the most financially lucrative way that contemporary sport organisations make their presence felt. Again, this topic is discussed in more detail elsewhere in the text but as an element of the SIMCM, sponsorship cannot be overlooked. According to Lagae (2005, p. 34), its integration into the promotional mix has increased greatly in recent years, making it a 'creative and powerful instrument of marketing communication'. Anyone you speak to in the world of sport will have a different interpretation of what sponsorship means. For a young, aspiring cricketer, sponsorship can mean that he gets a 30% reduction on his equipment, which is significant when his preferred cricket bat costs more than £200! To the professional cricket team chief executive, sponsorship can mean the long-awaited building of the new stand. In fact, any sport organisation (and player) will tell you that sponsorship is critical to their success, and it is, but there is also much to do with contemporary sports sponsorship that causes strong feelings of antipathy.

Lagae (2005) describes sponsorship as a business agreement between two parties, based on reciprocity. This means that both parties get something from the exchange, which is usually demonstrated by the sponsor providing funds, resources or equipment to the individual or team in return for some form of association or user rights, which can be then used to the sponsor's commercial advantage. In other words, through the benevolent and high-profile association with sport, organisations are able to reach out to a range of potential audiences and markets that they may not be able to reach through other marketing communications techniques. Mainly through the medium of television, modern sport consumers have become used to sponsorship being a very visible element of sport, but this has not always been the case. Sponsorship as a marketing communications technique for sport is a relatively new concept, although it is within sport that sponsorship has developed most rapidly within recent years, and it is exactly this fact that has caused some observers to look more critically at the influence that sponsorship may be wielding in contemporary sport business. It used to be, and still is the case for many amateur sport organisations, that a local entrepreneur would provide the junior football team's strips because his son played for the team and it was a good way of achieving relatively low-cost promotional activity.

Nowadays, according to Slack and Amis:

> Sponsorship is different from philanthropy: it is a strategic action from which the sponsor expects commercial benefits to accrue...(which) can come at a cost to the sport and often involve broader social costs. (2004, p. 285)

In March 2005, Brian Lara, the talismanic captain, and six other players from the West Indies national cricket team were dropped just before the start of the first test against South Africa. The reason? All seven players have lucrative sponsorship agreements with Cable and Wireless, which had been, until July 2004, the official sponsors of the West Indies Cricket Board (WICB). The new WICB sponsor, Digicel, which is a rival telecoms company to Cable and Wireless, was not happy with the prospect that such high-profile players could conceivably appear on a world stage wearing the logos of both companies. Because a compromise between the two sponsoring organisations could not be agreed, both the game of cricket and the fans suffered. The people of the West Indies are particularly dependent on their cricket team for bringing tourism and the associated wealth into their countries, some of which are still trying to rebuild after hurricane damage in 2004. In 2007, the West Indies will be hosting the Cricket World Cup and questions surrounding the WICB's ability to achieve this successfully, particularly if they are unable to resolve sponsorship quarrels, are already being asked.

CASE 11.1   Twenty20 cricket at Durham County Cricket Club

In common with the other 17 First Class County Cricket Clubs in the UK, Durham County Cricket Club had its first, memorable experience of the Twenty20 Cup in July 2003. This new national competition of twenty overs per side with all 18 First Class teams competing occurred during the two weeks from 2nd July 2003 with three groups of six teams playing on a regional basis. The semi-finals and final were played on the same day to sell-out crowds at Trent Bridge on 19th July. On all levels, the experience was a resounding success and at the time of writing, the Club is eagerly awaiting the start of the 2005 tournament. This case study shows how Durham CCC approached the new tournament as a sport marketing communications exercise.

When the Twenty20 Cup was launched it was described as the 'most revolutionary step since the advent of one-day cricket 40 years ago'. With accolades like that, it was clear that much was expected of the new tournament and there was much written and spoken in the media about this being make or break time for County cricket. Well, Twenty20 became THE sporting success story of 2003 and it is to the credit of those with foresight and courage involved in the game and the determination of the Counties to put the fun back into cricket that the Twenty20 Cup is going from strength to strength to the extent that even Cricket Australia are making room for it in their 2006 schedule.

So how did Twenty20 win round the cricket fans of North East England? From the start, the core product – the tournament – was given an identity which was communicated consistently and coherently through the use of an integrated communications strategy in which the following techniques were implemented: local radio advertising, editorial in the local press (publicity), consumer database (members), generic mailing through a local 'What's On?' guide, targeted direct mailings, trailer advertising and the Durham County Cricket Club website (eNews).

Publicity centred on the concept that Twenty20 was not cricket, that entertainment was the primary objective and that spectators' demand to be entertained would be satisfied.

The Twenty20 brand values were core to the communications strategy and though they were common to the generic product, each County was encouraged to stamp its own identity on the home games. The core brand values were that the new game was, above all, intended to be exciting and the language used to communicate with the new target audiences for the game was different to that perhaps more usually associated with cricket. The vocabulary of the Twenty20 lexicon included words such as fun, fast, frantic, competitive, captivating all of which helped develop an image for the new format.

Another aspect that was emphasised was the social aspect built around the summer carnival atmosphere theme, watching cricket after work with your mates, bringing the family for a picnic and some fun which would be generated by the noise and pace of the new game. Because one of the major challenges to overcome was cricket's perceived elitism, accessibility and a game that can be enjoyed by anybody, that starts and finishes at a reasonable time and is played at a ground near you emerged as the new core brand values. The brand imagery was very much focused on big crowds, many of whom would be wearing fancy dress, lots of noise, entertainment, colour, social activity (drinking, eating and cheering) and participation.

Clearly, these images were designed to appeal to a non-traditional audience. Cricket matches lasting less than three hours, coloured clothing, a white ball, the next players in sitting on the boundary, players miked-up and engaging in banter with the commentators during the live broadcast matches, each player running out to bat to his chosen theme song were all new, overtly appealing techniques most of which had never been used in cricket before. If there had been any doubts that Twenty20 cricket was just going to be more of the same, these were swiftly dispelled and replaced with a quite feverish interest in the new format. This new approach to marketing cricket was such a success because, according to James Bailey who was then Marketing Manager at Durham County Cricket Club, it recognised the intangible qualities of the game – cricket cannot be physically owned, touched, tasted or smelt, it can only be experienced. There was a need to 'tangibalise the intangible' through creating an image of service quality, the management of the physical surroundings, brand development and the understanding that spectators should leave the game with tangible products whether that took the form of a painted face, a replica shirt or a player's autograph on a child's cricket bat.

Though the generic Twenty20 brand values were set by the England and Wales Cricket Board (ECB), each county was encouraged to develop its own personalised version of the game. Durham's strategy was to make each game start at 6.00 pm ensuring that as many people as possible could attend after school and work. The language Durham used to promote 'the Durham Twenty20 Experience' included words such as innovative, surprising, inclusive, accessible, creative, entertaining, enjoyable, young people, women, buzz and sell-out – again, words not traditionally associated with cricket. This focus on individuality allowed Durham to create a product which consumers said they wanted to see.

An excellent marketing communications strategy was essential in achieving a successful outcome to the new product launch at Durham. The Sport Integrated Marketing Communications mix was fully utilised with a particular emphasis being placed on relationship management. The overall aim was to ensure that customers who bought into Twenty20 cricket had an enjoyable and memorable experience which could potentially lead to a life long interest in cricket. The whole range of marketing communications tools were implemented including radio advertising, targeted mailings, outdoor advertising, e-newsletters, atmospherics and personal contact. The outcome of all this activity was an unparalleled success for Durham County Cricket Club. The measurable results for the 2003 Twenty20 tournament showed a dramatically different profile for cricket attendance. The average crowd for each game was 5300 with some matches being a complete sell-out, the average age of the consumer was 34 compared with the average age of 53 usually found in the County Championship audience. The Male/Female ratio was 77:23, again comparing extremely favourably with the usual 86:14 ratio for cricket.

Twenty20 cricket clearly caught the imagination of a non-traditional cricket audience as similar results were returned by all 18 county clubs at the end of the 2003 season. 2004 saw further developments to the format and results were even better. It remains to be seen what the results of the 2005 season will show but there is the widespread conviction that Twenty20 will go from strength to strength because cricket has successfully extended its product to become something with which people actively want to engage.

Questions

1. What challenges did Durham County Cricket Club have to meet in promoting Twenty20 cricket to the sports-loving North East of England?

2. Identify the range of communications techniques used and describe the degree of integration that was evident in the execution of Durham's SIMC strategy.

3. Do you think that this approach could work with other sports? Give your reasons.

Conclusions

Getting your message across to your targeted audiences sounds easy, but it is clear that the reality for people involved within promoting sports and sport organisations is rather more challenging. It is evident that for any sport organisation intent on maximising its full potential as a business in the contemporary sports environment, a business focus is essential. A thorough understanding of the benefits of a well-planned, strategic SIMCM has to be fundamental to successful long-term business planning. In today's increasingly competitive environment in which competition might be in the form of an afternoon spent at the local out-of-town shopping centre rather than giving support to the local opposing team, sport organisations cannot afford to neglect the power of communications. As identified in this chapter, there are plenty of examples of sport organisations adopting excellent strategic SIMC thinking that is making measurable differences to their existence.

Having an understanding of some of the theory that underpins the SIMC is also extremely useful for those charged with the job of communicating on behalf of sport organisations. Basing communication strategies on the principles of the SIMC process model can be much more cost effective than relying on the ad hoc, shoestring approach that has been characteristic of sport organisations in the past. It should be evident from this chapter that a strategic approach is a business approach and such an approach will bring rewards.

Some knowledge of the characteristics, advantages and disadvantages of the SIMCM tools and techniques means that those engaged in developing effective sport communications strategies can have a much better understanding and insight into how each of the distinct techniques can be used synergistically to greatest effect. It also allows individual sport organisations to stamp their own unique personality on the generic sport product, as demonstrated by Durham County Cricket Club's approach to Twenty20 cricket. Although the basic core sport product might be generic, publics and audiences do not always see it that way, and effective marketing communications can exploit this view in a way that is beneficial to all parties in the sport marketing exchange process.

Marketing communications in sport presents an exciting and challenging area in which to work. It is frequently the case that when sport integrated marketing communications forms an important part of the overall sport marketing strategy, sport organisations that engage with it are those that enjoy the most satisfactory and lucrative relationships with their publics. The often-used phrase that 'success breeds success' is entirely relevant within the sporting context – if the sport organisation concentrates its communications efforts on the relationships it needs to develop, then the eventual outcomes will tell their own story. Equally, if sport integrated marketing communication strategies are ignored or relegated in terms of their importance, the long-term consequences could be very expensive, indeed.

Discussion questions

1. For any sport of your choice, identify all the different elements that could be called the sport product. Think about what it is that makes your chosen sport product different from any other consumer product with which you are familiar.
2. For your chosen sport product, analyse how each of the elements of the SIMCM can be used to promote the product.
3. Think about any memorable sporting event you have attended or seen on TV and consider how each of the elements of the SIMCM were implemented and how they contributed to the success of that event.

Guided reading

There is generally very good coverage of the subject of marketing communications in all the widely used sport marketing texts but, as yet, it is difficult to find a text that deals with the integrated philosophy of sport marketing communications. The most comprehensive coverage of sport marketing communications can be found in Mullin, Hardy and Sutton (2000), Irwin et al. (2002) and Shank (2005). Although written very much from the US perspective, there are plenty of useful examples and case studies that help the reader to understand the requisite theoretical underpinning. Shilbury, Quick and Westerbeek (2003) provide a very useful dimension on the role of public relations in sport marketing communications.

In order to understand the thinking behind sport integrated marketing communications, it is necessary to know the fundamentals of marketing communications. A very good source from which to acquire a thorough understanding of the principles of integrated marketing communications is Pickton and Broderick (2005). This is a very readable text that tells you everything you need to know about integrated marketing communications; however, it is a general business and marketing text, so it does not focus on the application to sport. Fill (2002) is another business-oriented marketing communications text.

A number of recently published sport business texts have much more of a United Kingdom or European perspective. Beech and Chadwick (2004) is up to date and very readable. Currently, the only available text that covers sports sponsorship and marketing communications is the one written by Lagae (2005). Both books by Smith and Westerbeek (2003, 2004) give an extremely interesting perspective on the recent developments in sport business and marketing. In addition, a trawl of the academic journals provides some interesting reading. Some useful sources are:

- *Journal of Marketing Communications*
- *Corporate Communications: An International Journal*
- *International Journal of Sports Marketing and Sponsorship*
- *Journal of Sport Management*
- *Sport Marketing Quarterly*

Keywords

Atmospherics; business acumen; communications theory; integrated marketing communications; marketing public relations; one-way communication; propaganda; reputation management; SIMC process model; sport integrated marketing communications mix; transactional; two-way symmetrical communication.

Bibliography

Barnes, S. (2005) At breaking point: The stars finding that more equals less, *The Times*, Friday 7 January 2005.

Beech, J. and Chadwick, S. (2004) *The Business of Sport Management,* Harlow: Pearson Education Limited.

Cutlip, S.M., Center, A.H. and Broom, G.M. (2000) *Effective Public Relations*, 8th edn, Upper Saddle River, NJ: Prentice Hall.

Duncan, T. (2005) *Principles of Advertising and IMC*, 2nd international edn, New York: McGraw-Hill/Irwin.

Fill, C. (2002) *Marketing Communications Contexts, Strategies and Applications*, 3rd edn, Harlow: Pearson Education Limited.

Grunig, J. (ed.) (1992) *Excellence in Public Relations and Communication Management*, Hillsdale, NJ: Lawrence Erlbaum Associates.

Gummesson, E. (2002) *Total Relationship Marketing*, 2nd edn, Oxford: Butterworth-Heinemann.

Hopwood, M.K. (2003) *Public Relations Practice in English County Cricket: A Case Study of Yorkshire County Cricket Club and Durham County Cricket Club*, Unpublished thesis, University of Stirling, Scotland.

Irwin, R., Sutton, W.A. and McCarthy, L.M. (2002) *Sport Promotion and Sales Management*, Champaign, IL: Human Kinetics.

Kotler, P. (1982) *Marketing for Nonprofit Organisations*, Englewood Cliffs, NJ: Prentice Hall.

Lagae, W. (2005) *Sport Sponsorship and Marketing Communications: A European Perspective*, Harlow: Pearson Education Limited.

Ledingham, J.A. (2000) Guidelines to building and maintaining strong organization-public relationships, *Public Relations Quarterly* 45(3):44–7.

Marconi, J. (2004) *Public Relations: The Complete Guide*, Mason, OH: Thomson Learning.

Mullin, B.J., Hardy, S. and Sutton, W.A. (2000) *Sport Marketing*, 2nd edn, Champaign, IL: Human Kinetics.

Peters, T. and Waterman Jr, R.H. (1982) *In Search of Excellence: Lessons from America's Best-Run Companies*, London: HarperCollins.

Pickton, D. and Broderick, A. (2005) *Integrated Marketing Communications*, 2nd edn, Harlow: Pearson Education Limited.

Shank, M. (2005) *Sports Marketing: A Strategic Perspective*, 3rd international edn, Upper Saddle River, NJ: Pearson Education.

Shilbury, D., Quick, S. and Westerbeek, H. (2003) *Strategic Sport Marketing*, 2nd edn, Crows Nest NSW, Australia: Allen and Unwin.

Slack, T. and Amis, J. (2004) 'A critical perspective on sports sponsorship', in *The Commercialisation of Sport*, Abingdon: Routledge.

Smith, A. and Westerbeek, H. (2004) *The Sport Business Future*, Basingstoke: Palgrave Macmillan.

Westerbeek, H. and Smith, A. (2003) *Sport Business in the Global Marketplace*, Basingstoke: Palgrave Macmillan.

Recommended websites

The best and most memorable way of learning about how sport organisations approach their marketing communications is to experience it for yourself. Visiting websites is a useful start, and many of the ones listed below have all been referred to in this chapter. Go have a look and critically evaluate them in terms of their communications appeal.

BBC Sports News
http://news.bbc.co.uk/sport/

Bradford Bulls Club
http://www.bradfordbulls.co.uk/index04.asp

Durham County Cricket Club
http://www.durhamccc.co.uk/

The England and Wales Cricket Board
http://www.ecb.co.uk

English Football Association
http://www.thefa.com

The Financial Times
http://news.ft.com/sportnews

The Guardian
http://sport.guardian.co.uk/

Manchester United Football Club
http://www.manutd.com/

Newcastle Falcons Club
http://www.newcastlefalcons.co.uk/3_6.php

Rugby Business World
http://www.rugbybusinessworld.com

Sport Business International
http://www.sportbusiness.com

The Twenty20 Cup
http://www.thetwenty20cup.co.uk/

Chapter 12

Direct, database and online marketing in sport

Paul Turner
Deakin University

Learning outcomes

Upon completion of this chapter, the reader should be able to:

■ Define the terms *direct marketing, database marketing* and *online marketing* and appreciate the nature of these activities.

■ Explain the importance of direct, database and online marketing from a sport marketing perspective.

■ Identify the wide range of sport organisation objectives that can be achieved through direct, database and online marketing.

■ Appreciate the major stages in the development of an effective sport database and online programme.

■ Highlight important issues relating to direct, database and online marketing activities.

Overview of chapter

A key feature of the current sport marketing environment is the increasing use of inter-activity. The more personal this interactivity is, the more persuasive and accepted it is. The concept of direct marketing and personal selling has been integrated within the sport marketing literature for a significant period of time. What has evolved is the changing face of direct and database marketing through new and innovative communication and information technology. It is now easier and more cost effective than ever before to have personal dialogue with customers, supporter groups, the media, sponsors and governing bodies. And these groups are increasingly expecting and demanding greater personal contact with each other.

This chapter begins with a definition and explanation of the terms *direct, database* and online marketing and relates them to the sporting context. Distinctions between direct marketing and personal selling are drawn at this point. Direct marketing introduces a one-to-one process of supplying information to customers with the intention of facilitating a sale. The methods used in a direct marketing campaign can be wide ranging and encompass the opportunity to be developed through a multitude of media.

Database management involves the creation, facilitation and maintenance of an organisation's customer information system. This customer information system can be represented by current users and interested or potential users. The database can be a simplistic alphabetic list of names through to a more sophisticated computer program involving comprehensive checking and cross-referencing.

Online marketing represents a 'new-media' form of communication, information dissemination and commercial opportunity. The development of a worldwide network of interconnected computer networks, widely known as the internet, has enabled the transmission and exchange of data to be communicated to audiences globally and cheaply. This development has presented opportunity for information dissemination and electronic commerce to expand on a scale unlike any other in history.

Each of these dimensions of direct, database and online marketing are addressed in turn. Case studies based on the practical experiences of well-known companies are introduced at regular intervals to illustrate core aspects of direct marketing, database marketing and online marketing. Several leading sporting organisations form the basis of case material. Important learning points are reinforced by the use of discussion questions that draw on case material or other issues and topics raised in the chapter.

Introduction

It can be argued that direct, database and online marketing are essential components of any competitive marketing strategy. The crucial outcome relates to the creation of an immediate sale, or to open a dialogue and develop ongoing relationships with potential customers in order to bring about a sale or series of transactions sooner (Kotler, Adam, Brown and Armstrong, 2003; Mitchell, 2003). The opportunity now exists within the information age for marketers to communicate with potential customers in real time, enabling immediacy of response and measured expenditures to be derived. An order can be filled immediately after it is placed, and databases can be developed and managed to store transaction details.

Direct and online marketing databases are used to identify prospects, determine which customers will receive certain types of offers, deepen customer loyalty, reactivate customer purchases and identify patterns and trends within the data ('data mining'). Although direct marketing in some shape or form has been around for a considerable period of time, the development of databases through advances in technology has made the process far easier to undertake. Principally, a key development in technology is the development of online methods of communication.

Each of the components of direct marketing, database marketing and online marketing is addressed in turn in this chapter, with case examples integrated throughout to support the context of the information presented.

Direct marketing

Direct marketing is defined as:

> ...non-personal and personal communications between a marketer and its publics that usually have the aim of gaining a direct response, such as sales, or even a vote at a forthcoming annual general meeting of shareholders. Such communications may be oral, mailed or electronic; an interactive system that uses one or more advertising media to effect a measurable response and/or transaction at any location. (Kotler et al., 2003, p. 495)

The impact of the definition presented is that direct marketing implements any or many different media and that a measure or response is sought from a measured input of expenditure.

Although direct marketing forms an integral component of the promotional mix, much of the focus on promotion is on advertising, sales promotions, personal selling and public relations or publicity. Although a great deal of attention is placed on these promotional mix tools, the opportunity to go direct with these same tools can generate an immediate behavioural response (Belch and Belch, 2004). Direct marketing is an integrated approach that uses the range of marketing attributes such as market research, segmentation, evaluation and conjunction with direct response media such as direct mail, telemarketing, interactive TV, print, the internet and so on.

The more personalised the interactivity is, the more effective and persuasive it is. Direct marketing has been around for decades, but the developing technology such as the internet is dramatically changing the way it is presented. It is easier and more cost effective to have greater personal dialogue with consumers, particularly those who represent the targeted audiences of a company. Equally, consumers are increasingly expecting and demanding personal contact with companies in return.

Direct marketing is effective in supporting the complete selling process from creating awareness of a problem or opportunity for customers to their purchase decision. The greatest impact is on closing the sale or enhancing the decision step. The other advantage in direct marketing is the capacity to enable organisations to measure their effectiveness quantitatively. The capacity to determine the cost coupled with the effectiveness of the sale is of paramount importance to an organisation (Duncan, 2002).

Within the field of direct marketing, a magnitude of terminology is used. Terms such as *one-to-one marketing, database marketing, loyalty marketing, e-marketing, interactive marketing, retention marketing* and *micro-marketing*, to name a few, are used (Kotler et al., 2003; Tapp, 2001). The common theme associated with direct marketing is that it involves activities that embrace one-on-one interaction between buyers and sellers. The concept of maintenance of a database, a relationship with the customer, and ordering and payment processes are observed.

In a sporting context, direct marketing is greatly enhanced in supporting consumption and communication. Sport consumers are extremely loyal and averse to brand switching (Shilbury, Quick and Westerbeek, 2003). A comprehensive and cohesive direct marketing campaign can ensure that information is readily updated and maintained, with sales being achieved and measured. Sport consumers seek to be involved and are extremely committed to their sports club, presenting a great opportunity to the marketers within a sporting organisation to achieve their goals. An extremely important feature of ensuring that sport consumers can be identified and successfully communicated with is through the maintenance of a database. A comprehensive and up-to-date database is a crucial element in a direct marketing approach, as is the concept of online marketing, which is an extension of direct marketing. Each of these areas is addressed in the following sections.

Although direct marketing represents the communication process with the customer, various media can be used in order to carry out a direct marketing campaign. These media are briefly identified below:

Telemarketing represents the use of the telephone to deliver an offer or take an order. This type of direct marketing is also strongly aligned to personal selling approaches. Telemarketing caters for a broad range of activities. It can be used to generate sales or assist in building a database, through to being developed in full account management practices. Often telemarketing can be used to coordinate customer service issues through mechanisms such as follow-up calls in order to ascertain customer satisfaction with a product.

Call centres comprise a bank of telephones staffed by sales representatives whose dialogue is guided by computer-generated scripts. The use of scripts ensures that the offer is presented in the correct order and the necessary response information can be recorded. These call centres can be used for soliciting sales and receiving orders, but extensions into surveys, appointment setting and customer service can also emerge.

Direct mail is presented in a number of formats from handwritten postcards to DVD recordings and sample packs. Often the direct mail message might piggyback other mailings such as including special offers or sales messages with utility bills or credit card statements. Although direct mail is an addressable medium, the majority of direct mailings are still impersonal. Although personalisation of direct mail is emerging, it is still largely cost prohibitive for most sporting organisations. The advantage is that it can be an accompaniment to customer reminders to renew memberships and such.

Catalogues are usually presented to customers as specialist offerings representing the particular items available at a store. The development of online catalogues, CD-ROMs and DVDs has added to the way in that information can be provided to the customer.

Infomercials represent programme-length advertisements that may run on the television for many minutes. The idea is to educate viewers about the product and then solicit potential sales. These infomercials can be cost effective in production compared with traditional television advertisements, given the cost of a single studio and presenter.

Direct print and reproduction represents the use of printed materials as a form of selected mailings in a targeted fashion to potential customers who have expressed interest in previous offerings.

Electronic dispensing and kiosks can extend from EFTPOS (Electronic Funds Transfer Point of Scale) machines through to emerging technology with telephones and computers to enable transactions to be carried out.

Direct selling involves selling directly to customers through door-to-door or more personal approaches. The costs associated with this type of selling are generally high through hiring, training and motivating salespeople.

Electronic shopping has emerged through the information age with telephones, interactive television programmes and internet services.

The advances in technology are creating increased opportunities for direct marketing to become an integral element of any sporting organisation's integrated marketing communications strategy.

CASE 12.1   The St George BRW Corporate Triathlon

The St George BRW Corporate Triathlon is a national series of triathlon competitions held at various Australian cities during March and April each year. Sponsored by the St George Bank and *Business Review Weekly* (BRW), the triathlon is managed and operated by an independent sport management company (Super Sprint Promotions). This company has experience in numerous triathlon events including responsibility for organising the 2000 Olympic Games Triathlon competition.

Now in its 17th year, the St George BRW corporate triathlon series has developed into a key feature within the Australian business community. The triathlon offers people with a wide range of abilities the opportunity to compete over a 400m swim, 10km cycle and 4km run. Events are presented in individual and team categories, with a strong emphasis on corporate team involvement. The competition dates for the 2005 National Series comprised:

Adelaide – West Lakes	6 March
Perth – Langley Park	13 March
Melbourne – Elwood Beach	20 March
Sydney – Mrs Macquaries Point	17 April
Gold Coast – The Spit	24 April

Entries into the Melbourne and Sydney series closed off in record time, while the other locations were patronised at record levels. Melbourne entries were closed two days after officially opening. The vast majority of entries were received online through a secure entry database. Entrants could opt to enter as an individual or corporate team. Entrants who missed the opportunity to enter the Melbourne event could enter through another triathlon event run by Super Sprint Promotions. The Gatorade Triathlon Series has 50 places on offer for teams who missed out on gaining a place in the Melbourne event. This is the 5th annual Corporate Qualifier which sees teams of 3 complete the 300m swim, 10km cycle and 3km run starting together with each member's time aggregated to give an overall team time. To enter you need to select the Brooks Fun Triathlon as the event and then the Corporate Qualifier as the race. The event is also the official warm up event for competitors who have gained a place in the Melbourne event. Competitors can compete as individuals in the Brooks Fun Triathlon with a 300m swim, 10km cycle and 3km run.

Due to the demand for the Melbourne and Sydney series a further entry opportunity was forwarded through a direct mailing to all St George Bank customers. Every St George Bank customer based in Victoria received, along with their bank statement, the opportunity to participate in the Melbourne event. The flyer below was part of a mail-out that was forwarded.

This opportunity was forwarded in a mass mailing, as part of the bank's normal mailing of statements to customers. While many people receiving this message would have little interest in the event, those Bank customers with any interest would be captured by the opportunity presented. The Bank can leverage its sponsorship by being the one organisation that has places available for this event. And these places are limited only to current customers.

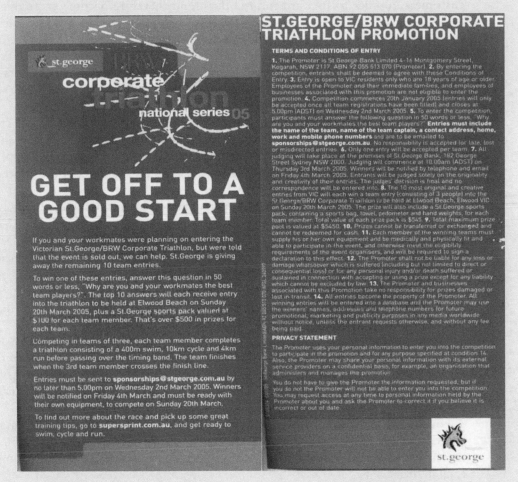

Source: Information from Super Sprint Promotions website. Retrieved 4 April 2005, from http://www.supersprint.com.au and St George Bank flyer

Questions

1. Is the direct mail approach through the use of a flyer such as this a suitable way to attract interest in this event?

2. What is the benefit of this direct mail to the sponsor (St George Bank)?

3. Would the cost of this direct mail campaign be justified?

Database marketing

Although it is theoretically possible to undertake a direct marketing strategy without a database, it is not entirely practical. Direct marketing achievements are a key result of the quality of the customer lists that they represent (Duncan, 2002). Because of the costs involved, direct marketers often do not make a profit on their first sale to customers. Therefore, they need to ensure that they have sufficient information on these customers in order to forward future offers (and therefore become profitable customers). A database aids this process while also enabling information about sales and measured outcomes to be achieved. Good databases are imperative in developing brand relationships because they allow marketers to identify the organisation's best customers, their value to the organisation and their needs and buying behaviours (visit Experian at http://www.experian.com for an example of an organisation that assists with database management opportunities).

The comprehensive development of an effective and functioning database is crucial in supporting the direct marketing efforts that are to be undertaken. It is pointless, however, in maintaining a database of significance if there is no understanding of how to use it. That is where it is essential to have a clear understanding of the direct marketing efforts to be employed.

The impact of database marketing is separated into two distinct roles (Tapp, 2002). The first represents an organisation's gaining a sense of the market needs and changes in order to retain an understanding of the customer. The second role is one of facilitation, in which marketers influence other functions' decision-making priorities to ensure that customer satisfaction is considered paramount. This second role is one in which the database marketer's role is to assist the company in its market sensing. The importance of the organisation's understanding its customer base is crucial in supporting the development and growth of its output and product lines.

Relational databases are now more commonly used in marketing. The data are entered via the internet and accessed by organisations. Data is stored in two-dimensional tables of rows and columns, with each row representing the attribute and each column representing the same attribute for all records. The tables are linked by common keys and can easily be reconfigured.

Four major categories of marketing strategies are pursued through the database (McClymont and Jocumsen, 2003). These four categories are customer retention, customer reactivation, product and service, and promotion strategies. Briefly examining each in turn:

Customer retention using database marketing is defined as building long-term business with customers through the gathering and storing of information about customer characteristics, purchasing patterns and satisfaction levels. It is generally considered more expensive to acquire a new customer than to service an existing one, and it is also potentially more profitable to develop an existing customer interest; therefore, the key customers who contribute to the organisation's profits should be developed fully.

Customer reactivation is closely aligned to retention, but the specific process of seeking to reactivate declining levels of loyal customer interest is one that may require the implementation of reactivation strategies. The process includes identifying which customers have defected, researching and analysing why they have left, and finally using this information to reactivate the customer when possible.

Product and service development occurs through the strategic use of database marketing. This process provides information for monitoring and assessing changing customer needs and wants. The process of developing new products to service these needs or revamping existing products is part of this process.

Promotion strategies involve the cross-selling (selling customers related or unrelated products) to an existing customer base or through prospecting (selling existing products to prospective buyers) to a new customer base.

Databases are implemented and developed over a period of time. Initial attributes associated with database management include:

■ *Identifying prospects* through advertising response features from which the database is built. The best prospects are then communicated with through a direct marketing approach to convert into customers.

■ *Deciding which customers to approach* in order to present a particular offer is undertaken through the database. This can enable customers most resembling the ideal type to be identified. Procedures can be implemented whereby the order can be filled and then a week later a thank-you note sent, 5 weeks later a new offer sent and 10 weeks later a special discount forwarded.

■ *Deepening customer loyalty*, which can be built through remembering customer preferences and forwarding appropriate information, gifts or other materials.

Extensions of the database can be achieved through reactivating customer purchases when product replacements, upgrades or complementary products can be identified in a timely fashion to support customer actions. Although reactivating customer involvement in an organisation is a key attribute associated with database management, the concept of data mining must be considered as a critical opportunity. Data mining involves maintenance of the database as a large warehouse of stored information. The database can be checked for patterns and trends that exist or may in fact develop connections between data items. Within the context of data mining is an additional process, that of 'web mining', which involves retrieving and converting information from websites into an organised database containing key variables of interest for better understanding customers. This process can be easily undertaken through the link between online activity and database activity, providing an organisation with valuable information about its customers or potential customers.

When using database technology, the intention is to engage in one-to-one dialogue and elicit a desired, measurable response in target groups and individuals (Kotler et al., 2003). These target groups form the database list of clients.

Web and email list database creation

Electronic database systems through which messages can be forwarded to customers via email are becoming increasingly more popular. The capacity to establish address books or email lists present greater opportunity to market products or services to interested sport customers. The opportunity for ready-made information dissemination on a personal or mass-produced level, targeted at niche segments or a complete membership list is now available to sporting organisations. As already stated, this is often supported through interested consumers readily requesting information online so they can 'belong' to their club or sport organisation.

Most clubs and sporting organisations, whether they are large or small, have members who join through the expression of an interest in the organisation. This interest can be developed through instant and inexpensive communication via the internet. Forwarding information to members through one consistent message can be done at the touch of a button. The message can be personalised if required, and the message can be accompanied by other promotional materials.

The effectiveness of these messages can be monitored through response and reply activities, either through return emailing or tracking purchase behaviours. Sporting organisations are in the enviable position of often requesting response information from interested consumers. Questions such as: 'Who will be the club's best player this week?' or 'Rate the service provided at the gymnasium', while providing invaluable information to the organisation, also enable a picture of consumer interest and behaviour to be developed.

Registration or membership to email lists is often free and readily accessible (see examples below of Melbourne Storm National Rugby League Club and of membership to Bomberland, the Essendon Football Club that plays in the Australian Football League). Registration is free, and subscribers to the service receive regular email updates from the clubs (weekly in the case of the Melbourne Storm; monthly in the case of Essendon).

The registration process is instant, provides access to restricted websites of the club, and provides the opportunity to receive regular updates and information packages. Newsletters are provided on a regular basis, but the opportunity exists for many other promotions and information services to be provided. The advantage is that the people

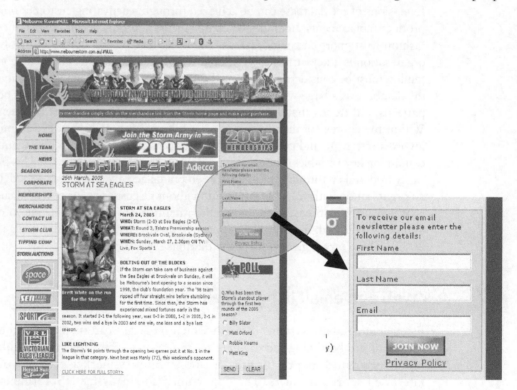

Source: Melbourne Storm. Retrieved 4 April 2005, from http://www.melbournestorm.com.au

who have registered for the site are often fans of the sporting organisation and therefore more receptive to promotions that involve the club.

Websites may offer users the opportunity to supply personal information to enable additional services to be provided, including allowing users to access restricted areas of the website, a response mechanism to users' questions by email or the provision of information to users. Consumers may also choose to complete online surveys or offer feedback to the persons responsible for maintaining the website. The issue of the maintenance and management of sport databases should be less worrying for clubs than for marketers of other generic products. Clubs have a ready-made brand-identifying market that will ensure a level of ongoing purchasing while also refraining from switching to another club.

Source: Essendon FC. Retrieved 4 April 2005, from http://www.essendonfc.com.au

CASE 12.2   Registering online for the Lawdons

The Essendon Football Club have a very successful membership recruitment and retention program. Club membership in the Australian Football League (AFL) is a very important component of club development, and one that provides a club with a ready stream of revenue. Within the context of the AFL, club membership is one of the few remaining activities that is not controlled or managed by the League. The clubs are responsible for attracting and retaining members, and as a result retain any revenue raised through membership.

While membership therefore becomes a major focus of the club, and the capacity to develop different streams and opportunity for members to be part of the club, there is a requirement to identify and develop alternative opportunities. These opportunities not only generate needed club revenues, but also enable databases to be developed about interested groups of people.

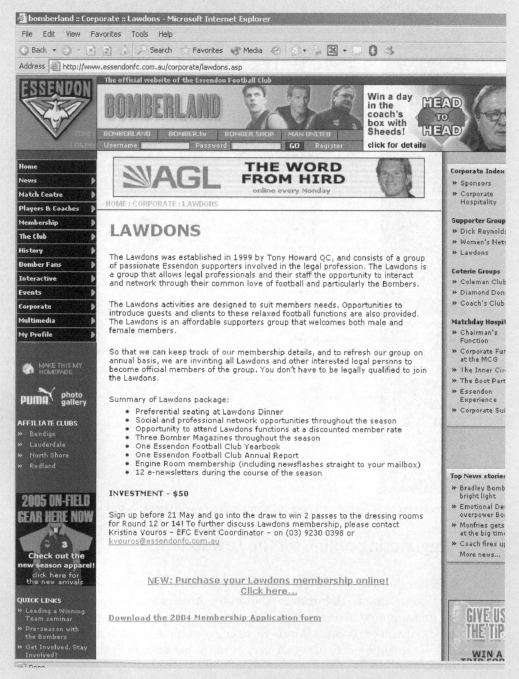

Source: Essendon FC. Retrieved 4 April 2005, from http://www.essendonfc.com.au

A novel opportunity to generate interest in the Essendon Football Club was introduced through their establishment of the Lawdons. The Lawdons involves a special membership to a key niche-oriented group of Essendon supporters. Membership does not obligate a person to attendance at club games, or any future commitment to club activities, but enables an interested supporter who may be too busy otherwise to regularly attend, to still feel that they are a valued club supporter. There are special activities conducted and information provided to these people, to ensure that they are provided crucial information about the club. The club can develop a relevant niche database on a core group of interested people, where regular updates and information can be presented to these people.

Questions

1. How effective or useful is a web registration site like this for a sporting organisation?

2. What are the implications of developing information gathered from subscribers to this site into a meaningful database?

3. Think of a sporting organisation that you are familiar with. How could a similar niche database be developed for this organisation?

Database privacy policies

Within many industrialised nations, the issue of personal privacy is something that is valued by members of the society. The ability of people to have their rights to privacy respected and not be bombarded with information that they have not requested is something that must be considered by any organisation developing responsible use of a database. The capacity to present information immediately and through many alternative media has required organisations to clearly state how they will use any information gathered. Many of these industrialised nations have a legal requirement to state the database privacy policy that is used by any organisation.

Key features of a stated privacy policy generally include:

1. A message stating the importance of the privacy of individuals. The general theme is that a person's individual information is important to the organisation and that the organisation collecting the information will endeavour to protect personal information and provide choice in how this information can be used.

2. The collection of personal information is undertaken to ensure development of products and services in order to enhance the experience. The critical issue here is not necessarily how the information will be used by the organisation but how the organisation may agree to disseminate information to other organisations. Personal information means information or opinions about a person that would reveal the identity of that person. It extends to information recorded in any format, including digital or electronic formats derived from computer access.

3. Preservation of privacy is stated in a way that any information regarding a person (e.g., name, address, email address and phone number) and products or services that

person may purchase from the organisation will not be given or sold to any outside organisation for use in marketing or solicitation, except with the person's consent. It should be stated, however, that information may be shared with agents or contractors of the collecting organisation for the purpose of performing services for the organisation. The use or disclosure of information is not to occur without a person's consent; however, an organisation may collect or disclose anonymous aggregate information regarding its stakeholders or the use of the organisation's services.

4. Promotional activities should only be conducted by the organisation responsible for collecting these materials. If an organisation wishes to develop market research opportunities, the subscriber to the database should be contacted. The organisation might also contact subscribers to see if they are interested in participating in market research. Once agreeable to receive marketing materials, the onus is on the consumer to request removal from the database in the future.

5. Storage and security associated with personal information should involve all reasonable steps to keep secure any personal information held while maintaining that this information is kept accurate and up to date.

6. Following any request, an organisation should provide a customer with a copy of any personal information held in accordance with obligations under the Privacy Act.

7. Problems or questions should be directed to the organisation's privacy officer.

A further mechanism that enables an organisation to obtain information about website access is through the development of cookies.

Cookies

A cookie is a small text file that is stored by a browser on a computer's hard drive. It has a limited lifetime, usually until the browser is shut down. This allows web servers to remember the user on subsequent visits without having to prompt them for the same information. This function may be disabled in the web browser if the user does not wish to accept cookies, but this may affect access to all parts of any visited website.

Cookies are used to store both personal and non-personal information. Examples of personal information are encrypted usernames and encrypted passwords required to access key sites. Examples of non-personal information include generic web servers that a user has authenticated into, the top-level domain name of the user's internet service provider, the date and time of a visit to the site, the pages accessed and downloaded, the address of the last site visited and the type of browser being used.

Cookies make it possible to identify registered users without needing to ask for registration details every time the user accesses a site. Using cookies makes accessing sites more convenient to the users because users do not need to remember their user names and passwords every time they enter the site.

Cookies can also be accessed to track users as they travel through a website. For instance, a site might use cookies to count the total number of unique users accessing the site over a particular period of time or to ensure that users do not see a particular advert more than once. This information is used purely for internal purposes. The use of cookies in this way helps to make systems more efficient. Many organisations also use this information for monitoring website use and to facilitate website management, development and planning.

Online marketing

Digital information systems are enabling new ways of doing business to emerge. Online marketing can be defined as the threefold role of the internet in commerce and government as a new media (communication) tool, knowledge media tool (the organisation learning about customers and employees, as well as customers and employees learning about the organisation), and a marketing channel (online transactions; Kotler et al., 2003).

The World Wide Web (WWW) has emerged as a significant mass communication medium in the past 5 to 10 years. Internet traffic is increasing exponentially, and the uses and opportunities emerging in a vast array of areas such as electronic commerce, online retailing, advertising and broadcasting are increasingly offering opportunities to sport and sporting organisations.

Sport marketers can use the WWW in presenting content and applications in areas such as ticketing, registration and membership, merchandise sales, sponsorship and advertising, newsletters, organisation contact details, player biographies and broadcasting, to name just few of the possible applications. With the advent of attributes such as streaming video, coaches are starting to use the WWW to instruct their athletes directly over the internet, major leagues are broadcasting competition fixtures through audio or audiovisual subscription services and real-time news reports are being presented to the fans. The internet is presenting sporting organisations with increased opportunities to develop databases and produce fully networked applications. This enables the removal of geographic restrictions, and through the use of security measures, a person can access membership databases from another geographic location, assisting the organisation to become far more competitive.

The internet also enables income and advertising to be generated through sport websites. This aspect continues to grow at an increasing rate. The National Football League's latest contract for internet rights is valued at $300m over 5 years (*Sport Business*, 2001c). Equally, Major League Baseball (MLB) recently entered into a $20m, 4-year deal with RealNetworks for live radio broadcasts of its games (*Sport Business*, 2001a). Global spending on the sponsorship of sport websites has been placed at $253m, according to joint findings reported by the Sport Business Information Resources Unit and Sponsorship Research International (*Sport Business*, 2001b). These research organisations have also estimated the online advertising expenditure on sport websites to be approximately $450m (Church, 2001).

The internet provides sport marketers with a continuous flow of timely and accurate business intelligence. For example, knowledge about potential customers (e.g., gender, marital status, age, interests, hobbies) is readily available and can be converted to consumer intelligence databases for marketing purposes. Discussions held in chat rooms, newsgroups and online bulleting boards provide an abundant source of market intelligence (e.g., consumer preference, evaluation of existing products, customer complaints). Competitor information and business direction can be gleaned from organisations' websites. Market surveys through the internet can present effective and efficient data-gathering opportunities for organisations (Lau, Lee, Ho and Lam, 2004).

CASE 12.3   Cyberhorse: marketing online

Cyberhorse, was established in 1995 as an internet business specialising in the Australian horse industry with a focus on Australian racing and breeding. The business is run from the property of Bill and Berni Saunders, Hollybrook Stud, situated in the heart of Victoria's thoroughbred breeding country near Emirates Victoria and The Independent Stallion Station.

Bill and Berni recognise that the horse industry is only just beginning to understand how to use the internet as a marketing and communication tool. As with all other media, its usefulness for advertising and promotion is dependent on getting to the right target audience in sufficient volume. Cyberhorse has based its business around creating high traffic services such as The Virtual FormGuide, The Virtual Saleyard and The Virtual Equestrian. These popular internet destinations attract thousands of visitors each day.

In turn, Cyberhorse's regular visitors ensure that clients for which it develops and manages websites, derive attention not only from their own audience, but are constantly exposed to potential new clients. The Virtual Saleyard software provides the mechanism to promote these other sites to Cyberhorse visitors and channel traffic to them. For example, a major thoroughbred stud received approximately 1000 hits per month before Cyberhorse redesigned their site and implemented its promotional strategy. During April 2002, only one year after the new site went live, traffic exceeded 250,000 hits in one month.

Cyberhorse promotes itself as a strategic partner for any horse industry business wanting to develop and implement an internet strategy. Cyberhorse sites have more than 250,000 unique visitors a month and over 10 million hits. Cross promotional capability is provided by The Virtual Saleyard's Featured and Enhanced Listings which prioritise advertisements in searches as well as allowing banner advertising.

There are 4 main listing categories:

- Horses (Featured, Enhanced and free text listings)
- Classifieds (Featured, Enhanced and free text listings)
- Stallions (Featured and Enhanced only)
- Products & Services (Featured and Enhanced only)

The Cyberhorse business is strategically split into three core components.

The Virtual FormGuide

The Virtual FormGuide is an Internet delivered range of information for Australian horse racing fans. Access to most of the services is via a membership application. Membership requires a positive balance to be retained in a member account. While membership is required to access The Virtual FormGuide, there is a mix of free and chargeable services. For form and ratings, subscriptions are available for periods from 1 day to a year. Alternatively, each form of data can be purchased as an individual pay-per-view file, paid for from the Member Account.

Free services include:

- Nominations and weights (includes prizemoney and last 4 start positions).
- Fields with jockeys.
- Realtime Odds including 3 TAB's odds on the same screen.
- Quickfind Search facility for all horses, jockeys, trainers, sires, mares and damsires currently online (usually 7 days).
- Virtual Stable allows for the creation of a stable of horses. An email message is forwarded to subscribers when they are running and/or they can be accessed directly from the web.
- Trainer, jockey and stallion statistics for all Australian runners for the past 5 years.

Chargeable services include:

- Form at Nominations service for all Australian TAB meetings. The NORM service provides a detailed 5 start form service similar to that for The Virtual FormGuide. NORM is available soon after nominations and is updated when weights are issued.
- 3 start, 5 start or 10 start form for all Australian TAB meetings. Depending on the level of service, includes all the normal information plus positions in running (metro races), actual prizemoney won per race, average prizemoney index, full owners list, first up and second up statistics, spells and let-ups. Form is available in zip file format for fast download and printing or interactively from the Real Time Odds screen.
- Cyberhorse Racing Clubs provide the opportunity to combine a form subscription with a low cost membership in a Club racing a well bred horse trained by Lindsay Park Racing Stables.
- Enhanced Virtual Stable allows form subscribers to add trainers, jockeys, stallions, mares and damsires to their stable.
- Base Ratings for all races issued at acceptance time and updated after scratchings on race morning.
- Plus Ratings for all races issued at acceptance time and updated after scratchings on race morning.
- Xtra Ratings for all races issued after scratchings on race morning.
- The Virtual Tipping Team – Professional ratings and selection providers with a complete track record of all previous tips.
- Enhanced Realtime Odds service which includes the recommended odds from the Cyberhorse ratings services (through subscription).
- By-A-Nose Data input. The free By-A-Nose selection software is available from Pineapplehead. The download of form and price data into By-A-Nose can be undertaken automatically from the web, through subscribing to Cyberhorse's customised service.
- Individual horse form for its complete racing career (email service)
- Detailed catalogue pedigrees for Australian and NZ thoroughbreds.

The Virtual Equestrian

The Virtual Equestrian is Cyberhorse's online destination for all equestrian sport fans. The site features reports and results for dressage, eventing, showjumping and showing. The Virtual Equestrian provides information to interested parties on horses, domestically and internationally with Olympic Games information and horse health tips and processes. Forums enable interested equestrian participants to discuss and acquire information, breeders to update facts, tax and accounting tips to be exchanged, a cyberfoal centre and a meet market where people with like interests can communicate with one another. Sections on dressage eventing showjumping and show ring have been developed, each of which present news, profiles, results and horse information.

The Virtual Saleyard

The Virtual Saleyard (TVS) was first developed by Cyberhorse in 1999. Since that time, Cyberhorse has listed thousands of horses worth more than $50m, making a justifiable claim to having the score on the board as the place to get horses sold. With reduced pricing, a more streamlined vendor interface and unique Featured Listings, which allow listings to be seen on web pages, The Virtual Saleyard is considered a 'must have' part of any horse sellers marketing campaign.

The Virtual Saleyard has been designed by Cyberhorse as an easy to use and economical service for those wishing to buy or sell horses or anything else which is horse related. Browsing through the listings is free and there is no charge for basic text advertisements in the Horses and Classifieds categories. Clients can take advantage of The Virtual Saleyard to earn income for themselves.

To list anything for sale it is necessary to register as a TVS Member. Registration is free and allows your contact details to be included when placing your advertisement(s). It is only necessary to register once even though you may have many listings across several categories. Cyberhorse promotes The Virtual Saleyard as being a popular destination in its own right but for advertisers, its selling power being greatly enhanced by the ability to have advertisements also appear as banner ads within the pages of Cyberhorse's popular content areas including The Virtual FormGuide, The Virtual Equestrian, Cyberhorse Forums and The Virtual Saleyard.

Cyberhorse identify that many of Australia's best performance horses are thoroughbreds who have raced. Sadly off the track thoroughbreds do not always find a loving equestrian home at the end of their racing days. The Cyberhorse Racehorse Outplacement Program is designed to cost effectively alert equestrian riders about the availability of ex racehorses and create a system where they can be rehoused and rehabilitated.

Source: Adapted from the website of Cyberhorse. Retrieved 4 April 2005, from http://www.cyberhorse.com.au

Questions

1. Do the services provided by Cyberhorse have widespread appeal?

2. Should the services being provided by Cyberhorse instead be provided by the governing sport organisations?

3. What are the benefits to be gained from providing a service such as this online?

Applications of the internet for sport

Sport websites are amongst the most widely accessed sites, with branded websites such as ESPN SportsZone and CBS SportsLine recording page hits in the millions every day. Branded sport sites receive great interest, as exemplified by IBM's official 1998 Wimbledon website, which recorded more than 106 million page views and more than 224 million server hits during the tournament (Turner, 1999). Sites such as NFL.com and NBA.com also receive heavy traffic and interest with the significant advantage of many of these sites being that the demographic profile of the average web user closely matches that represented by the viewers of the four major American professional sporting leagues (Brown, 1998).

Another advantage associated with sport websites is that viewers of a particular sporting programme often respond to the commentator's reference to the site by accessing these sites during the contest itself. This is exemplified by the promotion of NBC's Olympic site (http://www.olympics.nbc.com) during the 1996 Olympic Games, whereby throughout the day, NBC's server activity by hour (hits) remained under 150,000 from 8 am to 8 pm. But after an on-air promotion of the NBC website, the hits exceeded 400,000 and remained above 300,000 until midnight (Turner, 1999).

A clear and significant benefit of the internet is the level and range of content that it can carry. Content elements range from simple textual information through to the capacity to present live radio and television broadcasts. These content applications present sporting organisations with significant opportunity to sustain and develop their customer base in a multitude of ways through using the internet as an advertising medium, a promotional tool, a medium for exposing their organisation to a broader audience, and even an exclusive content application. Turner (1999) states that the internet has the capacity to develop a significant sport following, with sport content being in primary demand: 'The content that can be featured on the internet enables any league, team, or association to be a publisher on the Web to the extent that most sports have official and unofficial websites' (p. 44). The influx of sport-based web content ensures that consumers will seek out branded sport websites in order to obtain their information.

Delpy and Bosetti (1998) discuss the marketing applications associated with use of the internet. These applications focus on the issues of ticket sales and sport event registration, merchandise sales, sponsorship sales, public relations and sport information, market research, sport tourism, scouting, athlete representation, broadcasting and sporting goods marketing, presenting this information in a framework to identify classroom applications for professors and students. Delpy and Bosetti (1998) also discuss the opportunities available for revenue generation via the internet through subscriptions and advertising fees. This analysis sought to provide sport managers with an overview of the broad marketing elements associated with the internet.

A similar approach to that identified above was developed by Duncan and Campbell (1999), who describe the functions the internet can perform for users. These authors identified four categories of the internet: cost or efficiency, performance improvement, market penetration and product transformation. These four categories were applied to sporting organisations, resulting in the identification of six functions of sport internet development: improving customer service, improving advertising, creating a distribution channel, handling communications, providing low-cost entertainment and managing information systems. The focus of the analysis is a framework that allows sport managers to better understand the applications associated with the internet.

Caskey and Delpy (1999) reflected on the actual description of site types, identifying five key categories of application for web-based sport sites. The categories represented include:

- **Content sites,** which incorporate information, sports news, scores and analysis
- **Team or league sites,** which reflect the official sites of college or professional teams and offer information about the players, team records, statistics and merchandise and ticket sales
- **Commerce sites,** which encompass sites designed to sell a product or service on the web through sport
- **Gambling sites** combining content and commerce with a view towards making money through sport
- **Fan sites** lacking official endorsement of the team, league, athletes or companies that they represent

Other research is presented by Beech, Chadwick and Tapp (2000), who examined English football clubs in developing a schema for their effective presence on the internet. This research identifies core features required by football clubs incorporating selling, information, promotional, communication, data collection and design features. These features represent and important consideration in developing the core attributes contained in sporting organisations' websites. The crucial aspect of what the website is used for requires careful consideration by an organisation.

One method of consideration that can accompany the design and development of an organisation's website is through the Nolan Norton Institute's (1998) e-commerce maturity model. This model was formed to identify the stages of development of e-commerce readiness in an organisation. This maturity model reflects these stages through the identification of the attributes of websites as they progress through stages of evolution. Stage 1 of this development is known as experimentation, stage 2 is known as ad hoc implementation and stage 3 is known as integration.

At stage 1 of development of the maturity model, the website tends to be an experiment by an organisation to establish an online presence. There tends to be little presence of e-commerce, and the pages use only basic web technology, are very static and information based, and have little or no interactivity.

At stage 2 of development of the maturity model, websites display electronic commerce product development. These sites begin to display more interactivity, and a two-way flow of information commences. Most organisations at this stage have realised that they can use the WWW to sell their products and begin to add functionality to the website in an ad hoc fashion.

A stage 3 of the maturity model, the website is fully integrated into the business operations of the organisation. The website 'becomes a managed process, yielding efficiencies and two-way information exchange' (Nolan Norton Institute, 1998, p. 12). These websites nearly always require the support of the executive or board and always require expenditure to set up. They tend to be informational, dynamic and highly interactive and use the latest web technology to sell their products. The maturity model points out that as websites progress from stage 1 through 3, the effectiveness of electronic commerce and interactivity increase.

Adapting this model to the content and application development associated with sporting organisation's web development, each stage can be identified and integrated into the online activities of sporting organisations. This representation is presented in Figure 12.1. Information is represented through the general content applied to a sporting organisation's website. This content reflects information about the organisation itself; information reflecting on the competitions and events in which the organisation is involved in or presents; and promotional activities undertaken by the organisation to promote itself or its activities.

The second stage can be represented by the inclusion of electronic commerce activities. Electronic commerce represents a further development of the website and involves any dealings between business, consumers, manufacturers, service providers and intermediaries over a computer network (Nolan Norton Institute, 1998). Sport organisations in this position are maturing from primarily using the web as an information tool to actually conducting business over the web. The scope of electronic commerce is substantial, and the ability to reach millions of consumers with a relatively small overhead can be very enticing to a sport organisation.

The third stage reflects the interactive and broadcasting elements incorporated into a website. Interaction represents the opportunity to incorporate elements in which the

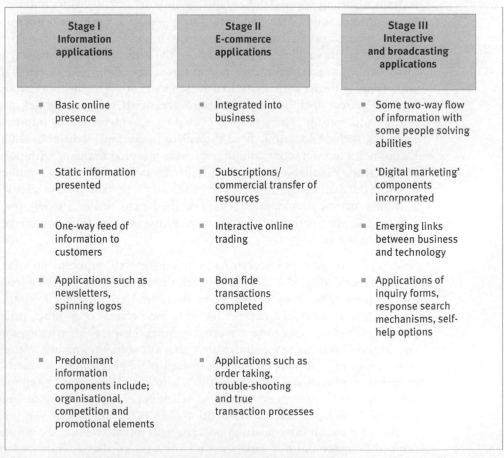

Stage I Information applications	Stage II E-commerce applications	Stage III Interactive and broadcasting applications
Basic online presence	Integrated into business	Some two-way flow of information with some people solving abilities
Static information presented	Subscriptions/ commercial transfer of resources	'Digital marketing' components incorporated
One-way feed of information to customers	Interactive online trading	Emerging links between business and technology
Applications such as newsletters, spinning logos	Bona fide transactions completed	Applications of inquiry forms, response search mechanisms, self-help options
Predominant information components include; organisational, competition and promotional elements	Applications such as order taking, trouble-shooting and true transaction processes	

Figure 12.1 **Adaptation of Nolan Norton Institute's e-commerce maturity model presenting application for sporting organisations**

consumer and organisation can develop a meaningful opportunity to receive immediate feedback on questions asked or activities being undertaken by the organisation. The implications associated with broadcasting technology also enable real-time viewing (or listening) to occur in relation to activities conducted by the organisation.

These stages simply illustrate the way that web development within organisations may be developed in the future and explains the logical progression from merely establishing a web presence to fully integrating the website into the standard business operations.

CASE 12.4   Sport organisations developing the internet for sport marketing

The application of the Nolan Norton Institute's model is developed within this case to encompass the website applications associated with a number of Australian sporting organisations. This approach is undertaken to ascertain the general content inclusions on most sporting associations' websites and the extension into a more dynamic and marketing oriented development of the site.

Initially focusing specifically on the development of website content by sporting organisations, Smith, Pent and Pitts (1999) present a report focusing on sport facilities' website content attributes. This research highlights that of the 35 facility sites reviewed, sports facilities can and do use the web to display a variety of information. The content features identified in this study comprised 22 items displaying a wide-ranging focus, with a calendar or schedule of events being the most prevalent form of content (included in 70% of sites reviewed), followed by ticket information (45%) and seating charts (41%). Other aspects identified as important content elements include location, field dimension, training facilities and club seating. E-commerce or interactive components were not predominant, with ticketing information readily available, but only 10% of the stadia reviewed had online access or a link to a purchasing agent. This outcome clearly reflects that these sites were in stage 1 of their website development (based on the Nolan Norton model), predominantly focusing on information applications, with little concern for e-commerce or interactive applications.

Brown (1998) presents research focusing on the web requirements of MLB teams. This approach adopted a process in which the content was identified from a marketing mix perspective. In total, 44 content inclusions were identified from the analysis of 24 MLB teams, with 35 categories linked to the elements of product, price, place and promotion and nine categories observed as being outside the marketing categorisation and recorded as other (e.g., information such as public/community relations, baseball links, front office). The findings presented highlighted that the team roster was included in all websites reviewed (100%), followed by player biographies (96%), ticket sales (96%), news releases (96%), schedules (92%), information about the ballpark (80%) and merchandise information (75%). The focus again was predominantly on the information dissemination process, with interactive and e-commerce applications in existence but not widely used. Only 21% of sites enabled ordering of merchandise to be undertaken, although 60% had online ticket purchasing capabilities.

Again, this analysis identified that these organisations were in stage 1 of website development, with information applications being dominant.

Focusing on the content and commercial elements associated with internet applications, the application of website requirements of sporting organisations was addressed. The components of content type used the Nolan Norton Institute e-commerce maturity model. This model was adopted in assessing the level of web content development when investigating the sporting organisations' websites reviewed. The second aspect involved the adaptation of the Nolan Norton model to reflect the key elements required by sporting organisations with respect to website development. This occurred from the perspective of identifying the core content aspects associated with these sites.

Content analysis of Australian State-based (SSO) and National-based (NSO) sporting organisation websites was undertaken. Twenty state-based sporting clubs (SSCs), 20 SSOs and a further review of 29 NSOs formed the basis of analysis. The content that appears on sporting organisations' websites is addressed from the perspective of the level of technical development in terms of general informational content through to requirements relating to interactive and e-commerce content. The development of content arises through application of an existing e-commerce maturity model developed by the Nolan Norton Institute (1998).

Much of the information gathered clearly indicates that the majority of sporting organisations are still currently at the point where their web presence is experimental and information based, primarily devoted to establishing a simple web presence. Very few organisations have taken the step up to using the higher forms of web technology, including e-commerce, and even fewer have moved to integrate interactive and broadcasting opportunities into the general operations of the organisation's online environment. Table 12.1 presents a summary of the major content attributes by level.

It is worth noting at the outset, however, that the web is a dynamic environment, and the sites of most organisations are changing on a daily basis. A review such as this should reflect that the needs of a particular organisation today do not necessarily reflect their requirements tomorrow, as technology continues to develop and the capacity of organisations to access this technology increases.

Table 12.1 presents the possible inclusions that sporting organisations might consider when developing their web presence. These inclusions have been categorised according to the requirements for information dissemination, e-commerce and interactive applications. The three key areas of development are:

1. Standard information content presented by organisational information, competition information and promotional information.
2. E-commerce web content is represented by seven items focusing on selling, merchandise and membership information.
3. Interactive web content represents 13 items focusing on sound and image interactive components.

A clear outcome arising from the content analysis is that many sporting organisations have used the web in the past predominantly as an information tool and are

Table 12.1 **Major sporting organisations' website content applications**

Level	Item
1. Information applications	
(a) Organisation elements	Organisation history
	Hall of fame or museum
	Organisation information
	Links (internal such as official team sites; external such as government support service)
	Direction or location information (e.g., stadium, offices)
	Member information
	Site map (stadium including upgrades of offices or seating)
	Contact information
	City information or tourism
	Prices (member, reserve seat)
	Specific event details
	Official sections (supporter groups, kids only, members only)
	Trivia section
	'Getting into the sport' information
	About the organisation
	Frequently asked questions
	Annual or special reports
	Staff information
	Jobs
	Contract information
	Accommodations
(b) Competition elements	Attendance record
	Team or player lists
	Player or coach bios
	Team or player stats

continued

Table 12.1 **Continued**

	Results (latest or archived)
	Special comments
	Competition standings or rankings
	Training or game schedules
	Selection systems
	Calendar
	League news
(c) Promotional elements	Sponsor banners, ads, links
	Supporter newsletter
	Media releases (current or archived)
	Media information
	Online publications
	Merchandise catalogue
	Community affairs or service
	Customer service
	Promotion
	Headline news
2. E-commerce applications	
	Merchandise prices
	Online merchandise purchase facility
	Online ticket purchase facility
	Online reserve seating purchase facility
	Competition entry
	Equipment suppliers link
	Online membership application
3. Interactive applications	
	Downloadable screen savers
	Fantasy competitions

Online chat, discussion forums

Mailing list subscriptions

Real-time updates

Audio broadcasting (live or archived)

Video broadcasting (live or archived)

Sport music themes

Online games

File downloads

Message board

Search facility

Fan polls

---

yet to fully explore the internet's e-commerce and interactive applications and opportunities.

Each of these content applications for different sporting organisations' websites offers some insight into the emergence of the WWW as a tool for sport marketing. The incorporation of site information and development is a key requirement for sport marketing personnel in understanding the development of the applications associated with the web. The development of an understanding of the key requirements of users of sport websites is potentially the next phase of understanding to be achieved.

Questions

1. Is the use of a model such as the Nolan Norton Institute e-commerce maturity model worth considering or relevant to the needs of sporting organisations when determining their website requirements?

2. Analyse the current website of a sporting club or organisation. Where would this website fit in terms of the Nolan Norton Institute model?

Conclusions

This chapter examined the impact of direct, database and online marketing in sport, including how to define the various terms associated with each marketing activity and appreciate the nature of the respective marketing activities. There is a widespread move by sporting organisations towards better data management concerning their customers, and with the emergence of new technologies, this process is now able to be managed and developed by these organisations.

There are a number of developments in mobile telephony, the internet and digital transmission methods that make the approach towards direct, database and online delivery more appealing and readily available to sporting organisations. Many sport consumers display a high degree of loyalty and readiness to consume in support of their sporting club or association. The opportunity to develop sales and update information on these consumers is enhanced by the development of online technologies, which enable data to be retained and used to support the functions of the sporting organisation. When a customer registers interest in the sport, then a detailed information database on this customer can be obtained and immediately accessed by the sporting organisation.

Discussion questions

1. Given a sporting organisation such as a local gymnasium, identify the possible direct marketing opportunities, database management strategies and online marketing activities that this organisation could initiate in terms of supporting its membership (retention or recruitment strategies).
2. Identifying new media technologies such as the internet, mobile telephony or podcasting, how does a sporting organisation access and incorporate these new technologies to assist in the organisation's direct, database and online marketing approach?
3. What is the difference between direct, database and online marketing?
4. How would you manage the database of a major sporting club such as a football club?
5. Take a look at a sporting organisation that you have some involvement with. What is the extent of its database, and how is it used for information gathering? How does the organisation use its database in a direct or online marketing sense?

Guided reading

Further information relating to the aspects relating to direct, database and online marketing can be found in the *Journal of Database Marketing and Customer Strategy Management*. This journal identifies key aspects relating to the techniques around database management. The *Journal of Database Marketing and Customer Strategy Management* is available online at http://www.ingentaconnect.com/content/hsp/dcsm.

Additionally, the textbook by Robert Bly titled *The Complete Idiot's Guide to Direct Marketing* provides a relevant and simplistic overview of the direct marketing approaches.

Keywords

Cookies; data mining; intermediaries; online marketing.

Bibliography

Beech, J., Chadwick, S. and Tapp, A. (2000) Towards a schema for football clubs seeking and effective presence on the Internet, *European Journal for Sport Management*, Special issue July: 30–50.

Belch, G.E. and Belch, M.E. (2004) *Advertising and Promotion: An Integrated Marketing Communications Perspective*, 6th edn, Boston: McGraw-Hill.

Bly, R. (2002) *The Complete Idiot's Guide to Direct Marketing*, USA: Penguin

Brown, M.T. (1998) An examination of the content of official Major League Baseball sites on the World Wide Web, *Cyber-Journal of Sport Marketing* 2(1), Retrieved 29 May 2006, from http://www.cjsm.com/previous.htm.

Caskey, R.J. and Delpy, L.A. (1999) An examination of sport Web sites and the opinion of web employees toward the use and viability of the World Wide Web as a profitable sports marketing tool, *Sport Marketing Quarterly* 8(2):13–24.

Church, R. (2001) Sponsorship slowdown: A new report suggests the boom could be nearing an end, *Sport Business* 58(June):9.

Delpy, L. and Bosetti, H.A. (1998) Sport management and marketing via the World Wide Web, *Sport Marketing Quarterly* 7(1):21–7.

Duncan, T. (2002) *IMC: Using Advertising and Promotion to Build Brands*, Boston: McGraw-Hill.

Duncan, M. and Campbell, R.M. (1999) Internet users: How to reach them and how to integrate the Internet into the marketing strategy of sport businesses, *Sport Marketing Quarterly* 8(2):35–42.

Kotler, P., Adam, S., Brown, L. and Armstrong, G. (2003) *Principles of Marketing*, 2nd edn, Frenchs Forest, NSW: Prentice Hall.

Lau, K.N., Lee, K.H., Ho, Y. and Lam, P.Y. (2004) Mining the web for business intelligence: Homepage analysis in the internet era, *Database Marketing & Customer Strategy Management* 12(1):32–54.

McClymont, H. and Jocumsen, G. (2003) How to implement marketing strategies using database approaches, *Database Marketing and Customer Strategy Management* 11(2): 135–48.

Mitchell, S. (2003) The new age of direct marketing, *Journal of Database Marketing* 10(3):219–29.

Nolan Norton Institute (1998) *Electronic Commerce: The Future is Here*, Research report, KPMG, Australia, Retrieved 5 May 2000, from http://www.kpmg.com.au/press_release/commerce.html.

Shilbury, D., Quick, S. and Westerbeek, H. (2003) *Strategic Sport Marketing*, 2nd edn, Crows Nest NSW: Allen & Unwin.

Smith, R.L., Pent, A.K. and Pitts, B.G. (1999) The World Wide Web as an advertising medium for sports facilities: An analysis of current use, *Sport Marketing Quarterly* 8(1):31–4.

Sport Business (2001a) MLB does the Real deal, *Sport Business* May(57):13.

Sport Business (2001b) Site sponsors hit $253m, *Sport Business* July(59):21.

Sport Business (2001c) NFL in $300m online deal, *Sport Business* August(60):2.

Tapp, A. (2001) The strategic value of direct marketing: What are we good at? Part 1, *Journal of Database Marketing* 9(1):9–15.

Tapp, A. (2002) The strategic value of direct marketing: Expanding its role *within* the company, Paper 2, *Journal of Database Marketing* 9(2):105–12.

Turner, P. (1999) Television and internet convergence: Implications for sport broadcasting, *Sport Marketing Quarterly* 8(2):43–9.

Recommended websites

Cyberhorse
http://www.cyberhorse.net.au

Essendon Football Club
http://www.essendonfc.com.au

Experian
http://www.experian.com

Footytips
http://www.footytips.com.au

Melbourne Storm
http://www.melbournestorm.com.au

Pineapple Head
http://www.pineapplehead.com.au

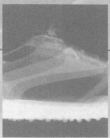

Chapter 13

Sponsorship, endorsements and naming rights

Michel Desbordes
University Marc Bloch, Strasbourg and ISC Business School, Paris
Gary Tribou
University Marc Bloch, Strasbourg

Learning outcomes

Upon completion of this chapter, the reader should be able to:

■ Profile the nature of the market for sponsorships, endorsements and naming rights.

■ Define and identify the nature of each of these activities.

■ Detail considerations relating to the organisation, implementation, management and evaluation of these activities.

■ Address issues relating to the practice and management of ambush marketing.

■ Consider the legal and ethical implications of sponsorship, endorsement and naming rights.

Overview of chapter

The chapter offers an introduction to sport sponsorship. The chapter's primary goal is to provide some general information rather than investigating all of the theoretical aspects that are connected to the concept. The chapter focuses on the historical aspects of sport sponsorship and examines when was it invented and why. After defining what sport sponsorship is and what the market is worth, the chapter analyses the different and various objectives of a sport sponsorship policy. As a foundation for this, it is assumed that sport sponsorship needs:

■ Financial means to publicise what is done in sport sponsorship by the brand. Buying rights is not enough.

■ To integrate sport sponsorship among the other means of communication.

- To engage an evaluation process to be sure the return on investment (ROI) was reached.
- To have an internal relay for sport sponsorship in order to associate all the employees involved in the company.

But sport sponsorship has also some limitations that are acknowledged in this chapter (e.g., ambush marketing or general behaviour of the event, champion or team sponsored). This chapter is original, insofar as it is illustrated with examples outside football. The approach is also voluntarily 'French' in the data, in the bibliography or in the theoretical concepts to give a more international vision of sport marketing and complete the other chapters that have a more Anglo-Saxon viewpoint.

Introduction

In France and across the world, 2002 was a turning point for the sport business market, which was historically developed by marketing agencies such as Jean-Claude Darmon's group or famous sport events organisers such as the Tour de France or the French Open. Several events such as the French national soccer team's poor performance in Asia, Kirch's bankruptcy (closely following that of ISL) and the financial difficulties of broadcasters in Europe could have stopped the market's expansion, but it did not. Sport marketing growth reached 10% (*Guide du Marketing Sportif*, 2003), and several advertising agencies such as Havas, Carat or DDB strengthened their position in the field. So, 2002 allowed companies to become conscious of what sport marketing and particularly, sport sponsorship, was: a real communication tool that entails risks. This reality influenced the maturing process of this means of communication. The year 2003 finally confirmed this tendency: Sports sponsorships had not started to fail, but they were becoming more closely scrutinised. Table 13.1 gives some examples of what took place.

As we can see, the market's evolution has brought about more reasonable fees for sponsorship properties being paid because company managers are now expected to prove a return on investment (ROI) for their sponsorship actions, in the same way as other means of communication have to. In this context, the chapter will analyse the general principles of sport sponsorship.

Table 13.1 Examples of sponsorship or TV deals signed in 2003

Increasing	Decreasing
Médiatis invested €5m on a 3-year contract with skipper Yves Parlier.	L'Oréal disengaged from the golfing tournament Trophée Lancôme that disappeared because of a lack of sponsors.
Adidas invested an estimated €60m on a 10-year contract with Olympique de Marseille.	9 Télécom disengaged from the catamaran championship Orma.
Marlboro signed a 4-year contract with the WRC team Peugeot for €50m	50% TV rights decrease for Formula 1 (€12m annually for TF1).
Nike signed a 7-year contract with Arsenal for €82m.	40% TV rights decrease for the Champions League (€33m annually for TF1).
Nestlé Aquarel signed a 6-year contract with the Tour de France for €24m.	

Source: Guide du Marketing Sportif (2004)

History

The roots of sponsorship are as old as ancient Greece or Rome. Roman games were used as commercial tools, even though most spectators could not read or write. Caesar used advertising and earned votes with gladiators' fights in 65 BC; he really was aware of the impact before organising this type of events. During the Renaissance period, most sponsors helped artistic creation. These patrons were aristocrats or high-ranking Church members.

Supporting an activity for commercial reasons is a more recent phenomenon that appeared during the 19th century. In 1861, the 'Spiers and Pond' company (a British catering company) sponsored the first Australian tour of the British cricket team and reached a £11,000 ROI. In 1864, a sport clothes producer based in Worcester, John Wisden, supervised the publication of the *Wisden Cricketers' Almanack*. Now, 143 years later, this is still the 'Bible' for the fans. In 1887, the French magazine *Vélocipède* sponsored a car race and, at the same time, the French company Michelin began offering tyres to the cycling racers to promote its products. Then, during the 20th century, these sponsorship activities became more and more common among big companies.

In the United States, sponsorship was already a widely used promotional tool, although investments did not increase in Europe until the 1960s and in Japan until the 1970s. The development of private radios at the beginning of the 1920s was possible thanks to the sponsorship of entertainment programmes and radio thus established itself a 'mass media'. Sponsorship became a must with companies supporting or even creating events that were broadcast live. 'Live from the Met' (supported by Texaco) began in 1940, and American tobacco companies became deeply involved in musical or sport sponsorship in the 1950s, long before restrictions on the broadcasting of such messages.

During the1960s, many companies considered sport sponsorship as a new opportunity. Supporting a team or an event could provide a significant media exposure in a positive and relaxed environment for an acceptable cost. During the 1970s, companies in other industrial sectors got involved in sponsorship for awareness or image reasons. The real growth in sport sponsorship occurred in the 1980s and continues today. The 1990s confirmed that sponsorship had become a real strategic tool in the communications policies of corporations, as the new century gave prominence to rationalisation and maturity.

Definitions

Sponsorship[1]

Sponsorship is a tool that allows an organisation to directly link a brand (or a company) to an attractive event or a specific audience (Sahnoun, 1989). Howard and Crompton (1995) go further by defining sponsorship as 'a business relationship between a provider

---

[1] For more details, see Tribou (2004).

of funds, resources or services and a sports event or organisation which offers in return some rights and association that may be used for commercial advantage'.

In fact, the most generic definition emerges from the International Chamber of Commerce (1992), which defines sponsorship as 'every communication action where a sponsor engages contractually to support financially (or other) in order to associate in a positive way its image, identity, brands, products or services to the event, activity, organisation or person it supports'.

Because the ultimate sponsorship goal is always the same – to increase its turnover – each marketing communications tool has its own specificity. According to Dambron (1991), advertising has a long-term effect by influencing the brand's awareness or image, and sales promotion has an immediate effect on sales. Whereas advertising is meant to change consumers' attitudes, sales promotion has an effect on their behaviour. The added value of sport sponsorship is in using a new language far away from the one used in advertising and one that enables an organisation to have a tighter link with a successful person, team or event.

Donation and patronage

Donation is an advantage (financial, material or otherwise) obtained without doing anything in return. As the distinction between sponsorship and patronage is less and less obvious, we can say that sponsorship is an advertising process that consists of financing totally or partly a sport, cultural, scientific, artistic, educational or humanitarian action by associating the name of a product to promote. In exchange, the product is promoted by the user. Therefore, the association is a medium of communication.

Patronage has a philanthropic dimension because only the company's name is mentioned, generally in a much less ostentatious way than in sponsorship. As with a donation, the patron does not receive anything in return. According to Biojout (1985), patronage has two key characteristics:

- The company exerts its activity in a field that has nothing to do with the person or the event supported.
- The expenses involved are irrational compared with the primary goal of the firm (i.e., maximisation).

If the first criterion is not fundamental, the second one is a characteristic of modern sponsorship, which frequently appears to be an irrational activity, although the times of unprofitable sponsorship ventures appear to now be over, except in some rare cases. Sometimes the border between sponsorship and donation can be blurred: A sponsorship that fails in terms of sales, awareness or image might be considered by managers as a donation (Copeland, Frisby and McCarville, 1996). But this is not the key point of the chapter, and we will now focus on the sponsorship market.

The sponsorship market

The global sponsorship market was worth approximately 30 billion US$ in 2002 (of which 33% and 5% were accounted for by the European and French markets, respectively), having risen in value from 23 billion US$ in 2000. The sport economics represents 1.5% of the gross domestic product in France (*Guide du Marketing Sportif*, 2003). Table 13.2 shows that estimations depend on the surveys: this reason for listing so many different valuations is that the definition of sponsorship is not clear.[2]

Table 13.3 shows that there was no real decrease in the sponsorship expense between 2002 and 2003 but that choice of property had become a much more rational decision.

Sponsorship has thus become a more mature tool for organisations to work with. But many sponsors are often disappointed with the results of sponsoring sport. There are undeniable risks attached to this type of communication (particularly with a team or an individual athlete), but failure[3] can also come from the weak specification of sponsorship goals before signing a contract. It is little wonder that sponsorship does not reach its objectives in situations when the objectives are not specified. However, most company managers have an intuitive feeling that sponsorship is essential in order to increase their brand's awareness. This is one of the opportunities presented by sport sponsorship that is discussed in the next section.

Table 13.2 **Sponsorship market data**

Market	Date	Value (€)	Source
World	1996	6 billion	Omnisports
Europe	1996	2.74 billion	Omnisports
United States	1996	1.68 billion	Omnisports
Asia-Pacific	1996	1.07 billion	Omnisports
Italy	1996	915 million	Omnisports
Germany	1996	640 million	Omnisports
France	1996	457 million	Omnisports
United Kingdom	1996	457 million	Omnisports
Spain	1996	274 million	Omnisports
Europe	1997	3 billion	Europub
Spain	2000	425 billion	Carat Spain
World	2000	25,3 billion	Les Echos
France	2000	1.1 billion	Les Echos
France	2001	3 billion	Taylor Nelson Sofres Sport
World	2005	17.73 billion	Arksports (Londres)
World	2010	21.1 billion	Arksports (Londres)
Europe	2005	5.17 billion	Arksports (Londres)
Europe	2010	6.23 billion	Arksports (Londres)

Source: Gdalia (2002)

---

[2] For example, when Salomon or Rossignol offers 100 ski pairs to a world cup racer, is it a promotion expense that has to be included in sponsorship or an R&D expense whose goal is to improve the product technically? For more details, see Desbordes, Ohl and Tribou (2004).

[3] This notion has to be discussed and is relative.

Table 13.3 **Evolution of the average expenditure on the sponsorship market between 2002 and 2003 (in million Euros per season)**

Sport	2002	2003
Formula 1	23 to 70[a]	55 (average 'team' sponsorship deal)
Cycling	4,5 to 7,6	3,50 (a team for a season)
		3,00 (TOP sponsor Tour de France)
Football	2,28 to 4,57 (Ligue 1[b])	3,5 (sponsorship for the shirt of a famous Ligue 1 team)
	0,3 to 1,07 (Ligue 2)	1,00 (idem for a medium Ligue 1 team)
		0,41 (idem for a medium Ligue 2 team)
Yachting	0,7 to 3,05	1,70 (a catamaran season)
		1,40 (a monocoque season)
		0,15 (others: Tour Voile, Solitaire du Figaro)
		0,06 (Minitransat)
Rugby	0,3 to 1,5 (top 16[c] teams)	0,60 (sponsorship for the shirt of top 16 team)
		0,20 (sponsorship for the shirt of pro D2 team)
Tennis	1,00	3,00 (top sponsor French Open)
		0,20 (average deal for other tournaments)
Ice skating	0,76 to 1,53	1,15 (title sponsoring on an event)
Basket-Ball	0,30 to 0,92	0,40 (sponsorship for the shirt of a Pro A[d] team)
Ski	0,38	0,25 (top sponsor of the French Skiing Union)
Roller	0,30	No data
Athletics	0,23	0,20 (sponsorship deal for a national event)
Golfing	0,01 to 0,03	0,20 (average sponsorship deal signed with the French Golfing Union)
Handball	0,12 to 0,23	0,18 (average deal)
Swimming	NC	0,15 (top sponsor of the French Union)
Volleyball	0,7 to 0,16	NC
Climbing	0,06	0,08 (top sponsor of the French Union)
Horse riding	0,04 to 0,3	0,20 (title sponsoring on an event)
Orienteering course	No data	0,06 (top sponsor of the French Union)
Outdoor activities	0,002 to 0,005	No data
Local sponsorship	0,002 to 0,05	0,01 (average deal for a non-professional small event)

[a] In 2002, it cost between €23m and €70m to be the main sponsor of an F1 team (e.g., Marlboro and Ferrari). In 2003, the average expense was €55m among the teams.
[b] Ligue 1 is the French equivalent of the English soccer Premier League. Ligue 2 is the second division.
[c] The 16 best French rugby teams belonged to the 'top 16' until 2005. In 2005, it became the 'top 14' championship. Pro D2 is the name of the second division.
[d] Pro A is the basketball first division.
NB: Definition of the 'average expense'. This was defined thanks to the data published by companies and to the TNS Sport expertise. As we can see, the variance is important among sport activities.
Source: TNS Sport published in *les Echos*, 28 March 2001, TNS Sport 2003

The objectives of sponsorship

There are many reasons to engage a sponsorship programme (Desbordes et al., 2004; Tribou, 2004), a majority of which fall into four main groups: awareness, image, sales and internal communication.

Awareness

One objective is to make the name of a brand or a company known in the minds of a specific target audience and therefore to bring, for example, a brand to the attention of potential consumers. Thanks to TV coverage of major events, this is particularly useful at an international or national level. In this case, sponsors focus more on indirect TV spectators than on direct spectators of the event (Desbordes and Falgoux, 2006). But this strategy does not concern companies that already have a high awareness rate. Indeed, if a brand or company's awareness rating is already high, a sponsorship investment can actually have an adverse effect on this rating. This is the case for worldwide companies such as Coca-Cola and Nike that were present at the beginning of sport sponsorship. Such companies have little interest in increasing awareness levels that are already close to 100%.[4] But these companies can still be concerned by the three other objectives.

Image

Being associated with someone or something famous is not always the ultimate goal of a sponsorship, although companies try to be associated with an interesting event or team in order to transfer their positive values on the company's image. Ries and Trout (1986) have defined a company's image as 'the sum of beliefs, ideas and impressions held by consumers about the company and its products'. Sponsorship cannot totally change a company's image, but if an association is relevant, the company will be able to transfer the positive values of the person, team or event into the consumer's mind. The legitimacy of a relationship plays a role in this transfer. For instance, Rolex is not engaged in ten-pin bowling sponsorship because the sport's image would not transfer well on to the Rolex brand.[5] The impact of image-related sponsorship can far exceed the message of traditional advertising and help to establish an effective link with consumers thanks to the sharing of values (McCarville and Copeland, 1994); this is often the particular sponsorship goal of companies involved in industrial sectors whose image is traditionally negative (e.g., tobacco, oil, nuclear, chemistry, pharmacy[6]).

Sales

As Roger Enrico (Pepsi-Cola president) said some years ago, 'In marketing, the goal is not to obtain free TV exposure but to increase sales' (Tribou, 2004). This point was reinforced by Michael Payne, International Olympic Committee (IOC) marketing director, who commented:

> . . . the days of patronage are gone. Corporate bosses are increasingly having to justify their marketing investments to their shareholders and can no longer just say being associated with the Olympics is good for a company – they will have to prove it with hard facts. (*Keeping the Olympics*, 1997, p. 32)

---

[4] That is one of the reasons the company changed its sponsorship policy. In 1996, Atlanta's brand started focusing more on its proximity with the consumer (Lardinoit, 2001). On the Tour de France, it is less visible.

[5] We have to be careful with some clichés. The reality of football, golfing, yachting or horse riding is more complex than the traditional stereotypes. That is why decisions to investigate a sport need to be prepared with ad-hoc surveys.

[6] We can notice that these industrial sectors are very active in the field of sport marketing.

The sales objectives of sponsors are varied. The company may wish to increase the sales of some products, stimulate the consumer to try a new product or motivate the commercial team working for a sponsor. In each case, sponsorship gives a more convivial dimension to communication, and the link to a target market therefore becomes friendlier. Many means of communication may underpin a sponsorship in this context, but the main one is to minimise the sponsorship effort by using point-of-sale promotions, adapting packaging, developing games or contests and, for example, inviting supermarkets or organising events. In other respects, increasing sales also involves a business-to-business relationship with clients; inviting them to prestigious events leads to a warmer relationship that can prove to be very useful. Whatever is involved, sponsorship has changed. Nowadays, achieving awareness is not enough, and companies must achieve an acceptable ROI.

If the ultimate sponsorship goal is always the same – to increase turnover – the objectives of sponsorship can vary considerably and depend to a large extent upon the sponsoring organisation's corporate objectives. When you consider sponsorship as a more general tool, sport sponsorship is increasingly used by public communities. Therefore, sales can not be considered as the objective, but this does not mean that these communities have a philanthropic vision of their support. Rather, they look for TV exposure, awareness, image and internal motivation, as private companies do, to reach an economic impact for their sponsorship action. We will now describe these objectives in the following sections.

Internal communication

Sponsorship can also have an internal effect that is unique or may combine with the three previous effects already discussed. It can be a cohesive tool whose goal is to gather people on a shared project. This has an important impact because it creates a feeling amongst employees that they are working on something 'extraordinary', high profile or glamorous thanks to the company's sponsorship activities. This can help develop 'team spirit' and assist in building organisation culture, depending upon the orientation of corporate policy and the sport sponsored by the company. Yachting sponsorships are often selected by some organisations because their values – team spirit, courage, performance, surpassing oneself, organisation, solidarity – are close to those of the business world.

Sponsorship and communication

Sponsorship does not replace advertising but is a complementary tool that has to be integrated into an organisation's global communication policy (Lardinoit, 2001; Walliser, 2003). Of course, the choice of the communication depends on the company's objectives. That is why companies support or create events outside the scope of their normal commercial activities in order to communicate differently. This can have an impact on the cognitive and attractive stages of consumer behaviour noted by Kotler, Dubois and Manceau (2003). The potential consumer reacts in the following process: sudden awareness, knowing (cognitive stage), attraction, preference, conviction (attractive stage) and consumption (compartmental stage).

Advertising

On average, a French consumer is exposed to 500 advertising messages every day compared with the 3000 messages in the United States.[7] In this context, sport sponsorship presents organisations with an opportunity because sport is high profile and very popular across the world and people tend to remember sponsorships rather than adverts (Figure 13.1). Different surveys confirm these conclusions but only when there is a coherent semantic link between the brand and the sport. Otherwise, sponsorship is also considered simply as a classical advertising operation.

Because advertising is a commonly used communications tool, companies sometimes use indirect ways to communicate. For example, the IOC noticed that candidate cities were using the Olympic Games image in order to obtain positive effects. The process is now more restricted, and cities now have to pay to be candidates. The IOC wants to avoid ambushing (see later in this chapter) and control the communication of its main product.

Because sponsorship and advertising are different tools, some companies make the choice to communicate about their sponsorship policy in order to make it known and better differentiate it in the market place.[8] Between 1992 and 2001, advertising investments increased by 92% in France (TNS Media Intelligence, 2002). Television is still recognised as being one of the most important media for classical advertising, but this has important implications for sponsorship.

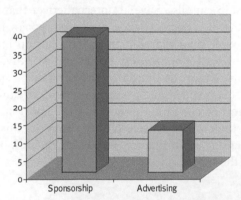

Figure 13.1 **Comparison between the memorisation of classical advertising and sponsorship (in %)**
Source: Desbordes (2004)

---

[7] According to David Stotlar, marketing professor at the Northern University of Colorado, USA, seminar of the MBA International management of sport, University Paris Sud 11, 2002.

[8] As the saying goes: 'For one euro spent on a sponsorship operation, you need three euros to make it known.' Companies that do not communicate with target markets about their sponsorship deals have a lower impact upon them.

Television

According to the SNPTV/IPSOS (2002) Image de la Télévision et de la Publicité survey, people watch television for 3 hours and 18 minutes per day, per person. This is the third most popular human activity after sleeping and working. More than 70% of the daily 3 hours and 35 minutes of free time each day that people have is therefore used for watching television. In 2001, 45.2 million people over 4 years old watched TV every day (Médiamat/Médiametrie, 2002) in France.

Sport programmes are amongst the most popular on television and consistently generate the biggest audiences across the world. A sponsor's brand may become part of a televised event and, in this way, television can provide a sponsor with:

- Media exposure for a minimal cost
- Reinforcement of other TV commercials because of consistent exposure
- Image transfer from sport to the product
- Presumption that the brand is used by stars involved in the event

The presence of sport on television is almost as old as television itself. The first televised event in France took place in 1948 with the Tour de France, and France–Sweden in 1949 was the first soccer game broadcast live. Sport began to take a significant place in the programming because of technological developments. Nowadays, one can speculate that the diffusion of television has reached a maximum. Its exposure has been significantly increased by the development of specialised networks, although there is a current tendency for TV groups to amalgamate. Given current market conditions, 'weak' sports find themselves fighting 'strong' sports for more exposure. Television networks are in the strong position of being able to choose the sports they wish to broadcast, and there is big competition among networks to acquire the rights to broadcasting these so-called 'major' sports. Details of the sports broadcast in France in 2003 are shown in Table 13.4.

Compared with a similar year (2001), the amount of sport broadcast on television offer appears to be stable except on Canal+ (1400 hours of sport in 1998 but less than 1000 hours in 2003, and many of its sports programmes are not broadcast by CanalSatellite). Alternatively, comparing 2003 with 1999 (the latter being the year in which the athletics world championships and the rugby world cup took place), the volume of sport programmes was also stable and four tendencies appeared to be emerging:

- The TV coverage of the world athletics championships was relatively weak (10 hours more than in 2002 but 30 hours less than in 2001).
- The diffusion of rugby increased and for tennis decreased. Formula 1 and ice skating also decreased because the basketball exposure is only because of the NBA coverage of Canal+ (there are otherwise too many late night broadcasts).
- Some surprises: Because of Canal+, ice hockey and American football had a good exposure, but handball (4 hours 4 minutes) and volleyball (0 hour 58 minutes) were neglected by the satellite networks, despite the various world and European championships that took place during 2003.

Many sponsors have thus used the broadcasting of big sport events to communicate with a power they could never have obtained (financially speaking) through traditional channels. This is the case with BNP Paribas, which used the opportunity of the French Tennis Open in 2000 to reveal its new international logo. Deborah Hughes,

Table 13.4 **Diffusion of sports on satellite TV channels in 2003 in France (specified in hours and minutes per year)**

Position	Sport	Total	TF1	France 2	France 3	Canal+	M6
1	Football	613h40	171h16	15h28	48h42	374h42	3h32
2	Rugby	312h21		123h49	49h18	139h14	
3	Cycling	165h56		113h59	51h57		
4	Tennis	152h36		115h20	34h58	2h18	
5	Basketball	101h01			0h19	100h42	
6	American football	87h56				87h56	
7	Ice hockey	77h55				77h55	
8	Athletics	69h57		34h29	35h28		
9	Golfing	55h01	1h04			53h57	
10	Boxing	37h06				37h06	
11	Formula 1	36h20	36h20				
12	Motorsport outside F1	35h15	10h04	8h50	16h21		
13	Ice skating	27h33		5h57	21h36		
14	Skiing	11h09		4h01	7h08		
15	Gymnastics	7h44		1h45	5h59		
16	Judo	5h50		2h53	2h57		
17	Bowling	5h28			5h28		
18	Motorcycle	4h27		1h02	3h25		
19	Yachting	4h24	2h16				2h08
20	Handball	4h04	1h37	0h45	1h37	0h05	
21	Horse riding	3h52			0h55	2h57	
22	Swimming	2h11		2h11			
23	Sport dancing	2h11		2h11			
24	Cyclocross	1h48			1h48		
25	Rowing	1h39		0h53	0h46		
26	Kick boxing or thaï boxing	1h39				1h39	
27	Mountain bike	1h36			1h36		
28	Fencing	1h26			1h26		
29	Paragliding	1h06		0h40	0h26		
30	Volleyball	0h58			0h58		
31	Table tennis	0h53			0h53		
32	Cross country	0h37		0h37			
33	Jetski	0h25	0h25				
34	Wrestling	0h22			0h22		
35	Archery	0h19			0h19		
	General programmes	206h25	0h30	98h34	43h01	46h54	17h26
	Total	**2043h10**	**223h32**	**532h49**	**338h18**	**925h25**	**23h06**

Source: Guide du Marketing Sportif (2004)

vice president of MasterCard International sponsorship, declared: 'In Asia, we would not have the financial means alone to reach so many consumers without the 2002 soccer world cup' (*Le Monde*, 31 May 2002).

■ International communication

As we have seen previously, the interaction between sport sponsorship and television gives an international dimension to sponsorship programmes. Therefore, big companies implement international strategies to benefit from scale economies. But to be successful,

Table 13.5 **Interest and practice of sport in five different countries[a]**

Great Britain		Spain		Germany		Italy		Poland	
Top 5 most popular sports	Top 5 most practiced sports	Top 5 most popular sports	Top 5 most practiced sports	Top 5 most popular sports	Top 5 most practiced sports	Top 5 most popular sports	Top 5 most practiced sports	Top 5 most popular sports	Top 5 most practiced sports
Football	Swimming	Football	Swimming	Football	Cycling	Football	Swimming	Football	Swimming
Rugby	Football	Basketball	Football	Formula 1	Swimming	Tennis	Football	Ice skating	Football
Tennis	Golfing	Tennis	Hiking	Athletics	Hiking	Athletics	Gymnastics	Athletics	Gymnastics
Athletics	Tennis	Swimming	Cycling	Tennis	Football	Formula 1	Tennis	Volleyball	Tennis
Cricket	Cycling	Cycling	Tennis	Skiing	Gymnastics	Swimming	Cycling	Basketball	Cycling

[a]Methodology: surveys were carried out by phone in November and December 2001 (except for Spain, where surveys were done December 2002). The sample (1000 people) was representative of each country.
Source: Guide du Marketing Sportif (2004)

the message transmitted through sponsorship or advertising needs to have a worldwide echo, at least for the target countries (e.g., the same logo and name). The main challenge comes in controlling the unique message being transmitted to target markets across a number of countries. As such, sponsors need to think about the following:

- Sociocultural context of communication (e.g., social references, historical references, cultural specificities)
- Economic context of communication (e.g., level of development, income per habitant)
- Administrative context of communication (e.g., administrative structure, political stability, procedures and reglementations)
- Mediatical context of communication (e.g., efficiency of the media used)
- Entrepreneurial context of communication (e.g., product life cycle, brand's awareness)

In an international sponsorship context, companies have to choose their sponsored activities carefully because even if some events have a universal dimension, many sports have a limited impact (e.g., cricket, sumo, bowling, pelota are good examples of this). Table 13.5 gives an idea of the interest and the practice of sport in five different European countries.

The limitations of traditional sponsorship

To be efficient, sport sponsorship must be underpinned by a long-term vision, so sponsorship is not always well used by every company. But sport sponsorship is only one part of a global communications policy that is essentially uncertain and thus risky. Here are several types of risks associated with a global communications strategy.

The main medium

One of sponsorship is the personality selected. In fact, some stars have such a personality they can eclipse the company with which they have a sponsorship or endorsement deal. Added to this, personalities such as Michael Jordan, Michaël Schumacher,

Zinedine Zidane and Tiger Woods are very expensive, are themselves considered as powerful brands and can not therefore be associated with just any brand. An alternative criticism can be that a company may be impeded by the low-profile image of the person being sponsored. However, matters could be worse, particularly when, for example, the champion is implicated in drug, doping or any other criminal affairs. In such a case, the sponsor can be faced with the negative effects of sponsorship. In such a situation, the brand can choose to support its athlete and therefore increase its risks if the athlete is proven guilty or be accused of a lack of loyalty if it wants to free itself from the contract. This can be considered as another limitation of sport sponsorship. As Cheng and Stotlar (1999) have concluded, a good sponsorship relation is like marriage: You need trust between the two partners, and you expect duration.

The disengagement

Although people love and admire world-famous sport stars, one of the major disadvantages of being associated with them is their relatively short career. Therefore, when they retire, brands need to find other communication solution. Disengaging from a property often becomes a necessity for the sponsor to avoid the saturation effects of advertising: After some years, awareness or qualitative variables do not increase anymore (Figure 13.2).

If there is a necessity to disengage, the challenge is to choose the right moment. Otherwise, it could have a negative impact on consumers' views of a company or a brand (e.g., they might suspect the firm of having financial difficulties).[9] So, disengaging has

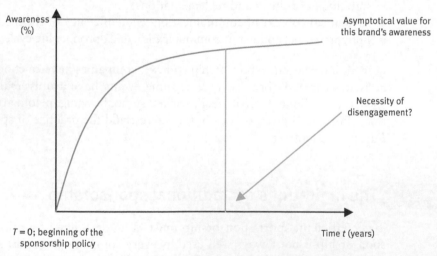

Figure 13.2 **When to disengage from a sponsorship policy?**
Source: Adapted from Tribou (2004)

---

[9] Disengagement may also be misinterpreted by sport participants. During the 1990s, La Poste, the French postal service, was the major sponsor of the mountain bike Union. In 1996, the organisation decided to focus on soccer and to quit mountain biking. Ten years later, this company is still thought to have betrayed this sport.

to be anticipated, planned and built into a communications strategy. Nevertheless, companies can minimise the risks of relations with personalities by sponsoring an event rather than a champion (e.g., bank Crédit Lyonnais for the Tour de France). But because the risks are smaller, the impact is also traditionally being viewed as weaker.

Congestion

Another recurrent problem is the increasing number of sponsors using the same medium. This may have a negative impact on the message communicated, especially in the way that consumers memorise it (both quantitatively and qualitatively). The singularising effect of sponsorship – for example, the benefits of exclusive rights to be associated with a property – may also suffer despite supposedly being an advantage of sponsorship. Sponsorship may also become commonplace because spectators are more and more difficult to reach because of the increasing number of television programmes being broadcast.

An example of some of the problems faced by sponsors is shown in Table 13.6. It is important to note that two types of conflicts can emerge in sponsorship. The first one occurs at the organisation level, and the second one occurs at the team level. The following two examples show how they occur:

- For the organisation of the 2003 athletics world championships, the organisation committee was looking for sponsors to balance the budget. But the IAAF (International Athletics Federation) had chosen its own sponsors, and that was a big limitation for the local organisation that could only find 'official suppliers' and no 'official sponsors'. Finally, even if the rights were different for each company with exclusivity rights for industrial sectors, consumers were confused by the number of official sponsors and suppliers. The rights of the 'local sponsors' were, of course, seen as being less important.
- Another example concerns again the French national soccer team, a sponsor of which is Adidas. Consequently, this sponsor has some rights concerning its visibility but because some players have individual contracts with other equipment companies

---

Table 13.6 Confusion during the 2002 soccer world cup

There are three mobile telephone companies in France: Orange, SFR and Bouygues Telecom. In 2002, during the soccer world cup in Asia, their sponsorship and advertising policies created confusion amongst consumers. On television, in less than 1 minute, spectators were frequently exposed to three different messages:

- A commercial for Orange that featured Zinedine Zidane (1)
- The daily highlight programme *Tous Ensemble* on TF1 that was sponsored by Bouygues Télécom with Bixente Lizarazu (2)
- A player from the French national team who was interviewed with a SFR logo on his shirt (e.g., Zidane or Lizarazu!) (3)

This confusion comes from the fact that consumers have difficulty in seeing the differences between an individual endorsement (1), the sponsorship of a TV programme (2) and a sponsorship deal signed with the French Football Union (3) (e.g., Nike and Puma), this sometimes leads to conflict between sponsors and confusion amongst spectators.[10]

The glorious uncertainty of sport

As underlined in Adidas' 2003 campaign with Zidane's 'Seule la victoire est belle' ('Only victory is great') campaign, a sponsorship policy is usually more efficient when it is associated with strong 'on-field' performances. Most companies want to be associated with the best teams or players in order to be themselves considered 'the best' or their sector's leader. The problem is that there can only ever be one winner. In the football World Cup, not all of them have chances to win – there will be 31 disappointed teams and one winner (Lardinoit, 2001). From this point of view, sport sponsorship is a gamble and does not present the same guarantees as a 'classical' advertising operation. As for disengagement, sponsorship managers always need to plan ahead, thinking about strategy in case the sponsored person or team perform badly.

The appropriateness between the sponsor and the sponsored

When a company decides to use sponsorship as a communication tool after having specified its objectives, it has to choose an appropriate medium (e.g., an event, a club, a team, a champion, a sport or a combination of these) through which to transmit messages. Very often, when the company has little experience in the field, it selects the medium before specifying the objectives. However, selecting an appropriate medium is essential for two reasons:

- The selected medium should consist with and help the sponsor to achieve their objectives.
- The link between the sponsor and the sponsored needs to make sense for the target audience. If not, the sponsor may fail to fulfil its objectives but might also risk changing its image unintentionally.

Except for sport equipment producers, organisations engaged in sport sponsorship may be involved in activities whose appropriateness to and synergy with sport media may not obvious. For example, insurance companies, banks and car companies often have no natural legitimacy to invest in sport.

---

[10] In February 2005, Robert Pires, who was disappointed not having played the game against Sweden in Paris, was interviewed the day after at the training centre. He was wearing a Puma sweater (Puma is his private sponsor), although he was supposed to be dressed with Adidas clothes (Adidas is the official sponsor of the team). Controversies also erupted during the 1992 Olympic Games when the US men's basketball team won the gold medal. Several members of the 'Dream Team' had endorsement contracts with Nike, yet Reebok had supplied the US Olympic Committee with its presentation uniforms. Just before the medal ceremony, some team members refused to display the Reebok logo during the medal presentations. A compromise was reached wherein players who objected could open the collars of their uniform to cover the logo or drape a US flag over the offending logo. As of 1998, the US Olympic Committee had established new, more restrictive, guidelines for logos on team apparel and revised their athlete-participation agreement.

The content of the message is also important because a sponsorship programme often uses the name or the logo of the firm as the only communication means. Therefore, the communication might be suboptimal, such as when this name has very low awareness amongst fans or consumers or when the message is not explicit enough (as in the case of LG and the French soccer national team).

How to address these matters is an important task facing sponsorship managers, particularly when seeking to engage with specific target audiences. But underpinning this is a further problem: ensuring that target audiences perceive the communication in the desired way.

Interference and denaturing

Some sponsors' objectives, particularly those associated visibility, may sometimes lead to behaviour that run counter to good ethics in sport. Even though the facts remain unconfirmed, Nike allegedly put pressure on the Brazilian coach to make Ronaldo play the 1998 World Cup final, despite his supposedly feeling ill. Whether this pressure was real or not does not matter; what actually does matter is the fact that people seemingly deemed such pressure to be acceptable. This reveals a lot about the behaviour of some sponsors that are ready to do anything to obtain a return on their sponsorship investment.

It is also interesting to note that some sport organisations have actually agreed to change the rules because of pressure from sponsors and the media. For example, volleyball modified the way points are counted and the clothing worn by female players; table tennis changed the size and colour of the balls; and judo introduced blue kimonos following sponsor pressure. We should nevertheless note that these evolutions were thought by some to correspond with the sport's needs (e.g., the International Judo Union wanted to change its traditional white kimono). Sponsors can be all powerful, but they can also help to improve sport and make it more attractive for spectators.[11]

Ambush marketing

Ambush marketing[12] appeared following the development of the sponsorship rights market associated with major events. The strategy involves trying to achieve outcomes similar to those available to an official sponsor but without having to pay an official right fee. Stotlar (2001a, 2001b) quotes Ukman[13] (1995) in defining ambush marketing as a 'promotional strategy whereby a non sponsor attempts to capitalize on the popularity/prestige of a property by giving the false impression that it is a sponsor. [This tactic is] often employed by the competitors of a property's official sponsors'.

During the 2002 football World Cup, Pepsi was found by an Argentinian court to have engaged in ambush marketing activities. The company had used some major

---

[11] For example, in soccer, the rules concerning the goalkeeper and the back pass lead to a faster game that is more attractive for the audience.

[12] For more details on ambush marketing, see three remarkable articles (Meenhagan, 1994, 1998; Sandler and Shani, 1989).

[13] Lisa Ukman is the founder and chairperson of the IEG (International Events Group). This company publishes the *IEG Sponsorship Report*.

soccer players in its commercials with the advertising slogan 'Tokyo 2002'. This was intended to make consumers think Pepsi was the official sponsor of the Fédération Internationale de Football Association (FIFA) world cup when, in fact, the Coca-Cola Company was. In France, TF1 recruited sponsors for its daily highlights programme 'Tous ensemble' (6:45 pm), including the official sponsors Fuji and Adidas, but also the mobile telephone operator Bouygues Telecom and some brands that are considered as having an 'ambiguous position', according to the FIFA Marketing's spokesperson. In other words, these brands entered the event without having paid the official rights (each one paid €1.7m to TF1 to have its name announcing the programme).

As the rights to secure major event sponsorships have become more expensive, ambushing problems increasingly confront the organisers of major events (Desbordes, 2002), to the extent that they now have to be prepared for 'marketing guerrillas'. One direct consequence of this is that international federations and governing bodies have as much need for legal experts in ambushing as they do for those with expertise in counterfeiting.[14]

Returns to sponsorship

For whatever reason – poor management, absence of objectives, ambushing – sport sponsorship offers no guarantees that positive returns will be achieved, whether they are raised awareness, enhanced image or sales generation. For instance, Table 13.7 illustrates how variable the returns can sometimes be.

Table 13.7 **Awareness survey after the UEFA soccer Euro 2000**

Sponsors	Suppliers	Spontaneous awareness (%)	
Carlsberg	Adecco	Adidas	41
Coca-Cola	Adidas	Coca-Cola	16
FujiFilm	Connexxion	Nike	14
Hyundai	KLM	Canal+	9
JVC	Lever Fabergé	McDonald's	7
EuroCard-MasterCard	Nashuatec	TF1	7
McDonald's	Nestlé Cereals	Crédit Agricole	6
Philips	Telfort	France Telecom	5
Pringles	TotalFina	National representative sample	
PSINet	Cisco Systems	(15 years old and over): 1000	
Playstation		interviews from July 6th to July	
Sportal.com		11th 2000	

Source: Institut Français de Démoscopie (2000) *Survey on Sport Sponsorship*, Paris

---

[14] Ambush marketing policies are increasingly sophisticated and it is thus almost impossible to prove. Only using a logo without having paid the official rights is reprehensible. What should we think of Reebok that organised daily press conferences under the Eiffel Tower during the 2003 athletics world championships? Therefore, the brand maintained the ambiguity it was perhaps a sponsor of the event.

The example shown in Table 13.7 highlights some important issues that readers should be aware of:

■ There are many brands that were neither sponsors nor suppliers of the event mentioned (Nike, Canal+, TF1, Crédit Agricole, France Telecom).
■ Many sponsors have not been recalled; this does not represent a failure for all of them because some were only interested in demonstrating or acquiring a technical competence rather than increasing awareness of their brands.
■ When sponsor's names were not recalled, this shows that being a sponsor is not enough to distinguish a brand from the group of other sponsors involved in sport sponsorship. This appears to confirm that effectiveness sponsorships require greater investment (or leveraging) to differentiate them from the programmes of other sponsors.
■ There was some confusion between broadcasters and sponsors.
■ For brands that have reached a sufficient awareness level, they have found it more interesting to reduce their sponsorship because they have had nothing else to gain. Adidas had the highest awareness level even though it was only an official supplier and paid less than the official sponsors.

The IOC decided to introduce the notion of 'parasite marketing' instead of ambush marketing to reverse the feeling of part of the population that attributes to this behaviour a more intelligent or inspired vision.

We laid down the principles of sport sponsorship in this chapter: It is an increasingly complex tool that can be optimised but also distorted. Therefore, the evaluation process becomes more acute for brands and for sponsoring companies.

CASE 13.1   Deutsche Bank tees off its US branding drive

Deutsche Bank tees off its US branding drive – The world's top bank is beginning a four-year deal with the PGA to sponsor a golf tournament, writes Adrian Michaels.

Five years after Deutsche Bank clinched its $10bn transatlantic merger with Bankers Trust, the German bank feels it is ready to launch its name in the US. Being America, it has chosen to do so on a golf course. Second-quarter results this month confirmed Deutsche as the world's number one bank, ahead of JP Morgan, in terms of investment banking trading and sales revenue. Fixed income, equities and foreign exchange business generated €2.7bn ($2.9bn) in the three months to June, up 30 per cent.

Yet the bank feels the need to boost its US profile with the first Deutsche Bank Championship tournament to be played at Boston's Tournament Players Club this weekend.

The event will be a welcome diversion at the bank from a run of bad news at financial institutions. Many headlines associated with Deutsche this year have been as a result of probes into alleged wrongdoing on Wall Street.

Just last week Deutsche was censured by the Securities and Exchange Commission for not disclosing conflicts of interest during last year's hotly contested merger between Hewlett-Packard and Compaq. Deutsche paid $750,000 and did not admit or deny wrongdoing.

The PGA Tour, which runs the pan-US network of TPC courses, also found a willing participant in Deutsche. Seth Waugh, chief executive officer of its Americas operations, said the bank was attracted by the holiday weekend timetable – which meant more TV airtime and a Monday finish, and the east coast locale, meaning easier travel for clients and executives from Europe. More than 12,000 of Deutsche's 69,000 employees are now based in the US, principally in New York.

The sponsorship will be accompanied by TV advertising, the bank's first in the US, as it attempts to put its name on a footing with its largest Wall Street rivals. The advertising, in print media as well, will continue at least until the end of the year, Mr Waugh said.

Of course, Deutsche is not the only bank that has latched on to sport. JP Morgan Chase is one of the main sponsors of the US Open tennis tournament currently being played in New York, and UBS was involved with the winner of this year's America's Cup sailing competition.

In spite of emblazoning its name everywhere this month, Deutsche is coy about how much it is spending. Golf industry experts say that title sponsorship typically costs $5m–$7m. Since the bank has signed up for four years, its total bill could be almost $30m.

About half of that goes on TV advertising slots during the tournament. The PGA pays most of the $5m prize money – the winner takes home $900,000 – and takes out the revenue from TV broadcast rights.

Meanwhile, Deutsche pays to run the tournament, but receives much of the gate revenue. About 25,000 spectators a day are due, paying $40. It has also defrayed costs by inviting 11 'founding' sponsors – including Tag Heuer, FleetBoston Financial and Fidelity Investments – to pay for entertainment space in the grounds and some brand visibility.

Deutsche has hired International Management Group, the globally-renowned sports management agency, to run the tournament. IMG manages many of the world's biggest golfers, such as Tiger Woods and Annika Sorenstam, the number one male and female players. But IMG's presence does not guarantee that Mr Woods will show up, which these days is a crucial ingredient for any sponsor. When Mr Woods plays, the TV audience is higher.

Tournament sponsors in the US, unlike Europe, are not allowed to pay appearance money either, but Deutsche has nonetheless secured Mr Woods' services in part by signing a four-year deal to give proceeds to the Tiger Woods Foundation, a charity run by the Tiger's father Earl.

Deutsche plans some heavy-duty schmoozing at the event too – which it sees a key benefit, and one of the ways it secured support from the whole organisation. Each part of Deutsche has a chance to bring some clients, and reserve some places in the professional-amateur golf day before the proper tournament starts. In all, 500 Deutsche clients a day will be there.

But Mr Waugh admits that measuring success will be difficult: 'You don't turn a brand on and off. They take years to build. We think this is going to be an excellent way to launch our new branding campaign in the US.' The US branding drive is part of a global marketing campaign, launched on Monday, with the tag 'A passion to perform'.

Source: A. Michaels, *Financial Times*, 28 August 2003

Questions

1. Why did Deutsche Bank sign a sponsorship deal on a golf tournament in the US? Do you think it will be efficient?

2. Which sports do banks usually choose?

3. Will this sponsorship be accompanied with other communication tools? Why?

4. A marketing agency will run the deal. Which one? Is it a good choice?

CASE 13.2   Sponsorship proves its pulling power

Beer brands have found that sponsorship refreshes parts of audience that ads no longer reach. When Euro 2004 is over, and we're reliving yet another penalty miss or fumbled goal, there will be significant numbers of Danes who will be happy, regardless of the result. Carlsberg's title sponsorship of the tournament is likely to ensure them a very profitable summer. After that it's Heineken's turn, as the relaunched Dutch lager sponsors the British Olympic team. Bud ploughs millions into sponsoring the football World Cup, and has already signed deals for 2006, as well as the Winter Olympics, also in that year.

We're used to sponsorship as a nice addition to the marketing mix, but sponsorship offers so much more than this. It's on the point of replacing advertising as the brand-building medium of choice.

Beer has always offered a fascinating perspective for anyone trying to keep abreast of marketing trends. Most leading lager brands are indistinguishable by taste, and their marketers are not allowed to talk about the most obvious benefit of their products, so marketing creates the only meaningful difference between leading brands. Brands such as Heineken and Carling pioneered funny, intelligent ads in the 1970s, and it is often said that with beer, people 'drink the advertising'.

Links between beer and football are nothing new. Brands have been using the game to sell a few more pints since it was first invented. When players still needed a second career after retiring, pub companies used to install them behind the bar to attract local fans. But Carling's sponsorship of the Premier League in the 1990s signalled a massive shift in emphasis away from advertising.

Through the period of the sponsorship, Carling grew in a declining market despite having negligible above-the-line spend. It became synonymous with football when football was suddenly fantastic. This kept it a relevant brand at a time when the growth of premium lager was making Carling's standard competitors look irrelevant.

Then, two years ago, Carling shifted from football to music, and now spends an estimated £20m a year promoting festivals, venues and tours. While Carling has returned to consistent TV advertising, the sponsorship budget dwarfs the ad spend. As well as renaming Reading the Carling Festival, Carling-branded venues are popping up around the country.

Advertising has made the Stella Artois brand incredibly successful. But Stella's association with film is now as readily recalled as its onscreen jaunts in Provence. This summer, some of the ad budget is being spent on advertising its screen tour rather than showing the cinematic-style brand ads. The idea of seeing The Hunt for Red October on board a Russian submarine, or Raging Bull in York Hall Boxing Club, has an intrinsic appeal that goes far beyond simple sponsorship of films on TV.

In Australia, Foster's sponsorship of Formula One is more readily recalled than its advertising. When the brand was felt to be losing touch in its heartland, the fix was not a glossy new ad campaign, but an expression of national pride via sponsorship of the 2000 Sydney Olympics.

The arguments in favour of this shift towards sponsorship are compelling. Beer brands are desperately trying to go global, and, on this scale, the gap is widening between what sponsorship and advertising can offer. It's notoriously difficult to develop advertising that crosses borders, especially in beer where so much of a brand's appeal is tied up with local pride. Traditional advertising can't even reach the audience it used to, because of media fragmentation.

By contrast, sponsorship and association allow brands to reach audiences that are growing bigger and more global. Sport and music, the lead associations, have a lot in common. Their appeal is universal, and they are watched by more people every year, especially those all-important 18–24-year-olds.

The choice of what to sponsor in the first place can create powerful and differentiated associations for the brand. Especially when you're young, a big football match or a live concert is a time to let rip. Any brand that can associate itself with the emotional intensity of these events is going to leave a bigger impact than one you just see on TV.

When a sponsorship is intelligently exploited, it creates a better experience for the consumer. Carling with its Homecoming gigs, and Stella with its free film events, create new experiences that would not have happened had they not decided to build these associations. Drinkers see that brands are giving something back, and regard this as a fair exchange for their loyalty.

But sponsorship is not without its drawbacks. Clutter in this arena is becoming a problem, sponsorships of sport and music are starting to look obvious, and all the big events are snapped up years in advance. Beer brands need to start looking for cleverer ideas that deliver strong associations across a broad range of experiences. What these might be is not immediately evident. But if the best minds in the ad industry can develop campaigns where advertising creates a promise, and events and third-party associations deliver on that promise, they can continue transforming the fortunes of brands in the sector.

Source: P. Brown, *Financial Times*, 1 June 2004

Questions

1. Why do beer companies become sponsors? Give some successful examples.

2. What did the beer companies change recently in their communication policy? For what reasons?

3. According to you, which trends should these brands follow in the following years? Is there a way to reach new customers through their communication policy?

Conclusions

In one sense, it can be said that sponsorship is an old communication medium that was much developed in the 1990s. It is now integrated among other communication media and has become more professionally planned and managed. Therefore, things have changed, and even if managers are fascinated by sport, they need to justify their investment with classical financial evaluations such as the ROI. In the future, the evaluation of sport sponsorship will thus become increasingly important. How should marketers evaluate the impact of sponsorship programme? How can modern technologies help this process?

These are some of the future challenges sport marketers will have to face in the next 10 years. This gives rise to two important conclusions:

- either sport sponsorship is a profitable communication means and property values and rights fees will therefore go up, or
- the surveys will show that sport sponsorship is risky and does not provide a financial guarantee meaning that companies could seek disengagement from it.

For now, it seems that the first option is the most credible one. But organisers of sport events have to be careful to offer reasonable prices and good service as part of their sponsorship programmes. Otherwise, companies will look for safer and more profitable communication strategies.

Discussion questions

1. Which goals can you reach because of sponsorship? Which can you not?

2. According to you, will sponsorship grow in the following years? In which countries in particular?
3. Which sports are risky when you want to become a sponsor? How can you convince brands to sign deals despite everything?
4. Which methods are used to evaluate sport sponsorship? Do you think some of them could be improved in the future?

Guided reading

Cheng, P.S.T. and Stotlar, D.K. (1999) Successful sponsorship: A marriage between sport and corporations for the next millennium, *The Cyber-Journal of Sport Marketing* 3. In this article, Cheng and Stotlar underline the dependence that exists between the brands involved in sport sponsorships and the events, teams or performers associated with them. The article suggests this is a similar relationship that bears some resemblance to a marriage because it requires trust and duration to be successful.

Desbordes, M., Ohl, F. and Tribou, G. (2004) *Marketing du Sport*, 3rd edn, Paris: Ed. Economica. Written in three parts (consumption analysis, sport services marketing and sport products marketing), this book provides a strong vision of what sport marketing is.

Lardinoit, T. (2001) (Re)construction de la proximité avec le consommateur: Le cas du parrainage de la Coupe du monde 1998 par Coca-Cola, in M. Desbordes (ed.), *Stratégie des Entreprises dans le Sport – Acteurs et Management*. Paris: Ed. Economica, pp. 31–59. In this chapter, Lardinoit analyses how the sponsorship strategy of the Coca-Cola Co. evolved after the 1996 Atlanta Olympic Games. The brand is now less visible but much more active in its search for a friendlier, closer relationship with consumers.

Meenaghan, T. (1994) Ambush marketing: Immoral or Imaginative practice, *Journal of Advertising Research* 34(Sept):77–88. Meenhagan investigates the concept of ambush marketing in this paper. This is arguably one of the most important papers he has written.

Tribou, G. (2004) *Sponsoring Sportif*, 2nd edn, Paris: Editions Economica. This handbook is extensive and provides general information about sport sponsorship for French-speaking readers. It is richly illustrated and uses numerous case studies.

Walliser, B. (2003) L'évolution et l'état de l'art de la recherche internationale sur le parrainage, *Recherche et Applications en Marketing* 18(1):65–94. Walliser undertakes one of the most important literature reviews in the field of sport sponsorship. This is a synthesis of what has been written on the subject in English, German and French and is a very useful tool for researchers.

Keyword

Ambush marketing.

Bibliography

Biojout, P. (1985) *Le sponsoring*, Limoges: Centre de Droit et d'Economie du Sport.

Cheng, P.S.T. and Stotlar, D.K. (1999) Successful sponsorship: A marriage between sport and corporations for the next millennium, *The Cyber-Journal of Sport Marketing* 3.

Copeland, R., Frisby, W. and McCarville, R. (1996) Understanding the sport sponsorship from a corporate perspective, *Journal of Sport Management* 10(1):32–48.

Dambron, P. (1991) *Sponsoring et Politique de Marketing*, Paris: Editions d'Organisation.

Desbordes, M. (2002) Vaches à lait, *Le Monde* 9–10 June:3.

Desbordes, M. (ed.) (2004) *Stratégie des Entreprises Dans le Sport*, Paris: Economica.

Desbordes, M. and Falgoux, J. (2006) *Les événements sportifs*, 3rd edn, Paris: Les Editions d'Organisation, Préface by Michel Platini, forthcoming.

Desbordes, M., Ohl, F. and Tribou, G. (2004) *Marketing du Sport*, 3rd edn, Paris: Ed. Economica.

Gdalia, G. (2002) *Le sponsoring : 1ère et 2ème génération*, MBA International management of sport, Final dissertation, under the direction of Michel Desbordes, University Paris Sud 11, France.

Guide du Marketing Sportif (2003) Hors-série de *Sport Finance & Marketing*, publication *Les Echos* et TNS Sport, December 2002.

Guide du Marketing Sportif (2004) Hors-série de *Sport Finance & Marketing*, publication *Les Echos* et TNS Sport, December 2003.

Howard, D. and Crompton, J. (1995) *Financing Sport*, Morgantown, WV: Fitness Information Technology.

International Chamber of Commerce (1992) *Sponsorship*, The World Business Organization, survey no. 523 (ISBN 92-842-2156-0).

International Olympic Committee (1997) *Keeping the Olympics*, survey written by Michaël Payne, Lausanne.

Kotler, P., Dubois, B. and Manceau, D. (2003) *Marketing Management*, 11th edn, Paris: Publi-Union Editions, p. 760.

Lardinoit, T. (2001) '(Re)contruction de la proximité avec le consommateur: Le cas du parrainage de la Coupe du monde 1998 par Coca-Cola', in M. Desbordes (ed.), *Stratégie des entreprises dans le sport – acteurs et management*, Economica, 31–59.

McCarville, R. and Copeland, B. (1994) Understanding sport sponsorship through exchange theory, *Journal of Sport Management* 8(2):102–14.

Médiamat/Médiametrie (2002) Annual report on television, Paris.

Meenhagan, T. (1994) Ambush marketing: Immoral or imaginative practice, *Journal of Advertising Research* 34(September):77–88.

Meenhagan, T. (1998) Ambush marketing: Corporate strategy and consumer reaction, *Psychology & Marketing* July: 305–22.

Ries, A. and Trout, J. (1986) *Marketing Warfare*, New York: McGraw-Hill, Inc., 216 pp.

Sahnoun P. (1989) *Le sponsoring: Mode d'emploi*, Paris: Chotard.

Sandler, D. and Shani, D. (1989) Olympic vs. 'ambush' marketing: Who gets the gold?, *Journal of Advertising Research* 29:9–14.

Stotlar, D.K. (2001a) *Developing Successful Sport Sponsorship Plans*, Morgantown, WV: Fitness Information Technology.

Stotlar, D.K. (2001b) *Developing Sport Marketing Plans*, Morgantown, WV: Fitness Information Technology.

TNS Media Intelligence (2002) *Annual report on advertising*, Paris.

Tribou, G. (2004) *Sponsoring Sportif*, 2nd edn, Paris: Editions Economica.

Ukman, L. (1995) *IEG's Complete Guide to Sponsorship*, Chicago: International Events Group.

Walliser, B. (2003) L'évolution et l'état de l'art de la recherche internationale sur le parrainage, *Recherche et Applications en Marketing* 18(1):65–94.

Recommended websites

Les Echos
http://www.lesechos.fr/lettrespro/presentation/sport/intro.htm

Sport and Technology
http://www.sportandtechnology.com

Sport Marketing Association
http://www.sportmarketingassociation.com

Sports Strategies
http://www.sportstrategies.com

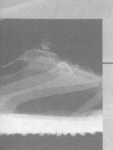

Chapter 14

Sports public relations

Maria Hopwood
Bond University, Queensland

Learning outcomes

Upon completion of this chapter, the reader should be able to:

- Identify the distinguishing characteristics of public relations.

- Consider the importance for sport marketers of understanding the distinct benefits that public relations can bring to sport marketing.

- Indicate how public relations can be integrated with the other elements of the sport integrated marketing communications mix presented in Chapter 11.

- Understand basic public relations theory and be able to apply it within the context of sport.

- Address issues pertaining to the effective use of public relations in sport.

Overview of chapter

Public relations is arguably the least understood of all the tools available to contemporary business and sport marketers. For all sorts of reasons, mainly to do with ignorance and lack of understanding, public relations is also the marketing communications discipline that attracts the greatest criticism and negative opinion. However, because of its unique characteristics, public relations, when it is carried out properly by people who understand its benefits, has a great deal to offer today's sport organisations.

In their book *Strategic Sport Marketing*, Shilbury, Quick and Westerbeek (2003) have devoted a completely separate chapter to public relations because, in their opinions: 'This book views the public relations function as a very important aspect of the promotional mix' (p. 8). This is an important endorsement for public relations because it gives recognition to the fact that public relations has special qualities that are of great value to sport and that, when efficiently implemented, can offer, amongst many other things, true competitive advantage in an overcrowded marketplace.

This chapter introduces some basic public relations theory, which is applied to the context of sport using examples and case studies to help clarify the concepts. It will become apparent as the chapter progresses that a surprising amount of what is being done under the umbrella term of *sport marketing* is, in fact, public relations and not strictly marketing at all. One of the greatest misunderstandings about public relations is that it is publicity and dealing with the media. But although these are indeed important parts of the practice, this is a very narrow vision of what public relations can achieve. Therefore, the chapter begins with a discussion of what public relations is and what it is not. A definition of *public relations* will be given together with a definition of *marketing*, which will serve as a mechanism for reminding sports communicators of the remit and objectives of the two separate and distinct functions. Practical sports public relations must be founded on a number of core principles that include analysing and understanding publics and stakeholders and applying the public relations planning process. These key elements of public relations theory will also be examined during the course of the chapter.

As the chapter progresses, it will become clear that although the close relationship between marketing and public relations is acknowledged and understood, it is important that the reader is able to appreciate the distinct qualities and benefits of public relations, which, in the context of sport particularly, have much to offer. As Pope and Turco (2001, p. 114) observe: 'The beauty of public relations is that it lends itself to many imaginative techniques that always offer new approaches.'

Introduction

Public relations is a field that is more often characterised by what it does rather than what it is (Ledingham and Bruning, 2000, p. xi). The overall aim of public relations is to create goodwill and good feelings about the organisation and its products. This can be done partly through the establishment of a sound corporate reputation and partly by getting people to think positively about the organisation's activities. Changing the way people think and feel about an organisation can be a long, drawn-out process, but when knowledge of public relations exists within the organisation and when public relations is a recognised and well-managed element of the overall communications function, public relations can lead to very real and measurable benefits. For a sport organisation, public relations can, if handled professionally, become its most cost-effective communications mechanism. To put it another way, public relations is all about making sure that the sport organisation does the right things at the right times and ensuring, when necessary, that those publics need to know what it is doing.

Very often, public relations is mistakenly seen as just being the responsibility of the public relations department or consultancy, but the reality is that everyone in the organisation has a vital role to play in public relations. This is perhaps especially the case for the sport organisation in which many employees carry an important public relations responsibility through their inherent visibility and public interest both on the field of play and in their personal lives. A useful perspective to start with about public relations is that it is the management of corporate image through the proactive and professional management of relationships with the organisation's publics and from that point, we can move on to considering some practical definitions and applications of public relations within the context of sport.

The scope of public relations

Before examining public relations more closely, it will be useful to consider the scope of the practice – in other words, to look at the kind of activities that are considered to fall within the remit of public relations. The following is a list of the typical areas covered by sports public relations:

- Media relations
- Publicity
- Publications
- Corporate communications
- Public affairs and community relations
- Lobbying
- Sponsorship and donations
- Events management
- Crisis management
- Research and analysis

It is immediately obvious that sports public relations has a broad remit that goes well beyond the purely commercial activities with which sport marketing is usually associated. More than anything else, public relations has the unique ability to build relationships, establish credibility and create understanding between the organisation and all its many publics, all of which are vital commodities to any sports enterprise. It therefore makes complete sense that anyone interested in a career in sports has an understanding of this essential element of the sport integrated marketing communications mix (SIMCM).

What is public relations?

When beginning to think about public relations, a good place to start is by dealing with some of the common misconceptions that surround the discipline. It is well beyond the scope of this chapter to engage in too much theoretical discussion, and anyone who would like further information on public relations should refer to the guided reading and website resources listed at the end. What public relations is certainly not, however, is spin doctoring. This is an immensely disparaging phrase that has unfortunately attached itself to public relations in recent years as a result of unscrupulous behaviour by individuals and companies that are not public relations professionals. Spin doctoring is concerned with covering up bad news and manipulating the truth during times of crisis. Public relations, when fully understood and practised professionally, can be a tremendous force for good within any organisation, and many organisations throughout the world benefit from having a strategic public relations focus. Sport organisations are no exception.

Because public relations is dogged with misconceptions, it makes sense to clear up these first. To do that, it is necessary to deal with some basic theory. We will start by attempting to answer the question, 'What is public relations?'

According to the Chartered Institute of Public Relations (CIPR), which is the professional body for public relations practitioners in the United Kingdom, public relations can be defined as:

Public relations is about reputation – the result of what you do, what you say and what others say about you.

Public relations is the discipline which looks after reputation, with the aim of earning understanding and support and influencing opinion and behaviour. It is the planned and sustained effort to establish and maintain goodwill and mutual understanding between an organisation and its publics.

Although other definitions exist, it is thought that this particular one contains much that is of relevance to the more specialised concept of sports public relations. When this definition is carefully deconstructed, a much better understanding of public relations can be gained.

Sports public relations as reputation management

Realising the fundamental premise of public relations often comes as a surprise – that is, no organisation can choose not to do public relations. This applies just as much to sporting as commercial organisations. Why is this? Well, as the CIPR definition states at the very beginning, public relations is about reputation. Everything the sport organisation says and does is public relations, whether that saying and doing happens on the field of play, in the boardroom or at the sport's central governing body. To explain this further, here is an example of how everything a sport organisation says or does can affect reputation: On Saturday 2nd April 2005, Newcastle United played Aston Villa in a normal Saturday fixture. The stakes were not especially high; however, the game will be long remembered, not because of the wonderful football being played but because two of the Newcastle players, Kieron Dyer and Lee Bowyer, had a fight on the pitch and had to be separated by their own teammates and the Aston Villa players. In a short but quite shocking space of time, those two players managed to seriously damage their own image and reputations as both individuals and players and bring the game into disrepute. They also severely injured the image of Newcastle United, whose manager, Graeme Souness, had to face the media and engage in extensive damage limitation public relations for some considerable time after the match. Once again, English professional football's image has been tarnished at a time when the national game is trying to overcome an already negative image created by the hooliganism engaged in by many of its fans and the questionable behaviour of some of its players and managers, both on and off the field. The attention of today's media is always drawn towards anything controversial and negative, so this particular example of 'bad sports public relations' has been played out in front of a global audience whose opinion of those players and their sport is significantly influenced by what they have seen on their televisions, in the newspaper and on the internet. In other words, it only takes a few minutes of literally taking one's eye off the public relations ball to create untold and quite possibly lasting damage to both personal and organisational reputation and credibility.

The above example shows that public relations is not something that just happens; it has to be worked at. It can take many years to create respect and a glowing reputation, both of which can be destroyed in seconds and at huge cost to the organisation if public relations is not fully regarded as a management function. Not only that, but knowing what public relations involves and how it is done requires the input of specialist communicators, people who are trained in the discipline of public relations and understand the clear distinctions that exist between public relations and marketing and the other elements of marketing communications.

Looking at the next part of the CIPR definition, which states that 'Public relations is the discipline which looks after reputation, with the aim of earning understanding and support and influencing opinion and behaviour', we can begin to debunk another myth. Understanding and support by publics has to be earned; it is not a given right for any organisation. Every sport organisation, whether amateur or professional, has what is referred to in public relations theory as a 'licence to operate'. This theory was developed from a business concept originally developed in 1966 (a very good year for English football!) known as Davis' iron law of responsibility, which states that 'those who do not take responsibility for their power ultimately shall lose it' (Kitchen, 1997, p. 135). Because of the very special nature of the sport product, sport organisations have many advantages that organisations in the commercial sector do not. But this does not mean that sport organisations can take their licence to operate for granted. Any business success, sporting or commercial, can only be sustained if it exists within a supportive operating environment, which underlines the necessity for effective public relations strategies that have 'earning understanding and support' as their main aim.

An important job of the sports public relations person is to be able to identify and know who and what grants this all-important licence to operate. All sport organisations have to develop and maintain relationships with a number of different but vitally important 'publics' who, even though they could be lifelong season ticket holders, need to be nurtured so that the licence to operate is renewed. Figure 14.1 shows a

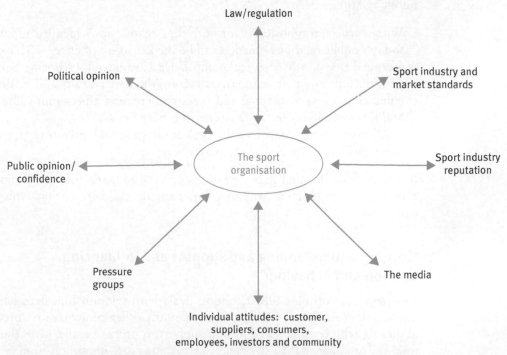

Figure 14.1 Key influences on the sport organisations' licence to operate
Source: Adapted from Kitchen (1997)

number of these key influences that, applicable to any organisation, need to be acknowledged and understood by the successful sport organisation.

Although not all of these influences are applicable to all sport organisations at all times, the majority of them are. If this model is applied to the Bowyer/Dyer episode mentioned earlier, public relations' role in sport becomes even more critical. Remembering the word of Davis' iron law (i.e., within the context of football, taking their publics, their tolerance and their continued support for granted, perhaps), even football's licence to operate gets tested from time to time. It is perhaps significant that Richard Caborn, minister for Sport and Tourism, drew attention to such responsibility in the aftermath of the Dyer/Bowyer when he said on Monday, 4th April 2005:

> We have a responsibility but it has to start at board level. The chairmen must get together and straighten it out. They must tell managers about their corporate and social responsibilities to the game and community as a whole. (http://news.bbc.co. uk/sport1/hi/football/teams/n/newcastle_united/)

In research conducted by the CIPR, Britain's industry leaders were recently asked about the most important factors they take into account when making judgements on companies. To them, the importance of financial performance is less significant than in 1997 (down 16 points to 59%), but factors relating to reputation have increased by 14 points to 60%. Although sport organisations are not specifically mentioned, there is no room for complacency. The increasing and sometimes intrusive attention that surrounds modern sport is enough of a reason in itself to ensure that reputations are upheld, maintained and regularly inspected. All of this can be achieved through excellent public relations. The CIPR points out the following helpful information about public relations:

> With a crucial responsibility for both the organisation's identity and its reputation, today's public relations function can be the key agent of change. This might include a critical role in achieving real competitive advantage by reducing barriers to competition, opening new markets, attracting the best recruits and business partners, enhancing access to funding and investors, creating a premium value for products and services and protecting business in times of crisis.
>
> All organisations big or small, local or international, private or public can benefit from good public relations. (http://www.cipr.co.uk)

It is clear from this that public relations go beyond marketing and promotion. Public relations, if conducted properly, can provide the roots from which marketing can grow.

■ 'Earning understanding and support and influencing opinion and behaviour'

The next part of the CIPR definition deals with relationship management through public relations. Sport, perhaps more than any other contemporary product, has the ability to achieve understanding and support. It unifies people, gives them an outside interest, can change their lives and can become more important to many people than other aspects of their lives. However, there have been far too many instances in recent years in which publics' understanding and support for sport have been sorely tested.

Hooliganism, cheating, drug abuse, player and manager behaviour (both on and off the field), player's salaries, violence, scandals, TV rights, expensive ticket prices, fan treatment, merchandising costs and lacklustre performance are all examples of issues that have led to reduced understanding and support for sport in recent times. Public relations, although it cannot paper over the cracks, can, if it is done properly, develop the relationships and consequent understanding and support that is vital to any sport organisation's continuing success.

Sports public relations as 'relationship management'?

Public relations has a much wider responsibility than just defending the sport organisation from attack and publicising its achievements. Public relations also has a key role in sports relationship marketing, in which it performs a long-term goodwill-building role that requires the implementation of a completely different strategy to that needed for the gaining of a quick sale. Many sport organisations use public relations solely for crisis management or as a tactical mechanism to deal with problems after something has gone wrong, which, as far as the sport organisation is concerned, frequently has to be handled in the full glare of publicity and media interest. This is a reactive approach to public relations that is usually far less effective than a proactive approach that seeks to avoid problems arising in the first place.

Whenever an organisation sets out to do business, it must know who it wants to do business with. In public relations, all of these groups and individuals are called publics, and sometimes, stakeholders. To be able to create understanding and support, the organisation needs to be able to identify its publics and stakeholders so that it can begin to communicate with them in the best possible way. After all, the organisation depends upon these publics for its survival. The typical publics for any organisation are consumers and customers, employees, investors, legislators, central and local government, the media, suppliers, pressure groups, competitors, the local community and society at large (as consumers of information about the organisation). We can see at once that this is an extremely diverse range of publics, all of which will engage with the organisation differently and have very different needs that the organisation has to try to fulfil. Some of these publics can be called stakeholders because they have a greater interest in the organisation than some of the other publics. For example, customers, employees and investors are all groups whose livelihood is intrinsically tied into the organisation. Perhaps the most important point to make here is that each of these publics can have a direct influence on whether or not the organisation is a success. It makes perfect sense, therefore, that time, effort and resources should be expended on developing mutually beneficial relationships with them.

It is exactly the same for sport organisations. Here are some of the typical publics for a UK Premier League football club, such as Middlesbrough Football Club (see Figure 14.2):

- Players (present, past and future)
- Supporters (present, past and future)
- Investors (financial publics, shareholders)
- Sponsors (current and potential)
- The media (press and broadcast, local and national)
- Other football clubs (both at home and abroad)

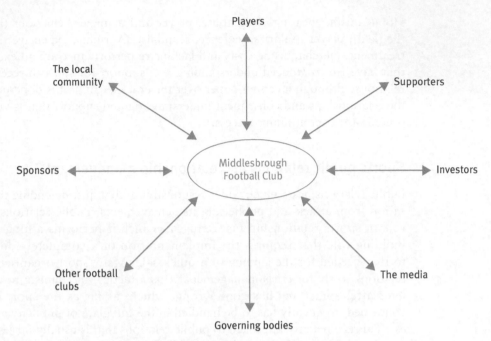

Figure 14.2 Typical publics for a Premier League Football Club

- The local community
- Football's governing bodies, both national and international (the Football Association, Fédération Internationale de Football Association, Union of European Football Associations).

Similar publics can be identified for any sport organisation, and again, some publics will be more significant than others. These are the stakeholders, all those people who are affected by the decisions, actions, policies, practices and goals of the organisation and whose decisions can affect the organisation (Kitchen, 1997, p. 93).

Relationship management, according to many contemporary public relations theorists, is the essence of public relations because public relations is often described as 'the management function that establishes and maintains mutually beneficial relationships between an organisation and the publics on whom its success or failure depends' (Cutlip, Center and Broom, 2000). Of all the communications techniques used by organisations, public relations is the one that focuses on the development of two-way communication strategies, those same communication strategies upon which the majority of human communications are founded. In diagrammatic representations, such as those above, the double-headed arrows reinforce this two-way communication. According to Davis (2004):

Relationships can develop from the least likely beginnings and some of the most fulfilling may be the least well planned or sought after. People, though, usually allow relationships to develop because they *want something out of them*, and the relationships that organisations cultivate with their customers and they in turn consider that they enjoy with those organisations are no exception. There is *calculation* afoot, often rather deep calculation, and it is *mutual*. (p. 101)

Although this statement describes the general principles upon which business relationships are founded, it can be argued that the relationships that 'customers' have with sporting organisations tend to be of a very different nature, so Davis' view is rather limiting within the sporting context. The relationship that a supporter has with his or her favourite team could well last a lifetime, and it is extremely likely that his or her allegiances will be transferred to other family members and even future generations. What supporters want out of their relationships with their club are likely to be much more intangible than something that can be satisfied by a bar of chocolate! What is it about the sport product that makes supporters renew their membership or buy their season ticket year after year when their club regularly finishes bottom of the league? If this was any other consumer product, customers would soon switch brands or go elsewhere if the service they were getting consistently failed to meet their expectations. The same thing rarely happens within the context of sport yet, for many sporting organisations, focusing on nurturing and developing such fantastically loyal relationships does not feature as an important part of their sport marketing communications strategies. However, as with any other relationship, the potential long-term damage of becoming complacent and taking people for granted should be understood and avoided; this is where excellent public relations can help.

It should also be remembered that not all the relationships that sport organisations have are with consumer publics. A major public, and one that is often overlooked by organisations, sporting and otherwise, is the internal public or the employees. From a public relations perspective, it is essential that the internal publics' needs are met because they are the organisation's most powerful public relations tool. Satisfied employees communicate positive messages about the organisation via one of the most effective public relations methods: word of mouth. Dissatisfied employees will do the same, and if a high-profile player or manager is involved, the damage to the sport organisation can be considerable. Sports public relations strategies, therefore, must be directed at both internal and external publics. Looking after player interests such as developing skills and education strategies for life and work after a playing career are examples of proactive internal sports public relations. Training and developing all staff to realise their public relations role is another. Remember, everything that the organisation says and does communicates a message; the way that message is interpreted is the job of public relations, whose job it is 'to facilitate positive communication between an organisation and its publics [and] that requires building relationships' (Ledingham and Bruning, 2000, p. 59).

■ 'Goodwill and mutual understanding'

According to Ledingham and Bruning (2000, p. 59) most, if not all, of public relations has to do with changing or building relationships. The all-important but intangible core features upon which public relations is built – openness, trust, involvement, investment and commitment – are all able to generate and influence perceptions of satisfaction with the organisation by all its important publics. For business owners and managers, Ledingham and Bruning argue, these perceptions of satisfaction can be more influential than variables such as price or product features in predicting consumer behaviour. In addition, research into relationship management has shown that the longer a relationship lasts also has a direct result on positive perception and satisfaction. This is clearly of significance to sport organisations because a great number of the relationships between organisations and publics that exist may well last a lifetime and beyond.

Regarding public relations as a relationship management tool is essential for sport organisations, and many are coming round to the same opinion. The end of chapter case study is about Newcastle Falcons Rugby Club and one of the techniques the organisation is successfully implementing as part of its relationship-building strategy. In creating goodwill and mutual understanding, effective public relations can facilitate a whole range of positive communication between an organisation and its publics. One aspect of this, which again is of increasing relevance to sport organisations, is the socially responsible role that the contemporary organisation has. Corporate social responsibility, or corporate responsibility, as it is becoming more popularly known, is an important dimension of business today. Sport, perhaps more than many other areas of business, has to take this issue very seriously. Sport participants and organisations become the focus of much adulation and hero worship, and as a consequence, they must become much more aware of their social responsibility, which, in proactive sport organisation, should be part of public relations efforts.

In 1988, the late Frank Jefkins, who was one of the United Kingdom's pioneers in public relations professionalism and education, devised a model that he called *the public relations transfer process*. In this, he clearly and straightforwardly illustrates the intended function of public relations (Figure 14.3).

The public relations transfer process shows us that professionally handled public relations has the power to convert a negative situation to a positive one. This process is achieved through creating relationships and dialogue between the organisation and its publics. It requires a complete knowledge of all the public groups, and it requires truth, openness, honesty and clarity in all communications between the organisation and its publics. Time after time, emotions such as those listed in the Negative situation box are converted, through the implementation of specific and well-thought-through public relations techniques, to those emotions and responses listed in the Positive achievement box.

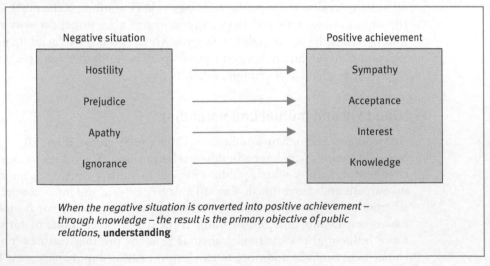

*When the negative situation is converted into positive achievement – through knowledge – the result is the primary objective of public relations, **understanding***

Figure 14.3 **The public relations transfer process**
Source: Jefkins (1994)

The theory underpinning public relations practice is continually developing, which is a reflection of public relations' relatively recent emergence as an academic discipline. Referring to public relations theorists is helpful in order to summarise the core features of public relations. For example, according to Kitchen (1997, p. 27) public relations:

- Is a management function.
- Covers a broad range of activities and purposes in practice.
- Is regarded as two-way or interactive.
- Suggests that publics facing companies are not singular (e.g., consumers) but plural.
- Suggests that relationships are long term rather than short term.

Wilcox, Ault and Agee (2003, p. 5) use the following words and phrases to encapsulate the nature of public relations:

- **Deliberate:** Public relations is always intentional, not haphazard.
- **Planned:** Public relations is organised, not short term.
- **Performance:** Public relations cannot be effective unless it is based on the actual performance of an organisation.
- **Public interest:** Public relations should be beneficial to both the organisation and the general public.

To develop the public relations concept still further, Wilcox et al. suggest that the following are also key elements of the practice

- Creating and reinforcing trust.
- Arousing attention.
- Creating and preserving communication and relationships.
- Articulating, representing and adjusting interests.
- Influencing public opinion.
- Resolving conflicts.
- Creating consensus.

So, we can now begin to see that there is a great deal more to public relations than might have previously been thought. Also, public relations offers much greater potential for sport organisations than simply being just a part of marketing. Uniquely, public relations gives sport organisations the opportunity to focus on relationship management and developing the two-way communication mechanisms that, in the long term, will produce measurable benefits upon which the sport organisation can capitalise. But this is the key to successful and effective public relations – it must be a long-term strategy and must be proactive, and this requires a very different mindset than that traditionally used in marketing.

Professional sports public relations

It will be useful here to revisit the CIM's definition of marketing in order that the differences between marketing and public relations can be further emphasised. The CIM website (http://www.cim.co.uk) defines marketing as 'the management process responsible for identifying, anticipating and satisfying customer requirements profitably'. Compare this with the CIPR's definition given earlier in the chapter that begins: 'Public relations is about reputation – the result of what you do, what you say and what others say about you.' We can see that they are indeed very different disciplines. In fact, when the two definitions are read together in this way, they do not seem to have much in common at all! There is, however, a symbiotic relationship between the two, which, when recognised and appreciated, can be hugely beneficial to sport organisations.

As successful business functions, marketing and public relations work to the best advantage for the organisation when they are treated as separate disciplines. In a study on public relations and marketing practices Ehling, White and Grunig (1992) found that:

> Both marketing and public relations are important functions for an organisation. Subsuming public relations into marketing, however, deprives the organisation of one of those two critical functions. Therefore, we believe that excellent public relations departments exist separately from marketing departments; or, at least, the two functions are conceptually and operationally distinct within the same department. (p. 390)

Unfortunately, the reality, especially within sport organisations, is very different. Of the two functions, marketing is the one that people feel more comfortable with, even if they are not entirely expertly trained in doing it. Identifying, anticipating and satisfying customer requirements and making money as a result is, after all, the raison d'être for most commercial organisations. It is also of great importance to sport organisations because even though the business is not always about making money, if people do not engage with you, then how can you be assured of your future success? But although making a profit or an immediate return on investment (ROI) is always to do with marketing, it is not always to do with public relations, which is why, although the two disciplines are enmeshed, they cannot and should not be dealt with in the same way by the same people.

Because of the competitive environment in which sport organisations now find themselves, it makes complete sense that people who are responsible for the successful operation of the business are competent business professionals. This means that staff need to develop expertise in, amongst other things, marketing and public relations. It is very obvious that the international sports governing bodies have developed a business acumen, which is gradually being disseminated through the varying sports structures and properly qualified people are being put in place. However, it is still too often the case that the critically important public relations function is at best lumped together as an adjunct of marketing or, even worse but more commonly, not bothered with at all. In January 2003, Durham County Cricket Club was the only one of the 18 UK first-class county professional cricket clubs that had a dedicated public relations professional (Hopwood, 2003). By April 2005, the number of first-class county cricket clubs with a public relations person had risen to six. In 3 months at the beginning of 2005, the following statements were made by prominent individuals involved in British sport business during personal conversation with the author:

> At Worcestershire County Cricket Club, PR is far more important than other forms of marketing and communications (Mark Newton, CEO, WCCC, April 2005).

> PR and relationship building is a vital part of FA media relations – key words are trust, honesty, truth. (Adrian Bevington, head of media relations, the Football Association, February 2005)

Our communications are all about real relationship building. (Stuart Duffy, media and public relations manager, Bradford Bulls Rugby League Club, March 2005)

These comments show that those who understand the business of sport understand and appreciate the value of public relations. It is also encouraging to report that professional public relations is being increasingly integrated into sport business at a number of different levels.

More about publics and stakeholders

According to Lagae (2005):

PR through sport also fits into an interactive communication strategy, making use of the various media to obtain understanding, attention and support for the values and aims of an organisation among clearly specified groups.

In public relations, these clearly specified groups are known as 'publics', and sports public relations can only really work effectively if the sport organisation's publics are clearly identified and understood. The term 'publics' is the preferred term used by public relations professionals to refer to the many target audiences, both inside and outside the sport organisation, towards whom communications efforts may be focused. All sport organisations, to a greater or lesser degree, depend on publics for their survival, so their importance really cannot be overestimated.

However, before examining publics in more detail, it is useful to distinguish between publics and stakeholders because these two words are often used interchangeably, both in the academic literature and everyday conversation. However, the terms have essential differences. A stakeholder literally has a 'stake' in the organisation, which usually takes the form of an interest that can be either direct or indirect, active or passive. Stakeholders might be aware or unaware of that stake, and it might be known or unknown, immediate or some distance removed. Stakeholders can take the form of large groups, sometimes even masses, and the language used to describe them tends to be generalised and non-specific. For example, players and athletes are stakeholders, as are supporters and sponsors, yet when spoken of in general terms like this, they become anonymous and amorphous. However, those same stakeholders can become publics if they become more closely identified with the sport organisation (e.g., Durham County Cricket Club's members; Middlesbrough Football Club's season ticket holders; Newcastle Falcon's first team squad; and Nationwide, sponsors of the England football team). It has been said, therefore, in an attempt to make a clear distinction between publics and stakeholders, that publics have importance attached to them because their interest and power in the organisation, both current and potential, is much more specific – that is, they can make or break an organisation.

Because publics exert such significant influence on organisations, public relations theorists have taken a close interest in how publics grow and develop to better develop relationship management techniques. In fact, a thorough understanding of publics means that public relations is more likely to be of the proactive and productive rather than the reactive and 'fire-fighting' kind that tends to be resorted to in times of crisis. American public relations theorist James Grunig developed his situational theory in 1984 to demonstrate that publics are not fixed entities. Rather, they are transient and, most importantly, organisations create publics when their operations have consequences for others. Publics form when there is something, usually a shared perceived problem that unites its members. If this is not recognised by the organisation then the public is considered to be latent: 'a potential public relations problem waiting to happen... Active publics are the only ones that generate consequences for organisations' (Grunig and Repper, 1992).

A distinctive view of publics that is of immediate relevance to sports public relations is that, according to Grunig and Repper (1992), members of active publics affect organisations more than passive ones because they engage in individual behaviours to do something about the consequence of organisational actions. They also join activist groups. In other words, they engage in collective behaviour to pressure the organisation or to resolve their problem in other ways. An example of such a situation in sport is the takeover of Manchester United Football Club by American business tycoon Malcolm Glazer, which was reported thus in *The Weekend Australian* dated 21–22 May 2005:

A bitter atmosphere threatens to spoil tonight's showpiece English FA Cup Final. Fans of Manchester United... plan to abandon their usual red scarves and joyful singing... in favour of black flags and protest. The focus of their ire is Malcolm Glazer, American shopping-mall tycoon and owner of the Tampa Bay Buccaneers, an American football team. This week Glazer declared victory in his long battle to buy United. Death threats have been made against him.

A common and very serious error made by non-professional communications personnel is the assumption that only one public, the general public, exists outside the organisation. In public relations, there is no such thing as 'the general public' because it is understood that publics are a highly diverse collection of groups that require specifically designed strategies in order to communicate with them effectively. In the sport business, it is evident that a great and varied number of diverse publics exist, each with different needs and requirements, have different relationships with sport organisations and expect that they will be communicated with in a way that suits them. For sports public relations strategies to work effectively, it is essential that the sport organisation is able to categorise its publics at any given time during the relationship. In public relations theory, the following four distinct publics have been consistently identified (an issue in this context is an event or occurrence):

■ **All-issue publics:** Publics that are active on all issues that affect them (e.g., traditionalist life members of a cricket club voicing their displeasure at the increasing number of Twenty20 cricket matches appearing in the season's schedule and voting against an increase in membership dues).
■ **Apathetic publics:** Publics that are inattentive to all issues (e.g., people who are just not interested in sport in any shape or form but who might well be part of the local community living near a football ground, for example, and who are therefore directly affected by what goes on at the football club).
■ **Single-issue publics:** Publics active on one or a small number of issues (e.g., NHL players going on strike during the 2004–2005 season in protest at attempts to curb their wages).
■ **Hot-issue publics:** Publics active only on a single issue that involves everyone in the population (e.g., Manchester United supporters demonstrating against the Glazer takeover bid).

Being aware that all these different publics exist offers a distinct advantage to people working in sport organisations because it means that they are more likely to engage in successful proactive public relations as a consequence. Such an awareness also shows that public relations is much more far reaching than is often suggested by sport marketing texts, which tend to only concentrate on the commercial and media aspects of sports public relations, if anything. Sports public relations can be divided into two categories: corporate public relations (CPR) and marketing public relations (MPR). The identification of publics and appropriate communications strategies falls within the remit of CPR, which aims to create goodwill and build long-term relationships with all those diverse public groups. A number of different types of public relations come under the corporate sports public relations umbrella such as media public relations, financial public relations and employee public relations.

MPR has the distinct aim of creating support for the sports brand and enhancing the sale of sport products and services. MPR can be described as the overlap area between marketing and public relations, an area that has been growing exponentially during the past 20 years. Pickton and Broderick (2004) describe MPR as:

> ...a healthy offspring of two parents: marketing and PR. MPR represents an opportunity for companies to regain a share of voice in a message-satiated society. MPR not only delivers a strong share of voice to win share of mind and heart; it also delivers a better, more effective voice in many cases. (p. 554)

For reasons such as these, contemporary sport organisations need to focus on the benefits of using public relations as the core component of their communications strategies. To facilitate this, a sports-specific dimension to public relations is proposed, which we will call sport marketing public relations (SMPR). SMPR is the parts of sports public relations that are most focused towards marketing-relevant activities (e.g., the use of a football club's website to communicate information about off-season activities, which are tied in with promotional offers such as early-bird season ticket purchase). Because of the public relations element, sport organisations can find that MPR activities are often more effective and cost efficient than other marketing communications activities. SMPR is much more of an integrated activity that fits very well with the concepts of sport integrated marketing communications dealt with in Chapter 11.

The sports public relations planning process

Having looked in some detail at sports publics, our attention will now turn to the process used to create and maintain those vital mutually beneficial relationships. To this end, the last section of this chapter will examine the sports public relations planning process, that is the way that strategic public relations can be implemented within the sport organisation.

It has been emphasised throughout this chapter that professional public relations is a carefully planned and strategic element of the integrated marketing communications mix. Sport organisations only truly reap the many significant benefits and advantages to be derived from public relations if it is professionally conducted. For this to happen, a trained public relations professional should be employed by the sport organisation to plan and implement public relations programmes because only trained public relations professionals have the detailed knowledge and understanding of the public relations planning process. In public relations theory, a number of different approaches to planning have been identified, but for sports public relations, Jefkins' six-point public relations planning model, which was originally devised in 1994, is considered to be the most user-friendly. The six elements of this model are:

1. Situation analysis
2. Defining objectives
3. Defining publics
4. Media selection
5. Creation of the budget
6. Implementation and control

When listing the elements in this way, one gets the impression that public relations planning is a linear process. But in reality, some of these elements occur simultaneously and end up looking more like the diagram shown in Figure 14.4. What often happens as well is that some elements of the process might occur 'out of sequence' in real-life situations. For example, it is more usual for a budget to be allocated before the planning process begins rather than being determined at a later stage, as this model suggests. However, it is usually considered helpful to follow a sequence of steps, at least in the initial planning stages, because that way it is easier to identify likely problems or difficulties.

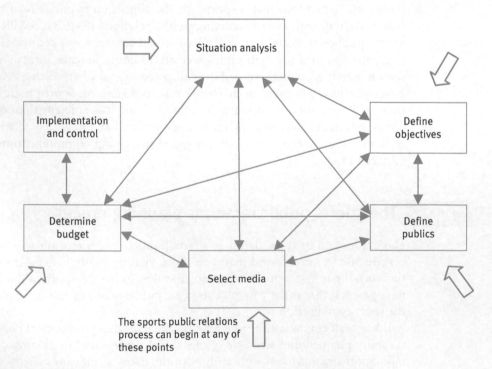

Figure 14.4 The six-point sports public relations planning process
Source: Adapted from Baines, Egan and Jefkins (2004)

One of the major challenges in sports public relations is the temptation to try to achieve much more than is actually possible. Mark Newton, CEO of Worcestershire County Cricket Club, observes that 'in my experience, over promising and under delivering are the biggest problems with public relations.' It makes perfect sense, therefore, that the professional sports public relations person always avoids such pitfalls.

Baines et al. (2004, p. 92) say that public relations can be extremely efficient in terms of ROI, and this is something that is widely endorsed by sports public relations practitioners. Stuart Duffy, media and public relations manager of the Bradford Bulls, is a strong supporter of what public relations can achieve with relatively little financial outlay. He cites word of mouth and people having a good time watching rugby league as powerful techniques for getting his message heard. There are many opportunities in sport in which public relations can be much more effective and economical simply because the other communications tools are not always the most suitable for a range of sports communications situations. The case study at the end of this chapter further endorses this view.

To better understand how the sports public relations planning process works, we will now briefly examine each of the six elements in turn.

Situation analysis

In public relations, situation analysis is sometimes called the *communications audit*. Having a detailed understanding of its present situation will reveal the current image of the sport organisation (i.e., how everything that the organisation says and does is perceived by its publics). In other words, if we do not know where we are now, it is pointless planning a public relations programme for the future. We can only find out what publics think of us by carrying out regular research. When we know what they think of us, we can implement positive strategies to ensure their long-term support and understanding.

Defining objectives

Sports public relations objectives should support the sport organisation's marketing objectives, which in turn should be consistent with the overall company objectives. Public relations objectives should be SMART: strategic, measurable, actionable, realistic and timely. Defining objectives is vital because only by doing that will it be possible to evaluate results and outcomes properly.

Defining publics

As already mentioned, all sport organisations have many different publics. Referring to the previous discussion on publics will clarify why defining them as part of the sports public relations planning process is essential.

Media selection

A significant proportion of sports-related public relations activity is spent on media relations. It is critical if public relations is to be successful that the correct media are used in order to best reach the various sports publics and meet their diverse communications needs. The word 'media' within the public relations context does not always refer to the mass media, however. Media are any of the methods through which communications messages are delivered to publics. For example, websites are becoming increasingly used as communications media by sport organisations.

The budget

One of the things that is often said about public relations is that it is free. Although some publicity may be gained at no or very little cost to the sport organisation, people's time and other public relations resources such as materials and expenses have to be carefully costed and estimated. It is, however, true that properly conducted public relations can be extremely cost effective, in both the short and long terms. Because finances are a constant limiting factor for most sport organisations, this is probably the most compelling reason for them to use public relations as the predominant element of the SIMCM.

Implementation and control

Management of the implementation of sports public relations activities is of crucial importance. Any public relations programme must be founded on substantial research and follow clearly set objectives. It must also be regularly monitored and evaluated in order to ensure that objectives are being met and that public relations activity is producing a measurable ROI. Keeping in touch with publics and adapting the public relations activity as necessary are also critical to achieving public relations success. This takes time and effort, but when lifelong relationships are at stake, it is certainly worth it. Yet another public relations myth says that public relations is intangible and cannot be measured. Twenty20 cricket, a game promoted almost exclusively through public relations, has placed many of the English first-class county clubs in the unique position of recording sell-out attendances before the 2005 season even began simply because the crowds wanted to see even more of the game that they had enjoyed so much the previous season.

The potential benefits to any sport organisation of implementing the six-point sports public relations planning process are considerable. Not least of these benefits is the enhanced reputation that the sport organisation will enjoy, which in turn will bring its own long-term financial rewards. Gregory (2000) says that public relations has a real job of work to do:

> If its [public relation's] task is guarding and managing reputation and relationships, this must have a demonstrable effect, and not just result in a 'feel-good' factor. (p. 4)

If a company has a good reputation, people are much more likely to engage with it, for example, in trying its new products, buying its shares, wanting to work for it, believing its advertising and supporting it in difficult times. Public relations has a proven track record of helping companies achieve all of these things and much more besides. Sports public relations, then, has rock-solid foundations upon which to build. The challenge now is for those involved in the business of sport to optimise this exciting communications technique to its full potential.

Some advantages and disadvantages of public relations

Just in case there are any remaining doubts concerning the benefits to sport organisations of learning about and implementing public relations, we will conclude with a brief summary of the major advantages and disadvantages that public relations can offer. When applied professionally, public relations can offer the following distinct advantages over other major marketing communications tools:

- **Credibility:** Unlike advertising messages, public relations messages are often generated by a source that is not the sport organisation. This is referred to as 'third-party endorsement' and is a very powerful way of gaining credibility for a message and thus the sport organisation. Having somebody else say good things about your organisation and your product is priceless, especially if that person is respected or recognised by your publics.
- **Cost:** As mentioned previously, public relations is considerably more cost effective than other communications tools.
- **Cutting through the clutter:** Public relations efforts frequently lead to publicity and are usually considered eminently newsworthy, particularly by the local news media. As a result, public relations messages are often in a class of their own and considered distinct from the proliferation of advertising and sales promotion messages, which can often overwhelm and confuse potential consumers.
- **Ability to reach specific groups:** Understanding publics and their behaviour, as discussed earlier in this chapter, allows for the implementation of specifically targeted communications and relationship-building strategies.
- **Image building:** The tireless development of effective public relations strategies can lead directly to the creation of a strong image and identity for the sport organisation. As already mentioned, this can result in very real benefits to the organisation, both financial and non-financial.

Public relations' main disadvantage is the lack of understanding that surrounds the discipline in some quarters and the uncontrollability of publicity. The more people involved in the business of sport learn about public relations, the better it will undoubtedly be for all sports generally. Unfortunately, no one can control human behaviour which can often result in negative publicity and negative information surrounding the sport organisation – the Dyer/Bowyer incident mentioned earlier in the chapter is a classic example of this. According to Halbwirth and Toohey (2005):

> Sport like any business is operating in a complex global marketing. Sport management needs to be adaptive to change, effectively manage risk, integrate technology advances and build stakeholder intimacy.

Embedding proactive and professional public relations within the sport organisation and integrating relationship-building strategies into the organisation's mission and long-term planning will undoubtedly make that significant and measurable difference.

| CASE 14.1 | Sports public relations in action: Newcastle Falcons Rugby Club community programme |

How is the organisation regarded by the people who live and work in the locality or the community at large?

(Baines et al., 2004)

Sports public relations incorporates an extensive range of communications objectives and activities, many of which are overtly linked to the sport organisation's commercial operations. Such public relations practice comes into the remit of MPR, which is where public relations is strategically linked to achieving marketing objectives. There is, however, another side to public relations, which is known as CPR. CPR, although not directly linked to commercial objectives, can, through long-term relationship building and keeping close to publics, contribute much to bottom-line success. sport organisations should think about nurturing and developing this aspect of public relations to a much greater extent because it is an extremely cost-effective method of developing and maintaining the sport organisation's image and identity and, very importantly, giving it the all-important competitive advantage that today's sport business demands. CPR can take many different forms, and this case study is an illustration of how one particular sport organisation is implementing one specific sports public relations technique to extremely profitable advantage.

Newcastle Falcons Rugby Club is based in Newcastle upon Tyne in North East England. Although only having been known as the Falcons since 1995, the Newcastle Falcons story dates back to 1877. The club, which was then called Gosforth Football Club, was formed by a group of old boys from Durham School (a private school also in North East England) who wanted to continue playing rugby whilst at the same time firmly rooting a club in their community. The period between 1877 and the present day has been one of both success and disappointment for the club. In 1995, Sir John Hall, a local entrepreneur who was then chairman of Newcastle United Football Club, finally realised his long-held ambition of establishing a Newcastle sporting club by acquiring Newcastle Gosforth rugby club, as it was then called. Bringing in some big-name players such as Rob Andrew, who became director of rugby as well as a star player, and All Black Inga Tuigamala, Hall initiated the transformation, which has become the Newcastle Falcons of today.

The Falcons' current homeground, where they have resided since 1990, is Kingston Park, which is a purpose-built ground situated on the outskirts of Newcastle. A visit to the ground shows immediately just how close the club is to its local community – only a road divides the two. Consistent with its original founders' intentions, the Newcastle Falcons are committed to being a part of this local community. To ensure that they are a good neighbour, the club works ceaselessly on its community relations strategies, which is a core element of its public relations planning. Club chairman Dave Thompson emphasises the Falcons' commitment to their community when he says, 'Our work in the community is at the very heart of everything we are about here at the Falcons, and developing rugby at grass roots level in the north east is every bit as important to us as having a successful first team.'

According to Mick Hogan, the club's commercial director, the Newcastle Falcons Community Programme is one of their most important initiatives and one with which everyone at the club, from the chairman to the groundsman, is involved and committed. As Hogan says:

For us, deciding whether or not to have a community programme is simply not an option. As a club, we are very much a physical part of the community and some of our neighbours love us and others don't. We have to accept that and work together with our neighbours, not against them, on managing our relationship.

Hogan explains that many real benefits from the community programme are now being noticed, both within the club and further afield. The community programme now employs four full-time members of staff, including a community education officer and a number of part-time workers, and has the enthusiastic support of the North East Rugby Football Union (RFU) regional manager. The Newcastle Falcons' community programme is predominantly focused on schools and rugby clubs and offers an extensive and exciting range of activities. As well as the immediate local community of Kingston Park, the community programme extends into the neighbouring counties of Northumberland, Tyne & Wear, Durham, North Yorkshire and Cumbria. During the 2003–2004 season, the Falcons' community programme made contact with more than 25,000 people, and the first team players made a total of 397 visits to the local community as part of the programme (http://www.newcastlefalcons.co.uk/40_39.php).

Hogan explains that the community programme is founded on four key principles:

- **Accessibility:** To ensure that professional players are accessible to the community and become involved in all elements of community work
- **Continuity:** To make sure that community relationships go beyond being short term or one-off experiences
- **Quality:** To make all programmes of the highest quality through management by qualified, skilled and motivated staff
- **Purpose:** To make all work worthwhile and congruent with the objectives of the Newcastle Falcons

The first thing that should be noted about these four principles is that each of them is founded on a real appreciation of public relations philosophy and a clear understanding that professional public relations must be long term and strategically focused. This understanding is particularly exemplified in the third principle, continuity. The first principle, accessibility, is worth examining more closely. The Falcons' director of rugby, Rob Andrew, is heavily involved in the community programme and insists that all the players, regardless of whether they are stars like Jonny Wilkinson or youngsters like Matthew Tait, get involved, too. In fact, every player has it written into his contract that he will commit to a set number of hours of community relations during the course of the season and that he will get the necessary interpersonal skills training to ensure that he becomes an excellent ambassador for both his club and his sport. Mark Foster, the Falcons community marketing manager, explains that 'every single player in the Falcons squad does at least three to four community visits each month, going out into the schools and clubs to meet the kids.' At the end of every season, a special community award is presented on awards night to the player who has contributed most to community relations. The current holder is Joe Shaw, who Foster describes as being a 'great ambassador for the club and for rugby in general.' For the Falcons players, this award is now equally as sought after as that of player of the year!

The 2005 community programme includes a number of initiatives, which are extensively detailed on the Falcons website at http://www.newcastle-falcons.co.uk. Community initiatives are divided into different categories and are aimed at both children and adults. The schools community package, for example, offers the following:

- **Coaching sessions:** These are offered by RFU qualified community coaches, who carry out the sessions at the school's premises both during and after-school hours.
- **Tag rugby coaching:** A non-contact version of rugby that introduces youngsters to rugby union.
- **Tackle learning scheme:** This programme was launched in 2005 and is designed to increase motivation in primary school children. The theme of rugby is used as a hook to link in with various subjects in the national curriculum.
- **Player visits:** First-team players visit local schools to support what is being taught and to talk to the children.
- **All-day visits:** The community team and first-team players spend whole days out in schools.
- **Stadium visits:** School visits to Kingston Park are provided, which include seminars in the club's facilities.

The Newcastle Falcons' community programme has won a number of awards in recent years, which is testament to the programme's success and achievement in making a real difference in the lives of its extensive and varied community members. In February 2005, an arguably even more powerful endorsement was given when the community programme was granted charity status. According to Hogan, this is a considerable achievement because it has the immediate benefit of giving enhanced credibility to the programme whilst at the same time attracting sponsorship and engagement from some high-profile companies such as Land Rover, Powergen and Hilton Hotels, which view their involvement with the community programme as a key part of their corporate social responsibility strategies. Charitable status has also resulted in a change of name to the Falcons Community Foundation, which has become a useful tool in Mick Hogan calls the 'community marketing' activities of the club, a real-life example of how sports public relations and sport marketing can work synergistically through SMPR.

Clearly, the Newcastle Falcons engage in proactive sports public relations through the Community Foundation, and the Falcons' publics derive a great deal from this relationship. But what do the Falcons get in return? Hogan describes how feedback from schools has been excellent and that the foundation is having to work hard to meet the ever-increasing demands for its offerings. Some of the many benefits to the club have been a measurable reduction in expenditure on advertising because public relations has become the dominant tool in the Falcons' integrated marketing communications strategy; extensive publicity in both the local and national media; national awards and recognition; player retention and motivation; increased staff motivation; increased number of season ticket holders; highly successful Easter and summer training camps; the ability to receive grants and gift aid on charitable donations to the foundation; and perhaps most importantly, successfully raising the profile of rugby in a region where football is very much the first and most popular sport of choice.

The Newcastle Falcons' experience tells us much about the benefits to sport organisations of developing a strategic public relations focus. By providing a classic study of how relationship management in sport can indeed be mutually beneficial on a number of different levels, the Falcons are an example definitely worth emulating.

Questions

1. What likely barriers did the Falcons have to overcome in gaining acceptance for their community programme?

2. Identify the aspects of the community programme that would appeal to you as a member of a Falcons' public. Give reasons for your choice.

3. Devise a community programme for a sport organisation of your choice. Give a clear rationale for your choice of activities.

Conclusions

Public relations within the context of sport has much to offer. Less visible and aggressive than some of the other SIMCM elements, it is the one communications discipline that should quietly work away in the background, not drawing attention to itself but continually functioning in order to establish and maintain relationships, create goodwill and understanding and ensure support for the sport organisation during both the good and the bad times. The CIPR's assertion that public relations is everything that the organisation says and does should be remembered at all times. It is when that responsibility is forgotten or taken for granted that problems occur. Everyone in the sport organisation, therefore, from the chairman and CEO to the cleaners and the groundsman, must understand their public relations roles because everything they say and do says a great deal not only about them but also their organisation.

Sports public relations must be planned and controlled in just the same way as any other business function. Proactive public relations for long-term relationship building is the key. The sport organisation cannot choose not to do public relations, so it makes sense to do it to the best of the organisation's ability. If public relations is attempted as an ad hoc, last-minute solution to a problem, it will not work, and the potential damage to the sport organisation's image will be considerable. As Shilbury et al. (2003) state:

It is important for the sport marketer to know how the sporting organisation's publics perceive the organisation and its product range. Knowledge of public opinion and how to influence opinion is vital in order to create proactive public relations strategies... Proactive strategies enable the sport marketer to 'control and adjust' public opinion, whereas reactive strategies always require changing negative public opinions. Prevention is better than repairing damage. (p. 267)

In 1982, Peters and Waterman coined the phrase 'staying close to the customer', and for sport organisations, it is an ambition that is perhaps even more pertinent today. In the face of increasing competition from other leisure pursuits and declining participation rates worldwide, it is extremely apparent that sport organisations have to find ways of engaging with and keeping their customers. It is clear that many involved with sport organisations at the highest level are very aware of the unique value of public relations, and some of their views have been highlighted in this chapter. However, there is much to be done in terms of implementing sports public relations in a more cohesive and professional manner. For sport organisations that come to understand public relations' benefits and are willing to invest time and engage in creating proactive public relations strategies, competitive advantage and long-term, mutually beneficial relationships between the organisation and its publics can be the reality, not merely the dream.

The main aim of this chapter was to outline the distinct and special role of public relations within the context of sport. It has been acknowledged that the remit of public relations is frequently misunderstood, but the definition of *public relations* and the subsequent exploration of how it operates are intended to clarify and dispel some common misconceptions. Some basic public relations theory relating to publics and the public relations planning process has been presented and analysed. The six-point sports public relations process that has resulted from this analysis is both realistic and can be implemented by any contemporary sport organisation. It is therefore hoped that the reader will be left with a more comprehensive understanding of the unique benefits that sports public relations can achieve if professionally implemented and practised and how this communications discipline combines with the rest of the SIMCM.

Discussion questions

1. Identify any recent examples of sporting events or organisations to which the public relations transfer process can be applied and where negative attitudes have been changed to positive ones through public relations.
2. For any sport organisation with which you are familiar, identify its key publics and suggest appropriate methods for communicating with each of them.
3. A new junior football club has just been admitted to your local Sunday league, and they have asked you to advise them on how to raise their profile. Use the six-point sports public relations planning process as the basis for a report to be compiled for the team management.

Guided reading

To date, very little has been written and published in sports public relations. In 2005, two articles were published on the subject by Hopwood, which can be found in the following journals: *Corporate Communications: An International Journal* (August 2005) and the *International Journal of Sports Marketing and Sponsorship* (April 2005). As public relations continues to develop as an area for academic study, some very good new publications on the subject have begun to appear. It is still the case that the 'classic theoretical' texts are those written by American authors such as Grunig and Hunt (1984) and Cutlip et al. (2000), which are listed in the bibliography. These texts are recommended for those who are especially interested in more rigorous public relations theory.

Good sources for specific sports public relations information are Lagae (2005) and Shilbury et al. (2003). Beech and Chadwick (2004) also have some more general coverage of sport marketing communications techniques that is useful for background information. General sport marketing authors such as Shank (2005) and Irwin, Sutton and McCarthy (2002) mention public relations within the context of marketing communications.

A very good and very readable text on public relations is Davis (2004). Although this book does not relate specifically to sports public relations, reading this will provide a sound understanding of contemporary public relations practice. The text by Baines et al. (2004), although slightly more theoretical, is also good.

Academic journals are always worth a look, and the following are very good for anything to do with sport marketing communications and public relations:

- *Journal of Marketing Communications*
- *Corporate Communications: An International Journal*
- *International Journal of Sports Marketing and Sponsorship*
- *Journal of Sport Management*
- *Sport Marketing Quarterly*

Keywords

Corporate public relations (CPR); licence to operate.

Bibliography

Baines, P., Egan, J. and Jefkins, F. (2004) *Public Relations: Contemporary Issues and Techniques*, Oxford: Elsevier Butterworth Heinemann.

Beech, J. and Chadwick, S. (2004) *The Business of Sport Management*, Harlow: Pearson Education Limited.

Cutlip, S.M., Center, A.H. and Broom, G.M. (2000) *Effective Public Relations*, 8th edn, Upper Saddle River, NJ: Prentice Hall.

Davis, A. (2004) *Mastering Public Relations*, Basingstoke: Palgrave Macmillan.

Ehling, W.P., White, J. and Grunig, J.E. (1992) 'Public relations and marketing practices', in *Excellence in Public Relations and Communication Management*, Hillsdale, NJ: Lawrence Erlbaum Associates.

Gregory, A. (2000) *Planning and Managing Public Relations Campaigns*, London: Kogan Page.

Grunig, J.E. and Hunt, T. (1984) *Managing Public Relations*, Fort Worth: Holt, Rinehart & Winston.

Grunig, J.E. and Repper, F.C. (1992) 'Strategic management publics and issues', in *Excellence in Public Relations and Communication Management*, Hillsdale, NJ: Lawrence Erlbaum Associates.

Halbwirth, S. and Toohey, K. (2005) *Leveraging Knowledge: Sport and Success*, Paper presented to the 12th World Congress of International Association for Sports Information, May 2005, Beijing.

Hopwood, M.K. (2003) *Public Relations Practice in English County Cricket: A Case Study of Yorkshire County Cricket Club and Durham County Cricket Club*, Unpublished thesis, University of Stirling, Scotland.

Hopwood, M.K. (2005) Applying the public relations function to the business of sport, *International Journal of Sports Marketing and Sponsorship* 6(3):174–88.

Irwin, R., Sutton, W.A. and McCarthy, L.M. (2002) *Sport Promotion and Sales Management*, Champaign, IL: Human Kinetics.

Jefkins, F. (1994) *Public Relations Techniques,* 2nd edn, Oxford: Butterworth Heinemann.

Kitchen, P. (ed.) (1997) *Public Relations, Principles and Practice*, London: International Thomson Press.

Lagae, W. (2005) *Sport Sponsorship and Marketing Communications: A European Perspective*, Harlow: Pearson Education Limited.

Ledingham, J.A. and Bruning, S.D. (2000) *Public Relations as Relationship Management: A Relational Approach to the Study and Practice of Public Relations*, Mahwah, NJ: Lawrence Erlbaum Associates.

Peters, T. and Waterman, Jr., R.H. (1982) *In Search of Excellence: Lessons from America's Best-Run Companies*, London: HarperCollinsBusiness.

Pickton, D. and Broderick, A. (2005) *Integrated Marketing Communications,* 2nd edn, Harlow: Pearson Education Limited.

Pope, N. and Turco, D. (2001) *Sport and Event Marketing.* Roseville NSW, Australia: McGraw-Hill Australia Pty Limited.

Shank, M. (2005) *Sports Marketing: A Strategic Perspective,* 3rd international edn, Upper Saddle River, NJ: Pearson Education.

Shilbury, D., Quick, S. and Westerbeek, H. (2003) *Strategic Sport Marketing,* 2nd edn, Crows Nest NSW, Australia: Allen and Unwin.

The Weekend Australian (2005) *The Economist* 21–22 May, p. 38.

Wilcox, D.L., Ault, P.H. and Agee, W.K. (2003) *Public Relations, Strategies and Tactics,* 7th edn, Allyn and Bacon.

Recommended website

Newcastle Falcons
http://www.newcastle-falcons.co.uk

Part Four

Getting sport products and service to the market

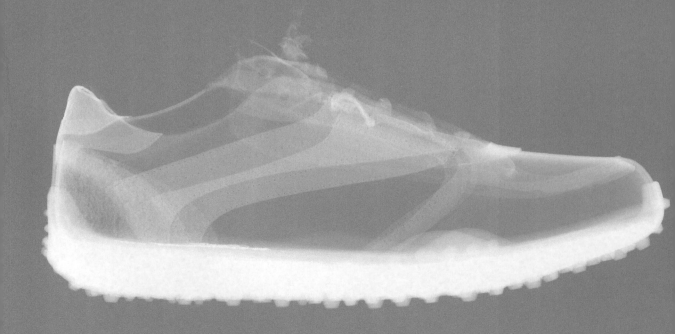

Chapter 15

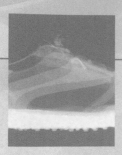

Pricing sports and sports pricing strategies

Rudi Meir and Dr Dave Arthur
Southern Cross University

Learning outcomes

Upon completion of this chapter, the reader should be able to:

- Recognise the role of pricing within the traditional marketing mix of sport organisations.

- Develop a pricing strategy that meets organisational objectives.

- Conduct research into relevant aspects of the organisation's market and use this information to develop a pricing strategy.

- Identify the most commonly used pricing methods within the sport and fitness industries.

- Recognise that price alone will not sell a poor product or service.

Overview of chapter

This chapter looks at the process of price determination and the strategies typically used in today's rapidly expanding and increasingly competitive sport and fitness industries. Few elements of the purchase decision influence the consumer quite as much as the actual monetary cost of purchasing a product or service. However, monetary value does not operate in isolation, and a range of factors play a part in this process from the consumer's perspective. For managers of sport or fitness organisations, this means having a good understanding of aspects that influence the price they set for their various offerings. To this end, this chapter provides the reader with a definition of 'price' and its function in establishing market share, competitive position and revenue for the organisation. The relationship between the consumer's perception of quality and value for money will also be closely examined. As with so many elements of the traditional marketing mix, the chapter will also consider the range of internal and external factors that sport marketers must factor in when deciding which method of pricing will be used by the organisation. Finally, a range of practical industry examples are presented to facilitate the reader's understanding of the pricing process and strategies used by sport marketers in a range of sports.

Introduction

No business, sporting or otherwise, would consider opening its doors without first giving some thought to a number of financial issues, including credit sales, credit collections, pricing, depreciation and relevant inventory levels. All have some impact on financial performance, but pricing and attendant pricing policies are typically given the least amount of attention and in some cases, viewed very simply by sport marketers. Yet it is argued that price is the only element of the traditional 4 Ps marketing mix that produces revenue, with the other aspects implemented at a cost to the organisation (Kotler and Armstrong, 2004). The 'price' paid for a particular good or service is often the single most important factor in the decision-making process for the consumer. For many sports fans, their decision to purchase a season ticket is based on a range of factors, not the least of which is their emotional attachment to the team they follow. On any given weekend, England's highways carry carloads of soccer fans who are willing to spend and invest significant amounts of time and money following the team of their passion to every home and away game. Consequently, brand loyalty in team sports has resulted in, as with other consumer goods that enjoy strong brand loyalty, price premiums being realised, which in turn aid professional sporting franchises to increase revenues and offset operational expenses (Aaker, 1991; Gladden and Funk, 2001). Yet this passionate support should not be taken for granted by the sport marketer nor should it be seen as an opportunity to 'milk' every last penny from fans blinded by their emotional attachment to their team. As with any purchase, there will be a limit to what consumers will tolerate in terms of the price they are willing to pay.

Typically, the approach used in pricing sport products is often different from that used in traditional consumer goods and services sectors. This is due in no small part to the many unique elements of the sport product, only some of which are related to price. Such elements are explained in greater detail elsewhere in this text but include the fact that many sports operate on a not-for-profit basis, operating out of taxpayer-funded facilities and have significant amounts of labour provided by volunteers, whose only motivation is to help the team they support and the opportunity to see them play for 'free' in exchange for their time. As a result, the price of the sport product (e.g., the cost of a single event ticket to watch a professional rugby team play) is small compared with the total cost paid (e.g., cost of venue and all associated running costs, cost of the team's playing salaries, cost of all team support and administrative staff) and finally that indirect revenues are greater than direct operating revenues (Mullin, Hardy and Sutton, 2000; Summers, 2003). For example, professional sport franchises no longer expect to recover all of their operating costs from the simple selling of tickets to fans, but this aspect of their revenue streams is increasingly surpassed by income from other sources (e.g., sponsorship, television, advertising, corporate hospitality). In effect, this subsidises the true cost of delivering the event to the fan, thus keeping ticket prices at acceptable levels for fans.

Price is a vital element of the organisational marketing mix and as such, should ideally be set at a level that reflects the true cost of putting on the event or match.

In addition, unlike food, clothing, utilities, fuel and the like, consumers purchase sport products and services on a discretionary basis – that is, from their disposable income – and in doing this, they may well be weighing up the value of the purchase against a wide range of other options readily available to them. This is of increasing importance when one considers that in American Major League Baseball (MLB), for every $1.00 spent on ticketing, the average fan will spend a further $1.03 on non-ticket expenditure (Raymond, 2001).

What is price?

Price is often a critical strategic marketing issue and is generally used to quantify the value of the good or service with which it is associated. Typically, price is simply the 'setting or adjusting a price charged to a customer in exchange for a good or service' (Shilbury, Quick and Westerbeek, 2003, p. 98). In this context, price is applied to a wide range of sporting goods and services (e.g., single event ticket, preferential seating in a venue, food and concession items, merchandise, sports equipment, venue hire, special events, personal coaching, corporate hospitality). In each example, the organisation sets a price based on what, in part, it believes is an appropriate expression of the product or service's value to the consumer while also providing a suitable return on investment (ROI) for the organisation, given its corporate objectives. Price, however, can also be a determinant of, for example:

- **Market share:** This may increase or decrease with changes in price (e.g., a personal trainer may decide to reduce the hourly fee in an effort to draw clients away from a competitor, thus increasing the share of the current market).
- **Competitive position:** Based on whether the product or service is priced above or below a competitor's product or service (e.g., a new gym, entering into a market already served by two existing gyms, offers a discounted price for casual visits, thus increasing pressure on the competitors to drop their prices).
- **Revenue:** A low price may increase total revenue (TR) but actually decrease profitability (because the product or service may be priced at a level below its original cost, resulting in the sales volume increasing markedly but meaning that a loss is achieved on these sales rather than a profit).

In economic theory, price, value and utility are related concepts (Stanton, Miller and Layton, 1994). Utility represents the characteristic of an item that enables it to satisfy consumer wants and has been defined as 'the attribute in an item that makes it capable of satisfying human wants' (Stanton et al., 1994, p. 10). Marketing essentially creates four types of utility intended to help satisfy consumer need:

1. **Form utility:** Production of the product using various elements that come together and make a product more valuable (for example, synthetic materials are brought together to produce sports shoes). This is production, not marketing, but as Stanton et al. (1994) point out, market research plays a role in the decision to make those shoes in a particular colour, design and so on.
2. **Place utility** is the place where the consumer wants the product, making it accessible to potential customers (e.g., the location of a fitness centre close to a large shopping district).

3. **Time utility** is getting the product to the customer when they want it. Fr example, transferring the English Super League competition in 1996 from its traditional winter schedule to summer has seen steady increases in attendance at matches and increased its appeal to younger fans. It could be argued that the fans at the time were resistant to this change; however, a condition of the lucrative commercial deal agreed to by the Rugby Football League with BSkyB required that the competition shift to a summer competition in order to fit with the satellite broadcaster's programming needs (in this context, the 'customer').

4. **Possession (or ownership) utility** is created when a customer purchases a product from a seller (e.g., a season ticket or fitness centre membership).

One of the most fundamental consumer perceptions links price with 'value', with price often used as a major positioning tool to differentiate a product (Yoo, Donthu and Lee, 2000). In short, price can be used by an organisation 'to send a message to the market about the firm and its products' (Dann and Dann, 2004, p. 303). Cheap products may be perceived as 'inferior', and a free product may be perceived as having little or no value at all. In contrast, a more expensive product may have a greater perceived value. Value is the quantitative worth of a product and is usually exchanged for money but might also be exchanged for other goods or services. Price is value expressed in monet-ary terms such as pounds and pence, dollars and cents or any other monetary medium of exchange. The price set for a good or service contributes towards shaping consumer perceptions regarding quality, value for money and the desire for particular products or services. Ultimately, consumer 'satisfaction', which will influence desire, is the product of purchase cost plus benefit received (Mullin et al., 2000). However, the 'cost' may be a combination of both the money exchanged and the time and effort needed to purchase the product or service. You may find a relatively cheap alternative but spend a considerable amount of time and effort locating it. As a result, this may have a negative impact in terms of your postpurchase analysis, leading to a low level of satisfaction with the purchase.

Stotlar (1993, p. 101) presents a matrix (Table 15.1) to help illustrate the relationship between price and quality for the sport marketer.

According to Stotlar (1993, p. 100), there are 'distinct advantages and disadvantages' associated with each position in the matrix. Examples are:

- **Low quality–low price (cheapie):** Quality is simply not an issue for some consumers, and the cheaper, low-quality alternative will do just fine. Particularly relevant for low-risk, 'throw-away' items such as practice balls for golfers.
- **Low quality–medium price (brand buy):** Low-end quality 'branded' item, in which the brand name is enough to convince the consumer to purchase the item.

Table 15.1 **Relationship between price and quality in sport**

Quality	Price		
	Low	Medium	High
Low	Cheapie	Brand buy	Rip off
Medium	Bargain	Equitable buy	Fad buy
High	Steal	Good value	Rolls Royce

■ **Low quality–high price (rip off):** This represents a 'risky' purchase. This might be reflected in a TV shopping channel purchase that promotes a product claiming to have numerous features, but once the purchase is made, the consumer then finds out that the product fails to deliver on the promise. As Stotlar (1993, p. 100) points out, these types of markets might be very profitable, but they tend to be relatively short lived.

■ **Medium quality–low price (bargain):** Everyone loves a bargain; the problem is finding them. The 'sale' purchase is often seen as an attractive option, particularly if backed up by quality service and good product benefits (e.g., discounted pair of running shoes from The Athlete's Foot® that provide durability and comfort).

■ **Medium quality–medium price (equitable buy):** A purchase made from this category can be done with some confidence that the product will 'deliver' in terms of both benefits and value. Stotlar says, 'You get what you pay for' (1993, p. 101).

■ **Medium quality–high price (fad buy):** Some consumers are willing to pay a bit more to be the first to purchase a particular product such as the latest mobile phone or plasma TV technology. Stotlar (1993) refers to this kind of purchase as a fad buy.

■ **High quality–low price (steal):** The 'Holy Grail' for many consumers! We all want products in this category, but they tend to be difficult to find.

■ **High quality–medium price (good value):** This is a pricing strategy often used as part of a 'penetration' strategy (referred to later in this chapter), and as Stotlar (1993, p. 101) states, can result in consumers who are impressed with the quality and price of their purchase, becoming repeat purchasers regardless, within reason, of future price increases.

■ **High quality–high price (Rolls Royce):** Obviously, some consumer markets are very demanding in terms of their expectations and are prepared to pay for this quality. This is typically associated with prestigious or exclusive products or services and is often linked to 'status seekers' who see such a purchase as reflecting something about them.

As can be deduced from Stotlar's (1993) price/quality matrix, price can be used as a strategy to manipulate marketing effect. There are three primary reasons for this strategy:

1. Price is a variable that is most readily changed, yet it is the least understood marketing element. If a price that has been set for a particular service or product is not accepted by consumers, then it can, if considered appropriate, be quickly changed.
2. In certain conditions, price can be one of the most effective tools in selling a product. However, remember, regardless of price, a poor product or service will not sell. Price is just one element of the four key elements of the classical marketing mix.
3. Price is highly 'visible'. Changes are easily communicated through a wide variety of communication media and can possibly lead to changes in consumer perception about the value of a product or service.

For example, in 1997, News Limited in Australia created a new rival professional rugby league competition, called Super League (SL), to compete with the traditional professional league operated by the original custodians of the game in Australia, the Australian Rugby League (ARL). The SL competition comprised teams that had defected from the ARL competition and a number of new teams that were needed in order for a viable competition to exist. The Hunter Mariners were one of the SL's new teams and were located in a stronghold of the ARL competition that was also the home of one of the ARL's most popular teams, the Newcastle Knights. The Mariners typically only attracted a few thousand spectators to their home games, and in an attempt to build bigger crowds, the team's management offered a family ticket (two adults plus two children) for just $40.00. Yet even at this price and despite the fact that tickets to ARL games were typically approximately $15 to $20 per adult, crowds were notoriously poor. Notwithstanding the strong local animosity that existed towards the Mariners from Newcastle's ARL traditionalists, there was also the lack of quality 'star' players and the relatively poor winning record of the team. These factors may have created the perception in the minds of potential fans that the ticket and the product it allowed access to were considered of low entertainment value.

Determining price

A range of internal and external factors influence the pricing decisions made by a sport organisation. These cannot be ignored and must be taken into consideration when setting the strategic pricing policy of the organisation.

Internal factors

Internal factors include the general and marketing objectives of the organisation, its cost structure and the marketing mix employed at the time price is determined.

Organisational objectives

In setting prices, sport marketers must consider the objectives of their own organisations, and these in turn are influenced by whether the organisation is a private (for-profit), public (government) or community-based (not-for-profit) organisation. According to Pride and Ferrell (1991), these objectives generally fall into seven categories: survival, profit, ROI, market share, cash flow, status quo and product quality. Organisational objectives might therefore relate to:

- **Efficient use of resources:** For example, a recreation centre operated by a local authority might 'price' to maximise the use of its facilities, seeing this as an important part of its service delivery to as many consumers within the community as possible.
- **Fairness:** What is a fair or equitable price given all environmental and organisational circumstances? For example, the Sydney Organising Committee for the Olympic Games (SOCOG) attempted this when they identified 1.5 million tickets for sale specifically to low income and disadvantaged community groups as part of their 'Olympic Opportunity' ticketing strategy for the Sydney 2000 Olympics. Similarly, a professional rugby league team based in a location with a large population of low-income earners might deem it appropriate to have a 'concession' price to selected seats in the venue (clearly, not the premium seats that readily command top price) rather than expect them to pay the normal premium price of entry to matches.
- **Maximum participation opportunities:** The provision of a range of price points throughout the product line, pricing products based on various features and benefits. As shown in Figure 15.1, a fitness centre might price a range of membership packages designed to target a wide range of segments based on their ability to pay: student concession, pensioner, unemployed, off-peak, sport teams and so on.

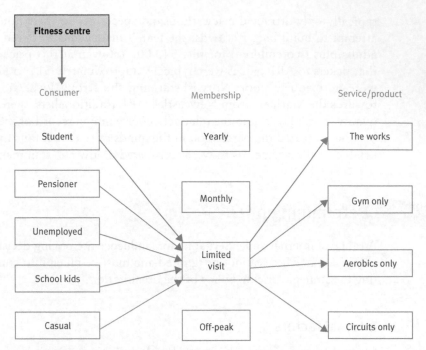

Figure 15.1 **Maximisation of participation opportunities**

- **Positive user attitudes:** As stated by Stotlar (1993), there is a general sense that you get what you pay for. Consumers who pay a premium price for a club membership, which they perceive as exclusive and prestigious, want exactly that! This is often referred to as prestige pricing. On the other hand, giving away excessive quantities of free tickets to events may also act to devalue the product in the consumer's mind. The Gold Coast Seagulls, which competed in the ARL competition from 1988 to 1995, struggled to attract crowds. During the club's chequered history, they only managed to fill its 14,000-capacity stadium on a handful of occasions. In an effort to attract bigger crowds and hopefully encourage new fans to sample their product and ultimately return as full paying customers, the club adopted a strategy of giving away large numbers of free tickets to every home game, yet over time, very few of these tickets were redeemed. This may have reflected a perception in the market that the tickets were easy to get and of low monetary value; the knock-on effect being that potential spectators perceived the game to be of low worth in terms of its entertainment value.
- **Profits:** Some organisations exist purely for the maximisation of profit. That is their goal and is reflected in their objectives.

Cost structure

Whatever its objectives, there is some necessity for the sporting organisation to 'break even', depending, of course, on whether it is a for-profit or not-for-profit organisation. The break-even point (sometimes referred to as the cost–volume–profit relationship) is the point at which the cost of providing the product or service is matched by the price charged and the volume sold. In short, it is the level of activity at which an organisation

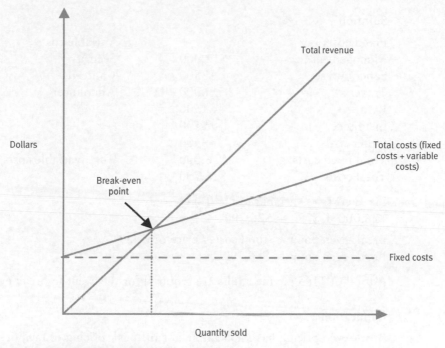

Figure 15.2 **The break-even point**

is making neither a profit nor a loss (Figure 15.2). Costs are generally referred to as fixed or variable. Fixed costs tend to remain the same for at least 1 year and include, for example, permanent staff salaries, rent and insurance. Variable costs, on the other hand, tend to change as the volume of business changes. Hourly wages paid to casual staff, advertising, telephone charges, utilities and consumables are generally considered to be variable costs (see Case 15.1).

CASE 15.1   Practical applications of the break-even point

Application 1

Your sporting organisation has decided to run a major event in a regional city. You have been appointed the coordinator for the event on a set consultancy fee of $12,000. Rent and lighting for the facility have been determined at $1500 and relevant insurance's at $500. Travel and accommodation for the two competing teams is calculated at $3000 per team and a fee ($2500) needs to be paid to the governing body to sanction the event. A number of casual staff are to be employed – five security guards ($10.00 per hour each), three canteen workers ($10.00 per hour each) and a ground announcer ($50.00 total). Security will be required for a total of ten hours and the canteen for eight hours. Other costs (marketing, telephone, consumables etc.) have been calculated at $3500 in total. Tickets for the event have been priced at $23.00 for adults with children admitted free of charge. How many tickets need to be sold in order for the event to break even?

Solution

Fixed costs		Variable costs	
Management Fee	$12,000	Security	$500
Sanction Fee	$2500	Canteen	$240
Travel	$6000	Announcer	$50
Rent	$1500		
Insurance	$500		
Other costs	$3500		
Total fixed costs	$26,000	Total variable costs	$790
Total costs	$26,790		

Fixed costs + Variable cost = Total costs
$26,000 + $790 = $26,790

Break-even point = Total costs / price of ticket
Break-even point = $26,790/23

A total of 1165 paying adults are required for the event to break even.

Application 2

Break-even pricing has implications for off-peak pricing of facilities (e.g., recreation and fitness centres). Such facilities could charge anything above variable costs during off-peak hours. This approach allows management to recover overhead costs from revenue that otherwise would not be received. A fitness centre might achieve this by having a special 'off-peak' membership restricted to the quietest time of the day, for example, from 11 am to 2 pm, as a means of attracting new members (e.g., house parents who have their children at school during this time). In the public sector during the 1970s and 1980s, there was a tendency by local authorities and state and federal agencies towards only recovering VC because FC (e.g., facilities, fields) were largely paid for by taxes. However, although to some extent this situation still exists, there is an increasing shift towards a 'user pays' philosophy resulting in the setting of more 'commercial' pricing policies.

External factors

External factors include demand within the particular target market, level of competition and broader factors such as the state of the economy. Pitts and Stotlar (1996, pp. 172–175) categorised these as the 4 Cs: the consumer, the competitor, the company and the climate.

The consumer

Consumers are price sensitive but consider more than this when making a purchase decision, including important aspects such as the product or service quality and consumer image. Of course, in the sport industry, the consumer's emotional attachment to the sport plays a vital role and goes some way towards explaining what to non-sports fans might appear to be irrational behaviour. Stotlar (1993) states that 'there is an obvious interaction effect with product and price'. There is a general sense that 'you get what you pay for' (p. 100). Typically, as we have already seen (some) consumers may perceive that higher priced products must be of better quality and conversely, that the lower priced alternatives are not. In fact, some consumers consciously avoid the cheaper alternative, fearing it is an inferior product and simply not worth buying (Stotlar, 1993). However, this may not apply to all categories of products or services. Dann and Dann (2004) believe there is also a 'reference price', a price that a given consumer will place on an item. This varies from consumer to consumer. For example, consumer A may think that $100 is a fair price for a tennis racquet; however, consumer B may be prepared to pay $250 for the same product. In addition to the buying decision, a decision-making process may involve the opinion of friends, family and salespeople. This process is influenced by demographic and psychographic factors.

The competitor

Competitors' prices and competitor pricing strategies are also important when determining price. This brings into play two factors in price consideration: (i) the consumer's perception of value in relation to that of a competitor and (ii) careful analysis of competitor prices. Sporting organisations need to consider how to set prices based on the proximity of both direct and indirect competitors within their market areas and the similarity of services or products that they sell to the same potential customers. For example, two fitness centres with similar facilities and levels of service and located within 5 minutes' drive of each other will likely have very similar prices for their various classes and memberships. However, if one offered a totally different level of service and facilities that clearly differentiated it from the other, then there may be more opportunity to price significantly above or below the competitor. Careful consideration must also be given to the total range of entertainment options available within the same market area from which, for example, spectators are drawn. An English Premiership football team does not compete simply with its geographically closest Premiership rival but rather with a potentially vast range of options for entertainment from which fans will select an option at a given time (e.g., cinemas, live music, theme parks or simply a night out with family for dinner).

The company

The third C is the sporting organisation itself. Ask yourself: 'What factors are peculiar to the organisation and might affect the price of our product or service?' For example, your organisation may have high labour costs or long-term leasing plans for equipment. Or it may own its own premises and have no rental obligations. Of course, some of this may relate to whether the sporting organisation is non-profit or profit oriented. Each type has differing cost structures that impact greatly on price determination.

The climate

The final C is the climate in which the sporting organisation operates. It includes factors that lie outside the direct control of the organisation, including the local and national political climate, government restrictions on pricing and the general economic climate. In Australia, for example, the Trade Practices Act ensures that unfair trade practices do not occur to exclude a particular producer from a market. This same act also limits things such as the length of membership that can be sold by a commercial fitness centre to its members.

Methods for setting prices

As soon as the parameters for pricing have been established, there are essentially three methods for setting of prices that are typically used within the sport industry. However, it should be noted that 'setting the final price is a complex decision based in part on ensuring that costs are met as well as achieving specific marketing goals' (Dann and Dann, 2004, p. 313).

Cost-based pricing

This type of pricing considers the total of fixed and variable costs and adds a percentage markup in order to make a profit. This method is common in the sport industry and is based on the following simple formula:

FC (fixed costs) + VC (variable costs) + Markup (desired profit) = Break-even sales

Example:

Arnie's Gym projects a yearly membership of 400
Total (FC + VC) costs = £120K/yr
Wants to achieve a profit margin of £25K/yr (which effectively becomes an FC)
Break-even sales revenue = £145K
Break-even sale price (average membership) = £362.50/yr

That is, the cost of some memberships will be more or less depending on use category (e.g., full facility use, aerobics only and so on). As long as the membership fees 'average' out to £362.50, then the target TR and profit margin will be achieved. Note that typically, there will be a range of other 'revenue' sources such as clothing, food and beverage sales, dietary supplements and so on. In this example, FC might include managerial salary, equipment lease, rent, loan repayments and so on, and VC might include a masseur who only attends when appointments warrant it (i.e., 'piece work') or a fitness instructor who is only employed to take classes on a casual basis.

For this approach to be effective, management needs timely and accurate information on both the fixed and variable costs. Such an approach is safe in that it ensures all business costs are met. However, competitors with different cost structures could have different prices, and this method takes no account of market pressures.

Going-rate pricing

When using the going-rate method, the organisation sets the price based on what its competitors are charging. To ascertain prices, the organisation would undertake an audit of all competitor businesses to determine the going rate and then set a price accordingly. As Dann and Dann (2004) commented, 'price is the only element of the marketing mix that competitors can copy exactly without any legal restrictions' (p. 303). Therefore, the major advantage of this method is that it is relatively easy to establish. However, it could be that audited competitors are using a different (e.g., cost-based) method of pricing. If the costs of your organisation differ markedly (e.g., you may be paying rent, but a competitor owns the premises outright, or you may have higher wage costs) the competitor may be making a profit at the price charged, but your organisation may not.

■ Demand-orientated pricing

This method is based upon ascertaining what particular target market segments are willing to pay. An example is variations in ticket prices for certain premium packages sold to either corporations or wealthy individuals at 'special events'. Some of the yachting tickets during the Sydney Olympics sold for £500/day and included catering on a luxury boat on Sydney harbour. Establishing this price can be achieved through consumer survey, by studying the competition or a combination of both. Factors influencing demand may include price, tastes and preferences, advertising, market demand, elastic demand and inelastic demand.

Price

In 2000, the Australian Rugby Union (ARU) played a test match against the Springboks for the first time in Melbourne at the (then) new Colonial Stadium (now called the TelstraDome). Just 34,042 fans turned up to watch the match in a stadium with a capacity of approximately 53,000. At the same venue the previous night, 34,567 fans turned up to watch a regular Australian Football League (AFL) match. The ARU set ticket prices starting at $53 rising to $130. The event was seen as an opportunity to promote international rugby in Melbourne, the traditional home of the AFL, and provide local football fans with a sampling opportunity for the sport. However, $53 was seen as too high a price and did little to change the perception of many that rugby union is an elitist sport and one that can only be afforded by those on moderate to high incomes.

Price of related goods

In a competitive market with numerous substitute products or services to choose from, consumers are unlikely to opt to purchase an overpriced version of the same or a similar product. In this situation, the lower priced version is most likely to be purchased by the consumer and therefore have a greater market share.

Consumer income

As previously stated, most sport products and services (e.g., season tickets, fitness centre memberships) are purchased from a consumer's discretionary income. Using census data and relevant market research, the sport marketer needs to establish the income levels of consumers within their target market(s). This information is then used to set a range of prices that take into consideration the general cost of living for households within the market area and provide a wide range of products at a price that is accessible by the full range of low to high income earners within that particular target market (see Case 15.2).

CASE 15.2   North versus south

In 1996, Wigan RLFC, the then English rugby league champions, played Bath RFC, the then English rugby union champions, in the first ever cross-code 'Rugby Challenge' event requiring each team to play a game under its respective code's rules. This was a unique event, and the marketers (the respective clubs) adopted a strategy that saw them set a different ticket price for tickets sold in the north of England than in the south. Therefore, a higher price was sought and tolerated by those attending the second game at Twickenham compared with the first game played at Manchester City's Main Road stadium. This was based on the notion that the south had higher levels of employment and household income than the north and therefore fans would pay a higher price than fans in the north to see this one-off spectacle. There were also different ticket options available based on where the seats were located within the respective venues. This is obviously a very common pricing strategy in professional team sports, with fans playing a higher price for the seats with a combination of the best facilities and most importantly, the best view of the action. A higher price might also be achieved for tickets in a high-quality venue such as English rugby's famous Twickenham stadium. The price structure for the 'Rugby Challenge '96' was:

Main Road, Manchester City FC

Kippax stand seats

- Upper tier: £15
- Lower tier: £13

Main stand seats

- All seats: £15

North stand seats

- Adults: £10
- OAP and juniors under 16: £6

Twickenham

Corporate seats: £35

Premier seats: £25

Main seats: £20

Family: £45 for 2 adults and 2 children under 16

Juniors, schools and clubs: £90 for 10 plus 1 adult

Tastes and preferences

Not everybody wants a seat in the best location in the stadium, and in fact, many traditional fans of sports such as football and rugby union prefer to stand on terraces with other like-minded fans (where this is still available). Others want access to parking close to the ground and comfortable seating out of any bad weather with a good view of all of the action. Increasingly, professional sport is catering to corporate clients who require high-quality facilities and service to watch their sport in the form of corporate boxes that have TVs, bars and full catering facilities available to occupants before, during and after the match along with an opportunity to perhaps rub shoulders with the team's 'star' players. As a result, these clients will happily pay a premium to see the same event as the fan on the terraces. It is all a matter of preference (and what they can afford!).

Advertising

Advertising can be a powerful medium that works to increase demand for sport events and services. In the lead up to the 2000 Sydney Olympics, the organising committee of the event promoted the Sydney Olympics as 'a once in a lifetime opportunity', helping SOCOG to sell 6.7 million tickets as well as gaining a price premium for many tickets. 'Being there' and experiencing the unique atmosphere of large sport events is a big part of the attraction for many sports fans, particularly at special events or occasions. As a result, many organisations use this as the theme of their advertising campaigns, appealing to consumers while also helping to justify ticket prices.

Market demand

As alluded to above, a major problem with both break-even and cost-plus pricing is that these methods do not take into account the most important factor in pricing decisions, that is, market demand. With limited income, consumers cannot simply buy everything they may want, which necessitates a balancing of needs against the price of those products or services for which the consumer has a preference. As previously established, a major consumer consideration is whether the price being asked for the product or service is thought to be the 'right' price. In a general sense, if the price of a product, say, casual attendance at aerobics classes, goes up, then the consumer may decide to attend less frequently. Conversely, if the price of attending these same aerobics classes goes down, the consumer may decide to attend more regularly. Elasticity of demand refers to the effect that unit price changes have on the number of units sold and TR. In many product categories, consumers can be very sensitive to changes in product price (Stotlar, 1993). For example, fair weather fans who support a team over an extended period of poor performance may be particularly sensitive to increases in their season ticket price from one season to the next, and as a result, they may choose not to renew their membership. The consumer reaction to price change is called price elasticity of demand.

In the context of price elasticity, more loyal consumers would be less likely to switch because of a given price promotion. Put simply, they would usually require a bigger discount to switch than a less loyal customer would (Baldinger and Rubinson, 1996). Loyalty is usually defined behaviourally and measured in terms of repeat buying patterns (repeat-choice measures of loyalty). As a result, it is strongly linked to market share state and price elasticity effects, demonstrating the importance of loyalty (Baldinger and Rubinson, 1996; Starr and Rubinson, 1978). Research by Dodson, Tybout and Sternthal (1978) found that offering a 'deal' can enhance brand switching. The withdrawal of a deal had a significant effect on the incidence of brand repeat purchasing.

Elastic demand

If there is a small change in price but a large change in demand, then demand is considered to be 'relatively elastic' – that is, consumers are very price sensitive and will not buy a product if this price is deemed too high. As a result, they are likely to seek out a cheaper alternative, possibly from a competitor. This might be the case when a fitness centre increases its casual aerobics price from £10 to £12 per class, causing a significant decrease in attendance rates and therefore TR. Conversely, a fitness centre may decide on a strategy that sees it decrease the cost of its casual aerobics class price from £10 to £8 per class, which results in a significant increase in attendance rates and also TR.

This latter example reflects a 'penetration pricing' strategy that can be used in this market condition in the belief that by pricing at the lower range of expected prices, there will be an increase in quantity purchased. However, as Stotlar (1993) states, 'The key issue in the area of price elasticity of demand is to determine if a price decrease will attract enough additional customers to maintain profits, while revenues from price increases must offset the calculated attrition of customers after the price change' (p. 98).

For example, an AFL team in Australia has a single match ticket price set at $10 for the season, and as a result, attracted a total of 320,000 fans to their matches (TR from ticket sales = $3.2m). However, the next year, they increase the ticket price to $12 per match but only achieved total attendance of 240,000 (TR from ticket sales = $2.88m). This represents a decrease in TR of $320,000. All things being equal, this would mean that demand is relatively elastic. To establish this, you simply examine the number of tickets (or units of an item) sold before the price change and again after the price change and compare it to the change in sales volume (memberships, tickets sold and so on).

Inelastic demand

If there is a large change in price, but a small change in demand, the demand is considered 'relatively inelastic'. As a generalisation, the demand for everyday necessities (e.g., petrol, milk, bread) tends to be inelastic (e.g., if petrol increases by 10 pence per litre the total volume sold will not change much). On the other hand, products purchased with discretionary income (e.g., luxury cars, furniture) are much more price sensitive (elastic). In a market condition such as the former, a 'skim pricing' strategy can be used in the belief that by pricing high in the expected range, greater TR will be generated.

For example, an AFL team prices a single match ticket at $10 for the season, and as a result, attracts a total of 320,000 fans to their matches (TR from ticket sales = $3.2m). However, the next year, they increase the price to $12 per match and saw total attendance drop by just 20,000 to 300,000 (TR from ticket sales = $3.6m). This would represent an increase in TR of $400,000, indicating that the new ticket price was relatively inelastic (i.e., fans were generally not sensitive to the price increase; see Case 15.3).

CASE 15.3   Price wars

In the Australian sport market, the National Rugby League (NRL) and ARU both compete within the city of Sydney's market of just over 4 million potential fans. Both codes use the 83,000-seat capacity Olympic Stadium (Telstra Stadium) to showcase their respective codes of rugby to fans. However, each has a very different pricing structure reflecting their respective fan base and their income levels. The ARL has a policy of ensuring that its tickets are priced so that its core fan base of lower- and middle-income families can afford to see the spectacle that is the national grand final.

Tickets for the 2004 event ranged from $35 to $125 plus a family ticket for $85 that includes transport to the venue by bus or train. For the ARU, the annual Bledisloe Cup match provides them with a significant source of income, with the code's more affluent fans prepared to pay higher ticket prices ranging from $64 to $149 to watch their national team play traditional rivals the All Blacks. In each case, the respective organisations have carefully considered their fans and what they determine they are prepared to pay to attend these hallmark events.

Questions

1. Which broad pricing approach is being used by each code to entice fans to its games?

2. Can you suggest alternative pricing approaches that can be used by the NRL and the ARU to market each code to new markets not currently attending matches?

In deference to general marketing in which loyal customers have found their relationship with a particular brand being strained as they receive little or no financial incentive to continue to purchase (Dann and Dann, 2004), sport marketers have generally paid great attention to this aspect of pricing (see, for example, Mullin et al., 2000). In an attempt to increase the link between the fan and the team, many professional sport teams have introduced loyalty programmes in an effort to re-establish a stronger relationship with their fan base. Rewarding customers who frequently purchase a product is not new and has been used to emphasise the benefits of a long-term purchase relationship that also shifts the emphasis away from price per transaction (Morrall, 1995). It has been suggested that an investment in loyalty programmes may lead to an increase in fan identification, attendance and merchandising sales (Pritchard and Negro, 2001). Sport franchises often use team merchandise to 'thank' fans for their loyalty (once they meet designated 'milestones' in attendance). Ultimately, the goal should be to develop truly loyal fans whose relationship with the team has become a significant part of their lives (Mahony, Madrigal and Howard, 2000, p. 22).

However, organisations can be lured into selling the sport consumer more than they really want (so-called upselling). In contrast, Spoelstra (1997) urged sport marketers to 'only try to sell a product that the customer wants to buy' (p. 109). A possible outcome of upselling a season ticket is that, upon reflection, the spectator becomes unhappy with the purchase and decides never to return to the seller again. As a result, the consumer will probably tell as many friends and family as they can about the 'unhappy' experience simply as a means of 'getting back' at the club.

CASE 15.4   The season ticket, single ticket conundrum

Many professional sport franchises appear to be guilty of upselling, primarily because they typically only sell the 'Full Monty!' (i.e., a full season ticket, either to the ground/terraces or main stand). Historically, clubs have a product range that is essentially limited to two categories of ticket: single game entry or full season ticket. Clearly, all clubs need season ticket holders – the more, the better. Season ticket holders are the lifeblood of any professional team because they pay up front, allowing budgets to be set in advance with a certain degree of income secured and in the bank while also guaranteeing (within reason) a minimum crowd attendance for each game.

The potential downside of selling season tickets is that some ticket holders may become disillusioned with their purchase over time. For example, they may not be able to attend all the games they have paid for. The advent of summer rugby in the English Super League competition means that some fans may plan their summer holiday during July and August and be away. As a result, they cannot attend some games, yet they have paid for them. Others might feel that the team's performance was such that they did not get the 'value' for money experience they had hoped for when initially purchasing the ticket in the hype of the preseason period. Given such scenarios, it is possible that once the season ticket holder reviews the purchase and is making a decision about renewing the ticket, these factors may lead the person to draw the conclusion that a season ticket is not worth the investment. As a result, the season ticket holder may not renew and may potentially become a defector, choosing to spend this disposable income in some other want-satisfying way.

Every year, there are numerous 'potential' season ticket holders out there for a professional sport franchise that:

1. Cannot afford the cost of a full season ticket purchase
2. Cannot afford the cost of renewal because their financial circumstances have changed
3. Cannot afford the personal time commitment associated with a full season ticket and therefore do not get the full purchase benefit
4. Only want to attend selected games
5. Have held a season ticket previously but have become 'defectors' because they were unhappy with the team's performance in the past
6. Combination of all of the above

Single game ticket purchasers are also important, in fact, very important. Given that few professional sport franchises, if any, enjoy 100% support from season ticket holders, single event attendees represent a significant source of match day revenue and cash flow. This segment of the market also potentially represents the season ticket holders of the future. The challenge is to get them to consume more and become regular repeat purchasers. However, they may not, for a range of reasons identified previously, want to purchase a full season ticket but would still like a product that would give them the benefits and privileges of such a package while also guaranteeing them entry to a range of games.

A possible solution is to develop a broader range of ticket products and a range of pricing options.

Strategy

Introduce a product that is pitched at those who in reality do not want to be forced into an upsell situation (i.e., do not want to purchase a full season ticket). In other words, provide a range of ticket products that will allow consumers to select one that is appropriate to their needs.

Philosophy

Do not try and upsell, and be prepared to downsell. In other words, do not try and sell fans something they do not want. Doing so might more effectively satisfy consumer needs and wants – the essence of good organisational marketing and the formula for long-term survival.

Potential benefit

In terms of current (and for that matter, past) season ticket holders, the professional sport franchise does not want to lose those who decide they no longer want the 'Full Monty'. The goal is to limit attrition.

As for current casual match attendees, the professional sport franchise wants to increase their commitment by progressively shifting them further towards full season ticket membership.

The products

A range of ticket packages that meet the individual's needs and wants. Find out what the fans want and what they can reasonably afford and provide it! Do some research.

Examples

- The 'pick-2' package combines an 'attractive' team with a less 'attractive' team together in the one package. Select a range of pick-2 products, grouping games according to expected attendance rates. The key here is to make the price structure attractive by offering a good discount off the face value of purchasing two separate tickets for the same games (e.g., 20% to 30%). The benefit is that the consumer starts to develop a commitment to the team, possibly leading him or her to sample more games. There is also the added benefit of gaining additional revenue for a game that may not normally be very attractive to fans and even if they do not turn up after purchasing the package, the club still gets revenue.
- 'Pick-4 or pick-6' – using the same approach as above package together tickets for 4 and 6 selected games. Again, there needs to be a significant benefit to the fan, which could be in the form of a saving on the normal price of entry along with some form of added-value benefit (e.g., discount on team merchandise).
- The 'mini-season ticket' package puts together a mini-season ticket of, for example, eight games. Again, a number of different package options may be available. English Super League team the Leeds Rhinos introduced an 'extra value 8' mini-season ticket package after being introduced to this concept in 1997, which simply

packaged the final eight home games of the season together. Similarly, the English Premiership soccer team Manchester City FC introduced a 'city super seven' ticket, packaging together the last seven home games of the 2004–2005 season. However, our view is that such mini-season packages need to be more flexible and imaginative and offer a wider range of options such as those outlined above and across the entire season.

Conclusions

Price is an important element of the marketing mix, yet it is often poorly understood within the sport and fitness industries. However, the reader should now appreciate and recognise the role of pricing within the traditional marketing mix of sport and fitness organisations. In particular, this chapter has provided a range of simple strategies that can be used to develop a pricing strategy that meets your organisation's objectives and fits within the overall marketing mix. To achieve this, sport marketers must make decisions about whether to use price as a tool for differentiating their product or as a means of maximising profit, increasing participation and the like. Issues such as the nature of the competition, overall market demand and general economic climate might all play a part in this process and need to be considered carefully. To this end, some form of research is necessary to examine a range of internal and external factors relevant to the organisation and its market. However, remember that price strategies alone do not guarantee a 'sale', and as a result, it is intimately related to others aspects of the marketing mix, which will ultimately work together in providing customers with a quality and value-added experience that will see them become long-lasting, loyal customers.

Discussion questions

1. Examine the various sporting websites referred to below and compare the prices charged for single event tickets, season tickets (full and mini type) and merchandise. What are the differences and similarities between the prices charged? Discuss why any differences exist in the context of the information provided in this chapter.
2. Describe three methods of setting prices in the sporting industry. Compare and contrast each in terms of appropriateness for a health and fitness centre.

Guided reading

Many generic marketing books provide interesting and informative information regarding pricing and attendant strategies. Examples are provided in the bibliography. Sport marketing journals provide limited readings on this aspect of sport marketing. The best include *Sport Marketing Quarterly* and *Sport Business International*.

Keywords

Fixed costs; penetration pricing; purchase cost; reference price; skim pricing; variable costs.

Bibliography

Aaker, D.A. (1991) *Managing Brand Equity*, New York: The Free Press.

Baldinger, A.L. and Rubinson, J. (1996) Brand loyalty: The link between attitude and behavior, *Journal of Advertising Research* 36(6):22–34.

Dann, S. and Dann, S. (2004) *Introduction to Marketing*, Australia: John Wiley and Sons.

Dodson, J.A., Tybout, A.M. and Sternthal, B. (1978) Impact of deals and deal retraction on brand switching, *Journal of Marketing Research* 15(1):72–81.

Gladden, M.J. and Funk, D.C. (2001) Understanding brand loyalty in professional sport: Examining the link between brand associations and brand loyalty, *International Journal of Sports Marketing and Sponsorship* March/April:67–94.

Kotler, P. and Armstrong, G. (2004) *Principles of Marketing*, 10th edn, NJ: Pearson Prentice Hall.

Mahony, D., Madrigal, R. and Howard, D. (2000) Using the psychological commitment to team (PCT) scale to segment sport consumers based on loyalty, *Sport Marketing Quarterly* 9(1):15–25.

Morrall, L. (1995) Golden handcuffs: Loyalty programs that retain customers, *Bank Marketing* 27(8):52–8.

Mullin, B.J., Hardy, S. and Sutton, W.A. (2000) *Sport Marketing*, 2nd edn, Champaign, IL: Human Kinetics.

Pitts, B.G. and Stotlar, D.K. (1996) *Fundamentals of Sport Marketing*, Morgantown: Fitness Information Technology, Inc.

Pride, W.M. and Ferrell, O.C. (1991) *Marketing Concepts and Strategies*, Boston: Houghton Mifflin Company.

Pritchard, M.P. and Negro, C.M. (2001) Sport loyalty programs and their impact on fan relationships, *International Journal of Sports Marketing and Sponsorship* 3(3):317–38.

Raymond, J. (2001) Home field advantage: Sports teams turn to loyalty programs to pitch new services to fans, *American Demographics* 23(4):34–6.

Shilbury, D., Quick, S. and Westerbeek, H. (2003) *Strategic Sport Marketing*, 2nd edn, St. Leonards: Allen & Unwin.

Starr, M.K. and Rubinson, J.R. (1978) A loyalty group segmentation model of brand purchasing simulation, *Journal of Marketing Research* 15(3):378–83.

Stanton, W.J., Miller, K.E. and Layton, R.A. (1994) *Fundamentals of Marketing*, 2nd edn, Sydney: McGraw-Hill.

Stotlar, D.K. (1993) *Successful Sport Marketing*, Melbourne: WCB Brown & Benchmark.

Summers, E.D. (2003) In J.R. McColl-Kennedy (ed.), *Services Marketing: A Managerial Approach*, Australia: John Wiley and Sons.

Spoelstra, J. (1997) *Ice to the Eskimos: How to Market a Product Nobody Wants*, New York: Harper Collins.

Yoo, B., Donthu, N. and Lee, S. (2000) An examination of selected marketing mix elements and brand equity, *Journal of the Academy of Marketing Science* 28(2):195–211.

Recommended websites

The Australian Football League
http://afl.com.au

The Australian Rugby Union
http://www.aru.com.au

Bath Rugby Union Football Club, England
http://www.bathrugby.com

Gloucester Rugby Union Football Club, England
http://www.gloucesterrugbyclub.com

Newcastle Knights Rugby League Football Club, Australia
http://www.newcastleknights.com.au

Leeds Rhinos, England
http://www.leedsrugby.com

Manchester City Football Club, England
http://www.mcfc.co.uk/index.asp

The National Rugby League, Australia
http://www.nrl.com.au

Wigan Rugby League Football Club, England
http://www.wiganwarriors.com

Trade Practices Act (Australia)
http://www.accc.gov.au/content/index.phtml/itemId/142

Twickenham Stadium, England
http://www.rfu.com/microsites/twickenham/index.cfm

Guinness Premiership, England
http://www.guinnesspremiership.co.uk/84–87.php

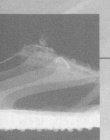

Chapter 16

Distribution channels and sports logistics

Leigh Sparks
University of Stirling

Learning outcomes

Upon completion of this chapter, the reader should be able to:

- Identify the most appropriate distribution channel choices for sport products.

- Define the components of the logistics mix and outline the management task in supply chain management.

- Make recommendations for the better management of sport product distribution.

- Understand the need to ensure appropriate channel behaviour and performance throughout the channel from production to consumption.

- Consider the logistics needs of major sporting events.

Overview of chapter

Products require distribution if they are to be used by consumers. Distribution channels have to be created and managed to satisfy consumer demands and marketing needs. Therefore, this chapter introduces two areas: distribution channels and the management and organisation of these channels. It achieves this by first examining some of the channel possibilities in sport marketing. Secondly, it considers channel management and in particular, draws on the logistics mix and ideas in supply chain management. It emphasises the critical importance of logistics and channel management in cost and service terms and at a time when channels of distribution are changing rapidly. These two sections are followed by an examination of some of the important issues in the area of channel management. In particular, controversial issues of product sourcing, including 'sweatshops' and price-fixing of replica shirts, are discussed. Issues around licensing, rights and exclusivity in distribution channels and particularly with regard to new media are raised. Finally, some concluding remarks and indications of the directions for future change are made.

Introduction

The marketing of sport products and services inevitably involves the distribution of these products and services and thus the development and maintenance of distribution channels. A distribution channel is the route along which a product (and its title or ownership) travels from production to consumption. In the past, distribution channels consisted mainly of sequential independent intermediaries used to push products towards the final consumer. As sports goods and services have become more fashion oriented and thus more subject to the fickleness of demand and as the nature of supply has changed, so consumer-focused rather than production-focused channels have emerged. The numbers and functions of intermediaries have reduced, and they are often now partners in a range of supply chain activities, rather than simply functional actors. Therefore, channels are no longer separated functionally; rather, they are integrated under concepts such as logistics and channel management. Channels are more focused on reacting quickly to known demand from customers, rather than simply supplying products that might perhaps be bought.

This new orientation is supplemented by an increasing breadth of sport products and services. Traditional sports such as football are now accompanied by extreme sports such as wakeboarding. Products such as tennis racquets have become more sophisticated. The market has expanded into leisurewear clothing in addition to traditional functional sports equipment. Women and children have been 'discovered' by the previously mainly male-oriented manufacturers and retailers. Information such as images and results have become sport products. Sports events and their consumers have become more complex and demanding (e.g., the scale of the Olympics). The sourcing of products and the matching of supply and demand now occur on a global scale and in a shortened time scale, rather than on a local scale and a relaxed schedule. There are now more opportunities to get distribution rights. There are also many more opportunities to get it wrong. Managing sports logistics appropriately is thus of considerable importance, and this importance is increasing.

Distribution channels

Distribution is about making products and services available. This availability occurs generally in two parts. First, products are made available for purchase. Secondly, they are made physically available for use or consumption. Making products available to a consumer can occur with the simultaneous transfer of sale and ownership and thus use. For example, a fan buying a replica shirt at a club store buys, owns and takes physical possession of the shirt immediately. Alternatively, however, the sale and consumption of a product can occur at different times. Purchasing tickets months before an event (e.g., for a Cup Final or international match) is one example. Tickets are bought at one place and time and consumed at a different place and time. Ordering a customised set of trainers on the internet and then waiting for delivery is another example of this separation. All of these examples have in common the need for flows of product and information to enable such transactions to occur. Customers need to know about the products available and to be able to physically 'use' or 'consume' them. These flows are organised in distribution channels (i.e., organisations and individuals involved in assembling and moving sport products from points of production to points of consumption). This assembly and movement includes information and product elements as well as other dimensions of risk, finance and so on.

Distribution channels take many forms in carrying out these, on the surface, comparatively simple activities. There are, however, many choices to be made and many potential channels to consider. A range of organisations and approaches may coexist and serve to meet demand and supply issues that arise. Some of these involve simultaneous availability and usage, but others take advantage of possible separability. Intermediaries (e.g., wholesalers, brokers) exist in these channels to provide aspects of finance, risk and physical movement management and control (e.g., inventory, storage, break of bulk deliveries).

Figure 16.1 represents a simplified diagram of possible interlinkages (product and information flows) in the distribution channel for branded sport products such as shirts and boots. Typically, such products are supplied to the consumer by a retailer. The retailer obtains the stock from the brand manufacturers or their representatives (e.g., importers). In some cases, the brand manufacturer may run the retail shop itself (e.g., Nike Town), but in others, the manufacturer supplies the product to the stores of various retailers (e.g., JJB Sports, Decathlon). The brand manufacturer may arrange

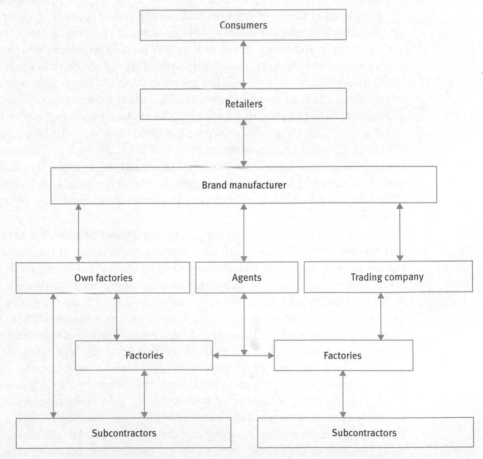

Figure 16.1 **Simplified distribution channel for branded sport products**

production in its own factories or in factories owned or organised by agents and trading companies with which the brand manufacturer has a contract. Depending on demand, some production may be placed with a hierarchy of subcontracted producers.

The channel in Figure 16.1 is not static. Change has occurred at the retail and brand manufacturer end of the channel as consolidation and concentration have occurred (e.g., the retailing and manufacturing sectors are now dominated by a smaller number of much larger businesses). At the manufacturing end of the channel, the locations for manufacturing have altered substantially through globalisation and the search for low-cost places of production. In some cases, this has led to abuse, often in the form of 'sweatshops'. The entire channel comes under stress as a consequence (we return to this issue later). Additionally, of course, the demand pattern from consumers has altered and is now more volatile and fashion oriented than before. This requires the channel as a whole to focus on issues of rapid response, information flows and cost reductions. The time taken from production to consumption will have reduced. Intermediaries such as wholesalers may have been removed from the channel to aid response and increase reward. Data capture and information dissemination (e.g., from a shop unit to a production facility) may thus replace previous physical product movements (i.e., the channel becomes one of rapid response using concepts such as 'just-in-time' logistics).

Figure 16.1 represents a single distribution channel. Distribution channels can also be considered in terms of breadth and alternatives. Figure 16.2 portrays a simplified set of channels for the supply of tickets for a major sporting event. A variety of choices are apparent in the figure. Some tickets will be sold to people who have rights to the seats (e.g., season tickets, corporate hospitality boxes or debenture holders). They have, in essence, pre-purchased the ownership rights. Some tickets might be supplied to consumers directly by their buying online, via the telephone or direct at club shops. A proportion of tickets will be allocated to exclusive agencies either for specific purposes (e.g., official hospitality company events) or to ease the handling burden on the host organisation (e.g., by using an official ticket seller such as Ticketmaster or a ticket broker). Some tickets will be allocated to participating clubs for them to distribute, and these could be added to allocations to players, officials and administrators. The channels are thus both real and virtual and 'sell' information, rights and products (the ticket).

These allocation mechanisms supply the initial distribution of tickets. For many consumers, obtaining the ticket will turn them into spectators at the event. For some who obtain tickets, however, a secondary market ensues as tickets are bought and sold. Some of this is informal (e.g., amongst friends). Some of this activity, however, is highly structured via 'ticket touts', who may obtain their tickets from a variety of sources. For major events, the presence of such 'ticket touts' is a visible indication of real-time dynamic matching of final supply and demand. Ticket touts attempt to make money from this separation of ticket availability and usage by leveraging demand. There is some evidence that the development of eBay may be affecting the viability of some ticket touting (in essence, individuals can sell more directly). Some tickets may go through many pairs of hands and be bought and sold at varying prices and by varying methods (phone, internet, face to face) before they are finally used by the spectator. Understanding the nature of supply and demand is critical in the allocation mechanism, with the host organisations seeking to maximise their revenue, satisfy various consumer demands and in most cases, avoid price gouging and profiteering by internal

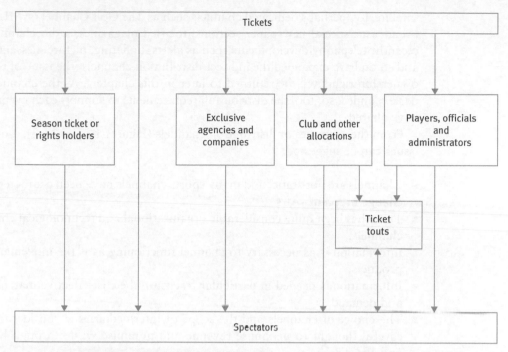

Figure 16.2 **Simplified distribution channels for tickets for major sporting events**

and external groups (e.g., players and touts). Product identification (e.g., tickets) with purchasers' names printed on them and product security (e.g., anti-forging measures) have become key considerations in the production and distribution of tickets. Information about ticket dissemination and use has thus become a vital component of such channels.

In the two cases above, distribution has been of physical products, albeit with different characteristics. In Figure 16.1 the channel combines consumer purchase with ownership and possession (use). In Figure 16.2, there are differing combinations or separations of purchase, possession and usage. Clothes (Figure 16.1) and tickets (Figure 16.2) are ultimately both physical products albeit that the physical ticket gives you a seat to watch a game (a service). Distribution in sport also occurs with non-physical products.

Figure 16.3 considers distribution channels for a sports event. A distinction is drawn in the figure between direct channels (involving spectators) and indirect channels (involving consumers). In the direct channel, the event is consumed by the spectators attending the event and seeing the game live. At the event, the spectator may both watch the game and various advertisements and entertainment and buy or use products and services such as programmes, food and drink vendors, toilets and so on. The indirect channel involves peoples viewing the game or event but not actually being there. This consumption could be 'live' in the sense of occurring at the same time as the 'real' event, or it could be 'delayed' as in watched or read about some time later.

Consumption and viewing patterns of drink, programmes (information) and advertisements differ. Distribution channels have to accommodate these various potential demands. In recent years, there has been tremendous effort placed on extending the indirect channels so as to enhance the 'reach' of the sports event. Developments such as satellite TV (perhaps dedicated channels such as The Golf Channel or MUTV), internet broadcasts, special newspaper sections, focused magazines, radio channels and more recently, telephony developments such as alerts, updating, picture messaging, club calls and so on have expanded the indirect distribution channels (the issue of telephony and ownership rights will be returned to later in this chapter). As the channel availability has expanded, so, too, the distribution requirements to support each event and channel have altered.

From the examples of distribution channels (Figures 16.1 to 16.3), a number of key issues can be suggested:

- Channels are not static, and many sports channels have been characterised by rapid change in recent years.
- There has been quite considerable organisational and technological change in many channels.
- Information is as necessary to channel functioning as is the movement of physical products.
- Information is needed in particular to ensure the cost-effective matching of supply and demand.
- The choice of channels and the scope of intermediaries is considerable and needs careful thought to maximise revenue and minimise waste through being efficient and effective.
- The scale (breadth and depth) of some channels is enormous.

Picking up on the last point, there are many dimensions of scale that could be considered. Scale is obvious in some of the major brand manufacturers (e.g., Nike, Adidas, Reebok) and in some of the product owners and event managers (including ticket distribution, e.g., Clear Channel, Ticketmaster). Within the United Kingdom, JJB Sports is a major retail business, and internationally, Decathlon or Foot Locker occupy similar positions. This scale and the proliferation of products and services to be marketed in the sports field makes a full classification of all channel possibilities difficult to achieve. This is seen in the simplified channel examples shown in Figures 16.1 to 16.3. From these examples, we can highlight and select four channel components as being amongst the most important and the most interesting (because of the changes that have occurred or are underway).

Retail outlets

The nature of the sport product is such that 'sports shops' have been a dominant force in distribution channels. Making products available to consumers is achieved by placing the products near to the market in purpose-built facilities (i.e., physical shops). These shops may be highly specialised (e.g., Tiso's Outdoor Experience), general sports retailers (e.g., JJB Sports) or could be general retailers selling some sport products (e.g., Asda, Wal-Mart). As with many channels, there is a choice to be made amongst exclusive (club shops), selective (official reseller deals) or intensive (all retailers) distribution opportunities. Such is the importance of this channel that it is the focus of Chapter 17.

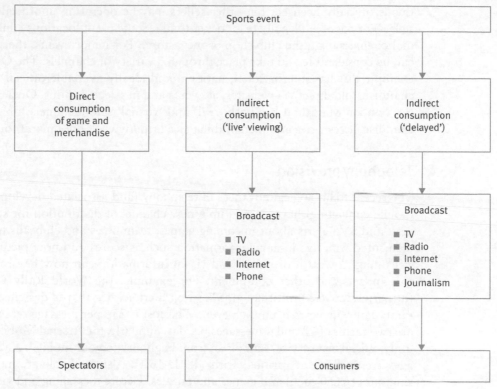

Figure 16.3 **Simplified distribution channels for sports events**

▨ Direct selling

For manufacturers, the use of retail outlets involves handing products over to another business and losing some of the value and profit on that product. Direct selling by manufacturers to consumers avoids this but at the price of raising operating costs for themselves. By selling direct, more control is maintained and more profit should be retained if consumers can gain access to the product. Direct mail order has been one distribution method (e.g., Cotton Traders), but recently, the internet has increased the potential for manufacturers to build direct relationships and services with consumers (e.g., standard products at http://www.reebokstore.co.uk or customised products such as mi-adidas or nikeid). Physical supply is still required, however.

▨ Event-based sales

Sport products are also often associated with particular sporting events. Items such as programmes and tickets are examples of event-specific products. These have particular issues around the demand patterns and obsolescence. Tickets have little value after the event has taken place. The event location may also contain event-specific items such as food and drink, 'ref link' systems and event-specific merchandise. Some of this is officially licensed, but other sellers may be operating unofficially (e.g., street sellers) or possibly illegally (e.g., ticket touts). Some event locations contain other formal channels (e.g., the club shop or megastore). For major events, the scale of selling can be considerable and take place through a variety of channels. The Olympics is one example that has international, national and locally available official branded merchandise, sold direct via websites, at events and in selected shops. On a different scale, the London Marathon has both 'real' and 'virtual' sales channels for technical merchandise, accessories and memorabilia (see http://www.londonmarathonstore.com).

Telephony provision

The recent technological advances in telephony (and associated developments such as mobile computing) have opened up a new channel of distribution for sport products. Text and SMS alerts about upcoming games, team news and clubcalls have been supplemented with live in-game information such as scores and now pictures and direct streaming. A wealth of verbal and visual information can now be provided directly to handsets and other equipment. For example, the World Rally Championship (http://www.wrc.com) offers an SMS text alert service that is designed to keep fans up to date with news from each event. The cost is 25p per message received, and there are two tariffs of 12 and 4 messages per day. Similarly, the Arsenal Mobile service is the 'only official text service, sent direct from Highbury to your mobile'. A variety of packages are available at various tariffs (Table 16.1). Also available are mobile auctions, ringtones (£2.50 each) and games and puzzles. Picture messaging and video clip distribution to handsets has emerged strongly recently, developing this channel further.

Table 16.1 **Arsenal mobile telephony services**

Service	Cost (per season)	Advertising example
News Extra	£19.99	Direct from Highbury, News Extra brings you the latest headlines from the press office, and general sale ticket news from the box office.
Matchday Away	£29.99	For the fan who attends home games, Matchday Away gives you goals & reports from away fixtures, plus line-ups, round-up and Wenger's thoughts.
Matchday	£29.99	Arsenal Matchday Text brings you the matchday essentials. Receive the team line-up, goal alerts plus half-time and full-time reports.
Matchday Extra	£39.99	Matchday Extra brings you the line-up, goal alerts, half and full-time reports, a post match round-up and comments from manager Arsene Wenger.
Arsenal Unlimited	£54.99	Want it all? Arsenal Unlimited brings you the team line-up, goals, news, ticket info, half and full-time reports, post match round-up and the Manager's thoughts!

Source: Retrieved 1 December 2004, from http://www.arsenal.com

The logistics mix and channel management

The discussion of selected channels of distribution provides some description of the way products are made available. This is often stated 'as getting the right products to the right place at the right time'. In all the examples earlier, there is a process of product production that requires (to a greater or lesser extent) some product distribution. In the case of physical products such as shirts or programmes, products have to be physically moved, so issues of stock, handling and transport come to the fore. In the case of telephony, information (capture, storing, sending and where to send it) is at the heart of the distribution channel. In terms of sports events, there may be particular requirements for equipment movement for participants, broadcast media, caterers, sponsors and so on.

In logistics and distribution terms, this last point is exemplified by thinking about the organisation needed to put on major events such as Formula 1 or the Olympics. The Olympics is clearly a major international sporting event, but it is not simply a case of various athletes turning up to compete. Case 16.1 considers some of the logistics aspects, as described by one of the major companies involved in the processes.

CASE 16.1 Schenker logistics: an Olympic discipline

Schenker is a subsidiary of Deutsche Bahn AG. Schenker was founded in Vienna in 1872, and its current head office is in Essen, Germany, supported by a worldwide network of local offices and facilities. It is a large (€6.9bn turnover) integrated logistics service provider, with well over a century of experience in handling global events ranging from exhibitions to major sports events such as the Olympics. Beginning with the 1972 Munich Olympics, Schenker has developed considerable expertise in managing the logistics for the largest global sports event. As a consequence Schenker is the official supplier to the International Olympic Committee for freight forwarding and customs clearance services for the Olympic Games. Its next major events are Torino 2006 and Beijing 2008, for which planning is already well advanced. In addition, national offices of Schenker may also be official partners of National Olympic Committees.

As the official provider of customs and freight forwarding services for the 2002 Salt Lake City Winter Olympics and Paralympics, Schenker handled the customs clearance and all related transportation services and catered to the logistics needs of 80 National Olympic Committees, 9000 media representatives and other participating associates and companies. Schenker transported 13,000 tons of freight just in time to Salt Lake City, ranging from sensitive sports and media equipment to clothing and specialist food (and including putting seals on 50,000 beer bottles for the Mormon State of Utah). Some 60 hours after the Games ended, most of the equipment was on its way back to more than 160 countries.

The Olympic Games require extraordinary logistics demands to be met. Massive investment in facilities and personnel are required. For Athens 2004, a specialist

12,000m^2 storage and distribution hub was required by Schenker with additional rental space as required. It is not just handling and movement, however. Information about products and customs clearance paperwork (carnets or electronic) are vital to allow on-time availability. Re-exporting requires similar paperwork. Additionally, there are both broad and specific security issues arising from general global threats to competitive concerns over equipment tampering. Security concerns thus require abilities to store and protect equipment and to verify delivery and quality.

For Athens 2004, there were 1000 road and rail deliveries, 800 sea containers and 1500 tonnes of air freight delivered to Athens and other venues by Schenker, most of which returned home after the Games. Some 70 container loads of sports boats, from sailing boats to canoes, also arrived. Schenker transported 255 horses to the Olympiad and another 78 horses for the Paralympics. More than 20,000 media representatives needed over 11,000 PCs, 600 servers and 2000 printers to be supplied, managed and re-exported. On the one hand, complete broadcast trucks for media partners had to be shipped whilst perhaps at the other extreme Special Infield Dirt with a special red colour (which could not be manufactured in Greece) was required from the United States for the baseball mound and warning track. Athletes' special equipment, clothing and specialist food are other detailed logistics requirements. In addition, for Athens 2004, Schenker gained contracts to:

- Supply the Games with beer.
- Provide furniture and mattresses for the Olympic and media villages.
- Organise the 'bed linen' washing, cleaning and resupply.
- Provide the infrastructure for ATMs at 15 venues.
- Supply all camera and digital printing equipment for Kodak in the press centre.
- Supply medical equipment for the Olympic Village Hospital.

The Olympics is an exceptional event and may be the ultimate sporting logistics challenge, but such logistics concerns are present at all major sporting events. There is a requirement for reliable logistics infrastructure, efficient information and communications technology, highly qualified human resources and specialist know-how to ensure the smooth functioning of such major sporting events.

Source: Adapted from http://www.schenker.com

Question

1. For a sporting event of which you have knowledge, list the elements that need to supplied logistically to ensure its occurrence.

Case 16.1 illustrates some of the complexity of handling an event such as the Olympics. The sheer scale of activities that have to be brought together is almost overwhelming. But even at smaller sports events, the conjunction of athletes and spectators (including media), with their disparate demands, require a variety of distribution channels and companies and organisations to work closely together to ensure that demands are met as closely as possible. Whether this is equipment, programmes or food, several channels have to converge to enable the activities to occur. Given the complications involved, it is hardly surprising that specialist logistics service providers such as Schenker have been engaged increasingly to manage, coordinate and undertake various distribution activities.

The very simplicity of the statement 'getting the right products to the right place at the right time' does not do justice to the effort that is needed to ensure things occur when and where they should, as Case 16.1 shows. Managing distribution channels is a complex activity that involves both anticipating and reacting to both known and volatile consumers and other demands.

Some other typical logistical challenges include:

- The production and provision of programmes for a major international sporting event requires that information is up to date and demand is accurately assessed. Programmes have little informational value after the game. Although some material can be printed and prepared in advance, team news may need to be inserted quite late, yet the programmes have to be available on the day in a narrow time frame.
- The launch of a new kit has high publicity value for a club. In many cases, this provokes a surge in demand that requires shops and websites to both be in stock and to respond quickly. The signing of a new 'galactico' or superstar changes demand patterns quickly, so retailers need to react. Overstocking, however, has its dangers, as Everton found out when it sold Wayne Rooney to Manchester United and were left with obsolete stock of personalised shirts (which they donated to the CAFOD charity for use in Liberia; see http://news.bbc.co.uk/1/hi/uk/3626874.stm).
- Text updates to mobile telephones have to be almost instantaneous in order to have value. Thus, there is pressure on the length of the message; the speed of response to, for example, a goal; and also on the accuracy of contacting the subscriber base. Tolerance of failure of these elements will be extremely limited.
- Major sporting series (e.g., Formula 1) have their own 'travelling circus' to ensure that the teams and their equipment get to the next event. This may occur by road or by air for different races. Additionally, broadcasting equipment, press accreditation, food and drink for corporate hospitality and a host of other elements have to be put in place for the 'right' time. The careful choreography of such events demands accurate logistics.

These examples demonstrate that the concern in channels is with both product and information flows. To make products or events available, the logistics of product movement and demand management have to be managed. This essentially requires the management of the 'logistics mix' (Table 16.2).

Inventory

Inventory (*aka* Stock) is often a necessary but unloved part of the channel activities. Stock generally represents capital that is tied up in unsold product. As such, businesses often try to minimise stockholding. However, stock is needed in order to meet demand

Table 16.2 **The logistics mix**

Item	Description
Inventory	Inventory is unsold physical product, also often referred to as stock. The amount, type and location of inventory are fundamental to the functioning of channels but involve considerable risks of management and obsolescence.
Storage facilities	Stock must be stored somewhere ahead of demand. These facilities might be warehouses or distribution centres and vary in location and scale as well as function.
Transportation	Most products have to be physically transported at some stage. This may involve air, sea, land or other transport modes and various components of each mode.
Unitisation and packaging	Products need packaging for sale and transit. Handling requirements can require particular sizes or combination of package sizes to ease distribution flow.
Communications	Information is vital to the functioning of distribution channels. The information itself also needs to be available, so communications networks are critical.

and to bridge the gap between production and sale, both in terms of distance and time. Businesses that are out of stock run the risk of consumers' selecting alternatives (e.g., different brands, retailers, channels). How much inventory to hold (and where) is thus a vital part of managing channel activities, as is managing the ownership of the stock and thus the risk profile for various intermediaries. A key component of stock management is thus the principle of postponement, whereby products are held in a neutral rather than a finished state until demand is certain (e.g., holding football shirts without names and producing customised shirts to order). Inventory can, however, also be beneficial and valuable, as, for example, when there is a scarcity of product or undersupply, whether generally or in specific situations.

Storage facilities

Stock requires being stored somewhere. The management of such facilities or locations is important in meeting both anticipated and unanticipated demand. These facilities may be traditional warehouses where product is stored and put away for later recall, or they may be distribution centres where the aim is not necessarily to store goods but is instead to immediately sort out incoming products (e.g., from suppliers) for allocation to outgoing destinations (e.g., retailers). Retailers and others may themselves have onsite storage areas at their own facilities (e.g., in the back room of a shop or at a stadium) in order to meet demand fluctuations.

Transportation

Most physical products require transportation at some time. Even telephonic products require a network over which to transport messages and images. Physical products often need to be transported over considerable distances, perhaps very rapidly. As such, organisations need to consider the appropriate mode of transport (e.g., air, road, sea, train). Issues such as the scheduling of transportation and the availability of the right vehicle (cubic capacity and weight availability) and driver are important because there may be restrictions on all elements (e.g., different countries have different legal restrictions on the weight and length of lorries and the hours for which drivers can drive). Scheduling is thus a major activity.

Unitisation and packaging

Most products require some form of packaging. This packaging may be part of the selling activity or might be needed for protection and handling during transportation. Generally, packaging also carries information that can be of use to the consumer (product content, instructions) or to others (e.g., bar codes for retailers or transportation). Products tend to be purchased by consumers in small quantities. Separate handling of these small quantities from production to consumption would be inordinately wasteful. Convenient combinations of products are thus assembled into regular sizes (unitisation) in order to aid handling (even automation) and transportation. Standardisation on generally agreed sizes helps channel efficiency. For example, a pair of running shoes comes in a box. This regularly shaped box assists handling, and set numbers of boxes make up cartons, pallet loads and even container loads for transportation. Regular, consistent, known shapes, sizes and weights allow for better planning and handling and reduce logistics costs.

Communications

Distribution channels are a method of joining production to consumption and thus overcoming space and time barriers. To work effectively, however, channels require to be informed. As such, the logistics mix is as much about data and information collection, dissemination and use as it is about product storage and movement. Data are needed to ensure that appropriate actions are taken and that linkages are made. For example, communication networks are needed to use the data captured on consumer demand in retail stores to reorder product from storage or to ensure further production to meet the demand. Without good information flows, the logistics mix will function more inaccurately and expensively and thus inefficiently.

Managing this logistics mix represents the core components of the logistics task (Figure 16.4), which has been defined as:

> The process of strategically managing the procurement, movement and storage of materials, parts and finished inventory (and the related information flows) through the organisation and its marketing channels in such a way that current and future profitability are maximised through the cost effective fulfilment of orders (Christopher, 1998, p. 4).

This definition points to the management of the core logistics tasks but also raises a number of other issues, also seen in Figure 16.4:

■ The emphasis on strategic management indicates the need to consider the choice of channels and the management of the logistics mix tasks very carefully.

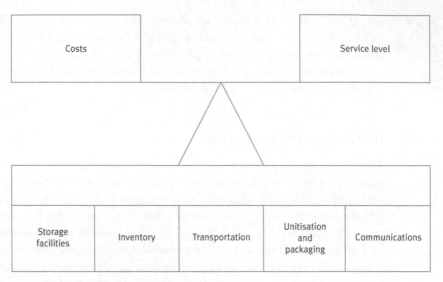

Figure 16.4 **The management task in logistics**

- The focus on cost effectiveness suggests that there is a balance to be struck between service and cost if the activity is to add value. Thus, although immediate delivery can always be promised, the cost of so doing may be too high. Having product available everywhere just in case someone wants it is ruinously expensive and inefficient. However, in some sports event logistics, the costs of not providing the right equipment (e.g., the beach volleyball court at the Olympics, the sponsors boards for the Champions League, or the timing equipment for a swimming meet) are too horrendous to imagine, so overprovision or early provision (at a cost) is normal to ensure the event takes place. The balance between cost and service varies, therefore, depending on the situation and the risk assessment.
- The management task involves the search for trade-offs in the mix, whereby suboptimal behaviour in one or more elements is balanced by optimal behaviour across the mix as a whole e.g., fewer distribution centres may be used, but more transport is therefore required in serving customers.
- These points come together in the concept of outsourcing, in which it might make sense for some of the distribution operation (e.g., transport or warehousing) to be outsourced to logistics specialists so as to gain from their expertise and other synergies. Case 16.1 is an illustration of this. In other cases, the equipment might be so valuable (e.g., a rowing eight's boat) that letting it out of sight is a major risk.
- Finally, the focus in the definition on raw materials as well as finished products emphasises the channel-long nature of the process. We need to be concerned about the components of products and how they are distributed because supply chains are only as good as their weakest link. Effectively, the chain as a whole competes with other chains, and problems in component sourcing impact overall efficiency. Whilst recognising this, much of this chapter does focus on the distribution of finished goods.

Issues in channel management

The management task in sport product distribution broadly consists, as noted earlier, of strategically managing distribution channels for sport products (in the widest sense). A wide range of issues could be identified in any discussion about sport product distribution, but here three have been chosen for particular discussion. This choice is based on the high profile and importance of these issues for the sport industry and to illustrate the interlocking and integrated nature of supply chains generally and sports supply chains in particular. In turn, attention is focused on:

- Product sourcing and sweatshops
- Price fixing in the area of replica shirts
- The role of licensing, rights and exclusivity in distribution channels, with particular reference to telephony

Product sourcing and sweatshops

The distribution of sport products represents the movement from production to consumption. At the consumer end of the channel, changing demands have intensified competitive structures. A key driver is to be able to offer consumers good-quality products at good prices. In recent decades, this has meant that there has been considerable pressure on prices. Discounting and low prices (e.g., for sports clothes and kit) are a large element of the market, particularly in the case of sports leisurewear.

The final price paid by the consumer is a function of a variety of cost inputs and profit taking (e.g., what profits do the producer, intermediary and retailer need)? Important components of this final price are the costs of production and the costs of distribution. As such, there has been real pressure to produce products cheaply and to distribute them rapidly and as cost effectively as possible. This process has been enhanced by developments in transportation (e.g., air freight) and by changes in communication systems. The ability to capture data and use them to control activity on a global scale has transformed the potential for production locations. Provided distribution can be carried out effectively, production is free to seek the least cost location. It is here that problems have occurred, both from the point of view of 'exporting jobs' and from 'exploiting child labour'.

The search for low-cost production capabilities has led to production in developing countries where labour laws and human rights may be less well observed (Frenkel, 2001). This production is linked to the market by modern communications systems, reflecting demand and order profiles, and rapid distribution systems when required. The distribution is a mixture of slow systems (e.g., containers by sea for base products) and regular demand and rapid systems (e.g., air for high value and dynamically demanded products). All, however, rely on a labour production point that is cheap and responsive. The weakest link in the channel is the conditions at the production point, often labelled 'sweatshops'. 'Sweatshops' have thus become a focus for campaigns against brand owners and globalisation generally (e.g., Klein, 1999).

The interactions between communications, distribution and production have also been affected by an increase in the volatility of consumer demand and in the more fashion orientation of many sport products. To manage demand, businesses are keen not to be overstocked and yet to be able to react rapidly to surges in demand. This puts pressure on the production facilities and on the physical distribution of the finished products. Information movement has become a key factor in supply chain interlinkages and efficiency.

Case 16.2 provides further details about sweatshops and the impact they have throughout the distribution channel. If channels of distribution are most vulnerable at their weakest point, then the damage to brand reputation by exploitative global supply chain practices has the potential to have a major impact. As a result, firms are concerned to attempt to ensure the production is responsible. However, the nature of the distribution channel means that in some cases, it is hard to pin down exactly what is being done and in whose name. Consumer awareness of and reactions to campaigns and approaches such as cleanclothes.org or nosweat.org.uk or to boycotts of sports brands remain to be fully assessed. Continuing pressure on such practices has implications for the global supply chain for sport products.

CASE 16.2   Sweatshops and the global supply chain

Western companies began to relocate manufacturing production to Asia in the mid-1960s. The pace and extent of this has subsequently accelerated. Low education levels, no legal employment age, poor working conditions and limited worker protection provided a low-cost, flexible manufacturing or production operation. Driven by the need to maintain and enhance profitability in an increasingly competitive market, sports goods manufacturers (as other garment manufacturers) have scoured the world for suitable low-cost production sites, either directly or through outsourced or subcontracted factories.

These factories have been categorised by many as sweatshops based on the harsh conditions of work, low pay and lack of (Western) standard rights. Most concern has focused on the hours of work, the low pay, the use of child or forced labour and the conditions or work themselves. Sweatshops are a focus of many campaigns, and particular targets have been major sports brands such as Nike and their athlete endorsers such as Michael Jordan and Tiger Woods. Although some of this concern is clearly based on the conditions and operation of sweatshops, some groups are also motivated by a desire to protect jobs in Western economies.

The business model at the heart of this process has a number of characteristics:

- Effective and efficient speedy delivery to retailers
- A focus on low production costs
- Reduction of inventory by applying just-in-time solutions to transport
- Shifting of reactions to consumer demand on to the suppliers through the use of communications technology

The 'sweatshop' answers a need for low-cost production so as to allow more flexibility in the system. The competitive driver focuses retail buyers to:

- Place smaller orders more frequently so as to avoid inventory and react rapidly to demand changes.

■ Reduce the lead times for delivery by using more rapid response modes and transport systems.

■ Lower the unit costs by seeking efficiencies throughout the production process, including reducing wage costs directly or by relocation.

Campaigns against brand manufacturers have had some impact in raising awareness and concern over sweatshops and the contrasts between workers' wages and the final price of the product. Companies have responded by introducing codes of conduct and emphasising corporate social responsibility. Practise, however, varies, and the chain of subcontraction can often be used as a screen to avoid direct compliance.

Source: Adapted from Klein (1999), LaFeber (1999), *Clean Clothes Campaign* (1998) and Fairolympics.org (2004)

Question

1. What are the linkages between sweatshops and sports logistics? To what extent do these matter to the final consumer?

■ Price fixing and replica shirts

The final price to a consumer for any product is made up of a variety of cost and profit decisions. Inefficiencies in the supply chain drive up costs and thus final prices. This could lead to adverse consumer reactions. There is thus competitive pressure to ensure supply chain efficiency by members of the supply chain working closely together.

However, there is a darker side to the interrelationships between producers and distributors that can have a different effect on consumers. If suppliers collude with a range of other actors in the channel (e.g., retailers) and the supply can be sufficiently regulated or controlled, then price fixing can be implemented. Thus, a supplier might agree with a number of retailers to distribute a particular item. They all agree a final price to the consumer and also agree not to discount this price. The agreed price does not represent supply and demand realities. It bears no relation to the costs of doing business and reduces competitiveness in the market. Retailers not privy to this agreement will find it hard to obtain supplies from official sources. Retailers who break the agreement may find that their sources of supply no longer agree to continue supplying them.

Such vertical restraints on trade and supply can occur in any distribution channel where manufacturers or retailers have power and are willing to abuse their position. When the product is licensed, such supply control is clearly more possible because the product has particular separate characteristics, and products are not substitutes (e.g., if you require an official Welsh rugby shirt, then an English shirt will not do). Licensing is perhaps more common in sports distribution than in some other channels, so the potential for price fixing is higher. Such agreements or collusion are illegal in the United Kingdom under the Competition Act because they are viewed as distorting competition and 'ripping off' customers.

Case 16.3 examines a recent high-profile instance of price fixing involving replica football kit. Some of the highest profile manufacturers, retailers and football organisations were involved. The competition authorities found that price fixing did occur, although JJB Sports and others still vehemently deny the accusations. The case illustrates the interactions and interlinkages that occur both vertically and horizontally in supply systems. It also suggests that there is a need to be vigilant over the activities of channel partners in order to protect the consumer.

CASE 16.3   Replica football kit price-fixing

In August 2003, 10 businesses were fined a total of £16.8m by the Office of Fair Trading (OFT) after an investigation into price fixing for Umbro replica football kit. This was a major breach of the Competition Act of 1998. The OFT found that the companies fixed the prices for various shirts through a number of agreements (e.g., the top-selling short-sleeved adult and junior shirt of the England team and for Manchester United). Other agreements involved replica kit for Chelsea, Celtic and Nottingham Forest. Most of the agreements covered key selling periods such as the launch of new kits or England's participation in Euro 2000. This was not the first such investigation of replica football kit price-fixing in the United Kingdom. The fines levied by the OFT were:

JJB Sports: £8.373m

Umbro: £6.641m

Manchester United: £1.652m

Allsports: £1.350m

Football Association: £0.158m

Blacks: £0.197m

Sports Soccer: £0.123m

JD Sports: £0.073m

Sports Connection: £0.020m

Sportsetail: Fine set at zero by leniency

The OFT initiated the investigation in August 2000 after a complaint from Sports Soccer that price-fixing was prevalent, despite assurances to the OFT after an earlier examination of the market. The formal investigation began in June 2001 and included unannounced raids on business premises and written and oral representations. The OFT investigation found evidence of agreement or concerted practice to fix the retail selling prices of shirts and other kit. Accordingly, fines were levied and companies told to cease such practices if they continued to exist.

JJB Sports was extremely annoyed by the decision, describing the OFT as a 'kangaroo court' and denying any wrongdoing or any involvement in price fixing. It launched an appeal against the decision and the fine, as did Allsports; others (Umbro and Manchester United) appealed against the level of the fine.

In October 2004, the Competition Appeal Tribunal found that JJB had been involved in some of the agreements (England and Manchester United), but there was insufficient evidence in the case of another agreement. The majority of the OFT findings were upheld. JJB continue to press its claim of innocence. Appeals about the level of the fines remain outstanding.

Source: Adapted from Office of Fair Trading (2003), Competition Appeals Tribunal (2004) and BBC (2003)

Question

1. Is price fixing against consumers' interest, or does it reflect business realities?

Licensing, rights and exclusivity in distribution channels

It should have become obvious by now that distribution channels are not neutral pathways down which products flow. They are instead a battleground of value distribution, mainly based on notions of power in the channel. This power tends to come from two sources:

- Knowledge of changing consumer demand patterns
- Ownership of products with attributes or characteristics demanded by consumers

The first power source is generally self-evident. Businesses that are close to the consumer and can understand and interpret their shifting reactions to products have the opportunity to position themselves better than the competition. So, closeness to the consumer provides benefits in rapid reactions to changing demands, less obsolescence of unwanted stock and in some cases, close relationship marketing opportunities (e.g., JD Sports' loyalty membership scheme). These advantages are, of course, subject to product or service availability. Demand might be identifiable, but can the product be created in time or delivered to the right place at the right time?

One of the ways that products are both created and controlled is through branding and licensing. Products are owned by somebody or some organisation, and this ownership is important to distribution channels. The licensing of products containing, for example, trademarks institutes a degree of control or even exclusivity into distribution channels, as Case 16.3 shows. So, a sports good retailer might be the only licensed reseller of a football club's merchandise as part of an exclusive deal. For suppliers or retailers without the licensing deal, knowledge of consumer demands is useless because the product is owned and exclusively available only through one channel. The specific product attributes and characteristics (e.g., brand name, badge, image) have been exploited in channel (and probably selling price) construction and management. Product ownership and thus the rights to resell have thus become key influences.

But it has become increasingly obvious that it is not simply product ownership that is important. Clubs, organisations and even individuals have become increasingly concerned to ensure that their intellectual property rights (IPRs) are protected. This may take the form of trademarks and brandmarks, but also includes aspects of image rights (e.g., of David Beckham or Jonny Wilkinson). For example, clubs are keen to protect the image rights of their players and of the ground and stadium. They are also becoming increasingly aware of the value in the ownership of the image rights to the game itself. These image rights provide product attributes that can then be distributed, either directly or indirectly.

In a distribution context, the issue of image rights is increasingly important in respect of the media. Clubs want to protect image rights so as to be able to use them on their own channels (e.g., club website, TV channel or clubcall or alerts to mobile phones). By 'owning' these rights, clubs can extract value from them by linking to dedicated fans, as seen in Table 16.1. The clubs may have to 'buy' these personal image rights as part of the salaries they pay their players. Other media owners (e.g., newspapers) are concerned that despite having photographers in the ground, they are going to be increasingly constrained over what they can print or use (words and pictures) and the time scales in which they can print or use 'their' images. Such concerns are not new but demonstrate the issues of ownership in distribution channels. These concerns are given an added urgency by the emergence of new channels through technological changes.

Another example of the ways that aspects of logistics and distribution can be manipulated or used to understand aspect of sport marketing is given by Lonsdale (2004). Lonsdale examines concepts of power and ownership in the context of value creation and capture in English football. The paper illustrates how although football clubs have seen a huge increase in revenue through broadcasting rights, this revenue has been captured at the top level by the players who have been able to appropriate the major share of value in the supply chain. Issues of power, scarcity, value and relationships are at the fore in the supply of this product, as others.

Conclusions

'Getting the right product to the right place at the right time' sounds easy. The reality in sport marketing is, however, rather more complex and difficult. Whether it is the distribution of physical products or the broadcast of sporting events, issues of availability, ownership, possession and use abound. From the buying of a programme at your local football club to the logistics needed to put the Olympics together (and to take them apart), there are major management issues in meeting demand and supply.

Distribution channels and logistics management bridges this gap between supply and demand. Sports distribution channels have to be efficient and effective in order to provide timely product availability. Sports channels are under considerable pressure because of the demands from consumers, which are increasingly volatile, and because of the changes in the nature of product supply. Volatility of demand and speed of supply are key issues that require good management of the basic logistics activities. Information and communications technology have thus become ever more important in the management of sports logistics channels.

Distribution channels can be complex and nuanced. They contain a host of intermediaries and choices to be made. The opportunities to get things wrong are endless.

Perhaps this helps explain the shadier sides of distribution channels, whether it is ticket touts, price fixing or 'sweatshops'. What they provide is a 'hedge' against error. The complexities are huge and the gains are considerable, so temptation to cut corners or to collude in unfair practices becomes great. On the positive side, customers are continually reinventing demand patterns and do not take kindly to being 'ripped off'. Distribution channels thus allow consumers to exercise their choices and to reward those who get it right and do it properly.

This reinvention emphasises the need for distribution and logistics practices to remain appropriate and aware of the potential to charge. Reaction to demand is a key focus, and technology has aided in this in terms of knowledge and time saving. Technological advances are also being felt elsewhere in distribution channels. If there is one key message for the future, it is that information capture and use will be every bit as valuable as product movement in distribution. Notwithstanding this, however, most sport products still demand a distribution channel to match production to consumption. Getting basic logistics management tasks right will remain fundamentally critical to successful sport marketing.

Discussion questions

1. To what extent is it possible to get the 'right products to the right places at the right times' all the time?
2. Taking any sport product of your choice, attempt to draw or map the distribution channel from production to consumption.

Guided reading

Given the importance of distribution and logistics to the delivery of products to consumers and events to spectators, there is remarkably little written on the topic of sports logistics and distribution channels. Standard sport marketing textbooks generally contain a brief chapter on the subject, although it is often combined with sports retailing. Sport marketing journals have little coverage of the subject of distribution. Logistics and supply chain books tend not to cover the sport sector. A web search of major journal databases turned up no relevant articles. Therefore, if you want to know more about the subject, you will need to do some groundwork yourself. In terms of supply chain and logistics, then a reasonable introductory chapter in a retail context is found in Sparks (2003). A good general logistics text is Christopher and Peck (2003). An advanced text on quick response is Lawson, King and Hunter (1999). Application of many of the logistics and supply chain elements discussed in this chapter in the retail field can be found in Fernie and Sparks (2004).

Specialist logistics and supply chain journals include:

- *Logistics and Transport Focus*
- *International Journal of Logistics Management*
- *International Journal of Physical Distribution and Logistics Management*
- *Journal of Business Logistics*
- *Supply Chain Management*

Keywords

Inventory or stock; logistics mix; logistics service providers; postponement; quick response; supply chain; sweatshops; touts; unitisation; warehouses.

Bibliography

BBC (2003) *Manchester United Fined for Price Fixing*, retrieved 12 November 2004, from http://www.bbc.co.uk/l/hi/business/3116353.stm.

Christopher, M. (1998) *Logistics and Supply Chain Management*, London: FT-Prentice Hall.

Christopher, M. and Peck, H. (2003) *Marketing Logistics*, 2nd edn, Oxford: Butterworth-Heinemann.

Clean Clothes Campaign (1998) *Nike case*, retrieved 11 December 2004, from http://www.cleanclothes.org/companies/nikecase.htm.

Competition Appeals Tribunal (2004) *JJB Sports and Allsports and Office of Fair Trading*, Case 1021/1/1/03, 1022/2/203, retrieved 12 November 2004, from http://wwwcatribunal.org.uk/documents/Jdg1021Umbro011004.pdf.

Fairolympics.org (2004) *Play Fair at the Olympics Oxfam, Oxford*, retrieved 12 November 2004, from http://www.fairolympics.org/en/report/olympicreporteng.pdf.

Fernie, J. and Sparks, L. (2004) *Logistics and Retail Management*, 2nd edn, London: Kogan Page.

Frenkel, S.J. (2001) Globalisation, athletic footwear commodity chains and employment relations in China, *Organization Studies* 22(4):531–62.

Klein, N. (1999) 'The Swoosh: The fight for good jobs', in *No Logo*, New York: Picador, pp. 365–79.

Lawson, B., King, R. and Hunter, A. (1999) *Quick Response*, Chichester: Wiley.

LaFeber, W. (1999) *Michael Jordan and the New Global Capitalism*, New York: WW Norton, pp. 102–9, 143–51.

Lonsdale, C. (2004) Player power: Capturing value in the English football supply network, *Supply Chain Management* 9(5):383–91.

Office of Fair Trading (2003) *Price Fixing of Replica Football Kit*, Decision CA98/06/2003, retrieved 12 November 2004, from http://www.oft.gov.uk/Business/CompetitionAct/ Decisions/Football+Kit.htm.

Sparks, L. (2003) 'Retail logistics', in P. Freathy (ed.), *The Retailing Book*, Harlow: FT-Prentice Hall, pp. 251–72.

Recommended websites

Arsenal
http://www.arsenal.com

Chartered Institute of Logistics and Transport
http://www.ciltuk.org.uk

Clean Clothes Campaign
http://www.cleanclothes.org

Competition Appeals Tribunal
http://www.catribunal.org.uk

Council of Supply Chain Management Professionals
http://www.cscmp.org

Cranfield University
http://www.som.cranfield.ac.uk/som/cclt/

Fair Olympics
http://www.fairolympics.org

Heriot Watt University
http://www.sml.hw.ac.uk/logistics/

London Marathon
http://www.londonmarathonstore.com

National Institute for Transport and Logistics
http://www.nitl.ie

No Sweat!
http://www.nosweat.org.uk

Office of Fair Trading
http://www.oft.gov.uk

Schenker
http://www.schenker.com

University of Cardiff
www.cf.ac.uk/carbs.lom/lerc/index.html

World Rally Championships
http://www.wrc.com

Chapter 17

Sports goods retailing

Leigh Sparks
University of Stirling

Learning outcomes

Upon completion of this chapter, the reader should be able to:

■ Demonstrate the importance of the retail sector to sport marketers.

■ Highlight the aspects of retailing that are of particular significance for sport marketers.

■ Outline the sports retail market structure and discuss how and why it is changing.

■ Understand the requirements of different forms of sports goods retail outlets, including high street and online stores.

■ Consider a range of management issues in designing and operating sports retail outlets.

Overview of chapter

Over the past two decades, there has been a transformation in the structure and composition of the UK sports goods market, as in many other countries (Mintel, 2004a). In the United Kingdom, a narrow market focused on 'games' equipment has been broadened and deepened as sport has taken a different place in the country's culture. The nature of sport has changed with a movement from traditional 'English' games such as cricket and tennis to a broad variety of sports ranging from personal health and fitness to extreme and adventure sports and from 'British' sports such as football to 'imports' such as American football. Female sport product requirements and purchasing have taken on greater significance as the nature of sport has changed. The explosion in media awareness and coverage of professional sports and the associated rise of celebrity sports stars have opened up new product and consumer markets. Sports clothing has developed from being a functional requirement needed to participate in 'games' into a globally branded fashion statement (i.e., there has been a movement from 'activewear' to 'casualwear'). As a consequence there has been an increased frequency of purchasing of sports clothing.

This interaction of media, sports and product globalisation and fashion has transformed what is sold and the ways it is sold. Sports goods retailing has undergone (and continues to undergo) quite radical change. The sports retailing sector is now of considerable economic and social significance in many countries. It also offers an insight into changing cultural roles and emphases in sport and sport marketing. This chapter therefore considers the changing characteristics, importance and operations of sports goods retailing. To meet this aim, the changing nature of the products that are purchased are considered first. Secondly, the structure of the UK sports retailing industry is assessed, both in terms of mainstream and more specialist retailing. These two areas are then combined into a consideration of various issues in sports retailing, including targeted consumer marketing, store design and experiential sports retailing and the internet as a retailing channel. Finally, conclusions are drawn.

Introduction

Retailing is concerned with the sale of products (normally, individual items or in small quantities) to the final consumer. Sports retailing is therefore the interaction amongst three components – sports, retailing and consumers – all of which have been undergoing considerable change. The change in the significance and marketing of sport has been considered in the earlier chapters of this book. What we identify as sport, our desires and abilities to participate in sport and our demands to associate with sport have all altered. The meaning we place on sport has been transformed. This is evident in many ways and forms, but is clearly reflected in the area of sports retailing. Retailing itself has been a sector undergoing considerable change. As identified in Chapter 16, the retail sector is no longer the innocent recipient of sport products from manufacturers produced in the hope that someone would need them to 'play the game'. Now, retailers are amongst the largest businesses in many countries. For example, Wal-Mart (which operates Asda in the United Kingdom) has sales (fiscal year to Jan 2004) of $256bn, through about 5200 stores, and employs about 1.5 million people worldwide. More than 138 million customers visit Wal-Mart stores each week. Similarly, retailers such as Tesco and Carrefour are significantly important and powerful organisations (Burt and Sparks, 2003). Such retailers are extending their ranges further into sports and leisure goods.

Although it is apparent in many countries and sectors that leading retailers have gained scale and power in distribution channels, it is also true that some manufacturers have also increased their relative position. This is often because of their development and maintenance of powerful brands. In sport, manufacturer brands have expanded enormously, and the sector contains some of the leading consumer brands in the world. Companies such as Nike, Adidas and Reebok are powerful global brands, and niche brands (e.g., Helly Hansen, Roxy, Ripcurl) also have strong consumer attraction. Power is perhaps more evenly distributed between retailers and manufacturers in sports retailing than in some other retail sectors.

Retailers, however, can use their knowledge of changing consumer demands to serve customers better and to reflect tastes, needs and wants. In the sports field, it is clear that customer demands have changed in a number of ways. For example:

■ The range of sports has expanded.
■ Equipment has developed through technology and safety enhancements.

- The gender balance of participants and consumers has become less biased towards male and middle-aged categories.
- Sports clothing has ceased to be a functional need and, in some cases, has become leisure-related casualwear.
- Style has become as important in some categories (of sport, equipment or clothing) as function.
- Demand around major sport events (e.g., Euro 2004, Rugby World Cup 2003, Ryder Cup 2004) has become larger and more volatile.
- Association and overt identification with sports teams, major brands and major sporting events have risen.

If customer demands and needs have altered in these (and other) ways, then it is to be expected that retailers should have responded to these changes by developing their retail operations. What sport products are bought and where we buy them has therefore been transformed. The sports retail shop of today looks different from sports retail stores of yesteryear. It merchandises and sells different products, services and experiences. This change has involved the creation of new businesses, approaches, brands and methods of operating. For example:

- There has been an increase in sports retailing specialists.
- Store design ideas and capabilities have developed.
- Club shops have expanded at the stadium and elsewhere.
- Experiential retailing, as at Niketown, ESPN Zone, or REI, has become more prominent.
- Internet-based sports goods retailing has expanded dramatically.

What do we buy?

The sports retailing market in product terms is normally divided into equipment, clothing and footwear components. Figure 17.1 provides some evidence of how the UK product market has altered in recent decades. The figure suggests that two main trends have occurred:

- The market as a whole has expanded enormously. Mintel (2004b) estimates that the current market size in the United Kingdom is c. £4.5bn, making it the third largest sports goods market in Europe in both total sales and per capita sales terms (Mintel, 2004a)
- Although this growth has occurred in all three categories, growth in clothing has been by far the most significant. There has been a switch in the market from an equipment focus in the 1970s to a clothing focus in the 2000s. This has also occurred elsewhere in Europe, although in France, equipment remains proportionately more important (Mintel, 2004a)

Before considering these three segments (clothing, footwear and equipment) in turn, the differences amongst the main sports goods markets in Europe are worth developing further. According to Mintel (2004a), France is the largest market in Europe in both total and per capita sales bases, probably because of the high levels of active participation in

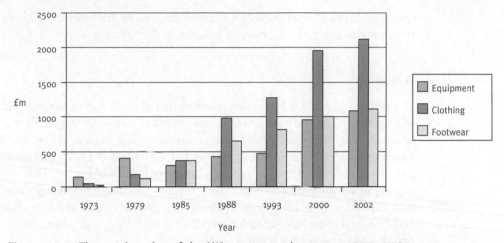

Figure 17.1 **The market size of the UK sports goods sector, 1973–2002**
Source: Selected Retail Business and Mintel Reports on UK Sports Goods Markets, 1979–2004

sports in that country. This high participation level in, for example, skiing and cycling makes the equipment segment of the market proportionately more important than in other countries. The second largest market in total sales in Europe is Germany, but on a per capita basis, Germany is the lowest of the largest six markets. A particular retail organisational form, the buying group, dominates the German sports retail market (discussed later). In contrast, the Netherlands is a small total market but has high per capita sales. As noted earlier, the UK market is third on both measures of sales, but it is biased towards casualwear and spectator leisurewear rather than participative (activewear) purchasing.

■ Clothing

Sportswear has become fashionable in the United Kingdom, and although clothing is needed to play sport (activewear), many clothing sales are fashion oriented (casualwear). This growth has been such as to outweigh expansion in the equipment market. Sports clothing holds a larger share of the market in the United Kingdom than in many other European countries (Mintel, 2004b). This share in the United Kingdom can be explained by the way that British consumers use sportswear as casual, everyday attire, probably based on perceptions of comfort, practicality and durability. Sports brands (Nike, Adidas and Reebok) and replica kit and club-branded leisurewear are ubiquitous, found across all ages and genders. For example, less than one-third of football kit sales are for participation purposes, reflecting the casual, fashion and associative dimensions of sports clothing. Sports leisurewear is also seen as fashionable by some because it can be well cut and flattering to certain (although not all!) body shapes. Fashion sports clothing may also be less durable and more 'disposable' than activewear.

A second and contrasting trend within sports clothing is the expansion of outdoor sports clothing. Used for practical reasons in outdoor sport pursuits and in some extreme sports, such clothing has become increasingly popular, both for active and leisure wear. Much of this segment is innovative (e.g., in its use and development of specialist fabrics), and although some items can be considered fashionable, changing technologies are perhaps more of a driver in this market.

Footwear

The choice of sports footwear for participants in sport has expanded. More fundamentally perhaps, the 'trainer' has become a fashion statement rather than a participatory necessity. Trainers are cultural icons (Garcia, 2003; Heard, 2003; Vanderbilt, 1998), seen everywhere. The footwear market has expanded considerably on the back of the use of the trainer and its derivatives for everyday, casual wear. This is now a fashion market in which product segmentation techniques (e.g., limited editions, retro styling and customisation) have been applied strongly. Similarly, the expansion of outdoor activities and sport has expanded the market for hiking and other boots, although these are also often used for everyday wear.

Equipment

The equipment market has not expanded as rapidly as the other segments, and proportionately in the United Kingdom, has become less important. Spending on sport equipment is a reflection of participation levels, the cost of equipment or kit needed and the quantity required to participate. Some sports require little by the way of equipment (e.g., swimming and aerobics), but other sports require some, if not substantial, investment (e.g., golf, fishing, skiing and some home fitness activities). For example, the golf equipment market is proportionately important because it has high participation levels, requires quite a lot of equipment, which can be quite expensive, and there is substantial product development. Specialist golf equipment retailers (e.g., the American Golf Discount Centre and Nevada Bob) have therefore thrived. But in some other sports, specialist equipment retailers are not as prevalent.

In the golf market, technological developments (e.g., club and ball development) can be important in encouraging new equipment purchase, but issues of branding and athlete endorsement can also be significant (e.g., Tiger Woods and Nike). Some similar issues may be found or are emerging in alternative and extreme sports in which equipment can be technologically demanding, but aspects of branding, design and style overlay this.

This brief review of sports goods products raises a number of implications for sports retailing:

- The switch from equipment to clothing suggests a need for a change in store design, layout and merchandise mix in retail outlets.
- The fashion orientation (and to an extent, concern over style) implies the need for a closer knowledge of the market and rapid adaptation to changes in demand. Volatility in this market has increased. More emphasis is thus placed on the management of the distribution and supply chain functions (see Chapter 16), with the retail shop being critical to capturing data on and understanding consumer behaviour.
- Segmentation in the product market (e.g., by gender, sport, equipment and clothing requirements) suggests the potential for segmentation in the retail market at the chain (e.g., female-oriented stores), product (e.g., specialist sport products) and in-store (e.g., separate specialist departments) levels.

Who do we buy from?

Many different types of retailers in the United Kingdom are involved in sports goods retailing. Mintel (2002) estimate that there are about 3500 sports shops in the United Kingdom, although definitional issues make accurate figures impossible. The market has undergone considerable change in recent years, as concentration processes have affected retailing generally and sports retailing in particular and as the nature of the sport product market has changed. Figure 17.2 demonstrates that specialist sports retailers have come to dominate the United Kingdom to an extent not seen elsewhere in Europe, except for France. Sport products are sold through many different types of retail outlets, but the main market in the United Kingdom is to be found in the specialist sector.

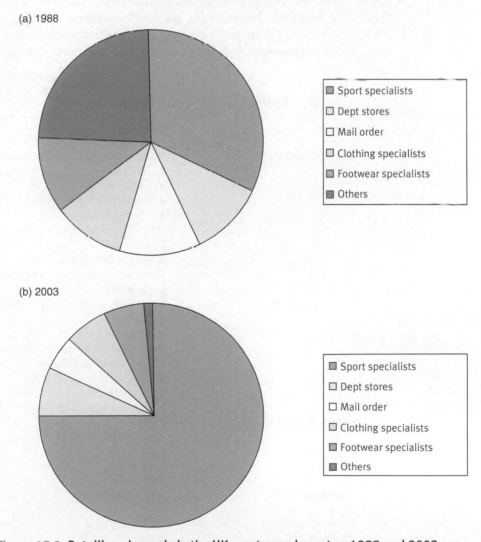

Figure 17.2 Retailing channels in the UK sports goods sector, 1988 and 2003
Source: Retail Business and Mintel Reports on UK Sports Retailers and Sports Goods Markets, 1988, 2004

Table 17.1 provides a typology by line of business and a listing of some of the major players in the sports retailing sector. The listing suggests that many of the leading retailers in the United Kingdom generally have some interest in the sport products sector (e.g., Marks and Spencer, Next, Tesco). They are not overall a major component of the sector, however, and indeed, in some categories (e.g., footwear), it is now less common to see national chains attempting to compete with the sports specialists. Table 17.1 identifies some of the top sports specialists (discussed in more detail later), but a number of further trends can be identified that are affecting this part of the sports retailing sector that include:

- The size and growth of the UK market has attracted a number of international retailers to the country. The American chain Foot Locker has expanded rapidly in the United Kingdom in recent years, and the French retailer Decathlon has six superstores in the United Kingdom.
- Smaller specialist chains focusing on particular markets have a strong position in the United Kingdom. For example, outdoor/adventure specialists such as Field & Trek, Cotswold Outdoor and Tiso have presence and considerable market reputation. A similar situation exists in board and extreme sports in which Blacks Leisure

Table 17.1 **Sports retailing: line of business typology**

Line of business	Examples
Sports specialists	Major sports retailing businesses
	■ JJB Sports
	■ Sports World
	■ John David Group
	■ Blacks Leisure
	Major brands with retail stores
	■ Niketown
	■ Adidas Performance Store
	Specialist sports brands with retail stores
	■ Quiksilver
	■ Fat Face
	■ Rip Curl
	■ Cotton Traders
	Niche or segmented sports retailers
	■ Club based (e.g., Rangers)
	■ Sport based (e.g., First XV)
	■ Sex based (e.g., sweatyBetty)
	■ Lifestyle based (e.g., Tiso)
Department and variety stores	Argos
	John Lewis Partnership
	Debenhams
Mail order	Littlewoods
	Argos
Clothing retailers	Marks and Spencer
	Next
Footwear retailers	
Others	Tesco
	Asda Wal-Mart

is the leader with a variety of fascias, but significant other players include White Stuff, Legends Surf Shops and Snow+Rock.

■ A number of specialist players have begun to explore the potential of multichannel retailing. Many of the retailers above would, for example, have both physical shops and sell over the internet. Other retailers, such as Cotton Traders, have emerged from a mail order leisure business into a multichannel physical and virtual retailer. As Case 17.1 shows, Cotton Traders is focused on the leisure end of the sport market. The company thus has a current requirement for locations that combine leisure-style situations and retail shop potential.

■ Despite the strength of the specialist sports retailers, the power of the manufacturers or sporting brands remains of importance in this market. Leading brands such as Nike, Adidas and Reebok have considerable product presence in sports retailers, but they also have outlets of their own. Similarly, sports clubs brands such as Manchester United have their own retail outlets (megastore, club stores, internet and mail order) as well as selling branded and licensed products through other retailers (e.g., Argos, Tesco, JJB Sports).

■ Spectacular consumption sites or experiential consumption outlets where products (e.g., clothing and equipment) can be tried in extreme conditions or consumption watched (e.g., ice wall climbing) have attracted considerable attention (e.g., Peñaloza, 1999). Major players in this market in the United States include Niketown, ESPN Zone and REI. Tiso, with its Outdoor Experience (Glasgow, Edinburgh), is attempting to provide experiential attributes to their largest stores (discussed later).

CASE 17.1   Cotton Traders

Cotton Traders was founded in 1987 by the former England rugby union captains Steve Smith and Fran Cotton, who thought there was a gap in the market selling rugby jerseys as leisurewear. Cotton Traders began (initially funded by venture capitalists 3i) by selling the rugby shirts through Sunday newspaper advertisements. It has now expanded into a multichannel retailer of a range of casual sports-based leisure clothing. The majority of the approximately £50m annual turnover comes from mail order sales, although there are now more than 40 retail outlets in the United Kingdom, and the catalogue products are available online. Cotton Traders employs more than 500 people in the United Kingdom. Next PLC has had a 30% stake in the company since 1996 (the remainder is held by Cotton and Smith). The company states its guiding principles to be quality, choice, customer service and value for money.

The concept of Cotton Traders was developed from the idea of expanding the rugby jersey into the leisurewear market. In the early 1980s, this was quite a dramatic step. Authenticity of the brand is maintained through continued supply of rugby shirts to leading clubs, including Sale Sharks, Leicester Tigers and The Barbarians. Cotton Traders had the contract to supply the England international rugby shirts, but Nike bought this out in 1997. A wide range of casual and leisurewear has been developed beyond the initial idea, as well as expansions into household items and formalwear (which was not successful). The Cotton Traders England replica jerseys use the 'old'

Cotton Traders: catalogues, website and shops

Photographs and Images © Cotton Traders 2005. Reproduced with permission

red rose emblem rather than the redesigned RFU/Nike logo, a right won in a court case in 2002, which decided that there are no protected rights in a national emblem.

Mail order is at the heart of the business, although 25% of sales are online. There are more than 800,000 customers in their database, and up to 30 versions of the catalogue are sent out each year. Being in the fashion/leisure industry, demand can be volatile, and variations in the supply and flow of product (all suppliers are based outside the United Kingdom) and orders can cause disruptions. Demand volatility can also be caused by demand increasing around major sporting events (e.g., Rugby World Cup 2003). To learn about likely demand, a preview catalogue is produced based on planned lines and sent to leading customers and others who are interested. They receive 20% off their orders for ordering in advance and thereby providing information about potential demand levels. This information is used to adjust the corporate buying of the other 60% of stock, not pre-bought ahead of the catalogue. Even so, buying decisions can lead to under- or overstocking because of unexpected demand fluctuations.

Almost inevitably, therefore, clearance stock becomes available from catalogues because of the imperfections in demand forecasting and ability to react to demand changes. To sell this stock, Cotton Traders initially opened a factory outlet shop in Altrincham. This success has led to further (about 30) factory outlet shops (e.g., Cheshire Oaks, Sterling Mills), although only 20% of the stock in these shops is now 'redundant', clearance or end of line stock. Prices in such outlets can be up to 70% cheaper than the original price in the catalogue.

Linked to the concept of leisure, Cotton Traders opened a store in Manchester Airport and has followed this with stores in other airports (Luton, Birmingham) and a test store in a Road Chef motorway service station (Evesham). Garden centres have also been used to obtain space in a leisure environment (e.g., Dobbie's at Lasswade). Some standard high street shop development has taken place but this is not seen as a priority.

Source: Adapted from Cuthbertson, C. (2004) This retailing life, *European Retail Digest* Summer:31–3; Jackson, P. (2002) 'War of Roses' leaves RFU in red to the tune of £1m, *Daily Mail* 27 March 2002:85; Retail Week (2004) Profile – Fran Cotton, *Retail Week* 6 February 2004; and Cotton Traders (http://www.cottontraders.co.uk)

Question

1. Outline and explain the Cotton Traders' store locational strategy.

Given their significance in the structure of the UK sports retailing market, Table 17.2 provides a brief description of the largest sports specialist retailers. There are a number of issues that arise from this table.

First, the considerable scale of these businesses is well demonstrated, with substantial sales volumes, number of retail stores and floorspace. Four of these retailers are ranked in the 100 largest retailers in the United Kingdom. It is also apparent from Table 17.2 that JJB Sports is by some way the largest player in the market, approaching £1bn in sales.

Secondly, the sector has been concentrating through natural growth and the strategic acquisitions that companies have made. Some of these acquisitions are noted in

Table 17.2 **Leading sports specialists in the UK**

Retailer	Description	Financial Details
JJB Sports (http://www.jjb.co.uk)	JJB Sports is the leading UK retailer of sports clothing, footwear, accessories and equipment, trading from high street outlets and increasingly out-of-town superstores (some jointly with health clubs). In 1998, JJB Sports acquired the then market leader Sports Division. The main aim is to supply high-quality branded sports and leisure products at competitive or discount prices. Recently started small chain of fashion sportswear (Icon).	Sales: £929.8m (2004) Pre-tax profit: £67.8m Stores: 448 (191 superstores) Selling space: 388,847 m^2 UK retail ranking: 36
John David Group (http://www.jdsports.co.uk)	John David Group is a leading specialist retailer of fashionable branded sports and leisurewear. It contains a sports division (JD Sport) and fashion division (Open, Size? and AthLeisure). There has been a rebranding of many stores (from First Sport – taken over in 2002 – to JD Sports), some store closures and expansion in superstores. The company sees its focus as higher-end sports fashion rather than a value-led strategy. JD Sports runs a loyalty card programme.	Sales: £458.1m (2004) Pre-tax profit: £2.1m Stores: 385 (333 Sports shops) Selling space: 133,300m^2 UK retail ranking: 59
Sports World (http://www.sports-world.com)	Sports World (formerly Sports Soccer) is a private operator of sports shops and superstores and the owner of sports brands that include Donnay and Dunlop Slazenger. The shops discount aggressively and promise 'unbeatable value and performance' on a range of leading brands, including their own. Sports World is a member of the German-based Sport 2000 International buying group. It also owns Lillywhites.	Sales: £397.6m (2002) Pre-tax profit: £46.1m Stores: 135 (about 30 superstores, 10 factory outlet stores) Selling space: 93,000m^2 (2001) UK retail ranking: 71
Blacks Leisure Group (http://www.blacksleisure.co.uk)	Blacks is a long-established business but with current interests in outdoor wear and equipment (Millets and Blacks) and boardwear (Free Spirit and Just Add Water). It has the UK rights for O'Neill, a world leading boardwear brand. In 2002, it sold its 209 shop Sport & Fashion division to JD Sports, thus exiting mainstream sports retailing. Millets and Blacks targets the outdoor sport market, occupying middle mass market and premium, enthusiast markets, respectively. Free Spirit and JAW target the aspirational, younger, fashion-led consumers and the hardcore extreme participant, respectively, in the boardwear market.	Sales: £255.5m (2004) Pre-tax profit: £15.6m Stores: 356 (246 Millets, 66 Blacks, 34 Free Spirit, 10 O'Neill) Selling space: 74,150m^2 UK retail ranking: 95
Allsports (http://www.allsports.co.uk)	Allsports is a mass or middle market fashion sportswear retailer focusing mainly on younger males. Its strapline has been 'where sportswear meets fashion'. It is a national UK retailer through smaller high street stores. With an emphasis on leading brands, Allsports prices are higher than value-oriented rivals. Clothing and footwear, as sports fashion, dominate the product range. It is owned by venture capital group 3i but is currently for sale.	Sales: £187.4m (2004) Pre-tax profit: £3.8m Stores: 272 Selling space: 51,300m^2 UK retail ranking: 114

Source: Mintel (2004a)

Table 17.2, but more details are provided in Table 17.3. Strategic acquisitions have been combined with significant store expansion programmes, occasionally also linked to some store closures and repositionings. Most acquisitions have been within the sector, but some have involved diversification outside the sector (e.g., JJB Sports' buying and then selling TJ Hughes, a discount department store chain). More sustainable perhaps are expansions into related fashion markets (e.g., JD Sports) and some internationalisation (e.g., Sports World), although JJB Sports has closed its shops in Spain (1997) and The Netherlands (2003). Although Table 17.3 contains a number of deals by the leading specialists, another theme is the purchases by smaller aggressive regional chains such as Hargreaves Sports and Gilesports. The takeover of the previously iconic sports retailers and brand Lillywhites is also significant.

Thirdly, Table 17.2 indicates that store formats and locations have been undergoing change. Fascias have changed as acquisitions have been made (Table 17.3), but much of the expansion has been focused on out-of-town superstores or in-town, larger stores. Scale is thus seen at both the organisational and the operational or store level. Out-of-town superstore or retail park development fits with broad consumer and retail trends. Format development at the smaller scale is also seen in Table 17.2 with segmented and focused chains being developed, particularly in expanding specialist markets (e.g., boardwear, outdoor sports).

Fourthly, Table 17.2 indicates that the sports retailing market is not in particularly good shape. The profits shown in the table are very small, and businesses are not necessarily sustainable at these levels. Price has become much more of a feature in this market recently. Market pressures have therefore been seen in the sales and takeovers of major chains and in some of the store closures. Despite overall growth in the market, it could be that there has been an overprovision of retail space, focusing price competition or the chains are too similar in their positioning.

Table 17.3 Recent changes in the UK sports retailing market

Date	Purchaser	Purchased
1998	JJB Sports	Sports Division (market leader, built in 1980s out of Olympus Sports)
1999	Blacks	The Outdoor Group (Air, Free, Millets)
2000	Gilesports	Sportsworld GB (15 stores)
2000	Hargreaves Sports	Terry Warner Sports (21 stores)
2000	JD Sports	Cobra Sports
2001	Associated Independent Stores (AIS)	Intersport GB Ltd (from receivership)
2001	Sports World	Disport (50%; 20 stores in Belgium and Luxembourg)
2002	Blacks	Famous Army Stores (from bankruptcy)
2002	JJB Sports	TJ Hughes (discount department stores)
2002	Sports World	Lillywhites (from Jeronimo Martins)
2002	JD Sports	First Sport (from Blacks)
2003	Blacks	Just Add Water
2003		Sports Connection (into administration)
2003	Gilesports	Dixons Sports (six stores)
2003		TJ Hughes Management Buy-Out (from JJB Sports)
2004	JD Sports	RD Scott (23 fashion stores)

Finally, the descriptions of the chains in Table 17.2 point to a recognition that there is need for differentiation in the main market. Different retailers have attempted to focus on fashion rather than value and on high quality rather than lower mass market goods. However, this is not an easy task because discounting and price awareness in the market are high. The differences amongst chains therefore may not be that great in the perceptions of consumers. Of the chains in Table 17.2, only Blacks is really positioned substantially differently because it has repositioned onto an outdoors and adventure/extreme sports basis.

Retailers can be classified in a number of ways by their organisational structures (i.e., how they are managed and organised). Table 17.4 provides details of four of these. Independent or single shop retailers are common numerically in many markets, but collectively they do not have significant market share. Cooperative or mutual retailers are important in some countries. The majority of retailers in many countries, however, are multiple or corporate retailers, running chains of stores under common fascias for profit. Another organisational type is the contractual chain, varying in type from franchises to affiliations of varying degrees and including buying groups. The key characteristic of contractual chains is that independent retailers essentially retain their independence but collaborate with each other in terms of branding, products, merchandising, marketing, distribution and so on. In this way, they gain some of the organisational and operational power that larger multiple retailers possess (e.g., collective buying or advertising).

In sports retailing, buying groups and affiliations are quite strong, particularly in some continental European countries. The largest contractual chains are the affiliated grouping of Intersport and the buying organisation of Sport 2000 International. In Germany, Intersport has about 50% of the sports retailing market, and as Table 17.3 notes, in the United Kingdom, this buying group and affiliated model has found less success, although the UK member of Sport 2000 International is Sports World. The legal

Table 17.4 Sports retailers: organisational typology

Organisational type	Description	Examples
Independents	Single store local shopkeepers	
Multiple or corporate retailers	Business operating a number or a chain of shops as a company or corporate entity. Can be private companies or publicly quoted businesses on the stock market. Vary enormously in size of business and numbers of shops.	JJB Sports (public) Sports World (private) Decathlon Gilesports Cotton Traders Tiso sweatyBetty
Cooperative retailers	Businesses owned by members run for mutual not shareholder benefits or profits. Strong in some countries such as Switzerland.	Edinburgh Bicycle Co-op REI
Contractual chains	Many independent retailers have become part of a contractual chain or a franchise whereby they are independent but are supplied or legally linked to a larger 'umbrella' organisation. They thus gain economies of scale, scope and some brand and distribution benefits. Can range in type of contract and degrees of support and control.	Eden Park (franchise) Intersport GB (affiliated group) Sport 2000 International (buying group)

distinctions amongst such organisations can be confusing. The buying group may be supplying a variety of organisational types in different countries and operating under a number of different store names or fascias. Given their importance in continental Europe, a brief description of the two contractual chain market leaders is provided.

Sport 2000 International

Sport 2000 International, which was founded in 1967, is a buying and marketing group serving cooperative associations of sports retailers in more than 30 European countries, mainly but not always under the Sport 2000 fascia (Mintel, 2004a). There are more than 3200 stores in its network, with Germany by far its largest market. Its central structure collates product orders from its member organisations and negotiates with brand suppliers. National organisations (members) are responsible for product promotion, distribution and finance. In some countries, whereas the product assortment selected at store level is compulsory through a franchise arrangement, elsewhere individual shops take on the responsibility for assortment selection themselves. Table 17.5 provides details of some of the member partners and store fascias in the organisation.

Intersport

Intersport has more than 4500 stores in more than 27 different countries and is essentially a global sports buying group that supports its retail partners. Martinez-Ribes (1994) provides some details of its operational structure using the example of Spain. Its focus is on expertise in sport rather than fashion in sport (Mintel, 2004a). The organisation is approximately 50 years old and is the largest European sports retail organisation, although within the organisation, there are very different national approaches (cooperatives, multiples, buying groups, affiliated groups). The common

Table 17.5 Sport 2000 International: selected partners and fascias

Country	Partner	Fascia
Germany	Nord-West-Ring	Sport 2000
UK	Sports World	Sports World
France	Sport 2000 France	Sport 2000
Austria	Zentrasport	Sport 2000
Italy	Sport Alliance	Sportler and others
Spain	Detall Sport	Base
Sweden	Team Sportia AB	Team Sportia
Denmark	Sport Denmark	Sport Master
Netherlands	Euretco Sport	Sport 2000
Finland	Wihuri Oy Sportia	Sportia
Norway	MX Sport	MX Sport
Greece	Hellenic Flame	Sport 2000
Others (e.g., Estonia, Lithuania, Hungary, Slovenia, Croatia, Bosnia, Serbia, Macedonia, Turkey, Russia, Belgium)	Mixed	Sport 2000 and others

Source: Mintel (2004a)

theme, however, is a grouping of affiliated independent retailers looking for combined strength and protection from multiple competition. Many of the stores are branded Intersport, but other store fascias are also in use (e.g., Sports Experts and Sport Leader in France; G-Sport in Norway). Retail members gain from scale, with integrated operations and enhanced buying. Intersport provides branding, distribution and marketing services as well as training, benchmarking and legal advice.

Issues in sports retailing

The description of the sports retailing sector thus far has focused on the structure and composition of the market and the way these have changed. This changing structure is a reflection of the nature of sport, the consumer market, consumers' perceptions of sport and business practicalities. The basic idea of a retailer is a simple one. The business acquires products and makes them available for sale to consumers. Retailers thus have to consider issues of shop location, consumer market segmentation and positioning, store design, buying and merchandising, staffing and customer service, as well as operational practicalities such as cash flow, security, product availability, and heating and lighting. Similar issues have to be considered by internet retailers.

Covering all of these aspects of sports goods retailing is impossible here. However, it was noted earlier that the market has a tendency towards similarity and that profit margins are currently low. This section therefore focuses on three particular aspects of sports goods retailing, all of which can be broadly considered as attempts to provide a differentiating proposition in the market. The three topics are:

- Approaches to the consumer
- Store design and experiential consumption
- Sports retailing and the internet

Approaches to the consumer

Retailers attempt to attract customers to visit their stores, make purchases and keep coming back. There are many ways to do this in sports retailing. It has to be recognised, however, that not all consumers will be attracted to stores by the same stimuli. Indeed, some consumers will actively be turned off some retailers by their approach (e.g., the in-store environment or the type, range, price and quality of the merchandise). There are trends in consumers' perceptions, desires and life stages that affect the level and nature of demand. For example, the positive feelings towards sports goods retailers by young teenagers are remarkably strong, but these reduce during later teenage years as participation rates in sport fall and other interests take over (Foresight, 2001). There are also differences between the genders in terms of perceptions of sports retailers. These are important not only because of the (increasing) scale of the female sport market but also because of the significant role women play in the purchase of sport products for and by men.

The Foresight (2001) report notes that sportswear as a category is viewed positively by teenagers, although this declines somewhat in the 16- to 19-year-old age group. Amongst all retailers, JJB Sports is the top retail brand overall for all teenagers. JD Sports was ranked seventh, and small and high street sports shops fifteenth, suggesting that for teenagers, sports and sports retailing are key components of image and identity. Teenage boys ranked JJB Sports first, but for girls, it was fifth after Top Shop,

New Look, Next and Boots. Fashion and health and beauty (cosmetics) are thus more critical for girls, but even so, fifth is a high overall ranking for a sports retailer. JD Sports appeared at fourth place for teenage boys. This Foresight (2001) report points to the significance of JJB Sports for this market and reinforces the market position of this company identified earlier. Case 17.2 therefore looks further at the market positioning and approach of JJB Sports.

CASE 17.2   JJB Sports

JJB Sports is the UK leading retailer of sports clothing, accessories and equipment. It has strong brand recognition, particularly among the youth market. Although the sports goods retailing market has been highly competitive and tough, JJB has grown in the past decade into a significant business. In recent years, however, it has, as with most of the mainstream sports retailing sector, come under pressure.

David Whelan (an ex-professional footballer) originally formed JJB in 1971 to take over a single sports shop. The store portfolio was built up gradually, although boosted by acquisitions in the 1980s. In 1994, JJB floated on the stock market, although the family retained a controlling interest. This interest was diluted in 1998, when JJB took over the then leading sports retailing business, Sports Division. The Whelan family, however, retains a significant (about 39%) stake in the business. The takeover was an excellent geographical and strategic fit and the combined group (stores rebranded to JJB Sports) has expanded rapidly since and now has almost 450 shops in the United Kingdom and Ireland.

JJB's main aim is to supply high-quality, branded sports and leisure products at competitive prices. The emphasis has been on active sports enthusiasts rather than the fashion follower and sports brands rather than casualwear labels predominate. This may be changing slightly as lifestyle and leisure become more important for the target market. JJB stocks major sports brands. There is an emphasis on partnerships with Nike, Adidas and Reebok, which in addition to their main ranges, also provide exclusive product to JJB. They also sell brands for which they have exclusive rights in the United Kingdom (Patrick, Lotto, Le Coq Sportif) and their own brand (Olympus). They are the 'official sports retailer for Manchester United'. JJB also has a recent agreement to develop and source Slazenger golf equipment. Clothing accounts for about 41% of sales; footwear, 31%; equipment, 12%; replica kit, 10%; and golf and cycles, 6%.

The company has increasingly focused on larger stores, both in the high street and out of town. Older high street stores have been gradually replaced. The larger stores in high streets are often located on the first floor of sites, with an escalator from the main street. This reduces rental levels. Recently, JJB has expanded its leisure division, which runs health clubs with attached JJB superstores. This 'activity concept' has the health club on the ground floor and a dedicated escalator to the first floor superstore. All superstores offer a women's sportswear and footwear area with dedicated changing rooms, as well as separate children's sports clothing and footwear areas. A branded leisure fashion chain (Icon) has also been developed and expanded slowly.

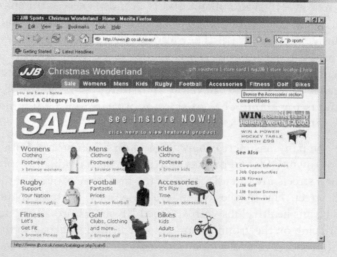

JJB Sports: shops and website

Photographs and web image © JJB Sports 2005. Reproduced with permission

JJB's sales space has grown in the past 5 years by approximately 35%, but sales have risen by about 150%, suggesting improving sales intensity and space productivity. Although profit has generally grown, profitability has declined.

JJB's website provides details of products and store locations as well as other business information. It is, however, not a transactional website. The JJB Sports head office is in Wigan, which is also the base for its centralised logistics operation. JJB has become synonymous with Wigan. The company sponsors Wigan Athletic Football Club (£174K in 2004), Wigan Warriors Rugby League Club (£347K) and Orrell Rugby Union Club (£45K) and buys the naming rights for the Wigan ground ('the JJB Stadium') at a current annual cost of £150k.

The company's quoted business strategy is:

■ Increase investment in the leisure division with the development of further health club and superstore sites.
■ Steady expansion into new superstore sites and gradual migration from small high street stores.
■ Consolidate position as United Kingdom's market leader in active sports retailing.
■ Strengthen relationships with key suppliers.
■ Develop and expand exclusive product ranges.

This results in a market position recently described thus: 'We don't set ourselves out to be a fashion retailer like JD Sports. We are trying to differentiate JJB from the likes of Tesco, Asda and Sportsworld – they are very much value-for-money players. We want to be in the middle ground.'

Source: Adapted from JJB Sports, *Annual Reports and Accounts*; Mintel (2001); Mintel (2004); *Retail Week* (2005) JJB Sports makes a bid for better performance, *Retail Week* 14 January 2005:8; JJB Sports (http://www.jjb.co.uk)

Question

1. Why do you think JJB Sports has been successful in attaining its number one position? What are the threats it currently faces?

However, JJB Sports is not a retail store that attracts everyone. Different reactions to different sports retailers occur. For women, for example, many sports shops are threatening environments that are viewed negatively as being overly male and aggressive. A typical viewpoint might be: 'Most sporting goods stores smell of stale sweat and old rubber and have techno booming loud enough to vibrate your diaphragm. They display their wares inelegantly, not to say indifferently, stacking them by activity: golf, jogging, swimming. A man's shopping environment if ever there was one' (Retrieved 23 December 2004, from http://www.cada.co.uk/articles/ar_1.htm).

Such stores do not meet the aspirations or requirements of many women in terms of sports goods products, shopping environments and customer service, nor do they fit with how women wish to shop generally. Some brands have recognised the issues that are raised by these 'standard' environments and by the growing demand from women for sport products. Nike, for example, has trialled NIKEGoddess (now renamed Nikewomen), which focuses exclusively on the female sport product market. These stores look and feel different from standard Nike stores, having different colours, layout, changing rooms, lighting, product presentation and so on. Niketown in London has a significant female component in its overall floorspace mix, based on learning from Nikewomen. This contrasts with many other retailers in which the approach could be considered to be tokenism ('apologetic product afterthoughts'), if women are considered at all. Nike also have a women-dedicated website (http://www.nikewomen.com). The important issue here is not to treat women differently because they are women (gender stereotyping) but to recognise that different consumer segments and markets have different aspirations and needs.

Case 17.3 takes this approach to a logical conclusion in discussing a retailer run by women for women. This women-only 'activewear boutique' sweatyBetty illustrates many of the differences between the genders, both in terms of sports goods retailing and retailing generally. It goes beyond that, however, in targeting particular requirements of the female market. Such differences need to be taken into account if retailers are to successfully position themselves for parts of the female (or the male, or both) market. Not all women react positively to sweatyBetty. The example, however, is used here to show how careful thought about shopping behaviours and aspirations can be taken into account in targeting specific sports and leisure markets. This has to translate into all aspects of the retail store location, design, product mix, merchandising and customer service, in order to create a strongly attractive environment for the target market.

CASE 17.3   sweatyBetty

sweatyBetty is a young, small, London-based women-only high street retailer ('activewear boutique'). It has been described as a highly targeted contemporary fusion of sportswear, swimwear, outdoorwear and gymwear. The founders believed that they had identified a gap in the market for women-only activewear, arguing that current sports retailers were not meeting women's needs and that women wanted particular things from a sports store. For many women, they felt, the feel-good factor and the overall health and well-being aspects of keeping fit were more important than winning. The retail store needed to reflect these attitudes.

The first store opened in November 1998, and there are now 10 stores (average floorspace, 700 sq ft), an in-store concession at Selfridges in London and (from 2000) a transactional website (which accounts for about 5% of sales). sweatyBetty sells activewear, combining fun with fashion and fitness, using superbrands such as Nike and Adidas and niche brands (including own brands) such as Pure Lime, Venice Beach and CandidaFaria. Celebrity endorsement by, for example, Elle MacPherson and Emma Bunton has helped raise the profile of the brand. Its values and beliefs statement encapsulates the company's sense of difference and of fun:

■ We believe in healthy living, having fun, Cornish clotted cream and cool tracksuits.
■ We welcome customers to share the sweatyBetty experience with us and to become our friends.

- We give our customers trusted advice and will deliver the perfect solution or even a magical transformation.
- A visit to sweatyBetty is sometimes unexpected, often memorable but always satisfying.
- Our products look gorgeous and perform well. We like comfort, great value and the WOW factor!
- We work with friends, we give each other support and achieve a balanced life. We aim to keep things simple and to stay in control.
- We value financial stability and growth so that we can share the sweatyBetty experience as widely as possible.
- We are building an amazing company, run by women for women to be the best!!!

To live up to these beliefs and the purpose of 'increasing the confidence and happiness of women by providing beautiful clothes and subtle inspiration to lead an active lifestyle,' the stores do not look like average sports shops. Stores are intensely feminine with soft lighting, spacious environments and fixtures and fittings more synonymous with an upmarket clothing store creating a pleasant boutique shopping experience. The colours are different – high white ceilings and loads of pink (also seen on the website). The mood is seductive rather than harsh sell. Changing rooms are prominent and large with flattering mirrors and lighting. This is a deliberately designed environment focusing on the feel-good, health and well-being aspects of keeping fit. Products are high quality and well presented as fashion, music is not overly dominant and the atmosphere is supportive and non-aggressive. Such details derive from the founders' belief that standard sports stores are often too male and threatening, treating women as second-class customers. As the founder of sweatyBetty, Tamara Hill-Norton comments, 'Why should women have to get advice on, or buy, a sports bra from a spotty male teenager?' Rather than conjuring up images of a typical sportswear store, it aims to position itself as a confidant or friend, someone to provide advice and guide exercisers in the right direction.

sweatyBetty therefore is best described as a niche activewear chain, selling clothing and footwear for yoga, the beach, skiing and the gym in addition to exercise-related accessories. It is a highly targeted offer that provides a stylish, attractive, feminine range of clothing that is intended for exercise but looks good generally. It is targeted at the busy young mother with an active home life and the young professional woman who works hard but has a highly disposable income to spend on looking and feeling good.

A vital aspect of the store offer, which brings together all components of the retail brand, is customer service. Staff members are carefully selected to reflect their target customers. Because the target customer is likely to recommend stores by word of mouth, service is paramount. sweatyBetty staff members are important to the store atmospherics, being enthusiasts themselves, keeping fit and leading active lives. They are personified as 'Betties', a device prominent on the website. The shop staff know their products and their uses. Their stories feature heavily on the website, which also has useful links to local gyms, running clubs, registered personal trainers and rollerblading evenings. Exercise is seen as fun – and stylish fun at that – but it is recognised that there are more important things in life as well.

sweatyBetty: shops and website

Photographs and web image © sweatyBetty 2005. Reproduced with permission

sweatyBetty is a small, expanding chain that in the coming years will face all the issues that normally confront such businesses. There are plans to expand the number of stores in the London area and then to consider other urban areas in the United Kingdom. Store expansion is needed to generate scale and improve profitability of the company, yet control issues will arise over a larger, more dispersed business. Moreover, with its distinct culture, the company is a reflection of the founder and the staff, and it is unclear how this ethos would survive a large expansion or even a takeover. Such issues will keep the business fully occupied in the next few years.

Source: Adapted from Business Europe (2004) *SweatyBetty – Shaping up for a peak performance* 4 February 2004, retrieved 20 December 2004, from http://www.businesseurope.com/cmn/viewdoc.jsp?cat=all&docid= BEP1_Feature_0000061983; *Retail Verdict* (2004) sweatyBetty expands to tone up financial muscles, *Retail Verdict* 20 February 2004; SGBUK (1999) Sisters are doin' it for themselves, *Sporting Goods Business UK* 14 October:43; *Telegraph* (2004) The shops we can't do without, *Telegraph* 24 January:4; sweatyBetty (http://www.sweatybetty.com)

Question

1. In what ways do you feel women shop differently from men for sport products, and how could this be reflected in sports shops?

■ Store design and experiential consumption

Consumers have become more discerning in their shopping behaviour. For some segments of the market, the retail experience is as much the driving force for behaviours as the product itself. This implies that much more attention has to be paid to aspects of store design. Retail outlets are planned and managed consumption environments (this is as true of a discount store as it is for the most exclusive boutique), so design has always been a feature, but recent years have seen considerably more attention paid to design.

Table 17.6 lists some of the key features of some of the world's leading sports shops in a design sense. The presence of some major manufacturer brand shops in the list is significant, as is the connection of some of the operations to major sporting events (e.g., Euro 2004, Athens Olympics). From the shop descriptions, it would appear that these stores focus very much on the ambience (visual, aural) and the presentation of merchandise for consumers. A key theme is the idea of consumer impact.

It is notable that in a number of instances in Table 17.6, the idea of the store as a destination is indicated (e.g., REI and Niketown). These retailers also have in common a pursuit of what might be called experiential or spectacular consumption. US retailer REI has become noted for having areas of the stores where consumers can try products. The highly visual climbing walls have become a distinctive feature of the store design and layout. Store atmospherics are a critical part of the approach of REI, and this is allied to a strong sense of social and environmental responsibility, including in-store design and materials use. Such environmental concerns and store atmospherics are considerable attractions to consumers (Ogle, Hyllegard and Dunbar, 2004). In the United Kingdom, Tiso has pioneered this approach to trying out products in store and turning the store into a destination in the sport market. Tiso's Outdoor Experience stores in Glasgow and Edinburgh are the subject of Case 17.4.

Table 17.6 **Sports stars: design showcases**

Retailer	Description
Galyans, Chicago	Outdoor pursuits specialist Galyans' 90,000 product-strong store is non-conformist, with product dangling precariously overhead. Campsite roomsets suggest a series of options for the uninitiated outdoor enthusiast, with everything except the campfire appearing ready to use. Galyans has similar outlets in 21 other US cities.
Quiksilver, Sydney	Quiksilver's newest and biggest store, at Bondi Beach, targets devotees of the 'urban ocean'. The 45 light boxes on the ceiling aim to give the store an underwater feel. The outlet combines historical and contemporary design, with giant graphics of famous surf heroes and a history of board-short prints illustrated on surfboards.
Alvalaxia, Lisbon	Alvalaxia was built for Euro 2004 as an additional post-tournament revenue stream. This complex of sporting shops uses neutral colours, with plasma screens, acrylic cones that project light across open spaces and padded vinyl seating pods, all giving the place a futuristic ambience.
Citadium, Paris	Opened a couple of years ago and just moving into profit, PPR-owned Citadium is a stone's throw from its parent Printemps store on Boulevard Haussmann. This is a sporting superstore designed in a circle, with a central atrium to allow curious visitors to peer between floors and people watch.
Double-Park, Hong Kong	The floor to ceiling map at the entrance sets the tone for Hong Kong's small but distinctive Double-Park. Primarily an exhibition space selling sports goods, product is displayed on scaffolding fixtures in this dimly lit, quasi-urban environment. Suspended monitors add weight to the noisy ambience and wall-product displays.
Studio R, Kuala Lumpur	Within this warehouse format, coloured backlit panels highlight individual brands. A large space is allocated to each product so they are not jostling for impact in a crowded house. The blue Skechers and pink Adidas areas are particularly distinctive.
The Olympic Store, Athens	The athletics roadshow has left town and Athens' Olympic Store now caters predominantly for tourists. Resisting the temptation to create a low-budget, high-density souvenir free-for-all, the store's designers have opted for bleached pine floors and simple merchandising units with considerably more than the usual 1.25m clearance between each one. Real interior space for shoppers and design restraint in the face of rampant commercialism.
REI, Seattle	Created by mountaineers in 1944, Recreational Equipment Inc (REI) boasts a 20m-high climbing wall inside a six-storey glass and metal structure. This flagship store houses a 1,950m^2 landscaped courtyard, nature trail, waterfall and a mountain bike test area. It is a destination in its own right.
Puma, Athens	This outpost of the Puma empire may come as a surprise. In place of the normal wall of shoes, customers are presented with a series of pods, each seeking to make a hero of the training shoe. What it lacks in display density, it makes up for in impact.
Niketown, London	One of Europe's cutting-edge stores, Nike's central London flagship brings the brand to life with a series of innovative product concepts and displays. Visual merchandising follows suit, with interactive merchandising units, including one that uses a line of vaults to feature selected shoe styles.

Source: Sports Stars (2004) *Retail World*, October:26–7

CASE 17.4   Tiso: the outdoor experience

Tiso is an Edinburgh-based retailer (established in 1962) with 14 stores across the United Kingdom, specialising in outdoor clothing and equipment combined with high-quality customer service. Expansion has been primarily through its specialist high street stores, but in recent years, Tiso has also developed two larger and award-winning 'Outdoor Experience' venues at Glasgow and Edinburgh. Tiso has developed contract sales to organisations such as rescue groups, local authorities, outdoor centres and expeditions.

The Tiso Outdoor Experience aims to be a destination retail venue. Tiso describe it as 'a unique retail experience that is the ultimate shopping environment' and as 'Europe's most exciting outdoor equipment and clothing store, where you can browse, buy, eat, climb and learn… all in one spectacular setting'. Amongst the facilities (as described on the company's website) at Glasgow are:

- The Cairn Café – bringing you delicious homemade food to eat in or take away.
- Alpine Bikes – for the beginner to the dedicated mountain bike rider, Alpine Bikes shop and hire centre has everything you need for hitting the trail.
- 40ft Climbing Wall – you can climb free on 'The North Face' climbing pinnacle. Whether you are looking to test new climbing equipment or simply want to try your hand at climbing for the first time, our expert staff are on hand to assist you. All climbing gear is provided. Children over age 8 are very welcome and can become a member of our Pinnacle Club on reaching the summit! Look out for event over the coming year for Pinnacle Club members.
- Windstopper Fabrics Chill Zone – Test the warmth of our range of windstopper fleeces and jackets in the −20°C Chill Zone.
- 20ft Ice Climbing Wall – Scale Europe's first indoor ice climbing wall and test out your crampons and ice axe. Everyone welcome from beginners to expert climbers. Age 18 minimum. All climbing gear provided.
- Private or Corporate Functions – If you are looking to hold a function or seminar in a slightly different environment, why not consider the Glasgow Outdoor Experience! We have our own Lecture Theatre which is able to accommodate up to 70 people. We also have free parking and the Cairn café can meet any catering requirements.

At Edinburgh, the facilities are described as:

- The Cairn Café – bringing you delicious homemade food to eat in or take away.
- Tonic Health – providing a fresh approach to health and well-being with a range of treatments including Massage, Podiatry and Osteopathy plus daily pilates and yoga classes.
- A dedicated watersports department for sailing and leisure watersports.
- An improved camping are with permanently pitched tents on display.
- An expanded boot room and separate footwear department. We are also the home of the United Kingdom's only outdoor boot repair workshop run by our fully qualified and experienced repairer Roger Galloway.
- Not forgetting that we still have a Gore-Tex Waterproof Test shower, Boot path, Rucsac Test Ramp, Stove Test Area, Ice and Crampon Wall, Harness Drop test and Mini-Climbing Wall, Carrymat Test Bed and free customer parking.

This transformation from a seller of products, albeit with good range, reputation and customer service, to an experiential retail destination reflects the changing needs

Tiso: shops and website

Photographs and web image © Tiso 2005. Reproduced with permission

of consumers and the requirement for retail stores to offer much more by way of information and support and to attract customers all year round.

Tiso has developed a range of contact methods that inform, educate and encourage participation. These methods include:

- Extensive club and organisation links on the website
- Lectures, workshops, clinics and courses by noted experts, explorers and adventurers, held both at the stores and in the field
- A magazine for customers providing information and reinforcing contact, and feeding in to database development
- Sponsorship of athletes, particularly climbers and skiers

Source: Adapted from Tiso (http://www.tiso.com)

Question

1. Tiso claims to allow customers to 'browse, buy, eat, climb and learn'. In what ways do they engage in these experiential consumption activities? Are there other retailers developing similar approaches?

It was noted above that the retail store has always been a designed or manipulated space. This has perhaps received its fullest expression in themed retail outlets such as Niketown (Peñaloza, 1999; Sherry, 1998) and ESPN Zone (Kozinets, Sherry, Storm, Duhachek, Nuttavuthisit and DeBerry-Spence, 2004; Sherry, Kozinets, Storm, Duhachek, Nuttavuthisit and DeBerry-Spence, 2001; Sherry, Kozinets, Duhachek, DeBerry-Spence, Nuttavuthisit and Storm, 2004). Niketown, Chicago is described by Peñaloza (1999) as 'a consumption venue, a fastidiously designed five-storey combination of merchandise, celebrity athlete memorabilia and corporate tribute' (p. 338). The consumption of spectacle at Niketown (and at ESPN Zone), where the consumers are part of the 'show', is the key component of the store. Spectacular consumption behaviour is participative in nature, involves knowledge of the production of the spectacle and its consumption and involves consumption of space, cultural meanings and products in what may be termed a hybrid store/museum. Consumers move (or are moved) through spaces and produce meanings of competition, performance, style, recreation and consumption. Through the design, they interact with displays of sports celebrities, products and corporate identifiers. As in ESPN Zone (Kozinets, Sherry, DeBerry-Spence, Duhachek, Nuttavuthisit and Storm, 2002), such flagship brand stores or themed retail brand stores both provide additional engagement with the product and the brand (engage by experience) and satisfies the need for shopping (the retail experience) to be more entertaining or leisure based. Such extreme combinations of themes, leisure, sport and consumption are at the cutting edge of retail store design. It has to be noted, however, that such 'shops' do not fit everyone's needs. As with other sports retailing, they may be seen as particularly (male) gendered experiences (Sherry et al., 2004).

Consumers need this engagement and involvement on occasion, but they also need functional sports goods shopping on other occasions. These examples suggest that the thematic space for sports goods retailers is much broader than might have been imagined by a quick look down the high street.

Sports retailing and the internet

Occasionally in this chapter, reference has been made to the presence of sports retailers on the internet or retailers becoming multichannel operators. This approach has emerged more strongly in recent years. Initially, many sports retailers operated informational rather than transactional websites. One argument was that consumers needed to see and touch the fabric of, for example, shirts in order to assess their quality. However, as the internet has become more sophisticated and as consumers have adopted the technology and shown a general willingness to purchase electronically, so many websites have become fully transactional, and this channel has expanded. As a result, many of the retailers mentioned in this chapter, although not all, have an online transactional presence. For example, of the five leading UK sports retailers identified in Table 17.2, although (JD Sports, Blacks and Allsports) three have transactional websites, neither JJB Sports nor Sports World have more than an informational site.

The sports retail internet presence thus to an extent mirrors the 'real' market. The degree of success is dependent on the standard retail and distribution attributes and effectiveness. There are general sports retailers online such as JD Sports, but there are also more specialist sports retailers such as Fat Face (fatface.com), Cotton Traders and sweatyBetty. But the internet also offers some additional features that add to consumers' opportunities to purchase sport products. Table 17.7 selectively lists some of the opportunities in sports retailing on the internet, although in reality, the potential to set up sites is almost endless. Whether such sites can survive commercially, however, is a rather different question. Consumers online are able to deal directly with some manufacturers and brand holders, use a standard retailer, search for the cheapest price and the exclusive item or could bid at an auction site. If price is important, then comparison sites are a very useful tool, even if it is only to find out the going market price before buying on the high street. If it is an exclusive or hard-to-obtain item, then a web search may be a good way of tracking it down. This has particular importance in

Table 17.7 **Sports retailing: internet opportunities**

Opportunity	Description	Example
Standard retailing	Web versions of shop businesses	jdsports.co.uk fatface.com
Branded 'outlet' operation	Sells end-of-line products from brands and suppliers	mandmsports.com
General retailers 'hidden' under web names	Providing broader range of products than in existing stores	sport-e.com (littlewoods)
Price comparators	Sites that search websites for prices to allow comparison	kelkoo.co.uk
Auction and memorabilia sites	General person-to-person or business sites selling sporting memorabilia	ebay.co.uk sportsicons.co.uk
Sport organisations branching out	Clubs or organisations adding to store presence at ground (and elsewhere) by online sales	rfu.com/therugbystore http://superstore.celticfc.net/
Event-based merchandise	Selling licensed products associated with the event	londonmarathonstore.com
Brand manufacturer sites	Brand manufacturer dealing direct with public	reebokstore.co.uk

the area of sports memorabilia and sport product collection in which specialist sites have emerged. If the item needs customisation (e.g., a replica shirt), this again could be arranged online. Customers may be more in control via internet retailing. Whether these sites, however, can match the facilities in store, particularly if store design is properly thought through, is unlikely, but as with 'real' shops, there are good and poor examples of website design. Some sites have extensive visual, aural and interactive features that engage users in the product and the site atmosphere. Others are very functional.

Some caution is needed online, however, because things may not always be what they seem. Some organisations have been less than careful in protecting their possible domain names. For example, although Reebok has an online store (reebokstore.co.uk), the sites adidasstore.co.uk and nikestore.co.uk are somewhat different from what you might expect.

Conclusions

Sports retailing has had to react to considerable changes in sport, the consumer market and retailing itself. There has been a transformation from an equipment product focus to a clothing orientation, which is strongly fashion or leisure based. The breadth of sports and products available has increased, as has the volatility of consumer demand.

Sports retailing in the United Kingdom is dominated by a small number of specialist sports retailers, amongst which JJB Sports is the market leader. The sector has concentrated through takeovers and acquisitions, but at the same time, niche markets have opened up, allowing smaller retailers to prosper in some situations. Keys to success in retailing are understanding the target consumer market and designing the shop proposition to meet these consumers' aspirations and needs. Differences amongst retailers in terms of their store positioning are thus emerging more strongly at the edges of the main market, particularly in specialist areas (e.g., outdoor wear), certain markets (e.g., women) and 'new' sports (e.g., extreme or adventure sports). Some of this is organised by the retailers, but in sports retailing, manufacturer brands continue to retain significance for consumers. More recently, the internet has broadened the sports retail propositions.

The future of the sports retailing market will be of considerable interest. Profitability in the United Kingdom amongst the largest businesses is slight because of the competition amongst themselves, new mass market retail entrants and the ability of niche retailers to erode the core market. This suggests that there are likely to be more takeovers and acquisitions at all levels in the sector and that there will be a continuing search for formats that closely meet consumers' demands. Closer adaptation to target markets, both in real and virtual stores, is likely to see new and tighter formats emerge as all aspects of the retail operation are aligned with consumer demands. Retail stores will continue to adapt from a purely functional product-based approach to one that involves all aspects of consumers' expectations about sport and sports retailing.

Discussion question

1. What changes are occurring in the sports retailing market in the United Kingdom?

Guided reading

The sports goods retailing sector is large and significant in retailing terms, with four sports goods retailers in the top 100 retailers in the United Kingdom and the largest sports retailer having almost £1bn in sales. It is remarkable therefore that there is so little coverage of the sector in mainstream retailing texts. This is even more curious given the sports participation and brand recognition rates of teenagers and other student markets. None of the leading five retail textbooks (Davies and Ward, 2002; Freathy, 2003; Gilbert, 2003; McGoldrick, 2002; and Reynolds and Cuthbertson, 2004) contain any coverage of sports retailing. They are, however, rounded texts on retailing as a whole and on retail operations generally.

The best sources of information are market research and consultancy companies that either specialise in the sector (e.g., SGI Europe at http://www.sgieurope.com) or provide regular detailed market updates (e.g., Mintel, 2004a, 2004b or http://www.mintel.com), although these come at a price. Many of the retailers mentioned in this chapter have their own websites, which provide basic corporate information (to varying degrees of detail and quality) and from which downloadable public reports may be available. Simply visiting retail shops or surfing their websites also provides additional viewpoints and information about their operations. The trade press in the United Kingdom is also a reliable source of sports retailing news items, whether from a retail (*Retail Week*, http://www.retail-week.com/), a sports goods (*Sports Goods Business*, http://www.datateam.co.uk/business_publications/sgb_uk.htm) or a sports business (*Sport Business International*, http://www.sportbusiness.com) perspective.

Specialist academic retail journals include:

- *International Review of Retail, Distribution and Consumer Research*
- *International Journal of Retail and Distribution Management*
- *Journal of Retailing*
- *Journal of Retailing and Consumer Services*

And in sport:

- *Sport Marketing Quarterly*

Keywords

Activewear; assortment; casualwear; multiple or corporate retailers; experiential consumption; factory outlet store; fascias; floorspace; independent retailers; internationalisation; internet retailing; out-of-town superstore; retail park; superstores.

Bibliography

Burt, S.L. and Sparks, L. (2003) Power and competition in the UK grocery market, *British Journal of Management* 14:237–54.

Davies, B.J. and Ward, P. (2002) *Managing Retail Consumption*, Chichester: John Wiley.

Foresight (2001) Destination retail: A survey of young people's attitudes towards a career in retailing, Retail E-Commerce Task Force, *Foresight*, retrieved 20th December 2004, from http://www.foresight.gov.uk/

Freathy, P. (ed.) (2003) *The Retailing Book*, Harlow: FT Prentice Hall.

Garcia, B. (2003) *Where'd You Get Them? New York City's Sneaker Culture 1960–87*, New York: Powerhouse Cultural Entertainment Books.

Gilbert, D. (2003) *Retail Marketing Management*, 2nd edn, Harlow: Pearson.

Heard, N. (2003) *Trainers*. London: Carlton Books.

Kozinets, R.V., Sherry, J.F., DeBerry-Spence, B., Duhachek, A., Nuttavuthisit, K. and Storm, D. (2002) Themed flagship brand stores in the new millennium: Theory, practice, prospects, *Journal of Retailing* 78(1):17–29.

Kozinets, R.V., Sherry, J.F., Storm, D., Duhachek, A., Nuttavuthisit, K. and DeBerry-Spence, B. (2004) Ludic agency and retail spectacle, *Journal of Consumer Research* 31(3):658–72.

Martinez-Ribes, L. (1994) 'Intersport Spain: The management of strategic change in groups of retailers', in P.J. McGoldrick (ed.), *Cases in Retail Management*, London: Pitman, pp. 113–28.

McGoldrick, P.J. (2002) *Retail Marketing*, 2nd edn, Maidenhead: McGraw-Hill.

Mintel (2002) *Sportswear Retailing UK*, Mintel Retail Intelligence, January 2002, London: Mintel.

Mintel (2004a) *Sports Goods Retailing UK*, Mintel Retail Intelligence, March 2004, London: Mintel.

Mintel (2004b) *Sports Goods Retailing*, UK Retail Briefing, June 2004, London: Mintel.

Ogle, J.P., Hyllegard, K.H. and Dunbar, B.H. (2004) Predicting patronage behaviours in a sustainable retail environment, *Environment and Behaviour* 36(5):717–41.

Peñaloza, L. (1999) Just doing it: A visual ethnographic study of spectacular consumption at Niketown, *Consumption, Markets and Culture* 2(October):337–400.

Reynolds, J. and Cuthbertson, C. (2004) *Retail Strategy*, Oxford: Elsevier Butterworth-Heinemann.

Sherry, J.F. (1998) 'The soul of the company store: Niketown Chicago and the emplaced landscape', in J.F. Sherry (ed.), *Servicescapes*, Lincolnwood, IL: NTC Business Books, pp. 109–46.

Sherry, J.F., Kozinets, R.V., Storm, D., Duhachek, A., Nuttavuthisit, K. and DeBerry-Spence, B. (2001). Being in the Zone: Staging retail theatre at ESPN Zone Chicago, *Journal of Contemporary Ethnography* 30(4):465–510.

Sherry, J.F., Kozinets, R.V., Duhachek, A., DeBerry-Spence, B., Nuttavuthisit, K. and Storm, D. (2004) Gendered behaviour in a male preserve: Role playing at ESPN Zone Chicago. *Journal of Consumer Psychology* 14(1–2):151–8.

Vanderbilt, T. (1998) *Sneaker Book: Anatomy of an Industry and an Icon*, New York: The New Press.

Recommended websites

British Retail Consortium
http://www.brc.org.uk/

Independent Sports Retailers Association
http://www.thesportslife.com/isra.htm

Institute for Retail Studies, University of Stirling
http://www.irs.stir.ac.uk

Online Sports Links Directory
http://www.sports365.co.uk/

Sport Business International
http://www.sportbusiness.com

Sport Industry Research Centre
http://www.shu.ac.uk/schools/slm/sirc.html

Sporting Goods Intelligence
http://www.sgieurope.com

Sporting Goods Manufacturers Association
http://www.sgma.com/

Sports Goods Business
http://www.datateam.co.uk/business_publications/sgb_uk.htm

Sports Textiles and Footwear Association
http://www.thesportslife.com/st&fa.htm

The Sports Industries Federation
http://www.thesportslife.com/

World Federation of the Sporting Goods Industry
http://www.wfsgi.org/

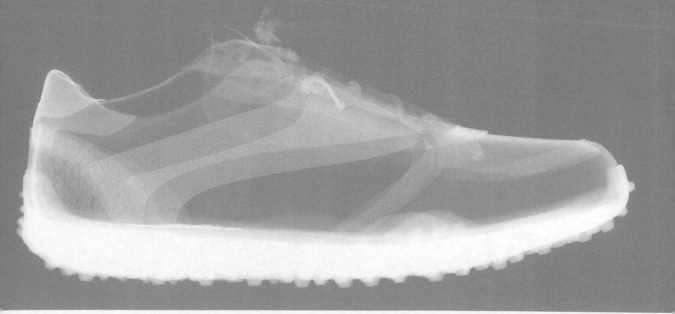

Part Five

Moving sport marketing forwards

Chapter 18

Strategic sport marketing

Dr Dave Arthur
Southern Cross University, Australia

Learning outcomes

Upon completion of this chapter, the reader should be able to:

- Define what is meant by strategic sport marketing, distinguishing it from a more operational perspective.

- Detail a model for developing a sport marketing strategy.

- Consider alternatives strategies sport marketers can implement.

- Explain the likely marketing, management and organisational implications of using different strategies.

- Undertake each of the above using a range of examples to highlight key areas for consideration by strategists in sport marketing.

Overview of chapter

This chapter looks at a range of issues associated with the process of developing sound sport marketing strategy. Central to the chapter is the proposal of a 'model for developing sport marketing strategy' composed of five distinct but overlapping stages. The model recommends a process to be undertaken by sporting organisations as they embark on a marketing strategy designed to achieve various marketing-related objectives. In addition, throughout the chapter, various examples of how sport marketers can apply the theoretical constructs are given with a view of guiding sport organisations to develop innovative and dynamic strategies that will enable them to compete in the marketplace.

Introduction

As Duan and Burrell (1995) indicate, 'There is a growing realization that survival and success in the future will come only from sound strategic planning and market preparation' (p. 5). That said, it is vitally important that the term 'strategy' is adequately understood. In broad terms, strategy is the process by which an organisation pulls all its resources together to fulfil its overall mission and objectives. Allen, O'Toole, Harris and McDonnell (2005, p. 186) advanced a number of key points about strategy:

- It is longer term rather than short term.
- It is not another word for *tactics*.
- It is based on careful analysis of both internal resources and external environments.
- It is essential to survival.

Marketing strategy is a process of planning, implementing and controlling marketing efforts to meet the goals of an organisation while at the same time satisfying consumer needs. In terms of sport marketing, it is a relatively simple step to use this definition provided the unique aspects of sport are taken into account during the strategic planning process. Mullin, Hardy and Sutton (2000) cautioned likewise in saying that every element of marketing required a significantly different approach when applied to the participant and spectator groups within sport. The major differences resulted from the unique aspects of the sport product and the unusual market conditions facing the sport marketer. According to Summers and Johnson (2000), these unique aspects relate to the:

- Market for sport products and services
- Sport product itself
- Price of sport
- Promotion of sport
- Sport distribution system

Mullin et al. (2000, p. 22) give a suitable definition of sport marketing strategy:

In its simplest sense, strategy entails setting long-term goals and developing plans to achieve those goals. This requires a continual analysis of the environment and the organisation. The challenges of today's marketplace have forced sport executives to think much more strategically.

Each of these aspects is addressed in this chapter via the proposition of a five-stage model of strategic sport marketing.

A model for developing a sport marketing strategy

There is no doubt that the marketing direction of an organisation, sporting or otherwise, should take its direction from the overall philosophy of that same organisation. In sport marketing terms, this is usually communicated via the development of a sport marketing plan. From the outset, however, it should be noted that it is essential that any plan, whatever its focus, be integrated into the larger strategic planning of the sporting organisation.

In marketing terms, Dann and Dann (2004) opine that 'effective marketing strategy depends on fully integrating the goals of the corporate, strategic, business and marketing plans of the organisation.' In sport marketing terms, Shilbury, Quick and Westerbeek (2003) intimate that the delineation between overall strategic planning and strategic marketing planning in sporting organisations is often indistinguishable.

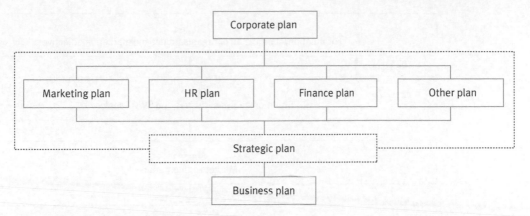

Figure 18.1 **Elements of the strategic plan**

As Figure 18.1 shows, other elements of the business plan include aspects such as finance, human resource management and asset management. Without such integration, there will be little conformation between the organisational functions responsible and little coherence between plans. Given this information, Figure 18.2 illustrates a five-stage model of strategic sport marketing used as the basis for further discussion in this chapter.

Stage 1: Formulation and clarification of organisational and marketing objectives

As alluded to previously, there should be a realisation that all strategic decisions flow from the overall mission of the organisation concerned. Nash (1988) believes a mission statement should be a central statement that defines what the business is and what it will become including, for example, major corporate goals. It is from the mission statement that strategy formulation takes its cue. Similarly it is from the mission statement that marketing objectives are formulated and consequently where marketing strategy emanates.

According to Reed (1997), the marketing objectives of an organisation can be divided into marketing stance objectives and marketing performance objectives.

Marketing stance is essentially a distillation of the mission statement with a focus on the parts that affect the overall marketing effort. Marketing performance, on the other hand, is related to the end product of the marketing effort – sales volumes, market share and profit. To be effective, any objective should be:

- **Specific:** Defines the end result to be achieved
- **Measurable:** You should know when it has been achieved
- **Attainable:** The objective is able to be achieved but should require effort
- **Relevant:** They must contribute to the organisation's goals
- **Trackable:** They must provide a 'yardstick' of achievement at given intervals

In addition, Reed (1997, p. 105) suggests that 'all sets of objectives should include two components: qualitative and quantitative dimensions.' Notwithstanding how marketing

Figure 18.2 The five-stage model of strategic sport marketing. SWOT = strengths, weaknesses, opportunities and threats
Source: Adapted from Shilbury et al. (2003)

objectives are constructed, they should guide the formulation of the marketing strategy to follow. In terms of a tennis club, marketing objectives could look something like this:

- To increase the enrollment of girls aged 11 to 15 in the 'Try Tennis' programme from 25 (2005) to 45 (2006).
- To increase to satisfaction levels of boys aged 11 to 15 in the 'Try Tennis' programme from average to above average.

Combined they conform to the SMART mnemonic and have qualitative and quantitative aspects.

After the marketing objectives have been satisfactorily set, the sporting entity can move through to the second stage of the strategic sport marketing process.

Stage 2: Situation analysis

Dann and Dann (2004) suggest that stage 2 should include an analysis of the current marketing conditions as they relate to the following 'situations' (p. 398):

1. Market situation
2. Product situation
3. Competitive situation
4. Distribution situation
5. Macroenvironment situation

Although this represents an 'ideal' approach, for practical purposes, this can be distilled into two distinct aspects: an issues analysis and a SWOT analysis.

Issues analysis

Sporting organisations should never be looked at as operating in some sort of vacuum, and marketing planning should always involve a robust analysis of the broader environment. The sport organisation's marketing system must work effectively within the framework of these broad forces despite the fact that they are largely not controllable by management. Such issues are wide ranging and ever changing, but some to consider with regard to sport include technology, foreign competition, an ageing population and women in sport.

Technology The impact of technology in the sport environment has increased markedly in the past decade. Access to international sport events via subscription television is now globally commonplace, and some major sport franchises have even established their own television channels as an additional revenue stream. Further technological advancements have seen the rise of both the internet and mobile telephones as delivery platforms.

Foreign competition Hand in hand with technological advancement has been an ability of non-traditional sports to compete in foreign markets without the necessity of playing games overseas. The National Basketball Association (NBA) has developed major merchandising markets in Europe that are in direct competition with local versions of the sport. Similarly, in Australia, the NBA competes for merchandising revenue with the National Basketball League (NBL).

An ageing population The development of a sport within a particular region is influenced by this factor. For example, this type of population has influenced the establishment of a new National Rugby League (NRL) franchise in the Gold Coast region of Queensland, Australia, because it has a population profile that is ageing because of the influx of sea changers and retirees to the area.

Women in sport Increased exposure of women's sport (e.g., cricket, netball, football and swimming) and the increasing role of women as a key target audience for traditional sports have seen sports undertake innovative sport marketing mixes as they reposition themselves in the marketplace.

The SWOT analysis

The SWOT analysis is an often used and well-known aspect that should be included as part of the situation analysis. Its use is widespread in sport marketing. It is so called because it involves the identification of the aspects of the sport organisation shown in Table 18.1.

Porter (1985) presents the five forces model that has been used by a number of authors as a framework for analysis of competition in particular and goes so far as to comment that 'the essence of strategy formulation is coping with competition' (Porter, 1985, p. 87). He suggests that organisations should consider these distinct forces:

1. Intensity of competition
2. Bargaining power of buyers
3. Threat of substitute products
4. Bargaining power of suppliers
5. Threat of new entrants

Table 18.1 **Generic SWOT analysis**

Internal	
Strengths may lie in the quality of staff, the organisation's financial structure or the high quality of its product range.	**Weaknesses** may lie in the organisation's lack of available capital, lack of club members or poor relationships with the media.
External	
Opportunities may include the development of new products, expansion to different geographic regions or a general growth in the size of the target market.	**Threats** may include changing trends within the target market, entry of competitors into the marketplace or global economic recession.

It is a good idea to develop a specific set of criteria that can be used to evaluate your sporting organisation in the marketplace and is necessarily quite subjective because it involves some manner of prediction or vision. Care should be taken with all aspects. Brooks (1994) emphasises this in saying 'outside your organisational structure is just as important as what happens inside' (p. 281).

CASE 18.1   SWOT analysis

You have been appointed as the marketing director for a large health and fitness facility operating in a major regional centre. An adequate marketing plan is in place, but it was written 3 years before you were appointed. Based on some of the information given above (and that referred to in other chapters), undertake a SWOT analysis for the facility (see the information below to help you):

Strengths	Weaknesses
■ Many product lines [e.g., circuit, spinning, machine and free weights, aerobics (variety of class types)]	■ Some obsolete equipment, class structure and types
■ Quality facilities (e.g., change rooms, spa, sauna, café, off-street parking)	■ Deteriorating facility (no maintenance of building)
■ Location	■ Facility too small
■ Strong market appeal across segments	■ No up-to-date marketing plan
■ Friendly staff	■ No market research programme
■ Management with good marketing skills and knowledge	■ Lack of qualified staff
■ Excellent reputation within the marketplace	■ Not enough staff to cope with demand
■ Cost advantages over competitors	■ Poor prior management and leadership
■ Good financial management and resources	■ Growth without direction
	■ High conflict between management and staff

Opportunities	Threats
■ Increasing population base	■ Shifting population
■ Emerging new market segments (e.g., elderly)	■ Increasing competition
■ Expanding product range (e.g., boxercise, pilates)	■ Change in consumer tastes and demand
■ Extend cost or differentiation advantages	■ Rise in new and alternative products
• Diversify into new areas (e.g., social club/bar/health food outlet);	■ New forms of industry competition (e.g., swimming centres developing aquarobics)
■ Overcome barriers to participation (e.g., child minding, females only times)	■ Potential for takeover
	■ Changing demographic factors
	■ Changes in economy
	■ Industry regulation
	■ Rising labour costs

At the completion of this stage, there is a need to briefly revisit stage 1 and when necessary, reassess the marketing objectives set in the light of the issues and SWOT analysis not previously considered. Mullin et al. (2000) believe that Nike has done this over the last 15 years as it moved from a focus on the running shoe market into sporting equipment ranging from replica jerseys to sunglasses and watches.

After this reassessment is done, the sporting organisation can proceed to the third stage of the strategic sport marketing process.

Stage 3: Market segmentation

This particular stage involves the practical use of previous market research methods to identify, describe and justify the target market segments chosen. Segmentation allows the tailoring of a marketing mix that will allow the sport marketer to design product benefits, set prices and develop promotional and distribution strategies to serve the needs of the target market(s). This means that instead of having a single product style or design, a single price, a single promotional programme and a single distribution strategy for all customers, the sport marketer could have separate marketing mixes for each segment or one marketing mix for a specific segment. There are three basic marketing segmentation strategies that can be used for sport:

1. **Undifferentiated marketing** focuses upon targeting what all or most of the consumers have in common and ignores the existence of segmentation within the marketplace;
2. **Concentrated segmentation** focuses upon a single target market with a single marketing mix.
3. **Multiple segmentation** focuses upon several distinct target markets and develops a separate marketing mix for each of the markets it wishes to reach.

In segmenting the target market, Mullin et al. (2000) use the following categorisations:

1. The consumer's state of being (demographic)
2. The consumer's state of mind (psychographic)

3. Product usage
4. Product benefits

They also emphasise the fluidity of the segments and that sport marketers would typically use cross-sections to describe particular segments. For example, rather than describe a segment as living within 5km of a facility, they would more likely be described as male, single professionals with high disposable income who have attended five netball games with their partner for social activity. In more detail, the general categorisations are demographic, geographic, psychographic and behavioural.

Demographic

Demographic segmentation refers to the target market in terms of, for example, what it earns, its gender, religion or stage in the lifecycle (e.g., single, married with children, empty nester). Whereas the promotion of rugby union in Australia has traditionally focused upon the 'white collar' professional, rugby league has been promoted as the 'blue collar' game. Similarly, a sport such as snow skiing has attracted a different social class than that attracted to darts.

Geographic

Geographic segmentation is not only concerned with where the particular segment is located but also incorporates logistical issues in serving the segment. Just because a particular person is located close to a stadium does not mean he or she will consume the sport 'live and in person'. The individual may instead prefer to consume vicariously such as, from his or her armchair watching pay television. Sport marketers have to understand that people's needs and wants are often influenced by geographic variables. For example, the place where they live may determine the sports they undertake, the sports they are exposed to and their access to facilities and events.

Psychographic

Psychographic segmentation attempts to explain consumer behaviour in terms of the reasons for purchase and the extrinsic and extrinsic needs purchase may meet. Lifestyle segmentation is often used by sport marketers to help refine a sport's promotional efforts by showing how a product will fit into a consumer's life. This provides an understanding of not only how consumers act but also how they think, and it is usually measured in terms of activities, interests and opinions.

Behavioural

Behavioural segmentation refers to the benefits and usages attributed to the purchase and subsequent consumption of the product or service. Different people seek different benefits in products. For example, whereas basketball appeals as a total family entertainment package, boxing is less likely to have such family appeal. Similarly, a person may attend a polo match not because he or she has a passion for horses or the sport in general but because it is 'the' place to be seen. In terms of usage, segments are divided into heavy, moderate and light categories. To the sport marketer, the heavy user is a highly valuable segment and often accounts for 80% of product usage.

Once the sport marketer has settled on the range of target markets, the organisation is ready to move to stage 4 of the strategic marketing process.

Stage 4: Development of an integrated marketing mix

In stage 4, an appropriate marketing mix is developed for each of the target markets identified previously. Reed (1997) suggests that there are two categories of marketing strategies available: industry-level competitive positioning strategies and marketing mix strategies.

The former are the 'grand strategies' that the organisation wishes to undertake in order to achieve its overall business objectives. Reed (1997) comments 'they are concerned with finding ways of effectively positioning the organisation against its competitors to create and maintain a sustainable competitive advantage' (p. 112). Marketing level strategies, although naturally following those at the industry level are, however, 'the strategic decisions concerned with products, prices, distribution and marketing communication'. Dann and Dann (2004) have developed an 11-point approach for setting marketing strategies. Broadly this encompasses:

1. Who exactly is the target market?
2. How is or how will the product be positioned in the marketplace?
3. What is the product line?
4. What pricing strategy will be used?
5. How will the product be distributed?
6. What sort of sales workforce will be required to distribute the product?
7. What service levels are required?
8. What is the general marketing strategy?
9. What sales promotions will be used?
10. What research and development will be required?
11. What sort of marketing research will be required?

The marketing-level strategies concerning product, price, distribution and promotion will be dealt with in the following section.

Product strategies

According to Summers and Johnson (2000), the sport product is distinct from others through its:

- Universal appeal
- Experiential nature
- Simultaneous competition and cooperation
- Lack of control over the core product
- Categorisation as both an industrial and a core product

Each of these factors brings unique challenges for sport marketers. At the core of the challenge is what Reed (1997) referred to as product item, or brand decisions. In terms of sporting goods, most major manufacturers of sports shoes have a range of products that ostensibly perform a similar function. This is referred to as the *product line*. In addition, those same manufacturers produce a range of products, not just sport shoes but also t-shirts, tennis rackets, caps and shorts. This is referred to as the *product mix*. As, for example an owner of a sports shop, you are faced with ongoing decisions as to which product lines to stock and further, which individual products (from a range of suppliers) form part of those lines.

To effectively develop a product strategy, there is an obvious requirement to understand the needs, wants, perceptions and attitudes towards the particular product. Kotler (1997) and Kotler and Armstrong (2004) suggest four alternative market strategies; market penetration, market development, product development and diversification.

Market penetration

Market penetration attempts to persuade *existing* consumers to consume at a higher rate. For example, a sporting organisation that attracts paying spectators could encourage current members to increase their frequency of attendance. Mullin et al. (2000) developed the 'attendance/participation frequency escalator' as an approach to facilitate this. The model operates on the principle that it is easier and cheaper to get existing consumers to buy more than it is to attract new ones.

Market development

Market development, on the other hand, attempts to increase the volume of products sold to *new* consumers. This can be achieved by getting a bigger share of existing consumers to purchase your product and service. You may classify your consumers in this approach in terms of their readiness to purchase your product. Here people move along a 'stages of readiness' continuum, typically by better or more promotions (Stotlar, 1993, p. 55).

Product development

Product development is expansion via the creation of new products or services to meet the needs of existing markets. An example of this is Nike, which has developed lines of sporting apparel to complement its initial range of sport shoes. In terms of new product development, there is an interesting challenge. In a fast-moving industry such as the fitness industry in which product life cycles are often short and the need to find new niches compelling, new product development can be an important and necessary revenue stream. Reed (1997) suggests a systematic, staged approach to new product development consisting of:

1. **Idea generation:** Emanates from and should reflect the mission statement
2. **Screening:** Sorts the 'prospects from the suspects'
3. **Idea evaluation:** Composed of concept testing and product testing
4. **Marketing strategy development:** A preliminary marketing strategic plan
5. **Product development:** Physical development of the actual product
6. **Test marketing:** Tests the developed strategies before a final yes or no decision is made
7. Commercialisation: If yes, a planned launch is enacted

Diversification

Diversification occurs when an organisation creates new products for new clients. For example, the National Football League in the United States diversified into logo licensing (clothing, souvenirs) in 1963 and now generates significant revenue through this source.

As alluded to in previous chapters, all products, sporting or otherwise, pass through a definite product life cycle. The product life cycle is composed of four stages – introduction, growth, maturity and decline – although some authors have added a further phase termed 'competitive turbulence' between growth and maturity. Sales tend to rise through the first two stages, peak in the maturity stage and decline thereafter. It is vitally important that sport marketers have an appreciation of where their products 'fit' at a given point in time and develop product strategies accordingly. In a fitness centre with a range of classes, profits will start to fall at some stage as, for example, a particular type of class fades in popularity and reaches the decline stage. At this point, there is a requirement to make cost reductions, and unprofitable parts of the product mix (i.e., the particular class) could be phased out altogether.

Pricing strategies

As with many aspects of the strategic sport marketing process, various pricing goals should be developed that conform with both corporate- and marketing-level objectives set as part of stage 1. According to Pride and Ferrell (1991) these objectives generally fall into seven categories: survival, profit, return on investment, market share, cash flow, status quo and product quality. In addition, such goals should take into account the supply and demand equation as it relates not only to the cost structure of the sporting organisation but also to the external environment in which the organisation operates.

Price sensitivity is measured by price elasticity of demand. If, for example, ticket prices to regular season matches are raised or lowered and there is no effect on demand, the market is said to be price inelastic. On the other hand, if a hike in price causes a fluctuation in demand (either up or down), then the market is said to be price elastic. The elasticity of demand varies according to product categories. Petrol and food staples such as bread and milk are relatively inelastic given that they are required for day-to-day existence. Sporting goods could be viewed as relatively elastic given that such items are usually purchased with disposable income and are not essential. This aspect links with identified market segments as some (e.g., single, male professionals with no children as opposed to unmarried mothers) would be able to more easily bear a price rise within their chosen sport.

Reed (1997) suggests there are also minimum and maximum prices that a potential purchaser is prepared to pay. For example, a tennis racket manufacturer has segmented the market and wishes to sell to club players who participate once a week during summer. If the racket is priced too, low target market perceptions regarding quality come to the fore and may cause consumers to reject it. Similarly, if the racket is priced too high, prospective buyers within the target market may feel it is aimed at a more serious participant and also reject it.

Sales do not, however, depend merely on unit price but also on other factors such as competitor pricing and the surrounding marketing activity. In addition, pricing decisions should also reflect the product's relative position in the product life cycle. For example, in the introductory phase 2, generic pricing strategies are usually taken into account. Firstly, the sport marketer could adopt a penetration strategy whereby the product is priced low. In pricing in this way, a high volume of sales is required, and the strategy is commonly used in which prospective buyers are price sensitive. Alternatively, the sport marketer could adopt a skimming policy whereby the product is priced high. Such a strategy sets a high reference point and quality perception in the minds of prospective purchasers and is a frequently used strategy to launch new products in which competitors are few and far between.

■ Distribution strategies

Strategies regarding where a particular sporting product can be purchased or consumed are termed *distribution strategies*. Put simply, it is all about getting the right product to the right customer at the right place at the right price (Reed, 1997). It is vitally important because significant competitive advantage can be achieved through an effective and efficient distribution strategy. Shilbury et al. (2000) suggest four variables associated with place: facility planning, physical evidence, process and people.

We will look here at the role of the facility and the role of traditional and non-traditional media. Shilbury et al. (2002) believe that the facility is the most important strategy for distribution; however, there are a variety of other strategies available for the distribution of the sport product. Organisations that combine to allow the distribution of the product are generally referred to as the *marketing channel*. The sporting facility is an essential facet of sport marketing mix and has become very important in the way sport is consumed. Nowadays facilities are well designed and able to handle vast numbers of spectators in comfort and safety with many now among the 'icon' structures of the modern world, especially when combined with 'icon' sports (e.g., test cricket from Lord's or the Melbourne Cricket Ground, rugby union from Twickenham or tennis from Flushing Meadow). Notwithstanding this, there is a comparatively simple distribution channel involved (Figure 18.3).

However, these channels become more complicated as the distribution of the sport becomes more widespread (Figure 18.4).

The media in its various forms has had a huge impact on the manner in which sport products are distributed. Not only do they open up hitherto unreachable target markets for sport but they can also provide significant revenue streams.

Figure 18.3 **The simple distribution channel for a Rugby Union event**

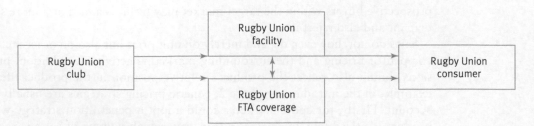

Figure 18.4 **The distribution channel for a Rugby Union event with free to air TV coverage**

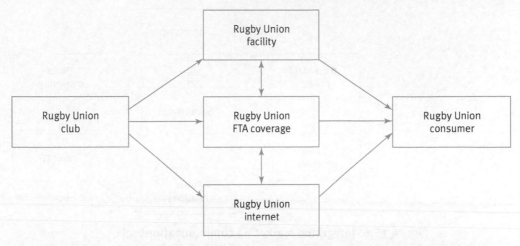

Figure 18.5 The distribution channel for a Rugby Union event with free to air TV coverage and internet coverage

Similarly, the emergence of new technologies has complicated the distribution channels even further (Figure 18.5).

The situation becomes even more complicated if the sport product is more tangible – a tennis racket as opposed to a particular game or event. Here the sport marketer may be faced with decisions regarding agents, wholesalers and retailers. In terms of deriving distribution strategies from marketing channels, Reed (1997) suggests the following steps be undertaken:

1. Conduct market research into customer needs and wants.
2. Choose distribution outlets.
3. Estimate costs.
4. Make a decision.
5. Implement the decision.

Marketing communication strategies

The major objective of any marketing communication strategy (Figure 18.6) is the integration of the various elements of the promotional mix into a structured, coherent integrated marketing communications programme that implicitly links to the marketing objectives set in stage 1.

The promotional mix (as illustrated in Figure 18.6) is composed of the following overlapping elements:

- **Advertising:** Perhaps the best-known element, this includes paid advertisements or commercials that appear in mainstream media such as newspapers, magazines, on radio or on billboards. Sport teams regularly advertise upcoming games, and peak bodies often advertise the benefits of regular participation.

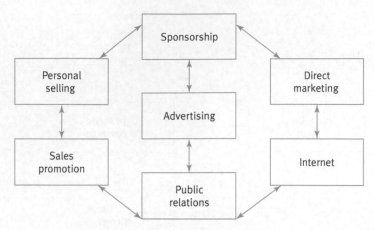

Figure 18.6 **Integrated marketing communications mix**

- **Sales promotions:** These are short-term incentives that encourage immediate purchase. Sporting organisations have become adept at sales promotion strategies such as buy an adult ticket and get a free child's ticket or a limited edition t-shirt or guest cards in fitness centres where a full member may bring a guest for a free trial of the facilities.
- **Personal selling:** This is selling through simple 'one-on-one' communication that, although comparatively expensive, is among the most effective promotional strategies. The selling of corporate sponsorship or venue hospitality suites are areas where personal selling is commonplace.
- **Sponsorship:** A highly visible promotional element that can be used to achieve a range of communication objectives, including increased awareness, changing public perception and employee motivation. A look at the front or sleeve of a team jersey gives many examples of its increasing use.
- **Public relations:** Used as a management tool to establish and maintain relationships between organisations and their various publics. Within sport public relations, public relations is increasingly used when crises have occurred and need to be addressed – for example, when racial vilification has occurred or when an athlete has been accused of a serious crime.
- **Direct marketing:** Composed of elements such as direct mail, telemarketing or even television, this promotional strategy communicates directly with target markets with a view to stimulating sales either in the short or long term. A good example is the use of a database to maintain and record contact with members. When opportunities arise (e.g., season ticket offers) the member can be easily reached through a mailout or via telephone and informed of the offer.
- **Internet:** This increasingly popular element of the promotional mix can range from a website where merchandise or tickets for sporting events can be purchased through to simple online brochures promoting an upcoming seminar.

The challenge for sport marketers is to determine how effectively and efficiently the various elements of the marketing mix can communicate with each target market to achieve the organisation's marketing objectives.

CASE 18.2   Rainbow Region Masters Games

The Rainbow Region Masters Games is a major, regional, multisport event that involves approximately 2500 people in participation, organisation and management. Originally conceived in 1997 as a means to promote the City of Lismore, it has evolved into a highly successful, well-patronised biannual event of significant regional importance. The economic value of the Games to the region has been estimated at approximately $1m. In the three games so far, attendance has risen, and post-event surveys have indicated exceptional levels of customer satisfaction. However, the most profit made by the Games was in the inaugural event, and key stakeholders are keen to make more money. Much of the event's non-financial success is directly attributable to a highly motivated organising committee composed of individuals with a deep practical knowledge of a variety of event-related issues. Alas, the organisers possess limited knowledge of strategic marketing and believe they would benefit from gaining some.

Questions

1. As a sport marketing consultant, you have been approached to recommend a framework with which the organisers can formulate a strategic marketing plan to take the event to the next level. You are also required to outline a range of strategies by which the organisers can increase awareness of the event, increase attendance at future events and increase the overall profit of the event.

2. Consider the model of strategic sport marketing proposed in this chapter and recommend to Games organisers exactly what they should do next and why.

Stage 5: Implementation, control and evaluation

Stage 5 is the ultimate stage in which the product, price, distribution and promotion strategies decided upon as part of stage four are put into practice in a coordinated manner. At this stage, it is important to consider the financial implications of the marketing planning strategies decided upon in stage 4. Reed (1997, p. 319) suggests that a 'broad brush view of the proposed marketing strategies is all that is required as detailed budget information is more appropriately specified in annual (operational) marketing plans.' That said, it is also wise here to look at the selection target groups and prioritise them if it has not been done before. This is because costs may need to be allocated to ensure that all the target groups are reached. It also allows the sport marketer to make decisions depending upon resources that are eventually available.

Implementation

Kotler defines marketing implementation as a process that 'turns marketing strategies and plans into marketing actions in order to accomplish strategic marketing objectives' (Kotler, 1989, p. 635, cited in Shilbury et al., 2002). Thus, the first stage is to prepare a comprehensive plan of action whereby personnel are assigned tasks to complete by a given date: Who does what by when? Effective implementation also depends to a great extent on the actual sport organisation, including its structure, culture and overall view of the marketing concept. Put simply, without a sympathetic organisation, implementation will be poor and the strategies will fail.

Control

The success (or otherwise) of implemented strategies should be evaluated. Marketing control involves measuring and evaluating performance and, when necessary, taking corrective action. A simple marketing control system may involve:

- Initial benchmarking against an appropriate standard
- The measurement of actual performance
- Evaluation of the actual performance against the benchmark
- The taking of corrective action where necessary

Evaluation

It is essential that any evaluation undertaken is related to the original objectives stated in stage 1 and is one reason that objectives should be stated in SMART terms.

Sport marketers should also be aware of and undertake some ongoing evaluation. This needs to be considered and identified, allowing the sport marketer to monitor the progress of the marketing strategy. This process includes asking and answering questions such as: What strategies are working during the campaign? Which ones need to be supplemented with more funds, time or resources? Regular reviews and reports will help in this regard. Evaluation in relation to all market segments should also be considered because, for example, some strategies may have had little or no impact on a specific target group.

Although specifically referring to the event industry, Getz (1997) identifies three key periods when evaluation is useful. They can be adapted to the strategic sport marketing environment:

1. **Pre-implementation:** Involves some manner of benchmarking and market research
2. **Monitoring:** Tracking the progress of the strategy during implementation
3. **Post-implementation:** The gathering of information after implementation and an analysis of them in relation to marketing objectives

At this stage, it is vital that the information gleaned from the various evaluations is fed back into the strategy process to enable responses to changing market conditions.

Further aspects of implementation, control and evaluation are dealt with in more detail in Chapter 21.

CASE 18.3   You've got to know what the goal is

Marketers have to be sure of what they want to achieve through links with football, writes Steve Hemsley. Vodafone's Mark Bond was probably the only Englishman in Lisbon to grab any crumbs of comfort from David Beckham's penalty misses against France and Portugal at Euro 2004. The brand's director of business marketing has recently negotiated a three-year extension of Vodafone's sponsorship of the world's most famous footballer, so he welcomed any additional column inches.

Bond has also secured a new contract for Vodafone's sponsorship of Manchester United, up from the £30m paid previously to £36m for a new four-year deal.

United have the most valuable club brand in Europe worth €288m according to FutureBrand, and as Beckham now plays for Real Madrid – Europe's second most valuable soccer brand, worth €278m – Vodafone has two of the main football bases covered as it uses the sport to retain and acquire customers globally.

Like its rival Siemens, which has branding deals with Real Madrid and Bayern Munich; and T-Mobile, an official partner at Euro 2004, Vodafone is happy to keep pumping money into football.

As top football brands increase their geographical and demographic reach, the potential for associated products to build a global customer base is huge. But so is the financial commitment involved if an advertiser is to stand out from the crowd in what can be a cluttered market. Marketers need to ensure that they don't get carried away by the goals and the glamour.

The question for the mobile operators now is whether they will start to demand exclusivity and begin to outbid other media owners to obtain certain rights. Bond insists he is more interested in good content rather than exclusivity. Indeed, Vodafone is considering launching a service where users would pay to be the first to hear post-match player interviews from the likes of David Beckham. Such an initiative would appeal to his thousands of fans at home and around the world, particularly in the Far East, and generate significant revenue in the process.

Bond says that football is being used by the mobile companies to drive brand preference. 'There are two reasons why mobile operators are getting into football. First, the sport enables them to connect customers with their passions and interact with people in personal moments when their side has scored a goal or won a game. Second, there are many additional revenue streams available from exploiting football content. Mobile is simply an additional form of communication,' he says.

The wider adoption of 3G technology will mean even more opportunities to market attractive mobile content. Vodafone and 3 will offer match highlights an hour after the final whistle from next month, following their joint rights deal with the FA Premier League, for instance.

But advertisers that are spending large sums on football sponsorship need to make sure that the millions of pounds they allocate actually generate additional sales as well as brand awareness. 'You must be clear about what you are trying to achieve through football sponsorship, and this must be aligned with the overall business and brand strategy if it is to provide real shareholder value,' says Marco Forato, head of brand analytics at FutureBrand.

This is important because brands can lose focus when getting involved in what is arguably the world's first global sport. There is the risk a company's message will be lost among the brand clutter that can suffocate major tournaments such as Euro 2004 or the World Cup where everything from perimeter boards, shirt sponsorship, big-screen commercials and programme advertising is screaming to attract fans' attention.

A survey by Sport Business Group demonstrates how brand messages can get diluted. It claims that after the last World Cup in 2002, more than 30 per cent of people questioned recalled Coca-Cola's sponsorship around the event. Brands such as Hyundai and JVC failed to reach 20 per cent. With this in mind, Coca-Cola, Hyundai and JVC, who are official partners of Euro 2004, welcomed UEFA's decision to reduce the number of official sponsors for the tournament in Portugal from 22 at the last European Championships to 18 this time.

'The winning brands will be those that can find new ways to stand out. Yet shareholders will always argue that companies will only get real value from their involvement in football if it is translated into more business,' says Forato. 'Brands must be more innovative to motivate fans who are surrounded by so many commercial messages when they attend a football match or watch a game on television.'

It is the power of television and the appeal of football across the globe which really gets brands excited when planning their global marketing strategy. The FA Premier League is the most successful league in Europe when it comes to raising commercial revenue, and when it recently renegotiated its television rights for territories outside the UK it generated £300m.

This represented a 60 per cent increase on the amount received last time these negotiations took place in 2001, as the Premiership is now watched by 15.2bn people on television every year, up from 13.8bn three years ago, according to Octagon Marketing, the sports marketing company.

Phil Carling, the former Football Association's commercial director, who is now head of football at Octagon, says there are two games being played in the football industry – a technical one on the pitch and a commercial one off it, although they are intrinsically linked. 'Brands know football can help them to achieve global objectives and they want to be linked with the most successful teams, such as Manchester United or Real Madrid, who have a worldwide fanbase. It means the elite teams will keep attracting the most money, and therefore the best players and will continue to dominate the game,' he says.

He adds that if brands are to take advantage of European football's worldwide appeal they must tailor their messages to how football is being consumed in different countries. 'In Asia, for example, it is a real social occasion to go to a bar to watch an English game on a Saturday night. Drinks brands should consider activity around these venues, such as holding Premiership-branded happy hours.'

Carling has been studying the area of football sponsorship for years and says the cleverest brands today will find ways to benefit from the integration of football and the world of entertainment. He says the celebrity status of players such as Beckham and new England hero Wayne Rooney is pushing football on to the newspaper front pages as well as the back, and into lifestyle and women's magazines. 'This trend is providing access to consumer demographics previously never associated with football, and this is where future growth will come from.'

Source: S. Hemsley, *Financial Times*, 29 June 2004

1. Using the model of strategy detailed in this chapter, how would you account for the involvement in football of organisations mentioned in the case study?

2. For marketers seeking to use football as a basis for the strategic development of their brands, what challenges are they likely to face, and what recommendations would you make in order for these developments to be successful?

CASE 18.4   Adidas: off the pace and more hurdles ahead

The World Athletic Championships in Paris this year generated one real surprise: the success of a skinny, lightning-quick sprinter who shuns weight-lifting and comes from St Kitts-Nevis in the Caribbean.

Kim Collins made the day for Adidas-Salomon, the German sportswear maker known for its three stripes logo. Sponsored by Adidas, Mr Collins stormed through the 100-metre finish wearing a black, retro-looking Adidas outfit and knee-high socks.

Adidas may be spending more money on soccer and basketball, but track and field is closest to its heart. With its US sales slumping dramatically and competition intensifying – even Adidas's once tiny neighbour Puma has become a potent rival – the group is taking advantage of demand for retro-style track and field shoes by stressing its 83-year-old athletics roots.

'Athletics goes back all the way for us – it is a fixed part of our philosophy to make products for all Olympic disciplines,' says Mike Riehl, who heads global sports marketing at Adidas.

In the run-up to the Olympic Games in Athens next year Adidas is ramping up its athletics credentials. Next year the company will sponsor 18 national teams, including Great Britain's and Germany's. Mr Riehl says the new focus on athletics is 'all about brand positioning and our claim to be the Olympic brand'.

But the company has a problem. Athletics is in the grip of what could become its greatest drugs scandal. The discovery of a new, previously undetectable steroid, tetrahydrogestrinone (THG), and the revelation that hundreds of top athletes may have been using the drug have tarnished the sport's reputation. Estimates vary on how many athletes may be excluded from the Athens Games for testing positive for THG but even cautious observers say the scandal could overshadow the Games.

The controversy has already touched Adidas. One of the athletes endorsed by the group is Dwain Chambers, a musclebound British sprinter who is among the fastest men in the world. But Chambers's reputation has been tainted by a recent positive test for THG.

The dilemma facing Adidas is how best to exploit its athletics credentials when the sport's integrity is being questioned. After all, it will become increasingly difficult to use top athletes to market its products if they are being banned for using illegal steroids, as will happen with Chambers.

Fortunately for Adidas, there does not appear to be a direct correlation between doping scandals and shoe sales. In fact, athletic shoes, which are far simpler in design and styling than basketball or tennis footwear, are experiencing a renaissance in Europe.

Unlike 1980s fads, such as wearing tennis shoes as street-wear or wearing oversized, untied basketball shoes, the retro trend has 'definitely found a market of itself', says Mr Riehl. If the retro trend is here to stay, Adidas hopes that Sport Heritage, its retro division and one of three brand categories, will contribute one in every three euros to group profits in five to 10 years. The division currently earns only 18 per cent of group profits.

'No other manufacturer has such a wide array of products that have written history,' says Erich Stamminger, Adidas board member responsible for marketing and distribution. 'Sadly, many manufacturers have abused the retro trend, but by comparison our past does not have an expiry date.'

The company's historic involvement in sport puts its younger rivals in the shade. Adidas first came to fame at the 1936 Games when Jesse Owens won four gold medals with shoes made by Adi Dassler, the company's founder. Twelve years later, Adi and Rudolf, the two Dassler brothers, went their separate ways and founded Adidas and Puma, respectively.

Since then Adidas products have been worn by a range of Olympic stars with its shoes coveted in equal measure by sports fanatics and the fashion-conscious. But while the trend for retro-styled athletics shoes may be popular in Europe, John Horan, editor of *Sporting Goods Intelligence*, the US sports trade magazine, says Adidas's focus on athletics could be a gamble in the US, where its growth strategy has temporarily run aground and 'where people only take interest in athletics once every four years.'

'They are definitely looking for a fix. They relied too much on certain products, particularly in the US, and they are now going back to their roots and athletic heritage,' he says.

Adidas's US growth campaign has stuttered since the beginning of the year and by late September the group's incoming orders were down 20 per cent. Herbert Hainer, the company's chief executive, admits Adidas has failed to cater for US consumers' taste. Massive discounting in the US market has further hit sales.

Then there is the tricky issue of the popularity of athletics in the US, where the sport lags behind professional disciplines such as basketball, baseball and American football.

'If interest in track and field comes and goes in Europe, it is basically non-existent in the US,' says Willi Holdorf, decathlon gold medal winner in Tokyo in 1964.

Mr Horan argues that Adidas's US problems stem from having the wrong products. 'In 2004, we must really see some hot new Adidas products out there,' he says, adding that Adidas lacks the 'must-have' products of competitors, such as Reebok's exclusive NBA-licence jerseys or Nike's bestselling Air Force 1 shoes.

He adds that Adidas needs to have more designers and product developers in the US, especially when it comes to products made for basketball.

But despite the problems facing athletics and its apparently lowly position in the US market, Adidas remains committed to the sport and stressing the company's track and field roots may be valuable in the run-up to the Olympics and benefit the company, as long as retro-styled shoes continue to be fashionable.

However, it is too early to gauge the impact of the THG scandal and Adidas will be hoping athletics recovers as quickly as it did from its last significant doping scandal, when an illegally turbo-charged Ben Johnson won the 100m gold at Seoul in 1988.

Source: M. Garrahan and U. Harnischfeger, *Financial Times*, 10 November 2003

Questions

1. In strategic terms, how would you account for Adidas's problems? What solutions would you suggest for these problems?

2. In the event of shocks such as drugs scandals, how do you think marketing strategists should handle them?

Conclusions

This chapter has dealt with a range of issues associated with the process of sport marketing strategy. Central to the chapter was the proposal of a model for developing sport marketing strategy. The model, which was predicated on congruence with the overall vision of the sporting organisation, was composed of five stages:

- **Stage 1:** Formulation and clarification of organisational and marketing objectives
- **Stage 2:** Situation analysis: Issues and SWOT analyses
- **Stage 3:** Market segmentation
- **Stage 4:** Development of integrated marketing campaign
- **Stage 5:** Implementation, control and evaluation

The model describes the process undertaken by sporting organisations as they embark on a marketing strategy designed to achieve a number of marketing-related objectives. It is not intended that this model be taken as definitive but rather a guide for a sport organisation to use as a foundation on which to build a range of innovative and dynamic strategies that will enable it to compete in the marketplace.

Discussion questions

1. Examine the various sporting websites referred to later and compare their approaches to the marketing-level strategies concerning product, price, distribution and promotion. Discuss why any differences or similarities exist in the context of the information provided in this chapter.

2. Describe each of the marketing communication strategies mentioned in this chapter. Compare and contrast each in terms of their applicability to the Rainbow Region Masters Games mentioned in Case Study 18.2.

Guided reading

A variety of authors have applied and adapted Porter's model to sporting situations. For example, see Brooks (1994, pp. 281–311) or Shilbury et al. (2002, pp. 22–5).

For an overview of the attendance/participation frequency escalator, students should read Mullin et al. (2000, pp. 214–20).

For a discussion of the relevant situations referred to under situation analysis, students are directed towards Dann and Dann (2004, pp. 398–400).

For further reading on new product development, students are directed towards Reed (1997, pp. 159–67).

Shilbury et al. (2002, pp. 97–114) present a very good analysis of the strategic pricing process.

Keywords

Commercialisation; issues analysis; sustainable competitive advantage.

Bibliography

Allen, J., O'Toole, W., Harris, R. and McDonnell, I. (2005) *Festival and Special Event Management*, 3rd edn, Australia: John Wiley and Sons.

Brooks, C.M. (1994) Sports *Marketing – Competitive Business Strategies for Sports,* Englewood Cliffs, NJ: Prentice Hall.

Dann, S. and Dann, S. (2004) *Introduction to Marketing*, Australia: John Wiley and Sons.

Duan, Y. and Burrell, P. (1995) A hybrid system for strategic marketing planning, *Market Intelligence and Planning* 13(11): 5–12.

Getz, D. (1997) *Event Management and Event Tourism*, New York: Cognizant Communication Corporation.

Kotler, P. (1997) *Marketing Management: Analysis Planning, Implementation and Control*, 9th edn, Englewood Cliffs, NJ: Prentice Hall.

Kotler, P. and Armstrong, G. (2004) *Principles of Marketing*, 10th edn, Upper Saddle River, NJ: Pearson Prentice Hall.

Mullin B.J., Hardy S. and Sutton, W.A. (2000) *Sport Marketing*, 2nd edn, Human Champaign, IL: Human Kinetics.

Nash, L. (1988) Mission statements – Mirror and windows, *Harvard Business Review* 66(2): 155–6.

Porter, M. (1985) *Competitive Strategy*, New York: The Free Press.

Pride, W. M. and Ferrell, O. C. (1991) *Marketing Concepts and Strategies*, Boston: Houghton Mifflin.

Reed, P. W. (1997) *Marketing Planning and Strategy*, 2nd edn, Sydney: Harcourt Brace.

Shilbury, D., Quick, S. and Westerbeek, H. (2002) *Strategic Sport Marketing*, 2nd edn, Sydney: Allen and Unwin.

Summers, J. and Johnson, M. (2000) 'Sport marketing', in J.R. McColl-Kennedy and G.C. Kiel (eds), *Marketing: A Strategic Approach*, Nelson ITP.

Stotlar, D.K. (1993) *Successful Sport Marketing*, Melbourne: WCB Brown and Benchmark.

Recommended websites

Adidas
http://www.adidas.com

Chelsea
http://www.chelseafc.com

Cricket Australia
http://www.cricket.com.au

Manchester United
http://www.manutd.com

National Basketball Association
http://www.nba.com

National Basketball League
http://www.nbl.com.au

National Football League
http://www.nfl.com

Nike
http://www.nike.com

Chapter 19

Achieving competitive advantage and leading strategic change in sport organisations

Ann Bourke
University College Dublin

Learning outcomes

Upon completion of this chapter, the reader should be able to:

■ Identify the ways sport marketing strategy can facilitate an organisation in achieving a competitive advantage over rivals.

■ Assess the relative merits of each of these strategies.

■ Explain how sport marketing can contribute to a process of strategic change within a range of organisations.

■ Establish how sport marketing as the focus for a process of strategic change impacts upon a range of sport organisations, including for-profit, not-for-profit, professional and amateur organisations.

Overview of chapter

The purpose of this chapter is to explain the essence of *strategic marketing and change* in the sporting context. Sports bodies and organisations depending on their ownership and type (for-profit, not-for-profit) aim to achieve strategic objectives such as increasing participation in their sport, raising the profile of the game and making efficient use of their key resources and capabilities. The attainment of these strategic objectives is influenced by developments (political, social, economic, and competitive) both within and outside the body or organisation. This chapter focuses on the key concepts associated with strategic marketing, competitive advantage, leadership and change. It is essential for a sports body or organisation (as for commercial enterprises) to accept that its strategy needs to be evaluated on a regular basis and changes introduced when and where appropriate.

Introduction

Marketing management, according to Kotler and Armstrong (1994), is the analysis, planning, implementation and control of programmes designed to create, build and maintain beneficial exchanges with target buyers for the purpose of achieving organisational objectives. Sport marketing has been defined as 'the specific application of marketing principles and processes to sport products and to the marketing of non-sport products through association with sport' (Shank, 2005). The impact of marketing and business strategy in the sports context in facilitating strategic change is considered in this chapter.

Sport marketing and strategy

A strategy provides a logic that integrates the different functions of the firm or organisation and points them in the same direction (Rogan, 2003). Strategy is about matching a company's resources with its capabilities (Grant, 1995). Strategy formation can be considered a conscious process through which a future plan is created and then acted upon, which is not to suggest it is independent of strategy implementation (Morgan, McGuinness and Thorpe, 2000). According to Barney (1997), a good strategy neutralises threats and exploits opportunities while capitalising on strengths and avoiding or fixing weaknesses. In any sporting situation – public, private or voluntary – there is a need to establish a strategy for ongoing management and future development of the organisation and the people in it. In many situations, the lack of strategic direction can be the downfall of the organisation, and although mission statements and visions may be seen as fancy management jargon, they are beneficial to the function of a successful organisation (Watt, 1998). According to Slack (1997), all sport organisations formulate strategies; they may be deliberate or emergent. Deliberate strategies are intended courses of action that become realised. Emergent strategies are those that are realised but not necessarily intended (Mintzberg, 1987). Senior Union of European Football Associations (UEFA) personnel presented proposals on local training in April 2005 to be considered at the following UEFA congress. It is proposed that as and from the 2008–2009 season, each professional football club will have at least four club trained and four association trained[1] players in its 25-man squad. The intended strategy here is to create a better balance in domestic competitions (http://www.uefa.com) and to prevent clubs from simply 'hoarding' players in squads and creating a system whereby locally trained players would be given an opportunity to play regularly in club sides. However, the unintended outcome may be increased recruiting across borders by leading professional clubs of talented youngsters at even an earlier age than is currently the case.

The main task of strategy is to determine how the organisation will deploy its resources within its environment to satisfy its long-term goals, and how it will

---

[1] A club trained player is defined as a player who has been registered for a minimum of three seasons with the club between the ages of 15 and 21. An association trained player is one who has been registered for at least three seasons by the club or by other clubs affiliated to the same association between the ages of 15 and 21.

organise itself to implement that strategy. According to Thompson and Strickland (1995a), the key factors that shape an organisation's strategy include:

- Societal political regulatory and citizenship considerations
- Industry attractiveness and competitive conditions
- Specific company opportunities and threats
- Organisational strengths, weaknesses and competitive capabilities
- Personal ambitions, business philosophies and ethical beliefs of managers
- The influence of shared values and company culture on strategy

Morgan et al. (2000) assess the contribution of marketing to business strategy formation. Their study findings suggest that the contribution of marketing to all strategy formation dimensions is significantly greater among high business performance organisations as distinct from low business performance organisations. Consequently, they advise that consideration must be given to decision aides used by managers to analyse and interpret market and competitive situations. They also note that managers must be aware that market-based management is multidimensional and its constituent elements need to be appreciated. According to Doyle (1994), marketing and innovation should be the foundation areas in setting the organisation's objectives. It is the organisation's performance in these areas that the customer pays for. If the company or organisation is not good at satisfying customers today and tomorrow, it will not make profits. The roles of production, personnel and finance are pertinent only in so far as those activities enhance the organisation's ability to satisfy customer needs. A marketing strategy is designed to achieve certain marketing objectives, including increased market share, entrance into a specific target market, improvement of brand awareness and the like. Doyle (1994) contends that the marketing strategy an organisation should adopt depends on three factors:

1. What is its competitive position? Is it a market leader or market follower?
2. What is its strategic position? Is it seeking market dominance or merely to carve out a profitable niche?
3. At what stage is the market? Is it in the early growth stage, or does it look to be in late maturity?

According to Grant (1995), strategy must be consistent with the organisation's goals and values, its external environment, its resources and capabilities and its organisation and systems. He maintains that four ingredients influence an organisation's ability to achieve success in strategy: (a) clear goals, (b) understanding the external environment, (c) appreciation of its internal strengths and weaknesses and (d) effective implementation. In Grant's (1995) opinion, strategy fulfils three key managerial purposes:

- It acts as a support for decision making and provides coherence within an organisation.
- It may be viewed as a vehicle for coordination and communication.
- It provides a focus (target) of where the organisation wants to be in the future.

An organisation's marketing strategy describes how the organisation will fulfil the needs and wants of its customers (Ferrell and Hartline, 2005). It may also include activities associated with maintaining relationships with other stakeholders (employees, supply chain partners). Marketing strategy is simply what the organisation does to achieve its objectives. The objectives vary according to business sector. The business objectives for UMBRO are outlined in the chief executive's review (UMBRO Annual Report, 2004) as follows:

- To be at least the number three brand in every market in which we operate as defined by on the field performance product
- To grow our branded business by 10% per annum[2]
- To develop a trend business (football/lifestyle and fashion) that directionally represents 5% of total global wholesale equivalent sales

On the other hand, the International Rugby Board (IRB) sets out its goals as follows:

a) To increase the number and competitiveness of Unions at Tier 1 (high performance level – the professional game)
b) To increase participation in rugby worldwide
c) To have Rugby rejoin the Olympic Games (http://www.irb.ie)

To achieve these goals or objectives necessitates planning, taking into consideration internal and external factors that have a bearing on the organisations' fortunes.

A marketing strategy can be composed of one or more marketing programmes (Ferrell and Hartline, 2005). Each programme consists of two elements – a target market (or markets) and marketing mix. In many cases, large organisations are composed of a number of businesses (often equating to divisions), each of which serves a distinct group of customers and has a distinct set of competitors. Each business or division may be strategically autonomous and form a strategic business unit (SBU). For example, the Goodyear Tire Company is a global organisation with a presence on six continents. Its SBUs are organised to meet customer requirements and serve geographic areas (Table 19.1).

Table 19.1 Analysis of Goodyear Tires

Strategic business unit	Products and markets	Geographic markets served
North American Tire	Original equipment and replacement tires for autos, trucks, farm, aircraft	United States, Canada, Export
Goodyear European Union	Original equipment and replacement tires for autos, trucks, tractors	Europe, Export
Goodyear Eastern Europe, Middle East & Africa	Original equipment and replacement tires for autos, trucks, tractors	Poland, Slovenia, Turkey, Morocco, South Africa, Export
Goodyear Latin America	Original equipment and replacement tires for autos, trucks, tractors	Central America, South America, Export
Goodyear Asia/Pacific	Original equipment and replacement tires for autos, trucks, farm, aircraft	Asia, Australia, New Zealand, Export
Engineered Products	Auto belts, hose, industrial products	Worldwide
Chemical Products	Synthetic and natural rubber, chemicals	Worldwide
Off the Road Tires	Original equipment and replacement tires for construction and other off-the-road vehicles	Worldwide
Aircraft Tires	Original equipment and replacement tires for private and commercial aircraft	Worldwide

Source: www.goodyear.com, retrieved 6 March 2005

---

[2] Branded business is defined as both branded footwear and apparel for both genders; see http://www.umbro.com

These organisations may find it beneficial to devise separate strategies for each SBU, subsidiary, division, product line or other profit centre within the parent organisation. The Adidas Salomon group strategy has five divisions or brands that aim to maximise consumer impact and enhance brand profitability (Figure 19.1). Business unit strategy determines the nature and future direction of each business unit, including its competitive advantages, the allocation of its resources, and the coordination of the functional business areas (marketing, finance, production, human resources). Within the organisation, there must be an information capability to support the SBUs, but in different ways.

The sport industry is a people-oriented service industry that exists to satisfy the needs of three distinct types of *consumers* – spectators (individual or corporations), participants (individuals or teams; amateur and professional; organised and unorganised groups) and sponsors (business organisations that choose to sponsor sport). A *sport product* is a good, service or any combination of the two that is designed to provide benefits to sports spectators, participants or sponsors. Sport marketers sell their goods or services based upon the benefits of these products to consumers. Sport products may be classified into four categories: sporting events, sporting goods, sports training and sports information. The primary product in the sport industry is the sporting event (US Open Golf, Olympic Games, Rugby Six Nations Championship) – this is needed to produce all the other related products in the sport industry. Athletes are participants who engage in organised training to improve their skills in particular sports. These performers can also be thought of as sport products because their performance can satisfy the needs of consumers, both on and off the field.

Sport marketers manage the complex and unique exchange processes in the sport industry by using the *strategic sport marketing* process, which consists of *planning*, *implementing* and *controlling* marketing efforts to meet organisational needs and satisfy consumer needs (Shank, 2005). Strategic marketing refers to the decisions taken to develop long-run strategies for survival and growth (Ashill, Frederikson and Davies, 2003). The marketing planning process begins by understanding the consumer needs, selecting a group of consumers with similar needs

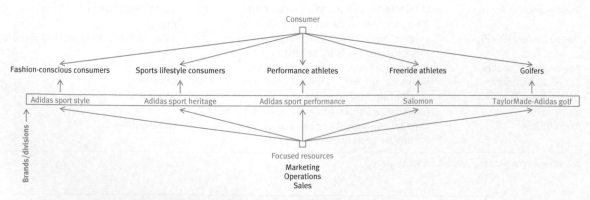

Figure 19.1 **Adidas consumer-oriented business model**

Source: Adapted from http://www.adidas-group.com/en/investor/reports/annually/2003/homepage.html

and positioning the sport product within this group of consumers as outlined in the following section.

Marketing planning

Marketing has been defined by Weerawardena (2003) as that function of the organisation's dealing with the mobilisation of an organisation's resources for the acquisition and integration of market-based knowledge to value creating activities of the organisation and the coordination of activities required for the organisation to reach its targeted customers with superior products and services. Organisations (including sports bodies) must possess or have access to marketing capability. This marketing capability refers to the integrative processes designed to apply collective knowledge, skills and resources of the organisation to the market-related needs of the business, enabling the business to add value to its goods and services and meet competitive demand (Weerawardena, 2003). The process of marketing planning involves a well-defined path from generating a *business mission* to implementing and controlling the resultant plans (Jobber and Fahy, 2003). The business mission is determined by the background of the company and the personalities of its senior management. In the case of a sports body or organisation (International Olympic Committee [IOC]), its mission is the general purposes of the organisation as put forth in the charter, annual reports, public statements by key executives and other authoritative pronouncements (Perrow, 1961, cited by Slack, 1997). For example, according to the Olympic Charter established by Pierre de Coubertin, the goal of the Olympic Movement (which includes the IOC) is to contribute to building a peaceful and better world by educating youth through sport practised without discrimination of any kind and in the Olympic spirit, which requires mutual understanding with a spirit of friendship, solidarity and fair play (http://www.olympics.org).

To develop a marketing plan, the organisation undertakes a *marketing audit*, which systematically examines the firm's marketing environment, objectives, strategies and activities, problem areas and opportunities. The purpose of the marketing audit (internal and external analysis) is to establish the future direction of the business. Brownlie (1999) notes that a marketing audit is completed to identify underachieving marketing resources and to generate recommendations about how those resources could be put to more effective use. The marketing audit is completed to impel action and to create an awareness of the need for change.

A SWOT (strengths, weaknesses, opportunities and threats) analysis is an effective tool in analysing environmental data and information. When performed correctly, a SWOT analysis not only organises data and information, but can also be especially useful in uncovering strategic advantages that can be leveraged (Ferrell and Hartline, 2005). It must be remembered that when using a SWOT analysis, relative strengths and weaknesses should be analysed, only resources valued by the customer should be included when evaluating strengths and weaknesses, and opportunities and threats should be listed as anticipated events outside the business that have implications for performance (Jobber and Fahy, 2003).

When the marketing audit and SWOT analysis are complete, marketing objectives may be derived. Two types should be considered: strategic thrust and strategic objectives (Jobber and Fahy, 2003: 282). The strategic thrust describes the future direction of the business and the basic alternatives as illustrated in Figure 19.2.

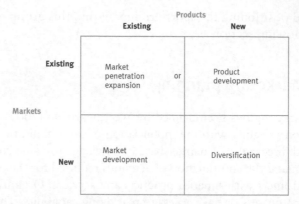

Figure 19.2 Product growth strategies: the Ansoff matrix

The product growth strategies are:

a) **Market penetration** involves taking an existing product in the existing market and attempting to increase penetration. Existing customers may become more brand loyal, new customers may begin to buy the brand, or both. Market penetration is achieved by using more effective promotion or distribution or by cutting prices.

b) **Product development** involves increasing sales by improving current products or developing new products for current markets. By improving style, performance and comfort, the aim is to get higher sales and market share amongst the present market (e.g., football boots, tennis racquets).

c) **Market development** is used when current products are sold in new markets. This may involve moving into international markets or moving into new market segments.

d) **Diversification** occurs when new products are developed for new markets. This is a risky strategy but may be necessary when a company's current products and markets offer few prospects of future growth. When there is synergy between the existing and new products, the strategy is likely to be successful.

In addition to product or market direction, strategic objectives for each product need to be developed. According to Jobber and Fahy (2003, p. 283), the four alternatives are build, hold, harvest and divest. Obviously, for new products or services, the intention is to build sales and market share. However, for current products or services, the strategic objective depends upon the particular situation. When the objectives have been formulated, a way to achieve them must be agreed upon. Core strategy focuses on how objectives can be accomplished and consists of three elements: target markets, competitor targets and establishing a competitive advantage. The choice of target markets is influenced by the outcomes from the SWOT analysis, and competitor targets are set based on the completion of an external analysis, profitability analysis and entry barrier analysis. Porter's (1980) five forces framework is commonly used to facilitate an external analysis. For a detailed review of strategy and environmental analysis in sport, see Parker (2004).

Strategies to gain competitive advantage

There is no common meaning for *competitive advantage*. Sometimes the term is used interchangeably with *distinctive capabilities* to mean relative superiority in skills and resources. Hill and Jones (1995) define competitive advantage as when a firm is earning profits which are higher than average for the industry. This superior financial performance, according to Porter (1985), is the result of inherent industry attractiveness in which the firm competes and its relative position. It grows fundamentally out of the value a firm is able to create for its buyers, that exceeds the costs of creating it.

Porter (1985) proposed three 'generic' strategies by which an organisation could achieve competitive advantage: overall cost leadership, differentiation and focus. These positions have to be related to the products and services on offer, the nature of the markets served and the potential for growth and competitive scope. The key to long-term profitability and success is that organisations choose their basic generic strategy or strategic foundation from one of these positions. To do so enables an initial clarity for organisation activities to be achieved. According to Pettinger (2004), many organisations do not do this and end up without clear direction.

Cost leadership strategy is where the organisation concentrates on being the lowest cost operator in the sector. To do so, it seeks out all sources of cost advantage. Organisation, production, marketing and distribution structures are all geared to achieve this. These organisations are likely to offer standardised, adequate and medium-quality products and services in markets in which these are the key characteristics required. The extent to the organisations' success depends upon the levels of price that can be commanded in the pursuit of this.

Differentiation strategies are those that seek uniqueness or identity for their products in ways that are widely valued by buyers other than price advantage. This involves conducting marketing, branding, advertising, promotions and public relations activities to give the organisation and its offerings a distinctive identity. Organisations that can achieve and sustain differentiation are likely to be above average performers in their sectors, provided that the price premium more than covers costs and charges incurred for being different.

Focus strategy is the phrase used when an organisation concentrates on a segment or segments within a sector and seeks to serve them to the exclusion of the rest of the sector. This requires a basic concentration on identifying, anticipating and meeting the needs of the segments and ensuring that this is accurately completed. Focus is then usually based on known, understood and accepted levels of product and service quality and certainty and continuity of the relationship. It is additionally usual to define *cost focus*, in which organisations serving specific sectors seek to do so on the basis of a cost advantage, and *focus differentiation*, in which organisations seek to service specific sectors in terms of brand advantage and consequent benefits of perceived and actual confidence, durability and quality.

Sources of competitive advantage

Porter (1987) draws a distinction between *corporate* and *competitive* strategy. Whereas competitive strategy concerns how to create *competitive advantage* in each of the businesses in which the organisation competes, corporate strategy poses two distinct questions: What business should the organisation be in? and How should the corporate office manage the array of business units? There are two types of competitive advantage: *low cost* and *differentiation*. A *cost* advantage may stem from such disparate sources as low-cost physical distribution system, a highly efficient assembly process or superior sales force utilisation. Organisations opting for low-cost advantage aim to supply the market place with a good or service that is cheaper than similar goods or services. This low-cost approach is designed to increase market share and hence a firm's profitability. A *differentiation* advantage may stem from diverse factors such as the procurement of high-quality raw materials, a responsive order entry system or a superior product or process design (Porter, 1985). Firms that offer a differentiated good or service do so with the objective of offering customers a unique product or service not offered by competitors. Customers will pay a higher price for the superior value on offer, thereby generating increased satisfaction and customer loyalty. The uniqueness is often embedded in the brand name (Nike, Adidas, Quicksilver, Lucozade) and cannot be replicated easily be existing or potential competitors.

Because the life expectancy of companies is smaller than human beings (Senge, 1990), there is an ongoing necessity to engage in the process of knowledge creation. When markets shift, technologies proliferate, competitors multiply and products become obsolete almost overnight, successful companies are those that consistently create new knowledge, disseminate it widely throughout the organisation and quickly embody it in new technologies and products. These activities define what Nonaka (1991) refers to as the 'knowledge creating' company but could also refer to the requirements needed by organisations to sustain their competitive advantage. According to Porter (1985), organisations have a sustainable competitive advantage (SCA) when their competitive advantage resists erosion by competitor behaviour or industry environment. The sustainability of the advantage depends of three forces:

1. The source of the advantage (higher or lower order advantage)
2. The number of distinct sources
3. Constant improving and upgrading

Hill and Jones (1995, p. 116) note that SCA depends on (i) the height of barriers to imitation (e.g., time and reputation with competitors), (ii) the capability of competitors and (iii) the general industry dynamism of the industry environment. SCA is the accumulation of attitudes and practices across an organisation (Coyne, 1993). The focus on time-based interdependence between an organisation's resources and its environment and the role strategy plays in creating these links, not passively but actively, influence the sustainability of the firm's competitive advantage (Williams, 1992).

Two schools of thought exist as to how organisations can gain competitive advantage (Petraf, 1993; Verdin and Williamson, 1994). One school views competitive advantage primarily as a function of industry attractiveness and the market position of individual organisations (Porter, 1985, 1980). This view extols the benefits of the organisation looking outward. The alternative view emphasises the bundle of resources in the form of tangible and intangible assets on which the organisation can draw. This framework notes that the differences in organisation resources will lead to differences in SCA (Black and Boal, 1994; Conner, 1991; Grant, 1991). It advises managers to build and develop their asset stock and capabilities as a basis for sustained competitive advantage.

Resources have been defined as anything that could be thought of as a strength or weakness of a given organisation or stocks of available factors owned and controlled by the organisation (Amit and Shoemaker, 1993). Hunt and Derozier (2004) define resources as the tangible and intangible entities available to the organisation that enable it to produce efficiently or effectively a market offering that has value for some marketing segment(s). These resources are not just land, labour and capital as in neoclassical trade theory. Instead, they include assets, capabilities, organisation processes, organisation attributes, information and knowledge controlled by the organisation, enabling it to conceive and implement strategies that improve its efficiency and effectiveness (Barney, 1991).

Resource bundles and capabilities are heterogeneous across organisations (Petraf, 1993), giving rise to superior production factors that are limited in supply. These resources and capabilities are the basis upon which an organisation's competitive advantage is built. Resources may be grouped into three categories – physical capital, human capital and organisational capital (Barney, 1991). Grant (1991) lists six categories: financial, physical, human, technological, reputation and organisational. To be a source of SCA, there are four essential requirements for a resource or skill (Barney, 1991):

- It must be valuable.
- It must be rare among the organisation's current and potential competitors.
- It must be imperfectly imitable.
- There must not be any strategically equivalent substitutes for this resource or skill.

According to Grant (1991), the characteristics of the organisation's resources that make them critical for gaining and sustaining competitive advantage are durability, transparency, transferability and replicability. Coyne (1993) points out that not only must an organisation have a skill or resource that its competitors do not have (i.e., there must be a capability gap), but also the capability gap must make a difference to the customer. In other words, for a business to enjoy SCA in a product market segment, the difference between the organisation and its competitors must be reflected in one or more product or delivery attributes that are key buying criteria. In addition, the key buying criteria and underpinning capability must also be enduring. Each organisation in the marketplace has at least some resources that are unique to it (e.g., very knowledgeable employees [Jonny Wilkinson, Roy Keane], efficient production processes) that constitute a comparative advantage in resources, which could lead to positions of competitive advantage (Hunt and Derozier, 2004). Some of these resources are not easily copied or acquired (i.e., they are relatively immobile); hence, such resources (culture and processes) may be sources of long-term competitive advantage. As noted above, central to the concept of SCA is the notion of durability or non-imitability. Barriers to imitation are endogenous and idiosyncratic (organisation specific). Organisations that occupy positions of competitive advantage can continue to do so if they continue to invest in the resources that produced the competitive advantage and if their rivals' acquisition and innovation efforts fail (Hunt and Derozier, 2004).

Organisational change

Marketing strategy overlaps significantly with business strategy. The strategic decisions in the functional areas of product, promotion, distribution, pricing and the sales force, although significantly developed in marketing, are frequent topics in business strategy

(Hunt and Derozier, 2004). Certain factors influence the successful implementation of an organisation's marketing strategy (e.g., the degree of autonomy that senior marketing decision makers possess, the extent to which a functional unit shares functional programmes and facilitate with other units in pursuit of synergies, the manner in which corporate-level managers evaluate and reward the performance of the functional unit). McDonald (1996) identifies a number of barriers that may inhibit the implementation of a marketing strategy such as the role of the decision maker, a lack of senior management involvement and a lack of cross-functional or top management support. The important role of the culture carrier (leader) in determining the level of support and involvement in strategic marketing planning has been highlighted by Leppard and McDonald (1991). In the context of corporate culture, marketing culture is characterised by what actually takes place in the organisation's marketing context. It is the way 'marketing' things are done in the organisation. Intertwined with the support climate for marketing strategy are the political undertones. Some authors (Hill and Jones, 1995; Thompson and Strickland, 1995b) consider strategy formulation to be a political exercise, suggesting that power dependency theory will enhance our understanding of the process. Implementing strategy frequently involves change, and the factors that help or hinder strategic change are considered in the following paragraphs.

Organisational competencies such as innovation, flexibility and responsiveness result from the collective cognition or sensemaking (Neill and Rose, 2006). An SCA derives from an organisation's capacity to successfully assimilate, negotiate and capitalise on complexities in its environment. According to Johnson, Scholes and Whittington (2005), organisations that display a tendency towards inertia and resistance to change suffer from strategic drift. In many cases, organisations continue to rely on the skills and capabilities that made them successful even when those capabilities do not match the current competitive environment (Hill and Jones, 1995, p. 409). Change involves much more than just introducing or suggesting changes; it means that old beliefs and values have to be broken down and that new directions have to be charted. Individuals within sport organisations can have a major input into this, both positively and negatively (Watt, 1998, p. 130). Organisational change is defined as the adoption of a new idea or behaviour by an organisation (Daft, 2000, p. 364). The forces contributing to organisational change exist both in the internal and external environment. Managers perceive a need for change when they note a performance gap, which is a disparity between existing and desired performance levels. The performance gap may stem from current procedures not being up to standard or because a new idea or technology could improve current performance.

There are many reasons for change within organisations such as resource efficiency and effectiveness, product and service ageing, staffing levels, expertise and mixes, reduced and eroded profit margins, increase in costs and attention to particular problems (Pettinger, 2004, p. 239). There are various barriers to change such as location, tradition, success, failure, technology, vested interests and management systems and bureaucracy. Pettinger (2004) maintains that behaviour barriers to change include – 'it cannot be done', 'there is no alternative', lack of clarity, fear and anxiety, and perfection. To reduce these barriers, communication strategies are crucial; these include briefing groups, plenary meetings, individual and group meetings, oral and written communications, the use of email and the internet, notice boards and other circulars.

Chapman (2002), drawing on Watzlawick, Weakland and Fisch (1974), notes that there are two levels of change: first-order and second-order change, which encompass the critical distinction between qualitative changes to the systems itself to adjustments within it. To add clarification to this distinction, Bartunek and Moch (1987, cited by Chapman, 2002) describe *first-order change* as a gradual modification that makes sense within an established framework. *Second-order change* involves alterations to the basic governing rules. Ford and Backoff (1988) see second-order change as a movement to a different plane of understanding, or a shift in deep structures; this is now commonly referred to as transformational change. According the Bartunek (1988, cited by Chapman, 2002), *transformational change* within organisations requires a basic shift in attitudes, beliefs and cultural values, reframing, or as Golembiewski (1979) stated, 'a redefinition of the relevant psychological space'. In other words, every person affected by the change is a *change agent* to the extent that his or her personal involvement in reframing contributes to a successful outcome, supplemented by involvement in structural and other changes.

Pettinger (2004) outlines the *four phases* of change – exploration, planning, action and integration, noting that these phases are clearly integrated rather than being linear. Each phase must be informed by the other. Exploration must be informed by the planning processes and the information gathering and other testing and piloting that should be completed. Action phases also have to do with testing, experimentation, planning in terms of reviewing product and service prototypes, identifying and assessing glitches in new information systems, addressing teething troubles in each area and attending to related issues such as new patterns of work. In order to facilitate strategic change in organisations, the role of resources (e.g., finance, personnel) is frequently reviewed. Kraatz and Zajac (2001) note that research on strategic change has neglected the issues of resource heterogeneity and has not considered how resource differences might affect an organisation's propensity to change. They acknowledge that a variety of factors may intervene and complicate the relationships between environmental shifts and strategic change. To the extent that organisational differences have been acknowledged, resources have largely been viewed as factors that impede or promote an organisation's necessary adaptation to environmental pressures.

According to Amis, Slack and Hinnings (2004), within the sport industry, increasing commercialisation, alterations to geopolitical boundaries, technological advancements and greater competition in the marketplace have resulted in pronounced changes to many organisations, often over very short periods. Three internal dynamics significantly affect the propensity of an organisation to successfully negotiate a programme of radical change:

1. The interests of different organisational subunits
2. The distribution of power within the organisation, which determines how disagreements over interests are resolved
3. The capacity for change, which is the competencies and capabilities with the organisation that can be used to guide it from one organisational design to another

Hill and Jones (1995, p. 409) maintain that power struggles and political contests take place at the top of an organisation as managers strive to influence decision making to protect and enhance their positions. The reality of how companies make decisions is often incomplete because politics and conflict influence the decision-making process and selection of organisational objectives. As stated previously, all organisations have a heterogeneous bundle of resources (physical, human, capital; tangible and intangible) and are composed of subunits or SBUs. Inevitably, there is considerable struggle among the units or groups to protect their individual interests. Organisations can be considered to be political systems in which power and conflict, rather than rules and authority, are the defining characteristics.

Strategic change has been recognised as an important phenomenon because it represents the means through which organisations maintain co-alignment with shifting competitive, technological and social environments that occasionally pose threats to their continued survival and effectiveness (Kraatz and Zajac, 2001). Pettinger (2004, p. 250) considers the following strategic approaches to the management of change:

- Force field analysis
- Unfreezing the organisation
- Phases of change
- Emergent change

No matter what approach to change is taken, it must be led and managed until the process is complete. *Change catalysts* are people, events or factors that bring the organisation to the realisation that it cannot go on as it is. A *change agent* is the person driving the change. The creator of the strategy may not be the change agent; he or she may instead rely upon others to take the lead in effecting change. The key role of the catalyst or agent of change is to gain universal understanding and acceptance of the need for constant change in all areas, including product and service quality, new product and service development, business operational and administrative processes, staff, expertise and technology output, returns on investment and cost base efficiency, effectiveness and development.

An organisation's capacity for change may be broken down into behavioural and technical components. There must be an ability to mobilise a commitment to change by creating excitement about the anticipated endpoint and convincing the organisation members that they will be better off as a result of the change (Amis et al., 2004). Amis et al. (2004) contend that there must be leaders to demonstrate they possess the technical expertise to bring about the change and understand what is required to operate in the changed state. In their view, leadership enables or constrains change. Gill (2003) maintains that change must be well managed; it must be planned, organised, directed and controlled. Change also requires effective leadership to introduce change. It is the leader who makes the difference. Gill's model proposes that the leadership of successful change requires vision; strategy; the development of a culture of sustainable shared values that support the vision and strategy for change; and empowering, motivating and inspiring those who are involved or affected. There is no shortage of prescriptions for organisational change processes and management in the literature. Nevertheless, the forces and factors driving change in every situation and context are different.

Impact on sport organisations

As noted by Slack (1997), sport organisations are not unitary entities that can be clearly defined. Rather, they are complex processes and sets of socially and historically constituted relationships, which include Nike, Quiksilver and Reebok on the one hand and the Gaelic Athletic Association (GAA), the Special Olympics and Women's

Tennis Association on the other. Their missions and organisational strategies and structures differ depending upon the context, as does their ability to embrace change. One major distinction to be made with respect to sports organisations is in relation to human resources: Whereas many sport organisations rely heavily on voluntary personnel to achieve their objectives, others are well endowed with human, financial and other resources. In certain cases, the over reliance on voluntary personnel may hinder change, but in other organisations, it may be a stimulus. Tennis Ireland (http://www.tennisireland.ie) depends on voluntary personnel (e.g., parents, coaches in local clubs) to provide the necessary support for the elite participants in the academy. Its strategic plan for the future development of Irish tennis and young players was implemented in 2003, which to date, has yielded some positive results.

Hums and MacLean (2004) focus on change in sport organisations, noting that it often stems from three sources: events occurring within the organisation, factors arising outside the organisation and an interaction of external and internal factors. The non-availability of Dublin's Croke Park (GAA's ultramodern stadium) for international rugby and soccer matches has been a contentious issue for many parties (government, members of the Association and other sporting bodies) over the years. However, because of the many forces (internal and external), change in the organisation's policy was achieved in 2005. It is a fitting example of a situation whereby the sources for the policy change were all three, as detailed by Hums and MacLean (2004).

In sport organisations, change can occur in four different areas: technology, products and services, structures and systems, and in people (Slack, 1997). Many sport bodies and organisations are in a constant set of change as new people join the organisation and others leave. In certain governing bodies, there have been changes at the senior executive level (e.g., the Football Association and the Football Association of Ireland). In others, changes in personnel are common at lower levels. Changes in personnel at the senior level are likely to have an impact on strategic initiatives and policy implementation.

The majority of suppliers of goods and services in the sport industry engage in market research to get insights on possible gaps in the market for their wares. To offset the growth of clones in golf clubs – and realising that golfers are not all cast in the same mould – many leading original equipment manufactures (OEMs), such as Ping, Slazenger, Nike, Callaway, TaylorMade and others, have begun offering custom fitting for golfers across the United States (http://www.worldgolf.com/products/component-golf-clubs-167). Advances in technology have facilitated major changes in product and service offerings (e.g., insurance, travel, information – fixtures and results, financial) within the sport industry. The replacement of the traditional wooden tennis racquet has not only had implications for tennis players, but also for the game. The modern game is now faster, but the newer racquet is lighter and accommodates elite and non-elite players. In addition, sports suppliers have altered their distribution strategy – several organisations use the internet to facilitate order and delivery processes and procedures. Many personnel in sport organisations are aware of the communication potential from technology and use it efficiently to inform key stakeholders of the latest developments. It was stated that Sir Clive Woodward would inform the players selected for the British and Irish Lions Summer Tour 2005 using text messaging; however, some of those selected asserted that they got news of their selection via Sky News!

CASE 19.1   The ring cycle is complete

Whatever happens at Athens, and I am confident it will be a great Olympic Games, the last 20 years have seen a remarkable turnround in the Olympic movement.

Today, the future of the Olympic Games has never seemed so secure. This year's Games in Athens will be broadcast to more than 220 countries, with a global audience of close to 4bn – making it the largest media event in the world.

Already the 2008 Games in Beijing is anticipated as one of the seismic political events of the new century; no fewer than nine of the most famous cities in the world announced their desire to host the 2012 Games, eventually five were shortlisted – London, Paris, Madrid, Moscow and New York.

In the early 1980s, it was a different story. Back then cities had to be cajoled into hosting the Games. Shortly before the Moscow Olympics in 1980 the Olympic Movement was staring into the financial abyss. The International Olympic Committee was on the verge of collapse. Written off by most commentators, it had less than $200,000 in cash and only $2m in assets.

How was this transformation – one of the most remarkable turnrounds of all time – achieved and what lessons does it have for other organisations? I was fortunate enough to witness much of it firsthand.

It began, quite clearly, with the appointment of a relatively unknown Spanish diplomat, Juan Antonio Samaranch, to the IOC presidency in 1980. Samaranch laid the foundations for the turnround in three ways. First, he made it clear that the IOC needed to stand on its own two feet financially. Given the IOC's parlous financial state there could be little debate about the need for it to become self-sufficient.

This financial imperative led to the creation of what became the most successful global marketing programme in the world. The programme operated under the code name TOP. This stood for nothing originally but eventually became The Olympic Partners. The idea of the TOP Programme was blissfully simple: to bundle all the rights together – the IOC, the Winter Olympic Games, the Summer Olympic Games and more than 150 national Olympic committees – into a single four-year exclusive marketing package, offering companies one-stop shopping for their global Olympic involvement. The programme now attracts the support of many of the world's leading blue chip organisations including Coca-Cola, Kodak, McDonald's, Visa, Swatch and Samsung. Single sponsors pay up to $70m – more than the total amount generated at the Lake Placid Winter Olympics – with 200 sponsoring corporations.

The second element of Samaranch's turnround strategy was to take control of the agenda. When he took over, the Olympic movement was a political football in the Cold War. It was powerless in the face of politically motivated boycotts. Samaranch set out to change this by creating a dialogue with influential people.

His idea was to avoid problems by anticipating and engaging with issues early rather than attempting to solve them at the last minute. He developed relationships with the world's political rulers. The Olympics became a force to be reckoned with.

The third element in Samaranch's recovery strategy was unity within the Olympic world – especially the NOCs and the International Federations. The entire Olympic movement faced a crisis, he explained, and it was only by working together that we could get out of it.

These three elements were the starting points. Others emerged as things were slowly turned around. Samaranch's leadership – long-term and strategic – was fundamental. He offered a clear vision. He wanted to modernise the Olympics while remaining true to their ideals; to commercialise without compromising. People tend to forget that he refused to sell European TV rights to Rupert Murdoch because reaching a larger audience through terrestrial channels was integral to the Olympic spirit. In doing so, the IOC accepted an offer which was $600m less than News Corporation's.

This underlines an integral part of the strategy. As a spectacle the Games are for everyone. Access and inclusiveness are vital to its stature as the world's pre-eminent sporting event.

Samaranch was patient. The Olympic movement works to long-term plans. It is not driven by quarterly results. At the same time, clarifying what constitutes success for the Olympics is an important element in its resurrection. The key measures of Olympic success are whether the Games are still the ultimate prize for athletes; whether they are true to their values, philosophy and brand; and the size of the broadcast audience.

Greater clarity about what matters for the Olympics has been matched by greater assertiveness about what the commercial success of the Games depends on. Defending its rights, its image and what it stands for is central to the Olympic turnaround.

Exclusiveness is key. Sponsors need to know that they can invest in the Olympic movement and be certain that they are not going to be undermined by a last minute surprise promotional campaign by their competitor.

If the IOC had sat back, and taken the easy option, turning a blind eye to the occasional borderline promotion or partner presence marketing indiscretion, the marketplace would have rapidly been cluttered and sponsorship fees would have stagnated at 1980 levels.

The Olympic Games allow no stadium advertising. The Olympic brand – the five rings logo that is the most widely recognised image in the world – is always the star. Official sponsors follow strict rules.

Ambush marketing is stamped on – hard. In Sydney, four days before the Opening Ceremony, we discovered that the catering services company, Aramark, had provided 30,000 uniforms to all the food service personnel with its logo prominently displayed on the left side of the chest.

This was a technical breach of TOP sponsor McDonald's exclusive rights. A team of seamstresses was quickly brought in to sew new patches on.

Such single mindedness has paid dividends in building and sustaining Olympic value.

In Lillehammer, 60 Norwegian spectators turned up to the cross-country events, with the name of an insurance company emblazoned across their clothes.

This was not accidental. It was a clearly orchestrated attempt to gain free publicity, with the insurance company probably paying for the cost of the spectator tickets.

The spectators were told that in order to enter the venues they had to cover up the advertising or take off their clothes.

As it was minus 20 degrees Celsius at the time, they were quickly able to find new jackets to cover up the offending advertising.

Source: M. Payne, *Financial Times*, 6 August 2004, p. 4

Questions

1. Outline some of the historic problems faced by the Olympic movement and by the Olympic Games.

2. Using the models detailed in this chapter, account for and explain the strategy used by Juan Samaranch to turn around the Olympics.

3. In relation to Question 2 above, identify what you think will have been the major challenges faced by the Samaranch and evaluate various ways these could have been addressed.

CASE 19.2   No style handicap

Sorry folks, but it appears you just don't mean a thing if you ain't got some swing. Golf swing, that is, not rhythm and blues. Yes, those deal making fairways frequented by (male) executives have now been driven into seriously glamorous – and unisex – territory. Anyone who's anyone – or wants to be someone – has to know their way around a driving range. Just think of actress Catherine Zeta Jones who, by wielding her clubs, manages to both decrease her handicap and increase her profile with a deftness befitting any (male) power-broking movie mogul. And stars such as Robbie Williams and Justin Timberlake are in on it too.

But it's not just trendy celebrities providing the glamour. Professional, if young, golf players are themselves shaking off the dead weight of all those loose-fitting woollen jumpers synonymous with the game, and are bringing style to the green. Tiger Woods is not the only person leading the way. Ian Poulter (aged 28) cuts a dash in Adidas tops teamed with vibrantly-printed trousers from William Hunt. 'I get loads of comments about how loud they are but that's all positive; if they're seeing them I know they're doing the job,' he says.

Nick Dougherty (23), of genetically improved Robbie Williams looks, jaunts about in Ralph Lauren loose-legged slacks in shades of baby blue and pink, and pin-stripes. Balancing the sexes is Annika Sorenstam (33), who is so glamorous that she was the subject of a recent American *Vogue* photoshoot. 'It's very important to a professional golfer to look right when on a golf course,' says Dougherty. 'Playing great golf is obviously the most important thing, but to have in mind "I'm feeling like a million dollars," to know you look the part, is great psychologically.'

These younger professionals are attracting a younger and broader interest. *GolfPunk*, a quirky magazine dedicated to golf was launched earlier this year, pitched specifically at 15- to 35-year-olds. Naturally, with a younger audience, more attention is being paid to appearance – and fashion – and everyone wants a piece.

Burberry introduced golf wear four years ago, and dresses both sexes; Ermenegildo Zegna offers hemp golf bags, lightweight cotton trousers, and quick-dry polo shirts; Nike have introduced Linkster, a range of golf-inspired trainers that boast rubber spikeless soles for on and off the golf course; Chanel introduced a range of double C logoed golf bags, clubs and balls to boost a sporting image to coincide with the launch of their Allure Home Sport fragrance; Tag Heuer, who sponsor Poulter, Dougherty and Tiger Woods, have introduced 100 limited edition Link Challenge watches that guarantee entry to the prestigious competition of the same name to be held in September, and are also developing a golf-specific watch. 'We are clear about the project but it won't be this year,' says Jean Marc Lacave, head of watches in the UK for LVMH.

Lacoste, who have been making golf wear for over 35 years and aim to dress everyone aged 'eight to 80', have started to place more of a stylish focus on designs, recently producing clothes 'that can make the transition to the street', according to Christian Kemp-Griffin, their international marketing director. Quirky pieces include photosensitive sun visors with peaks that change colour to match the headband.

Golf wear is, in many ways, easier to make fashionable than almost any other genuine sports wear because it doesn't need to be performance wear. 'Golf is a physical sport, but not to the same degree as running or rugby,' says Dougherty. 'You just need some freedom to move for your golf swing, which isn't a very complicated move.'

And that means it's easy for companies such as Dior to enter the fray with their new range of traditionally styled clothes with modern, almost grafitti, patterns. 'The style of the collection is based on the aristocratic elegance of the 1930s combined with the modern day Dior street chic style,' says John Galliano, creative director. So brightly patterned diamond checks emblazoned with Dior appear on plus fours and golf bags; pullovers have Dior spelled out in bobbled pompoms across the front; polo T-shirts come in pale pinks with red trim. They've even launched a Dior Malice Golf watch with wide strap bracelet to co-ordinate with the clothes.

'I wanted to create a great weekend line for the Dior clients,' explains Galliano of his new fashion obsession. 'They come to Dior looking for casual dresses and suits but I've known for a while that we needed to offer them more luxury casual wear.'

His inspiration came when he found an old book on golf. 'I basically used golf as a theme to play around with. I've always been interested in decontextualising things, a saddle for a handbag for example, and never being too literal. Golf is the traditional sport of the bourgeoisie and the privileged, and we enjoyed bringing it to street level.'

Interestingly, it's been the philosophical as much as the fashionable that's been at the forefront of the modernisation of golfing style. Johan Lindeberg, a keen golfer himself, is largely credited with starting the revolution in 1996 when he created his own fashion and golf wear ranges. 'I thought if I could change golf, I could change the world,' says Lindeberg. 'As the establishment really took over golf, as so many decision makers play golf, I thought if I could make them more modern, they would make more modern decisions.'

Lindeberg approached Swedish golfer Jesper Parnevik who he thought 'looked terrible but somehow under all his chunky clothing I thought he had the potential to be a sexy guy', and asked to dress him in his colourful, fashionably cut kit made from cutting edge fabrics. 'He was very brave as at the time golf was stale and so conservative. People laughed at him and the comments on TV were unbelievable,' recalls Lindeberg.

But they stuck it out and together 'we created a movement'. Lindeberg's philosophy is simple. 'I don't want to protest, I want to inspire, to connect the fashion world with the golf world,' he says. 'It's all part of the new modern lifestyle and I'm trying to create clothes that fit in with that. If you drive to your country club in your modern car, it's hard to step out of it wearing pleated chinos and a jacquard shirt.'

Heather Dixon, meanwhile, is concentrating only on ladies' golf wear with her range of femininely cut T-shirts, trousers, skirts and accessories. 'I'm giving a young feeling to a sport that had been regarded as either masculine or more mature. Our first collection was for me a statement of femininity in golf. I want to make equality in golf a little more happening,' she says.

Dixon, a former health spa developer, came to her task by accident. When her stolen car was returned to her by police, it came back with a set of golf clubs. She kept them and was taken by a friend to a driving range.

'But I wasn't allowed on the course as I was wearing jeans and trainers – I didn't have any idea about golf etiquette. I went to look in the course shop but there wasn't much choice, and what was there was for men.' Not long afterwards she gave up her job and started to fill the gap in the market. Now her range is stocked in top resorts worldwide (www.heatherdesign.com).

At Pringle, they've been trying hard to lose the old image of Nick Faldo and baggy diamond print jumpers, for both their men's and women's ranges. But while they've been shaking up their fashion image, 'golf wear was put to the side a little bit,' says Simon Mills, sales director for golf wear. 'But over the last six months we've started to relaunch golf wear with new fresher looks, obviously using influences from the fashion collection.' Though the completed results of the makeover won't be in stores before autumn, current styles are still more body-conscious, though 'not a completely fashion fit', and new fabrics such as Dryfit are coming.

Technological fabrics are playing a key part in the golf makeover. 'Golf will always be based around polo shirts and a pair of golf slacks,' says Nick Waddington, head of golf wear at Dunhill. The house has recently updated its golf wear, first introduced in 1985. 'What's changed most over the last 20 years is the functionality of the garments, with the technological advances. Stylistically, it's in the modern spirit because it's the most technically forward part of our range so it makes sense to make the styling fit a more modern design.'

As all this fashion hits the fairway, clubs are having to move with the times. Gleneagles recently relaxed its clothing rules: now if you turn up in jeans, as long as you're wearing the right shoes, you're allowed to play. New courses, such as The Grove in Hertfordshire, are deliberately all inclusive, non-exclusive. There is no club membership – play is on a strictly turn-up-and-pay policy, and no clothing rules. 'We want the customer to feel comfortable whether on the course or in a restaurant,' says club spokeswoman, Helen McDonnel. 'They can be in jeans and an open neck shirt. There's no formal attire for the golf course, none of that outdated stuff.'

In turn that means that designers are more free to create. 'Believe it or not I'm making my first mini skirt now,' declares Dixon. 'I call it a cullotte, really – it looks like a skirt but has hotpants underneath. I wouldn't have done it a year ago, but the demand is coming from the US and Dubai. People there are living in the sun and they don't want to be covered up,' she says.

What can top mini skirts on the golf course? Well, how about some bling-bling? Diamond Touch Golf Plc have produced a driver with a 20 carat diamond insert.

Source: E. Ings-Chambers, *Financial Times*, 19 June 2004

Questions

1. What are the main strategic issues identified by this case study?

2. To what extent do you think the issues identified in the case are problems for golf rather than for the sports clothing companies?

3. To what extent do you think the golfing authorities and the sports clothing companies could or should strategically collaborate?

Conclusions

The dynamic nature of strategy has been widely documented in the literature (Barney, 1991; Johnson et al., 2005; Porter, 1985; Thompson and Strickland, 1995a). Many organisations have periods of relative continuity during which strategy remains largely unchanged or changes incrementally, followed by periods of flux and transformational change. Should strategy progressively fail to address the strategic position of the organisation, then performance deteriorates (Johnson et al., 2005). Carrillat, Jaramillo and Locander (2004) distinguish between *market-driven* and *market-driving* organisations. The former have to the ability to understand, attract and keep valuable customers, and the latter can gain an SCA by changing the structure or composition of a market or behaviour of its players. In the business arena, Ikea is frequently cited as a player that has changed the marketplace for furniture; in the sport industry, many commentators would probably include Nike in that category.

Hums and MacLean (2004) deal with the many issues associated with governance in sport organisations. These authors maintain that sport organisations need to review the governance structure on a regular basis in order to maintain pace with market developments and need to put in place a structure that will best facilitate the advancement of the organisation's strategic objectives. Strategic marketing embraces many activities and organisational tasks (as detailed in this chapter) in the context of understanding the nature of external opportunities and threats and internal strengths and weaknesses. Various strategies have been detailed in relation to market positioning adopted by organisations in order to gain a competitive edge over rivals. Many factors impact on the level of strategic change implemented by sport organisations – a key one being resource availability (e.g., human, financial, technological). It is essential for senior executives to be current with national government policies in relation to sporting matters and European Union directives on legal, labour mobility and competition issues. It is now widely acknowledged that domestic and multinational sport organisations (governing bodies, clubs, federations, firms) need a marketing capability to promote their mission. The topic of organisational change in the sport industry is now getting greater attention, but it is essential that the focus be on those bodies that influence directly the sport market, its players and its future development, bearing in mind the roles and responsibilities of key stakeholders.

Discussion questions

1. Frequently, the council of sport organisations (membership and size) are mentioned as factors that prevent strategic change in such bodies. Do you agree with this assertion? Explain your viewpoint.
2. Sport organisations are service providers, and information is critical for them in gaining and sustaining a competitive edge. Select two such organisations (operating in a different sport sector) with which you are familiar and detail the source of each organisation's competitive advantage. Detail the possible threats to this advantage and how they might be circumvented by each organisation.

Guided reading

For detailed reading on strategy and strategic change, the reader is referred to Pettinger (2004) and Johnson et al. (2005). Parker (2004) is also recommended as an interesting analysis of strategy in the sport environment is provided. Governance issues are pertinent for change in organisations, and the reader is directed to Hums and MacLean (2004), which takes a US perspective yet is insightful on organisational change issues.

Keywords

Cost leadership strategy; marketing audit; organisational change; strategic drift; strategic objectives; strategic thrust.

Bibliography

Amis, J., Slack, T. and Hinnings, C. (2004) Strategic change and the role of interests, power, and organizational capacity, *Journal of Sport* 18:158–98.

Amit, R. and Shoemaker, P.J.H. (1993) Strategic assets and organizational rent, *Strategic Management Journal* 14(1):33–46.

Ashill, N., Frederikson, M. and Davies, J. (2003) Strategic marketing planning: A grounded investigation, *European Journal of Marketing* 37(3/4):430–60.

Barney, J. (1991) Firm resources and sustainable competitive advantage, *Journal of Management* 17:99–120.

Barney, J, (1997) *Gaining and Sustaining Competitive Advantage*, Reading, MA: Addison Wesley.

Bartunek, J.M. (1988) 'The dynamics of personal and organizational reframing', in R.E. Quinn and K.S. Cameron (eds), *Paradox and Transformation: Towards a Theory of Change in Organization and Management*, Cambridge, MA: Ballinger.

Bartunek, J.M. and Moch, M.K. (1987) First-order, second-order, and third-order change and organization development interventions: A cognitive approach, *Journal of Applied Behavioural Science* 23(4):483–500.

Black, J. and Boal, K. (1994) Strategic resources: Traits, configurations and paths to sustainable competitive advantage, *Strategic Management Journal* 15:131–48.

Brownlie, D. (1999) Benchmarking your marketing process, *Long Range Planning* 32(1): 88–95.

Carrillat, F. Jaramillo, F. and Locander, W. (2004) *Market Driving Organisations: A Framework*, Retrieved 5 February 2005, from http//www.ansreview.org/articles/carrillat052004.pdf.

Chapman, J. (2002) A framework for transformational change in organizations, *Leadership and Organization Development Journal* 23(1/2):16–25.

Conner, K.R. (1991) A historical comparison of resource based theory and five schools of thought within industrial organization economics: Do we have a new theory of the firm?, *Journal of Management* Aug:121–54.

Coyne, K. (1993) Achieving a sustainable competitive advantage, *Journal of Business Strategy* 14(1):3–10.

Daft, R. (2000) *Management*, Orlando: Dryden Press.

Doyle, P. (1994) *Marketing Management and Strategy*, London: Prentice Hall.

Ferrell, O.C. and Hartline, M. (2005) *Marketing Strategy*, Thompson, South Western.

Ford, J. and Backoff, R.H. (1988) 'Organizational change in and out of the dualities and paradox', in R.E Quinn and K.S. Cameron (eds), *Paradox and Transformation: Towards a theory of Change in Organization and Management*, Cambridge, MA: Ballinger.

Gill, R. (2003) Change management or change leadership?, *Journal of Change Management* 3(4):307–18.

Golembiewski, R.T. (1979) *Approaches to planned change Part 11: Macro level Interventions and Change-agent Strategies*, New York: Marcel Dekker.

Grant, R. (1991) The resource based view of competitive advantage, *California Management Review* 33(3):119–35.

Grant, R. (1995) *Contemporary Strategy Analysis*, Malden, MA: Blackwell Business.

Johnson, G., Scholes, K. and Whittington, R. (2005) *Exploring Corporate Strategy*, Harlow: FT Prentice Hall.

Hill, C. and Jones, G. (1995) *Strategic Management Theory: An Integrated Approach*, Boston: Houghton and Mifflin.

Hums, M. and MacLean, J. (2004) *Governance and Policy in Sport Organizations*, Scottsdale, AZ: Holcomb Hathaway Publishers.

Hunt, S. and Derozier, C. (2004) The normative imperatives of business and marketing strategy: Grounding strategy in resource advantage theory, *The Journal of Business and Industrial Marketing* 19(1): 5–22.

Jobber, D. and Fahy, J. (2003) *Foundations of Marketing*, Berkshire: McGraw-Hill Education.

Kotler, P. and Armstrong, G. (1994) *The Principles of Marketing*, Englewood Cliffs, NJ: Prentice Hall.

Kraatz, M. and Zajac, E. (2001) How organizational resources affect strategic change and performance in turbulent environments: Theory and evidence, *Organization Science* 12(5): 632–57.

Leppard, L. and McDonald, M. (1991) Marketing planning and corporate culture: A conceptual framework which examines management attitudes in the context of marketing planning, *Journal of Marketing Management* 7:213–36.

McDonald, M. (1996) Strategic marketing planning: Theory, practice and research agendas, *Journal of Marketing Management* 12:5–28.

Mintzberg, H. (1987) Crafting strategy, *Harvard Business Review* July/August:66–75.

Morgan, R., McGuinness, T. and Thorpe, E. (2000) The contribution of marketing to business strategy formation: A perspective on business performance gains, *Journal of Strategic Marketing* 8:341–62.

Neill, S. and Rose, G. (2006) The effect of strategic complexity on marketing strategy and organizational performance, *Journal of Business Research* 56(1):1–10.

Nonaka, I, (1991) The knowledge creating company, *Harvard Business Review* November/ December: 96–104.

Parker, C. (2004) 'Strategy and environmental analysis in sport', in J. Beech and S. Chadwick (eds), *The Business of Sport Management*, London: FT Prentice Hall.

Perrow, C. (1961) The analysis of goals in complex organizations, *American Sociological Review* 26: 854–66.

Petraf, M. (1993) The cornerstones of competitive advantage: A resource based view, *Strategic Management Journal* 14:179–91.

Pettinger, R. (2004) *Contemporary Strategic Management*, Hampshire: Palgrave Macmillan.

Porter, M. (1980) *Competitive Strategy*, New York: Free Press.

Porter, M. (1985) *Competitive Advantage*, New York: Free Press.

Porter, M. (1987) From competitive advantage to corporate strategy, *Harvard Business Review*, May/June: 43–59.

Rogan, D. (2003) *Marketing: An Introduction for Irish Students*, Dublin: Gill and Macmillan.

Senge, P. (1990) *The Fifth Discipline – The Art and Practice of the Learning Organization*, London: Century Business.

Shank, M. (2005) *Sports Marketing: A Strategic Perspective*, Upper Saddle River, NJ: Pearson Education.

Slack, T. (1997) *Understanding Sport Organisations*, Champaign, IL: Human Kinetics.

Thompson, A. and Strickland, A. (1995a) *Crafting and Implementing Strategy*, Chicago: Irwin.

Thompson, A. and Strickland, A. (1995b) *Strategy Formulation and Implementation*, Chicago: Irwin.

Verdin, P.J. and Williamson, P.J. (1994) 'Core competences, competitive advantage and market analysis: Forging the links', in G. Hamel and A. Heene (eds), *Competence Based Competition*. Chichester: Wiley.

Watt, D. (1998) *Sport Management and Administration*, London: E&FN SPON.

Watzlawick, P., Weakland, J.H. and Fisch, R. (1974) *Change: Principles of Problem Formation and Problem Resolution*, New York: Norton.

Weerawardena, J. (2003) The role of marketing capability in innovation based competitive strategy, *Journal of Strategic Marketing* 11:15–35.

Williams, J.R. (1992) How sustainable is your competitive advantage?, *California Management Review*, 34(3):29–51.

Recommended websites

International Olympic Movement
http://www.olympics.org

International Rugby Board
http://www.irb.ie

Tennis Ireland
http://www.tennisireland.ie

Umbro
http://www.umbro.com/corporate/doc/accounts04

Union of European Football Associations
http://www.uefa.com

World Golf
http://www.worldgolf.com/products/component-golf-clubs-167

Chapter 20

International sport marketing and globalisation

Dr Susan Bridgewater
University of Warwick

Learning outcomes

Upon completion of this chapter, the reader should be able to:

- Understand the drivers of the globalisation of sports.

- Understand the key challenges arising from this globalisation.

- Identify the key aspects of creating global brands.

- Understand global marketing mix issues in sports.

Overview of chapter

This chapter reviews the major drivers of the globalisation of sports, such as the creation of star players as global icons, the cost of building a successful team, international legislation on transfers and mobility of sports players and the globalisation of media, such as the internet and digital broadcasting. Given this globalisation, the chapter reviews the major discussions of international marketing literature and considers the extent to which we can learn by applying these to sport marketing. The chapter then considers the development of global brands in sport marketing. How can clubs develop these, and should the marketing strategy be standardised or adapted to the needs and wants of particular markets? In expanding into international markets, clubs must decide how best to internationalise.

The chapter then explores the different types, or modes, of international operation – for example, export, franchise and foreign direct investment (FDI) – and the pros and cons of each of these in terms of control, risk and ability to expand successfully. Some of the main theoretical underpinning, such as Dunning's (1988) eclectic paradigm and oligopolistic reaction theory, are applied to sport marketing to offer insights into the challenges facing firms as sport marketing globalises.

Introduction

Sports, such as football, are no longer simply 'beautiful games' but are businesses with stakeholders, global brands and global market expansion opportunities. There are many indicators of the increased importance of the international environment on sports. European sports clubs must comply with European competition law – as in the Bosman ruling, in which the European Union is interested in whether broadcasters should be allowed to sell collective media rights to the Premier league, players and sports personalities, the key assets of sport businesses, transfer in large numbers between countries and sports personalities can become global icons.

With this acceptance comes the question of which of the key managerial debates from international marketing can meaningfully be extended to gain understanding of the professional sport market.

Drivers of globalisation in sport

Any chapter on global marketing, regardless of the sector, tends to begin with consideration of the global imperative for marketers. The global market may seem remote to players, and clubs lower down the levels of sporting prowess. Yet changes in international legislation, global television coverage, the internet and other changes in the sporting environment mean that the global imperative impacts on all participants in sports.

CASE 20.1 Formula 1: global entertainment and what of the future?

Bernie Ecclestone's involvement in Formula 1 over a period of 25 years has seen that sport has become a global entertainment and advertising medium. The 1990s saw the arrival into the sport of global automotive firms such Mercedes, Toyota, BMW and Honda. Multinational corporations brought hundreds of millions of US dollars into this increasingly high-tech sport, creating great wealth in grand prix racing. This vision reached its peak in 1997 when the sport reached its height of popularity. Yet a more problematic future lay ahead as the multinational corporations' shareholders began to question the reasons why they receive only 40% of revenues of Formula 1 despite their heavy investment in the sports development. When Ecclestone began to sell 75% of SLEC, the company that owns the commercial rights to Formula 1, in 1999, the deal foundered with the fortunes of German TV company EM-TV. Fellow German buyer Kirch Media also hit trouble, and the shares came into the possession of three global banking giants, Bayerische Landesbank, Lehman Brothers and JP Morgan, which had funded the purchase of the shares. In 2004, these banks won a high court judgement that changed the balance of power in Formula 1 and allowed them a right of representation on the company that controls the sport's commercial rights.

The big strategic decisions facing the future of the sport will now be subject to a greater level of scrutiny and the involvement of a number of new global stakeholders.

After the present contract expires in 2007, GPWC, a splinter group created by the motor manufacturers, proposes running its own world championship.

A further challenge to the future of Formula 1 lies within the field of global sponsorship of Formula 1 cars after claims late in November 2004 that the method previously used by Ecclestone's management group inflated the number of viewers watching each race by around 130 million. Based upon the most common method of calculating sponsorship value on the amount of 'media equivalent airtime', that is the equivalent costs of gaining that much airtime via other media such as global adverts, this would have a significant impact on the amount of money that global sponsors are prepared to pay to put their names on the cars.

Source: Adapted from 'Motor racing: Ecclestone forced into new deal', *The Guardian*, 7 December 2004; 'F1 struggles to get back on track', *Marketing (UK)*, 18 March 2005, p. 15; 'F1 admits to 'misleading' TV audience numbers' *Marketing Week*, 11 March, p. 7; 'F1 global viewers recount could hit sponsors' deals' *Marketing (UK)*,11 March 2004, p. 1

Questions

1. What major changes can be identified in the nature of the global stakeholders who play a role in Formula 1?

2. What challenges do these changes pose for the future development of Formula 1 as a global sport?

3. To what extent do you believe the doubt over audience figures for Formula 1 will influence future global sponsorship deals?

Global stakeholders

The above account of the development of Formula 1 into a global sport and the challenges it now faces are a clear illustration of the way that global players can shape the face of sport. Global car manufacturers, global investors, including banks and other firms, global television coverage, global sponsors and international law, all feature in the above case history.

An analysis of the competitive environment surrounding many sports would see an increase in the number and the influence of the international players who have an impact on the development of different sports. As the competitive arena becomes more global, so do the challenges facing global marketers in the sporting field.

Amortising the costs of global competitive advantage

Developing a new drug can take between 8 and 10 years. The firm must commit money to research and development for this lengthy period before it can begin to recoup its investment and then only if the drug successfully makes it to market and offers a benefit over and above existing treatments for whatever medical condition. The firm then has a similar period in which it can patent, or legally protect, its innovation and command a premium price before competitors can come into the market with cheaper generic drugs offering the same benefit. In this situation, it is easy to understand that the pharmaceutical firm will be pushed to expand rapidly into as many international markets to amortise, or offset, the setup costs. Because many medical conditions affect only a small proportion of the population of the company, the pharmaceutical firm targets a niche market across as many markets as are accessible, have a sufficiently large number of sufferers and can afford to pay.

The costs of global competitive advantage in sports may put the same pressure on sports clubs to expand globally. Consider the example of football. The population of a country has a certain proportion of people who like football, those who prefer other sports and those who support none. Although it may appear that the chanting mass in the stadium contains a large number of fans, most football clubs are technically small businesses in terms of their turnover and profit. The football fan base is intensely loyal and unlikely to switch to supporting the rival team, regardless of how poor the run of results. Therefore, the market of Manchester United, Real Madrid or Boca Juniors is a niche market. Gaining success in international competition involves investment in quality international players. Player wages are high – the financial crisis in English football was largely fuelled by the escalation of player wages. In 2002–2003, these were, in many cases, more than 100% of the turnover of the club. Revenue from gate receipts is limited with the capacity of stadia. Funding the ambition of clubs and fans, therefore, is often only possible if a club can find a benefactor or tap into revenue from groups of supporters in other countries.

Global media

One of the greatest strengths of sports is their unique nature as live entertainment with uncertain outcomes. For other entertainment types such as movies or theatre, the ending is often known. The Titanic always sinks! In sports events, however, uncertainty of outcome makes for compulsive viewing. The same competitors may face each other in a rematch in the league, or the World Championships after the Olympics, but each can be equally gripping. Indeed, the element of wreaking revenge can add to the spice of subsequent encounters.

One important development that has helped sports clubs with their international expansion is the growth in the availability of global communication media. Although the market potential for global satellite channels, and especially pay-per-view coverage of sporting events may have been overestimated (figures), the increasing international coverage of sporting events fuels demand in new international markets. Whether via global channels, such as Sky and CNN, or on local channels purchasing the rights for an individual market, fans can increasingly satisfy their appetites for mainstream and specialist sporting events. The availability of multiple channels and 24-hour coverage has brought a much wider range of sporting events to the global market. This makes sports more attractive to sponsors looking to boost international awareness of products and services.

The internet

The advent of new media has brought a whole new set of challenges for global marketers of sports. The late 1990s saw the internet heralded as bringing a global marketing revolution. Commentators and practitioners recognised the internet's capability to offer global connectivity; to provide real-time interaction; and to break down the barriers of geography, time and cultural distance. The low costs of the internet as a medium to access global markets is seen to level the playing field for small firms to compete with larger multinational rivals across many sectors. In sports, the internet has allowed clubs to communicate with fans on a global scale at relatively low costs. The later rollout of broadband connections into the market increased the potential for online club-specific TV channels offering events highlights and exclusive access to interviews with star players. It has also resulted in a proliferation of fan websites and web boards to facilitate interaction between fans on a global scale.

Alongside the obvious opportunities presented by the internet, however, is a set of new challenges arising from the technology. Global connectivity means that any information disclosed on the internet is globally accessible. Many small firms that post a website become 'unintentional internationalists'. The firm may find itself dealing with customers in a diversity of markets. If physical distribution of goods and services is required, the firm may need to form alliances with partners who are able to handle this side of the business for them. Global online banking systems – such as PayPal – may help to facilitate online currency conversion and secure banking, but logistical and resource implications of transacting on a global scale remain.

The internet has particular value in breaking down barriers to international markets for goods and services that can be digitised and distributed online. Much of the revenue for sports brands comes from this type of coverage, including video and audio coverage of matches and interviews. Merchandise, however, may be less easily transacted online. Serving international markets has effectively pushed some sports brands into establishing international franchise outlets such as the Manchester United retail stores in the United Kingdom, Singapore and the United States and other strong franchises established by AC Milan, Juventus, New York Yankees and Washington Redskins.

The open nature of the technology has other implications for global marketing of digital media. Despite advances in internet security, protection of intellectual property online is difficult. There is a potential issue with grey markets (buying in cheaper markets and switching across borders) and potential for damage to global brands. Turnbull's risk assessment applies to football – damage to the brand reputation. The difficulty of controlling what is written on independent websites and the ease with which viral emails and information can be distributed on a global scale increase the extent to which brands can be damaged by negative publicity about star players or events.

Global entrepreneurs

Investment in sports brands across national borders appears to be on the increase. English football, for example, has seen a number of landmark events in recent years. In summer 2003, Russian Oligarch Roman Abramovitch made a massive investment in Chelsea Football Club that has turned around the on- and off-field performance of the club. Liverpool Football Club was linked with a potential investment by the Thai prime minister, Thaksin Shiniwatra, and Malcolm Glazer, American owner of the 2003 Super Bowl winners Tampa Bay Buccaneers, has just launched his third bid to take over Manchester United Football Club.

This type of investment shows that global investment flows are as much part of the competitive environment in sports as they are in other business sectors. Strong sports performance and strong brand development attract more money into clubs from investors around the globe. The phenomenon is interesting on a number of levels. Firstly, this increases the potential rewards of success. In addition to the short-term benefits, this may attract new international investment and have longer term impact. If it does so, however, the cultural and strategic implications for the club or team are significant. The strategic intent behind the investment may be that the investor wants to be involved in the game, as with Abramovitch. It may be to develop the brand in the investors host market, as would seem to have been the case with the potential investments in Liverpool and Manchester United. In the last case, it does not appear that Glazer is a particular fan of football as a game, let alone of Manchester United, but is attracted by the business potential of the brand. This type of investment increases the significance of the global marketing strategies and strength of sports brands.

The following section considers the major issues involved in developing and maintaining successful global sport marketing strategies.

Global marketing strategy in sports

The emergence of global brands

Brands are important on a number of levels. Firstly, depending on the nature of the market, up to 70% of an organisation's earnings can be attributed to brands. Secondly, customers tend to build loyalty to strong brands. Finally, brands now provide the guiding principles for market-oriented organisations. Over time, research attention has shifted from a focus on brand image (Boulding, 1956) to the creation of brand identity (Harris and De Chernatonay, 2001; Kapferer, 1997). The former centres on understanding what customers value in a brand, whilst the latter also encompasses the process of ensuring that employees' values and behaviour towards customers and other stakeholders is consistent with these.

The growing importance of image to sports clubs (Ferrand and Pages, 1999) suggests that it may be effective to consider professional sports clubs and events as brands. Within sport marketing literature, there is a growing volume of work in the areas of 'fan identification with clubs' (Sutton, McDonald, Milne and Cimperman, 1997; Wann, 1995) and with loyalty to particular teams or sports personalities (Fullerton, 1995; Wakefield and Sloan, 1995).

When measuring the value of these brands, Aaker (1996) suggests that the measures should cover the full scope of the brand equity, including awareness, perceived quality, loyalty and associations. A number of these aspects have been addressed by studies of involvement in professional sports.

In terms of perceived quality, economic studies (see Baade and Mattheson, 2004) suggest that fans are more loyal to teams that are successful. Success translates into higher average attendance and lower variability of attendance. Awareness in professional sports is contributed to by the extent to which the club is covered by television and other media. In addition to fans that regularly attend sporting events, a much larger fan base may be involved in the brand via a variety of other media. Sports coverage is unique among televised entertainment in that the outcome is unknown and that coverage is live and unrehearsed (Gantz, 1981).

As with other types of brands, the value placed upon the brand is not only based on awareness and perceived quality, but the level of loyalty is influenced by intangible, emotional associations with the club. Sociologists have long studied the reasons and outcomes of being a sports fan (Edwards, 1973). 'Being a fan fulfils the needs of sharing, feeling and belonging. It provides an acceptable outlet for exhibiting emotions and feelings' (Gantz, 1991, p. 264). Sports psychologists point to the complex relationship between fans and professional sports brands by suggesting that being a fan is relatively low risk. When the team does well, the fan shares success and considers himor herself to have played a role in this. When the team does not do well, the fan tends to externalise this and attribute the blame to the players, manager or other external agents (Zillmann, Bryant and Sapolsky, 1979).

In addition to the emotional side of fan support of professional sports, Melnick (1993) suggests that many fans support professional sports clubs for the social and entertainment opportunities they present. Loyalty becomes part of the pattern of behaviour of sports fans and therefore the potential for loyalty to this type of brand is considerable.

A useful summary of the attributes of brand equity in professional sports can be found in Sutton et al. (1997), who classify the determinants of fan involvement as team performance, organisational ability, emotional affiliation and activity links.

The scope of attachment to a sports brand is, however, very local in some cases. The emotional dimension may be strongest for a 'home team' with which the history, symbols, venue and local connections may be a source of emotional pride. With the advances in technologies of travel and communication, however, the geographic scope of brand attraction may increase. The following example contrasts the global reputation of two English football clubs of very different size and fortunes, both of which benefit from international marketing activities.

CASE 20.2   A tale of two football clubs

Stockport County plays in the English League One, although the club currently languishes at the bottom of the division and may go down through the trapdoor of relegation at the end of the 2004–2005 football season. From this relatively lowly position to the European Competition–challenging Premiership heights of near neighbour Manchester United may seem like some distance. Manchester United, the world's wealthiest sports franchise, may appear to overshadow its smaller rival. Yet many miles away in China in cities such as Shenyang, Wuhan and Beijing, Stockport County draws crowds of 25,000. Its home gate in England reaches only 6500 at best.

The team's international marketing manager, Steve D. Bellis, puts Stockport's success in China down to smart marketing and the desire to be entrepreneurial in exploring the scope of new sources of marketing revenue. In May 2005, the club will be the first professional soccer team of any nationality to play in China's remote Urumqi province.

The global soccer industry is a $12 billion sector. Professional soccer leagues are emerging in countries from the Baltics to China. This global popularity has brought fame and fortune to iconic players such as David Beckham and has attracted investment from billionaires into the game. About 80% of the game's global revenue comes from Europe, but the gap between rich and poor is immense. Relegation from Italy's Serie A costs a team around 40% of its revenue. So, the rich get rich and the poor get poorer. Should there be regulation of the global game to control this disparity? Regulated French teams struggle to compete against teams from unregulated Spain and England, so a more international scale of agreement would be needed. The French market is only just beginning to allow clubs to list on the Bourse, the French Stock Exchange.

So, as with smaller firms in many sectors, part of the answer may lie in global expansion. Even Europe's smaller players can attract interest in vast nations such as China. Stockport now makes 10% of its revenue from China, although the efforts and frequent trips increase the pressures on the team and commercial staff. Stockport has recently bought 50% of a Shenyang-based football club, now called Stockport Tigers. What will the future hold for the innovative international marketing strategy of Stockport and its international namesake?

Source: Adapted from 'Madness of crowds', *Forbes* 173(4): 120, 12 April 2004; 'Liverpool's Thai-Up', *The Economist* 371 (8375): 57, 15 May 2004

Questions

1. Evaluate the potential of Manchester United and Stockport County to develop brand awareness in China.

2. What challenges does each club face in growing its brand value in China?

3. To what do you attribute the success of Stockport County in China?

Sports brands can be 'clubs' or teams (e.g., Real Madrid, Udinese, Ajax) or sports personalities (e.g., Ellen MacArthur, Johnny Wilkinson, Lance Armstrong).

These brands differ in their values as with any other type of brand. Young and Rubicam's Brand Asset Valuator approach identifies four aspects of brand equity; differentiation, knowledge, esteem and relevance.

- **Differentiation** is the extent to which a product of service is different or better. In sports terms, this suggests that successful teams and successful players have greater differential advantage and create stronger brands.
- **Knowledge** is the extent to which a customer is aware of the brand and what it stands for. In sports terms, television and internet coverage of sports has vastly increased access and knowledge of sports and should have strengthened the global brand potential.
- **Esteem** is the extent to which fans 'like' or feel emotionally attached to a brand. Esteem is high for sports brands because a strong emotional attachment is present. This can be culturally specific. The appeal of David Beckham in Japan during the 2002 Football World Cup was based not only on his footballing ability and appearance but also the extent to which his image as a clean-cut family man appealed to Japanese fans.
- **Relevance** is the extent to which a brand appeals to a target market. Sports brands are not relevant if the sport is not widely understood or supported in a country.

Relevance in sports can, for example, be boosted by signing a player who would appeal to a particular target market (see Japanese example).

CASE 20.3   Junichi Inamoto

Star Japanese football player, Junichi Inamoto was a hero to Japanese fans in the 2002 World Cup. His appeal was greatly enhanced by his time playing in the English Premiership with Arsenal. His subsequent moves to Fulham, Gamba Osaka back to West Brom in August 2004 attracted less attention. The player has not been helped by injuries and recently moved on a one month loan to Coca-Cola Championship side Cardiff in an attempt to regain match fitness.

From an international marketing perspective, the fortunes of the player and the impact of his exploits in English football are fascinating, and the motivations behind his football moves may be as much about marketing as they are about football.

Midfielder, Junichi Inamoto joined Championship winning Arsenal for around $5m in July 2001 from J-league club, Gamba Osaka. A true star in his own national team, Inamoto was unable to have an impact on the Arsenal first-team, prompting speculation that he might have been signed to boost interest in Arsenal in Japan, rather than for his football prowess. Inamoto attracted global attention after helping Japan to win two consecutive Asian cups and soon had a number of European clubs keen to sign him. Arsenal manager, Arsene Wenger had worked in Japan and saw his performances whilst working there as a TV Analyst.

Yet the chances did not come for Inamoto at Arsenal and, despite his Japan team reaching the last 8 of the 2002 World Cup, he was released from his contract. Inamoto was still keen to remain in European football. His football fortunes have been mixed since. Likened to Japan's Michael Owen – Nakato who plays at Fiorentina is likened to Beckham and Ina is nearly as big a name – 25 Japanese journalists and six TV crews attended the press conference to mark his transfer to West Bromwich Albion. Analysts suggested that his signing was a real winner, but not just on the pitch. Previous club Fulham became a massive name in Japan, although Inamoto was not a regular starter. In global marketing terms, therefore, team selection and signings may be of far greater significance than just on the pitch results.

Source: Adapted from *Japanese Times*, 28 December 2004; ESPN Soccer Base www.espnsoccernet.com, www.sportinglife.com/football/worldcupfinals2002/team_sections/japan.html; 'Favourite son: Inamoto is an icon back in Japan', *Sports Argus*, 18 September 2004

Questions

1. How might the signing of Inamoto fit with Arsenal's international marketing strategy?

2. What are the dangers of linking market development strategies to a particular player or celebrity?

3. To what extent do you think Inamoto's relative lack of success on the pitch might affect Arsenal's brand image in Japan?

The pattern of internationalisation of sports brands

International marketing shows two main models of how firms become international. The first, traditional, model based on research from the Nordic studies of the Uppsala School shows organisations reaching a critical mass and then expanding gradually, both in terms of the level of investment in each market – from export to franchises and other knowledge agreements towards FDI – and into markets that are progressively more different from the host market. A more recent challenge to the Uppsala model, however, shows more rapid international expansion. 'Early internationalists' may even be international from inception and expand into parallel markets simultaneously and may enter culturally different markets before those more similar to the host.

A study of international marketing in sports shows an interesting combination of influences on the way that sports clubs and events have become international. Some events, such as the Olympics or the World Cup, have been international from inception. These are the equivalent of the big global brands because they face the changing face of the global market as global players. For many domestic sports clubs, however, international exposure came only after they had become big players in their home market. The pace and nature of global exposure in sports has changed with the advent of global media, such as global satellite channels, the internet and digital radio. Domestic players such as Manchester United, Real Madrid, the All Blacks and others have become global brands. Despite their high level of visibility, the value of these brands remains, in international marketing terms, underdeveloped in many markets. The next stage of development is to assess the next tier of target markets for these brands.

The previous section explains that global sports brands largely target niche markets. Three explanations are commonly proposed for the behaviour of rapid internationalists. They may internationalise rapidly because of the nature of the markets in which they operate. These are narrow and specialist and to grow beyond a certain size, firms must seek out similar target markets in other countries. They may internationalise rapidly because of the nature of the entrepreneurs or founders of the business. Some entrepreneurs transfer useful knowledge from other international ventures, and they are often charismatic leaders with ambition and drive. Finally, early internationalists may have firm-specific capabilities that mark them out from other firms. They may be better at managing, marketing, spotting talented staff and so on.

If this learning from the broader international marketing field is transferred to the internationalisation of sports, the following issues arise.

The nature of sport markets

With most sectors, if a brand fails to deliver in terms of its quality or otherwise loses its appeal, customers will switch to a competitor brand. Sports fans are very loyal to particular clubs, sports individuals or events. Although there are some sports fans with a general interest in sports, most have a preference for some types of sports and usually an allegiance to certain sports clubs. No matter how bad a season Real Madrid may have, the club's fans are unlikely to switch allegiance to Valencia or Barcelona. Many rivalries between fans of different clubs are firmly entrenched, often antagonistic and tribal. Research suggests that poor performance of sports brands results in a general lessening of interest in the brand and maybe of sports in general. The perceived level of success of a fan's chosen team or favourite star is felt very personally. A bad result may mean that the fan goes out of his or her way to avoid reading about sport or does not watch sports news channels to avoid this source of discomfort.

Given the nature of the market for sports brands, there is limited potential to grow a domestic market, although good performance helps to draw in those who are not usually interested in sport or in that particular sport. Many English sports fans and non-sports fans became interested in rugby after the World Cup, but this type of fan tends to drift away again. Core support is easier to gain by horizontal diversification into new international markets.

Segmenting the global sport market

How widespread the appeal of the sport is and how uniform the nature of support determine whether there is a globally standard target market. Global homogenisation of tastes is proposed as favouring the ability to supply standardised products or services to world markets (Levitt, 1983). Global standardisation, in turn, is attractive to international marketers because it reduces the cost and complexity of creating a global marketing offering.

The global market for cricket, for example, is limited by the fact that the sport is most prevalent in Commonwealth countries. Moreover, its complex rules make it difficult to expand that appeal. Having tried, in vain, recently to explain the attraction of cricket to Italian sports fans, this became very apparent. Similarly, US baseball does not travel very well in terms of global appeal. The rules of this transferability are not very clear, but it would appear to relate to the level of complexity of the sport, the immediacy (both cricket and baseball are lengthy sports and not particularly well suited to 'trial' or people dipping into them to see whether they like the experience) and the extent to which the sport is played and understood in the local market. In contrast, because early forms of soccer were played in many regions, the duration is relatively short, the level of drama is high and the complexity is relatively low, the sport has a relatively global appeal.

Yet even if the sport itself has an appeal, regional variations may mean that the marketing offer has to be adapted to local market conditions. Soccer in the United States is mainly played by women and children, which may limit the appeal of the European men's football teams. Although some sports stars become global icons or global brands in their own right (e.g., Lance Armstrong, David Beckham, Magic Johnson), others are strong only in a particular country or region. Good examples of this local appeal are cyclist Roberto Heras in Spain or Bangladesh cricket captain Habibub Bashar, although they may not have attracted particular attention from global media.

International marketing mix

Sports as a media for global communication: global sponsorship

Recent decades have seen significant growth in the use of sponsorship as a marketing communication tool (Tripodi, Hirons, Bednell and Sutherland, 2003, Walliser, 2003). The global sponsorship market stood at $30 billion by 2002. There is significant evidence that sponsorship can improve the bottom line for companies by increasing sales, decreasing marketing communications costs and strategic targeting of a specialised target audience (Clark, Cornwell and Pruitt, 2002).

The potential of sponsorship as part of a strategic communications strategy is that it allows the sponsor to link the company or brand name with a place or event and allows the company to share in the image of the place itself (in the same way that a product can share the image of a celebrity who endorses it).

This 'co-branding' has a number of values for the company:

- Publicity opportunities
- Breaks free from traditional media 'clutter'
- Builds awareness of the corporate or brand name
- Helps to position the brand as innovative and creative
- Enhances the brand image
- Enables cost-effective communication with target markets
- Provides positive impact on consumer recall of the brand
- Reaches a diversity of publics
- Renews interest and vitality of the corporate or brand name
- Develops goodwill in the local community

The growth in global sports sponsorship deals suggests that this media is one of those that effectively travels across borders. Global marketing literature suggests a rank ordering of the extent to which global advertising messages travel (Bovee and Thill, 1995).

Travel well

1. Product facts and functions
2. Basic emotions
3. Universal myths and symbols
4. Topical events
5. Humour and idiom

Travel poorly

Distillers Diageo recently appointed a top sport marketing director to head its global sponsorship activities, fuelling speculation that it intends to increase its usage of sports sponsorship. McDonalds Corporation sponsored the Athens Olympics and has already signed up to sponsor World Cup 2006.

CASE 20.4   Coke's global sponsorship activities

Coca-Cola's portfolio of global sports sponsorships is impressive. Sponsors of the Olympic Games since 1928, Coca-Cola now sponsors athletes from about 200 countries in return for exclusive sponsorship opportunities for Powerade and Classic Coke. Coca-Cola has also been a Fédération Internationale de Football Association partner since 1974; has sponsored the women's football World Cup in 1999 and 2003; sponsors a range of other global sports events, including Copa America, the Asian Football Federation, the Paralympics and the Rugby World Cup; and has a 100-year agreement for Sprite to be the official drink of the US National Basketball Association.

Some sponsorships are very global in scope, and others tailored to sports with more local appeal and associations. Coca-Cola recently declared, for example, that it was to invest a further £7m on top of its initial £15m to position Coca-Cola as a drink of lower division footballers in England.

Sports stars have been used in Coca-Cola's adverts from as early as 1903 when the company used images of world champion cyclist Bobby Walthour. Today, it is the biggest sports sponsor in the world, spending around $1 billion a year on sports sponsorship. The associations between Coca-Cola and sports stars and teams can be based on global icons as well as more locally recognised stars.

Coca-Cola's range of sports and levels is intended to help the company to be locally responsive as well as globally recognised. Accordingly, the targets for sports sponsorship span different international markets, interest groups and ages of fans. Sponsorship of football is perhaps the largest single area of sponsorship. The men's football World Cup is the largest single global sporting event in terms of viewing figures. At the other end of the scale, in considering the launch of special edition packs in the colours of successful league or cup teams, Coca-Cola appeals to their particular supporters.

The power of the global image – the New Zealand All Blacks' haka in a Coca-Cola advert, or an Olympic gold medal winning performance – transcends global boundaries, but global sports sponsorship can also provide a medium for tailoring the image to those that will create local associations with the brand.

Source: Adapted from 'Cokes good sports', *Ad Age Global*, 2 March 2004, p. 7; 'Coca Cola Pours £7m into football campaign', *Marketing Week*, 22 July 2004, p. 14

Mode of international operation

The type of operation that firms use in international markets has been a central topic in economics, international business and international marketing literature for the past 30 years. In this section, we refer, from now on to the type of operation, such as export, licensing or FDI as the 'mode' of international operation.

Theories of mode of international operation

In his eclectic paradigm, Dunning (1988) identifies three types of influences on the decision to invest and locate the investment in a country: country- or location-specific advantages, firm-specific advantages and ownership-specific advantages later referred to as internalisation-specific advantages.

- **Country-specific advantages:** These are advantages that the firm can gain from the availability of raw materials, labour, large population, geographic location or other advantages of a particular country. Large population size might, for example, be the motivation for the current interest of European football clubs in developing links in China.

■ **Internalisation advantages:** Theory argues that 'firm-specific advantages' come from superior marketing skills or management ability (Kindelberger, 1969), the ability to differentiate products (Caves, 1971) or from continuous research and development activity (Hirsch, 1976). In sports clubs, a clear form of differentiation lies in on the field, or track, performance. A successful team brings in attendance revenue, sells merchandise, increases uptake of match or event coverage from a variety of media and may even bring in investment.

Economists argue that the environment facing firms operating in international markets is more uncertain than that in the home market. Clubs or teams may wish to protect themselves against the uncertainty of the different market environment by taking a greater level of control over their activities. For example, if digital video images of players or matches are a prime source of revenue, a club might be very concerned about the extent to which intellectual property rights are protected in a country. This might result in a reluctant to work with an internet partner in whose security systems they have less confidence than in their own. The concept of taking ownership, or control, of activities is referred to as 'internalisation'.

■ **Ownership advantages:** This type of advantage results from the way the firm is structured. This governance of the firm may, for example, involve partnerships in different markets. Liverpool football clubs have an alliance in Shanghai, China. This alliance might give them a better understanding of what works in the Chinese market than their rival European football clubs.

Oligopolistic reaction theory

Proposed by Knickerbocker (1973), oligopolistic reaction theory focuses on the FDI behaviour of multinational corporations. According to this theory, firms in the same industry tend to enter an international market at around the same time. After the market leader has entered, other firms in the sector follow soon after. This clustering of entry has been seen in a number of industries, and most recent examples include the patterns of entry by international players into emerging markets such as Eastern Europe and China.

The reasons why this clustering takes place are not entirely clear. One suggestion is that industry rivals are watching each other's actions. Each firm's decisions may be triggered by a competitor's. This could be for fear of missing opportunities in a market. Alternatively, the lead firm might be assumed to have better market intelligence systems than its rivals and may be first to enter a new market because of superior ability to assess its potential. The knowledge that a competitor views a market as attractive may increase its attractiveness in the eyes of competitor firms.

When viewed in the light of oligopolistic reaction theory, some interesting insights can be gained into the behaviour of players in sport markets. Often sports are oligopolies – that is, there are a few strong rivals. In football, for example, the top three or four clubs in a country win entrance into international competitions and are rewarded with higher television fees and gate receipts. As a result, there is a tendency for the gap between rich and poor clubs to increase.

In spotting new opportunities, these strong rivals do appear to be studying and responding to the same market opportunities. Football is strongly attracted by the market potential of China. The first few entrants into the market cluster together.

■ Transaction cost analysis

Williamson (1975, 1981) proposes that choices between different modes of inter-national operation could be measured using transaction costs. These are theories that suggest ways of calculating the cost of performing an activity within the firm (e.g., owning your own retail outlets) or having the activity performed by a partner (e.g., joint venture or franchised retail outlets).

A number of factors may increase transaction costs of using a partner:

- Bounded rationality: Managers do not have perfect knowledge. International marketing managers, when looking at ways of entering a country whose culture, politics, economy or geography they do not understand, may not make the best decision.
- Opportunistic behaviour: Individuals or groups within an organisation may make decisions for reasons of self-interest.
- Small numbers bargaining: Based on supply and demand arguments, the choice of potential partners may be restricted or transaction costs may be higher if there are few potential partners.

■ Exploring control and risk tradeoffs in international mode choice

Although critics have expressed concern about the difficulty of operationalising trans-action costs, the concept is often used together with other of the above theories of international mode of operation to make choices on optimal type of international operation.

Transaction cost analysis forms the basis of many studies of international mode choice (e.g., Anderson and Gatignon, 1986; Jarillo, 1988; Klein and Roth, 1989). Anderson and Gatignon (1986) use transaction costs to explore the relationship between control and risk. To gain control – for example, to take 100% ownership of an operation – firms have to commit financial and human resources. This creates risks. If the venture does not succeed, either for external reasons (e.g., civil war, earthquake or shortages of raw materials) or internal reasons (e.g., poor understanding of the international market), the firm stands to lose more than if it makes a lower level of investment. The alternatives are to export to the market from the home country so as to try out the market potential with a lower level of investment or to form a partner-ship with another firm to share the risks.

These alternative modes of operation, although involving lower levels of invest-ment, have drawbacks. For example, in entering China or India, a firm could benefit from lower labour and raw material costs, rather than producing material at home and exporting. However, the firm may also fail to gain a good understanding of the export target because it does not have enough contact and miss significant market opportunities. Similarly, use of a partner means that the firm's brand or service qual-ity may be damaged if the partner does not deliver the product or service to an appro-priate level.

Applied to the global sport market, similar tradeoffs exist. Manchester United has the strongest global sports brand. This can partly be developed by exporting audio and video coverage of matches and interviews with its main personalities. Merchandise can be bought via the internet. To reach the mass market in a particular country, the club has decided, however, that it needs a greater presence. This can be gained by opening retail outlets such as those in Singapore (see boxed example).

The club has two choices. It can own its outlets or establish them as a franchise. In a franchise, the money to set up and run the outlet comes from the franchisee, but in return, the franchisor (in this case, Manchester United) gives the franchisee the right to use the brand, sell branded goods and use other advertising materials with club images to promote the outlet. Use of a franchise operation allows the club to expand more rapidly but provides lower control over each operation.

A classic example of an organisation that has managed this kind of tradeoff is that of the McDonalds Corporation restaurants. McDonalds is mainly a franchise operation, which has allowed it to spread rapidly across the globe. When it enters a new international market that it considers uncertain, McDonalds takes a controlling interest in a joint venture. This was the case with its successful restaurants in Moscow. After the concept is established and the firm believes that it fully understands what works in the market, it will then expand further using franchises.

Conclusions

The increasing globalisation of sports is here to stay and will continue to accelerate. This new global environment poses challenges for sport marketers. If they wish to survive and thrive, they must enhance their understanding of the dynamic and complex global sport market. To do so means understanding the implications of the broad international context of sports. This includes, for example, the impact on sports of rapidly growing economies such as China; the challenges posed by international competition law, especially for broadcasting; and the opportunities and pressures posed by new global technologies such as the internet.

International sport marketers must also look at the strengths and weaknesses of their own organisations to identify firm-specific advantages, which will allow them to compete in this global marketplace. As can be seen in the Stockport County example, smaller sport organisations can also compete effectively on the global stage. This may be a country-of-origin effect whereby Chinese fans make a positive association between Stockport County as an English football team and other more successful English teams. Indeed, as a result of the internet and global satellite television coverage, many sports now operate on an international stage. Clubs have become 'unintentional internationalists', and not all realise both the opportunities and threats that this poses. The transferability of the appeal of minority sports and smaller clubs may be greater then they recognise, although it will take commitment of time and resources to analyse international markets and formulate effective marketing strategies. Conversely, however, competition for the attendance and viewing time of national sports fans increases, and audiences and fan bases may be eroded. Although analysis of international market opportunities, study of the extent of fan interest in a particular sport or club may and formulation of strategies to capitalise on market potential may seem onerous to busy management teams, the potential benefits are clear. Manchester United has become the world's largest global brand. Malcolm Glazer may have had to pay £800m to acquire the business, but this value is largely attributable to the strength of the brand. On a smaller scale, Stockport Country now earns 10% of revenue from China, despite a lowly league position in its home country, and this international revenue may play a vital role in determining the future of the club.

Discussion questions

1. Analyse the trends that are drivers of globalisation in a sport of your choice.
2. Who are the main stakeholders in the global market for this sport?
3. What are the main opportunities and threats arising from the diverse interests of clubs, sporting bodies, broadcasters and fans of a sport of your choice?
4. Analyse the extent to which there is an international segment of fans that values your chosen sport (remember, this will require analysis of the extent to which the sport is played, viewed and has values that appeal to the target market).
5. Take a player who you consider to be a global icon, and use Y&R's brand equity framework to analyse the characteristics of the icon's personal brand which contribute to their global appeal.

Guided reading

Dunning, J.H. (1988) The eclectic paradigm of international production: A restatement and some possible extensions, *Journal of International Business Studies* 23(3):1–27.

A seminal contribution to understanding of the modes of operation used by multinational corporations.

Levitt, T. (1983) The globalization of markets, *Harvard Business Review* May/June:92–102.

A polemical article arguing for standardisation of global marketing.

Keywords

Amortise; bounded rationality; country- or location-specific advantages; firm-specific advantages; foreign direct investment; homogenisation; internalisation; internalisation-specific advantages; mode of operation; oligopolies; oligopolistic reaction theory; ownership-specific advantages; transaction costs.

Bibliography

Aaker, D.A. (1996) Measuring brand equity across products and markets, *California Management Review* 38(3):102–20.

Anderson, E. and Gatignon, H. (1986) Modes of foreign entry: A transaction cost analysis and propositions, *Journal of International Business Studies* 12(3):25–34.

Baade, R.A. and Matheson, V.A. (2004) The quest for the cup: Assessing the economic impact of the World Cup, *Regional Studies* 38(4):343–55.

Boulding, K.E. (1956) *The Image,* Ann Arbor, MI: University of Michigan Press.

Bovee, C.L. and Thill, J.V. (1995) *Global Marketing Communications,* Prentice Hall.

Caves, R.E. (1971) International corporations: The industrial economics of foreign investment, *Economica* February:1–27.

Clark, J.M., Cornwell, T.B. and Pruitt, S.W. (2002) Corporate stadium sponsorships, signaling theory, agency conflicts and shareholder wealth, *Journal of Advertising Research* 42(6):16.

Dunning, J.H. (1988) The eclectic paradigm of international production: A restatement and some possible extensions, *Journal of International Business Studies* 23(3):1–27.

Edwards, H. (1973) *Sociology of Sports,* Homewood, IL: The Dorsey Press.

Ferrand, A. and Pages, M. (1999) Image management in sport organisations: The creation of value, *European Journal of Marketing* 33(3/4):387–401.

Fullerton, S. (1995) An application of market segmentation in a sports marketing arena: We can't all be Greg Norman, *Sport Marketing Quarterly* 4(3):43–7.

Gantz, W. (1981) An exploration of viewing motives and behaviours associated with television sports, *Journal of Broadcasting* 25:263–75.

Harris, F. and de Chernatonay, L. (2001) Corporate branding and corporate brand performance, *European Journal of Marketing* 35(3/4):441–56.

Hirsch, S. (1976) An international trade and investment theory of the firm. *Oxford Economic Papers* 28:258–270.

Jarillo, J.C. (1988) On strategic networks, *Strategic Management Journal* 9(1):31–41.

Kapferer, J.N. (1992) *Strategic Brand Management,* London: Kogan Page.

Kindelberger, C.P. (1969) *American Business Abroad: Six Lectures on Direct Invesment,* New Haven, CT: Yale University Press.

Klein, S. and Roth, V.J. (1990) Determinants of export channel structure: The effects of experience and psychic distance reconsidered, *International Marketing Review* 7(5):27–38.

Knickerbocker, F.T. (1973) *Oligopolistic Reaction and the Multinational Enterprise,* Cambridge, MA: Harvard University Press.

Levitt, T. (1983) The globalization of markets, *Harvard Business Review* May/June:92–102.

Melnick, M. (1993) Searching for sociability in the stands: A theory of sports spectating, *Journal of Sport Management* 7(1):44–60.

Sutton, W.A., McDonald, M.A., Milne, G.R. and Cimperman, J. (1997) Creating and fostering fan identification in professional sports, *Sport Marketing Quarterly* 6(1):15–22.

Tripodi, J.A., Hirons, M., Bednell, D. and Sutherland, M. (2003) Cognitive evaluation prompts used to measure sponsorship awareness, *International Journal of Market Research* 45(4):435.

Wakefield, K.L. and Sloan, H.J. (1995) The effects of team loyalty and selected stadium factors on spectator attendance, *Journal of Sport Management* 9:153–72.

Walliser, B. (2003) An international review of sponsorship research, *International Journal of Advertising* 22(1):5–25.

Wann, D. (1995) Preliminary validation of the sport fan motivation scale, *Journal of Sport and Social Issues* 19:377–96.

Williamson, O.E. (1975) *Between Markets and Hierarchies: Analysis and Antitrust Implications,* Macmillan.

Williamson, O.E. (1981) The economics of organisation: The transaction Cost approach, *American Journal of Sociology* 87(November):548–77.

Zillmann, D., Bryant, J. and Sapolsky, B.S. (1979) 'The enjoyment of watching sports contests', in J.H. Goldstein (ed.), *Sports, Games and Play: Social and Psychological Viewpoints,* Hillsdale, NJ: Erlbaum.

Recommended websites

British Broadcasting Corporation
http://www.bbc.co.uk

Know This
http://www.knowthis.com/internl.htm

Skysports
http://www.skysports.com

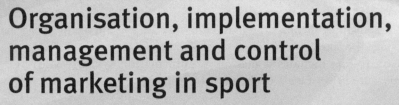

Chapter 21

Organisation, implementation, management and control of marketing in sport

Dr Dave Arthur
Southern Cross University, Australia

Learning outcomes

Upon completion of this chapter, the reader should be able to:

- Identify, consider and explain the importance of a range of marketing organisation issues for sport marketers.

- Identify, consider and explain the importance of a range of marketing implementation issues for sport marketers.

- Identify, consider and explain the importance of a range of marketing management issues for sport marketers.

- Identify, consider and explain the importance of a range of marketing control issues for sport marketers.

- Undertake the above with specific reference to the contents of this book and the specific nature of sport organisations.

Overview of chapter

Many of the chapters preceding this one have, to a large extent, concentrated on aspects of planning in sport marketing. This chapter takes much of this material and demonstrates how, within the construct of a sporting organisation, marketing planning is actually implemented. Initially, the chapter suggests a 'model' sport marketing plan and what should be included therein, and from there focuses on the vexing issues of implementation, control and evaluation. Brooksbank (1996) developed a useful process called BASIC that encompasses the interaction between planning and the operational aspects of the sport marketing process. It is composed of five phases:

1. Business customerising in which the entire organisation is examined and, when necessary, a marketing orientation is adopted (this approximates to stage one of the model of strategic sport marketing referred to in Chapter 18).

2. Analysing involves market research and various analyses (stages 2 and 3 of the model).
3. Strategising includes the setting of the strategic outlook of the sporting organisation (stages 1 and 4 of the model).
4. Implementing includes the marketing mix and organisation of the marketing effort (stage 4 of the model).
5. Controlling includes a marketing information system (MIS) and performance measurement (stage 5 of the model).

This chapter deals with the final two aspects in some detail.

Introduction

The process and framework for the strategic marketing planning process was discussed in Chapter 18. Gray (1991) states that the tangible result of the strategic marketing process is the development of a sport marketing plan. He goes on to say that such a document should become the framework for the sport marketing process, and the sport manager will become most effective when the plan becomes systematic and formalised. Therefore, it is important to consider exactly how and why such plans are essential and suggest a basic framework for one.

Benefits of a sport marketing plan

There are a number of benefits to having a sport marketing plan. A plan:

1. Provides a roadmap for the development of the sport or sport business, which, depending upon the organisation concerned, may focus on the short term, long term (strategic) or as Shilbury, Quick and Westerbeek (2002) imply, a mixture of both. Without it, the sporting organisation will simply lack direction:

   'Would you tell me, please, which way I ought to go from here?' 'That depends a good deal on where you want to get to,' said the Cat. 'I don't much care where' said Alice. 'Then it doesn't matter which way you go,' said the Cat. 'So long as I get somewhere' said Alice. 'Oh. You're sure to do that,' said the Cat, 'if you only walk long enough.' (Lewis Carroll, *Alice in Wonderland*)

2. Encourages the sport organisation to think ahead by recognising its strengths, weaknesses, opportunities and threats (SWOT).
3. Ensures that the appropriate marketing activity takes place along with the assignment and responsibility of tasks.
4. Sets performance standards by monitoring the marketing activities of the sporting organisation. These can then be checked against the objectives and changes made to make sure the marketing objectives are met.
5. Helps you prepare for change by becoming proactive (after your SWOT analysis) rather than reactive. In this manner, it can assist in identifying the resources you will need for your sport's development.
6. Promotes the efficient use of resources, including people, facilities and finances.

Table 21.1 **Components of a marketing plan**

1. Executive summary	6. Marketing objectives
2. Table of contents	7. Marketing strategies
3. Introduction	8. Marketing tactics
4. Situation analysis	9. Implementation and control
5. Analysis of target markets	10. Summary

After the necessity for a sport marketing plan has been established, the sporting organ-isation needs to consider ways of actually constructing it. Generic marketing specialists advocate a number of marketing plan 'models', each of which contain various compon-ents. For example, some authors (Cohen, 2002; Kotler and Armstrong, 2004) advocate the use of an executive summary. Some refer to action plans (Proctor, 2000), and others call for marketing tactics (Cohen, 2002). According to some, a marketing plan for sport can include a background or introduction to the plan, a positioning statement, some marketing objectives and strategies, merchandising strategies and finally media strategies. It can become very confusing indeed! Therefore, it is important to remember that no 'one size fits all' framework for a sport marketing plan is 'correct' and that as sport marketers may be required to apply different components at different times in different situations. In this chapter we use the sport marketing plan components listed in Table 21.1, explain-ing each element in turn.

Components of a marketing plan

Executive summary

Usually the first part of the sport marketing plan to be read and the last to be written, the executive summary is a synopsis of the proposed marketing actions with an emphasis on overall strategy, major activities to be carried out and expected results. In short, the executive summary should describe:

- What the organisation is going to accomplish with the plan
- If the plan costs anything to implement
- An indication of when the plan could be implemented
- The value of the plan to the organisation

Table of contents

A good table of contents provides the reader, who may be outside the particular func-tional area, with a shortcut to the relevant area he or she wishes to peruse.

Introduction

The introduction is distinct from the executive summary in that it sets the scene for the remainder of the plan by describing the broad project for which the plan has been developed. This should include an analysis of the product or service and should reflect the organisation's mission statement. It should also include items such as the unique aspects of the product or service and how it fits into the market.

Situation analysis

Dann and Dann (2004) suggest that this section should include an analysis of the current marketing conditions as they relate to the following 'situations' (p. 398):

- Market situation
- Product situation
- Competitive situation
- Distribution situation
- Macroenvironment situation

Two aspects usually included in situation analyses are an issues analysis and the SWOT analysis. Both are explained in detail in Chapter 18.

Analysis of target markets

This particular part of the sport marketing plan involves the practical use of previous market research methods with a view to identifying, describing and justifying those target market segments chosen.

Example analysis for a given sporting event may include:

- **15–25-year age group:** Typically interested in high-profile, fast-paced sports; however, encouraging attendance with family and friends will enable them to learn more about the sport. There is also a lot of peer pressure influencing this group and with social aspects likely to appeal.
- **Female 25–35-year age group:** This group may wish to attend the event for the social atmosphere and may become interested in the sport as a casual player. This group is typically influenced by time; they do not like to plan. They will most likely attend the event 'at the spur of the moment'.
- **35+ age groups:** This segment typically has young children and may want to attend the event as a family to socialise and learn more about the game. This may encourage them to become involved at a recreational level.

This aspect is also explained in detail in Chapter 18.

Marketing objectives

Vitally important are the initial statements of intent within a sport marketing plan. Dann and Dann (2004) discuss the two types within such a plan:

1. **Financial objectives,** which define how much money should be made and usually expressed in terms of return on investment and profit.
2. **Marketing objectives** in which the desired financial outcomes are translated into marketing action.

Example objectives for a given sporting event may include:

- Increase revenue in 200* by 25% over the 200* event.
- Contribute 10% of profit to grassroot development programmes.
- Generate a licensing contract that produces an additional $50,000+ in revenue for the event in 200*.

- Generate a 20% increase in awareness of the event and a 10% increase among younger markets (15–25- and 25–35-year age groups).
- Increase overall event attendance by 20%, including a 15% increase in the numbers of women and 15–25-year-olds attending the 200* event.

This aspect is referred to in more detail in Chapter 18.

Marketing strategies

In Chapter 18, it was suggested that there were two categories of marketing strategies available: industry-level competitive positioning strategies and marketing mix strategies. The former strategies are the 'grand strategies' that the organisation wishes to undertake to achieve its overall business objectives. The marketing-level strategies concern product, price, distribution and promotion.

An example of a distribution strategy for a given sporting event is as follows. Tickets will be available for purchase through the following means:

- Ticketek: A ticketing and sales agency
- The dedicated event website
- Through event sponsors
- Via an 800 telephone number

Ticket sales in the lead-up to the event will be closely monitored via weekly reports with the general goal to generate a high level of pre-event ticket sales to ensure commitment and monitor interest in the event. Tickets will also be available at the event entrance on all days of competition (where available).

Marketing tactics

Marketing tactics are general implementation aspects that are specific to the sporting organisation but should include what will be done, when, by whom and how much it will cost.

Implementation and control

Arguably the most important part of a sport marketing plan, this section outlines exactly how it will be put into practice, monitored and controlled. Meldrum (1996) states: 'One of the concerns about marketing as a management discipline is the ability of organisations to put into practice the policies devised in its name' (p. 29). Furthermore, as strategies are implemented, they must also be controlled (Lussier and Kimball, 2004, p. 101). Both are central topics in the remainder of this chapter.

Summary

According to Dann and Dann (2004), this is the final section that concludes the plan while emphasising its advantages, profits, costs and the competitive advantage that will be gleaned over its competitors.

CASE 21.1   The great softball plan

You have been appointed as the marketing director of the state association that is charged with running an interstate softball league. The executive director of the association has asked you to make a presentation to the board of directors regarding sport marketing in general and sport marketing plans in particular. Although some members of the board are conversant with the need and rationale for plans, others are still quite naïve regarding them and therefore need some convincing. However, the board is well aware of the need for the interstate league to make a profit to finance the operations of the national side and to ensure the operation of the league in the future.

The **league** is the major association in the state and consists of eight teams. The regular season has 20 games per team with a top four finals competition and average attendance figure approaching 3000 per week over the season as a whole. All grounds have passed rigid criteria with excellent media, spectator and catering facilities of the norm. Media coverage is lacking, with only sporadic coverage on television and radio and almost no print media exposure. A recent bequest has left approximately $500,000 to be spent by the state association to 'improve the marketing of softball locally and nationally'. You as marketing director have been asked to formulate a plan to do exactly that. The board would like this presented to them in plain English at its next meeting.

Questions

Using information presented anywhere in this book:

1. Outline the steps you would take to formulate a strategic marketing plan.

2. Outline the setup of the marketing plan in point form.

3. Broadly discuss the various objectives and strategies you would recommend to achieve the general aim of the bequest.

   Remember that not all of the board is conversant with marketing terminology; some are highly sceptical, and all require the presentation in plain English.

As soon as the sport marketing plan and all that it entails (e.g., objectives, strategies and budgets) have been approved by senior management, then the practical application of strategic marketing management can commence. The marketing plan will then provide a reference point between where the organisation wants to progress to and where it actually is. The next section describes the process of implementation.

Implementation in sport marketing

Summers, Gardiner, Lamb, Hair and McDaniel (2003) opine that 'implementation is the process that turns marketing plans into action assignments and ensures that these assignments are executed in a way that accomplishes the plans' objectives' (p. 468). In short, implementation is where an action plan is developed whereby who is to do what, by when is clearly delineated and acted upon. In trying to implement a plan, the sport marketer may meet some obstacles that may impinge on the success of the strategies and tactics embodied within it and may cause the plan to be redesigned to suit them. Whatever the barrier, it is vital that it is overcome. McColl-Kennedy, Kiel, Lusch and Lusch (1992) believe that 'without proper implementation the plan is virtually useless' (p. 526), and Reed (1997) believes 'in too many cases, poor implementation has contributed to marketing failure' (p. 320). Finally, Schermerhorn, Campling, Poole and Wiesner (2004) emphasise that 'no strategy, no matter how well formulated, can achieve longer-term success if it is not properly implemented' (p. 230). It is clear that implementation is vital!

Simkin (2002) examined a range of core barriers to implementation as well as some that had arisen over the past decade that, either in isolation or in combination, had the effect of undermining the strategic marketing plan. In summary, the barriers were:

- Inadequate communication within the organisation
- Insufficient resources devoted to implementation
- Inadequate involvement by management
- Lack of integration of the plan and attendant process into the organisation
- Overemphasis on short-term (tactical) rather than longer term (strategic) planning

Some of these hark back to various stages of the model of strategic sport marketing proposed in Chapter 18. Without congruence between corporate-level vision and objectives and marketing-level issues, there is a good chance that the whole strategic sport marketing process (and consequently, the sport marketing plan) will be ineffective. Lussier and Kimball (2004) give a simple reason why plans fail: They 'often end up buried in bottom drawers and no action is taken to implement a strategy' (p. 101).

Without the organisation contributing the required resources, a similar fate would ensue. McColl-Kennedy et al. (1992) concur that a key requirement for implementation was the commitment of both financial and human resources to achieve the stated objectives. Thus, the culture of the sporting organisation as well as its structure contribute to effective implementation. In terms of finance, there may be a need to purchase or lease new equipment to facilitate the marketing objectives. This may include things such as customer databases or new machines to produce existing or new products. In terms of human resources, as with most aspects of business, there is an opportunity cost involved whereby employees could easily be used elsewhere other than on planning or, in this case, marketing implementation. In addition, the implementation of the plan may lead to the employment of new personnel in, for example, front office roles or selling corporate sponsorship. Summers et al. (2003) summed it up succinctly: 'It is not enough to give everyone a job; if insufficient money, people or time is allocated to doing the job, then all the planning will have been in vain' (p. 468).

Most authors also seem to agree that implementation is organisation-dependent – that is, without buy-in and support from the entire organisation, implementation and indeed control are hard to achieve. Lussier and Kimball (2004) feel that 'successful implementation of strategies requires effective and efficient support systems throughout the organisation' (p. 101). Thus, there is a requirement for the entire organisation to adopt a marketing orientation and embrace the marketing concept. The marketing orientation 'proposes that the social and economic justification for an organisation's existence is the satisfaction of customer needs and wants while meeting organisational objectives' (Summers et al., 2003, p. 460). The marketing concept expands on this and includes focusing on these needs and wants to distinguish it in the marketplace and the integration of all activities to satisfy needs and wants. Without such, the implementation of a plan is difficult.

In terms of overcoming the barriers to implementation, a number of strategies can be enacted. Dann and Dann (2004, p. 412) suggest the following methods:

- **Internal marketing:** The basic premise of internal marketing is that all employees, whether or not they are involved in 'sport marketing' per se, should be kept informed and abreast of marketing developments. For marketing strategy to be most effectively implemented, it simply must be supported by all staff.
- **Infrastructure requirements:** For implementation to be given its best chance of success, there needs to be adequate resourcing of all elements.
- **Facilitation of the implementation:** Ongoing support from management is crucial to successful implementation. Simkin (2002) suggests five methods of ongoing facilitation: audits and appraisal, specification and support, orientation and communication, authorisation and empowerment and reviews and remedial action.

An example of a simple sport marketing implementation plan for an event is shown in Table 21.2.

For the last word on the subject of implementation, we will turn to the words of Shilbury et al. (2002): 'Implementation is often difficult – more difficult than determining the strategies. It is easy to dream up a range of creative strategies; however, when it comes to the actual implementation it may be found that they are totally unrealistic or impractical' (p. 304).

Table 21.2 A sample action plan for an event

When	Strategy	Who
August 200*	Event planning, goals and objectives	Event manager
	Location selection	Event manager and general manager
	Discussions and agreement made with facility	Event manager
	Marketing plan created, including advertising, promotions and budgeting information	Event, marketing and financial managers
September–December 200*	Sponsorship secured	Event manager
	Media rights sold and coverage deal secured	Event manager
	Licensing secured for on-premise sales	Sales team and
	Retail licensing contract(s) secured (event merchandise production)	marketing manager
	Merchandise products selected and initial product run begins	
January to February 200*	Second production run of merchandise	Sales team and marketing assistant
	Contact prospective retailers and provide them with information about the merchandise.	Sales team and marketing assistant
	Secure agreement with specialty stores to stock merchandise and distribute to stores	Event manager and computer company
	Launch 200* website	
March 200*	Event announced after European Championship	General manager
	Sponsorship partners announced	General manager
	Launch publicity campaign; press release	Marketing manager

	Event tickets on sale	Marketing assistant
	Begin selling merchandise online on websites	Sales team
April 200*	Direct mail campaign to members and mailing lists	Marketing assistant
	Advertising plan actioned – radio, newspaper and television, increasing frequency 4 weeks before event	Marketing and events manager
	Billboards and poster advertising	Marketing assistant
May 200*	Review current ticket sales	Financial manager and sales team
	Review player list	Event manager
	Determine whether additional advertising and promotion are required to enhance interest in the event and increase ticket sales	Marketing manager and events manager
	Announce event media coverage schedule	TV media and marketing manager
June 200*	Publicity campaign begins – radio and television announcements	Marketing assistant
	Launch of cross-promotional activities	Marketing manager and sponsors
	Press releases and pre-event news conference	Marketing manager
June 20–26, 200*	Event	
	Spectator survey at event entrance	Marketing assistant
	Competitions, prizes and giveaways throughout event	and event staff
July–September 200*	Post-event analysis, including information about ticket sales, consumer and sponsor feedback	Market researchers
	Celebrate success of event	All event staff
	Post-event spectator survey distributed and analysed	Market researchers
	Begin preparations for the 200* event – use information from event analysis to make appropriate improvements to future events	Event, marketing and financial manager

■ Marketing information systems

To aid in the implementation of sport marketing strategies and as a link into the next section of control, we will now look at the use of MIS. Such a system is seen as integral part of the marketing process and as such should form a basic foundation for ongoing sport marketing management. Stanton et al. (1995, cited in Shilbury et al., 2002) suggest that an MIS is 'an ongoing organised set of procedures and methods designed to generate, analyse, disseminate, store and later retrieve information for use in decision making' (p. 57). Mullin, Hardy and Sutton (2000, p. 81) summarised the characteristics of an ideal MIS as:

- **Centralised:** All information should be located in a single place.
- **Integrated:** Various databases (e.g., sales, consumers, accounting) should be able to be merged and compared with each other.
- **Easy to use:** The user must be able to retrieve information in a form that enables effective decision-making processes.

To develop such an MIS, three types of data must be collected:

- **General market data** relating to the broad environment in which the sport operates. This includes, for example, the size of the market, the geographic extent of the market area, demographics of the market area, purchase behaviours of those living within the market area and data on future trends.

■ **Individual consumer data**, including, for example, names, addresses, contact numbers and email addresses; purchase patterns; and frequency of attendance on which to base future marketing strategies.

■ **Competitor data** containing information about the competition in general (e.g., price lists, promotional strategies) as well as information regarding who actually consumes competitor's product or service.

Data sources for a marketing information system

Data for a sport MIS can come from two major sources. *Internal data* are generated and held within the particular sporting organisation, and *external data* include information from outside the organisation. Internal sources include items such as sales records, inquiries and accounting records. External data is termed either *primary*, which include studies initiated by the organisation itself, or *secondary*, which refers to whether the data is already published, for example, a census report (the Australian Bureau of Statistics), a trade association or through syndicated research services (such as Sweeney Sport or Sport Marketing Surveys).

Sporting organisations have become quite adept at collecting various forms of data for future use in marketing activities. For example, the use of competitions and coupon redemptions in which names, addresses, mobile telephone numbers and increasingly, email addresses are collected and put into a draw are commonplace. Marketing staff can then input this data into a designated MIS and use either immediately or in the future for a particular marketing campaign.

Control in sport marketing

With a sport marketing plan in place and implemented, the most important aspect of the sport marketing management becomes that of control. Essentially, whereas 'control' means knowing what is happening in comparison with preset standards or objectives, 'controlling' establishes mechanisms that ensure that objectives are achieved. Without proper control, it is unlikely that the marketing process (or indeed, any process within the organisation) will be wholly successful. As Mullin et al. (2004) say, 'Marketing control must be incorporated into an overall strategic plan' (p. 349). In terms of a suitable definition for control, Schermerhorn et al. (2004) believe 'controlling is the process of measuring performance and taking action to ensure desired results' (p. 185). Allen, O'Toole, Harris and McDonnell (2005) believe the process of control is 'complex' (p. 317) and describe it in three broad steps:

1. Establishing standards of performance
2. Identifying deviations from standards of performance
3. Correcting deviations from performance

Lussier and Kimball (2004) take this a little further with four albeit similar steps:

1. Establish the standards against which performance is to be evaluated.
2. Create the measuring and monitoring systems that indicate whether or not the targets are being achieved.

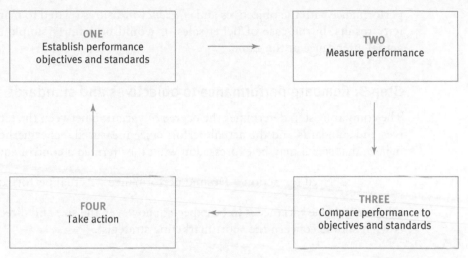

Figure 21.1 **The marketing control process**

3. Compare actual performance against the established targets.
4. Initiate corrective action when it is decided that the standards and targets are not being achieved.

Figure 21.1 illustrates the typical control process for a sport organisation. However, before describing the process, it is important to note that to be effective, marketing controls should be an integral facet of ongoing planning and incorporate four component parts, according to Mullin et al. (2004, p. 349):

1. Mission statements and objectives
2. A sympathetic organisational structure
3. Employee performance standards that link to said performance to objectives
4. Methods to adjust all of the above in the light of performance.

Step 1: Establish performance objectives and standards

Lussier and Kimball (2004) suggest setting both 'big picture' standards, which they regard objectives to be, as well as 'little picture' standards, which tend to be more detailed and specific. For completeness, they suggest that five criteria should be addressed when framing standards: quantity (how many), quality (how well), time (when), cost (how much) and behaviour (which). Reed (1997) calls this stage benchmarking and suggests that there are two types, *comparative* (compared with industry standards or historical performance) and *ideal* (what is thought to be best practice). In sport marketing terms, this may involve the sale of a range of tickets for an international fixture in which a 'sell-out' crowd would be required as opposed to 20,000 out of a possible 50,000 patrons for a lesser fixture.

Step 2: Measure performance

According to Woodburn (2004) 'Marketing has habitually avoided performance measurement' (p. 63); however, in this case, it is an essential requirement. Reed (1997) suggests they could be divided into *effectiveness measures* related to a comparison of performance with the objectives and *efficiency measures* related to marketing product-ivity results. In the case of ticket sales, it would be a fairly simple measurement of actual attendance at the game.

Step 3: Compare performance to objectives and standards

The comparing step determines the degree of variation between the established object-ives and standards and the actual performance measured. Schermerhorn et al. (2004) believe that step 3 may be expressed in what they termed a control equation in which:

$$\text{Need for action} = \text{Desired performance} - \text{Actual performance}$$

Obviously, some variance is to be expected; however, the size and direction of variance is what should concern the sport marketing strategist.

Step 4: Take action

Robbins, Bergman, Stagg and Coulter (2003) indicate that management has a choice of three possible courses of action in step 4: take no action, correct the performance or revise the original stand-ards; however, the control equation indicates that the greater the variance from the benchmark, the greater the need for managerial action. Dann and Dann (2004) believe that whenever results deviate from the expected, it is a managerial imperative to find out why. In sporting terms, correction of the performance may involve dismissal of staff – for example, a marketing manager could be dismissed if ticket sales fell below those expected. In the future, however, the performance standard may be revised to reflect the historical data, and the expected ticket sales would be sim-ilarly decreased.

Types of control

There are a number of controls categorised on the basis of when they are actually implemented:

- **Feedforward, preliminary or predictive controls** are those implemented before the sport marketing activity takes place. Robbins et al. (2003) believe these are pre-ventative in nature because they ensure, for example, that the correct resources or correct directions are in place.
- **Concurrent or steering control** takes place during the particular sport marketing activity. For example, in a sport marketing campaign, a particular coupon redemp-tion strategy may be poorly performing; steering control allows action to be taken prior to the completion of a task. Similarly, if an event has not reached corporate sponsorship targets, steering control allows marketers to take restorative action.
- **Feedback, post-action or rework controls** are implemented after a sport marketing activity is completed. Such controls focus on the end product. An exit survey of pur-chasers of concessions at a venue may tell the sport marketer how good (or bad) the customer service was. Feedback allows for future changes such as the implemen-tation of a customer training education programme or a rewards programme for quality service.

Timing of controls

Not all controls are used all of the time. Some, referred to as *constant controls* are in continuous use and include self-control and standing plans. *Periodic controls*, however, are used on a regular, fixed basis such as weekly, monthly, quarterly or annually and include regularly scheduled reports, budgets and audits. Finally, *occasional controls* are used on a needs basis. They include observation, special reports and project controls.

Control methods

Although the three control methods referred to here are treated as separate, it should be noted that they also act in unison. The measurement of a financial goal (e.g., an increase in profit for a health and fitness centre) can be viewed as a financial control; the knock-on effect may be to increase market share in a particular market segment. If measured, this would be a marketing control.

Financial control

One of the most common control methods is financial control. According to Lussier and Kimball (2004): 'Budgets and financial statements are important tools. The information they contain is key in making decisions of all kinds' (p. 386). Perhaps the best known of these is a budget, but it could also include items such break-even analysis (see Chapter 15 for an explanation of this financial control method), *financial statements* such as the income statement (which shows the company's revenues and expenses and its profit or loss for a stated period), the *balance sheet* (which lists assets, liabilities, and owners' equity) and the *statement of cash flows* (which shows cash receipts and payments for a stated period).

An example of financial controls for a given sporting event may include:

- **Event ticket sales** for the event will be examined on a fortnightly basis in the lead up to the event. Ticket sales are the primary indicator of interest in the event. Ticket sales will be monitored according to how and when they are purchased. This information provides insight into consumer preferences and allows the event organisers to determine additional methods for increasing advance ticket sales. Additionally, daily and total event ticket sales will be determined and compared with those from previous events.
- **Monitoring event budget** through the fortnightly release of progress statements from event organisers. The information will be used to determine whether the event is 'on track', both financially as well as at an organisational and planning level.

Table 21.3 provides a sample budget for an event.

Human control

Lussier and Kimball (2004) also emphasise the importance of human controls. In particular, coaching is used to give employees motivation and feedback to maintain and improve performance. These authors believe human control is vitally important because without motivated employees, it is hard to maintain productivity. Human control also includes the well-used generic management technique of management by walking around (MBWA) whereby managers listen, teach and facilitate.

Table 21.3 **A sample budget for a given event**

Strategy	Expenditure	Strategy	Income
Promotions		**Sponsorship**	
Member/Mailing list	$5000	Primary sponsors	$1,500,000
direct-mail campaign		Secondary sponsors	$650,000
		Media sponsors –	
Under 14s free	$100,000	television rights	$2,000,000
Total	**$105,000**	**Total**	**$4,150,000**
Market research		**Licensing**	$50,000
Surveys of event participants	$50,000	Contract plus royalties from	
and analysis of information		sale of event merchandise	
Purchasing statistical information	$15,000		
Total	**$65,000**	**Total**	**$50,000**
Promotions		**In-kind donations:**	
Television	$1,500,000	Caps	$2500
Radio	$500,000	Under 17s lunch	$4000
Newspaper	$400,000	Spectator giveaways	
Posters, billboards	$100,000	and competitions	$10,000
Website	$20,000		
Total	**$2,520,000**	**Total**	**$16,500**
Public relations		**Event ticket sales**	
Television (in kind)	$25,000	Practice	$350,000
Radio (in kind)	$10,500	Championship	$550,000
Newspaper (in kind)	$15,000	Flex Book	$600,000
		Season	$500,000
Total	**$50,500**	**Total**	**$2,000,000**
Event hosting			
Venue			
Equipment			
Media centre			
Staffing			
Player-only areas			
Approximate total	**$2,000,000**		
Total	**$4,740,500**		**$6,216,500**

Marketing controls

Marketing controls can be used to determine whether marketing objectives have been achieved (it is why they should always be stated in measurable terms). However, marketing controls should also include determination of the effectiveness of, for example, positioning strategies and the various marketing mix strategies developed.

An example of marketing controls for a given sporting event:

- Determining the amount of media coverage and publicity the event attracted. This will be calculated for print, television and radio media, and appropriate financial values will be applied to determine an approximate dollar value of publicity achieved. The information collected will be compared with previous events and will provide insight into changes in awareness of the event. This can also be done on a weekly basis to ascertain if pre-event marketing methods are working effectively.

■ Effectiveness of sponsorship that includes gathering feedback from sponsors regarding product sales, brand associations with the event and consumer recall information.

■ Tracking the sale of event merchandise before, during and after the event to determine whether licensing was effective for both the manufacturer and the event. The sale of individual items and how they were purchased (online, in store or at the event) will be tracked and the information will be used to identify popular products and when consumers typically purchased event merchandise. It will also allow the event organisers to develop new strategies to increase sale of merchandise and offer new products at future events.

■ Collection of statistical data from the event organisers, sporting bodies and clubs to be used to determine post-event changes in participation and memberships at local and national levels. Additionally, the event will also collect consumer feedback via surveys to further determine the impact of the communications strategy.

CASE 21.2   Japanese fans form a new major league

'At last!' screamed one headline from a Boston newspaper after its home-town baseball team, the Red Sox, won the World Series last month. The victory ended a legendary 'curse' that has kept the Red Sox from a World Series title since 1918.

Baseball fever may, at last, be subsiding in the US, but the buzz is resuming in Japan, where 28 top US Major League baseball players are this week competing against stars from Nippon Professional Baseball.

The eight-game All-Stars series, which will be played in five Japanese cities including Tokyo, Osaka and Nagoya between November 5 and 14, is part of an effort by MLB to stoke Japanese enthusiasm for US baseball and continue the effort to export baseball as far afield as Australia, South Korea, Germany and the UK.

As well as exhibition series, MLB has started youth programmes, mentoring for coaches, camps, training clinics and ambassador programmes that send players overseas. MLB is even planning a baseball World Cup for 2006 with teams from 16 countries.

Baseball has been played in Japan since the 1890s but appetite for the game has exploded since two of Japan's players joined the US major leagues. MLB is keen to take advantage of this burst of popularity.

Hideki Matsui, the home-run hitter formerly with the Yomiuri Giants, joined the New York Yankees last year with a three-year contract worth $21m (£11.4m). The success of Mr Matsui, nicknamed 'Godzilla', follows that of superstar Ichiro Suzuki, who joined the Seattle Mariners in 2001.

Since Mr Matsui and Mr Suzuki joined MLB, revenue from the company's international arm has tripled.

International revenue from television, sponsorships, licensing and events last year came to about $100m, with about half coming from Japan, compared with $10m in 1989. MLB opened its first Asian office this year in Tokyo.

Other businesses are cashing in on Japanese enthusiasm for baseball. In March, New York's tourism bureau launched a multi-million dollar marketing campaign in Japan to promote travel to New York. The effort appears to have worked: NYC & Co said Mr Matsui helped boost travel there from Japan by 40 per cent in the first six months of the year.

There are lucrative rewards in TV advertising, corporate sponsorship and licensing. Last year MLB International signed a deal with Dentsu, a big Japanese advertising group, to license television rights to show baseball games in Japan. The six-year contract was worth roughly $300m and greatly expanded Dentsu's previous five-year $13m contract.

TV viewing numbers in Japan have rocketed. An estimated 15m Japanese viewers watched game seven of the play-offs between the Red Sox and the Yankees, which was shown at 8am in Japan.

Companies are even advertising within US baseball stadiums in an effort to reach Japan's TV audience. Nintendo bought Japanese-language signs behind the home plate at Seattle's Safeco Field, a spot that can cost millions of dollars per season.

MLB is now looking beyond Japan to South Korea, Taiwan, Australia and China. In China it is training coaches and launching school development programmes to groom the next generation. 'We're very excited about what's going on in China,' said Paul Archey, senior vice-president of MLB. 'It's a place where we want to be as a business, just like any other business.'

Major League Baseball aims 'to grow the game and business of baseball throughout the world to make Major League Baseball the premier professional sports league in the world'. Its initiatives include:

■ A youth development programme that introduces schoolchildren aged 8–12 to baseball through the physical education curriculum in Australia, Germany, Italy, Mexico, South Africa and the UK. Since 1994 it has reached more than 2.5m children in 6,000 schools.
■ A coaching development programme that brings coaches to the US for two weeks of instruction with MLB coaches. Since 2000, 60 coaches from 11 countries have participated.
■ An agreement covering youth and coach development in China.
■ 'Sabor a Beisbol', a 20-episode TV special broadcast directly to Spanish-speaking audiences in Latin America.
■ Spring training, regular season games and all-star tours overseas. This year MLB held games in Puerto Rico, Japan and Mexico.
■ Sending coaches overseas to teach baseball. Last year MLB trained more than 23,000 players.

Source: A. Yee, *Financial Times*, 12 November 2004

Questions

1. Given the global development of baseball, what are the major organisation, implementation, management and control issues facing MLB marketers?

2. In the face of competition from other sports such as basketball and football, what recommendations would you make to the MLB regarding the effectiveness of its marketing effort?

CASE 21.3   Centre court to centre stage

Tennis is fast becoming a round-the-clock business – and there is no let up even if you are one of its most bankable stars.

The day after Maria Sharapova's 18th birthday – and a long evening dancing at a New York disco   the Russian Wimbledon champion completed countless media interviews.

After these, she was whisked away for a long photo shoot for *People* magazine, which selected her as one of the world's 50 most beautiful people – placing her in the company of the actresses Julia Roberts and Penelope Cruz.

It was all business, business, business – even the supposedly 'pleasure' part. The previous night's party had been thrown by Sony Ericsson, the new sponsor of the Women's Tennis Association Tour.

The party, the interviews, the photo shoot, these were all part of a big push – organised by IMG, the sports marketing firm that also represents Tiger Woods – that is meant to establish Ms Sharapova even more firmly in the popular imagination.

It is also the latest evidence that the Women's Tennis Association wants its stars to be available for off-court promotional activity as never before.

After her win at Wimbledon last year, Ms Sharapova – who was born in Siberia and emigrated to the US when she was six in order to train at the famous tennis academy run by Nick Bollettieri – was catapulted from relative anonymity into the world of big-money endorsements. Since then, she has raked in a reported $23m (£12.6m) in sponsorships from blue-chip companies such as Motorola, Canon and Honda. Her marketing potential also helped the WTA secure its record-breaking $88m deal with Sony Ericsson.

Ms Sharapova, who comes across as self-confident and professional with none of the traits of the spoiled tennis brat, appears to have taken it all in her stride. She admits that thinking of herself as a brand is 'very strange', but she has a clear idea of what the Sharapova brand is – or should be – all about. 'I want it to be what I am,' she says. 'It's about having the qualities of a champion.' It is noticeable that she emphasises her game rather than her looks. And, by doing so, she obliquely blocks the inevitable comparison with Anna Kournikova, another striking Russian tennis player who won lucrative endorsements despite having never won a tournament.

Ms Sharapova does not disguise her ambition nor her competitive drive – all part of what makes her the champion admired by tennis fans and business chiefs. At 16, she had objected to the WTA's rules limiting the number of tournaments that players under 18 could play. 'If there's a line,' she says, 'then I want to be in front of the line.'

Ms Sharapova was bombarded with offers after Wimbledon – but her managers were selective. IMG's strategy was to sign deals with a handful of sponsors, allowing her to get back to concentrating on her game.

It knows that there is a balance to be struck between the time spent on promotional activity – which is favoured by business sponsors and the WTA – and the time spent on practising and playing the game. Ms Sharapova is currently ranked second on the WTA tour, behind Lindsay Davenport. So far this year, she has won $805,527 in prize money.

The fact that the income she raises from her commercial endorsements far outweighs the amount she raises from her court activities is a clear indication of the importance of her business commitments.

It means that for Larry Scott, the WTA tour's chief executive, the task of raising the profile of women's tennis is that much easier. As he says: 'In terms of the product, it's a bit of a golden age for women's tennis.'

As a Harvard graduate himself, Larry Scott welcomed an offer from its business school to do a case study on the WTA tour. The study was carried out by Jay Lorsch, a Harvard Business School professor, and Ashley Robertson, a research associate. It discussed challenges Mr Scott faced in getting the WTA's board to focus on the long-term health of women's tennis. It also examined the WTA's Roadmap 2010, a long-term strategic plan. Highlights of the plan include:

■ Shorten the season
■ Implement mandatory commitment of top players to top-tier events
■ Implement stronger player withdrawal penalties
■ Restructure the bonus pool
■ Improve the ranking system
■ Improve co-operation among other governing bodies

Source: C. Grimes, *Financial Times*, 24 May 2005

Questions

1. In the context of the issues discussed in this chapter, discuss the advantages and disadvantages of using a sports celebrity such as Maria Sharapova as the focus for a marketing strategy.

2. In the event of, for example, Sharapova being injured and having to retire from tennis, what are likely to be the organisation, implementation, management and control issues facing marketers involved in tennis?

Conclusions

The issues of management, implementation and control can be very important in the overall sport marketing process. Readers should now appreciate and recognise the issues involved. In particular, this chapter has provided the student with a basic outline (together with examples) of a sport marketing plan as well as the way the plan and its attendant strategies can be effectively implemented and managed within a sporting organisation. After that discussion, control and controlling became a central theme with a simple model of the process of control being presented together with a range of control methods discussed in light of various sport event–related examples. However, as you progress through your career as a sport marketer and gain further practical insight into the medium, you should remember that it is an ever-changing environment. What once worked extraordinarily well may not be quite as effective or efficient in the future. However, by applying the basic tenets supplied here, you will put yourself in the best position to confront these challenges head on.

Discussion questions

1. Discuss, with reference to the unique requirements of sport marketing, the barriers to the effective and efficient implementation of a sport marketing plan.
2. In relation to a sporting organisation that you know well, discuss how would you overcome these barriers.
3. Choose a favourite professional sporting team and outline a strategy that the team could use to develop an MIS. What available sources of data could the team use in this development?
4. Outline the methods of control available to sporting organisations and comment on their applicability to a health and fitness centre. For the examples of control for a given sporting event referred to in this chapter, categorise each as a feedforward, concurrent or feedback and give reasons for your choice.

Guided reading

Chapter 2 of *Sport Marketing* by Mullin et al. (2000) provides a very good summary of marketing management in sport. In particular, it presents in graphical format the marketing management process in sport (p. 25).

For an excellent overview of issues regarding the implementation of marketing strategies, students are directed to Meldrum (1996).

Most generic management books have sections about control. For a good overview, students are advised that Robbins et al. (2003, pp. 455–483) provide excellent reading. Lussier and Kimball (2004, pp. 391–398) provide an overview of human control in particular coaching.

Keywords

Break-even analysis; strategic marketing management.

Bibliography

Allen, J., O'Toole, W., Harris, R. and McDonnell, I. (2005) *Festival and Special Event Management*, 3rd edn, Milton, Australia: John Wiley and Sons.

Brooksbank, R. (1996) The BASIC marketing planning process: A practical framework for the smaller business, *Marketing Planning and Intelligence* 14(4):16–24.

Cohen, W. (2002) *The Marketing Plan*, 3rd edn, Australia: John Wiley and Sons.

Dann, S. and Dann, S. (2004) *Introduction to Marketing*, Brisbane, Australia: John Wiley and Sons.

Gray, D.P. (1991) 'Sport marketing', in B.L. Parkhouse (ed.), *The Management of Sport: Its Foundation and Application*, St Louis, MO: CV Mosby, pp. 311–20.

Kotler, P. and Armstrong, G. (2004) *Principles of Marketing*, 10th edn, Upper Saddle River, NJ: Pearson Prentice Hall.

Lussier, R.N. and Kimball, D. (2004) *Sport Management: Principles, Applications, Skill Development*, Mason, OH: Thomson South-Western.

Meldrum, M. (1996) Critical issues in implementing marketing, *Journal of Marketing Practice: Applied Marketing Science* 2(3):29–43.

McColl-Kennedy, J.R., Kiel, G., Lusch, R.F. and Lusch, V.N. (1992) *Marketing: Concepts and Strategies*, Melbourne: Thomas Nelson.

Mullin, B.J., Hardy, S. and Sutton, W.A. (2000) *Sport Marketing*, 2nd edn, Champaign, IL: Human Kinetics.

Proctor, T. (2000) *Essentials of Marketing Research*, Harlow: FT-Prentice Hall.

Reed, P.W. (1997) *Marketing Planning and Strategy*, 2nd edn, Sydney: Harcourt Brace.

Robbins, S.P., Bergman, R., Stagg, I. and Coulter, M. (2003) *Foundations of Management*, Australia: Prentice Hall.

Schermerhorn, J.R., Campling, J., Poole, D. and Wiesner, R. (2004) *Management: An Asia Pacific Perspective*, Australia: John Wiley and Sons.

Shilbury, D., Quick, S. and Westerbeek, H. (2002) *Strategic Sport Marketing*, 2nd edn, Sydney: Allen and Unwin.

Simkin, L. (2002) Barriers impeding effective implementation of marketing plans – A training agenda, *Journal of Business and Industrial Marketing* 17(1):8–24.

Stotlar, D.K. (1993) *Successful Sport Marketing*, Melbourne: WCB Brown and Benchmark.

Summers, J., Gardiner, M., Lamb, C.W., Hair, J.F. and McDaniel, C. (2003) *Essentials of Marketing*, Victoria: Nelson Thomson Learning.

Summers, J. and Johnson, M. (2000) 'Sport marketing', in J.R. McColl-Kennedy and G.C. Kiel (eds), *Marketing: A Strategic Approach*, Melbourne: Nelson ITP.

Woodburn, D. (2004) Engaging marketing in performance management, *Measuring Business Excellence* 8(4):63–72.

Recommended websites

Australian Bureau of Statistics
http://www.abs.gov.au

Sports Marketing Surveys
http://www.sportsmarketingsurveys.com

Sweeney Sport
http://www.sweeneyresearch.com.au/sports.asp

Ticketek
http://www.ticketek.com.au

Chapter 22

Managing service quality and innovation in sport

Gary Tribou
University Marc Bloch, Strasbourg, France
Michel Desbordes
University Marc Bloch, Strasbourg, France & ISC Business School, Paris (France)

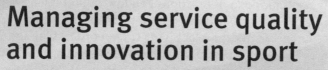

Learning outcomes

Upon completion of this chapter, the reader should be able to:

■ Provide a definition of innovation in sport.

■ Distinguish between minor innovation and major innovation.

■ Point out the link between an innovation and service quality.

■ Locate innovation in the mix marketing by service suppliers.

Overview of chapter

This chapter shows the place of innovation in the quality management of sport services. The chapter begins by proposing a definition of sport services that relies on a fundamentally uncertain quality because of their intangibility and their emotional characteristics, their variable environment and the more or less cooperating relationship between the active consumer and the service production. The chapter then explores the idea that an innovation policy can allow sport marketers to reduce risks and to guarantee a certain quality standard. To do so, the chapter discusses a definition of innovation in sport, which embraces more than the attributes of services but also their environment and their image by consumers.

The chapter ends with the cases of two French companies in the leisure market: the Club Méditerranée, an international commercial company working in 36 countries, and the *Union Nationale des Centres Sportifs de Plein Air* (National Union of Outdoor Sport Centres, or UCPA), associations focusing on the French market whose aims are both commercial and social. The comparison of their innovation policies shows a relative similarity for the quality of a service being subjective; innovations then represent points of reference for consumers.

Introduction

A sport service is a specific good. It functions as a low capital-intensive production, of which the main factor is work, making it easy to adapt itself to a variable demand (Bateson, Eiglier, Langeard and Lovelock, 1981; Desbordes, Ohl and Tribou, 2004; Pitts and Stotlar, 1996). Service organisations are able to manage their service range in an innovative and reactive way because from a technical point of view, capital is restricted to some equipment in combination with a flexible workforce. Investments are low and the indebtedness is cheap; the workforce consists of an important part of workers with precarious jobs (short-term contracts, many trainees) who may be deployed quickly after receiving a rapid training. These conditions allow service organisations to innovate constantly in order to respond to the continuously shortening lifespan of their products, partly under the influence of the changes in fashion, partly in order to develop loyalty among particularly fickle consumers.

Sport services and quality management

This chapter presents a three-point analysis of sport services quality management. Given the fundamentally uncertain quality of sport service, the chapter tries to demonstrate how an innovative policy can bring marketing solutions. Finally, we will underpin our demonstration by describing the cases of two French companies active in this particular sector of activity: the Club Méditerranée and the UCPA.

The quality of a sport service is fundamentally uncertain

Four factors with a direct impact on marketing policy may define a service (Berry, 1980; Flipo, 1984; Holbrook and Hirschman, 1982)

- **A service is an intangible product** (Levitt, 1976, 1981). Consumers can neither look at it nor compare it and decide to buy it on the basis of the organisation's promise written down in a booklet, a catalogue or expressed face to face. This obliges a producer to display its credibility and capacity to respond to consumers' needs (much more than a producer of goods). Hence, communication policy is based upon trust by presenting the image of a specialist, and product policy focuses essentially on making the service tangible (e.g., a good associated with a service).
- **A service is an unstorable product that will be totally lost if not consumed when offered.** In the absence of buffer stocks between a continuous offer and an irregular and unpredictable demand, an obvious problem of service management will arise over time. Under such conditions, the organisation has to be reactive in order to respond as quickly as possible to demand fluctuations; this requires that production factors – mainly the workforce – be highly flexible. A price policy may bring some solutions by differentiating the price, raising it in periods of shortage and lowering it when sales are poor.
- **A service is a product of variable quality.** The consumer's perception of quality can be modified by many different environmental elements. Consumers will inevitably sanction a skiing holiday without snow or a show in the pouring rain. They are rarely prepared to distinguish between the organisation's responsibility and what is

beyond the organisation's control. Product policy offering an appropriate service must, therefore, be flexible in order to offer services adaptable to difficult situations (e.g., snowshoe walking as an alternative to skiing when there is shortage of snow) or adding compensating services (a warm drink to counterbalance nuisance caused by rain). In the end, the consumer will remember that the organisation made a gesture and will report the experience positively to others.

■ **Services are produced and consumed simultaneously and require the consumer's participation** (Eiglier and Langeard, 1987). Let us take the example of a show to underline that the audience's more or less enthusiastic participation is part of the service. If a spectator enjoys the show, she will have the feeling that she is fully consuming the service, and the service gains in quality through the effect of interaction (a lively audience stimulates an actor's performance). The active role played by the consumer, contributing to the production of what she is consuming, in such a way that some services are more or less self-produced (e.g., running a marathon), does not exist in the consumption of regular goods. This is a difficult factor to include in product policy, with the exception of peripheral attributes (e.g., skills used for creating a group atmosphere, as taught at Club Med).

The definition of a sport service includes these four factors. But in an even more specific way, these factors have a direct impact on the consumer's perception of quality. We can define quality as a factor of efficiency in the market: Products are efficient when they respond better to the demand of the consumers than competing products or earlier products that have become obsolete. Quality in sport services is, therefore, mainly linked to the consumers' conception and in a secondary way to objective technical attributes (e.g., comfortable accommodation, reliability and performances of sport equipment, the instructor's teaching ability).

The emotional component of quality in sport services

The intangible characteristic of sport services is coupled with a highly emotional one, bringing more strength to the service (Jeu, 1987, 1992; Pons, Laroche, Nyeck and Perreault, 2001).[1] A sport show will inevitably be less interesting if it is not accompanied by enthusiastic comments of a journalist or by the public expressing its emotions. For example, watching two tennis players in a match on television without any comments is not interesting. Comments and atmosphere are an integral part of sport services (Holt, 1995). Likewise, the enthusiasm of practising a sport, such as playing tennis, can disappear quickly if one does not convince oneself that one is living intense moments, meeting interesting people and improving one's physical condition. But it is also the role of the organisation to encourage and motivate athletes who can get tired quickly. Endless returning of a tennis ball is not interesting at all. Transforming this repetitive and exhausting exercise by adding the spirit of competition can turn this otherwise monotone exercise into an emotionally rich game. The wish to take one's revenge on the opponent, to conclude a match with a tie-break or to successfully strike a volley are emotions that require the player's active participation.

---

[1] Bernard Jeu (1992, pp. 20–21) wrote that 'sport is perceived as a beautiful story . . . a real field of emotional strength, a constant invitation to the imaginary, where the wish to win is guided by passion.' According to him, 'sport has a poetic function.'

Moreover, sport service consumers are particularly sensitive to a trusting relationship with the supplier. An interactive, high-quality relationship provides added value to the service, for which the customer is ready to pay a premium. A survey in fitness clubs in Strasbourg has revealed that sharing the same sport passion and ethics establishes a trusting relationship between organisation and client. It becomes, in some cases, a means of persuasion and of developing loyalty among customers (Tribou, 1994). In this case, the service consumed exceeds the simple sport dimension (being in good condition) and becomes part of the emotional and ethical dimension, which has an influence on the price policy: There can be no question of money between people sharing the same passion for sport – 'in love, one doesn't count'.

It must be noted that, in general, the emotional character of practising a sport gets amplified with the element of conflict. Whether one fights an opponent (in a squash game), nature (off-piste skiing) or oneself (when running a marathon), the physical exercise becomes more meaningful partly through challenge and confrontation (Elias and Dunning, 1986).[2]

The quality of a sport service depends on its environment

The environment in which sport is practised has a big influence on the sensation of pleasure and the degree of satisfaction of the practising consumer. We may even say that environment is an integral part of the service (Minquet, 1992), and this makes its quality uncertain and variable (Mullin, Hardy and Sutton, 2000; Shank, 1999). Indeed, whether a sport show (e.g., an indoor windsurf or acrobatic skiing[3] show) or any other kind of practice (indoor or outdoor), the intangibility of the service requires that the environment is taken into account. Attending a stretching course in a dark and dismal little room does not produce the same satisfaction as enjoying the exact same course in a bright and spacious place: The two products are not the same. In a similar way, playing golf near a motorway or in a pastoral environment does not produce the same pleasure.

Pretending that the influence of the environment is proper to sport services would, of course, be excessive (there are many other examples of the environment's being decisive: theatre, dining and so on), but a sport service requiring that the participant makes a physical effort, not only as a player but also as an 'active' spectator sitting on the tier of a stadium, must fully integrate the service's environment (Andrews and Jackson, 2004). The consumer of a sport event is not comparable to the passive consumer of a car repair. On the one hand, a sport event without decorum could seem in itself poor and without sense: What entertainment would football or running be without it? A car

---

[2] Jacques Defrance quotes Elias (1976, pp. 20–21): Sport 'is the kind of fight that provides pleasure without hurting the conscience...the reinforcement of control on customs of illegally used violence and the correlated intensification of its rejection have also eliminated from everyday life in industrial Nation States a large part of what was in the past obviously, a strong source of pleasant sensations. Corporal suffering has diminished, but so have the pleasure and the joy of living.'
[3] Sport events organised at the Palais Omnisport of Paris-Bercy are shows where the conception of the environment has no doubt as much importance as the sport show itself. These events are also musical performances with light effects, choreographic interludes, comments by celebrities and so on.

repair, on the contrary, is obviously useful. On the other hand, as the consumer is a co-producer of the service by bringing in his own energy, he expects that the organisation will offer him at least a pleasant environment to participate in. The environment of a car repair is less important than the quality of the repair itself. This leads us to the third point of a sport service, with a direct impact on its quality – co-production.

The quality of a sport service depends on the consumer's attitude

A sport service is also particular because of the cooperating relationship between the active consumer and the service production (Eiglier and Langeard, 1987). Through involving his or her body in the event – in sweat and dust and sometimes pain – the consumer consumes the service. The individual's own energy, efforts and resources (not those of the organisation) give substance to the service. The body is in a way the principal production tool (Pigeassou and Garrabos, 1997). But the co-production of sport services limits the quality. The success of the sport production is highly dependent on the athlete's level of physical and technical control and of his or her objectives in sport. An athlete in bad shape and who is technically poor will co-produce a performance of less sport quality than an athlete of a fair level, independent of the organisation's managerial level of competences. If a beginner does not make progress, he or she will turn rapidly into a disappointed and defeated consumer. On the other hand, a fair-level athlete will renew the consumption that boosts him or her.

In a more subtle way and when dealing with collective practising, one can say that satisfaction depends also on the partners' service and their social closeness. Indeed, if the partner is a better player but his way of playing brings value to oneself (by well returning the balls in order to have longer exchanges but taking into account what is at stake at sport level), one will feel more satisfied than if the partner plays in a more personal way (by serving at maximum power and shortening the exchanges with volley strokes at the risk of humiliating his opponent).

Furthermore, we have noticed that in clubs selecting their members on social criteria, members' satisfaction is superior compared with the satisfaction of members of non-selective clubs in which the members are socially heterogeneous. In the first case, the club spirit and the social image can be considered as being part of the consumed service: in the second case, members have the impression of an incomplete service, and they feel a certain frustration as they want to gain a social position through sport (Ohl, 1994, 2004). If the practice is also socially shared, there is thus a co-production of sport pleasure by the players, the other partners and the organisation.

The fluctuating and uncertain quality of sport services obliges organisations to innovate continuously with new attributes or, more radically, with new services, in order to convince consumers to continue purchasing.

The place of innovation in the quality management of sport services

Innovation applied to sport is a notion that needs clarification because different degrees of innovation exist with increasing economic risks (Figure 22.1). The proportion of strong innovation for both the innovating company and the consumer is estimated at less than 10% (Kotler and Dubois, 1986; Gallouj, 1994). This means that for nine of 10 innovations, the risk is relative: Either the company is just limiting itself

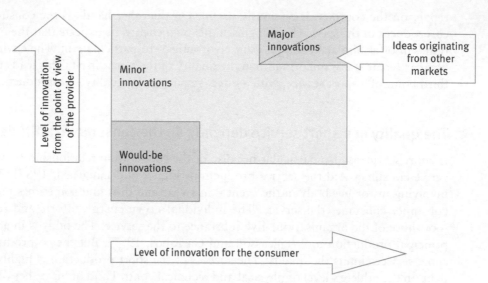

Figure 22.1 **The various degrees of innovation at growing risks**

to improving products it has already experimented or the products are already present on the market but produced by other brands.

Defining innovation in sport

The first innovation degree concerns only the company. It uses a new product idea of another company. For example, a stretching service provided in fitness clubs can inspire VVF to offer a similar service in its villages; the risk is limited because the service has already been experimented with elsewhere. A mere renovation of existing practices can also be considered as a small innovation: the service is offered with little changes and some striking attributes. For example, the Club Méditerranée gives the new name 'beach volley' to the leisure volleyball traditionally played on the beach. If holidaymakers get carefully equipped with balls in 'beach' colours and by obeying to the dress and language codes of the new practice, they will have the impression that they are consuming a novelty, without much risk or cost for the organisation. The important element is, of course, that the consumer or user has the impression of novelty, whereas the product is familiar to the supplier (Van de Ven, 1989). Fitness clubs have become masters in the art of more or less artificial and mainly semantic innovation: Aero step, cardio funk, step slide with low- or high-low impact represent the various possibilities of endurance training, in the same way as pump or body sculpt are simple muscle-building exercises. Those in charge of fitness clubs explain the innovation inflation by the high turnover of their clientele; undecided customers must continuously be seduced with numerous artificial tricks (Tribou, 1994).

There is a second more risky level of innovation consisting in transforming an existing practice into a new product for both the organisation and the consumer. The example of street ball is striking. It originates from indoor basketball of which rules, environment and practising conditions have been modified. The game was imported from the United States, and teenagers freely developed it in urban areas. Then local authorities took over and used it as a means to implement their sport education policy (by making playgrounds available for free). Industries organised promotional events around street ball (the 'Adidas Street ball Challenge' competing with the Reebok's 'Black Top'), and the French Basketball Federation itself started its own itinerant event as from 1994 (the 'French Basket Tour').

The third level of risk and innovation launches on the market a totally new practice for both the organisation and the consumer (e.g., paragliding in the 1980s; kite surf in the late 1990s), even if the innovation remains relative. Indeed, elements from other fields of activity can be used. Snowboarding is, for example, a derivative product of water surfing in the same way as paragliding comes from parachuting. In such cases, the risk comes from the target groups: Who will be interested in gliding? Parachutists wishing to practice in a different way or people coming from other similar disciplines or at least motivated in a similar way? The answer must take into account the people's culture and lifestyles. Paragliding is considered to be a slide sport and mainly attracts customers who are already introduced to other slide practices. Those practising parachuting, which finds its origin in military practice, will be less easily attracted (Loret, 2004). On the other hand, we have noticed that only part of the snowboarders (and the urban street skaters as well) were surfers who went from the waves to the snow. The majority were alpine skiers who have adopted the cultural codes of sliding practices.

Innovation is relative because it can be reduced to a simple amalgamation of existing activities. The current enthusiasm for triathlon is a good illustration of how a new practice comes up. Swimming, cycling and running are associated (three classic activities and in mature stage). To clearly demonstrate that the activity is new and to avoid confusing the image, the triathlon-practising athlete carefully uses a look very different from the ordinary swimmer during swimming exercise (special neoprene swimming costume), from the ordinary cycling competitor (her bicycle's technology is very different from that of other bicycles) and from the ordinary marathon runner (a running outfit that reveals the body much better).

Therefore, innovation in sport uses existing services, which undergo more or less significant changes:

- Some attributes (rules, details in materiel equipment or outfits)
- The practising environment (moving from indoor to a natural environment or the other way round)
- The image that will be associated with other social representations (in general, the transition from a middle-class to an anti-conformist symbolic)

Innovation is also the result of a change in the target group. Surfing, for example, was limited to some groups of marginal young people in top form and required a high level of technical skills. Body boarding seems to have been created, therefore, to reach, for enrolment in a several-day introductory course, categories of older, less athletic and impatient people.[4] The objective of reaching more customers explains the innovative elements.

Innovation is usually associated with technological innovation of products with a view to become more visible in the marketplace. Indeed, a mere modification of only

---

[4] Innovation in sport was initially very controversial, and there continues to be on the one hand practising handcrafts men wishing to make their practice evolve and on the other hand industrials looking for novelty (Hillairet, 1999).

one aspect of the practice without any changes in equipment or outfit, would, in fact, not be considered as a complete innovation.

The process follows a marketing logic of extending the market or the non-market sphere of the practice. In general, its dissemination starts from the non-market sphere at the initiative of a handful of pioneers and is directed towards the market area as soon as the practice becomes profitable. In the mid-1970s, for example, fun board practice in France was in the hands of small handcraft firms, responding to a wild practice. In the beginning of the 1980s, the multinational Bic Company incorporated it before it appeared in the catalogues of such service organisations as the UCPA or the Club Méditerranée. It took the sport movement a long time to react by integrating the innovation. Wind surfing thus became an Olympic discipline in 1984, but the variants of fun board are still not recognised.

Innovation and quality

The double innovation movement – equipment and practices – allows quality improvement of the service supply. The customer's interest (always seeking for new sensations and social distinction) is boosted by the innovation of practice innovation (Ohl, 1994). As soon as a discipline is massively broadcast, it may become obsolete because it no longer brings any kind of distinction. From this point of view, a new attribute would mean an incentive to join it. Carving, for example, has boosted the practice of traditional alpine ski. It has attracted both skiers who were getting bored and new athletes looking for distinction through sport. At the same time, an innovation in the equipment provides visibility to the innovation of the practice. The new shorter carving skis with wide tips have, therefore, contributed to the success of the new practice.

However, if supported by a promotional campaign, a slight or even artificial innovation can better reach the consumer than a string innovation. The success of street ball as an example is more linked to the athletes' clothes than to new practice rules. The sport fundamentals continue to be those of basketball, but the culture is different (ethics, language, dress codes, musical references).

The success of an innovation depends on how the consumer perceives it. This perception can be measured using the SERVQUAL (Parasuraman, Zeithaml and Berry, 1988). The SERVQUAL instrument measures the difference between customers' minimum expectations (adequate service level, meaning the minimum level of service customers are willing to accept) and their perception of those services as delivered (desired service level, which is a realistically ideal level of service). The SERVQUAL instrument focuses on five customer-valued dimensions of service:

1. **Empathy:** Caring, individualised attention the organisation provides its customers
2. **Assurance:** Knowledge and courtesy of employees and their ability to inspire trust and confidence
3. **Responsiveness:** Willingness to help customers and provide prompt service
4. **Reliability:** The ability to perform the promised service dependably and accurately
5. **Tangibles:** The appearance of physical facilities, equipment, personnel and communication materials

The Club Méditerranée and the UCPA are two French companies of which the positions on the sport and leisure market relies on hard innovation policies. One is a commercial multinational company, and the other is an association that focuses on the French market. We found it interesting to compare their product policies (Tribou, 2001).

CASE 22.1   The product policies of Club Méditerranée

The Club Méditerranée was founded in 1950 as a 2300-member association. Its mission was to provide happiness to its member after the years of war. Several years later, the first tent villages were replaced by Polynesian huts, launching the 'Club Med' style. GOs ('gentle organisers') would welcome GMs ('gentle members') at the village and share, for the time of the consumers' holiday, their Tahitian way of life.

In 1957, the Club Med became a limited commercial company, and each member received a share in return of a subscription. In the same year, the first snow village opened in order to compensate for flawing turnover during the slack winter season. Basic concepts are created at the same time. The 'collier bar' (necklace bar) allowed people to consume freely within the village without any money constraints (referring to the myth of Tahiti). GMs were requested to fill in the 'Oscar', a questionnaire on the quality of services provided by the Club Med.

Club Med already cultivated its image of an organisation, wishing to bring quality. During the 1960 and 1970s, the company became international. It developed villages in Japan, Brazil, Malaysia and New Caledonia with a view to conquering South American, Australian and Asian markets. In 1980, the first American village opened in Copper Mountain, Colorado.

The company is restructuring in order to confront globalisation. Four large geographical sectors were defined in the framework of decentralising activities: Europe/Africa, based in Paris; Northern America and the Caribbean (New York); South America (Rio); and Asia/Pacific (Tokyo and Singapore). In 1986, a new concept is experimented in Vienna: the 'city club', an urban village where conferences and seminars may be organised. This concept has been revived in 2000, and big cities established 'Club Med World'.

Globalisation continued during the 1990s: The Aquarius Club took over in order to attract a less wealthy clientele, followed by the charter company Minerva (before withdrawing from air transportation and focusing the activities again on tourism). New products were launched: Club Med One, followed by Club Med Two, making cruises available to a new, particularly Japanese clientele.

Today, Club Med provides hotel services with entertainment in more than 120 villages spread over 36 countries. About 9500 GOs are employed and among them 1800 sport instructors (average age: 28 years). Its clientele (1.5 million of GMs) is composed of 69% Europeans (mainly French, Germans and Italians), 14% North Americans, 11.5% Asians (Japanese in particular) and 5.5% South Americans. With each nationality having different holiday periods (the Germans in June and September, the French in July and August, the Belgians in July), the villages enjoy a relatively well-balanced reservation rate.

The characteristics of the clientele have changed: The average age was 18 to 20 during the 1950s but is now 35 to 40. Young singles (28%) have been replaced by families with children (44%); moreover, 16% of the GMs are children under age 12. To satisfy this new family clientele, 75% of the Club Med villages are especially intended for families, and some of them offer entertainment facilities for children. Another type of customers is emerging: Seniors are encouraged to choose their stays during the low season. On the other hand, people in liberal professions remain the over-represented socioeconomic group.

Club Med supplies five products, namely

1. The traditional holiday villages (120 villages)
2. The hotels with cultural, sport and tourist entertainment
3. Tour operator activities (around 40 tours)
4. Cruises (in the Mediterranean in the summer and in the Caribbean in the winter)
5. Urban leisure activities in the 'Club Med World(s)' proposing dining, shows and sport

Questions

1. What are the innovations that allowed Club Méditerranée to develop its supply?

2. How might innovations allow the company to respond to demands from customers such as senior citizens and families?

3. Explain the link between innovation, service quality and a supplier's image.

CASE 22.2   The product policies of Union Nationale des Centres Sportifs de Plein Air

The *Union Nationale des Centres Sportifs de Plein Air* (National Union of Outdoor Sport Centres) (UCPA) was founded in 1965. It is a non-profit association with the social mission to make sport accessible to the largest number of young people during their holidays. Sport should financially, but also technically, be accessible through providing courses and adequate equipment. It should also be culturally accessible by democratising activities that were so far reserved to a few initiated people.

The competition context has obliged management to evolve towards more competition and efficiency in the market. By setting up, in 1992, a marketing department and implementing a marketing plan, the association changed its strategy and equipped itself to actively fight its competitors.

The individual clientele is young as a consequence of the association's principle of not accepting people over 40. The core target group is composed of people

16 to 25 years old, particularly students and pupils. The other social categories are employees (20%), middle managers (10%) and senior managers (15%). Those under age 18 (10% of the clientele) are welcomed separately in a 'junior' department (7 to 17 years old) where specific products are offered. Another clientele group consists mainly of school groups, enterprise committees, sport clubs and student associations.

UCPA centres are primarily located in France (most of them, 60%, in the Provence-Alpes-Côte d'Azur region). The internationalisation process started in 1991 with nautical products in Spain and Greece and subsequently in Tunisia, Crete, Morocco, and Turkey (i.e., countries on the Mediterranean Sea). There are 68 'winter' and 79 'summer' centres, as well as 11 peri-urban recreation centres. The sport services proposed – ball sports (tennis, golf, badminton), horse riding, air sports (paragliding, gliding), cycling sports (mountain bike, motor trial, bi-crossing, tour cycling) – currently exceed the traditional activities of the 1960s: nautical activities (30%) and mountain activities (representing more than 40% in the winter and less than 15% in the summer).

The services proposed are mainly sport stays in France and abroad, neighbourhood leisure sport (residential, in partnership with local authorities) and since 1993, adventure sport stays abroad (hiking, horseback riding, mountain biking and so on in about 30 countries). Three distinctive product lines are offered for three kinds of customers and motivations:

- The 'passion sport' line intended for the original UCPA target group, real athletes expecting intensive practice (over-40 activities)
- The 'relaxing sport' line geared to a less practice-oriented clientele more in comfort
- The 'adventure sport' line intended for travel and discovery sport enthusiasts

In parallel, UCPA offers services intended for young people from underprivileged classes (30,000 young people every year). Similar to Club Med, the UCPA provides 'all-in' stays guaranteed by a service quality chart, concerning mainly the teaching quality. This is at the roots of the UCPA reputation and contributes largely to its image and position.

Questions

1. What part does innovation play in UCPA's product policy of passion sport, relaxing sport and adventure sport?

2. How does innovation allow the company to better reach its core target group (people 16 to 25 years old)?

3. To what extent can innovation be a means of sport democratisation?

Innovation policies

Going beyond the simple finding of a convergent marketing policy between these two service organisations that compete in the same leisure market, we will notice some differences.

Firstly, concerning the mere conception of sport services, Club Med displays a clear commercial attitude. The service appears to respond to a segmented demand. On the other hand, the service proposed by the UCPA does not only take the demand into account but also the mission of the association – making sport accessible to the largest number. One does take into consideration the evolution in taste such as by increasing the proportion of leisure sports and by reducing tough practices. However, educational ethics are preserved. We deal with two product policies of which the underlying philosophy remains different, despite competition. Even though Club Med is an old association, its logic is utilitarian: selling stays with a view to developing profit and increase market shares. Sport ethics and shared sport passion are only commercial arguments used as a means to reach economic objectives. The associative status of the UCPA is, on the contrary, much more based on a civic policy of sport democratisation intended for young people in the name of general interest ethics. This policy bears, however, the risk of seeing the young people leaving and consuming elsewhere; hence, the marketing concern of attracting them and developing their loyalty is a very competitive market. This is reached by continuous innovation.

We can notice a relative convergence with regard to minor innovation choices. Both organisations aim at innovating in the sphere of 'well-being' by creating peripheral attributes related to the reception, the conviviality and the comfort of the stay. They agree that consumers – whether they are customers or members – will grant their satisfaction in accordance with how they remember the service in its totality and not exclusively in relation to the sport instruction and equipment; the smile of the instructor is as important as the quality of his instruction.

Concerning major innovations in sport, everyone knows how important these innovations are in terms of image. Fly surf, for instance, cannot be missed in the catalogues of these companies wishing to demonstrate that they are following big current trends. There is also agreement on the necessity of innovation as a factor facilitating access to sport practices and, therefore, making them available to more potential clients. Whereas one would call it market massification, the other would rather use the term democratisation, but the approach is similar. However, UCPA has built its reputation partly on a particularly dynamic innovation policy. Some key dates in the development of UCPA are show in Table 22.1.

Table 22.1 **Key dates in the development of UCPA**

Year	Event
1969	The 'UCPA method' was established: an evolutionary method for learning alpine skiing
1980	Launching of the first mono-skis in snow resorts; launching of hang gliding in summer resorts
1982	UCPA instructors take part in designing the first snowboards
1982	Launching of golf with a view to facilitate its democratisation (10,000 golf players per year)
1983	Launching of wild water rafting
1984	Invention of oversaddle to facilitate learning of horseback riding; Oscar award given at the horse fair
1984	Launching of canyoning and mountain bike
1986	Launching of paragliding
1993	Launching of skwal

Innovation processes are similar. Information on the need for novelty is coming from the basis – clients and instructors give their opinion, directors of villages or centres add their analyses – and is moved to the top of the hierarchy where the decisions on the marketing strategy are made. The UCPA seems, however, to apply the concept of 'shared marketing' by attaching more importance to instructors being in direct contact with clients whereas Club Med is more interested in reacting on 'feeling' when it experiments with more risky operations.

But there is a difference between the UCPA and Club Med in their relations to sporting goods producers and their product innovation policies. For Club Med, equipment must be of high quality and of recent manufacture because these are key elements for Club Med's image and position. From this point of view, the industrial brand enhances the organisation's reputation. Hence, it is essential to select brands that will boost the image and communicate the choice. Relations with manufacturers are important to obtain equipment in accordance with the announced high quality of the service.

The UCPA maintains relationships with the manufacturers that are not limited to the quality of their goods. The association considers these partnerships to be strong communication assets that exceed the synergy of the image. Clients test new materials, and their opinions are heard. Moreover, brands are pre-selected with a view to be used by different categories of clients: beginner or advanced, junior or adult. Advantage is taken from the image of the manufacturer to strengthen the UCPA's image in the various carefully differentiated categories of clients. But the image is also strengthened by the reputation of the sport instructors trained in the UCPA's educational centres.

The marketing policies of the two organisations tend to converge because they are intended for a very similar public. Indeed, Club Med is particularly interested in a young and sporty clientele (traditionally, the UCPA's public), and the UCPA tries to attract a category of older customers with better purchasing power and a less rigorous approach of sport practice (Club Med client). But this analysis must be put in the context of the global sport services supply, in which other service organisations intervene and influence marketing decisions. For example, Terre d'Aventures has contributed to directing supplies to more nature-oriented sport services; VVF has influenced the conception of new services intended for all family members.

Innovation in sport services must be considered as directly related to the evolution of the market on the one hand and to the supply structure on the other. Sport practice has widely emancipated itself with regard to the federal educational movement and has become consumption among other leisure consumptions. Every physical activity is called 'sport' nowadays, and this has largely contributed to opening the possibilities for innovation. In the past, it was limited to traditional practices. There is no 'real' sport or 'third-rate' sport anymore, but all are more or less physical activities to occupy free time. As a consequence, the market has exploded. On the other hand, the supply has also changed. From an educational supply offered by associations, the supply has become largely commercial and integrated into the economy. Under the condition of a massive demand and integrated supply, innovation policies are from now on part of market logic. All what is not profitable will be excluded, even if it presents a real sport interest (from the point of view of sport ethics, in terms of public health, social integration and so on). All that may increase the turnover increase will be developed, even if the relation with sport is merely semantic.

Conclusions

A sport service is, therefore, not a product like others. Its quality is uncertain and obliges organisations to innovate constantly in order to guarantee customers' renewed satisfaction. The perception of the quality of a service is subjective. Innovations represent, therefore, a point of reference with a high visibility.

Discussion questions

1. What is the specificity of a sport service?
2. Why is the quality level of a sport service so difficult to master?
3. How can an innovation policy answer to the uncertain quality of a sport service?

Guided reading

Eiglier, P. and Langeard, E. (1987) *La Servuction. Le Marketing des Services*, Paris: McGraw Hill.

The authors develop the idea of a specific services marketing, partly different from goods marketing, showing in particular that consumers are actively taking part in the production process.

Hilllairet, D. (1999) *L'innovation Sportive. Entreprendre pour Gagner*, Paris: L'Harmattan.

Hillairet shows that innovation is of a major importance in the production of sports products, especially when small-sized companies are concerned, which are often pioneers in this field.

Loret, A. (2004) *Concevoir le Sport pour un Nouveau Siècle*, Grenoble: Presses Universitaires du Sport.

Loret proposes a prospective analysis of sports supply that relies upon the hypothesis that the way we practice sport today – (a body practice) can move to more virtual ways (cybersport).

Tribou, G. and Augé, B. (2006) *Management du Sport: Marketing et Gestion des Clubs Sportifs*, Paris: Dunod.

The authors show there is a specific management of sports clubs, from a marketing point of view as well as concerning their financial and accounts management.

Keywords

Major innovation; minor innovation; quality of sport service.

Bibliography

Andrews, D. and Jackson S. (2004) *Sport, Culture and Advertising*, London: Routledge.

Bateson, J., Eiglier, P., Langeard, E. and Lovelock, C. (1981) *Services Marketing,* Cambridge: Marketing Sciences Institute.

Berry, L. (1980) Services marketing is different, *Business* 80(5–6):24–30.

Desbordes, M., Ohl, F. and Tribou G. (2004) *Marketing du Sport*, Paris: Economica.

Eiglier P. and Langeard E. (1987) *La Servuction. Le Marketing des Services*, Paris: McGraw Hill.

Elias, N. (1976) Sport et violence, *Actes de la Recherche en Sciences Sociales* 6:20–1.

Elias, N. and Dunning, E. (1986) *The Quest of Excitement, Sport and Leisure in the Civilizing Process,* London: Basil Blackwell.

Flipo, J.P. (1984) *Le Management des Entreprises de Services*, Paris: Ed. & Organisation.

Gallouj, F. (1994) *Economie de L'innovation dans les Services*, Paris: L'Harmattan.

Hillariet, D. (1999) *L'innovation Sportive, Entreprendre Pour Gagner*, Paris: L'Harmattan.

Holbrook, M.B. and Hirschman E.C. (1982) The experiential aspects of consumption: Consumer fantasies, feelings, fun, *Journal of Consumer Research* 9(2):132–40.

Holt, D. (1995) How consumers consume: A typology of consumption pratices, *Journal of Consumer Research* 22(1):1–16.

Jeu, B. (1987) *Analyse du Sport*, Paris: PUF.

Jeu, B. (1992) Sport, philosophie, histoire, *Revue Française du Marketing* 138:19–26.

Kotler, P, and Dubois, B. (1986) *Marketing Management*, Paris: Publi-Union.

Levitt, T. (1976) The industrialization of services, *Harvard Business Review* September/October:63–74.

Levitt, T. (1981) Marketing intangible products and products intangibles, *Harvard Business Review* 59:94–102.

Loret, A. (2004) *Concevoir le Sport Pour un Nouveau Siècle*, Grenoble: PUS.

Minquet, J.P. (1992) Le produit sport, *Revue Française du Marketing* 138:27–35.

Mullin, B., Hardy, S. and Sutton, W. (2000) *Sport Marketing. Promotion and Sales Management*, Champaign, IL: Human Kinetics.

Ohl, F. (1994) La consommation sportive, *Revue Française du Marketing* 150:17–32.

Ohl, F. (2004) 'Staging identity trough sporting goods', in D. Andrews and S. Jackson (eds), *Sport, Culture and Advertising*, London: Routledge, pp. 241–62.

Ohl, F. and Tribou, G. (2004) *Les Marchés du sport. Consommateurs et Distributeurs*, Paris: Armand Colin.

Parasuraman, A., Zeithaml, V.A. and Berry, L. (1988) SERVQUAL: A multiple-item scale for measuring consumer perceptions of service quality, *Journal of Retailing* 64(1):12–40.

Pigeassou, C. and Garrabos, C. (eds) (1997) *Management des Organisations de Services Sportifs*, Paris: PUF.

Pitts, B.G. and Stotlar, D.K. (1996) *Fundamentals of Sport Marketing*, Morgantown: Fitness Information Technology Inc.

Pons, F., Laroche, M., Nyeck, S. and Perreault, S. (2001) Role of sporting events as ethnoculture's emblems: Impact of acculturation and ethnic identity on consumers orientation toward sporting events, *Sport Marketing Quarterly* 10(4):132–46.

Shank, M. (1999) *Sports Marketing: A Strategic Perspective*, Upper Saddle River, NJ: Prentice Hall.

Tribou, G. (1994) Le marchés de la remise en forme: Stratégies marketing, *Revue Française du Marketing* 150:35–46.

Tribou, G. (2001) Politiques d'innovation sportive. Les cas du Club Méditerranée et de l'UCPA in M. Desbordes (ed.), *Stratégie des Entreprises dans le Sport: Acteurs et Management*, Paris: Economica, pp. 123–42.

Van de Ven, A.H. (1986) Central problems in the management of innovations, *Management Science* 32(May):5.

Recommended websites

InfoSport
http://infosport.org

Marketing du Sport
http://marketingdusport.com

The Sport Journal
http://thesportjournal.org

Sports Strategies
http://sportsstrategies.com

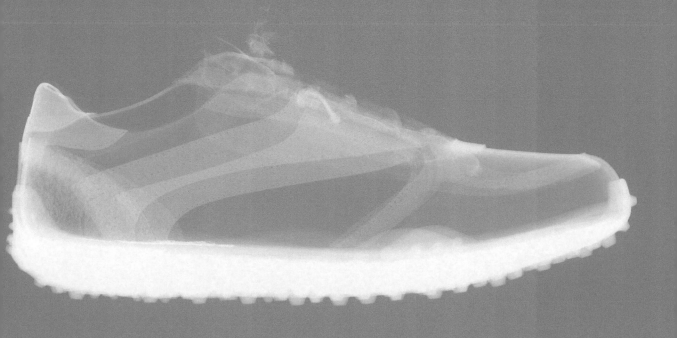

Part Six

Assessing the future for sport marketing

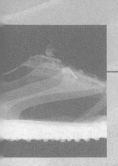

Chapter 23

The future of sport marketing

Simon Chadwick
The University of London
John Beech
Coventry University

'Prediction is very difficult, especially if it's about the future.'

Niels Bohr, Danish physicist (quote of unknown origin)

Learning outcomes

Upon completion of this chapter, the reader should be able to:

■ Explain the nature of a variety of techniques sport marketers can use to predict the future.

■ Identify sources of information available to sport marketers seeking to predict the future.

■ Identify emerging trends and challenges facing sport marketers.

■ Suggest how sport marketers might address these trends and challenges.

■ Highlight opportunities for the development of managerial practice and academic research as a result of this book.

Overview of chapter

This chapter begins by briefly highlighting how sport has developed in recent years. This sets the scene for an examination of the techniques that can be used to predict the future for sport marketing and the sources of information that enable this process. Drawing from a number of expert views, options for promoting the uncertainty of outcome in a variety of sports are then considered. Beyond this, specific potential developments are considered in each of the five areas covered by this book: the distinctive nature of sport marketing, meeting the needs and wants of sport markets, communicating with the sport market, getting sport products to the market and moving sport marketing forwards. The chapter concludes with two cases: the marketing of sport in China and the apparent decline in the popularity of professional boxing.

Introduction

If one reflects upon the history of any sport, in a majority of cases, the first game would have been played as a form of leisure pursuit. Inevitably, the sport would then have developed and become bound up in the social, political and cultural structures of its country of origin. Consider football in England, cycling in France or Australian Rules football, and one gets the picture of how these sports have become so intertwined with the historical development of these countries. Throughout the process of codification, professionalisation and commercialisation (Beech and Chadwick, 2004), performers and elite athletes have been at the heart of sport – and rightly so. Without these highly skilled individuals and teams, sport would still be nothing more than a leisure pursuit. But it is now something much more than that. Sport is now variously seen as one of a number of leisure alternatives, a consumer preference, a revenue-generating opportunity – a big business. What happens on the field of play, the pitch or the court is still important, but what happens off the field is becoming increasingly as important. Structuring a league to ensure its attractiveness is now within the domain of the sport marketer, yet so, too, is the sale of replica merchandise, the pricing of tickets and the exploration of new markets. From being highly product-focused, sport is now changing by seeking to satisfy the needs and wants of a global, often highly sophisticated, marketplace. The question is: Will this trend continue?

Predicting the future

The English economist John Maynard Keynes once said that, in the long run, we are all dead. In this respect, the future is both inevitable and predictable. However, the practice of predicting what might happen in the meantime is rather less precise. The recent dash for a share of the Chinese sport market (detailed later in Case 23.1) illustrates that what we think might happen and what actually does happen are often two different things. Alternatively, consider the global popularity of soccer: Whether in Brazil, England or Malaysia, the game is hugely popular. Yet despite several attempts to market the game to an American audience (in the 1970s by buying in stars such as Pele and George Best; in the 1980s by winning the bid to stage the World Cup; in the 1990s by introducing a new league, the Major League Soccer), interest remains relatively weak. But there have been notable successes for sport marketers. In an attempt to address the decline of a supposedly outdated, Anglo-Saxon colonial sport, the marketers helped to introduce Twenty20 cricket (Twenty20 Cricket, 2005). So successful has been this derivative that some commentators are now suggesting that it is not only the saviour of the sport but will actually be the future. No one could have predicted this.

Trying to predict the future would therefore appear to be a difficult task, although choosing not to think about it is not really an option. Indeed, Glendinning (2001) points out that sport organisations that fail to consider what might happen at a later date are left exposed to all kinds of problems. Not least of these are financial difficulties and, potentially, ultimate closure. As such, sport managers need to consider how they can use a range of business forecasting techniques to help them predict the future. Finlay (2000) distinguishes between two types of predictive technique: forecasting and scenarios. The former focuses on the near and middle future, when existing information can be used as the basis for identifying possible trends and developments. The latter is more frequently used when identifying the long-term future, for which there is no information and no precise indication of what might happen.

A forecast can be described as a statement containing projections about the future, and may be undertaken in a number of ways. These include:

a) Time series forecasting, which primarily involves collecting past and current data and then extrapolating it into the future. For example, if we identify that the match ticket prices at Premier League football clubs have increased by 2%, 4% and 6% in each of the past 3 years, we may forecast next year's price increase to be somewhere in the region of 8%. This form of forecasting is often used, primarily because it uses existing data and is relatively easy to use as a basis for projection. The biggest problem with the approach is the extent to which the past can help to form an accurate picture of the future.

b) Causal forecasting takes a similar approach to time series forecasting by using past and current data as the basis for predicting the future. The main difference is that it uses observations about cause-and-effect relationships between two or more variables to highlight what might happen in the future when a similar relationship is evident. For example, in the past, when advertising expenditure rose by 5%, it may have been observed that the purchase of merchandise rose by 10%. In such a case, the sport marketer might conclude that spending more on advertising leads to increased sales of, for example, replica team shirts. As with time series forecasting, this approach is useful because it is based upon existing data, but it adds elements of previous experience, particularly in relation to the impact that two variables can have on each other. The two main problems with this are the extent to which a past relationship ever really existed between the variables and whether a continuing association can be assumed to exist in the future.

c) Judgemental forecasting is often used when the data needed for a time series forecast are unavailable or where there is little experience of a specific set of circumstances. In such a case, experts make judgements based upon their knowledge and experiences. For example, the growing interest in English football in China is such that we might expect the country to become a major export market for branded football club merchandise because the Chinese population is both large and fanatical about football. This is a good technique for building on the competencies and specialised knowledge of many sport managers. Many of them know 'their' sport well, and most have network contacts who keep them informed about important developments. The main concern is that the technique is largely subjective and, as such, predictions may be inaccurate or biased.

Scenarios are pictures of the future developed by those with an understanding of a business or an industry and are often used to predict the longer term – that is, a time in the future when past or current data may not be applicable. The precise nature of what might happen to a sport organisation becomes incredibly difficult to pinpoint. Therefore, scenarios can be used to develop logical and coherent views of the future, in which sport marketers attempt to establish the way things might turn out. In the case of motor sport, given that tobacco advertising in Europe is due to become illegal, teams are already thinking about likely scenarios such as lose revenue and cease to operate, seek alternative forms of sponsorship, continue to be sponsored by a tobacco company or display the name and logo outside Europe but think creatively about the sponsorship and advertising inside Europe. In this respect, scenarios force sport managers to think about the long term. In turn, the process enables them to begin thinking about the likely ramifications of their observations. Nevertheless, although scenarios can be methodically and professionally developed, what will happen in 5 or 10 years' time can never really be accurately identified.

A number of other techniques can also be used for generating information about the future and for making predictions. The former includes brainstorming and Delphi, and the latter embraces practices such as model building and impact analysis. Brainstorming is a well-established technique that involves groups of creative or insightful people meeting to assess future trends. Extending beyond this rather unstructured practice, Delphi is a more systematic technique in which, through an iterative process of discussion, managers reach a consensus about the future. Both techniques are likely to generate qualitative information and may involve observations being made about issues such as the likely future use of the internet by sport managers or proposals for reforms in sport governance.

This is in contrast to modelling, which often uses sophisticated computer software to generate hard quantitative data. Modelling primarily focuses on identifying trends and patterns, and making predictions based upon the influence of a number of key variables that are input into the software by managers. For example, when planning a service delivery process, sport managers should be able to generate a computer-based model of the process that can identify the impact of, for example, an increase in the cost of producing merchandise or a decrease in demand for tickets. Modelling may even be able to gauge the impact of rain on an event or competition. Impact analysis may also use computer software but may equally rely on qualitative data analysis.

Sources of information

The techniques noted above will never generate a completely accurate picture of the future. Yet the sport manager will still need to ensure that forecasts are as close as possible to what, ultimately, might actually happen. Clearly, the use of a technique such as modelling demands a high level of statistical competence on the part of those using it. Similarly, although Delphi is widely used by managers across industries, it nevertheless requires them to have a detailed understanding of their industrial sector. Therefore, a consideration common to all forecasting techniques is the quality of information fed into the forecasting process. Unless sport managers have accurate information about trends and patterns, they can never convincingly construct a time series analysis. And if they work uninformed, they cannot expect to make authoritative judgements about the future state of their sport. The way that information is gathered and analysed is therefore fundamental not only to forecasting but also to a general understanding of how different sports are changing.

One of the most interesting recent developments in predicting the future is known as the 'power of crowds' (Surowiecki, 2004). Surowiecki suggests that large groups of ordinary people are actually better than small groups of bright people at identifying what is going to happen in the future, humorously noting that:

> If, years hence, people remember anything about the TV game show 'Who Wants to Be a Millionaire?', they will probably remember the contestants' panicked phone calls to friends and relatives. What people probably will not remember is that every week 'Who Wants to Be a Millionaire?' pitted group intelligence against individual intelligence, and that every week, group intelligence won…those random crowds of people with nothing better to do than sit in a TV studio picked the right answer 91 percent of the time.

Using techniques such as online discussion forums and stock market games, it is thought that crowds are particularly adept at identifying correct answers to questions (e.g., whether or not a sport business should open up a new retail outlet in a particular location). What the technique appears to be unable to do is replicate skilled tasks; therefore, crowds are much poorer than individuals at, for example, implementing and managing a strategic marketing plan.

Two different types of information can be used to assist in the forecasting process: information gathered from primary sources (information collected specifically for the purpose of the forecast) and information from secondary sources (information collected for another reason but that may be used for the purposes of forecasting). Saunders, Lewis and Thornhill (2003) provide a good overview of the differences between the two sources of information and discuss some of the advantages associated with each. For a more detailed commentary on the specific sources of information available to sport managers, Scarrott (1999) is an excellent resource.

The future of sport

The first chapter of this book set an agenda for the future of sport marketing by placing the uncertainty of outcome at the heart of sport. On this basis, the way that sport continues to be marketed should be based upon the sporting contest. Emphasising the nature of the core product by promoting uncertainty is of paramount importance, but we now know that this creates additional opportunities and challenges for the marketing of tangible, augmented and potential sport products amongst organisations both directly and indirectly related to sport.

Clear evidence indicates that sport marketers have already embraced this notion. The Xtreme Football League (Willoughby, 2003) is a recent example in which a sport business developed a new sport product in response to market pressures. Set up by the owners of the World Wrestling Entertainment brand (formerly the World Wrestling Federation), the product was a modified version of American football, designed to speed up the game, increase excitement and stimulate crowd interest. This is an interesting case for two reasons: firstly, it clearly represents an attempt to strategically manage the sport product in order to satisfy the needs and wants of the marketplace; secondly, the product failed after just 1 year of the league's operations. The organisers forgot one thing: Sport is not just about entertainment. As we now know, to many sports fans, it is something much more. Nevertheless, in the same vein, consider some of the other proposals made in Tables 23.1 and 23.2 for enhancing the uncertainty of outcome, and so the marketability, of sporting contests.

Table 23.1 The *Observer* newspaper's view of the future in sport

Expert	Comments on the future of the sport
Nigel Mansell, former racing driver	**'Get rid of driver aids**. Technology has taken so much away from the cars and driver aids shouldn't be allowed. I don't even bother to watch races any more.'
John McEnroe, former tennis player	**'Bring back wooden rackets**. The sweet spot is smaller so players need to be more precise. Play let serves: they quicken the pace and add excitement.'
Steve Davis, former snooker player	**'Make snooker more like bar billiards**. I've had enough of watching players clear the table in one visit. Placing a bar billiards-style mushroom between the blue and the pink spots would give snooker that x-factor it lacks.'
Barry McGuigan, former boxer	**'Same day weigh-ins**. Weigh-ins should be put back so fighters can't cheat the scales. At the moment they take place at 2pm the Friday before a fight, which gives boxers more than 24 hours to binge and put weight back on.'
Stuart Barnes, former rugby player	**'Ban tactical substitutions**. When you allow tactical substitutions (and these days it's seven per game) then you are giving too much importance to the coach and not enough to the mental courage required by a player to take him through that pain barrier in the last 20 minutes.'
John McCririck, British horse racing commentator	**'Ban whips**. In 2004, you cannot hit the wife, your kids, or your dog. Yet jockey's hit horses. You cannot justify hurting animals.'
David Elleray, former football referee	**'Introduce sin bins**. I would like to see the sin bin used instead of yellow cards. First, I think it would serve to improve standards of discipline. Second, it makes the system of punishment more just.'
Gavin Newsham, golf magazine editor	**'Make the hole bigger**. Rather than Tiger [Woods]-proof every course in the world, why not throw the game wide open and double the size of the hole, from four and a quarter inches to an almost wok-sized eight and a half?'

Source: Adapted from *Observer Sport Monthly* (2004)

Table 23.2 The BBC's view of the future in sport

Sport	Comments on the future of the sport
Tennis	'Cyclops [the electronic eye] is all very well for helping line judges decide whether a serve is in or not. But it cannot be used once a rally is in progress. And hey – why not get rid of line judges altogether? They don't always get it right [and] they cost money to employ. By underlaying the entire court with sensors and using balls in-laid with a special conductive material, it would be possible to judge with complete accuracy whether a shot was in or out.'
Athletics	'The long jump is all very well. But the plasticine marker used to judge fouls on the take-off board has got to go. And why should athletes jump from one small area, anyway? Surely the event should be a test of who can jump the furthest, not who can jump the furthest from one particular point. A chip in the athlete's spikes could be used to give a perfect indication of take-off point from the runway. And replacing the out-moded sand pit would be an impact gel which retains the shape of the jumper for a few moments to allow measurement before morphing back to its original shape for the next jump.'
Motor sports	'Cars have air-bags to protect drivers in the event of a crash. Moto GP riders often come off their bikes and injure themselves. Put them together and what do you have? The personal airbag-suit. Okay, so the name's not too catchy, but the concept is good. When a rider is thrown from their bike, their suit instantly inflates and cushions their impact on the tarmac.'
Cricket	'The use of the third umpire to adjudicate on run-outs and stumpings is now an accepted part of the game. But why not extend the range of decisions that technology can clarify? Not sure whether a batsman has nicked a delivery to the wicketkeeper? A sensor built into the edge of the bat could send an instant signal to the umpire's ear-piece if it makes contact with the ball.'

Source: Adapted from Fordyce (2004)

The distinctive nature of sport marketing

Let us revisit the very first quote that was made in this book: 'Sport is the only entertainment where, no matter how many times you go back, you never know the ending' (US playwright Neil Simon quoted in Pickering, 2002). This quote is a good one because it captures the essence of what sport marketing is all about. But it needs to be clarified in two ways. Firstly, sport is not simply a form of entertainment, and secondly, in some sports, the outcome of the sporting contest is rather more predictable than many would like. To say that sport is not entertainment would be naïve. Despite the pain and anguish some people suffer when they watch sport, many others do find sport entertaining at a number of levels. However, unlike a film which after you have seen it the ending is predictable, the uncertainty never goes away, even after repeated consumption of it. Staying with the film example, many new productions are also test marketed first. This means an invited audience watches the film and is then invited to suggest how it should be modified for the mass market. But sport simply is not like this; a football match or a boxing bout cannot be played out and then, in the light of feedback from fans, be staged again. Nor can sport merely be equated with other forms of entertainment. Although it is clear that sport is in competition with the arts, cinema, theatre and so on, the pure sport product is not the same as an entertainment product. The current difficulty in some sports, such as European football and Formula 1 motor racing, is that the uncertainty of outcome is not guaranteed. The task of the sport marketer in the future will therefore be to ensure that these and other sports remain attractive by retaining their uncertainty of outcome. Because many sports are embedded within social, cultural and political institutions, abandoning a sport and replacing it with something else is not an option; fans would object. The process of marketing the future of sport would therefore seem to be an evolutionary rather than a revolutionary one. Indeed, if one looks at ill-fated attempts to manufacture sport entertainment products (Xtreme Football) or export sport products with distinctive cultural associations (American Football being played in Europe), the results have often been poor. The future for sport marketing would therefore appear to be one of adaptation and gradual introduction.

Meeting the needs and wants of sport markets

Sport should not change! For those who are passionate about sport, this is inevitably and invariably true. Rugby in south-western France, football in Catalonia, cricket in England – these sports are a way of life, steeped in history and tradition. But the latter example has some salutary lessons for the whole of sport. Attend any major English domestic cricket match (they often take place mid-week) and you will find that the grounds are largely empty, with whatever crowd there being skewed towards the more 'mature' end of the market. Added to this is the fall in membership many clubs are encountering, and there are the ingredients for serious financial problems, possibly even the demise of the sport. One response of the cricket authorities has been to develop a new competition based around the traditional game: Twenty20 cricket. This has been hugely popular, attracting large crowds, stimulating television and media interest and producing exciting contests. It is an excellent example of how marketing can help to boost sport. But some traditionalists in cricket strongly disapprove of this new development, believing it to be the gauche, commercial exploitation of a once fine game. This begs the question: What does the marketplace think? Clearly, fans love Twenty20 cricket and are prepared to back this up by spending money to watch it. There is no reason nevertheless why the traditional form of cricket should not function and flourish alongside it. But the problem is, at the moment, evidence indicates the market no longer wants the traditional version (at least in its current form). Although this does not necessarily present a case for the abandonment of a historic sport, it does present a hugely persuasive case that cricket marketers need to address what is happening to their sport. Why are people not attending games? Of those who do attend, why are they there? What could be done to improve the game? How can more people be persuaded to buy tickets? To some, the task may seem huge, but sport is now about much more than setting up a game between two teams. Understanding the market within which you operate is essential. In a complex and ever-changing world, nothing is sacrosanct. Not being in tune with the needs and wants of fans and other customers therefore is at best naïve and at worse tantamount to suicide. Sport marketing in the future will not be a case of exploitation or the corruption of sport, it will be a case of necessity in order to survive.

Communicating with the sport market

Lance Armstrong, the American professional cyclist and six-time winner of the Tour de France, has a reputation for being cold, aloof and arrogant. Armstrong is often thought to retort by claiming that he needs to be in order to ensure he remains successful. It is not for us to discuss here whether this is the case or not – sport marketers are not necessarily elite performance psychologists, and performers and sport marketing need not be so closely linked. However, many sport organisations do take the on-field mentality of their performers as the basis for conducting their off-field operations. This sometimes means that teams and clubs have an almost monolithic stature amongst their various stakeholders. However, unlike the on-field performers, marketers need to adopt a rather different approach to their relationships with others. At one level, there is a need to communicate the existence of sport products to the marketplace. Having asked fans and customers what they want from you, yet then not inform them that you have responded to their demands seems a slightly strange notion. At another level, sport marketers should work to create and foster bonds with key stakeholders, whether they are fans, sponsors, suppliers or the media. This helps to build affinity, promote understanding and enhance retention of valued partners. But ask yourself: When did you last see a club or team advertisement on television or in the newspapers aimed at persuading you to attend a game? How many clubs and teams are locked into short-term, often uneasy, relationships with sponsors? When have you seen co-promotional offers (e.g., 'buy a full-priced meal at the club restaurant and get a half-price ticket for next game') being presented in sport? Do sport organisations really know who sat in their stadiums, really know their names, address, sociodemographic profiles, purchasing habits, tastes and preferences? In many sports across the world, the answer to all of these questions is probably 'no'. Sport marketers in the future, if sport is to compete with other products, will have to become more communication savvy.

Getting sport products to the market

Whether you are a spectator at a surfing event at the Banzai Pipeline in Oahu, you are standing in Casino Square in Monaco watching a Ferrari speed past, you are amongst the massive crowds waiting to see the Tour de France go over the top of Luz Ardiden or you stand on the terraces of the Maracana Stadium in Brazil, the sporting spectacle created by each guarantees that the live sporting contest can never be replaced, no matter what sport marketers might think. The way that the sport product is distributed to the marketplace may, however, change. For example, television schedules have recently led to English soccer matches being rescheduled, although not without dissent amongst fans, and without notable success. The way that technology facilitates the distribution of sport products is an area where sport marketers will come to develop new or innovative distribution strategies. Some clubs and teams already have their own dedicated television channels through which exclusive footage is sold to customers. But this is set to grow more in the future and represents a significant opportunity for sport marketers. Third-generation handsets that allow fans and customers to purchase content will be one way forward; being able to buy and watch the edited highlights of your favourite game on your mobile phone when you are 5000 miles away is not very far away. Add to this the advent of digital and interactive television and radio and the importance of MP3 technology, and one begins to see that there are immense new markets opening up to sport. Technology is not the only way forward. New international markets are also already an important focus for sport. The American National Basketball Association series has already targeted new market entry into China, using figures such as Yao Ming as figureheads, and American Major League Baseball is collaborating with diary producer Yoplait to promote baseball in Europe by using the 'Frubes' brand. New segments within existing markets are also important. For example, football club financial services products are a new way to get sport products and brands into the marketplace, and weekend diners represent a way of using existing and often idle stadium facilities to generate revenue. In other words, sport marketers need to start thinking laterally about their product offerings and about how to get them to the marketplace. Simply relying on traditional distribution channels – the stadium and the club or team shop – denies the importance of broader distribution changes across numerous other markets and fails to capitalise upon the opportunities that new technologies and new marketplaces represent.

Moving sport marketing forward

Everybody wants their team or club to well *now*, although there are many examples in sport where organisations have been long term and strategic in their thinking. Nantes Atlantique (a French soccer team) and Argentinian tennis are two examples. The problem is, too many sport organisations are short term in their thinking about on-field success, failing to account for the longer term development of their performers or teams. This mentality has permeated the marketing activities of many sport organisations in which the objectives are often based around short-term sales and revenue generation. At the same time, some sports clubs appear to hold their customers in complete disregard: It is the performers who are important – they are the ones who win trophies. As a result, the service that some fans have therefore encountered has not always been of the best quality. Bernie Ecclestone's recent threat to remove the British Grand Prix from the Formula 1 calendar was, for example, partly motivated by his desire to improve the facilities on offer to spectators. But it is glib, if not ignorant, to suggest that sport should simply change. Many sport organisations often have few staff and little marketing competence and are structured around on-field performance. Moving forward with a more strategic view of their operations is therefore likely to be culturally and organisationally difficult. A long-term view of marketing is important, but helping marketers to establish the conditions in which such an orientation can flourish will be just as important in the future.

CASE 23.1 **China's sports fans open their hearts – but not their wallets**

When Stockport County went to China just under four years ago, they were the 39th best football team in England and Wales – hardly the most promising position for building a global brand.

But when they turned up in Guang'an City, birthplace of the late Chinese leader Deng Xiaoping, they drew a crowd of 25,000. Some spectators travelled for four days to get there.

Things have not improved for Stockport, but the club's reception is symptomatic of a much wider trend in Chinese society: from basketball to auto racing, American and European sports have become hugely popular, prompting teams and leagues to make significant investments in the hope of new revenue streams.

But despite the fervent support, these foreign investors are finding that passion for their products in the world's most populous market is not leading to the commodity they most need to sustain their marketing efforts – hard cash.

An insider at Real Madrid – Europe's most successful football club and employer of David Beckham, England captain and global sports icon – estimates that just 4–5 per cent of its €303m (£209m) of ordinary revenue is derived directly from Asia, with China providing perhaps 40–50 per cent of this.

At Manchester United – the English club with the highest international profile – China is thought to account directly for about £1m of its £160m annual turnover, despite the fact that the club estimates it has 20m committed fans in China's main urban centres – twice the UK total.

'If you measure success by how many people are watching, that's no problem,' says Guangyu Li, a Shanghai-based associate principal with McKinsey, the management consultant. 'But deriving financial returns is much more difficult.'

One problem for foreign leagues is the lack of competition in the TV rights market. This has kept rights fees, which have escalated sharply elsewhere, very low.

The English Premier League puts the value of its three-year deals in China and Hong Kong at something over $100m, or about $5m per club. But a good three-quarters of this is generated by Hong Kong.

'If the television market opened to competition, China could become for sports such as basketball and volleyball what India is for cricket,' says Emmanuel Hembert,

London-based manager at AT Kearney, the management consultant. But it would be surprising to see significant loosening before 2008's Beijing Olympics.

Merchandising sales are also limited because the price of official team kits and other branded items puts them in the luxury bracket, making sales volumes disappointingly low.

The US's National Basketball Association has a five-year partnership covering Asia with Reebok, the sports goods company that in turn has a multi-year agreement with Yao Ming, the 7ft 5in tall NBA star who is China's biggest sports celebrity. A Reebok spokesman was quoted last year as saying that the group had $30m in annual sales of athletic shoes and apparel in China.

Considering that the NBA generates an estimated $3bn in annual revenues, those numbers are a mere drop in the merchandising bucket, even with Yao's help.

The one area where foreign sports continue to see financial support is in ticket sales, even with high prices for some premier events.

The inaugural Formula One Grand Prix in Shanghai last year saw 150,000 tickets snapped up at more than £200 each. But even there, experts are cautious. McKinsey's Mr Li believes demand for elite sporting events is driven in part by status rather than love of sport, making it vulnerable to shifting fashions.

More encouraging is the impact China has had in luring sponsorships from multinational companies, which are equally eager to get their brands known in Asia.

Michael Payne, the former Olympic marketing chief now with Formula One, argues that for some global events 'corporate interest in China would account for 30–40 per cent of the total return on investment for many sponsors.'

Germany's Siemens, in deciding to end its sponsorship of China's football Super League, said it would 'use our sponsorship of other teams, for example Real Madrid, to keep our profile high in China'.

Even with the difficulties of generating revenues, there is no sign of Big Sport abandoning its efforts to crack China. Andy Anson, Manchester United's commercial director, says: 'I would like to think of us generating between £5m and £10m a year in China within 10 years.'

An executive at another top European club adds: 'If you want to compete in the football business in 10 years' time, you are either in China or you are dead.'

Source: D. Owen, *Financial Times*, 21 February 2005

Questions

1. Compare and contrast the various techniques that are available to sport marketers seeking to predict the future of sport in China.

2. For marketers in non-Chinese sport organisations, what specific factors do you think they will need to account for when marketing sport to this country in the future?

3. For a sport of choice (e.g., football or basketball), identify and explain three possible future scenarios for marketing sport in China.

CASE 23.2   On the ropes with Peckham's finest

Anyone who grew up in the 20th century following sport will have had their lives punctuated by world heavyweight title fights. As a child, my father listened to Jack Dempsey v Georges Carpentier on a 'cat's whisker' radio.

I grew up during the great days of Muhammad Ali, the most famous man in the world, heard him beat Sonny Liston on my transistor, and went to cinemas at 3am to watch him fight Joe Frazier.

For any British sporting enthusiast, the idea that one of our boys might some day avenge dear old Henry Cooper and become the champ was a fantasy far more potent than winning the World Cup of anything. You did not have to like the idea of grown men whacking each other to be infected by this. It just mattered.

Tonight in Las Vegas, Danny Williams of Peckham will be challenging Vitali Klitschko of Ukraine for the title. No radios or cinemas necessary; it's on pay-per-view. Hands up those who know. Hands up those who care.

Boxing's decline as a serious sport has been in inverse proportion to the number of world champions. There used to be eight, and their names were general knowledge. Now there are at least six competing 'governing' bodies, of varying degrees of seriousness, each recognising different champions in 17 weight divisions. This arrangement suits everyone: a world title contest is going on somewhere on the planet at pretty much any given moment, and some poor saps are being suckered into paying to watch.

If I formed the Universal Boxing Association (assuming it doesn't yet exist), got some fancy letterhead, and persuaded two big blokes from the pub to have a punch-up on the lawn for the UBA title, I dare say we could rake in a bit of gate money and a low-key cable TV contract.

But it wouldn't be like the days when the world held its breath. Squeamishness is another factor in the decline. The sight of Ali, the cleverest and prettiest of all, reduced to a mumbling hulk by the punches he took should be the final proof for most intelligent people that boxing is no sport.

And, quite simply, boxing needs to be box office. It thrived on the clash of personalities, and the heavyweight division has failed to provide one since Mike Tyson's boxing became as flawed as his psyche. Apologists will tell you there is really good stuff lower down the weights. But for these fighters to be more than home-town heroes, recognised by the locals and some quasi-official body only slightly more real than the UBA, they have to manufacture an image for themselves, like 'Prince' Naseem or Chris Eubank.

The Vegas fight is for the World Boxing Council title, the least unconvincing of those on offer. And one of the combatants is intriguing. For this Klitschko is no ordinary pug. He is a PhD (in sports science); he speaks four languages (four more than some past champs); and he comes from Ukraine, where he and his brother Wladimir, himself a leading heavyweight, have been prominent supporters of the orange-clad protesters on the streets of Kiev. To Ukrainians, his success matters.

But though he is the first man in boxing history to use the word 'geopolitical' at a pre-fight press conference, that is not the most significant fact about him. He is also more than 6ft 7in tall and hits like billy-oh, which is why the bookmakers make him about 5-1 on to win.

Williams is not, as things stand, even the most famous man in Peckham. Earlier this year, he lost his British title to one Michael Sprott but became a contender in July after knocking out Tyson, who had lined him up as a patsy; whether that makes him credible is another question – beating the husk of Tyson no longer counts for much.

However, Williams too is a big, big man: six inches shorter than Klitschko but at 19st 4lb at yesterday's weigh-in, 20lb ahead of his rival. Klitschko is not without flaws: there were allegations of steroid use in his amateur days; he lost to Lennox Lewis because he cut badly; and his only other defeat, against Chris Byrd nearly five years ago, came when he simply gave up. 'Klitschko has a yellow streak in him,' Williams taunted the other day, desperately trying to make it sound like a grudge match to drum up interest.

Actually, both men seem rather admirable. Williams's entourage in Vegas has consisted of just two – a trainer and a cook – and he has been spotted in his little rented house folding his own clean laundry.

Outside Vegas, Ukraine and maybe Peckham, no one is that bothered who wins. But I hope neither giant gets hurt.

Source: M. Engel, *Financial Times*, 11 December 2004

Questions

1. To what extent can sport marketing arrest the decline of boxing?

2. As a sport marketer, what recommendations would you make for the future of boxing?

3. 'Boxing is not about the uncertainty of outcome, it's about power, aggression and violence.' Discuss with reference to your answer to Question 2 above.

Conclusions

Some people insist that the only thing predictable about change is change itself. So at least we know that sport and sport marketing are not going to remain the same. This does not mean sport marketers should be casual about change; sport as we traditionally know will increasingly come under pressure from other forms of leisure expenditure, changing customer tastes and service expectations and the challenges posed by managerialism, corporatism, globalisation and new technology. Therefore, the key over the next 5 to 10 years will be how sport organisations respond. Many already have; there are good examples amongst small organisations (e.g., Bedford Rugby Club in England, which has worked hard to increase membership through marketing) and amongst large organisations (e.g., Manchester United, which continues to increase profitability at an unprecedented rate). Even in the not-for-profit sector, governing bodies, community groups and charities are enhancing the effectiveness of their operations through sport marketing. For those organisations yet to embrace its importance, the necessity is becoming ever-more pressing. In some respects, sport marketers must demonstrate that they can generate a tangible return. But sport organisations must also change their orientation to create organisations that can address the marketing challenges they face by building more effective relationships with their stakeholders. Although it is hard to imagine 'big' sports such as soccer and motor racing disappearing, it is more disturbing that other smaller and less mainstream sports are now really struggling to remain in business. As one leading consultant recently claimed, 'The clock is ticking for them.' Sport marketing can help, but this requires focus and a strategic direction that one hopes will preserve the special place that sport has for many of us.

Discussion questions

1. Discuss the statement: 'The future for sport marketing will be less about ensuring an uncertain outcome to a sporting contest and more about guaranteeing that customers receive high-quality products, even if it means that we know who the winner of the contest will be.'
2. For a sport of your choice, construct a plan to indicate from where you should gather information in order to that the marketing of this sport remains up to date and relevant.
3. Using the logic of 'the power of crowds', what future do you predict for the marketers of a sport with which you are familiar?
4. To what extent do you think that 21st century sport marketing will be a competition for global dominance between European and North American sport brands?

Guided reading

For students wanting to familiarise themselves with business forecasting techniques, a standard textbook on strategic management, such as Lynch (2003), should be sufficient as an introduction. For those seeking a more detailed commentary, Finlay's (2000) book on strategic management examines a range of forecasting techniques and highlights key issues for those who intend to use the techniques mentioned. In cases in which students require a more quantitative approach to forecasting, Waters' (2001) book contains information about the statistical procedures underpinning some of the techniques mentioned in this chapter. The area of business forecasting is also well served by journals such as the *Journal of Business Forecasting Methods & Systems*. This is a good source of information on current forecasting practices, and students might find articles by Chase (1998) and Lapide (2002) interesting overviews of recent developments in forecasting.

Further resources relating to business forecasting can be found on the Institute of Business Forecasting's website, which provides links to other forecasting resources.

Journals in the area of strategy and planning, including *Long Range Planning*, can also prove to be useful reading and are sometimes good sources of information about potential future developments in the business world.

For sport marketing–related information, the reader's specific attention is drawn to the Academy of Marketing's Sport Marketing Special Interest Group and to the Business of Sport Management Blog.

Also, an increasing array of sport business–related information, including journals, websites and current issues publications, is available. A number of relevant websites are listed on page 518, but students will find that the *International Journal of Sports Marketing and Sponsorship, Sport Marketing Quarterly* and the *International Journal of Sport Management and Marketing* are useful starting points. Market intelligence publications such as Mintel and Keynote are immensely helpful to sport marketers, although the major downside of these publications is that, unless you have free access through a library, they are very expensive to buy.

Students may also find it useful to monitor developments associated with the European Association of Sport Management, the Sport Management Association of Australia and New Zealand and the North American Association of Sport Management. Each of these organisations holds an annual conference at which academics and practitioners present papers of current interest. Their websites are also good sources of information about current and potential future developments in sport marketing.

Keywords

Causal forecasting; Delphi; judgemental forecasting; modelling; power of crowds; scenarios; time series forecasting.

Bibliography

Beech, J. and Chadwick, S. (2004) *The Business of Sport Management*, Harlow: FT-Prentice Hall.

Chase, C.W. (1998) The role of life cycles and forecast horizons in a forecasting system: Reebok's perspective, *Journal of Business Forecasting Methods and Systems* 17(1): 23–9.

Finlay, P. (2000) *Strategic Management: An Introduction to Business and Corporate Strategy*, Harlow: FT-Prentice Hall, pp. 54–80.

Fordyce, T. (2004) *What Will the Sports We Love Look Like in 2050?*, Retrieved 1st October 2005, from http://212.58.226.40/sport1/hi/front_page/3696988.stm.

Glendinning, M. (2001) Preparing for trouble in paradise, *Sport Business International* 1(July):6.

Lapide, L. (2002) New developments in Business Forecasting, *Journal of Business Forecasting Methods and Systems* 21(2): 11–14.

Lynch, R. (2003) *Corporate Strategy*, 3rd edn, Harlow: FT-Prentice Hall.

Observer Sport Monthly (2004) *10 Ways to Shake Up Sport*, Retrieved 3rd October 2005, from http://observer.guardian.co.uk/osm/story/0,6903,1315431,00.html.

Pickering, D. (2002) *Cassell's Sports Quotations*, London: Cassell and Co.

Saunders, M., Lewis, P. and Thornhill, A. (2003) *Research Methods for Business Students*, Harlow: FT-Prentice Hall.

Scarrott, M. (ed.) (1999) *Sports, Leisure and Tourism Information Sources*, Oxford: Butterworth Heinemann.

Surowiecki, J. (2004) The *Wisdom of Crowds: Why the Many Are Smarter Than the Few and How Collective Wisdom Shapes Business, Economies, Societies and Nations*, New York: Little Brown.

Twenty20 Cricket (2005) Twenty20 Cricket Homepage, Retrieved 1st March, from http://www.thetwenty20cup.co.uk.

Waters, D. (2001) *Quantitative Methods for Business*, Harlow: FT-Prentice Hall, pp. 262–99.

Willoughby, K. (2003) The inaugural (and only) season of the Xtreme Football League: A case study in sports entertainment, *International Journal of Sports Marketing and Sponsorship* Oct:227–35.

Recommended websites

Business of Sport Management Blog
http://businessofsportmanagement.blogspot.com

Business of Sport Management Companion Site
http://www.booksites.net/download/chadwickbeech/index.html

ESPN Sports Business
http://espn.go.com/sportsbusiness/index.html

European Association for Sport Management
http://www.easm.org

European Sport Management Quarterly
http://www.meyer-meyer-sports.com/en/produkte/zeitschrift/esmq.htm

Institute of Business Forecasting
http://www.ibforecast.com

International Journal of Sport Management and Marketing
https://www.inderscience.com/browse/index.php?journalID=102

International Journal of Sports Marketing and Sponsorship
http://www.imr-info.com/#goIJSM

Journal of Sport Management
http://www.humankinetics.com/products/journals/journal.cfm?id=JSM

Long Range Planning
http://www.lrp.ac

North American Association of Sport Management
http://www.nassm.com/

Sport Business International
http://www.sportbusiness.com

The Sport Journal
http://www.thesportjournal.org

Sport Management Association of Australia and New Zealand
http://www.gu.edu.au/school/lst/services/smaanz/

Sport Marketing Quarterly
http://www.smqonline.com/

Sport Marketing Special Interest Group
http://sportmarketingsig.blogspot.com/

SportQuest
http://www.sportquest.com/resources/index.html

Sports Business and Industry Online
http://www.sportsvueinc.com/

Sports Business Daily
http://www.sportsbusinessdaily.com

Sports Business Journal
http://www.sportsbusinessjournal.com/

Sports Business News
http://www.sportsbusinessnews.com/

Chapter 24

The marketing of sport: a practitioner perspective

Nick Wake
Former Head of Marketing, Sport England

Challenges and trends

As a sport marketing practitioner for one and a half years with David Lloyd Leisure and 3 years with Sport England, I have gained an insight into the challenges, issues and trends within this broad, diverse and growing business sector. In the increasingly congested private health and fitness market, the challenge was fairly clear-cut: member retention and new member sales. The measures of success were there for all to see. At Sport England, it was a little more complex in terms of the need to work in partnership across so many agendas, but then also perhaps a little more varied – marketing the benefits of a more active lifestyle; supporting the governing bodies of sport, when appropriate, in marketing their sports; communicating opportunities and processes related to lottery funding; and communicating the unique role of Sport England as a non-departmental public body (NDPB). There were many differences in the two roles, not the least of which is, that as a government body, you are not entirely in control of your own agenda because governments change. However, the broad principles of understanding your audiences, developing objectives and strategies, implementation and evaluation remain the same, as they do in all areas of marketing.

As illustrated above, the precise nature of the sport marketing role varies enormously according to where you sit – that is, what your precise business is, what type of market you operate in, how the major stakeholder(s) sees marketing and where you, as an individual, sit in the organisation. Thus, any one sport marketing practitioner may be a specialist in research, product development, communications strategy, communications delivery, sponsorship, brand management, partnership development, business development, event management, athlete representation, hospitality and more. The fact is there are many different sport marketing roles that lie behind a range of job titles, often without the word 'marketing' in them.

Indeed, a case could be made that 'marketing' in the job title should only occur at opposite ends of the spectrum. The big marketing teams that go along with big sports brands such as Nike and Adidas are typically headed up by a 'marketing director' (who manages a team of specialists, probably a mix of in-house and external agency personnel, covering the different areas outlined above) and the 'marketing manager' or 'executive' (who is effectively a one-person band, a jack of all trades, who at best has some external agency support but needs to 'do it yourself' pretty much on the whole process).

So where is sport marketing at now? What are the challenges and what are the trends? As highlighted above, the answers to these questions depend largely on where you sit in the sporting landscape and what you are seeking to achieve. Are you a sports governing body or a club? Are you wealthy and can afford the services of highly paid professionals, or are you poor and heavily reliant on the services of unpaid volunteers? Are you operating in the private sector with a national market or in the public sector, serving the needs of a distinct local community? Is your market international, domestic or just the local town? 'Sport' is a wonderful world, but it is also complex, with many different types of organisation operating in many different contexts. The good news for everybody who works in sport is that, despite the odd overpaid footballer, greedy agents and the drama that befell Leeds United, there is much to celebrate in the generic concept of sport. And there is much evidence of great marketing happening at all levels in sport.

What follows is a reminder of the inherent value of sport and just a few examples of good marketing practice in different contexts.

Sport is valuable for society

For the individual, involvement in sport can foster self-esteem, confidence and general well-being. Sport helps us understand what it takes to be a winner, and when we do not win, the value that comes from simply taking part. These are the kinds of lessons that stand us in good stead throughout our lives. For a few, sport can be an all-consuming passion that drives them on, making huge sacrifices along the way, to seek success and recognition at the highest level.

For society as a whole, sport and physical activity, in the widest sense, can foster economic value, social cohesion, regeneration, crime reduction and quite literally, the health of the nation, unquestionably one of the biggest debating issues of this time. With one in four adults and one in five children reportedly obese, pushing the health value of participation in sport has, quite simply, never been more important.

For brands operating outside sport, the opportunity to associate with typical sport values of passion, drama and excitement, to capitalise on fan and spectator loyalty and to achieve efficient customer reach are among reasons why sports sponsorship, in recent years, has grown its share of the marketing communications mix. No wonder that many traditional advertising and public relations agencies, in recognition of the trend, have been quick to set up their own specialist sports divisions. For practitioners reaching the top of their profession, dealing with the issue of which lucrative sponsorship offer to countenance, when and under what circumstances, is one that will shape the rest of their lives. There is, of course, no shortage of 'experts' waiting to offer advice. And once it gets going, the marketing process surrounding the compliant and willing sports star is likely to generate more column inches than their sporting deeds.

However, lest we forget, consumer demand drives the whole shebang. Everyone who plays sport, at whatever level, has his or her sporting heroes. We grew up with them. They are what inspired us to have a go. And when we got onto the field, we tried to imitate their style. (My languidness at the crease, however, was generally attributable to ineptitude rather than anything remotely resembling David Gower.) Sadly, in my formative years, the media was all too ready to tear down our sporting heroes as quickly as they built them up, and there is not much sign of that changing. Paula Ratcliffe will testify to this, as might any England footballer by the end of this summer. But then again, the world of the media is in the marketing game, too.

Sport is changing in line with social trends

In order to sustain and grow their sport, there is some evidence of sport marketers evolving and adapting their core product in response to changing macro trends in society. Sport organisations are recognising that people are living and working longer, the number of single person households is increasing, and in dual adult households, fewer parents are caring for children on a full-time basis.

We are more time conscious than ever before and, consequently, more demanding of our leisure time. We expect choice, instant gratification, excitement and escapism. The younger generations can, and do, seek their thrills sitting on the sofa. Play Sport has to compete with PlayStation. For those who do have the time and the inclination, the choice of 'how' to be active has paradoxically also never been greater.

So, those involved with promoting sport have had to get smarter and more sophisticated. They have had to research their customers, segment them into meaningful and targetable groups, develop new product, create strong new brands based on differentiated propositions, seek out beneficial partnerships, communicate, measure and learn. In short, they have had to get better at marketing. And it is happening.

Marketing a more active lifestyle

The marketing of sport as a generic brand, or more precisely, the marketing of the benefits of leading a more active lifestyle, is one that Sport England, as a government agency, has sought to explore. The process began with a huge research exercise, commissioned by Sport England and undertaken by the Henley Centre, in response to the government's strategy for sport, Game Plan, published in early 2003. The Henley Centre work identified a number of key drivers of participation and areas to be addressed if the lofty goal of 70% of the population to be by active (defined as 5×30 minutes of moderate exercise a week) were to have any chance of being attained. One of these key areas highlighted was promotion and marketing. Further research was then conducted to examine how social marketing campaigns in other areas had impacted on social behaviour in this country (e.g., wearing seatbelts, drunken driving, smoking and throwing fireworks). Examples of marketing campaigns promoting physical activity in other countries were also examined. Evidence was uncovered to suggest that sustained campaigns in countries such as Australia, Canada, Germany and Scotland had gone some way to making people aware of the benefits of a more active lifestyle and had indeed shifted attitudes.

In response, the Sport England Main Board agreed to drawing up a brief for a marketing campaign and conducting a test in the North East region, identified as having among the lowest participation rates in the country, yet a region that was also very passionate about its sport. Although the obesity debate raged, this was Sport England's contribution, backed by the government and other key stakeholders, to providing further insight that might inform the development of a national campaign.

London-based agency Team Saatchi responded to the brief with their concept, Everyday Sport. The idea was a simple one: It really was not difficult to build a little more activity into one's daily routine in a way that suited each individual. The pay-off was that 'every body felt better for it'. With an emphasis on fun, the creative poster executions suggested that taking the stairs instead of the lift and getting off the bus one stop early had been officially recognised as sports. The TV commercial featuring the odd North East celebrity mixing in with normal everyday people doing normal everyday things, added to the notion that increasing activity levels was within everyone's grasp. The above-the-line work was underpinned by a robust programme of public relations initiatives designed to engage local organisations to actively show their support for and participate in the campaign. 'Ban the lift weeks', Office Games and the Everyday Sport awards were just some of the activities that took place.

The initial research results appeared to offer some encouragement. First of all, the target audience of adults with infrequent activity patterns 'got the campaign idea'. In other words, they understood it was about doing a little more each day in a way that suited them as individuals. Concerns expressed by some agencies around the potential negative connotations of competitive sport were thankfully absent. On the contrary, there was enough evidence of positive attitudinal change among those aware of the campaign and enough governmental interest in the campaign overall to prompt significant discussion on the role of further campaigning in the government White Paper on health, published in November 2004.

Start with research

So much for the big picture, but direct results of marketing initiatives are perhaps more easily identified at individual sport and club level. In early 2003, vice chair of Plymouth Argyle and ex–London advertising agency executive Peter Jones persuaded his board that more could be done to drive financial growth, regardless of on-field performance. He committed the club to invest in professional market research amongst the fan base to find out what they thought about the club experience and then, just as importantly, acted on the results. A quantitative questionnaire was designed and distributed to fans at the ground, via the website and in the local newspaper, the *Plymouth Herald*. A host of data was gathered, but there were some clear key themes to emerge: The fan base was older than average, there was a commitment to the club that suggested a season ticket sales opportunity, steward attitudes on match days were less than engaging and significantly, there was a gaping opportunity to build more in-depth relationships with loyal spectators. At that point, the only formal contact season ticket holders got with the club was a renewal letter! The focus groups that followed were rewarding not just in terms of the added insights but also in the gratitude expressed by fans for the club's interest in their views. At these focus groups, of the various insights gathered around some marketing ideas to add value, the most powerful one was the notion of 'membership', building on the passion and loyalty felt by the fans. It is interesting to compare this with the way that health clubs market themselves to 'members', rather than 'customers'. Member, it seems, implies a more in-depth, ongoing and involved relationship than customer. It was this type of relationship with the fan base that Plymouth sought to cultivate.

Having gathered the data, Jones and his fellow board directors were not slow in acting. A number of short-term and longer term actions were identified. Stewards were given customer care training, and fans were subsequently advised of a number and contact for comments on the stewarding. The old-style season ticket was replaced by four levels of membership: green, tangerine, white and junior green, with each level offering options on the number of tickets, added value and depth of contact. The fresh way of relating to the fan base was reflected in the membership communication materials, implying that each fan was a '12th member' of the team and that the Plymouth brand was 'run by the fans for the fans'.

And what were the results? Like any integrated marketing programme, the impact needs to be measured over time, but the short-term impact on ticket sales was a resounding success: Green membership increased by 35% against the old season ticket, and tangerine and white added more than 1000 additional members. Even the stewarding complaints went down. More significantly still, the brand building around the notion of a club 'run by the fans for the fans' helped to stabilise the club in the wake of the shock departure of the popular manager, Paul Sturrock, as the club challenged for promotion to Division 1. What could be more devastating to a club on a mission? Despite this setback and perhaps a reflection on the newly created brand strength of the club, Plymouth Argyle still achieved the Sought-after promotion.

The Plymouth Argyle experience illustrates well much of the marketing process outlined earlier: research the customers, segment them into meaningful and targetable groups, develop a new product, create a strong brand based on a differentiated proposition, communicate, measure and learn. A simple, logical plan, developed, agreed and beautifully (in green, tangerine and white) executed.

Product development in sport

Making it happen and making it happen 'fast' can be relatively straightforward when you have a tightly knit leadership team. But at a national governing body level, owing largely to outdated committee structures and complex decision-making forums, making progress on good marketing initiatives can be a little slower. However, with the advent of Twenty20, the English and Wales Cricket Board (ECB) eventually got there. The writing had been on the wall for some time: Attendance at county matches was in long-term decline, less cricket was being played in school and many clubs were either merging or shutting down altogether. The game was ready for a fresh new format. A shorter, more colourful and flamboyant version of the game that could attract new, younger and more time-pressed spectators was badly needed. Now with two seasons of Twenty20 behind it, the ECB is able to claim one of the most successful product innovations in recent years in one of the most traditional of sports. Even Lords, the home of the game – 'central HQ', as it is fondly referred to by some elder statesmen – was witness last season at the fall of each wicket to the new batsmen running out to the square with their personal signature tune ringing around the ground.

Another traditional sport has also caught the mood, but this time the objective is more geared towards participation than people in seats. Having already developed Mini Tennis for 6- to 10-year-old children and Play Tennis to encourage the adult market to 'have a go' during the summer season, the Lawn Tennis Association (LTA) has launched a new brand of the game targeted at the elusive teenage market. Raw Tennis taps into a need to have street credibility with a touch of glamour and seeks to fit into the already congested lifestyle of the aspiring adult. It is widely known that participation in sport drops sharply with the arrival of adolescence. Getting this market to stay active is a tough challenge that will only be overcome by astute product development that taps into the emotional psyche of the target audience. As the marketing message goes: 'You don't need to be the best to give Raw Tennis a go. You just need a racquet, attitude and willpower.' Raw Tennis is a laudable initiative and another step in the right direction for a governing body trying to broaden the appeal of its sport.

Segmentation in private health and fitness

In the private health and fitness sector, although private equity firms have bought up a number of competitors, the Whitbread owned-David Lloyd brand has continued to thrive and is now expanding into Europe. The membership concept described earlier has been practised for some time in the David Lloyd clubs, where general managers are encouraged to hold regular member forums and to drive member retention, or 'stickiness', through the development of clubs within the club. Research has identified the brand's core markets as the young at heart, tennis enthusiasts, families and young, affluent adults. The product has been adapted over time and by location to ensure that the offering meets the needs of these target groups. This has included the introduction of targeted activity programmes for different age groups, much of which takes place in multisport areas that have been reconfigured from former tennis courts. In the gym area, customer insight has ensured that team members understand the motivations of different types of gym visitors, whether it is to train for an event, to lose weight, to look good or simply to feel better. Furthermore, the David Lloyd 'coaches' are encouraged to flex their behaviours towards these groups in recognition of their individual reasons for being there. It is this kind of attention to detail that enables David Lloyd to live up to its brand promise of 'expertise'.

The marketers at David Lloyd Leisure have also not been slow to recognise the opportunity presented by the current wave of publicity around increasing levels of obesity and have invested in a marketing partnership with the organisers of the Great North and Great South Runs, Nova International. This partnership aims to get a million people doing a mile run by staging 'fun runs' in advance of the regular half marathons already put on by Nova around the country. Not only can this initiative be presented in positive public relations terms, but it also enables David Lloyd to take the brand outside the club, build brand awareness through TV coverage of the events and stimulate trial of the local club through giving out passes to mile-run participants.

Sport in the community

Taking the sport outside the stadium is now commonly practised by all the leading sports, both at national governing body and at the club level. The wealthier sports have become experts at taking their games into the shopping centres, onto the streets and into the schools in the shape of their star attractions, inflatable arenas and increasingly sophisticated school packs that hit all the right curriculum buttons. For virtually every club outside the football premiership, establishing a 'brand experience' within the local community is essential to the club's prosperity. The increase in the number of paid community sport development officers, whether at national governing body, club or local authority level, is testimony to the fact that creating a thriving grassroots environment for sport is being tackled from a number of directions. And to my mind, the 'development' part of the job title could just as easily be substituted with 'marketing'.

In England, Sport England has coordinated much of the activity at grassroots level through consultation and working with partners and with the support of the Department for Culture Media and Sport. In early 2004, the organisation published the framework for Sport in England, setting out the strategic direction and policy priorities that sit behind the vision of making England an active and successful sporting nation.

The community sport investment strategy now encourages a longer term and more rounded approach to facility development. The traditional notion of single sport clubs at single sport venues has to change, and indeed, it is happening. There are many great examples of the development of multisport club environments where facilities are shared across a variety of user groups, and the users themselves are able to engage in a variety of activities. Multisport clubs are the norm in much of the rest of Europe, and evidence suggests they are key to sustainability at the grassroots level, both of assets and participation. At the professional level, there are already many examples in the sport of rugby of ground sharing. What price Everton and Liverpool going down this road? Unthinkable to those driven by the traditional passion for their club, but undoubtedly something to be considered by those with a more clinical business perspective.

Bringing sport and business together in the community

Some of the best marketing of sport at the grassroots level almost invariably involves the government's sponsorship incentive scheme, Sportsmatch. Sportsmatch funding acts as an incentive for small businesses and local branches of larger businesses to get involved with community sport by offering to double the money they might put into a scheme on a pound-for-pound basis. The scheme is there to help not-for-profit groups deliver sport in their community. These include sports clubs, schools and colleges, charities, governing bodies of sport, local authorities and voluntary groups.

Projects can be capital or revenue, although priority is given to revenue (e.g., coaching, competition, equipment and facility hire). A recent survey of 500 grassroots sport organisations revealed that one in two organisers would have been unable to attract commercial sponsorship without Sportsmatch funding. Two-thirds of grassroots sport sponsors surveyed confirmed this, saying they would not contribute to community sport or would give significantly less without Sportsmatch funding.

Since its inception in 1992, Sportsmatch has generated £80m for grassroots community sport. Award totals can vary from £500 to £50,000 with the average award being around 8000 and involving just over 1000 participants, 90% of whom are under 18.

The best Sportsmatch schemes are celebrated during an annual awards scheme at the end of each year. In 2004, the top award went to the Cumbrian LTA. 'Serving Tennis to Schools' provides primary and secondary and special needs schools with equipment, taster sessions and training for teachers to introduce young people to the sport and opportunities to continue their interest at clubs and tennis centres. Local car firm PV Dobson and Sons have committed £7750, which when doubled by Sportsmatch, enables the programme to run for 3 years. Similar to many of the other 5000 businesses that have engaged with sport in the community, this scheme enables PV Dobson and Sons to generate positive awareness amongst their core family audience whilst positioning themselves as a socially responsible business at the heart of the community. For the regional arm of the LTA, the scheme helps them achieve their marketing objective of introducing more children to the sport and changing the image of tennis as game for the well heeled only.

Conclusions

So the business of sport marketing is certainly, in my experience, a very broad and diverse church. At one end of the scale – the unpaid one – it can be as simple (or not) as selling an advert in the fixture card to generate much-needed club funds. In my volunteer marketing role for my local cricket club in Tring, I certainly understand this process and the value that it brings, as do many thousands of others throughout the United Kingdom. At the other end, it can mean an intricate web of stadia and image rights deals that play a crucial role in the complex financial matrix of a major sport brand. What it should not involve is endless and overpopulated committee meetings where the prevailing mood is one of looking back, rather than looking forward. Harnessing the unquenchable enthusiasm of the volunteer with a professionally driven, single-minded focus on the customer feels like a winning combination for the individual sport. And, as I have shown, there is much evidence that the generic brand of sport is a healthy one with good marketing at all levels.

With the recent introduction of the first-ever sport marketing qualification through the Chartered Institute of Marketing and Cambridge Marketing Colleges, there is now the opportunity for those wishing to make a career in this field to enhance and add weight to their credentials. The arrival of this qualification is also a sure sign that the vital contribution that good marketing can and does make to sport, in all its shapes and sizes, is becoming more widely recognised. This can only be a force for good.

Recommended websites

Chartered Institute of Marketing
http://www.cim.co.uk

David Lloyd Leisure
http://www.davidlloydleisure.co.uk

Department of Culture, Media & Sport
http://www.culture.gov.uk

English and Wales Cricket Board
http://www.ecb.co.uk

Lawn Tennis Association
http://www.lta.org.uk

Plymouth Argyle
http://www.pafc.premiumtv.co.uk/page/Home

Sport England
http://www.sportengland.org

Sportsmatch
http://www.sportsmatch.co.uk

Tring Park Cricket Club
http://www.tringpark.play-cricket.com

Glossary

Activewear: Sports clothing that is worn to participate in sport activities.

Affiliation: Attachment or connection.

Allegiance: Loyalty.

Ambush marketing: A promotional strategy whereby a non-sponsor attempts to capitalise on the popularity or prestige of a property by giving the false impression that it is a sponsor. Often employed by the competitors of a property's official sponsors.

Amortise: Offset or absorb costs.

Assortment: The mix of products that a retailer sells in a shop.

Atmospherics: The ambience of the shop, encompassing visual, aural, olfactory, tactile, physical and human (staff) attributes designed to provide an overall sense of the shop.

Audiences: Anyone who is on the receiving end of a marketing communications message.

Behavioural segmentation: The division of a market according to the benefits a consumer wants from a product or the degree of usage they make of a product or service.

Bounded rationality: The fact that managers and other individuals cannot know everything.

Brainstorming: A technique for generating, refining and developing ideas that can be undertaken by individuals; more effective when undertaken by a group of people.

Brand: Consists of the name, logo, symbol and other marks associated with an organisation, company or person that distinguish that entity from others in the same category.

Brand associations: Feelings, emotions, thoughts and ideas consumers hold for a brand.

Brand awareness: Consumers' ability to recall a brand when the competitive landscape in which the brand competes is mentioned.

Brand equity: The 'added value' that a brand name provides to a product.

Brand extensions: New products and services offered by a brand in a category different from the one already served by the brand.

Brand loyalty: A brand's ability to attract consumers and to keep them.

Brand management: The design and implementation of marketing programmes and activities to build, measure and manage brand equity.

Break-even analysis: A method of determining what volume of sales must be attained before total revenue equals total costs.

Business acumen: Having a keen perception and insight into business operations.

Business markets: The markets for goods and services, local to international, bought by businesses, government bodies and institutions for incorporation, consumption, use or resale.

Buyclass: A buying situation.

BuyGrid model: This model reflects the process through which buyers pass as they make their purchasing decision.

Buyphase: An activity performed during an organisation's procurement process.

Buying centre: The group involved in purchasing decisions; also referred to as the decision-making unit (DMU) in business-to-business buying situations.

Buying group: An organisational form whereby smaller businesses collaborate formally to pool resources and thus gain economies of scale, particularly in product purchasing.

Casualwear: Sports clothing that is worn generally rather than for a specific sporting purpose.

Causal forecast: A forecasting technique used to identify the relationship between two or more variables whereby a change in one variable causes a change in one or more of the other variables.

Causal research: Research that examines whether changing the level of one variable causes a change in the level of another when the problem is very clearly defined.

Celebrity endorsement: The capitalising on hero status of athletes through endorsement messages.

Co-branding: The development of two or more brands that are associated with each other.

Collaborate: Formal pooling of resources by two or more organisations in order to gain economies of scale.

Commercialisation: The process increasingly found in sport in which a business or businesses from outside the sport have become significant stakeholders in the sport in order to make a direct or indirect profit.

Communications theory: The scientific ideas and thinking behind how human communication works and upon which sport integrated marketing communications is based.

Competitive advantage: The ability of an organisation to deliver the same benefits to customers at a lower cost or deliver benefits that exceed those of competitors.

Competitive strategy: The basis on which a business unit might achieve competitive advantage over competitors in the marketplace.

Concentration: The process by which more of the market is shared by fewer businesses, i.e. the large get larger.

Consumer behaviour: The processes or actions individuals, groups or organisations use to obtain, use and dispose of products, services or experiences to satisfy needs.

Consumer decision-making: The patterns of behaviour that precede, determine and are resultant on the decision-making process for the attainment of need-satisfying products, ideas or services.

Consumer product: Anything that is designed to be consumed by an end user; a consumer product does not necessarily have to be something that has been bought.

Consuming: A mode of action in which people make use of consumption objects in a variety of ways.

Context: The setting in which the business environment takes place. Context can be seen as a combination of historical, economic and social factors that can guide courses of action.

Controlling: The process of measuring performance and taking action to ensure desired results.

Cookies: Small text files stored on a computer to enable access to web sites to be remembered and readily accessed upon a return visit to that web site.

Corporate public relations (CPR): Public relations activities engaged in with and by organisations that are not commercially driven.

Corporate strategy: The overall purpose and scope of an organisation and how value will be added to different parts (business units) of the organisation.

Cost leadership strategy: A pricing strategy whereby a firm offers an identical product or service at a lower cost than its competitors.

Country- or location-specific advantages: Advantages that result from the natural resources or developed capabilities of a country.

Database: A manual or electronic mechanism that aids in the gathering, retention and processing of information that can be used to support the marketing functions employed by an organisation.

Database privacy: Ensuring the privacy of individuals who access, use and register their personal details; maintained by a database operator.

Data mining: Using a database to identify information that can be of value to an organisation.

Delphi technique: A technique for generating information about the future involving a number of iterative stages through which managers gain a consensual view of what might happen to a business.

Demographic segmentation: The division of a market according to potential customers' age, race, gender, income, family life cycle and so on.

Descriptive research: Research that describes the characteristics of a targeted group by asking questions such as who, what, where, when and how problem is clearly defined and also when exploring relationships between two variables (e.g., age and likelihood of becoming a season ticket holder).

Differentiation strategy: A strategy whereby a firm takes advantage of its real or perceived uniqueness on elements such as design, reputation or after-sales service.

Direct marketing: Methods of providing information to people in a direct and targeted fashion through oral, mailed or electronic communications.

Distribution: The activity that makes products physically available for use by consumers.

Distribution channels: The routes along which products (and their ownership) move.

Dyad: Two actors in a relationship.

Dynamic interaction: The process of relationship building and evolving.

Ecological or ethical environment: The external sphere of influence on an organisation that arises through growing organisational and consumer concern regarding the natural environment and ethical trading.

Economic environment: The external sphere of influence on an organisation from macro- or microeconomic forces.

ETOP analysis: A system for analysing the likelihood of external environmental impact on an organisation arising from a SWOT (strengths, weaknesses, external opportunities and threats) analysis.

Experiential consumption: A form of consumption where the consumer is part of the process of product construction.

Exploratory research: Research that is useful when problems are unclear and vague in order to gain a better understanding of a particular problem.

Face validity: Whether the data collection instrument makes sense in terms of whether the items intended to measure a concept do, on the face of it, look like they measure the concept.

Factory outlet centre: An out-of-town shopping centre containing a preponderance of retailers that are selling end-of-line or clearance merchandise at substantial discounts to regular prices.

Fan: A fervent and passionate follower of a certain sporting activity.

Fan identification: The personal commitment and emotional involvement customers have with a sport organisation.

Fascia: The trading name(s) under which a retailer operates shops.

Feedback: The direct interpretation of a response in a manner useable to the marketer.

Firm-specific advantages: Advantages that result from an organisation's assets and capabilities.

Fixed costs: Costs that tend to remain the same for at least one year.

Floorspace: The size of the shop, normally identified as net (the area the customers can access) or gross (the total size of the shop unit).

Foreign direct investment: An equity investment in another country.

Format: The type of shop (e.g., superstore).

For-profit organisation: Private or public organisation that returns a dividend or payment to an owner or group of stakeholders.

Franchise: A contractual agreement to use the brand names and marketing strategy of another firm for a fee.

Geographic segmentation: The division of a market according to location such as by region, city, country or continent.

Governance: The system by which organisations and firms are directed and controlled. It refers to the systems and structures in place at the centre of the organisation for decision making, accountability, controls and behaviour.

Heterogeneity: Services that are difficult to standardise because they are based upon the interaction of employees and customers.

Homogenisation: The process of becoming more similar to each other.

Independent retailer: A retail business owned and operated by one individual.

Industrial marketing: All activities involved in the marketing of goods and services to firms, which use them in the production of consumer or industrial goods and services. It is also referred to as business to business marketing.

Inseparability: When service production cannot be separated from its consumption.

Intangibility: A service product that cannot be touched, seen, tasted or smelt.

Intangible: Something that cannot be touched, tasted or smelt (e.g., emotion in sport).

Integrated marketing communications: A concept of marketing communications planning that recognises and appreciates the added value of combining the range of communication disciplines (e.g., advertising, public relations, sales promotion, direct marketing, personal selling) in order to achieve consistency, clarity and maximum communications impact for messages.

Interaction: The communication and exchanges that take place between a marketer and an active customer or other stakeholder.

Intermediary: An organisation or business (e.g., wholesaler) that provides support functions in linking distribution activities.

Internalisation: Performing a function within a firm.

Internalisation-specific advantages: The advantages an organisation can gain from protecting a function within the organisation. For example, the organisation might produce goods itself to avoid disclosing technological secrets to a joint venture partner.

Internationalisation: The process of entering and expanding in international markets.

Internet retailing: Retailing on the world wide web.

Inter-organisational: Between organisations.

Intra-organisational: Within an organisation.

Inventory or stock: Unsold products.

Issues analysis: An analysis of the broader environment that impacts on a sport organisation's marketing system.

Judgemental forecast: Forecasting technique involving the use of opinion, experience and judgement; often used when there is little information about a specific set of circumstances.

Just-in-time: A set of processes by which supply reacts to known demand, keeping down labour and production costs.

Legal or regulatory environment: The external sphere of influence on an organisation that arises through government legislation enacted as law.

Licence to operate: Support and interest from an organisation's publics that allows the organisation to exist and function.

Line extensions: New products or services offered by a brand in a category that is already being served by the brand.

Logistics: The strategic management of products and information in distribution channels.

Logistics mix: The activities of inventory, storage facilities, communications, unitisation and packaging and transport, which require management to meet cost and service demands.

Logistics service provider: An organisation that provides logistics management activities to other organisations.

Major innovation: An innovation that leads to a rupture in the market, including a new segment and new consumers (e.g., carving in skiing).

Market research: The systematic process of collecting, analysing and reporting information to enhance decision making throughout the marketing process.

Market share: An organisation's sales as a percentage of total sales within that industry.

Marketing audit: A systematic examination of the organisation's marketing environment with a view to identifying key strategic issues, problem areas and activities.

Marketing information system (MIS): A system of procedures that generates, analyses, disseminates, stores and retrieves information for use in decision making.

Marketing mix: Marketing variables (e.g. product, price, place, promotion, people, physical evidence and process) used to tactically manage a product to fit a specific customer group.

Marketing plan: The framework for the sport marketing process composed of written statements of the strategy, tactics, timetables and objectives of the sporting organisation.

Marketing public relations (MPR): The overlap area between marketing and public relations when public relations is used to achieve marketing objectives.

Marketing strategy: A plan for selecting and analysing a target market and creating and maintaining an appropriate marketing mix.

Markets as networks: The view that all firms are linked to each other via direct or indirect relationships.

Minor innovation: An innovation that allows for better service (e.g., a nutritionist's advice within a sports club).

Mnemonic: An abbreviated term that can aid memory.

Mode of operation: The type of international operation used.

Modelling: Forecasting technique normally involving the use of computer software; software is used to identify the nature and strength of relationships between variables contained in sets of data.

Motivation or motives: Reasons for behaviour, which are interactions of internal and external factors within which numerous drives are combined.

Multiple or corporate retailer: A retail organisational form in which chains of stores are operated together for profit under one or more fascias.

Network perspective: A perspective that focuses on the interaction with clusters or relationships rather than on a single marketing relationship.

New product development (NPD): A set of activities that describes the process of how new products are brought to the market.

Not-for-profit organisation: An organisation that returns surplus funds back into specific development or charitable programmes in the community.

Objectives: SMART statements of direction and intent for the sport organisation.

Oligopolistic reaction theory: The tendency of competitors in an oligopoly to enter a country one after the other in close succession.

Oligopoly: The existence of a few strong suppliers within an industry sector.

One-way communication: An overtly persuasive method of communication in which the sender has total control and that does not have any mechanisms for feedback built in. One-way communication campaigns are frequently based upon incomplete messages and untruths. Propaganda is an example of one-way communication.

Online marketing: Provision of the internet and other new technologies in disseminating information, obtaining knowledge and conducting e-commerce.

Organisational buying: The decision-making process carried out by individuals, in interaction with other people, in the context of a formal organisation.

Organisational change: The adoption of a new idea or behaviour by an organisation.

Out-of-town retailing: Retailing that is located away from the town centre, often on the edge of town or on greenfield sites.

Outsourcing: The use of logistics service providers to provide some or all of the overall sense of a shop.

Ownership-specific advantages: Advantages that result from the way a firm is organised and owned.

Packaging: Material used to protect a product in distribution or to inform, particularly in product purchasing.

Parent brands: Products that are produced for and branded by a retailer for their sole use. More accurately termed *retailer brands*, although *private labels* is the term used in the United States.

Penetration pricing: Setting a low price for a product or service in order to overcome barriers to adoption and gain market share.

Perceived fit: The extent to which a consumer sees a brand extension as a logical offering of the parent brand.

Perceived quality: Consumers' evaluation of a brand when considering the overarching purpose of the product as well as alternative options.

Perishability: A service that exists in real time and cannot be stored for future use.

Phenomenology: An inductive approach to research in which data are collected and theory developed as a result of data analysis.

Political environment: The external sphere of influence on an organisation from either political ideology or level of government.

Positioning: The decisions and activities that an organisation pursues in order to maintain its desired concept in the minds of customers.

Positivism: A deductive approach to research in which theory and hypotheses are tested to produce generalisations similar to those produced by physical or natural scientists.

Postponement: The activity of storing partially completed rather than finished products until demand is known.

Power of crowds: A technique, often involving electronic market places and discussion forums, through which large groups of people reach a consensual view of the future.

Price: What is given up in exchange for a particular product or service, usually in the form of monetary exchange.

Pricing: The process by which an organisation decides upon a price for a product or service.

Primary data: Data collected specifically for a purpose; sources may include questionnaires, interviews and focus groups.

Product: A physical good or a service produced by an organisation to satisfy a customer need.

Product life cycle (PLC): A conceptualisation of the stages a product goes through during its life length.

Product management: The task of coordinating each element of the marketing mix to satisfy organisational objectives.

Propaganda: Information, especially of a biased or misleading nature, used to promote a cause or point of view.

Psychographic segmentation: The division of a market according to factors such as customers' lifestyles and the degree of their involvement with a product or service.

Public relations: A planned and sustained effort to establish and maintain goodwill and mutual understanding between an organisation and its publics.

Publics: The different individuals or groups upon which the success of a sport organisation depends; frequently used in the context of public relations.

Purchase cost: The combination of money exchanged and the time and effort needed to purchase a product or service.

Pure product: An offering that is sold only with tangible elements.

Pure service: An offering that has no tangible elements.

Quality of sport service: Partly conditional upon the consumer's social representations and how he or she remembers the activity.

Qualitative data: Data based upon meanings expressed through words and collected in no-standardised form requiring classification into categories.

Quango: An organisation that receives its funding from government but is intended to remain independent in its operations and decision making (quango is derived from [qua]si [n]on-[go]vernmental organisation).

Quantitative data: Data based upon meanings derived from numbers, analysed through diagrams and statistics and presented numerically and in standardised form.

Quick response: The rapid production and distribution of finished product to meet known demands.

Reference price: The price that a consumer uses as a comparison to judge whether it is cheap, expensive or reasonable.

Relationship marketing: Identifying, maintaining and building durable relationships with customers for the mutual benefit of both sides using interactive, personal and value-adding contact.

Relationship perspective: A growing perspective on marketing that focuses on the customer or other stakeholder as an active participant who interacts with a brand or organisation.

Reputation management: Also known as corporate image management; involves using public relations to create and protect the image of an organisation or individual.

Resource-poor organisation: 'Largely amateur' not-for-profit sporting organisations that do not generate large surpluses through their operations.

Resource-strong organisation: 'Largely professional' sporting organisations that generate large surpluses through their operations.

Retail park: A collection, often centrally managed, of out-of-town retail superstores (also known as a retail warehouse park).

Retailing: The sale of products, normally individually or in small quantities, to a final consumer.

Reward measurement theory: The traditional expectancy model of motivation that focuses on the rewards systems of the organisation.

Satisfaction: The product of purchase price plus benefit received.

Scenario: Pictures of the future developed by those with an understanding of a business or an industry; these are often used to predict the longer term – that is, a time in the future when past or current data may not be applicable.

Secondary data: Data collected for a purpose other than the one a forecaster may use it for; sources may include newspapers, press releases and market research reports.

Segmentation: The process of dividing markets into groups of customers with common characteristics for the purpose of developing an apt marketing mix that more precisely fits the needs of individuals in target segments.

SERVQUAL: An instrument that measures the difference between customers' minimum expectations and their perception of those services as delivered.

Service: Provision of services to consumers rather than tangible goods.

Shop, store or outlet: The business location at which retailing takes place.

SIMC Process Model: The Sports Integrated Marketing Communications Process Model is an adaptation of the integrated marketing communications process model. The main function of the SIMC Process Model is to identify each variable in the sport marketing communication process with the intention of understanding how each impinges on the other and how they engage with communications.

Skim pricing: Setting a high price for a product or service that is newly available in the market.

Sociocultural environment: The external sphere of influence on an organisation from either shifts in societal tastes or changes in cultural beliefs and attitudes.

Specialist retailer: A retailer that sells products drawn from only one retail product sector.

Spectator: Someone who watches and observes sports events.

Sponsorship: Cash and/or in-kind fee paid to a property in return for access to the exploitable commercial potential associated with the property; based on a mutual exchange between a sport entity and an organisation.

Sponsorship objectives: An array of benefits that can be pursued through sport sponsorship, including increased awareness, enhanced image, growth of sales, corporate hospitality and improved employee motivation.

Sport consumers: Participants (athletes), spectators, sponsors and commentators.

Sport integrated marketing communications mix: The Sports Integrated Marketing Communications Mix is the combining of a range of communication disciplines in order to achieve maximum communications impact. Because of the special nature of the sport product, the SIMC Mix comprises different components to the general IMC Mix.

Sport marketing: An ongoing process through which contests with an uncertain outcome are staged, creating opportunities for the simultaneous fulfilment of direct and indirect objectives amongst sport customers, sport businesses and other related individuals and organisations.

Sport marketing domain: The directly related and indirectly related organisations to which sport marketing can be applied.

Sport product: A good, service or any combination of the two (intermediary or final) designed to provide benefits to a sports spectator, participant or sponsor.

Sport promotion: Products and services related to marketing sport. Sport media, merchandising, sport sponsorship, and athlete endorsements are all examples of economic activity in this category.

Stakeholders: People who are affected by the decisions, actions, policies, practices and goals of an organisation and whose decisions can affect the organisation.

Standardisation: Using standard international marketing strategies to serve all international markets.

Static marketing situation: Applied to the traditional approach to marketing, this suggests that marketing looks only at a single exchange and not at the buildup of exchanges over time in a relationship.

Strategic change: The means by which organisations maintain co-alignment with changing competitive, technological and social environments that occasionally pose threats to their continued survival or effectiveness.

Strategic drift: Process that occurs when strategies progressively fail to address the strategic position of an organisation and performance deteriorates.

Strategic marketing management: The implementation of systems to enable the implementation of marketing philosophy and to provide a framework for the development of specific marketing tactics.

Strategic objectives: Product-level objectives relating to the decision to build, hold, harvest or divest products.

Strategic thrust: The future direction of the business and the basic alternatives that exist.

Strategy: The direction and scope of a firm or organisation over the long term in order to achieve competitive advantage over its rivals through its configuration of resources and competencies designed to fulfil stakeholder expectations.

Superstore: A large, sometimes free-standing, normally single-storey retail superstore; also known as a retail warehouse park.

Supply chain: The organisations involved in the production and distribution of support functions in linking distribution activities.

Sustainable competitive advantage: Advantage an organisation or firm has when its competitive advantage resists erosion by competitor behaviour or the industry environment.

Sweatshops: Factories often in low-cost production countries where harsh conditions of work, low pay and lack of standard rights combine to exploit labour and keep production costs down.

SWOT analysis: A marketing planning tool whereby the sport organisation examines its internal strengths and weaknesses and external opportunities and threats.

Target market: A group of people for whom an organisation creates and maintains a marketing mix.

Targeting: The process by which an organisation selects the segments it wishes to concentrate resources upon (mass marketing, single segment or multisegment).

Technological environment: The external sphere of influence on an organisation that originates from advances in the technological rate of change.

Time-series forecast: Forecasting technique that uses past and current data as a basis for extrapolating about the future.

Tout: An individual who buys and sells tickets with the aim of profiting from high demand and fixed supply.

Trade-offs: The known incurring of additional costs in one area of the logistics mix or supply chain with the aim of increasing overall logistics or supply chain operational efficiency.

Transaction: A single sale or marketing encounter.

Transaction costs: Costs involved in performing a particular operation.

Transactional: The traditional approach to marketing as opposed to the relationship perspective.

Two-way symmetrical communication: A form of communication founded on dialogue that generates feedback and can lead to organisational adaptation and change.

Uncertainty of outcome: The core product in sport; the unpredictability of the sporting contest and the foundation upon which the marketing of sport is built under a common fascia.

Unitisation: The development of standard unit sizes or loads to aid the physical handling of products.

Validity: Whether results are really about what they appear to be about (internal validity) and their generalisability to the external environment (external validity).

Value: The quantitative worth of a product or service.

Variable costs: Costs that tend to change as the volume of business changes.

Vertical extensions: New products or services offered by a brand, resulting in the upward or downward manipulation of price and quality.

Warehouse depot or distribution centre: A facility where inventory is stored or is sorted for onward distribution.

Index